Jesus Christ

Source of Our Salvation

Teacher's Wraparound Edition

ave maria press notre dame, indiana

Online Resources

There are many resources for this text, including Chapter Tests and Handouts, available online. Go to www.avemariapress.com and follow these steps:

1. Click on the "High School Textbooks" link at the top of the page.
2. Choose "Classroom Resources" from the pull-down window.
3. Click on *Jesus Christ: Source of Our Salvation.*

Founded in 1865, Ave Maria Press is a ministry of the United States Province of Holy Cross.

Engaging Minds, Hearts, and Hands for Faith® is a trademark of Ave Maria Press, Inc.

www.avemariapress.com

ISBN-10 1-59471-189-5   ISBN-13 978-1-59471-189-3

Project Editor: Michael Amodei.

TWE Lesson Plan Author: James Bitney.

Cover and text design by Andy Wagoner.

Printed and bound in the United States of America.

Contents

- Our Mission to Divine Pedagogy iv
- Introduction to *Jesus Christ: Source of Our Salvation* 1
- 1 God's Good Creation: The Beginning of Salvation History 14
- 2 The Fall and the Promise of a Savior 42
- 3 The Coming of the Messiah 70
- 4 The Ministry and Message of Jesus Christ 98
- 5 The Passion and Death of Jesus Christ 126
- 6 The Resurrection of Jesus Christ 152
- 7 Redemption through the Paschal Mystery 178
- 8 Living the Paschal Mystery: A Call to Holiness 206
- 9 Discipleship: Following in the Footsteps of Jesus 232
- 10 Prayer in the Life of a Disciple of Jesus Christ 262
- Appendix 291
- Reproducible Pages 293

Our Mission to Divine Pedagogy

Ave Maria Press, a ministry of the Congregation of Holy Cross, carries on the tradition of our founder, Bl. Basile Moreau, as "educators in the faith." Our textbooks seek to form the "hearts, minds, and hands" of students to know, love, and serve Christ in his Church.

Inspired by the *National Directory for Catechesis*, Ave Maria Press seeks to use "God's own methodology as the paradigm, and with that divine pedagogy as the reference point, chooses diverse methods that are in accord with the Gospel" (*NDC* 29). Following the pattern of divine Revelation, our textbooks seek to communicate the Word of God and the creed of the Church, and to lead students "on the journey toward the Father in the footsteps of Christ under the guidance of the Holy Spirit" (*NDC* 28). As they progress through their high school years we seek to both evangelize and catechize them, to strengthen their faith and encourage an ongoing change of heart to follow Christ more closely. This process of formation involves four key dimensions: knowledge of their faith, participation in the community of the Church especially through its liturgy, Christian living in service to others and in the promotion of justice, and growth in prayer and reflection (*NDC* 28).

Our textbooks employ two complementary methods: the experiential or inductive method and the kerygmatic or deductive method. Because "human experience is a constitutive element in catechesis" (*NDC* 28), our method begins by engaging students in reflection on their lives through comparison with and application to both the saints and heroes of the past and their own contemporary experience. Our texts build on this foundation by helping students understand how the principles and truths of the faith give meaning and purpose to their lives. Through the study of Scripture, the Creed, the Church, the liturgy and the Sacraments, and Christian morality they are led progressively to a deeper understanding and practice of their faith.

Our goal is not only to prepare students for further study of theology in college should that opportunity be a possibility for them, but more importantly to form them in the faith that will guide and strengthen them in the next stage of their lives, whatever that may be.

Introduction to *Jesus Christ: Source of Our Salvation*

"Truly, this man was the Son of God!" (Mk 15:39). This was the proclamation of the Roman centurion who witnessed Jesus Christ taking his last breath. For the first time in Mark's Gospel, a human being recognized Jesus as the Son of God. This profound truth was revealed in the key moment of Christ's life: the Paschal Mystery. Through his suffering, Death, Resurrection, and Ascension, Christ brought Salvation to the world. These events, foretold in the Old Testament and proclaimed in the Gospels, are the cornerstone of faith.

Jesus Christ: Source of Our Salvation is written in light of the outline for Course III—"The Mission of Jesus Christ (The Paschal Mystery)"—from the *Doctrinal Elements of a Curriculum Framework for the Development of Catechetical Materials for Young People of High School Age,* unanimously approved by the United States Conference of Catholic Bishops. The primary focus of this course is to emphasize Christ's saving work in the Paschal Mystery and its effects on the Church. Students return to an examination of Sacred Scripture in the context of the Paschal Mystery and explore the implications for those events on the world.

The *Framework* acknowledges that "the definitive aim of catechesis is to put people not only in touch but in communion, in intimacy, with Jesus Christ" (5). The strong Christological focus of the *Framework* is evident in this third book in the *Jesus Christ* series and in the other core and elective courses in this sequence.

As catechists and teachers, we have something of incalculable value to offer students: the joy of knowing Christ through the Sacred Tradition and Sacred Scriptures. This Word of Salvation centers on the person of Jesus Christ. He calls each of us—teachers and students—into friendship with him and leads us in "the way and the truth and the life" (Jn 14:6).

Additionally, *Catechesi Tradendae (CT)* and the *National Directory for Catechesis (NDC)* call for a deeper focus on Christocentricity in catechesis. This means many things, including:

- Jesus is the center of catechesis. "Everything else is taught in reference to him—and it is Christ alone who teaches" (*CT*, 6). "Jesus Christ is the energizing center of evangelization and the heart of catechesis" (*NDC*, Introduction, 1).
- Christ-centered catechesis presents "Christ first and presents everything else with reference to him, for he is the center of the Gospel message. He is the center of Salvation History" (*NDC*, chapter 3, A).
- Catechists and teachers imitate Christ the Teacher, whose methodology was multidimensional. "The whole of Christ's life was a continual teaching: his silences, his miracles, his gestures, his prayer, his love for people, his special affection for the little and the poor, his acceptance of the total sacrifice on the Cross for the redemption of the world, and his Resurrection are the actualization of his word and the fulfillment of revelation" (*CT*, 9).
- Catechesis on Jesus will "draw its content from the living source of the word of God transmitted in Tradition and the Scriptures" (*CT*, 27).

For teaching about Jesus Christ to be effective and authentic, catechists and teachers must be devoted disciples themselves. "The integration of culture and faith is mediated by the other integration of faith and life in the person of the teacher. The nobility of the task to which teachers are called demands that, in imitation of Christ, the only Teacher, they reveal the Christian message not only by word but also by every gesture of their behavior" (*The Catholic School*, no. 43). No teaching about Jesus will ring true with students unless we are in love with the Lord, who has called us to proclaim his message. Our commission is to share our faith to help enliven and strengthen the faith of our students. We have been invited into a personal relationship with a living Lord. As catechists, we have accepted his gift and—in the name of the Church—share with our students Jesus' invitation to a fuller life. The goal of Christocentric catechesis includes both knowledge *about* and knowledge *of* Jesus.

Focusing on the Religious Experience of Students of High School Age

Church documents and contemporary research on the religious experience of students of high school age have underscored the need to focus on both evangelization and catechesis with the objective of leading teens to a loving relationship with the Lord and a life of committed discipleship.

High school theology teachers know only too well how difficult it is to evangelize and catechize teenagers in a culture that is strongly driven by popular media and developing technology. Additionally, the family structure of students in Catholic high schools is different from earlier eras. Religion teachers cannot assume that all of the students' parents accept what the Church teaches or that the parents even practice the faith. This course follows up on an introductory course on Jesus and the Bible by offering a deeper look at how God reveals himself and how humans respond to the Revelation with faith. It teaches that as Jesus is the fullness of God's Revelation,

we are called to a life of discipleship in him. The Mystery of the Incarnation and the events in Jesus' life teach us how to be fully human. In learning about Jesus' mission and his ministry, we come to understand that the concrete goal for this life and the next is to live in him.

When everything is said and done, the task for a high school religion teacher, and specifically for a teacher of younger adolescents, is formidable. Religion teachers can't solve all the problems of youth and certainly can't reach all the students, some of whom are for this moment alienated from religion or find it boring or irrelevant. But what you can do is offer the person and message of Jesus. The Gospel is a genuine alternative to today's culture. Jesus joyfully tells of our dignity and worth. He invites everyone into a personal relationship with him, one that can transform our lives, giving them meaning and direction. Pope John Paul II stated it well in speaking of providing a genuine faith education for adolescents:

> The revelation of Jesus Christ as friend, guide, and model, capable of being admired but also imitated; the revelation of his message which provides an answer to the fundamental questions; the revelation of the loving plan of Christ the Savior as the incarnation of the only authentic love and as the possibility of uniting the human race. . . . (*CT,* 38)

Jesus Christ: Source of Our Salvation builds on the scriptural introduction provided in *Jesus Christ: God's Revelation to the World* and delves deep into the life of Jesus that was the focus of *Jesus Christ: His Mission and Ministry*. Students will enter into Salvation History beginning with creation and find its fulfillment with the coming of the Messiah and ultimately in the Paschal Mystery. The Paschal Mystery—the Passion, Death, Resurrection, and Ascension of Christ—is the climax of all Salvation History. It enables us to live a life of holiness and prayer in Christ. More than any other events in the Scriptures, students need to understand the power of the Paschal Mystery in their lives.

The second part of the task is to help teens separate from an atmosphere of hesitation, uncertainty, and insipidity through participation in the Catholic Church, where Christ and his Holy Spirit dwell. In the Church, all people can uncover the Good News of Salvation and determine with God's help their calling for life as disciples of Jesus Christ. The Church offers the holy signs and rituals that will unite us to Christ and enable teens to live grace-filled lives, as well as a rich tradition of prayer that will help them on their spiritual journey to the Father.

To accomplish this task, it is important for religion teachers to incorporate a comprehensive "ministry of catechesis" as much as possible within the setting of this course. This ministry of catechesis for adolescents has several distinct features, as described in the *National Directory for Catechesis* (201–202). Specifically, it:

- teaches the core content of the Catholic faith as presented in the *Catechism of the Catholic Church.* This text has been found in conformity with the *Catechism.*
- provides developmentally appropriate content and processes around key themes of Catholic faith that respond to age-appropriate needs, interests, and concerns.
- integrates knowledge of the faith with opportunities for liturgical and prayer experiences.
- utilizes the life experiences of adolescents, fostering a shared dialogue between the life of the adolescent—with his or her joys, struggles, questions, concerns, and hopes—and the wisdom of the Catholic Church.
- engages adolescents in the learning process by incorporating a variety of learning methods and activities. Among those suggested in this Teacher's Wraparound Edition are media options, dialogues, plays, games, and semester-long projects related to different learning styles (see pages 10–13).
- involves group participation in an environment that is characterized by warmth, trust, acceptance, and care so that young people can hear and respond to God's call.
- provides for real-life application of learning by helping adolescents to apply their learning to living more faithfully as Catholic adolescents—considering the next steps that they will take and the obstacles they will face. For example, this course—as did the previous two courses—offers a variety of Ongoing Assignments for each chapter. These projects allow, first, for the students to choose applications that fit their interests and learning styles and then serve as opportunities to live out the lessons they have learned.
- promotes a family perspective in catechetical programming. In the case of this text, the Church—which had its origins at the beginning of time, was cultivated in the experience of the Chosen People of the New Testament, and was expanded at Jesus' invitation to include all people—is represented as the "Family of God."
- promotes Christian attitudes toward human sexuality.
- recognizes and celebrates multicultural diversity in the Church.

- incorporates a variety of program approaches. Many opportunities for large and small group learning are suggested throughout this course.
- explicitly invites young people to explore the possibility of a personal call to ministry and the beauty of the total gift of self for the sake of the Kingdom based on prayerful reflection with the celebration of the sacraments.

As a ministry of the Congregation of the Holy Cross, Ave Maria Press and its high school textbooks are committed to a ministry of education that is simultaneously academically sound, reflective and prayerful, and committed to witness and service. The founder of the Congregation, Bl. Basile Moreau, wrote that:

> An education that is complete is one in which the hands and heart are engaged as much as the mind. We want to let our students try their learning in the world and so make prayers of their education.

This commitment is evidenced in student activities and assignments in each chapter of the Student Text with focus in the areas of knowledge, prayer, and service.

The Presentation of Jesus Christ and His Message

The criteria for an authentic presentation of the Christian message that forms the basis for this course has been outlined in the *National Directory for Catechesis*. The material is drawn from the normative instruments of catechesis including Sacred Scripture, the *Catechism of the Catholic Church*, the writings of the Church Fathers, the teachings of the Church councils (particularly the Second Vatican Council) and from the Core Curriculum points of Course III, "The Mission of Jesus Christ (Paschal Mystery)" of the USCCB's *Doctrinal Elements of a Curriculum Framework for the Development of Catechetical Materials for Young People of High School Age*. A preliminary outline was drawn from the *National Directory for Catechesis* that teaches that the Christian message:

- *Centers on Jesus Christ* This text focuses on the centrality of Christ in the Gospel message and its application through the life of the Church. For example, Chapter 2 focuses on the covenants of the Old Testament and their culmination in the person of Christ.
- *Introduces the Trinitarian dimension of the Gospel message* As the *National Directory for Catechesis* teaches, "the Christian message is inherently Trinitarian because its source is the incarnate Word of the Father, Jesus Christ, who speaks to the world through his Holy Spirit" (77, B). The central Mystery of the Blessed Trinity is explicitly is referred to throughout the text.
- *Proclaims the Good News of Salvation and liberation* The text emphasizes several points that were prominent in Jesus' teaching: that God is a loving Father, that Salvation is offered through Jesus' preaching of the coming of the Kingdom. Chapter 4 presents Jesus' ministry in reference to the coming Kingdom of God, and Chapter 7 explicitly focuses on the experience of Salvation for the human race.
- *Comes from and leads to the Church* The ecclesial character of catechesis is essential because it is the Church who first received the Good News, "understands it, celebrates it, lives it and communicates it" (*NDC*, 80). Chapter 9, which focuses on discipleship, explains what it means to be a disciple in the Church.
- *Has a historical character* The Gospel message of Salvation was unwoven in history. From the various stages of Revelation in the Old Testament, to the life and teachings of Christ as recorded in the Gospels, to the history of the Church, Christ continues to reveal the work of Salvation until he comes again. *Jesus Christ: Source of Salvation* traces God's Revelation in history from Creation to the Israelites and to its pinnacle in the Paschal Mystery of the New Testament.
- *Seeks enculturation and preserves the integrity and purity of the message* The Good News is for all times, places, and cultures. This particular text incorporates the profiles of Christian heroes, including saints, and tells their stories while applying their example to the universal and timeless call to live the Gospel.
- *Offers the comprehensive message of the Gospel and respects its inherent hierarchy of truths* Among these themes and truths covered in the text: God revealed himself as the Creator (Chapter 1); the loss of Original Justice and Original Holiness (Chapter 2); Christ's commitment to the Kingdom (Chapter 3); the focus of Christ's ministry on the Kingdom of God (Chapter 4); the Passion and Death (Chapter 5); the Resurrection and Ascension (Chapter 6); humanity's Redemption (Chapter 7); the call to holiness (Chapter 8); the path of discipleship (Chapter 9); the importance of prayer in discipleship (Chapter 10).
- *Communicates the profound dignity of the human person* Jesus' respect for the dignity of all people is well represented in the Gospels; the foundation for this respect and compassion for all is laid in the Old Testament (e.g., Chapter 1 and 2).

- *Fosters understanding of the language of faith* The text takes pains to introduce both the technical and the common language of faith, particularly as it is contained in the *Catechism of the Catholic Church*. An extensive glossary of terms highlighted in the text is a feature of *Jesus Christ: Source of Our Salvation.*

Suggested Catechetical Methods for a Christocentric Faith Synthesis Course

The *National Directory for Catechesis* reminds catechists that in the sharing of faith, "the Church does not rely on any single method." This teacher's manual recognizes this statement and has suggested a variety of ways to communicate the faith for those presenting a course about Jesus and his mission among us.

- *Learning through human experience* Jesus is the center of our catechesis. Pope John Paul II wrote in *Catechesi Tradendae*, "Everything else is taught in reference to him—and it is Christ alone who teaches" (6). There is opportunity for teachers to share their personal relationship with Jesus Christ, both in deed and word. In the name of the Church, our example calls the students to a deeper life with Christ.
- *Learning by discipleship* The *National Directory for Catechesis* teaches that the ongoing Christian formation supported by catechesis increases in us our "capacity to understand those truths more deeply later in life and disposes [us] to live Christ's message more faithfully" (29B, 99). This course offers regular opportunity for individual reflection and common prayer. An integrative prayer is offered with each chapter, calling the students to both reflection and resolution.
- *Learning within the Christian community* As the parish is a necessary place for all to participate in liturgy, learn hospitality, and be nourished in faith, this course draws from that strength both in the actual parish community and by extension through the intentional community formed in a school setting. The course is not stagnant in either setting. The high school youth are encouraged to investigate, live, and support the ongoing life of the Church.
- *Learning within the Christian family* The warmth of the Christian family is to be re-created in the school or parish setting. Lesson openers are designed to connect the experience of family and to make a religion class much different from that of another academic subject. Programmatic catechesis models the "church of the home" by creating a similar environment of love and warmth and by building on lessons about prayer, traditions, and moral formation, for example.
- *Learning through the witness of the teacher* As mentioned above, teachers make the words of Christ their own. They call on Jesus and accept the guidance of the Holy Spirit to share the Gospel faithfully both in their words and actions. At the same time, the teacher should cultivate a serious academic setting for this course, which includes tests, assignments, and projects that are challenging and should rank as a similar scholastic discipline to other subjects high school youth take in school.
- *Learning by heart* The *National Directory for Catechesis* points out that "while the content of the faith cannot be reduced to formulas that are repeated without being properly understood, learning by heart has had a special place in catechesis and should continue to have a place today" (29F, 96). The text includes objective Review Questions at the end of each major section designed to elicit a recall of the important names, terms, and topics covered in the text. A set of Explaining the Faith questions in each chapter is also applicable to a variety of testing methods, including memorization.
- *Making a commitment to live the Christian life* As previously mentioned, a variety of Ongoing Assignments are offered in each chapter. This course calls for students to choose and complete at least three of these assignments during the time of study and discussion of that particular chapter. These assignments, while testing knowledge, are truly a call for application of the Gospel to everyday life. Similarly, features labeled with heart and hand icons are explicitly connected to Christian service.
- *Learning by apprenticeship* This method of catechesis is modeled in the catechumenate as a catechumen's faith is modeled to him or her by a sponsor. This course encourages dialogue among peers of varying degrees of commitment, practice, and membership in the Christian faith as a means to further the faith development of all the students.

About this Course

Jesus Christ: Source of Our Salvation is intended as a one-semester course focused on the Paschal Mystery of Jesus, especially as suggested by Course III, "The Mission of Jesus Christ (Paschal Mystery)" according to the *Doctrinal Elements of a Curriculum Framework for the Development of Catechetical Materials for Young People of High School Age*. The text and course is intended as a study of the Paschal Mystery, which was introduced in the two previous books of the series but is brought onto center stage here. The

course is designed to review the topics of *Jesus Christ: God's Revelation to the World* and *Jesus Christ: His Mission and Ministry* by placing them in the context of Christ's Paschal Mystery.

This course consists of the following components:

1. Student Text
2. Teacher's Wraparound Edition (TWE)
3. Online text files at www.avemariapress.com

It is strongly recommended that for this course the students keep a personal copy of the Bible with them. Both the Student Text and TWE quote from the *New American Bible with Revised New Testament.*

Scope of the Course

Jesus Christ: Source of Our Salvation is a companion for reading and learning about the Paschal Mystery and Salvation. The text is dotted with numerous Scripture references from the Old and New Testaments. The text is intended to help students clearly understand the stages of Divine Revelation, culminating in the Life, Death, and Resurrection of Jesus Christ. The major focus of the text is on the Paschal Mystery as the pinnacle of God's Revelation.

- Chapters 1 and 2 present the reason that Salvation is necessary: namely, the Fall of Man from Original Holiness and Original Justice.
- Chapter 3 introduces the Gospels and the early events of Jesus' life.
- Chapter 4 focuses on the teaching and healing ministries of Christ and their focus on the Kingdom of God. Each of these chapters builds up to the greatest events of Jesus' life—his Paschal Mystery.
- Chapter 5 and 6 invite students into a deeper appreciation of the suffering, Death, Resurrection, and Ascension of the Lord Jesus Christ through a thorough examination of the Gospel accounts of these events. Then, students will delve into a deeper understanding of the effects of the Paschal Mystery on their lives.
- In Chapter 7, students will examine their Redemption, life after death, and the resurrection of the body. Then they will discover what it takes to be a disciple: a life of virtue (Chapter 8), self-sacrifice (Chapter 9), and prayer (Chapter 10).

Course Sequence

The sequence of the course focuses on the Fall, the life of Christ, his saving work, and the Paschal Mystery's effect on discipleship. A complete chapter-by-chapter sequence of the course follows. Also, please note that the teaching objectives for each chapter are listed in the Chapter Introductions of the TWE. The Main Ideas at the end of each chapter of the Student Text also list important teaching points for each chapter.

1: God's Good Creation: The Beginning of Salvation History

- **Model of Compassion**
  The saving deeds of our Lord in the Paschal Mystery reveal God's love, forgiveness, and compassion.
- **Origins of the World and Humankind**
  Natural questioning about the existence and meaning of life leads us to answers from Divine Revelation, God's free gift of self-communication by which he makes known the mystery of the divine plan.
- **How Scripture Is Interpreted**
  Special attention to the literary forms and the intention of the sacred authors are among the ways we can understand the meaning of Scripture.
- **The First Creation Account (Genesis 1:1–2:4a)**
  The first creation account contrasts ancient creation myths by expressing the inspired belief in the one, true God—Yahweh—who entered their history in a radical new way.
- **The Second Creation Account (Genesis 2:4b–25)**
  The second creation account was written by the Yahwist author who portrays God as anthropomorphic—that is, with human qualities.
- **The Theme of Creation in Theology and Scripture**
  The theme of creation is the foundation of God's saving plans and is the subject of Catholic theology and found throughout all of Scripture.

2: The Fall and the Promise of a Savior

- **Creation and De-Creation**
  The consequences of Original Sin remain a part of our lives today.
- **The Effects of Original Sin**
  Pains of childbirth, backbreaking work to eke out a living, shame as a result of nakedness, and death: these are some of the effects of Original Sin.
- **Was Original Sin a Historical Event?**
  The Fall of Adam and Eve in Genesis does not have to be interpreted in a literal way, but we must believe that there was a real historical event behind it.
- **God Remains Faithful in Times of Sin**
  Cain and Abel, the Great Flood, and the Tower of Babel are three Scripture stories that tell us that the spread of sin was immediate and had dire consequences for humanity.
- **Covenants in the Old Testament**
  The covenant between God and Noah was the first of three major covenants in the Old Testament. In biblical covenants between men, God is the witness to the agreement.
- **God Remains Faithful to His Promises**
  The time of the Israelite monarchy showed how God remained faithful to his promises, in spite of the continued sinful behavior of the leaders and the people.

3: The Coming of the Messiah

- **Jesus: Our Hope and Salvation**
  Through his Paschal Mystery, Jesus Christ has won salvation for humanity.
- **Gospel Portraits of Christ's Origins**
  Taken together, the four Gospels paint the most complete picture of the saving deeds of Jesus, beginning with the events surrounding his origins and birth.
- **Learning from the Life of Christ**
  The events at the beginning of Jesus' public ministry set the stage for communicating the mysteries that form a foundation for our salvation.
- **The Beginning of Jesus' Ministry**
  The central theme of Jesus' preaching right from the beginning is that the Kingdom of God is at hand.

4: The Ministry and Message of Jesus Christ

- **What Is Really Important**
  Rather than gather up worldly possessions, Jesus says that we should focus on growing rich in the sight of God.
- **Jesus Announces the Kingdom of God**
  At the beginning of his public ministry Jesus proclaimed that the Kingdom of God is at hand.
- **Jesus Teaches about the Kingdom of God in Parables**
  Jesus' parables—stories that used common images to teach an important lesson—told about the requirements of the Kingdom for the present and promises of the Kingdom for the future.
- **Jesus' Miracles: Signs of the Kingdom of God**
  The "wonders, words, and signs" of Jesus that accompanied his words are dramatic evidence to the coming of God's Kingdom.
- **Two Great Miracles of Jesus**
  The Transfiguration of Jesus provides a glimpse into the glory of Jesus, the Son of God. His institution of the Eucharist is the source of our nourishment for this world and beyond.

5: The Passion and Death of Jesus Christ

- **So Another Might Live**
  St. Maximilian Kolbe gave up his own life so that another man could live. Jesus Christ, our innocent Savior, gave up his life for us so that we could be saved.
- **Christ's Redemptive Death**
  The theological and historical understandings of the events surrounding Christ's Death help to reveal its meaning.

- **Overview of the Passion Narratives**
  Each of the evangelists shaped the events of Christ's Passion in order to emphasize certain theological points.
- **Tracing the Events of Our Salvation**
  The Paschal Mystery of Christ's Passion, Death, and Resurrection is the central part of God's eternal plan and is revealed in each of the Gospels, including Matthew 26–27.

6: The Resurrection of Jesus Christ

- **The Fog Lifted**
  With Christ's Resurrection, the clouds of despair lifted and his disciples were able to understand more fully God's plan.
- **Redemption Accomplished and Promise Fulfilled**
  Christ's Resurrection, part of the Paschal Mystery, is both a historical event and a transcendent event.
- **The Resurrection Accounts in the Four Gospels**
  The Resurrection accounts in the four Gospels have some differences in detail that in fact highlight their authenticity as well as their many similarities.
- **Our Participation in Christ's Resurrection**
  The Resurrection of Jesus gives new meaning to our lives. Death does not have the final word.
- **The Ascension and Glorification of Jesus Christ**
  Jesus' glorification consists of his Resurrection, his Ascension into Heaven, and Pentecost—the day when the Father and Son sent the Holy Spirit to the Church.

7: Redemption through the Paschal Mystery

- **The Wonders of Our Salvation**
  Jesus Christ, the Wonder of all Wonders, redeems us by his life, Death, Resurrection, and Ascension into Heaven.
- **The Presence of God in Creation**
  Human beings are the pinnacle of God's creation. Jesus Christ, God's Son, shares in the joys and sufferings of being human.
- **Good News: The Kingdom of God Is at Hand**
  The Kingdom of God, ushered in by Christ, provides the structure and goal for our life in the Lord.
- **Forgiveness of Sins**
  Jesus preached repentance of our sins—the turning from sin and the embracing of God's Kingdom.
- **The Paschal Mystery Wins Our Redemption**
  Christ's work of Redemption is principally accomplished by the Paschal Mystery.
- **The Last Things: Christian Death and the Resurrection of the Body**
  We believe that our loving God will judge us fairly and compassionately after our deaths and look forward to eternal life in both body and soul.
- **More About Eternal Life**
  Our particular judgment will confirm whether we will merit the eternal reward of Heaven, need to be purified of our sins in Purgatory, or deserve punishment in hell.

8: Living the Paschal Mystery: A Call to Holiness

- **The Light of Christ**
  A mark of holiness is to let Christ's light shine through in our lives.
- **Living a Life of Virtue**
  The habitual and firm disposition to do good—the meaning of living a virtuous life—empowers us to perform good acts and give the best of ourselves.
- **God Helps Us Grow in Holiness**
  Growth in holiness is a difficult but not impossible task as long as we rely on God's help, including through sharing of his grace and the seven gifts of the Holy Spirit.
- **Essential Elements of Holiness**
  Our God-given gifts of human reason, free will, and conscience impact our moral decision-making and allow for growth in holiness.

9: Discipleship: Following in the Footsteps of Jesus

- **The Fellowship of the Unashamed**
  It takes bold action and sometimes dramatic response to be a disciple of Jesus Christ.
- **Discipleship Means Following Jesus and His Teachings**
  Being a follower of Jesus involves learning from him, entering into a personal relationship with him, and imitating his example of sharing the Good News with all.
- **Following Jesus' Commands**
  We are called to keep the Ten Commandments and to incorporate the Beatitudes into our lives as disciples of Christ.
- **More Requirements of Discipleship**
  Disciples of Christ are both evangelists of God's Word and stewards of his gifts.
- **Putting Discipleship into Practice**
  Love is the main "job" of Christian discipleship.

10: Prayer in the Life of a Disciple of Jesus Christ

- **An Invitation to Prayer**
  Jesus instructs us to pray constantly: "Ask and it will be given to you; seek and you will find; knock and the door will be opened to you" (Mt 7:7).
- **Defining Prayer**
  Prayer is our response to God who seeks us. We must pray without ceasing.
- **How to Pray**
  We can pray in several ways, including vocally, through meditation, or mental prayer. Any effort at prayer is prayer itself.
- **Praying with Sacred Scripture**
  Many Catholic prayers come directly from the Bible or are partially based on Sacred Scripture.
- **Two Special Prayers for Jesus' Disciples**
  The Lord's Prayer is the preeminent Christian prayer. Next to the Our Father, the Hail Mary is a favorite Catholic prayer that calls on Mary for her intercession on our behalf.

Catholic Handbook for Faith

Glossary

Index

Organization of the Student Text

The Student Text is organized around several common elements in ten chapters. The common elements are described below.

Chapter Openers

A chapter outline of the main topics and the major headings is located at the beginning of each chapter. A Scripture quotation or prayer related to the major topic of the chapter is also in the opener. *Catechesi Tradendae* reminds us that Sacred Scripture along with Sacred Tradition "make up a single deposit of the word of God, which is entrusted to the Church" (27).

Main Chapter Features

Each chapter is divided into four or five main sections. Generally, these main sections make up one class lesson. Within each main section are several recurring features:

- *Opening activities* help to center the information in the student's own life experience.
- *Explaining the Faith* provides an apologetics-style format to respond to several frequently asked questions students have about their faith.
- *Faithful Disciple* highlights a saint or other notable Catholic who has enacted an element of the faith introduced in the chapter.
- *"Mind" Exercises* are cognitive exercises, projects, and features that are designed to strengthen the students' knowledge of the topic and are designated by this icon:

- *"Heart" Exercises* are presentations and activities that promote prayerful reflection and discernment. They are designated with this icon:
- *"Hand" Exercises* are practical applications that encourage service and witness to the faith. They are designated by this icon:
- *Separate features* further break down the running text material, often adding a historical or contemporary perspective.
- *For Review* questions help summarize each main section.
- *For Reflection* starters provide the basis for discussion and/or journal writing.
- *Vocabulary* terms, boldfaced in the text, are defined in the Glossary.

Chapter Quick View

A chapter summary section allows for a review of the chapter and other means for enrichment. These are the regular elements of this section:

- *Main Ideas* are chapter summary statements with page numbers that refer the students back into the chapter for further depth.
- *Terms, People, Places* is an exercise designed to aid students in reviewing the highlighted vocabulary terms in the chapter.
- *Primary Source Quotations* gather material from Scripture, Church documents, and saints and other teachers. A suggestion for further investigation related to these quotations is also offered.
- *Ongoing Assignments* are individual and group applications related to the chapter material. It is suggested that students choose up to three of these assignments to work on through the lessons of the chapter. An opportunity to share their work is scheduled in Chapter Review lessons.
- *Prayer* is an appropriate way to conclude the chapter. Students are offered the opportunity for reflection and to make a resolution for action.

Catholic Handbook for Faith

The *Catholic Handbook for Faith*, included in the Appendix of the Student Text, includes prayers, teachings, creeds, and information on Church history, the sacraments, and practices that are important to Catholics. This material can be used for review and enrichment.

Organization of the Teacher's Wraparound Edition

The TWE provides suggestions for teaching the course, including lesson ideas for every content page of the Student Text. Each chapter includes the following regular elements:

- *Introduction* A brief overview of the chapter that highlights its central points.
- *Chapter Objectives* Lists the major goals the chapter hopes to accomplish with the students. These objectives may be both intentional and affective.
- *Advance Preparations* Reminds teachers of extra materials and preparations like photocopying that will be involved in the chapter.
- *Chapter Handouts* These pages may be photocopied and given to the students. Handouts include supplemental activities and exercises related to suggestions in the lesson plans. Online versions of these materials are available at www.avemariapress.com.
- *Testing Program* Tests with both objective and subjective questions follow each chapter. Tests are based on a one-hundred-point scoring system. However, points may be weighted based on teacher preference. For example, a teacher may choose an all-objective test or a test with all essays and short answers. Tests are based on both material in the Student Text and additional material introduced in the TWE.

Lesson Plan Organization

The lesson plans are the most important feature of the TWE. Complete lessons are included for each of the main chapter sections. Lesson plans include the following elements:

- *Bell Ringers* These are arrival activities, assignments, discussion questions, and the like. The purpose of the bell ringers is to introduce the lesson material, to serve as an icebreaker, or to review homework or previous class lessons and assignments.

- *Teaching Approaches* This is the main element of the lesson plan. It offers several specific, creative approaches for teaching the Student Text material page-by-page. As much as possible, the approaches correspond directly to the material on the facing Student Text pages. Review or re-teaching ideas and homework assignments are also included in this main lesson plan.
- *Homework* It is essential for the students to read ahead in the text and to be prepared for the next lesson. The TWE helps teachers assign text readings, day-to-day and long-term assignments, and offer reminders for bringing necessary supplies to class.
- *Background Information* Primarily for teachers, these panels include a more detailed exposition of a particular topic of the lesson. Often this material can be shared with the students or incorporated into an enrichment or extra credit assignment.
- *Extending the Lesson* While the Teaching Approaches are geared toward offering a method for fifty-minute class sessions, the Extending the Lesson ideas are intended to provide alternate assignments and approaches that can be done in lieu of the main lesson, as homework, or for additional class periods.
- *For Enrichment* This panel offers individual or group assignments the students can undertake outside of class to explore the topic further or for extra credit.
- *For Review* Answers to all the objective For Review questions are included in the TWE.

Testing and Evaluation

Tests for each chapter are included in this TWE. Each test is weighted on a one-hundred-point scoring system. There are a combination of true/false, matching, fill in the blank, short answer, and essay questions. Answers for the tests are included in the TWE; the tests, starting on page 291 of the TWE, can also be accessed online at www.avemariapress.com. The testing material can also be supplemented by repeating the Review Questions from each main chapter section for a particular unit. These questions are organized in units in the Test Question Bank, also found online at www.avemariapress.com.

Theology courses in Catholic high schools are part of a rigorous curriculum that is mostly part of a college preparatory track. Evaluation and grades are important to students and teachers alike. They help communicate to students the seriousness of the course. Without testing and other means of evaluation to hold both students and teachers accountable, students especially will take the message that the four-year theology curriculum is less important than curricula for other fields of study.

The Chapter Tests included in the TWE, as well as ones that you will create yourself, offer one means of evaluation. (The Chapter Tests may be redesigned and adapted to fit material you have added or deleted from the study of each chapter.) Besides testing, other ways to judge the effectiveness of your teaching and student learning include observing student attention in class; participation in class discussions; the quality of student questions and responses; journal entries; fidelity to homework assignments; the gathering, reporting, and oral presentation of research; participation in service projects; cooperation with you and fellow students; participation in prayer; personal interviews with each student; and informal interaction.

Theology courses teach to the cognitive ("head" knowledge), affective ("heart" knowledge), and behavioral ("hands" or action knowledge) domains. Student performance in all these areas should be reflected in the grade you assign for the course.

Assigning grades is a key way to emphasize the importance of this course. However, grades should never be used to manipulate, control, or intimidate students. In Christian charity and justice, many opportunities should be given for students to do well. Understanding of cognitive content should not be the exclusive criterion for grades. Rewarding students for effort, participation, and cooperation helps create a loving and just classroom.

Additional Teaching Approaches

There are many different kinds of assignments that can help you to bring variety to a course on Jesus and Sacred Scripture. Some suggestions are listed below:

- *Article reading* Consider assigning magazine articles that are related to each topic, including those from national and worldwide news magazines. Popular magazines like *Catholic Digest*, *St. Anthony Messenger*, *Liguorian*, *America*, and *U.S. Catholic* also have articles pertinent to the topics discussed in the text. As part of the reading assignment, have your students write a summary and evaluation of the article and report on it to the class.
- *Small- and large-group discussions* Discussion builds Christian community in the classroom and often leads to faith-sharing among students. For Reflection suggestions can initiate this type of sharing. After small groups have discussed a topic, call on one person from each group to summarize the major points of the discussion for the entire class.
- *Faith sharing* Evangelization and Christian witness is a central part of this course and curriculum with the objective of stirring students to a relationship with Jesus beyond providing information about him.

- *Guest speakers* Well in advance, arrange for speakers who may also provide Christian witness and testimony about the Lord, as well as speakers who can speak on the academic topics of the course, including Scripture study, beliefs about Jesus, means for Christian discipleship, and vocation. Make sure the presentation is orthodox in its Catholic presentation.
- *Internet* There are many links to relevant websites both in the Student Text and in the TWE. You can also offer suggestions for Internet searches on particular topics or for specific assignments.
- *Journal keeping* Students can collect many of their written reflections in a journal separate from their class notebook. Journal writing can also be a helpful way to pray. Choose some journal assignments to collect and read for a grade. Allow other assignments to be private, though you can glance at the page to make sure the students wrote for the private assignments. The For Reflection panels offer regular suggestions for journal entries.
- *Prayer* Besides the specific prayer opportunities listed at the end of each unit, you can add to the course's prayer by using the Scripture quotations that begin each chapter as well as other prayer ideas offered in the TWE.
- *Text reading and chapter summary* Throughout the course, students will be instructed to read the Student Text, usually as a homework assignment. It is preferable for material to be read prior to its being discussed. Students should be instructed as to how to note the most important points in a text section and to highlight those points for later study. The Review Questions at the end of each main section provide a source for testing and review. They can be assigned as homework or reserved for a closed-book quiz. The Main Ideas bullet points provide a way to review the material for the Chapter Tests.

Also note the multiple intelligences learning styles listed below and their relationship to the Ongoing Assignments in each chapter as well as other approaches to learning that take place inside and outside of the classroom.

Projects and Assignments Using Multiple Intelligences Learning Styles

Multiple intelligences is a term used to describe the ways that people learn. Developed by Howard Gardner, a professor at the Harvard School of Education, the multiple intelligences allow eight ways for a student to learn that fit his or her preferred learning style. The eight learning styles with sample activities related to each are:

- Bodily/Kinesthetic (dance, gesture, movement, drama, clowning, mime, puppetry)
- Interpersonal/Relational (games, competitions, discussions)
- Intrapersonal/Introspective (reflection questions, prayer, journal writing)
- Logical/Mathematical (games, research, constructing scale models)
- Musical/Rhythmic (singing, music, raps, poetry)
- Naturalist (architecture, photography)
- Verbal/Linguistic (oral presentations)
- Visual/Spatial (art projects, working with textiles)

Though people learn using all these different styles, each person has preferred ways of acquiring and processing information. The best learning takes places when teaching methods offer processes, assignments, and projects for all eight learning styles with opportunities for students to access their preferred learning style and to proceed from their chosen strengths.

This section offers a brief description of Gardner's eight multiple intelligences and information about which methods students who learn in each of these styles prefer.

Bodily/Kinesthetic Intelligence

Bodily/Kinesthetic Intelligence involves the capacity to use one's whole body to express ideas and feelings. It specifically involves using one's hands to create things or to skillfully manipulate objects. A concrete way to think of people who learn in this style is that they must be active and engaged in a "learning-by-doing" assignment or project. Methods include:

- developing and performing role plays
- participating in a theater arts performance
- creating and/or demonstrating a use of a relevant tool, instrument, or utensil
- exercising or competing in athletics

Interpersonal/Relational Intelligence

This intelligence involves the ability to perceive and appreciate the feelings, moods, intentions, and motivations of other people. These types of learners flourish working in groups, teams, or with a partner. Learning methods include:

- brainstorming ideas
- playing cooperative games
- dialoguing with others
- working on a group project

Intrapersonal/Introspective Intelligence

Intrapersonal/Introspective Intelligence is the ability to base one's actions on self-understanding. Being in touch with one's dreams, feelings, moods, intentions, motivations, and spirituality is a key aspect of this intelligence. People who learn best in this intelligence usually prefer to work alone on self-directed assignments. Examples of learning methods are:

- writing reports or research papers
- keeping a journal
- explaining the personal connection of some given information
- identifying with characters in a story

Logical/Mathematical Intelligence

Logical/Mathematical Intelligence includes the skill to work well with numbers and to use reason to solve problems. Persons who learn well in this style are adept at categorizing and exploring relationships within a set of data. They tend to find it difficult to function in an environment that is chaotic or one in which the goals are not clearly defined. Methods that work well in this learning style are:

- categorizing names, places, and events
- outlining bodies of material
- exploring patterns and relationships
- problem solving

Musical/Rhythmic Intelligence

The ability to distinguish rhythm, pitch, and melody is a characteristic of this intelligence. People who prefer to learn in this style often express themselves in musical forms. They enjoy being surrounded by sound and rhythm and understand these as learning tools. Some methods preferred by learners in this style are:

- making and playing instruments
- setting stories to music
- creating or performing in a musical
- writing new lyrics for familiar tunes

Naturalist Intelligence

A person with a Naturalist Intelligence learning style is at home in the natural environment. He or she appreciates the joys of nature and is comfortable raising and caring for plants and animals. This person would also enjoy events in the lines of camping, hiking, and many other outdoor activities. A person with a preference for learning in the Naturalist Intelligence learning style appreciates methods like:

- experimenting in a lab setting
- classifying elements in the natural world
- "digging" or any simulation of an archaeological experience
- demonstrating proper procedure and care for gardens or animals

Verbal/Linguistic Intelligence

Verbal/Linguistic Intelligence involves aptitude with both the spoken and written word. A person who learns best with this intelligence appreciates being able to see things in print, hear spoken words, and say things aloud. Memorization is also a key learning method. Other methods preferred by this type of learner are:

- debating
- reading and summarizing the material
- memorizing and repeating many facts
- writing essays

Visual/Spatial Intelligence

This intelligence caters to people who learn by visualizing and dreaming about concepts and ideas. Learners in this style incorporate both sight and mental images. Whereas printed materials may frustrate these learners, visuals in the form of charts, pictures, graphs, and maps help them to grasp a topic. Other methods that work well for these learners include:

- drawing, painting, and sculpting
- creating collages, posters, and murals
- designing maps and graphs
- producing videos

Scheduling the Course

Jesus Christ: Source of Our Salvation is primarily intended as a one-semester course (sixteen weeks), but it could be adapted to fit a shorter unit. In a school setting, the course is based on coverage of three to five lessons per week. These daily lessons are forty to sixty minutes in length. There are four to seven lessons provided for each chapter. This includes one chapter review lesson and one period reserved for the administration of a chapter test. Suggestions within some lesson plans are made for utilizing more than one class period.

The TWE has organized the material into lessons lasting approximately one hour. This means it is possible to cover most lessons over the course of one to two class meetings.

Several of the lessons in the TWE offer chances for enrichment, including media projects, role plays, discussions, and short films. Using or removing these suggestions will impact the number of periods necessary to cover a chapter.

No matter the given number of days allotted for chapter coverage, it is absolutely necessary to assign chapter reading to the students prior to the material being addressed in class. There is an expectation that many of the other assignments (e.g., For Review questions, For Reflection, Ongoing Assignments) will also be assigned as homework.

Chapter 1: God's Good Creation: The Beginning of Salvation History

Introduction

In the beginning, God.

—**Genesis 1:1**

Creation is the foundation of our Salvation. Stop for a moment to think about that. Salvation was never a divine addendum inserted into our history by a munificent deity, after a rather egregious human whoop. No, Salvation was always the driving force in the divine scheme. From *the beginning*, God was plotting for us a course to Salvation, a course that would find its fulfillment in the Life, Death, and Resurrection of the One we call "Savior," Jesus the Christ; and its finale in our welcome into eternal life with God. Because our road to Salvation begins at the beginning, this study of Jesus the Savior begins there, too.

The first chapter begins with a story about compassion and goes on to draw from the students' understanding of what compassion means to them. They recall how others have acted with compassion toward them and how they have acted compassionately toward others. Formulating their own definition of compassion prepares them to meet the compassionate God of creation who fashions all things out of love. As in the first two volumes of our study of Jesus, this volume goes on to involve the students in questioning and striving to understand who and whose we are. It leads them to recognize that in searching for truth, they are involved in a holy act. And yet, God is still beyond our reach. God must bend. God must reach out to us. And God does just that and in a way we understand best: in a person, the person of Jesus, God-with-us. To appreciate fully the person, the gift, and the Salvation that is Jesus, the students look to the beginning, where our Salvation began.

The students examine the formation of the Bible—God's self-revelation to us. They begin by discovering how to identify literary forms of the Old Testament, the human biblical authors' intent, and what God wanted to reveal. Focusing on the structure and composition of the Pentateuch—the first five books of the Bible—students discover how it was composed in stages and was derived from four major sources.

The students discover that the first creation story is drawn from ancient myths and tells the truth about God in concrete ways. The creation story is not a scientific rendering of creation but a poetic declaration that all things come from the hand of a God who is one, compassionate, and good. Even more, the story also makes it abundantly clear that all creation is good.

In the second creation story, the students discover the intimate relationship between God and his creation before the Fall. It likewise speaks of the intimacy between men and women, their Original Holiness and Original Justice, their equality, and their summons by God to be the compassionate stewards of all of creation. Finally, the students look at the theme of creation, which, like some golden thread, winds itself through the warp and weave of the tapestry of theology and Scripture.

Advance Preparations

Prepare or have on hand:

For Lesson 1

- Blank sheets of paper
- Copies of Chapter 1, Handout 1, "Contemplating Compassion"
- A variety of art supplies

Chapter Objectives

To help the students:

- recognize that from the beginning God has been—and remains—a God of compassion.
- appreciate that the Paschal Mystery is the zenith of God's compassion for us.
- appreciate the role of reason in finding God.
- recognize the reasons for Revelation.
- learn the meaning and elements of the Deposit of Faith.
- understand how to approach and read the Scriptures.
- explain how the first five books of the Bible developed.
- recognize the *religious* truths revealed in the creation stories of Genesis.
- explore the theme of creation in theology and Scripture.

- Bibles
- A digital camera (optional)

For Lesson 2

- Bibles
- Copies of Chapter 1, Handout 2, "Why O Why O Why-O?"
- Copies of the quotation from the *Dogmatic Constitution on Divine Revelation*, 9 (optional)

For Lesson 3

- Bibles

For Lesson 4

- Bibles
- Copies of Chapter 1, Handout 3, "Sources of the Pentateuch"

For Lesson 5

- Bibles
- Lyrics and music or recordings and a player for the following or similar hymns, all of which are available at GIA:
    - "How Great Thou Art"
    - "All Things Bright and Beautiful"
    - "The Works of the Lord Are Created in Wisdom"
    - "Creator of the Stars of Night"
    - "How Wonderful the Three-in-One"
    - "When the King Shall Come"

For the Chapter 1 Review Lesson

- Equipment necessary for students to make PowerPoint® presentations
- Lyrics and music or a recording and a player for "Canticle of the Sun" by Marty Haugen (GIA) (optional)

For the Chapter 1 Test Lesson

- Copies of the Chapter 1 Test (starting on page 291 of the TWE and also online at www.avemariapress.com)

Chapter 1 Handouts

- Handout 1, Contemplating Compassion—The students define compassion.
- Handout 2, Why O Why O Why-O?—The students discuss and ask "Why?"
- Handout 3, Sources of the Pentateuch—The students study the sources of the Pentateuch.

Chapter 1: God's Good Creation: The Beginning of Salvation History—Lesson 1

Bell Ringers

- Begin this first session by warmly welcoming the students. Introduce yourself and be ready to explain classroom guidelines and to answer any initial questions the students might have. Distribute copies of the student text and allow the class a few moments to examine it. Ask the students to predict what topics they will learn about in the course. Discuss their predictions (or write them on the board).
- If the students do not know one another, consider using the following introductory activity:
  - Pass out sheets of paper.
  - Have the students draw a framework of squares similar to that of a tic-tac-toe diagram, but with the same number of squares as there are students.
  - Then invite the students to mill around the room, interviewing each classmate in turn. Tell them that when they are being interviewed, they should share their name plus something about themselves, different with each interviewer, and that others may not know. For example, "My name is Emma Wecht, and I have a pet salamander."
  - Direct the interviewer to write the interviewed person's name and shared information in one of the squares and then move on to interview someone else. When finished, everyone will have a different name and something interesting written in each square on their papers.
  - Gather the class together and ask for a volunteer to be the focus of attention. Have other students share, in turn, what they learned about the volunteer. Continue until everyone has been the focus of attention.
- Introduce this session's main topic by writing the word **compassion** on the board. Then, to help the students discover what they already know about compassion, have them brainstorm the term. List ideas on the board. Afterward, distribute copies of Chapter 1, Handout 1, "Contemplating Compassion." Give the students a moment to read over the quotations on compassion. Use a show of hands to vote on which quotation best illustrates the meaning of compassion for them.

Model of Compassion

Professional golfer Roberto De Vicenzo is perhaps best known for a mistake he made in signing a scorecard. In the final round of the 1968 Masters Tournament De Vicenzo signed an incorrect scorecard that had been prepared for him by his caddie. The scorecard incorrectly stated that he made a par on the seventeenth hole when, in fact, he birdied it, that is, shot one under par on the hole. His birdie would have tied him with the eventual champion, Bob Goalby. However, under the Rules of Golf, when a player signs an incorrect scorecard, the score stands. Due to this error, De Vicenzo came in second. A lesser man would have been embittered by this mistake and the unbending rules of golf, but not Roberto De Vicenzo. He accepted full responsibility for not checking the accuracy of his scorecard before signing it. He simply said, "What a stupid I am."

Roberto De Vicenzo continued his career by playing superb golf. Worldwide, he won a remarkable 230 tournaments, including the prestigious British Open. Along the way, he garnered many honors including the Bob Jones Award for distinguished sportsmanship in golf.

The mark of his character shines forth in an incident that happened late in his career. As De Vicenzo left the clubhouse after winning another tournament, a young woman approached him and congratulated him on his victory. She then began to cry and tell him that she was jobless and had a baby who was near death. She said that she could not afford a doctor or hospital bills. De Vicenzo paused a moment and then asked, "May I help your little girl?" He endorsed his winning check, handed it to the woman, and wished her and her sick baby well.

A week later, a Professional Golfers' Association official told De Vicenzo that the lady in the parking lot had defrauded him. She was childless and told her sad story to fleece him out of his money. De Vicenzo asked the official, "You mean there is no dying baby?" The golf official said, "That's right." De Vicenzo face lit up with a huge smile, "Well, that's the best news I've heard all year."

Roberto De Vicenzo's relief and compassion in the face of an evil that had befallen him reminds

The Goodness of Creation

Genesis 1–3 reveals important theological truths about the origins of creation, humans, and sin. Among these truths is that God creates a good and orderly world (Gn 1:31). This includes the natural world: the sky and sun, the moon and the stars; lakes and rivers, waterfalls and rainbows; trees and flowers, fields and mountains; all kinds of animals; and human beings most of all. "God willed creation as a gift addressed to man, an inheritance for and entrusted to him" (*CCC*, 299). Many times the Church has had to defend God's gift of creation, including that of physical creation. Related to the teaching of the goodness of creation, complete the following assignment and reflection.

Assignment

With a digital camera, take five photos that represent the goodness of creation. Print out your favorite photo and adhere it in your journal. Write a paragraph explaining how this picture makes you feel.

Reflection

- How happy are you with the way that God made you?
- What is the best thing about you?
- If Jesus were to tell someone about you, what might he say?

Lesson 1 Objectives

The students will:

- discuss the meaning of compassion.
- define compassion.
- create symbols of compassion.
- examine a model of compassion.
- recognize that from the beginning God has been—and remains—a God of compassion.
- recognize that the Paschal Mystery is the zenith of God's compassion for us.

Lesson 1 Preview

In this first lesson, the students learn what it means to be a person of compassion. They discover how God has been compassionately concerned for them since the beginning and how God's compassion culminated in the flesh of Jesus and his saving Paschal Mystery.

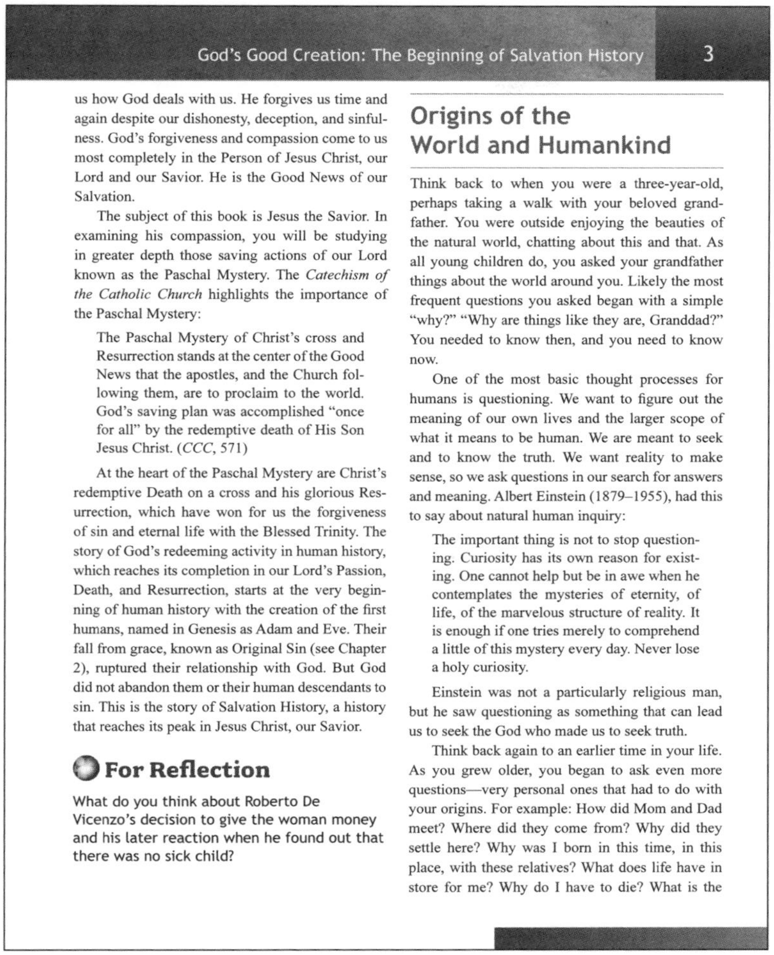

us how God deals with us. He forgives us time and again despite our dishonesty, deception, and sinfulness. God's forgiveness and compassion come to us most completely in the Person of Jesus Christ, our Lord and our Savior. He is the Good News of our Salvation.

The subject of this book is Jesus the Savior. In examining his compassion, you will be studying in greater depth those saving actions of our Lord known as the Paschal Mystery. The *Catechism of the Catholic Church* highlights the importance of the Paschal Mystery:

> The Paschal Mystery of Christ's cross and Resurrection stands at the center of the Good News that the apostles, and the Church following them, are to proclaim to the world. God's saving plan was accomplished "once for all" by the redemptive death of His Son Jesus Christ. (*CCC*, 571)

At the heart of the Paschal Mystery are Christ's redemptive Death on a cross and his glorious Resurrection, which have won for us the forgiveness of sin and eternal life with the Blessed Trinity. The story of God's redeeming activity in human history, which reaches its completion in our Lord's Passion, Death, and Resurrection, starts at the very beginning of human history with the creation of the first humans, named in Genesis as Adam and Eve. Their fall from grace, known as Original Sin (see Chapter 2), ruptured their relationship with God. But God did not abandon them or their human descendants to sin. This is the story of Salvation History, a history that reaches its peak in Jesus Christ, our Savior.

For Reflection

What do you think about Roberto De Vicenzo's decision to give the woman money and his later reaction when he found out that there was no sick child?

Origins of the World and Humankind

Think back to when you were a three-year-old, perhaps taking a walk with your beloved grandfather. You were outside enjoying the beauties of the natural world, chatting about this and that. As all young children do, you asked your grandfather things about the world around you. Likely the most frequent questions you asked began with a simple "why?" "Why are things like they are, Granddad?" You needed to know then, and you need to know now.

One of the most basic thought processes for humans is questioning. We want to figure out the meaning of our own lives and the larger scope of what it means to be human. We are meant to seek and to know the truth. We want reality to make sense, so we ask questions in our search for answers and meaning. Albert Einstein (1879–1955), had this to say about natural human inquiry:

> The important thing is not to stop questioning. Curiosity has its own reason for existing. One cannot help but be in awe when he contemplates the mysteries of eternity, of life, of the marvelous structure of reality. It is enough if one tries merely to comprehend a little of this mystery every day. Never lose a holy curiosity.

Einstein was not a particularly religious man, but he saw questioning as something that can lead us to seek the God who made us to seek truth.

Think back again to an earlier time in your life. As you grew older, you began to ask even more questions—very personal ones that had to do with your origins. For example: How did Mom and Dad meet? Where did they come from? Why did they settle here? Why was I born in this time, in this place, with these relatives? What does life have in store for me? Why do I have to die? What is the

- Draw on the quotations and the brainstorming ideas to help the students develop their own definition of compassion. As the students work to arrive at a definition, encourage them to:
  - think about what compassion might sound, feel, smell, and look like;
  - consider whether their definition would explain the meaning of compassion to a visitor from another planet;
  - recognize that compassion is more than an emotion, and incorporate that recognition in their definition.

  Finally, have the students write the definition in the space provided on Handout 1.

Teaching Approaches

Model of Compassion (pages 2-3)

- Have the students read (or reread) the story of the golfer Roberto De Vicenzo (pages 2–3). Afterward, ask how De Vicenzo showed compassion *according to their definition.*
- Before moving on, point out that De Vicenzo's compassion enabled him to detach himself from what we might think someone like him would need: in the first instance, fame; in the second instance, fortune. His compassion toward others allowed him to realize that neither fame nor fortune defined him as a person.

Lesson 1 Homework

1. Make sure the students have a notebook for use as a journal for this course. Explain that they will use their journals for self-reflection, to help them analyze and evaluate what they learn, to develop writing skills, and to organize and retain key ideas. Have the students complete the following activity for their next session:
   - a description of a time someone showed them compassion
   - a description of a time they showed compassion to someone
   - a brief description of a person—living or dead—who they believe to be a person of compassion
2. Direct the students to read "Origins of the World and Humankind" (pages 3–9) in preparation for their next lesson.
3. Have the students turn to Ongoing Assignments on page 25. Point out that they are to choose any three of the listed assignments to complete prior to the conclusion of this chapter. (*Note*: Consider grading the students' work based on the particular assignment's degree of difficulty. In any case, encourage the students to choose and begin working on their assignments ASAP.)

Background Information

For some wonderful insights into the meaning of compassion, read and share the book *Compassion: A Reflection on the Christian Life* by Henri Nouwen, Donald P. McNeill, and Douglas A. Morrison, available from Doubleday. The authors begin by examining the nature and mission of Christ and what he reveals about the Father. Next, they look deeply into community to discover the ways of living the compassionate life. Finally, the authors set out a way to compassion through patience, prayer, and action.

- Take a few moments to discuss compassion as it relates to teenagers. Use questions like the following to get the ball rolling:
  - For the most part, do you think teenagers are compassionate or are they mostly self-absorbed? Give reasons (examples) for your answer.
  - How do you feel when others demonstrate compassion toward you?
  - How do you feel when you are compassionate toward others?
  - To what extent would you inconvenience yourself for another person?
  - Roberto De Vicenzo let go of fame and fortune in order to act with compassion. What would you be willing to let go in order to act with compassion toward another? (e.g., money, social position, reputation, etc.)
- Have the students work individually to create a symbol of compassion. Explain that they may draw a picture or create a collage or write a poem or compose a song/rap (using an existing melody if they wish) or choreograph and present a dance. Allow ample time for them to create their symbols and then to present them to the class.

philosophy
The investigation of truths and principles using human reason.

pantheism
The belief in opposition to Christian doctrine, that God and nature are one and the same.

polytheism
The belief, in opposition to Christian doctrine, that there are many gods.

Redemption
A word that literally means "ransom." Jesus' Death is ransom that defeated the powers of evil.

Salvation History
The story of God's saving actions in human history.

Divine Revelation
The way God communicates knowledge of himself to humankind, a self-communication realized by his actions and words over time, must fully by his sending us his divine Son, Jesus Christ.

meaning of life—of my life? Where did everything come from?

You are in good company if you ask questions like these because you are indeed engaged in a holy activity—that of thinking and searching for truth. Through the ages, men and women have tried to make sense out of reality, to seek meaning in the world around them. This helps explain the existence of **philosophy**, the name for the systems of thought that try to provide rational explanations of why things are the way they are and how we know and should conduct our lives. Most of these systems of thought have concluded that behind the life we see and experience there must be a source of all life—something or someone greater than we are who brought life into existence and sustains it. When asked whether he believed in God or not, Albert Einstein replied,

> I am not an atheist. . . . We are like a little child entering a huge library filled with books in many languages. The child knows someone must have written those books. It does not know how. It does not understand the languages in which they are written. The child dimly suspects a mysterious order in the arrangement of the books but doesn't know what it is. That, it seems to me, is the attitude of even the most intelligent human being toward God. We see the universe marvelously arranged and obeying certain laws but only dimly understand those laws.

Down through the centuries, various religions and cultures have tried to discern the origin of the world and all creation. Using only human reason, different religions have come up with many diverse, and often conflicting, theories. For example, Hinduism holds that the universe is the same as the force that created it. This is known as **pantheism**, the religious belief that the material world and God are one and the same. Other ancient religions (e.g., Zoroastrianism) held that there are two equal spirits in the universe, one evil and the other good, who are constantly engaged in a cosmic struggle. Still other religions are based in **polytheism**, that is, they believe there are many gods who are responsible for the creation of the world.

Although by studying his works by the natural light of human reason we can come to know the one true

For Enrichment

Have the students use the computer to examine the "Charter for Compassion" at www.charterforcompassion.org/share/about. The Charter is the work of the Council of Conscience, a multi-faith, multi-national group of religious thinkers and leaders. To develop the "Charter for Compassion," they gathered from people of every nation, contributions on the meaning and importance of compassion.

The Charter affirms that:

- all religions and spiritual and ethical traditions celebrate compassion.
- compassion calls us to treat others as we wish to be treated (i.e., the Golden Rule).
- it is necessary for all people to refrain from inflicting pain either physically or emotionally.
- compassion should be restored to the center of morality and religion.

Extending the Lesson

Direct the students to the Primary Source Quotations section on page 25. Have them read the quotation from St. Simeon the New Theologian. Then, give the students copies of the following words of St. Teresa of Avila, or write them on the board:

> **Christ has no body on earth but yours, no hands but yours, no feet but yours. Yours are the eyes through which Christ's compassion for the world is to look out; yours are the feet with which he is to go about doing good; and yours are the hands with which he is to bless us now.**

Invite the students to discuss the challenge St. Simeon and Teresa set before us. Have the students name *specific* ways they can act as Christ's compassionate eyes, hands, and feet in their home, school, parish, neighborhood, city, and world.

God with certainty, it is not the whole story, because human reason is limited. Various philosophies based on human reason and other religions are limited too. Catholics respect the beliefs of these other religions about God and the origins of the world. The Church's perspective on these life questions is unique and unequaled. Catholics and other Christians believe that the Divine Author is a loving Father who has sent his only Son to live among us, to teach us about the Father, to show us how to live, and to redeem us so that we can one day go to a blessed home of happiness and joy in Heaven. The Second Vatican *Council's Declaration on the Relation of the Church to Non-Christian Religions* taught:

> The Catholic Church rejects nothing that is true and holy in these religions. She regards with sincere reverence those ways of conduct and of life, those precepts and teachings which, though differing in many aspects from the ones she holds and sets forth, nonetheless often reflect a ray of that Truth which enlightens all men. Indeed, she proclaims, and ever must proclaim Christ "the way, the truth, and the life" (John 14:6), in whom men may find the fullness of religious life, in whom God has reconciled all things to Himself. (*Nostra Aetate,* No. 2)

While the Church does respect other religions, she has been entrusted with the truth of the Gospel of Jesus Christ. She must share with others the Good News that he is the "way, the truth, and the life." St. Ambrose (340–397) explained the Gospel message this way:

> When we speak about wisdom, we are speaking of Christ. When we speak about virtue, we are speaking of Christ. When we speak about justice, we are speaking of Christ. When we speak about peace, we are speaking of Christ. When we speak about truth and life and Redemption, we are speaking of Christ.

St. Ambrose understood that all that is important in life is the Person of Jesus Christ. This text focuses especially on Ambrose's last point—**Redemption**. Jesus is our Redeemer. He is the one who will make it possible for us share in God's own life:

> It pleased God, in his goodness and wisdom, to reveal himself and to make known the mystery of his will. His will was that men should have access to the Father, through Christ, the Word made flesh, in the holy Spirit, and thus become sharers in the divine nature. (*CCC,* 51, quoting the *Dogmatic Constitution on Divine Revelation,* 2)

Understanding Divine Revelation

Out of God's infinite mercy and love, he stepped into human history to disclose who he really is. He did this through the events of **Salvation History**, that is, the account (of both deeds and words) of God's saving activity for humankind. In other words, God *revealed* himself to the world.

Lesson 2 Objectives

The students will:

- appreciate the need to ask "Why?"
- understand how humankind has sought answers to life's crucial questions, including the origin of the world and humankind.
- discover how reason can lead us to an understanding of God.
- recognize that God had to reveal himself.
- appreciate Christianity's unique take on Revelation.
- recognize that we know what God has revealed through the Deposit of Faith.
- understand the meaning and elements of the Deposit of Faith.
- appreciate that the Magisterium of the Church is responsible for preserving and handing on the Deposit of Faith.

- Invite the students to open their Bibles to 2 Corinthians 1:3. Ask one of the students to read the verse aloud: (*"Blessed be the God and Father of our Lord Jesus Christ, the Father of compassion and God of all encouragement."*) Note how God is described as a parent—a loving, encouraging father who is compassionate toward his children. To say God is compassionate is to say that God is *one with us, sympathetic toward us,* and *lovingly acts on our behalf.*
- Go on to write the term **Paschal Mystery** on the board. Ask the students what it means (*Jesus' Passion, Death, Resurrection, and Ascension*). Tell the students that the Paschal Mystery is the way God is compassionate toward us. Reinforce this theme by having the students read the quotation from St. Leo the Great in the Primary Source Quotations section on page 25. Go on to point out that while the divine compassion culminated in Christ's Paschal Mystery, it was never withheld from humankind. From the dawn of creation, God has been with us, has been one with us, and has acted with compassion on our behalf.
- Call attention to the opening activity, "The Goodness of Creation" (page 2). Read through it with the students. Explain that the students are to complete the activity as a homework assignment. (*Note:* Since it is likely that not every student may have access to a digital camera, either make one available or allow the students to find a magazine photo that speaks to creation's goodness.)

Chapter 1: God's Good Creation: The Beginning of Salvation History—Lesson 2

Bell Ringers

- Ask three or four students to share their picture representing the goodness of creation, their explanation of how the picture makes them feel, and their responses to the three Reflection questions (see page 2). Afterward, collect all the students' pictures and paragraphs.
- Call on different students to share how they described:
    - a time someone showed them compassion;
    - a time they showed compassion to someone;
    - a person—living or dead—who they believe to be a person of compassion.

Teaching Approaches

Origins of the World and Humankind (pages 3-9)

- Introduce this lesson by distributing copies of Chapter 1, Handout 2, "Why O Why O Why-O?" Have the students read the funny but facetious "Why?" questions. Then invite them to add their own humorous questions to the list.
- Call attention to the quotation from Bernard Baruch on the handout. Then ask the students why it is so important for us to ask "Why?"
- Write the word **philosophy** on the board. Explain that the word comes from the Greek, meaning lover (*philos*) of wisdom (*sophia*). Note the definition of philosophy in the text (*the investigation of truths and principles using human reason*).
- Write the following questions on the board:
  - **What's going on?**
  - **Why am I here?**
  - **Where am I going?**
  - **Which is the best way to go?**
  - **How should I be living?**
- Tell the students that these are some basic questions that philosophers seek to answer. Note too, that they are also questions that all human beings eventually come to ask. Explain that our asking "Why?" is, as Einstein said, "a holy curiosity"—an inquisitiveness that can be satisfied completely only by a holy answer.
- Have the students turn to the For Reflection section on page 9. As a class, discuss the two questions. Before moving on, invite the students to write their biggest "Why?" question in the space provided on Handout 2. Ask students to share their questions with the class. (*Note:* Don't be concerned about providing answers to the students' questions. Rather, simply encourage the questions. Likewise assure the students that there are no stupid questions in this class. Challenge them to have inquiring minds.)
- Point out that in humanity's search for answers regarding the origin of all things, people of different religions have arrived at different theories. Ask the students to describe *pantheism* and *polytheism*. Ask how these theories differ from Catholic belief.
- Go on to stress that the Catholic faith realizes that God is a God beyond reason. While our reason can lead us to God, it cannot encompass God. Write the following quotation from St. Augustine on the board:

6 Jesus Christ: Source of Our Salvation

Deposit of Faith
"The heritage of faith contained in Sacred Scripture and Tradition, handed on in the Church from the time of the Apostles, from which the Magisterium draws all that it proposes for belief as being divinely revealed" (*CCC*, Glossary).

Sacred Tradition
The living transmission of the Church's Gospel message found in the Church's teaching, life, and worship. It is faithfully preserved, handed on, and interpreted by the Church's Magisterium.

Sacred Scripture
The inspired Word of God; the written record of God's Revelation.

inspiration
The guidance of the Holy Spirit that enabled the human authors to record faithfully, and without error, what God wanted revealed to us for our beliefs.

Magisterium
The official teaching office of the Church. The Lord bestowed the right and the power to teach in his name to Peter and the other Apostles and their successors. The Magisterium is the bishops in communion with the successor of Peter, the Bishop of Rome (Pope).

Recall that **Divine Revelation** is God's free gift of self-communication by which he makes known the mystery of the divine plan. God's divine plan is to communicate his own divine life to the men he freely created, in order to adopt them as his sons in his only-begotten Son. In brief, this is the answer to the ultimate question of why we are here. We are here because God created us to know him, to love him, and to be called in communion with him (*CCC*, 27). Jesus reveals most fully what that communion means: adoption as sons and daughters into the divine family.

How do we know what God has revealed? Divine revelation is contained in a single **Deposit of Faith**, which Christ turned over to the Apostles after his Ascension into Heaven. The Apostles, under the inspiration of the Holy Spirit, handed on this deposit, or "heritage of the faith," to the Church. They did this through their oral preaching and their writings, both done under the inspiration of the Holy Spirit. This is why all generations since the Apostles can hear about God's love for us in Jesus Christ until he returns in glory at the end of time. We find the single Deposit of Faith in Sacred Tradition and Sacred Scripture.

The word *tradition* means "handing on." **Sacred Tradition** is the living transmission or "handing on" from one generation to the next of the Church's Gospel message. **Sacred Scripture**, consisting of the Old and New Testaments, is the written record of Revelation. It is "the speech of God as it is put down in writing under the breath of the Holy Spirit" (*Dogmatic Constitution on Divine Revelation*, No. 9, *CCC*, 81). Jesus Christ is the unique Word of Sacred Scripture, both its starting and ending points. His presence is revealed in human words of both the Old Testament and New Testament. The Scriptures tell us that the Word of God became man and saved us from sin.

We can rely on the truth of Sacred Scripture because it is inspired. God used the human authors and their unique talents to put into writing exactly what he wanted written, and nothing more. Likewise, we can only understand the meaning of Scripture when it is "read and interpreted in the light of the same Spirit by whom it was written" (*CCC*, 111, quoting *Dei Verbum*, 12 § 3). This is the meaning of **inspiration**.

> The books of the Scripture firmly, faithfully, and without error teach that truth which God, for the sake of our salvation, wished to see confided in Sacred Scriptures. (*Dogmatic Constitution on Divine Revelation*, No. 11, *CCC*, 107)

When Christ entrusted the Deposit of Faith to the Apostles, he authorized them to interpret God's Word authentically. This authority keeps the Church free from error and guarantees that Christ's Gospel is passed down authentically to future generations. Jesus gave this teaching authority to the Apostles' successors—the Bishop of Rome (the pope) and the bishops in communion with him.

Lesson 2 Preview

This lesson helps the students appreciate that they are part of a long history of Salvation that is marked by God's loving care and saving activity. The students also discover that that divine revelation in the Deposit of Faith has been carefully preserved and handed on by the Church (Magisterium) through the Sacred Scriptures and Sacred Tradition.

Lesson 2 Homework

1. Direct the students to respond in their journals to the nine For Review questions on page 8.
2. Direct the students to read "How Scripture Is Interpreted" (pages 9–12) in preparation for their next lesson.
3. Remind the students to continue work on their chosen Ongoing Assignments (page 25).

"God is not what you imagine or what you think you understand. If you understand you have failed." Tell the students that Augustine is reminding us that a God small enough to fit our minds is too small. God is more than our reason can hold.

- Point out and read aloud the following sentence (from page 5 in the text):

  > *Catholics and other Christians believe that the Divine Author is a loving Father who has sent his only Son to live among us, to teach us about the Father, to show us how to live, and to redeem us so that we can one day go to a blessed home of happiness and joy in Heaven.*

- Reinforce this point by having the students turn to the quotation by St. Bonaventure in the Primary Source Quotations section on page 25. Remind the students that Jesus is God's compassion for us in the flesh, and that Jesus' Paschal Mystery, more than any philosophy, answers the question why we are here—to know, love, and serve God in this world and, as St. Bonaventure says, to *delight* in him in the next.
- Draw attention to the text section "Understanding Divine Revelation" (pages 5–9). Begin by pointing out the definition of Divine Revelation (God's self-communication which helps us understand God's plan for us). Stress that it is pure gift. Likewise, call attention to the term "Salvation History." Explain that it refers to the story of God's saving presence and activity on our behalf.
- Write the term **Deposit of Faith** on the board. Draw on material in the text to explain that the term refers to the body of truths Jesus handed to us through the Apostles. Go on to explain that the Deposit of Faith is contained in Sacred Tradition and Sacred Scripture. Note the definitions of both terms in the text (page 6).
- Briefly explain each term:
  - *Sacred Tradition*: Tell the students that after Jesus' Resurrection and Ascension, the Apostles began handing on the faith through preaching, teaching, and shared worship.
  - *Sacred Scripture*: As time passed, Christ's teachings were preserved by the Apostles and eventually written down. Along with the books of the Old Testament, these writings are the written record of Revelation.
- Point out the term "inspiration" on page 6. Ask a volunteer to read aloud the quotation from the *Dogmatic Constitution on Divine Revelation.* Ask the students

Faithful Disciple

ST. IRENAEUS OF LYONS

The life of the Christian is essentially knowing Jesus Christ. It is also in being known yourself. No one is intended to live life in isolation. You must both know Christ and his Father and be known by them. These essential insights of our faith were gleaned by St. Irenaeus, a Father and Doctor of the Church, who was bishop of Lyons in Asia Minor in the late second century.

Irenaeus was born around the year 125 in a seaside province in Asia Minor. He likely had the chance to hear the Gospel directly from one of the Apostles or their immediate disciples. Irenaeus was ordained a priest and served under the bishop, St. Ponthinus. In 177, Irenaeus was sent to Rome. While he was gone, the Church in Lyons faced severe persecutions. St. Ponthinus and other Church leaders were martyred. Eventually Irenaeus was sent home to replace Ponthinus as bishop.

Irenaeus was left to face another challenge in the region that was affecting the entire Church, the heresy of Gnosticism. This was the name for movements in the second century that claimed secret, revealed knowledge of God had been transmitted to either the Apostles or the leader of a Gnostic sect.

St. Irenaeus answered the Gnostics in his treaty *Against Heresies*. He also highlighted the importance of Church Tradition for arriving at religious truth. He wrote that the source of right teaching and belief resides with the Roman Church because the Church was founded by Jesus and entrusted to St. Peter.

It was in *Against Heresies* that Irenaeus wrote about the glory of God being witnessed in the person who is fully alive:

> The glory of God gives life; those who see God receive life. For this reason God, who cannot be grasped, comprehended or seen, allows himself to be seen, comprehended and grasped by all, that he may give life to those who see and receive him. It is impossible to live without life, and the actualization of life comes from participation in God, while participation in God is to see God and enjoy his goodness.

For Enrichment

When St. Irenaeus said, "The glory of God is man fully alive," he said a mouthful. The saint wanted us to recognize that God is glorified when men and women are fully alive in Christ. Like other early Church Fathers, Irenaeus talks about the "great exchange," how the Son of God became man so that men and women could become sons and daughters of God. To have that life of Christ in us means to be fully alive. As Christ himself reminds us, "I came so that that they might have life, and have it more abundantly" (Jn 10:10). To have the abundant life is to be fully alive in Christ. To live abundantly in Christ is to allow God's grace and power to fill our souls and our lives so that the glory of God shines through us.

to discuss how the unique talents of human authors could be used by God to develop the text. Remind the students that the Scriptures teach *without error* the truth that God wants us to know.

- Finally, draw attention to the term "Magisterium" (page 6). Tell the students that as successors to the Apostles, the pope and bishops have the ministry and possess the authority to teach and ensure the faithful handing on of the Deposit of Faith. Read the following to the students (or make copies):

> Sacred Tradition and Scripture are bound together in a close and reciprocal relationship . . . Scripture is the utterance of God as it is set down in writing under the guidance of God's Spirit; Tradition preserves the Word of God as it was entrusted to the Apostles by Christ our Lord and the Holy Spirit, and transmits it to their successors, so that these in turn, enlightened by the Spirit of truth, may faithfully preserve, expound, and disseminate the Word by their preaching. (*Dogmatic Constitution on Divine Revelation*, 9)

- Summarize the lesson by explaining to the students: (1) God reveals the Deposit of Faith through Scripture and Tradition; (2) the Magisterium preserves,

8 Jesus Christ: Source of Our Salvation

This authority is known as the **Magisterium**. The Holy Spirit guides the pope and bishops so that they can serve the Word of God, listen to it faithfully, preserve it through the ages, and explain it to the Church so that we can live according to Christ's teachings.

The first eleven chapters of Genesis are vital in the story of Salvation History because they reveal important truths about the creation of the world and of humans, of the relationship between males and females, of God's intentions for us, of Original Sin and the fall from grace, and of God's promise of a future Redeemer. This next section focuses on the first two chapters of Genesis. Before Genesis 1–11 are discussed as a whole, it is necessary to first address the figurative, symbolic language used by the authors of Genesis so that we can correctly interpret what religious truths God wants us to learn from this opening book of the Bible—a book that answers many important *why* questions about human existence.

For Review

1. What questions are humans naturally conditioned to ask?
2. What does philosophy attempt to do?
3. Define *pantheism* and *polytheism*.
4. What is unique about the Christian belief about Revelation?
5. Define *Salvation History* and *Divine Revelation*.
6. Briefly state God's divine plan of Salvation for human beings.
7. Define the *Deposit of Faith*.
8. What is the relationship between Sacred Scripture and Sacred Tradition?
9. What special role does the Magisterium play in relationship to the Deposit of Faith?

QUESTIONS AND ANSWERS ABOUT CREATION

- **Why did God create?**
  God did not have to create. He is complete perfection in himself. He created the world to manifest his glory. God did not create to increase his glory, which is impossible, but to show forth and communicate his goodness, truth, and beauty.
- **What does the glory of God mean?**
  "Glory" is the recognition and praise of someone's excellence. Applied to God, it means recognizing God's absolute goodness, love, beauty, power, majesty, holiness, and perfection.
- **Why did God create humans?**
  God created us out to share his love and goodness and "to be his sons through Jesus Christ," that is, to adopt us into the divine family and share his eternal life with us.
- **How do we humans glorify God?**
  St. Irenaeus said, "The glory of God is man fully alive." We are fully alive when we know, love, and serve God; when we offer back to him in thanksgiving all of creation in this world; and when we are raised up to eternal life with him in Heaven. We are truly human when we become other Christs, the perfect Man, the Son of God, who is the perfect image of God.

For Review Answers (page 8)

1. Answers may vary, but they should reflect an understanding that humans ask "Why?" questions—questions that lead to the truth.
2. Philosophy tries to provide rational explanations of why things are the way they are as well as how we should act.
3. Pantheism is the belief that all things are divine—that God and nature are one and the same. Polytheism is the belief that there are numerous deities.
4. Regarding Revelation, Christians believe that God (the Divine Author) is a loving Father who sent his only Son to be one with us, to teach us about the Father, to show us the way to live, and to redeem us and so enable us to live forever with God.
5. Salvation History is the account of God's saving words and acts on our behalf. Divine Revelation is God's gift of self-communication that makes known the mystery of the divine plan.
6. Answers may vary, but should evidence understanding that God made us to know, love, and serve him in this world and to be called into communion with him.
7. The Deposit of Faith is the heritage of faith contained in Sacred Scripture and Tradition, handed on in the Church by the Apostles, and preserved by the Magisterium.
8. Sacred Scripture is the written word of God (Old and New Testaments); Sacred Tradition is the living transmission and interpretation of the gospel message.
9. The role of the Magisterium is to authoritatively interpret the Word of God, to keep the Church free from error in its teachings, and to pass down Christ's Gospel authentically to future generations.

For Reflection

- What questions about the meaning of life do you have? List some steps you can take to find some answers to these questions.
- The typical human cell has forty-six chromosomes. A single human chromosome contains twenty billion bits of information, the equivalent of about three billion letters or five hundred million words. Assume further that there are three hundred words on a page of written text; this would correspond to about two million pages of text on one chromosome! Imagine how rich a library of information goes into making one human being. Discuss one other phenomenon from the natural world that would lead you to believe there is a Creator-God.

How Scripture Is Interpreted

The inclusion of *two* creation stories in the first two chapters of Genesis presents a quandary. You might question why there are two accounts of the same event. You might also wonder how these stories came to be since there was no one around at the time of creation to record them! Similarly, in Genesis 3, we have the story about a serpent (Satan) talking to Eve in the Garden of Eden, tempting her to eat the fruit of a tree. It is certainly valid to ask: could a snake really talk in the Garden?

Reading the Bible with understanding requires us to recognize that it deals with a time, people, and culture that are foreign to us. To interpret it correctly requires that we gather some background information on the text, including being able to distinguish between figurative and symbolic language and what should be taken literally.

The Second Vatican Council offered guidelines on how to interpret Sacred Scripture:

> However, since God speaks in Sacred Scripture through men in human fashion, the interpreter of Sacred Scripture, in order to see clearly what God wanted to communicate to us, should carefully investigate what meaning the sacred writers really intended, and what God wanted to manifest by means of their words.
>
> To search out the intention of the sacred writers, attention should be given, among other things, to "literary forms." For truth is set forth and expressed differently in texts which are variously historical, prophetic, poetic, or of other forms of discourse. The interpreter must investigate what meaning the sacred writer intended to express and actually expressed in particular circumstances by using contemporary literary forms in accordance with the situation of his own time and culture. For the correct understanding of what the sacred author wanted to assert, due attention must be paid to the customary and characteristic styles of feeling, speaking and narrating which prevailed at the time of the sacred writer, and to the patterns men normally employed at that period in their everyday dealings with one another (*Dei Verbum*, 12).

Note the meaning of this teaching of the Second Vatican Council. First, God used humans and human language to communicate his message. Therefore, we must first figure out what the authors of the texts really meant

Lesson 3 Objectives

The students will:

- appreciate that interpreting Scripture correctly entails paying attention both to what the human author wanted to say and to what God wanted to convey.
- investigate various literary forms found in the Bible.

Lesson 3 Preview

In this lesson, the students will investigate the Catholic understanding of the interpretation of the Scriptures. They will discover the dual focus of interpretation and some of the principles necessary for interpreting God's self-revelation in the Scripture.

interprets, and hands it on; and (3) all the faithful have a share in the Deposit—the treasure that is our faith.

- Have the students turn to the text section "Faithful Disciple: St. Irenaeus of Lyons" (page 7). Point out how St. Irenaeus championed both the role of the Magisterium and the critical importance of Sacred Tradition in the quest to discover religious truth.
- Direct attention to the section "Questions and Answers about Creation" (page 8). Suggest that the students review these questions in preparation for reading the stories of Genesis.

Chapter 1: God's Good Creation: The Beginning of Salvation History—Lesson 3

Bell Ringers

- Call on different students to offer their responses to the nine For Review questions on page 8, paying special attention to the final three (answers are on page 22 of this text).
- Continue the review by asking the following:
  - What term do we use to refer to God's action over time on our behalf? (*Salvation History*)
  - What do we call God's self-communication to us? (*Divine Revelation*)
  - What do we call the written record of God's self-communication? (*Sacred Scripture*)
  - What do we call the authority that hands on both Scripture and Tradition, so that we may come to and grow in faith? (*the Magisterium*)

If the students have any further questions or concerns, take time to discuss them as a class.

Teaching Approaches

How Scripture Is Interpreted (pages 9–12)

- Direct students to skim through the creation stories in Genesis 1–3. Instruct them to make a list of the parts of the stories that seem impossible or improbable (e.g., a snake talking). Record the responses on the board. Explain to the students that when we read Scripture, we must first investigate the background information of the text: the author's intention, the literary forms that were used, and the culture within which the story was written.

- Point out how the text (page 10) offers the example of the difference in literary form between a fable and a news story. Then direct the students to turn to For Reflection on page 12. Direct them to choose a familiar fable: the tortoise and the hare, the wolf in sheep's clothing, the ant and the grasshopper, the boy who cried wolf, the fox and grapes, etc. Ask students to write out the important truth for living that the fable conveys. Then have the students rewrite the fable as a news story. Afterward, share stories, inviting the students to comment on how changing the original's literary form changed its meaning or the impact of its meaning.
- Have the students turn to the text section "More on Literary Forms" (pages 10–12). Take a few moments to run through the examples in the text, noting how each form colors the meaning of the particular passage. Go on to do the same for the literary forms listed in the text section "More Examples of Literary Forms in the Bible" (see page 12), and have the students look up and read each listed Scripture passage. Finally, have the students complete the Assignment (page 12) by reading and identifying the literary form of 2 Samuel 12:1–4 (*parable*).
- Go on to point out that the second task in interpreting Scripture is to try to discover what the Divine Author wanted to convey. This we do first of all by reading the text in the spirit it was written. Explain to the students that this means we have to consider the content and unity of Scripture *as a whole*, recognizing that the Scriptures don't contradict themselves and that Scripture's ultimate purpose is to deepen our relationship with God. When interpreting Scripture, we have to be careful that our interpretation of this or that particular passage does not run contrary to what the rest of Scripture says. If we disregard Scripture's ultimate purpose, we will not find a proper explanation of the texts.

by their written words. To do so requires that we pay close attention to literary forms, that is, the different kinds of literature (literary genres) that appear in the Bible. For example, we would interpret a fable differently than a piece of news reporting. The fable might present an important lesson on how we should behave using an imaginative story, whereas a news story would present "just the facts" as they occurred. We could learn the truth about some aspect of human behavior from the lesson the fable is trying to teach without having to believe the story took place as written.

Also, we should pay attention to the customs and ways of speaking, feeling, and passing on information that took place at the time the sacred author was writing. For example, a teaching of the creation stories is that the human person, created in God's image and likeness, is a being with both corporal (bodily) and spiritual aspects. The way the biblical author drew out this point in the second creation account was to say that "the Lord God formed man out of the clay of the ground and blew into his nostrils the breath of life, and so man became a living being" (Gn 2:7). In these words the biblical author revealed this truth: "Man, whole and entire, is therefore *willed* by God" (*CCC*, 362).

After identifying the literary form, we must ask the further question: What did God want to teach by way of these words, that is, by using these literary forms? To answer this question, we must read the text in the spirit in which it was written. *The Constitution on Divine Revelation* continues:

> But, since Holy Scripture must be read and interpreted in the sacred spirit in which it was written, no less serious attention must be given to the content and unity of the whole of Scripture if the meaning of the sacred texts is to be correctly worked out. The living tradition of the whole Church must be taken into account along with the harmony which exists between elements of the faith. (12)

What this means is that the Holy Spirit has inspired the sacred writers to reveal the truths of our religion in both the Old and New Testaments. Together, they are a unity and express the speech of God in human words. Finally, the Magisterium of the Church has the task of drawing on Sacred Tradition as it "carries out the divine commission and ministry of guarding and interpreting the word of God."

More on Literary Forms

The teaching of the Second Vatican Council that "Sacred Scripture must be read in light of the same Spirit by whom it is written" (*Dei Verbum*, 3) is an essential starting point for the interpretation of biblical texts. Also, it is important to interpret Scripture from two main senses—the literal and spiritual. These two ways for looking at and interpreting Scripture shape the way the Bible is to be understood.

The first way is to look at the literal sense of Scripture. The literal sense refers to the literal meaning conveyed by the words and discovered by **exegesis**. The goal of exegesis is to lead or bring out the biblical author's intentions, purpose, and meaning related to the writings. The precise literal sense refers to what the written words mean as they are written. There are several types of literary forms in the Bible. Examples from the Old Testament include:

Lesson 3 Homework

1. Have the students respond in their journals to the two For Review questions on page 12.
2. Direct the students to read "The First Creation Account (Genesis 1:1–2:4a)" (pages 12–17) and "The Second Creation Account (Genesis 2:4b–25)" (pages 17–19) in preparation for their next lesson.
3. Remind the students to continue to work on their chosen Ongoing Assignments (page 25).

For Review Answers (page 12)

1. It is important to pay attention to literary forms when reading the Bible because different forms will affect the way the passage should be interpreted.
2. Answers will vary. See pages 10–12 of the student text.

- *Anthem.* An anthem is a joyful song or hymn. The beginning of Psalm 27 is an example of an anthem:

  The Lord is my light and salvation;
  whom should I fear?
  The Lord is my life's refuge;
  of whom should I be afraid? (Ps 27:1–2)

- *Census.* A census is an official numbering of the people of a country or district. See Numbers 1–14.
- *Debate.* A debate discusses a problem in a back-and-forth way. The debate in Job 4–30 starts with his curse and includes discussions with his friends. The debate ends when God intervenes.
- *Epigram.* An epigram is a short poem, often making a caustic point at the end. Note the example in Proverbs below. The first two verses give advice; the third verse tells what will happen if you do not follow it.

  Hear, my son, and be wise,
  and guide your heart in the right way.
  Consort not with winebibbers,
  nor with those who eat meat to excess;
  For the drunkard and the glutton come to poverty,
  and torpor clothes a man in rags.
  (Prv 23:19–21)

- *Etiology.* An etiology is a story that gives the cause of something. In Genesis 32:23–33, for example, an explanation is given for why "the Israelites do not eat the sciatic muscle that is on the hip socket."
- *Genealogy.* A genealogy provides a list of ancestors and their descendants. Genesis 5 gives the descendants of Adam up to the time of the sons of Noah.
- *Maxim.* A maxim is similar to a proverb. It states a brief practical principle for daily living. For example: "Two are better than one: they get a good wage for their labor."
- *Parable.* A parable is a vivid short story told to convey religious truth, usually with a surprise ending. For example, Isaiah 5:1–6 tells the story of a vineyard that yielded only wild grapes, so it was destroyed. Verse 7 interprets the parable by comparing the vineyard to the nation of Israel.

There are many other literary forms in both the Old and New Testaments. One starting point for understanding the biblical text is to be able to identify the form and how the sacred author wanted his words understood by his audience. A second way of interpreting Scripture involves not just looking at the words themselves, but also at what the words signify. The spiritual sense can be divided into three subdivisions:

1. Allegorical, that is understanding Scripture by recognizing its connection and significance with Christ. For example, the story of Jonah in the belly of the large fish references the three days Christ spent in the tomb.
2. Moral, or how the Scripture ought to lead us to act more justly. For example, Ruth teaches us the importance of loyalty in our relationships.
3. Anagogical (Greek for "to lead"), reminding us that the sacred words are intended to lead us to eternal life.

It is the task of everyone from biblical scholars to everyday Christians to judge, interpret, and read a biblical literary form according to these senses of Scripture and to do so ultimately subject to the judgment of the Church, "which exercises the divinely conferred commission and ministry of watching over and interpreting the Word of God" (*Dei Verbum 12 § 3, CCC,* 119). Only then will we know the truths God wished to convey through the human authors and their literary styles.

exegesis
A Greek word meaning "to lead." It is the study or the explanation of a biblical book or passage.

- Remind the students that just as we need to read an individual Scripture passage in the context of the whole of Scripture, so too we have to read Scripture within the whole of Church Tradition. Emphasize that because Scripture and Tradition are the *two* forms of the *one* Word that God speaks, any interpretation that would find one form contradicting the other would be denying the truth of God's Word.
- Finally, point out that it is the mission of the Magisterium to ensure the *union* between Scripture and Tradition.
- Conclude this lesson by writing the phrase **Scripture is inerrant** on the board. Make sure the students understand that this phrase does not affirm the accuracy of historical or scientific data included in the Scripture. It does, however, affirm that the Scripture contains no errors when it comes to matters of faith or spiritual teaching.

For Enrichment

Scripture and Prayer

St. Augustine wrote: "When we pray, we speak to God; when we read Scripture, God speaks to us." Augustine's words tell us that praying and reading Scripture go hand in hand. Our prayer puts our reading of Scripture in the context of a *relationship* with God. Prayer reminds us that we are about to enter into a conversation with a *person*, and that the point of our reading or listening is not simply to know things *about* God, but to know *God himself.* Prayer joined to our Scripture reading challenges us to recognize that our ultimate goal is not to discover answers to questions or even to obtain theological information, but to put on the mind of Christ so as to *become* the answers to the questions of our time and world.

Suggest to the students that they use the following prayer of St. John Chrysostom before reading or listening to the word of God:

Lord Jesus Christ,
open the eyes of my heart,
that I may hear your word
and understand and do your will,
for I am a sojourner upon the earth.
Hide not your commandments from me,
but open my eyes, that I may perceive the wonders of your law.
Speak unto me the hidden and secret things
of your wisdom.
On you do I set my hope, O my God,
that you shall enlighten
my mind and understanding with
the light of your knowledge,
not only to cherish those things
which are written, but to do them;
that in reading the lives and sayings
of the saints I may not sin,
but that such may serve for my restoration, enlightenment
and sanctification, for the salvation of my soul,
and the inheritance of life everlasting.
For you are the enlightenment of those
who lie in darkness,
and from you comes every good deed
and every gift.
Amen.

Chapter 1: God's Good Creation: The Beginning of Salvation History—Lesson 4

Bell Ringers

- Ask students to offer their responses to the two For Review questions on page 12 (answers are on page 24 of this text). Be sure to allow the students to ask any other questions they may have.
- Ask the students to write versions of the creation stories in a genre taken from the list of literary genres on pages 10–12. Ask students to share their responses.

Teaching Approaches

The First Creation Account (Genesis 1:1-2:4a) (pages 12-17)

- Call attention to the feature "An Overview of the Pentateuch" (pages 14–15). Write the words **Pentateuch** and **Torah** on the board. Explain that *Pentateuch* comes from the Greek and means "five scrolls"; *Torah* comes from the Hebrew and means "instruction" or "law." Make sure the students recognize that both terms refer to the first five books of the Bible: Genesis, Exodus, Leviticus, Numbers, and Deuteronomy. Likewise, make sure they realize that these books relate the accounts of:
    - God's creation of all that is
    - God's covenantal love for the Hebrew people
    - God's call of the Hebrews out of slavery
    - God's gift of the Law to the Hebrews

  (*Note:* While the figure of Moses looms large in the Pentateuch, the claim that he is its author is cast into doubt not only by the composite nature of the Pentateuch but also by the fact that Moses lived about five hundred years before the existence of any form of written Hebrew.)
- Drawing on the information in the feature, "An Overview of the Pentateuch," outline the four stages in which the Pentateuch was likely composed. Likewise, point out that the entire Pentateuch is a composite work—the work of many inspired human authors—that accounts for duplication and even contradictions in the text (e.g., two creation accounts).
- Write the letters **JEDP** vertically on the board. Explain that these letters are designations scholars use to identify the component traditions or sources that

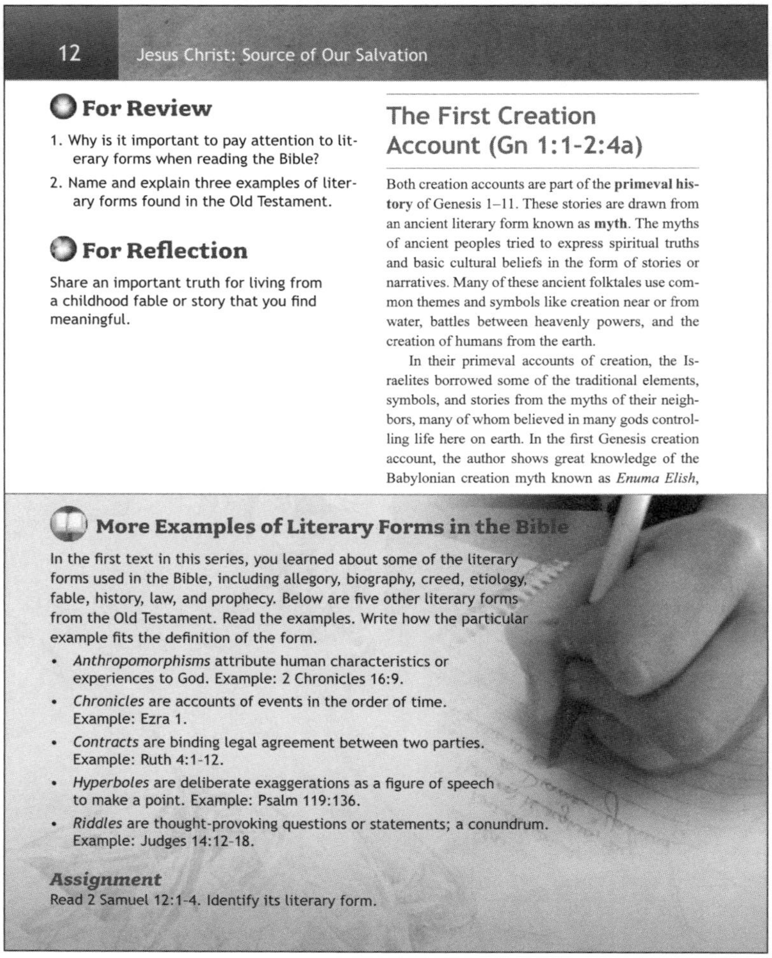

12 Jesus Christ: Source of Our Salvation

For Review

1. Why is it important to pay attention to literary forms when reading the Bible?
2. Name and explain three examples of literary forms found in the Old Testament.

For Reflection

Share an important truth for living from a childhood fable or story that you find meaningful.

The First Creation Account (Gn 1:1-2:4a)

Both creation accounts are part of the **primeval history** of Genesis 1–11. These stories are drawn from an ancient literary form known as **myth**. The myths of ancient peoples tried to express spiritual truths and basic cultural beliefs in the form of stories or narratives. Many of these ancient folktales use common themes and symbols like creation near or from water, battles between heavenly powers, and the creation of humans from the earth.

In their primeval accounts of creation, the Israelites borrowed some of the traditional elements, symbols, and stories from the myths of their neighbors, many of whom believed in many gods controlling life here on earth. In the first Genesis creation account, the author shows great knowledge of the Babylonian creation myth known as *Enuma Elish*,

More Examples of Literary Forms in the Bible

In the first text in this series, you learned about some of the literary forms used in the Bible, including allegory, biography, creed, etiology, fable, history, law, and prophecy. Below are five other literary forms from the Old Testament. Read the examples. Write how the particular example fits the definition of the form.

- *Anthropomorphisms* attribute human characteristics or experiences to God. Example: 2 Chronicles 16:9.
- *Chronicles* are accounts of events in the order of time. Example: Ezra 1.
- *Contracts* are binding legal agreement between two parties. Example: Ruth 4:1-12.
- *Hyperboles* are deliberate exaggerations as a figure of speech to make a point. Example: Psalm 119:136.
- *Riddles* are thought-provoking questions or statements; a conundrum. Example: Judges 14:12-18.

Assignment

Read 2 Samuel 12:1-4. Identify its literary form.

Lesson 4 Objectives

The students will:

- discover how the first five books of the Bible developed.
- compare and contrast the Biblical creation accounts and other similar myths of their time.
- recognize the *religious* truths revealed in the Bible's creation stories.

Lesson 4 Preview

In this lesson, the students investigate the creation stories of Genesis. Because these stories are so familiar, it is all too easy to miss their revolutionary nature. It is important, then, that you help the students see beyond the literal detail of the creation stories to the important religious truths the stories convey. Be sure to read the accounts in the first two chapters of Genesis yourself as well as both the student text and this lesson plan, so that you will be comfortable explaining the stories' religious themes and dealing with any questions your students may have.

though the Genesis story does not accept its view of many gods, all springing from the gods of fresh and salt water. Marduk emerged as the hero in the story as he created the heavens out of the carcass of the goddess Tiamet whom he slayed. He also created humans out of the blood of another god to be slaves so that the gods could rest. The Israelites, inspired by the Holy Spirit, changed these traditional stories and symbols to convey their belief in the one true God—Yahweh—who entered their history in a radical new way.

Contrast this Babylonian myth with the forceful, stately, and grand style of Genesis 1:1–2:4a where creation is the result of an awesome, dramatic act by a glorious and majestic God. The intention of the author was to show the Jews who were in captivity in Babylon, or had just recently returned to Jerusalem, that their God is the only true God. Yahweh is the God who creates only goodness. He is totally unlike the false gods of Babylon, who were believed to have created humans to be slaves to the gods. A clear telling of the first creation account to the Israelites was: "God has selected *you* as his Chosen People. He has been faithful to *you*. Therefore, *you* must be faithful to him."

In composing the story of the origins of the world, the author may have drawn on the Israelites' tradition of a seven-day week, in which the seventh day, the Sabbath, was a day of rest and prayer. Creation takes place in six days, with each day representing a higher level of creation. Humans are at the peak of God's design. The refrain "God saw how good it was" delineates each day. It also stresses the goodness of everything God made, in contrast to the Babylonian and other ancient myths that held that some creatures were evil.

The author seems to have used a brilliant parallel construction to distinguish between separation and decoration: God divides on the first three days, he decorates or "adds to" on the next three days:

Separation	Decoration
Day 1: light from darkness	Day 4: bodies of light—sun, moon, stars
Day 2: sky from water	Day 5: birds and fish
Day 3: land from water	Day 6: life on land—animals and humans

Note how in this first creation account both males and females are created at the same time. God creates both man and woman in the divine image:

> Then God said: "Let us make man in our image, after our likeness. Let them have dominion over the fish of the sea, the birds of the air, and the cattle, and over all the wild animals and all the creatures that crawl on the ground."
>
> God created man in his image;
> in the divine image he created him;
> male and female he created them. (Gn 1:26–27)

By saying God rested on the seventh day, the biblical author reminds the Jews of their own obligation to

primeval history
Stories or myths about the origins of the earth, humans, other creatures, languages, and cultures.

myth
Symbolic stories that express a spiritual truth or a basic belief about God.

were used to compile the five books of the Pentateuch. Next to the letters write the full names of each source: **Yahwist, Elohist, Deuteronomist, Priestly**. Next, summarize each source with the topics each source is most concerned about: **Patriarchs, Prophets, Law, Temple**. The board should show:

J (Yahwist) = Patriarchs
E (Elohist) = Prophets
D (Deuteronomist) = Law
P (Priestly) = Temple

- Distribute copies of Chapter 1, Handout 3, "Sources of the Pentateuch," and use the table on the handout as a summary of the information in the text (pages 14–15). As you go through the table with the students, explain the following if necessary:
    - the differences between "Yahweh" and "Elohim" as names of God
    - the difference between the Northern and Southern Kingdoms and their origins and history
    - the emphasis/theme of the Priestly source, which focused on the concerns of priests serving in the Jerusalem Temple. Concerns included technical record keeping and legal traditions (census lists, genealogies, dates, etc.) associated with the proper functioning of the Temple and its related activities.
- Before moving on, point out that realizing that the Pentateuch derived from a combination of sources over time does not lessen its claim to be God's Word. Rather, understanding the "dynamic" nature of the Pentateuch can actually help us to recognize the Word and work of God as dynamic in the Hebrew community of faith as it strove throughout history to come to terms with God's self-revelation and put it into practice in their lives. The development of the Pentateuch helps trace the progression of Salvation History.
- Call on different students to read aloud Genesis 1:1–2:4a. Afterward, point out that this account is termed *primeval history*: that is, it's a story about the origins of things—the universe, earth, people, cultures, etc. Go on to explain that *myth* is a metaphoric or symbolic story that tells the truth in a non-scientific but very concrete way. Myths in the Bible relate basic spiritual truths and/or beliefs about God.
- Write the following question on the board: **Polytheism/Pantheism or Monotheism: what'll it be?** Tell the students that this is the essential question addressed in the first creation story. Remind the students that as the Pentateuch was developing, temptations to idolatry abounded. Israel was surrounded by

polytheistic nations who believed that all the various regions of *nature* were divine: sun, moon, stars, etc. There were sky gods and earth gods and water gods; gods of light and darkness, rivers and vegetation, animals and fertility. In addition to all the nature gods, pharaohs, kings, and heroes were often seen as sons of gods, or at least as special mediators between the divine and human spheres. Stress to the students that this polytheistic onslaught made a monotheistic faith difficult to sustain.

- Remind the students that the creation story was written down when the Hebrew people were returning from years of exile in Babylon—hence the author's knowledge of the Babylonian creation myth. Ask, "What does this story say about the Hebrews' God in contrast to the gods of Babylon?" (*It declares that God creates not out of evil but out of goodness; it asserts that God has loved humankind first and has chosen the Jews to be his people; it speaks repeatedly of all creation being good.*)
- Draw attention to the chart on page 13 that delineates the first creation story's parallel construction showing how the one true God separates the elements on the first three days of creation and then adds to them on the final three days. Ask, "How does the telling of this story in a seven-day format make it easy to remember?"

AN OVERVIEW OF THE PENTATEUCH

To understand the Book of Genesis, it is necessary to understand how it fits within the entire Pentateuch. The Pentateuch (meaning "five scrolls" in Greek) contains the Torah, that is, the Law of the Jewish people. The other four books of the Pentateuch are Exodus, Leviticus, Numbers, and Deuteronomy. The Pentateuch is also known as the "Book of Moses," or the "Five Books of Moses," because ancient Judaism and early Christianity believed that Moses authored them. Even the New Testament assumes this, for example, when Jesus refers to the Pentateuch as "the Book of Moses" (Mk 12:26).

However, the Church understands that the first five books of the Bible only took their final form after centuries of telling, retelling, adapting, and reinterpreting the many stories of Yahweh's dealings with the Chosen People. It is true that Moses is the central figure of the Pentateuch since God delivered the Ten Commandments to him on Mount Sinai and he led the Israelites out of Egypt. The Israelites naturally looked to him as the source of the laws and traditions recorded in the Torah. However, Moses certainly could not have written *everything* in the Pentateuch. For example, Deuteronomy 34:5-12 gives an account of Moses's death.

Pentateuch
A Greek word meaning "five scrolls." It is used to refer to the first five books of the Bible—Genesis, Exodus, Leviticus, Numbers, and Deuteronomy. The books contain the Jewish Law, the Torah.

Torah
The Law handed down to the Chosen People by God that they were to live in response to his covenant with them. A summary of the Torah is found in the Ten Commandments.

The Pentateuch was likely composed in stages, probably proceeding this way:

- *Stage 1:* The core incident in the Pentateuch is the strong personality of Moses, the lawgiver, and the events of the Exodus, God's deliverance of the Israelites from Egypt.
- *Stage 2:* Various laws, speeches, stories about human origins and the patriarchs, reflections, liturgical celebrations, and so forth, were handed down orally from generation to generation. Some of these were committed to writing as well.
- *Stage 3:* Authors and editors began to collect their sources into a continuous narrative.
- *Stage 4:* Sometime during the fourth and fifth century BC under the leadership of the priestly scribe Ezra, the various traditions were brought together into the five-volume document we know as the Pentateuch.

Most scholars believe there were at least four major sources that went into the composition of the Pentateuch. Because the Pentateuch (including Genesis) is a composite work, later authors and editors did not always try to reconcile all the differences in the stories and traditions that came down to them. They simply included their stories right along with the stories of other authors. A most notable example of this is the two creation accounts that appear right after each other in the first three chapters of Genesis.

The four major traditions or sources that are behind the Pentateuch are:

- *Yahwist (J).* This tradition originated around 950 BC in the southern kingdom of Judah. Its name comes from its frequent use of "Yahweh" (or "Jahweh" in German) for God's name. This source emphasizes the divine promises made to the patriarchs and provides the basic outline for the Pentateuch: human origins, patriarchs, slavery in Egypt, the Exodus, the desert wanderings, the covenant on Mount Sinai, and entrance to the Promised Land.
- *Elohist (E).* Traceable to the northern kingdom of Israel, which uses "Elohim," a generic name for "god" in Hebrew, this source came about one hundred years

after the Yahwist. The E source emphasizes prophecy (especially the message of Elijah and Elisha) and the theme of covenant. It is more abstract than the J tradition. Abraham is a central figure in the Elohist narrative. Additionally, many scholars believe that around 750 BC an editor combined J and E into one narrative without bothering to drop repetitions or contradictions.

- *Deuteronomist (D).* The name Deuteronomist is derived from a Greek word meaning "second law." First composed in the northern kingdom at the shrine at Shechem in approximately 650 BC, it may have been completed in Jerusalem. This source refers to God as "Yahweh" and emphasizes morality and living the Law. "Listen, Israel" is a constant refrain. Central also are several long speeches by Moses.
- *Priestly (P).* This source originated during the Babylonian Exile and was likely completed around 400 BC. The Priestly account refers to God in the formal "Elohim," like the Elhoist, and is interested in census lists, genealogies, numbers, dates, liturgical procedures, Temple ceremonies, ritual cleanliness, and so forth. It also emphasizes worship because it sees God's action in the history of Israel as a liturgy. Because P was the last tradition, it gave a coherent framework to the Pentateuch. Priestly editors under Ezra gave the first five books of the Bible their final form.

worship God on the Sabbath (from sundown on Friday to sundown on Saturday). Sabbath observance helped captive Jews maintain their identity as God's Chosen People among a foreign people with pagan beliefs. They believed they should offer thanks and praise to God each week because he is the source of all that is good.

Religious and Theological Truths of the First Creation Account (CCC, 290-373)

This first creation account is not a scientific explanation of the beginning of the universe. Rather, God inspired its author to draw on the knowledge of the people of his time to construct a story that reveals important *religious* and *theological* truths about creation, including these:

1. *There is only one God.* The biblical authors wrote that God is eternal and gave a beginning to all that exists outside of himself. The priestly author of this first creation story firmly rejects the vindictive false gods of the Babylonians portrayed in their creation myth, Enuma Elish.
2. *God planned creation.* Creation did not result from anything else like chaotic forces, warring gods, fate, or chance. God created the world in an orderly way to share his being, wisdom, and goodness with us. God creates by his Word, decreeing what is to be and establishing limits.
3. *God created an ordered and good world out of nothing.* Material creation is good and not the result of magic or the workings of false gods. The Babylonian creation story told how humans emerged from the rotting corpse of a god. Ancient peoples believed that much of material reality is evil and constantly at war with the spiritual elements in the universe. In contrast, Jews and Christians see in Genesis a positive view of created reality. The biblical

- Go on to point out that each "day" of creation also takes on two principal deities of polytheism of the time, and declares that these are not gods at all, but creatures that come from the hand of the *one* true God.
    - Day 1 dismisses the "gods" of light and darkness.
    - Day 2 banishes the "gods" of sky and sea.
    - Day 3 puts the "gods" of earth and vegetation in their place.
    - Day 4 rejects the divinity of the sun, moon, and stars.
    - Days 5 rebuffs any notion that anything in the animal kingdom is divine.
    - Day 6 reveals that all human beings—not just pharaohs, kings, and heroes—are made in the divine image and likeness.
    - Day 7 makes it absolutely clear that all creation comes from the *one* God who is not to be confused with his creation. The creation is good, but it is not divine. Therefore, it is only this one, loving, and creating God who is worthy of worship.

- Review with the students the section "Religious and Theological Truths of the First Creation Account" (pages 15–16). Help them make connections between the six truths and their reading of Genesis 1:1–2:4a. Encourage questions. Finally, lead the students in discussing the two For Reflection questions on page 17.

The Second Creation Account (Genesis 2:4b-25) (pages 17-19)

- Call on different students to read aloud the second creation story from the Bible. Review the concept of anthropomorphism from the text. Ask:
    - What are some anthropomorphic ways in which God is portrayed in this story?
    - When are humans created in this account of creation? How does God create them?
    - What does Genesis 2:25 say about the original relationship between God and humankind?
    - What does Genesis 2:18, 22–24 reveal about God's creation of human beings? (*Note*: Look for answers like those that follow. List responses on the board.)

16 Jesus Christ: Source of Our Salvation

author tells us that God was pleased with everything he made, especially human beings made in God's own image and likeness and entrusted with responsibility for the rest of creation.

4. *God creates man in his own image, male and female.* We are unique because:
    - We possess great dignity, value, and worth. Man is "the only creature on earth that God has willed for its own sake" (*CCC*, 356, quoting *Gaudium et Spes*, 3). We are able to know and love God. We are predestined to share in the eternal goodness of God himself by reproducing in our own lives the image of Jesus Christ, God's Son made man, the "image of the invisible God" (Col 1:15).
    - Human nature unites both the spiritual and material worlds. Humans are endowed with bodies and souls, the spiritual principle in us.
    - God created males and females as perfect in equality as human persons, with inalienable dignity. They are privileged to share in God's great gift of creation by being given the power to procreate life, to "be fertile and multiply" (Gn 1:28).
5. *God gave humans a place of honor in creation, making them stewards over what he created.* We are responsible for taking care of and developing the many gifts of creation God entrusted to us.
6. *God blessed the Sabbath and made it holy.* The priestly writer tells how God rested on the seventh day. Obviously, God does not need to rest. But we, God's creatures, need to take time to be renewed by ceasing from ordinary activities one day out of the week. Furthermore, we need to recognize a kind and loving God as the source of our existence and worship him in prayer and thanksgiving. Catholics keep Sunday holy, the first day of the week and the day of Christ's Resurrection by participating at Mass and refraining from unnecessary work.

These six truths emerge from the magnificent first creation story. They highlight our belief in the one, powerful, good, wise, and loving God who shares his life with his creatures.

For Review

1. Define: *Pentateuch* and *Torah*.
2. Summarize the stages involved in composing Genesis and the other books of the Pentateuch.
3. Briefly identify the four sources that are behind the Pentateuch.
4. What is the purpose of the ancient literary form known as *myth*?
5. Discuss at least three religious and theological truths that emerge from the first creation account.

Keeping Sunday Holy

In commemoration of the day of our Lord's Resurrection, Catholics are obligated to gather to celebrate the Eucharist to thank God for all the good gifts he has bestowed on us, especially the gift of Salvation won for us by Jesus Christ, our Savior. Catholics also rest from regular work and activity on Sundays. Analyze how you spent the past two Sundays. In your journal, note what activities you engaged in that showed you take "Sabbath rest" and the "Sunday obligation" seriously. If your review shows that you have neglected to "keep holy the Lord's day," write out some resolutions on how you might observe it more faithfully this coming weekend.

Lesson 4 Homework

1. Have the students respond in their journals to the five For Review questions on page 16 and the three For Review questions on page 18.
2. Direct the students to read "The Theme of Creation in Theology and Scripture" (pages 19–23) in preparation for their next lesson.
3. Remind the students to begin wrapping up work on their chosen Ongoing Assignments (page 25).

For Review Answers (page 16)

1. Pentateuch means "five scrolls." Torah means "law." Both refer to the first five books of the Bible.
2. Answers should reflect the information on the four stages outlined on page 14 of the text.
3. The four sources behind the Pentateuch are: (1) Yahwist, which emphasizes the promise to the patriarchs and offers the Pentateuch its basic outline; (2) Elohist, which emphasizes prophecy and the theme of covenant; (3) Deuteronomist, which emphasizes morality and living out the Law; and (4) Priestly, which emphasizes worship and priestly concerns of Temple service.
4. The purpose of myth in the Bible is to express spiritual truths and basic cultural beliefs in the form of stories.
5. Answers should include at least three of the six religious truths outlined on pages 15–16.

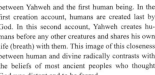

For Reflection

- What does it mean to you to have been created in God's image?
- How has your understanding of God been enhanced by reading and praying with the Book of Genesis?

The Second Creation Account (Gn 2:4b-25)

The second creation account is written in a more down-to-earth style and portrays God as *anthropomorphic*, that is, with human qualities. Some scholars attribute the second account to the Yahwist (J) author and have dated it some time in the tenth century BC.

The account images God as a potter who molds Adam's body like a delicate sculpture. Into this form Yahweh breathes his spirit, the breath of life. This intimate picture reveals the loving relationship between Yahweh and the first human being. In the first creation account, humans are created last by God. In this second account, Yahweh creates humans before any other creatures and shares his own life (breath) with them. This image of this closeness between human and divine radically contrasts with the beliefs of most ancient peoples who thought God was distant and to be feared.

The author describes a compassionate God who cares for Adam by making him a garden and sending him animals for companionship. God puts Adam in charge of creation by permitting him to name the animals. (In the ancient world, the power to name gave one control over what was named.) However, animals do not fulfill Adam's basic human need for companionship.

This is why the author gives a further story, the creation of Eve from Adam's rib. This highlights a rich image of the dignity of women and their equality with men. This second story provides an etiology of marriage, that is, why men and women leave their parents to form their own family. The story reveals that Yahweh wants the couple to "become one

Preserving the Earth

There is rightful concern today about ecology and the degradation of God's good creation. The challenge is to be part of the solution and not part of the problem. You can do a lot to make people aware of the need to conserve precious resources. Try one of the following recycling projects. Advertise your project on an approved Internet network. Consider the following examples for projects:

- Begin a paper-recycling contest between classes at your school. (Recycling one ton of paper saves seventeen trees, 380 gallons of oil, three cubic yards of landfill space, 4,000 kilowatts of energy, 7,000 gallons of water, and sixty pounds of air pollutants.)
- Recycle Styrofoam cups and trays.
- Establish stations around the school for recycling batteries.
- Start a campaign to eliminate drinking bottled water. Encourage people to refill their personal bottles or cups from a tap or other common water dispenser.

- God created men and women to be equal partners and companions.
- God put into the hearts of the human beings a longing for intimacy with one another.
- God intended sexual intercourse to bond husband and wife as one body, so as to become partners in creation through procreation.

- Call attention to the paragraph on page 18 ending in italics. Encourage the students to write the sentences in italics in their journals. Suggest that an easy way to remember what the two creation accounts reveal is by learning the following simple rhyme:

  God alone made all that is.
  Made of God's love,
  we all are his.

  Write the rhyme on the board. Invite the students to copy it in their journals and commit it to memory.

- Present the material in the text section "Truths of the Second Creation Account" (page 18). Take a moment to explain that Original Holiness and Original Justice refer to the state of perfection in which God created human beings so that they might share in his life. Emphasize that this state was one of perfect harmony among humans and between humans and God.

For Enrichment

Music

Consider playing selections from a recording of Franz Joseph Haydn's *The Creation* as the students read the creation accounts in class.

Video

If your students have not seen the Academy Award winning documentary *An Inconvenient Truth* consider presenting it to the class. The film speaks of global warming as a great moral challenge facing our global civilization. It is available on DVD.

- Invite the students to turn to the feature "Preserving the Earth" on page 17. If your class is not already involved in ecological, earth-friendly activities, be sure to discuss and decide on a class project the students might undertake to help preserve the earth.
- Write the two For Reflection questions from page 17 and the one question from page 19 on the board:
  - **What does it mean to you to have been created in God's image?**
  - **How has your understanding of God been enhanced by reading and praying with the Book of Genesis?**
  - **How do you imagine the Garden of Eden before sin? Describe in detail.**

  Discuss as a class.

Original Holiness and Original Justice
The state of man and woman before sin. "From their friendship with God flowed the happiness of their existence in paradise" (CCC, 384).

body," to enter into a close relationship that mirrors God's own relationship with them. Man and woman are equal and complementary, intended by God to be true companions.

The author who is sometimes associated with the Yahwist or "J" understanding tells us that Adam and Eve felt no shame, even though they were naked. Their natural condition of intimacy with God and each other was one of total openness. Only when sin entered the picture did human beings feel ashamed and want to hide.

After examining these two creation accounts, we can better understand why the final editor of Genesis was inspired by God to include two different creation accounts. Together they reveal something very important about our God: *Yahweh, the awe-inspiring sole creator of the universe (story 1) is intimately concerned with the man and woman he made the jewels of his creation (story 2).*

Truths of the Second Creation Account (CCC, 369-379)

The second creation account emphasizes both the equality and differences between man and woman that are willed by God. It teaches that God created humans in friendship with his Creator and in harmony with themselves and all the creation around them.

The second creation account also teaches that Adam and Eve were born in a state of **Original Holiness and Original Justice**.

The Church, interpreting the symbolism of biblical language in an authentic way, in the light of the New Testament and Tradition, teaches that our first parents, Adam and Eve, were constituted in an original "state of holiness and justice." This grace of Original Holiness and Original Justice was "to share . . . divine life." (*CCC*, 375)

Original Justice and Original Holiness involved the inner harmony of the human person, the harmony between man and woman, and the harmony between our first parents and all of creation. As long as the first humans remained in intimacy with God, they would not have to suffer or die. Work was not a burden but a share in perfecting God's visible creation.

Man and woman were created for each other, for companionship, to be helpmates to each other, and to share in God's work of creating new life. Furthermore, they were to love everything God created for them and to responsibly care for the world he entrusted to them.

For Review

1. Name at least one difference between the two creation accounts.
2. Name three anthropomorphisms in the second creation account.
3. Name a religious and theological truth revealed in the second creation account.

For Review Answers (page 18)

1. Students may point out that in the second creation story God is portrayed as anthropomorphic, humans are created before all other creatures, and God shows intimate concern for humans.
2. Answers will vary, but could include God breathing life into Adam, God molding Adam as though God were a potter, and God walking in the Garden.
3. In the second creation account, God's intent is for humans to be in friendship with him and in harmony with one another, all of creation, and their inner person.

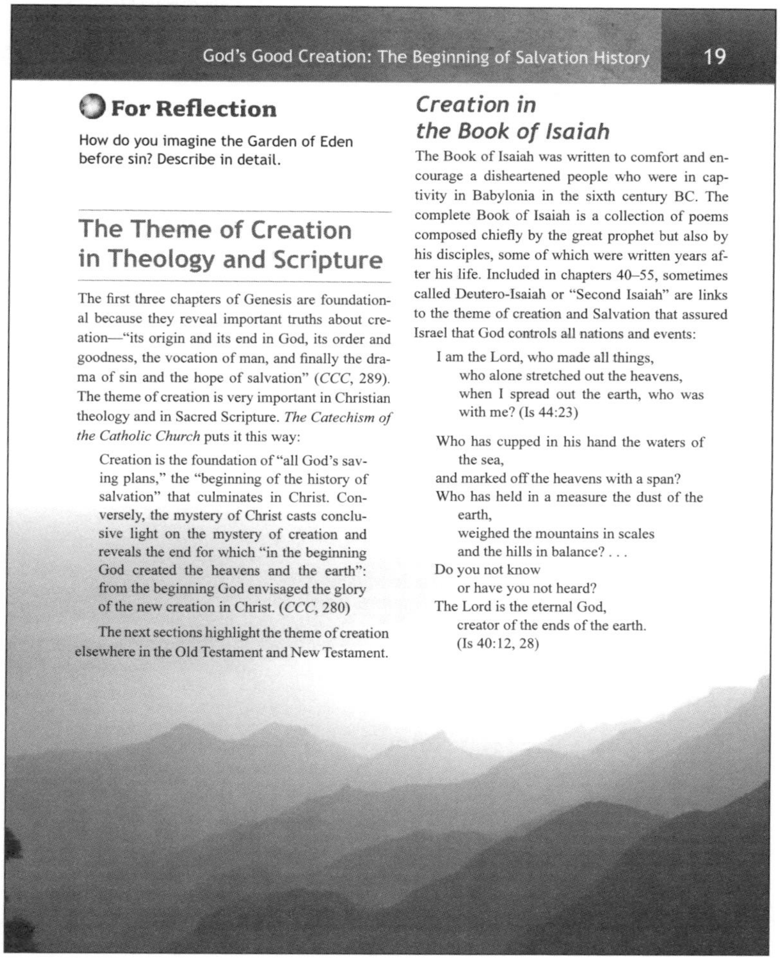

God's Good Creation: The Beginning of Salvation History 19

For Reflection

How do you imagine the Garden of Eden before sin? Describe in detail.

The Theme of Creation in Theology and Scripture

The first three chapters of Genesis are foundational because they reveal important truths about creation—"its origin and its end in God, its order and goodness, the vocation of man, and finally the drama of sin and the hope of salvation" (*CCC*, 289). The theme of creation is very important in Christian theology and in Sacred Scripture. *The Catechism of the Catholic Church* puts it this way:

> Creation is the foundation of "all God's saving plans," the "beginning of the history of salvation" that culminates in Christ. Conversely, the mystery of Christ casts conclusive light on the mystery of creation and reveals the end for which "in the beginning God created the heavens and the earth": from the beginning God envisaged the glory of the new creation in Christ. (*CCC*, 280)

The next sections highlight the theme of creation elsewhere in the Old Testament and New Testament.

Creation in the Book of Isaiah

The Book of Isaiah was written to comfort and encourage a disheartened people who were in captivity in Babylonia in the sixth century BC. The complete Book of Isaiah is a collection of poems composed chiefly by the great prophet but also by his disciples, some of which were written years after his life. Included in chapters 40–55, sometimes called Deutero-Isaiah or "Second Isaiah" are links to the theme of creation and Salvation that assured Israel that God controls all nations and events:

> I am the Lord, who made all things,
> who alone stretched out the heavens,
> when I spread out the earth, who was with me? (Is 44:23)
>
> Who has cupped in his hand the waters of the sea,
> and marked off the heavens with a span?
> Who has held in a measure the dust of the earth,
> weighed the mountains in scales
> and the hills in balance? . . .
> Do you not know
> or have you not heard?
> The Lord is the eternal God,
> creator of the ends of the earth.
> (Is 40:12, 28)

Chapter 1: God's Good Creation: The Beginning of Salvation History—Lesson 5

Bell Ringer

- Ask students to offer their responses to the five For Review questions on page 16 and the three For Review questions on page 18 (answers are on pages 30 and 32 of this text). Again, be sure to encourage further questions.

Teaching Approaches

The Theme of Creation in Theology and Scripture (pages 19-23)

- Read aloud the passage from the *Catechism of the Catholic Church* on page 19. Note that this textbook series is titled *Jesus Christ* because of Christ's central role in Salvation History. Introduce the lesson by sharing with the students that they will be tracing the theme of creation through many different books of the Bible culminating with Christ in the New Testament.
- "Creation in the Book of Isaiah" (pages 19–20). Tell the students that the theology in Genesis 1 and the passages quoted from Second Isaiah are essentially the same. Actually, both are from the same time period, and therefore part of the same cultural

Lesson 5 Objectives

The students will:

- investigate the theme of creation in theology and books of the Bible other than Genesis.
- compare and contrast the creation stories of Genesis and the accounts of creation in other books of the Bible.
- show that Christ is the culmination of the theme of creation that can be traced throughout Scripture.
- draw on hymns to discover and celebrate the theme of creation.

Lesson 5 Preview

Recognizing that students learn through a variety of (multiple) intelligences, including musical intelligence, this lesson employs numerous hymns in the Teacher's Wraparound Edition to illustrate and reinforce learning. Since the students may not be familiar with some of the songs, try to have lyrics available as well as a pianist to accompany singing. If that is impossible, try to have recordings of the hymns, so that the students can sing along or, at the least, listen to them—the words of the chosen hymns are important to the lesson. If you are unable to find the listed hymns, choose others appropriate to the themes. In order to keep the flow of the lesson, feel free to sing or play the songs at the end of the lesson.

context. Explain that the Assyrians had conquered all of Palestine, except for Jerusalem (ca. 722 BC). And more than a century later, the Babylonians had, in turn, conquered all of the Middle East including Palestine and Jerusalem. The last remnant of Jewish autonomy had been overrun, the Holy City invaded and burned, the Temple destroyed, and most of the people carried off into exile. The prophet Isaiah responds to the disheartened condition of captive Israel by applying creation theology to the people's attitudes and actions. He highlights God's greatness, power, sovereignty, and mercy, reminding Israel that God is the creator, the one who stretched out the heavens and the earth. Isaiah heartens Israel by reassuring them that the powerful, sustaining creator is on their side, comforting them and promising to restore them.

- Direct the students to read Isaiah 45:18. (*"For thus says the LORD, The creator of the heavens, who is God, The designer and maker of the earth who established it, Not creating it to be a waste, but designing it to be lived in: I am the LORD, and there is no other."*) Ask, "What do Isaiah's words tell us about God's position on earth care? What do they challenge us to do?"
- Ask the students to compare Isaiah's depiction of God to the first and second creation stories. Ask, "Does Isaiah use anthropomorphic images?" Ask, "What are some similarities?"

The poet intended for a discouraged people to know that God is in charge. He is both almighty Creator and Savior. He will renew the face of the earth by creating rivers in the desert and making crooked paths straight. The passage is intended to let the people know that just as God delivered the Israelites from slavery in Egypt, made a covenant with them, and created them as a people, he will rescue the captives from the Babylonians. Also, God will renew the people just as he renews creation:

> I am the Lord, there is no other;
> I form the light, and create the darkness. . . .
> Let justice descend, O heavens, like dew from above,
> like gentle rain let the skies drop it down.
> Let the earth open and salvation bud forth;
> let justice spring up!
> I, the Lord, have created this.
> (Is 45:7–8)

Creation in the Book of Psalms

The Psalms are "songs of praise" to God. The book of Psalms is a source of inspiration, instruction, hope, consolation, and instruction for both Jews and Christians. Creation is a central theme in many Psalms, stressing God's uniqueness, power, and majesty, while reminding us that we should worship God. Psalm 8 is an example of a hymn of praise that highlights God's greatness. The psalmist is awestruck at God's creative activity and especially at God's marvelous creature—humans: "You have made him little less than the angels, and crowned him with glory and honor" (Ps 8:6).

Another example of the theme of creation is found in Psalm 104, a majestic hymn that praises God's creative wisdom and power. The psalmist's heart leaps to the heavens, praising God's majesty:

> Bless the Lord, my soul!
> Lord, my God, you are great indeed!
> You are clothed with majesty and glory,
> robed in light as with a cloak.
> You spread out the heavens like a tent;
> you raised your palace upon the waters.
> You make the clouds your chariot;
> you travel on the wings of the wind.
> You make the winds your messengers;
> flaming fire, your ministers. . . .
> How varied are your works, Lord!
> In wisdom you have wrought them all;
> the earth is full of your creatures.
> (Ps 104:1–4, 24)

Creation in the Book of Proverbs

All wisdom has its source in God. Wisdom is an expression of God's own nature. The Book of Proverbs personifies wisdom and praises it as God's helper in the act of creation. Specifically, Proverbs 8 stresses the role of divine wisdom at the beginning of creation. God's wisdom was responsible for an orderly, intelligent, and joyful creation:

> "The Lord begot me, the first-born of his ways,
> the forerunner of his prodigies of long ago; . . .
> When he established the heavens I was there,
> when he marked out the vault over the face of the deep;
> When he made firm the skies above,

Lesson 5 Homework

1. Have the students write out their responses to the five For Review questions on page 22.
2. Assign the For Reflection activity (page 22). Tell the students not to complete it in their journals. Rather, they are to complete it and hand it in at their next session.
3. Remind the students to bring and turn in their completed chosen Ongoing Assignments at the next lesson.
4. Direct the students to read over the Chapter Quick View section on pages 24–26. If they have any questions, tell them to write them out and bring them to the next session.

For Enrichment

Evolution or Creationism—A False Dichotomy

Today's popular media often portray the creation vs. evolution question as a debate between science and religion, with creation being "religious" and evolution being "scientific." The debate always seems to center on whether the Genesis accounts of creation and/or the evolution theories regarding the origin of life should be presented in the classroom. That focus, however, is misleading. To suggest that the first chapters of Genesis ought to be taught in the classroom as an alternative to evolutionary theories is NOT pitting biblical understanding against evolutionary theories. Rather, it is pitting *literalist* theories of biblical interpretation against *evolutionary* theories. Doing this is not even like comparing oranges and apples; it is more like trying to compare oranges and orangutans.

when he fixed fast the foundations of
the earth;
When he set for the sea its limit,
so that the waters should not transgress
his command;
Then was I beside him as his craftsman."
(Prv 8:22, 27–30)

Christ and Creation

With the coming of Jesus Christ, the Son of God, we have access to the fullness of Divine Revelation. We learn from St. Paul that "Christ [is] the power of God and the wisdom of God" (1 Cor 12:24). The Letter to the Colossians proclaims the identity of Jesus Christ:

He is the image of the invisible God,
the firstborn of all creation.
For in him were created all things in heaven and on earth,
the visible and the invisible,
whether thrones or dominions or principalities or powers;
all things were created through him and for him.
He is before all things,
and in him all things hold together.
He is the head of the body, the church.
He is the beginning, the firstborn from the dead,
that in all things he himself might be preeminent.
For in him all the fullness was pleased to dwell,
and through him to reconcile all things for him,
making peace by the blood of his cross (through him), whether those on earth or those in heaven. (Col 1:15–20)

These remarkable verses, perhaps originally an early Christian hymn, proclaim our Lord to be:

- the *Agent of Creation* ("in him were all things created"),
- the *Wisdom of God* ("the firstborn of all creation," as in Proverbs 8:22),
- the *Sustainer* ("in him all things hold together"),
- and the *Savior* (God reconciles everything through him).

The Gospel of John tells us Christ is also the Word of God who spoke creation into existence. Everything was created through him:

In the beginning was the Word,
and the Word was with God,
and the Word was God.
He was in the beginning with God.
All things came to be through him,
and without him nothing came to be.
What came to be through him was life,
and this life was the light of the human race;
the light shines in the darkness,
and the darkness has not overcome it.
(Jn 1:1–5)

The Holy Trinity and Creation (CCC, 290-292)

New Testament passages like Colossians 1:15–20 and John 1:1–5 reveal very clearly that God created everything by the eternal Word, the Son of God. In addition, the Church professes belief in the creative activity of the Holy Spirit. He is the "giver of life" and "the source of all good" as proclaimed in the Catholic creeds.

The Old Testament Hebrew word for spirit is *ruah*, which can be translated as both "wind" and "breath." Recall the mighty wind in Genesis 1:2 that swept over the waters when God created the heavens and earth. This image powerfully points to the creative activity of the Holy Spirit from the very beginning. In the New Testament, the Holy Spirit came to the Apostles on Pentecost Sunday in a strong driving wind (Acts 2:2). His descent on them emboldened Christ's disciples and formed them into

- Conclude by having the students sing or listen to a recording of the hymn "How Great Thou Art" (GIA).

- "Creation in the Book of Psalms" (page 20). Help the students appreciate that the psalms use creation theology to stress God's majesty and God's glory. Creation themes like those in Psalm 8 and Psalm 104 demonstrate God's greatness and God's authority over nature, human beings included. They also point to human responsibility on behalf of creation.
    - Read Psalm 104:1–4, 24 as a class. Discuss its similarities to the creation stories of Genesis.
    - Conclude by having the students sing or listen to a recording of the hymn "All Things Bright and Beautiful" (GIA), or simply have the students pray Psalm 8.
- "Creation in the Book of Proverbs" (page 20). Read aloud the first and second sentences in this text section: *("All wisdom has its source in God. Wisdom is an expression of God's own nature.")* Note how Proverbs 8 describes wisdom as if it were a person. Point out, however, that the passage fixes wisdom's origin in God himself, assuring that it is fundamentally a divine attribute, belonging to the Creator God's being.

Extending the Lesson

Becoming Better Stewards

Tell the students that scientific studies tell us that every hour, three species of life become extinct: that's seventy-four a day, more than 27,000 a year. If every global citizen lived like the average US citizen, we would need five extra Earths to sustain our lifestyle. Given facts like these and recent findings regarding global warming, the Church asks us to recall our mission to act as good stewards of creation. To help the students in that stewardship, introduce them to the National Federation for Catholic Youth Ministry (NFCYM), which offers numerous ways to help young people in parish and school groups learn more about the environment and then engage in actions that make a positive difference in the world. Have your students check out NFCYM's website at www.climate.nfcym.org/index.htm. There they can take the first step to becoming part of the Catholic Climate Covenant by taking the St. Francis Pledge (see below), and then begin to do—or increase doing—their part to act as responsible stewards of creation.

The St. Francis Pledge

I/We pledge to:

PRAY and reflect on the duty to care for God's Creation and protect the poor and vulnerable.
LEARN about and educate others on the causes and moral dimensions of climate change.
ASSESS how we—as individuals and in our families, parishes and other affiliations—contribute to climate change by our own energy use, consumption, waste, etc.
ACT to change our choices and behaviors to reduce the ways we contribute to climate change.
ADVOCATE for Catholic principles and priorities in climate change discussions and decisions, especially as they impact those who are poor and vulnerable.

- Before moving on, have the students sing or listen to a recording of the hymn "The Works of the Lord Are Created in Wisdom" (GIA).

- "Christ and Creation" (page 21). Go through this section carefully with the students, pointing out the four declarations made by Colossians 1:15–20 regarding Christ. Note that both the passage from Colossians and the passage from John's Gospel indicate that it is Christ who stimulates, sustains, saves, and sums up creation.
  - Read the passage from John 1:1–5 aloud, substituting "Christ" for "the Word." Emphasize that John declares that even before all things existed, the "Word" (Christ) not only *was with* God, but actually *was* God, and was the *source* of all that is.
  - Conclude by having the students sing or listen to a recording of the hymn "Creator of the Stars of Night" (GIA).

the Church that would proclaim the Resurrected Lord to the ends of the earth.

"Breath" is also an apt image for the creative activity of the Holy Spirit. To live, we must breathe. Thus, the Holy Spirit is a life-giver. The psalmist knew this well when he wrote about God's creative activity:

> When you send forth your breath, they are created,
> and you renew the face of the earth.
> (Ps 104:30)

This image of God sending his Spirit to bring life also reminds us how the Spirit was present at the creation of the first man, when God breathed life into Adam (Gn 2:7).

In conclusion, then, we must understand that when God said, "Let us make man in our image, after our likeness" in Genesis 1:26, the words suggest the activity of all Three Persons of the Blessed Trinity. Only God alone can reveal himself as Father, Son, and Holy Spirit. This is the teaching of the Church—that creation is the work of Father, Son, and Holy Spirit.

> The Old Testament suggests and the New Covenant reveals the creative action of the Son and the Spirit, inseparably one with that of the Father. This creative co-operation is clearly affirmed in the Church's rule of faith: "There exists but one God . . . he is the Father, God, the Creator, the author, the giver of order. He made all things by himself, that is, by his Word and by his Wisdom," "by the Son and the Spirit" who, so to speak, are "his hands." Creation is the common work of the Holy Trinity. (*CCC*, 292)

This chapter presented an overview of the biblical accounts of God's creation. Creation is the first stage of Salvation History, revealing God's glory and his existence. The psalmist said it so well when he proclaimed, "The heavens declare the glory of God; the sky proclaims its builder's craft" (Ps 19:2). And in the words of the famous poet Gerard Manley Hopkins, "The world is charged with the grandeur of God." As the astronaut Frank Borman observed, "The more we learn about the wonders of our universe, the more clearly we are going to perceive the hand of God."

God's hand is in creation. He is the master builder who made human beings in his image to share life with him. God's creation is very good. From the beginning, humans were meant to be in communion and harmony with our loving God. However, the tragic consequences of Original Sin remain with us. But God did not abandon us. He promised a Savior who would redeem us from sin and death. We turn to that promise and God's fidelity to it in Chapter 2.

For Review

1. Share one example of how the creation theme is present in an Old Testament book other than the Book of Genesis.
2. What role does Christ have in creation?
3. How is the Holy Spirit involved in creation?
4. Why do Catholics believe that creation is the work of the Blessed Trinity?
5. What does the Church believe about evolution?

For Reflection

- Write your own song of praise to God for the gift of creation. Read Psalm 148 as inspiration.
- "The glory of God is man fully alive." Given your own talents, write how you might use them to glorify God.

For Review Answers (page 22)

1. Answers should include reference to Isaiah, Psalms, or Proverbs.
2. Christ is the agent of creation; everything was created and fulfilled through him.
3. The Holy Spirit is the powerful, creative "wind" at the dawn of creation and the "breath" of life infused (*inspir*ation) into the first human beings.
4. We believe that creation is the work of the Holy Trinity because although we often ascribe the work of creation to the first Person of the Trinity (Father), all three Persons of the Trinity act as *one* and thus are fully present in *all* the works, redeeming, sanctifying, and creating.
5. The Church takes no official stance except to say that scientific truth and religious truth are not contradictory and that each individual soul is created by God and does *not* evolve from some created matter.

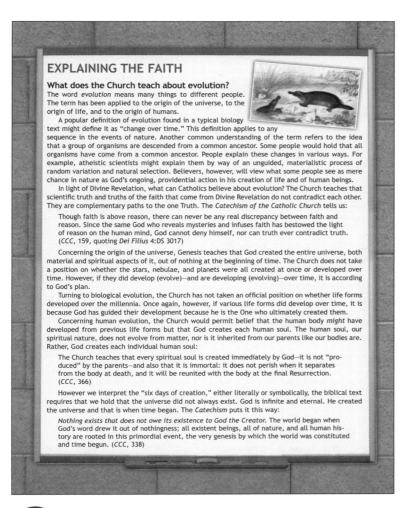

EXPLAINING THE FAITH

What does the Church teach about evolution?

The word *evolution* means many things to different people. The term has been applied to the origin of the universe, to the origin of life, and to the origin of humans.

A popular definition of evolution found in a typical biology text might define it as "change over time." This definition applies to any sequence in the events of nature. Another common understanding of the term refers to the idea that a group of organisms are descended from a common ancestor. Some people would hold that all organisms have come from a common ancestor. People explain these changes in various ways. For example, atheistic scientists might explain them by way of an unguided, materialistic process of random variation and natural selection. Believers, however, will view what some people see as mere chance in nature as God's ongoing, providential action in his creation of life and of human beings.

In light of Divine Revelation, what can Catholics believe about evolution? The Church teaches that scientific truth and truths of the faith that come from Divine Revelation do not contradict each other. They are complementary paths to the one Truth. The *Catechism of the Catholic Church* tells us:

> Though faith is above reason, there can never be any real discrepancy between faith and reason. Since the same God who reveals mysteries and infuses faith has bestowed the light of reason on the human mind, God cannot deny himself, nor can truth ever contradict truth. (*CCC*, 159, quoting *Dei Filius* 4:DS 3017)

Concerning the origin of the universe, Genesis teaches that God created the entire universe, both material and spiritual aspects of it, out of nothing at the beginning of time. The Church does not take a position on whether the stars, nebulae, and planets were all created at once or developed over time. However, if they did develop (evolve)—and are developing (evolving)—over time, it is according to God's plan.

Turning to biological evolution, the Church has not taken an official position on whether life forms developed over the millennia. Once again, however, if various life forms did develop over time, it is because God has guided their development because he is the One who ultimately created them.

Concerning human evolution, the Church would permit belief that the human body *might* have developed from previous life forms but that God creates each human soul. The human soul, our spiritual nature, does not evolve from matter, nor is it inherited from our parents like our bodies are. Rather, God creates each individual human soul:

> The Church teaches that every spiritual soul is created immediately by God—it is not "produced" by the parents—and also that it is immortal: it does not perish when it separates from the body at death, and it will be reunited with the body at the final Resurrection. (*CCC*, 366)

However we interpret the "six days of creation," either literally or symbolically, the biblical text requires that we hold that the universe did not always exist. God is infinite and eternal. He created the universe and that is when time began. The *Catechism* puts it this way:

> *Nothing exists that does not owe its existence to God the Creator.* The world began when God's word drew it out of nothingness; all existent beings, all of nature, and all human history are rooted in this primordial event, the very genesis by which the world was constituted and time begun. (*CCC*, 338)

- "The Holy Trinity and Creation" (pages 21–22). Introduce this section by having the students turn to Primary Source Quotations section on page 25 and read the quotation by Bl. Julian of Norwich. Then draw on the information below to help the students understand how the Holy Trinity is active in creation by reviewing our understanding of how the Holy Trinity acts in our lives.
    - Ask the students to describe how they picture the Holy Spirit. What images do they think of when they hear "Holy Spirit"? Discuss the ways the Holy Spirit acts in the creation stories to add to or solidify their images of creation.
    - Stress that although we ascribe these works separately, all three Persons of the Trinity act as *one* and are fully present in *all* the works.
    - Conclude this section by having the students sing or listen to a recording of the hymn "How Wonderful the Three-in-One" (GIA).

Extending the Lesson

Celebrating God's Grandeur

Have the students present the Gerard Manley Hopkins's poem "God's Grandeur," as outlined at the end of the Primary Source Quotations section, on page 25. A copy of the poem is below.

The world is charged with the grandeur of God.
  It will flame out, like shining from shook foil;
  It gathers to a greatness, like the ooze of oil
Crushed. Why do men then now not wreck his rod?
Generations have trod, have trod, have trod;
  And all is seared with trade; Bleared, smeared with toil;
  And wears man's smudge and shares man's smell: the soil
Is bare now, nor can foot feel, being shod.
And for all this, nature is never spent;
  There lives the dearest freshness deep down things;
And though the last lights off the black West went
  Oh, morning, at the brown brink eastward, springs —
Because the Holy Ghost over the bent
  World broods with warm breast and with ah! bright wings.

- Before concluding the lesson, draw attention to the Explaining the Faith feature, "What does the Church teach about evolution?" (page 23). Note that the Church has not taken an *official* stance except to say that scientific truths and the truths of faith are not contradictory since both emanate from God who *is* truth. The Church, however, does insist that whether or not the scientific theory of human evolution (humans having developed from previous life forms) is true, the human soul does not evolve from some created matter. Rather, God creates each and every individual soul, a soul that is immortal and is reunited with the body on the last day.
- Wrap up this lesson by having the students read Romans 8:19–23. Note the common "groaning" (or "yearning" or "longing"). Not only humankind but all creation groans for Redemption—for a return to Original Holiness and Justice. Tell the students that clearly human destiny and cosmic destiny are now and always have been inexorably linked.
- Finally, have the students sing or listen to a recording of the hymn "When the King Shall Come" (GIA).

Chapter 1 Quick View

Main Ideas

- The story of Redemption begins at the beginning of human history, at creation. (pp. 2–3)
- Human reason can come to know God by studying his works, though that is not the whole story, because human reason is limited. (pp. 3–5)
- God disclosed who he is through the events of Salvation history. (pp. 5–6)
- We know what God has revealed through the gift of the Deposit of Faith, Sacred Tradition, and Sacred Scripture working together. (pp. 5–6)
- The Deposit of Faith is entrusted to the Magisterium. (pp. 6–8)
- To read the Bible with understanding, we must recognize that it deals with a time, people, and culture that is foreign to us. (pp. 9–10)
- There are dozens of literary forms in the Bible, including anthem, epigram, etiology, parable, and more. (pp. 10–12)
- The Book of Genesis is part of the Pentateuch that contains the Torah, that is, the Law of the Jewish people. (pp. 12–15)
- Both Genesis creation accounts are part of primeval history recorded in Genesis 1–11. (pp. 12–15)
- The first creation account changed traditional stories and symbols of ancient myths to convey the Chosen People's belief in one, true God—Yahweh. (pp. 15–16)
- The second creation account portrays God as anthropomorphic, that is, with human qualities. (pp. 17–18)
- The second creation story also highlights the fact that the first humans were born in a state of Original Holiness and Original Justice, the grace of which was to share the divine life. (p. 18)
- The theme of creation is present in Catholic theology and Sacred Scripture as the foundation of all of God's saving plans and the beginning of Salvation History. (pp. 19–22)
- With the coming of Jesus Christ, we have access to the fullness of Divine Revelation. (pp. 20–21)
- Creation is the work of the Holy Trinity—Father, Son, and Holy Spirit. (pp. 21–22)
- The Church teaches that scientific truth and the truths of faith that come from Divine Revelation do not contradict each other. (p. 23)

Terms, People, Places

Match the following terms with the definitions below.

A. inspiration
B. polytheism
C. Deposit of Faith
D. Divine Revelation
E. philosophy
F. Magisterium
G. myth
H. Torah
I. Original Holiness and Original Justice
J. Redemption

1. The official teaching office of the Church.
2. The guidance of the Holy Spirit to help in the recording of Sacred Scripture
3. A word that means "ransom."
4. A summary is found in the Ten Commandments.
5. God's self-communication.
6. Symbolic stories that express a spiritual truth or a basic belief about God.
7. The state of man and woman before Original Sin.
8. Contained in both Sacred Scripture and Sacred Tradition.
9. A false belief that there are many gods.

For Enrichment

Words of the Holy Father

God's creation is one and it is good. The concerns for non-violence, sustainable development, justice and peace, and care for our environment are of vital importance for humanity.

—Pope Benedict XVI, World Youth Day, June 2008

All that exists carries the imprint of the Most Holy Trinity, because it all comes from love, tends toward love and is driven by love, naturally with different degrees of awareness and freedom. The best evidence that human beings are made in the image of the Trinity is that only love makes us happy, because we live to love and to be loved. Using an analogy suggested by biology, we would say that the human being carries in his very "genome" the profound trace of the trinity, of God-love. God's presence in all of creation is well expressed in Psalm 8: "Lord, our Lord, how awesome is your name through all the earth!"

—Pope Benedict XVI, Address on the Feast of the Most Holy Trinity, June 7, 2009

God's Good Creation: The Beginning of Salvation History 25

10. The investigation of truth and principles using human reason.

Primary Source Quotations

Our Creator God

The Trinity is our maker. The Trinity is our keeper. The Trinity is our everlasting lover. The Trinity is our endless joy.
—Bl. Julian of Norwich

In God alone there is primordial and true delight, in all our delights it is this delight that we are seeking.
—St. Bonaventure

The Lord Lives in Our Life

Invisible in his own nature God became visible in ours. Beyond our grasp, he chose to come within our grasp.
—St. Leo the Great

Poor creature though I be, I am the hand and foot of Christ. I move my hand and my hand is wholly Christ's hand, for deity is become inseparably one with me. I move my good and it is aglow with God.
—St. Simeon the New Theologian

Search for the poem "God's Grandeur" by Gerard Manley Hopkins, S.J. Prepare a dramatic reading of the poem. Consider setting the reading to music. Share the poem with your classmates.

Ongoing Assignments

As you cover the material in this chapter, choose and complete at least three of these assignments.

1. Research various theories on the probable location of the Garden of Eden. Present your findings in a PowerPoint presentation.
2. Conduct and record interviews on the subject of belief in God with one of the following audiences:
   - Five children under the age of ten on what they believe about God. Identify any statements they make that reveal wisdom that goes beyond their years.
   - Five believing adults on why they believe in the existence of God. Note any common reasons they might give.
3. Research a Native American religion. Find answers to these questions:
   - What is its concept of the Almighty?
   - What do they believe about how humans came to be?
   - How do they view the reason for human existence?
   - What are their beliefs about human destiny and concepts of the afterlife?
4. Prepare a PowerPoint presentation on how humans have abused the environment. Show how thoughtlessness is contrary to the biblical concept of good stewardship.
5. Prepare a PowerPoint presentation on Psalm 104. Use pictures from nature to accompany the words. Choose suitable background music.
6. Report on George Sim Johnson's article, "How to Read the First Chapter of Genesis" *Lay Witness* (September 1998). Report on the story of the Catholic priest behind the "big bang theory" of the origin of the universe. See Mark Midbon, "'A Day Without Yesterday': Georges Lemaitre & the Big Bang" *Commonweal* (March 24, 2000): 18–19.
7. Research and report on the subject of science and creation.
8. Research and report on the creation myth from a religion and culture other than Christianity.
9. Report on what three early Church Fathers and theologians taught about Genesis.
10. Research the topic "Ecological Footprint." Take one of the quizzes you discover to see how much of the earth's resources you consume.

Chapter 1 Quick View

Chapter 1: God's Good Creation: The Beginning of Salvation History—Review Lesson

Bell Ringers

- Review the last lesson by inviting the students to share responses to the five questions in the For Review section on page 22. Then share journaling on the For Reflection section from page 22.
- Collect the For Reflection activities from the previous lesson (page 17).
- Collect the students' Ongoing Assignments for Chapter 1 (page 25). Allow time for those who chose #4 or #5 (creating PowerPoint presentations) to make their presentations to the class.

Teaching Approaches

Chapter Quick View (pages 24-26)

- This section is provided for the students to review the chapter material. Although it is helpful for the students simply to read and study the list of Main Ideas, more creative use of the list might help the students retain the information. For example, make copies of

Review Lesson Objectives

The students will:

- review Chapter 1 in preparation for the chapter test.
- join in prayer together.

Terms, People, Places Answers (page 24)

1. F	3. J	5. D	7. I	9. B
2. A	4. H	6. G	8. C	10. E

Review Lesson Homework

1. Reread Chapter 1.
2. Study for the Chapter 1 Test.
3. Complete any unfinished Ongoing Assignments.

the list with some of the key words and/or phrases blocked out. Use this as a quiz to help students evaluate areas they need to examine more carefully or use simply as a study sheet.

- Call attention to Terms, People, Places on page 24. Have the students use the section as a vocabulary study tool by having the students complete the matching exercise. (See answers on page 39.)
- Take some time to go over any material the students may have overlooked in their review or that you feel needs more attention. Allow time for the students to ask any questions they may have.
- As time allows, invite various students who handed in written Ongoing Assignments reports to share their information with the group.

Prayer Service

- Begin by gathering the students in a circle. Light a candle. Ask the students the Reflection question from page 26: (*"What is it in God's creation that you are most grateful for?"*) Go around the circle, allowing each student to respond.
- Point out the Resolution on page 26. Encourage the students to make it and keep it.
- Lead the students in praying St. Francis of Assisi's "Canticle of Brother Sun" (page 26). (*Note*: If you wish, have the students sing a version of St. Francis's hymn: for example, "Canticle of the Sun" by Marty Haugen [GIA].)
- Conclude by sharing a sign of peace.

Chapter 1 Test Lesson

Teaching Approaches

- Allow sufficient time for the students to work on the Chapter 1 Test (starting on page 291 of the TWE and also online at www.avemariapress.com). Collect tests as the students finish.

Chapter 1 Quick View

26 Jesus Christ: Source of Our Salvation

Prayer

St. Francis of Assisi (1182–1226) is one of the most popular Catholic saints. He is the patron saint of ecology due to his great love of God's beautiful creation. He wrote the following prayer toward the end of his life. It is a wonderful hymn of praise to God the Creator and Father of us of all.

Canticle of Brother Sun

Most High, all powerful, good Lord,
Yours are the praises, the glory, the honor, and all blessing.
To You alone, Most High, do they belong, and no man is worthy to mention Your name.
Be praised, my Lord, through all your creatures,
especially through my lord Brother Sun,
who brings the day; and you give light through him.
And he is beautiful and radiant in all his splendor!
Of you, Most High, he bears the likeness.
Praise be You, my Lord, through Sister Moon
and the stars, in heaven you formed them
clear and precious and beautiful.
Praised be You, my Lord, through Brother Wind,
and through the air, cloudy and serene,
and every kind of weather through which
You give sustenance to Your creatures.
Praised be You, my Lord, through Sister Water,
which is very useful and humble and precious and chaste.
Praised be You, my Lord, through Brother Fire,
through whom you light the night and he is beautiful
and playful and robust and strong.
Praised be You, my Lord, through Sister Mother Earth,
who sustains us and governs us and who produces
varied fruits with colored flowers and herbs.
Praised be You, my Lord,
through those who give pardon for Your love,
and bear infirmity and tribulation.
Blessed are those who endure in peace
for by You, Most High, they shall be crowned.
Praised be You, my Lord,
through our Sister Bodily Death,
from whom no living man can escape.
Woe to those who die in mortal sin.
Blessed are those whom death will
find in Your most holy will,
for the second death shall do them no harm.
Praise and bless my Lord,
and give Him thanks
and serve Him with great humility. AMEN.

- *Reflection*: What is it in God's creation that you are most grateful for?
- *Resolution*: In the coming days, focus on each of the five senses in turn. For example, one day choose the gift of sight. Several times a day, stop and concentrate on this gift of sight and all the beautiful things it enables you to see. Recite a short prayer of praise and thanksgiving to God for this gift. On subsequent days, focus on the other senses in turn, praising and *thanking* God for what they enable you to perceive.

Test Lesson Homework

1. Read the following text sections of Chapter 2: "Creation and De-creation" (pages 30–32) and "The Effects of Original Sin" (page 32).
2. Examine the Chapter 2 Ongoing Assignments on page 52–53.

God's Good Creation: The Beginning of Salvation History 27

Chapter 1 Quick View

Chapter 1 Test Answers

Part 1: Matching. (3 points each)

1. D 2. C 3. A 4. E 5. B

Part 2: True or False. (3 points each)

1. F 2. T 3. F 4. F 5. T 6. T 7. T 8. T 9. F 10. T 11. F 12. T 13. F
14. F 15. F 16. T 17. T 18. T 19. T

Part 3: Fill in the Blanks. (3 points each)

1. pantheism 2. Torah 3. Holiness; Justice 4. philosophy 5. Mystery

Part 4: Essays.

1. See pages 10–12 of the student text for literary genres. (6 points)
2. Compare student definitions of compassion to the story of Robert De Vicenzo in the opening section of the chapter. (3 points)
3. Answer should stress the anthropomorphic differences in the second creation account, the difference in the order of creation, or the difference in their sources. The comparisons between the Genesis creation accounts and other books of the Bible will vary. (4 points)

Chapter 2: The Fall and the Promise of a Savior

Introduction

Music can noble hints impart,
Engender fury, kindle love,
With unsuspected eloquence can move,
And manage all the man with secret art.

—Joseph Addison

In the movies, the background music alerts us when something dire is about to take place. If you were making a movie of the Book of Genesis, the very first sentence of Genesis 3 would signal a sinister shift in tone. Check it out: "Now the serpent was the most cunning of all the animals that the Lord God had made." The major key modulates to minor key, forewarning us that "something wicked this way comes." And just as the creation stories ring with harmony—between humankind and God, with creation, and with one another—the stories that follow ring with discord and dissonance.

In the story of the Fall, the students see how our first parents' free choice resulted in the loss of Original Holiness and Justice. This Original Sin stripped them of their divine birthright and replaced it with a state of disharmony, suffering, death, and sinfulness into which all future generations would be born. Even so, there is good news among all the bad. The students discover that although Adam and Eve turned their backs on God, God would not do likewise. Rather, God promises to send a savior—a *New Adam*—who will restore our birthright by reconciling us to God, to one another, and to all creation as well.

The next stories in Genesis present a clear depiction of the effects of sin. The dispute between Adam and Eve's children, Cain and Abel, reveals the depth of the effects of Original Sin. Brother turns against brother. Jealousy morphs into murder. God marks the murderer but does not turn away. Sin continues to overcome the human race and God decides to cleanse the world by flooding the earth. He remains faithful to Noah and his descendants and promises never to flood the earth again. Yet, humankind continues to sin. The story of the Tower of Babel reprises the story of humans choosing self over God. Communication breaks down exacerbating even further the alienation and separation that is sin. Still, God refuses to abandon humankind. He will continue to make covenants with his people.

The students investigate the divine covenants with Abraham, Moses, and David. They discover how God promises faithful and obedient Abraham a future that includes a nation of descendants, a blessed name, and the assurance that all the earth will be blessed through him. Through Moses, God creates a *people*, rescues them from slavery, and establishes a covenant that offers value-laden guidelines for living in harmony once again with God, with one another, and with all creation. Finally, in the covenant with King David, the students learn how God promises him a descendant who will be a Messiah for all humankind.

Although God does not turn away from his people, the people continue to turn away from God. So, the Father sends prophets to warn the people to turn back to him, to honor his covenants. The students look at the prophecies of Amos, Jeremiah, Ezekiel, and Isaiah. In Amos they hear a powerful voice for social justice. In Jeremiah, they discover the promise of a new and very personal covenant with God. In Ezekiel, they visit a vision filled with a new in-spiration, a divine re-creating breath. In Isaiah, they meet a servant whose suffering will save us all. In all the prophets, they encounter a message that rebukes and reconciles, cautions, and comforts.

Chapter Objectives

To help the students:

- review their understanding of the purpose of myth in the Scriptures.
- recognize that a historical event lies behind the story of the Fall.
- examine Original Sin and its consequences.
- examine the spread of sin as recorded in the stories of Cain and Abel, the Flood, and the Tower of Babel.
- appreciate how God remained faithful even in times of sin.
- understand and appreciate the meaning and impact of the Old Testament covenants.
- discover the role of the biblical prophets.
- investigate the Servant Songs of Deutero-Isaiah.

Finally, the chapter concludes with an abbreviated history of the Hebrew people as they suffered and survived under the rule of mightier nations. This was a people longing for Salvation, for the fulfillment of the covenants, for the coming of a Messiah. This was a people listening for the background music to change. And that change was coming *prestissimo.*

Advance Preparations

Prepare or have on hand:

For Lesson 1

- Corrected copies of the Chapter 1 Test
- Bibles
- A recording of Joni Mitchell's song "Big Yellow Taxi" and player (optional)
- Construction paper

For Lesson 2

- Bibles
- Copies of Chapter 2, Handout 1, "The Exultet"
- Copies of recent newspapers and/or news magazines, scissors, glue, art paper

For Lesson 3

- Bibles

For Lesson 4

- Bibles

For Lesson 5

- Bibles
- A recording of the spiritual "Dry Bones" and player (optional)
- Copies of Chapter 2, Handout 2, "Prophetic Voices"
- Copies of Chapter 2, Handout 3, "Isaiah x 3"

For the Chapter 2 Review Lesson

- Equipment necessary for students to make PowerPoint presentations
- A recording and a player for a song of repentance and reconciliation: e.g., "Healer of Our Every Ill" (Haugen, GIA)

For the Chapter 2 Test Lesson

- Copies of the Chapter 2 Test (starting on page 291 of the TWE and also online at www.avemariapress.com)

Chapter 2 Handouts

- Handout 1, The Exultet—The students examine the Exultet to discover how the prayer describes Jesus as the new Adam.
- Handout 2, Prophetic Voices—The students read the prophets and write their own prophetic message.
- Handout 3, Isaiah x 3—The students examine the three-part Book of the Prophet Isaiah and discover how the Fourth Servant Song refers to Jesus.

Chapter 2: The Fall and the Promise of a Savior—Lesson 1

Bell Ringers

- Distribute the corrected Chapter 1 Test. Go over the test with the students, using it as a means to review the previous chapter. Address any remaining questions or concerns the students may have.
- Write the word **myth** on the board. Take a few moments to review the students' understanding of the term. See to it that the students recognize that a myth is a story whose main purpose is to express a great spiritual truth or insight into reality. Emphasize that while myth is truth, it grapples with the reality in a *story* rather than with a schematic proposition; myth addresses questions about the *meaning* of events that are part of the human experience.
- Explain that the two creation myths of Genesis speak to the following crucial questions—write on the board:
  - **How did everything come to be?**
  - **Who are we?**
- Invite the students to respond to the two questions. Look for the following understandings:
  - *Everything came to be through the action of a compassionate, loving, and self-existent being (God) who existed before the material universe and is distinct from it.*
  - *Fashioned in God's image, human beings are the pinnacles and stewards of creation, called to share in God's creative act.*

Teaching Approaches

Creation and De-creation (pages 30-32)

- Have the students read Genesis 3:1–13 on their own. While the students are reading, write the following on the board: **Why is there evil in God's good world?** When the students finish reading, ask them to answer the question. Point out that the mythic story of the Fall is the Genesis response to this crucial question, a question they will investigate further in this chapter. Challenge the students to think deeply about this question. Discuss what this makes them think about God. Conclude the discussion by offering the following quotations:

30 Jesus Christ: Source of Our Salvation

Creation and De-creation

An anonymous satirical poem titled "De-creation" graphically contradicts the beautiful creation accounts in the Book of Genesis by showing how sin is destroying the world:

In the beginning was the earth,
and the earth was beautiful.
But the people on the earth said,
"Let us build skyscrapers and
expressways."
So they paved the earth with concrete and
said, "It is good!"
On the second day,
the people looked at the rivers and said,
"Let us dump our sewage into the waters."
So they filled the waters with sludge
and said, "It is good!"
On the third day,
the people looked at the forest and said,
"Let us cut down the trees
and build things."
So they leveled the forests
and said, "It is good!"
On the fourth day,
the people saw the animals and said,
"Let us kill them for sport and money."
So they destroyed the animals
and said, "It is good!"
On the fifth day,
the people felt the cool breeze and said,
"Let us burn our garbage
and let the breeze blow it away."
So they filled the air with carbon
and said, "It is good!"
On the sixth day,
the people saw other nations on earth and
said,
"Let us build missiles
in case misunderstandings arise."
So they filled the land with missile sites
and said, "It is good!"
On the seventh day,

the earth was quiet and deathly silent,
for the people were no more.
And it was good!

This poem is a sad, if not accurate, view of creation today. "De-creation" takes place because human beings have turned from God and put their own self interests above those of their Creator, other humans, and the beautiful world God has entrusted to us. De-creation takes place because of human pride and sin, causing alienation from self, others, God, and creation itself. It all started with the **Original Sin** of Adam and Eve described in Genesis 3:1–24. However, God never abandoned sinful humanity. From the beginning, God promised a Savior, a Redeemer, who would make all things new. In the midst of the story of the fall of humanity, God

Lesson 1 Objectives

The students will:

- review Chapter 1.
- review their understanding of the purpose of myth in the Scriptures.
- recognize Original Sin and its consequences.

Lesson 1 Preview

This lesson introduces the students to the biblical story of the Fall and to the concept of Original Sin and its consequences. To help the students understand the material in this chapter, be sure to lay the groundwork by re-emphasizing the meaning and purpose of myth and mythic language.

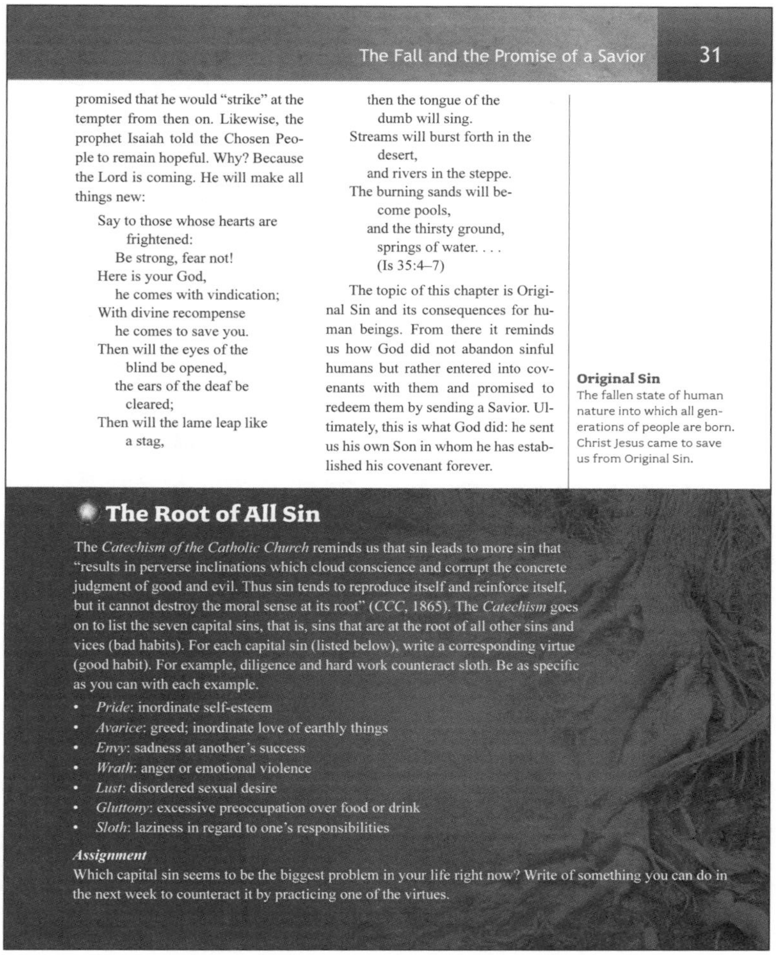

The Fall and the Promise of a Savior 31

promised that he would "strike" at the tempter from then on. Likewise, the prophet Isaiah told the Chosen People to remain hopeful. Why? Because the Lord is coming. He will make all things new:

> Say to those whose hearts are
> frightened:
> Be strong, fear not!
> Here is your God,
> he comes with vindication;
> With divine recompense
> he comes to save you.
> Then will the eyes of the
> blind be opened,
> the ears of the deaf be
> cleared;
> Then will the lame leap like
> a stag,
> then the tongue of the
> dumb will sing.
> Streams will burst forth in the
> desert,
> and rivers in the steppe.
> The burning sands will be-
> come pools,
> and the thirsty ground,
> springs of water. . . .
> (Is 35:4–7)

The topic of this chapter is Original Sin and its consequences for human beings. From there it reminds us how God did not abandon sinful humans but rather entered into covenants with them and promised to redeem them by sending a Savior. Ultimately, this is what God did: he sent us his own Son in whom he has established his covenant forever.

Original Sin
The fallen state of human nature into which all generations of people are born. Christ Jesus came to save us from Original Sin.

The Root of All Sin

The *Catechism of the Catholic Church* reminds us that sin leads to more sin that "results in perverse inclinations which cloud conscience and corrupt the concrete judgment of good and evil. Thus sin tends to reproduce itself and reinforce itself, but it cannot destroy the moral sense at its root" (*CCC*, 1865). The *Catechism* goes on to list the seven capital sins, that is, sins that are at the root of all other sins and vices (bad habits). For each capital sin (listed below), write a corresponding virtue (good habit). For example, diligence and hard work counteract sloth. Be as specific as you can with each example.

- *Pride*: inordinate self-esteem
- *Avarice*: greed; inordinate love of earthly things
- *Envy*: sadness at another's success
- *Wrath*: anger or emotional violence
- *Lust*: disordered sexual desire
- *Gluttony*: excessive preoccupation over food or drink
- *Sloth*: laziness in regard to one's responsibilities

Assignment
Which capital sin seems to be the biggest problem in your life right now? Write of something you can do in the next week to counteract it by practicing one of the virtues.

Lesson 1 Homework

1. Tell the students to turn to Ongoing Assignments on pages 52–53. Have the students choose any three of the listed assignments to complete prior to the conclusion of this chapter. Tell them the assignments are due on the day they gather for their chapter review.
2. Have the students read, "Was Original Sin a Historical Event?" (pages 32–38) in preparation for their next session.

  - "God permits evil, in order to draw forth something greater, even after sin."—St. Thomas Aquinas (*CCC*, 412)
  - "I sought whence evil comes and there was no solution"—St. Augustine (*CCC*, 385)
- If possible, play a recording of Joni Mitchell's song "Big Yellow Taxi" (also covered by the group Counting Crows under the title "They Paved Paradise"). If you're unable to get a recording, read, distribute, or write the following lyrics on the board:

  They paved paradise
  And put up a parking lot
  With a pink hotel, a boutique
  And a swinging hot spot.
  Don't it always seem to go
  That you don't know what you've got
  Till it's gone?
  They paved paradise
  And put up a parking lot.

- Call on different students to read aloud the poem "Decreation" (page 30). Point out that each "day" speaks to a result of human sinfulness.
- Divide the students into six small groups. Assign to each group one of the days of De-creation. Direct each group to respond to two questions regarding its day. Tell the students that for each question they should offer as many answers/solutions as they can.
  - Group 1: Why should we be alarmed over urban sprawl?
    What can we do to reduce urban sprawl?
  - Group 2: Why should we be concerned about water pollution?
    What can we do to keep our waters clean?
  - Group 3: Why should we protect the forests?
    What can we do to protect the forests?
  - Group 4: Why should we strive to preserve wildlife?
    What can we do to preserve wildlife?
  - Group 5: Why should we keep air pure?
    What can we do to keep air pure?
  - Group 6: Why should we worry about nuclear proliferation?
    What can we do to stop nuclear proliferation?
- Have each group write its ideas on a sheet of construction paper. Then have the groups present their ideas to the class. Post the sheets in the classroom. Have the entire class decide on the most convincing reasons to protect the earth and the best ways to

accomplish what they propose. Encourage specificity. Finally, note how the responses and ideas speak to our role as stewards of creation.

- Write the term **Original Sin** on the board. Point out its definition in the text (page 31). Remind the students that Original Sin often refers to a historical event represented by the sin of Adam and Eve, who abused the freedom God gave them by choosing to follow their own wills, not God's. Explain that this chapter will delve into the meaning and consequences of this first sin as well as God's refusal to abandon us to sin's effects.

The Effects of Original Sin (page 32)

- Have the students turn to the text section "The Effects of Original Sin" on page 32. Review the terms Original Holiness and Original Justice. Make certain the students understand that these terms refer to the state of perfection in which God created human beings so that they might share in God's life, experiencing harmony within themselves, with others, and with all of creation (Original Holiness) and not suffer pain or death (Original Justice).
- Note some of the effects of Original Sin listed in the text (page 32). Tell the students they will further investigate these effects and others in their next lesson.
- Note how sin is that which *alienates* and *separates*. Stress that Original Sin alienated/separated human beings:

For Reflection

How would you define "de-creation"?

The Effects of Original Sin

Genesis 3 describes Original Sin and its effects. From it, we learn important truths about the human condition. Recall that God created us good from the start; we were meant to be happy. Adam and Eve enjoyed Original Holiness and Original Justice with God. The grace of original holiness meant human beings were created to share in God's own life. Adam and Eve were meant to be in friendship with God, living in harmony with him, with each other, and with all other creatures. Being in the state of original justice meant that humans would not die or experience suffering or pain.

After losing the state of Original Holiness and Original Justice, human beings suffer many effects of the loss. Women now suffer the pains of childbirth, men (and women) do back-breaking work to eke out a living, nakedness causes shame, and death is the fate of humans. All of these sad outcomes are the result of Original Sin. By disobeying God's commands, the first humans chose themselves and their own wills rather than submit themselves to the will of a loving God. Friendship with God required them to respond to him. By asserting their own wills instead of responding to the Lord in friendship and obedience, Adam and Eve sinned: "Sin is an abuse of the freedom that God gives to created persons so that they are capable of loving him and loving one another" (*CCC*, 387).

Was Original Sin a Historical Event?

Did the Fall of Adam and Eve take place as depicted in Genesis 3? The *Catechism of the Catholic Church* teaches:

> The account of the fall in Genesis 3 uses figurative language, but affirms a primeval event, a deed that took place at the beginning of the history of man. Revelation gives us the certainty of faith that the whole of human history is marked by the original fault freely committed by our first parents. (*CCC*, 390)

We are not required to interpret the story about the Fall of Adam and Eve in Genesis in a literal way, but we must believe that there was a real historical event behind it. After all, where did sin and evil come from? God, who is all-good, cannot be the source of sin. Yet, human wickedness, moral evil,

Extending the Lesson

Myth-Making

Help the students better their understanding of how myth addresses questions about the *meaning* of events that are part of the human experience. Invite them to create a myth of their own. Have the students form small groups, and then lead them through the following procedure:

- Develop a statement of a problem or a question from their life experience (e.g., Why do hurricanes happen? Why can't parents understand what their kids are saying? What's the deal with acne?)
- Brainstorm the setting, characters, and a storyline that will explain the question or statement.
- Write, illustrate, or present (act out) the myth.

For Earth's Sake

Have the students investigate the website for Earth Protect (www.earthprotect.com), an overall social networking environmental website that allows users to upload and download videos and films on environmental issues and solutions. Earth Protect's goal is to help people and organizations worldwide become aware, informed, committed, and empowered to take action to protect the earth and achieve a sustainable and healthy environment.

and sin are here. The great Catholic writer, G. K. Chesterton, said that you could prove the truth of the doctrine of Original Sin by simply reading the daily newspaper. Sin is part of the human condition from the beginning. "Sin is present in human history; any attempt to ignore it or to give this dark reality other names would be futile" (*CCC*, 386).

As Divine Revelation unfolded throughout history, it reached its fulfillment in the Life, Death, and Resurrection of Jesus Christ. Only then could God's People understand the full meaning of Original Sin.

> [T]his story's ultimate meaning . . . is revealed only in the light of the death and Resurrection of Jesus Christ. We must know Christ as the source of grace in order to know Adam as the source of sin. (*CCC*, 388)

Temptation Leads to Original Sin

Temptation is defined as "an attraction, either outside oneself or from within, to act contrary to right reason and the commandments of God." Genesis uses the symbol of the serpent to tell us about the seductive influence of a fallen angel who tempted Adam and Eve to choose themselves over their God. This fallen angel is known as **Satan**. Like all angels, Satan and other demons were created good by a loving God. They became evil by their own design by making a free choice. They: radically and irrevocably rejected God and his reign. We find a reflection of that rebellion in the tempter's words to our first parents: "You will be like God." The devil "has sinned from the beginning"; he is "liar and the father of lies." (*CCC*, 392)

Satan, in the guise of a serpent, did great harm by seducing and tempting Adam and Eve. Created good in God's image and likeness, man was deceived into letting his trust in his Creator die in his heart and, abusing his freedom, disobeyed God's command. This is what man's first sin consisted of. All subsequent sin would be disobedience toward God and lack of trust in his goodness (*CCC*, 397).

Genesis 2:16–17 mentions the tree of knowledge of good and evil and God's command not to eat its fruit on pain of death. The serpent distorted the truth and deceived Adam and Eve. He promised that if they ate of the forbidden fruit, they would be like God. The forbidden fruit symbolizes knowledge only God should have—the knowledge of good and evil. Through their own willful choice, both by disobeying and defying God, Adam and Eve tried to make themselves gods. They sinned by preferring themselves to God. In so doing, they scorned God and did not recognize that they were creatures. They wanted to be like God but not in accord with his own plans for them (*CCC*, 398).

Satan
A fallen angel or the devil; the Evil One (CCC, 391, 395, 2851).

- from God
- from one another
- from themselves
- from all the rest of creation

- Tell the students that this alienation caused a gap that could be closed only by God. Only the God who made all things could make all things anew. Have the students turn back to page 31 in their text and read the passage quoted from the Book of Isaiah (Is 35:4–7). Tell the students that these inspired and inspiring words speak of re-creation, re-generation, reconciliation, and restoration to Original Holiness and Justice.
- Move on to the opening activity "The Root of All Sin" on page 31. Read aloud the quotation from the *Catechism*, 1865. Use a metaphor or simile to help the students better understand what the *Catechism* is saying. For example, tell them that sin is like an oil slick that oozes and spreads, polluting all it touches.
- Go on to have the students read Proverbs 6:16–19 in their Bibles. Then point out the list of the seven capital sins on page 31. Explain that these sins are based in part on the passage from Proverbs.
- Have the students work in pairs to write the antithesis of each sin. Afterward, share responses. Look for opposites similar to the following:
  - Pride: humility/modesty/meekness
  - Avarice: generosity/charity/liberality
  - Envy: kindness/gratitude/brotherly love

Extending the Lesson

Just for Fun—"The Seven Deadly Virtues"

Have the students listen to a recording of the song "The Seven Deadly Virtues," from the musical *Camelot* by Lerner and Loewe and sung by the villain Mordred. You may be able to find a version of the song on YouTube. Ask students to share what they know about Camelot, King Arthur, and Mordred. Distribute the lyrics to the students and discuss the meaning of the words after you listen to the song. The lyrics are as follows:

> The seven deadly virtues, those ghastly little traps.
> Oh no, my liege, they were not meant for me
> Those seven deadly virtues were made for other chaps
> Who love a life of failure and ennui.
> Take courage—now there's a sport
> An invitation to the state of rigor mort
> And purity—a noble yen
> And very restful every now and then.
> I find humility means to be hurt
> It's not the earth the meek inherit, it's the dirt.
> Honesty is fatal, it should be taboo,
> Diligence—a fate I would hate.
> If charity means giving, I give it to you,
> And fidelity is only for your mate.
> You'll never find a virtue unstatusing my quo or making my Beelzebubble burst.
> Let others take the high road, I will take the low.
> I cannot wait to rush in where angels fear to go.
> With all those seven deadly virtues free and happy little me has not been cursed.

- Wrath: serenity/compassion/patience
- Lust: chastity/purity/wholesomeness
- Gluttony: temperance/moderation/self-control
- Sloth: diligence/zeal/persistence

- Before dismissing the students, allow time for them to journal their response to the Assignment on page 31.

Chapter 2: The Fall and the Promise of a Savior—Lesson 2

Bell Ringers

- To review what the students learned about sin and its pervasiveness in the last lesson (see "The Root of All Sin" on page 31), help them recall the simile of the spreading oil slick that surrounds and defiles all it touches. Explain that the polluting and pervasive nature of sin is explained in the doctrine of Original Sin.
- Tell the students that perhaps no Christian doctrine is more controversial or more consequential than that of Original Sin. Then write the following question on the board: **Original Sin—Are we bad to the bone?** Allow the students to respond.
- Go on to remind the students that the Church teaches that because of Original Sin, all human beings inherit the sinful tendencies and structures passed on to us by

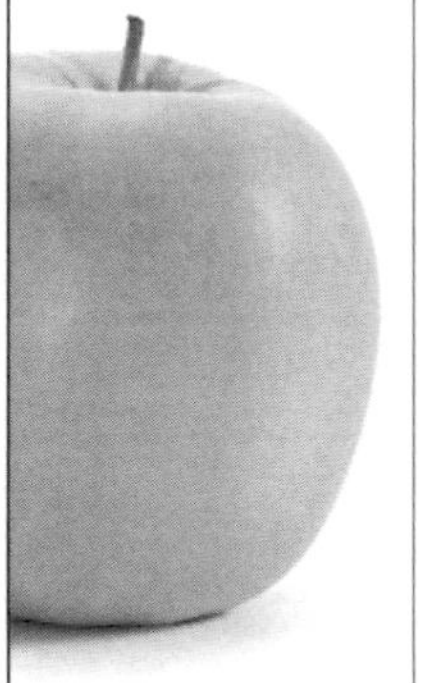

Protoevangelium
A term that means "the first gospel," which is found in Genesis 3:15, when God revealed he would send a Savior to redeem the world from its sins.

New Adam
Announced in the Protoevangelium, a name for Jesus Christ who through his obedience in Life and Death makes amends for the disobedience of Adam.

Consequences of Original Sin

The sin of Adam and Eve did in fact bring them new knowledge, namely the knowledge of shame and guilt. They realized they were naked and sewed fig leaves together to make loincloths to cover their nakedness. This action symbolized how their sin caused alienation between them. More importantly, their sin led to their alienation from God, the loss of Original Holiness. They tried to hide from God because they were "afraid of the God of whom they have conceived a distorted image—that of a God jealous of his prerogatives" (*CCC*, 299). The Yahwist author uses intimate language when talking about the Lord God who walks in the Garden looking for the man and the woman "in the breezy time of the day" (Gn 3:8). When questioned about why he ate the forbidden fruit, Adam blamed Eve. When Eve was questioned, she also made an excuse for her behavior: "The serpent tricked me into it, so I ate it" (Gn 3:13). Blaming and making excuses does not negate what Adam and Eve really did—freely and defiantly choosing to contradict God's command.

The *Catechism* lists the following outcomes that resulted from the Original Sin:

> The harmony in which they had found themselves, thanks to original justice, is now destroyed: the control of the soul's spiritual faculties over the body is shattered; the union of man and woman becomes subject to tensions, their relations henceforth marked by lust and domination (Gn 3:7–16). Harmony with creation is broken: visible creation has become alien and hostile to man (Gn 3:17, 19). Because of man, creation is now subject "to its bondage to decay" (Rom 8:21). Finally, the consequence explicitly foretold for this disobedience will come true.... Death makes its entrance into human history (Rom 5:12). (*CCC*, 400)

All humans are implicated in the sin of Adam and Eve. Through Original Sin, we have inherited a fallen human nature, are deprived of Original Holiness and Original Justice, and are subject to death. St. Paul taught that, "through one person sin entered the world, and through sin, death, and thus death came to all, inasmuch as all sinned" (Rom 5:12).

Exactly how does Original Sin affect all of humanity? St. Thomas Aquinas observed that the human race is in Adam "as one body of one man." There is a unity of the human race that results in our sharing in Adam's sin, just as we all share in Christ's Salvation. The transmission of Original Sin is fundamentally a mystery, but Divine Revelation does make it clear that Original Holiness and Original Justice was given to Adam not only for himself but also for all humans to follow. By giving into temptation, Adam and Eve committed a *personal*

For Enrichment

The following quotations are taken from the United States Conference of Catholic Bishops' statements on the environment. Read the quotations as a class and discuss their implications for everyday life.

> All people on this globe share a common ecological environment that is under increasing pressure. Depletion of soil, water and other natural resources endangers the future. Pollution of air and water threatens the delicate balance of the biosphere on which future generations will depend. The resources of the earth have been created by God for the benefit of all, and we who are alive today hold them in trust. This is a challenge to develop a new ecological ethic that will help shape a future that is both just and sustainable.
>
> ***Economic Justice for All: A Pastoral Letter on Catholic Social Teaching and the US Economy***

> At its core, global climate change is not about economic theory or political platforms, nor about partisan advantage or interest group pressures. It is about the future of God's creation and the one human family. It is about protecting both 'the human environment' and the natural environment.
>
> ***Global Climate Change: A Plea for Dialogue, Prudence and the Common Good***

previous generations, beginning with our first parents. Because we're *born* into sin, we must be *re-born*. This we cannot do on our own. God must come and restore us into new life through his Son and his sacraments. Put simply, Original Sin tells us: "We're broken. We need fixing. We can't do it ourselves."

The Fall and the Promise of a Savior 35

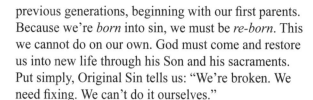

sin. This personal sin of theirs "affected the *human nature* that they would then transmit *in a fallen state*" (*CCC*, 404). The wounded human nature is passed on through propagation to all succeeding generations. We are deprived of Original Holiness and Original Justice, lost by the sin of our first parents. The *Catechism* teaches that Original Sin is "'contracted' and not 'committed'—a state and not an act" (*CCC*, 404).

Adam and Eve's sin did not totally corrupt human nature. However, it weakened it. This means that we are subject to the temptations of Satan. Our wounded human nature also subjects us to ignorance, suffering, and death. Moreover, it inclines us to sin, a condition known as concupiscence. St. Paul knew this condition well when he wrote, "What I do, I do not understand. For I do not do what I want, but I do what I hate" (Rom 7:15).

The effects of Original Sin are obvious to anyone who has eyes to see. Think of all the problems that exist in the world: greed that leads to exploitation of the poor and destruction of the environment; wars in which nations are bent on destroying other nations; abortions that snuff out the lives of innocent children; prejudice that denies people basic human rights; marital discord that leads to broken families; lust that results in sexual perversion and life-threatening diseases; the list is truly endless. Something is wrong with human nature. Things were not meant to be this way. Human beings are seriously wounded and in need of help.

The Protoevangelium

God did not abandon Adam and Eve and their descendants after the Original Sin. Immediately after Adam and Eve offered their excuses for their disobedience, the Lord God revealed his plan of Salvation. This plan would conquer evil and death, restore humanity from the Fall, and bring into harmony once again all relationships, especially the relationship between humans and their loving God.

The announcement of God's plan of Salvation appears in Genesis 3:15. God speaks to the serpent (Satan), who had deceived Adam and Eve and led them into sin:

I will put enmity between you and the woman,
and between your offspring and hers;
He will strike at your head,
while you strike at his heel. (Gn 3:15)

This verse is known as the **Protoevangelium** (translated "first gospel"). It predicts a future Messiah and Redeemer, a battle between the serpent and the woman, and a final victory of a descendant of hers. Christian Tradition sees in this passage the announcement of the **New Adam**. The New Testament tells us "the Son of God was revealed to destroy the works of the devil" (1 Jn 3:8). Jesus Christ did this by "becoming obedient unto death, even death on a cross." His obedience made up in a superabundant way for Adam's disobedience. Church Fathers have identified the woman in this passage as the Blessed Mother, the new Eve. Her offspring, of course, is Jesus Christ.

Lesson 2 Objectives

The students will:

- recognize that a real historical event lies behind the story of the Fall.
- investigate the meaning and effects of Original Sin.
- represent the effects of Original Sin in today's world.

Lesson 2 Preview

In this lesson the students examine the significance and consequences of Original Sin. Given the weight of this material and its importance for understanding the mission of Jesus, consider allowing more than one class period to cover the material.

Teaching Approaches

Was Original Sin a Historical Event? (pages 32–38)

- Point out that the Church holds that *a real historical event* lies behind the story of the Fall. Explain that this position is rooted both in Scripture and in Tradition.
    - Scripture—We know that the literary form of Genesis is a mythic story. That understanding does not, however, deny the intrinsic truth of a deliberate rebellion initiated at a specific time by the first human beings.
    - Tradition—The historical nature of Original Sin is an essential part of Church doctrine, because it defines the problem of evil as a specific willful rebellion against God. This rebellion resulted in separation and guilt. The action of God through the atoning work of Christ repairs this separation and washes away guilt.
- Ask one of the students to read aloud the last paragraph of the text section "Consequences of Original Sin," including the passage from paragraph #388 of the *Catechism.* (See page 33.) Then distribute copies of Chapter 2, Handout 1, "The Exultet." If the students are not familiar with it, explain that it is the great proclamation sung at the Easter Vigil. Go on to read and discuss the Exultet with the students, paying particular attention to the phrases that are printed in boldface italics. Ask:
    - What is the mood of the prayer?
    - What is being proclaimed? (*Jesus' Resurrection and our Redemption*)
    - How does this proclamation relate to the celebration of Easter? (*It describes the night God freed us from sin.*)
    - To what does "Adam's sin" refer? (*Original Sin*)
    - Why is Adam's sin called a "happy fault"? (*As the Catechism states, without it, the "source of sin," we would not know Christ, "the source of grace."*)

- Call attention to the final highlighted phrases of the Exultet, beginning with *"the power of this holy night"* and ending with *"we are reconciled to God!"* Note carefully all that was lost due to Original Sin and all that was gained by Christ's Resurrection.
- Take a moment to review again the students' understanding of myth. It should be similar to this: Myth addresses questions about the *meaning* of events that are part of the human experience. Myth answers the question "Why?" and helps us to accept the world as we experience it.
- Have the students reread Genesis 3:1–7. Then ask:
    - What questions do you think this story answered for the people of Israel? (List all replies on the board—to be referred to later on—for example: *Why is there evil in God's good world? Why do we do what is wrong? Why do we have to work so hard? Why do we have to die?*)
- Write the word **temptation** on the board. Challenge the students to come up with a definition of temptation—something similar to the following: *the inclination to do what we know is not right.* Then ask:
    - What is the agent of temptation in the Genesis story? (*the serpent*)
    - Of what/whom is the serpent symbolic? (*evil, the devil, Satan*)
    - Why do you think the biblical author chose a serpent to be the tempter? (*Both temptation and the serpent are fascinating, stealthy, artful, insinuating, scary, etc.* Note: *Explain that Israel's pagan neighbors used serpents in worship, thus making the serpent the antithesis of the one true God.*)
- Take a few moments to further analyze the temptation story with the students.
    - Ask: What did the Serpent convince Eve to desire? (*To be like God*)
    - Genesis 3:4–5—Note how in her imagination, Eve sees God's prohibition as God being selfish, not caring. Resenting the restriction, Eve grasps at what she thinks will make her like God.
    - Genesis 3:6–7—Ask, "What happened when Adam and Eve's eyes were opened? (*They realized they were naked and they were ashamed. Now that they were deprived of Original Holiness, their vision was influenced by sin.*)

36 Jesus Christ: Source of Our Salvation

Jesus' Death on the cross won for us Salvation and Redemption. It atoned for the Original Sin of Adam and Eve and all the sins people have committed down through the centuries. Mary was the first person to benefit in a unique way from Christ's victory over sin. She, the Mother of God, "was preserved from all stain of original sin and by a special grace of God committed no sin of any kind during her whole earthly life" (*CCC*, 411).

Christ's Death is the source of our Salvation. St. Paul writes, "But God proves his love for us in that while we were still sinners Christ died for us" (Rom 5:8). Christ is God's instrument for the great reversal. He is our Salvation: "For just as through the disobedience of one person the many were made sinners, so through the obedience of one the many will be made righteous" (Rom 5:19). It is through the Church that we receive the gift of Salvation. All Salvation comes through the Body of Christ, the Church, from Christ. As Christians, we enter into the life of Christ when we receive the Sacrament of Baptism. The water symbolizes death to an old life of sin, cleansing, and rebirth into a new life, the life of Christ. The Holy Spirit guides our new life in Christ.

God has raised us up through Jesus Christ—the Good News of Salvation History. "The doctrine of original sin is, so to speak, the 'reverse side' of the Good News that Jesus is the Savior of all men, that all need salvation and that salvation is offered to all through Christ" (*CCC*, 389). Good can come out of bad. Victory can be won out of defeat. No greater good and no greater victory could possibly happen to humanity than the coming of Jesus Christ, the Redeemer.

> But why did God not prevent the first man from sinning? St. Leo the Great responds, "Christ's inexpressible grace gave us blessings better than those the demon's envy had taken away." And St. Thomas Aquinas wrote, "There is nothing to prevent human nature's being raised up to something greater, even after sin; God permits evil in order to draw forth some greater good. Thus St. Paul says, 'Where sin increased, grace abounded all the more'; and the Exultant sings, 'O happy fault, . . . which gained for us so great a Redeemer!'" (CCC, 412)

The Protoevangelium is the first announcement of the Gospel of Jesus Christ. Reading the Old Testament in this way—discerning persons, events, or things that prefigure and serve as a prototype of the fulfillment of God's plan in the Person of Christ—is known as *typology*. This type of reading of the Old Testament is practiced in many examples that will be introduced both in this chapter and in Chapter 3. However, for God's plan to unfold, he first had to form a nation—Israel—from whom the Savior would be born. God entered into covenants with his

Origins of Names, Types of Sins

- Read Genesis 2:7 and Genesis 3:20 to guess the meanings of the names Adam and Eve. Then research to find out if you were right. Also, check the meaning of your baptismal name. Does the description fit your personality in any way? You may wish to check your middle name as well.
- There are several examples in the Old Testament of how the Chosen People "missed the mark" in keeping their covenant with God. The prophets had a special role in the history of the Chosen People to call people away from their sins. Speaking for God, they told of the offenses the people had committed. Read these four passages from the prophets Isaiah, Jeremiah, and Hosea and identify the sin that is being criticized: Isaiah 1:2; Jeremiah 2:29; Hosea 7:13; Hosea 8:1.

Lesson 2 Homework

1. Have the students journal their responses to the Reflection activity on page 37.
2. Direct the students to write their responses to the ten For Review questions on page 38.
3. Ask the students to read "God Remains Faithful in Times of Sin" (pages 38–41) in preparation for their next lesson.
4. Ask the students to finish their "Consequences Collage."
5. Remind the students to continue to work on their chosen Ongoing Assignments (pages 52–53).

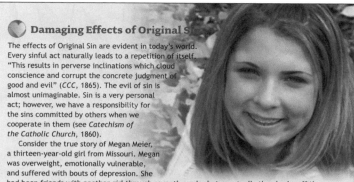

Damaging Effects of Original Sin

The effects of Original Sin are evident in today's world. Every sinful act naturally leads to a repetition of itself. "This results in perverse inclinations which cloud conscience and corrupt the concrete judgment of good and evil" (*CCC*, 1865). The evil of sin is almost unimaginable. Sin is a very personal act; however, we have a responsibility for the sins committed by others when we cooperate in them (see *Catechism of the Catholic Church*, 1860).

Consider the true story of Megan Meier, a thirteen-year-old girl from Missouri. Megan was overweight, emotionally vulnerable, and suffered with bouts of depression. She had been friends with another girl through seventh grade, but eventually they broke off the relationship, or so Megan thought.

Sometime after the relationship ended, a guy name Josh showed up on Megan's MySpace page asking to be added as a friend. He began to chat with her, saying she was cute and saying other nice things about her. This, of course, helped Megan's self-image. For a time, things went well. But then Josh started to say he didn't want to be friends with Megan anymore. He claimed that Megan talked behind the backs of her friends and that no one liked her. Obviously, Megan was very upset by this turn of events. What could possibly have happened to bring this on?

Josh continued to send mean notes. Moreover, he had been sharing other nasty messages with others online—messages that called Megan the most derogatory of names. Megan was devastated, especially when one night Josh wrote that everyone hated her and the world would be better off without her.

Tragically, Josh got his wish; later that night Megan hanged herself.

Weeks later the truth of the whole affair came out. There was never a "Josh." Lori Drew, the forty-nine-year-old mother of Megan's ex-friend, was accused of fabricating Josh and creating a false identity on MySpace in order to seek revenge on Megan for ending the friendship with her daughter.

Reflection Questions

- How did this story make you feel?
- Where does such evil come from?
- Have you heard other examples like this?
- What should the law do about the parents?

Assignment

Research more about the life of Megan Meier. Use her life as an inspiration to find ways to eliminate cyberbullying among your peers. Propose a list of dos and don'ts for Internet use that addresses this problem.

Background Information

What about Limbo?

The Church sees Baptism as washing away the stain of Original Sin. "Limbo," which comes from the Latin word *limbus* meaning "hem," "border," or "edge," was the term used by medieval theologians to describe a state or place reserved for people (especially babies) who die unstained by personal sin but also unbaptized. While Limbo was never part of Church doctrine, and is not mentioned at all in the *Catechism of the Catholic Church*, the notion was, at last, formally dispensed with by the Church's International Theological commission in 2007 in its pronouncement "The Hope of Salvation for Infants who Die Without Being Baptized." (See www.vatican.va/roman_curia/congregations/cfaith/cti_documents/rc_con_cfaith_doc_20070419_un-baptised-infants_en.html.)

- Point to the students' answers you listed earlier on the board. Explain that the temptation story in Genesis responds to all these "Why?" questions by saying, "Because the first human couple sinned."
- Call attention to the word and definition of "temptation," written on the board. Then share with the students the following quip (attributed to Oscar Wilde): "I can resist anything but temptation." Ask:
    - Did the devil make Eve and Adam sin?
    - Can the devil make us sin?

  Make sure the students realize that the answer to both questions is "No." Sin is a result of a freely made decision on our part, just as it was for Eve and Adam. While the devil may tempt us to sin, if we give in to the temptation, the sin is ours. We can never say, "The devil made me do it." Ultimately, the responsibility for sin rests on us, as do its consequences.
- Have the students reread Genesis 3:7–24. Then ask, "How does the story show that the first couple loses its original unity, harmony, and wholeness after sinning?" (*Feeling shame, they cover their nakedness, and they hide themselves from God.*) Emphasize to the students that the first two consequences of sin related to the loss of Original Holiness are: alienation from themselves (they were no longer okay with themselves), and alienation from God (they were no longer at home in God's presence). Note, too, that when God seeks out the couple to give them the opportunity to own up to their sin, they play the blame game—Adam blames Eve, and Eve blames the serpent.
- Encourage the students to notice how Genesis 3:14–24 documents the nitty-gritty of the human condition:
    - broken relationships among people and between people and the rest of creation
    - pain and suffering
    - toil for survival (alienation from nature)
    - the inevitability of death
- Call attention to the third paragraph of the text section "Consequences of Original Sin" (on page 34). Point out in the text where the *Catechism* mentions these same consequences. If you wish, list them on the board.
- Note that these consequences speak quite clearly to the human condition into which we are born. Emphasize this point by creating a "Consequences Collage." Have copies of recent newspapers and/or news magazines available. Tell the students to find and cut out headlines or stories that they feel describe

the consequences/effects of evil/sin in today's world and then to place them on a bulletin board. This project could also be assigned as homework.

- Direct the students to the feature "Damaging Effects of Original Sin" (page 37). Ask the students to relate the story of Megan Meir in their own words. Afterward, use the Reflection Questions on page 37 to discuss this sad account. Before moving on, note the Assignment on page 37. Have the students complete it as part of their homework
- Call attention back to the collage, pointing out how the first couple's *personal* sin has affected all of humankind. That is, we all share in their fallen nature. Tell the students that the theologian Reinhold Niebuhr put it this way: "Original Sin is that thing about man which makes him capable of conceiving of his own perfection and incapable of achieving it." Or, as mentioned above, "We're broken. We need fixing. We can't do it ourselves."
- Have the students read Romans 6:23 from their Bibles: ("For the wages of sin is death, but the gift of God is eternal life in Christ Jesus our Lord.") Tell the students that while sin is our condition, death is not our lot. Then have them turn to the text section, "The Protoevangelium" (pages 35–38). Make sure they understand what *Protoevangelium* means (*first Gospel—first Good News*). Ask, "Why is this a fitting

38 Jesus Christ: Source of Our Salvation

people and never abandoned his promise to bring humanity a Savior, even though the people fell into their sins time and again.

For Review

1. What did it mean for Adam and Eve to have been created with Original Holiness and Original Justice?
2. Define *Original Sin*.
3. Define *sin*.
4. How was Adam and Eve's sin also a personal sin?
5. How did Satan tempt Adam and Eve?
6. List three effects of Original Sin for Adam and Eve.
7. How does Original Sin affect all humans?
8. Define *concupiscence*.
9. What is the Protoevangelium?
10. Who are the woman and her offspring alluded to in Genesis 3:15?

For Reflection

- How has your personal sinfulness resulted from the abuse of freedom?
- Cite several examples of the tendency to blame one's sins on something or someone else.

God Remains Faithful in Times of Sin

Humanity's sinful behavior expanded after the personal sin of Adam and Eve. Once Original Sin entered human history, it spread like a virus. The effects of sin on human beings are harmful and destructive, yet God never abandoned the creatures he made. This point is made in three other stories in Genesis. The Yahwist stresses God's judgment on sinners but also his mercy. This theme is brought to fulfillment in Jesus' attitude toward sinners.

Cain and Abel (Gn 4:1-16)

The story of the first offspring of Adam and Eve reveals how sin leads to fratricide, the murder of a brother. Out of jealousy toward Abel, whose offering was more pleasing to the Lord, Cain killed his brother. Beforehand, God told Cain that he could master his sinful urges, but Cain, like all sinners, did not resist the temptation (Gn 4:7).

Sin deserves punishment, so the Lord banished Cain from the land and condemned him to a life of wandering. He also "put a mark on Cain, lest anyone should kill him at sight" (Gn 4:15). God's punishment is swift and just, but even the commission of such an evil crime as the murder of one's brother did not mean abandonment by the Lord. Faithful and loving to his beloved creatures, the Lord wished to refashion humanity, a humanity that will be redeemed in the fullness of time by the New Adam, Jesus Christ.

The Great Flood (Gn 6:5-9:29)

A careful reading of the account of the Great Flood reveals many repetitions and discrepancies. A possible explanation may be that the story interweaves both the so-called Yahwist (J) and Priestly (P) versions. Compare Genesis 6:19–20 to Genesis 7:2–3 for an example of this repetition. Also note in these verses a major discrepancy in the number of animals Noah is to take onto the ark. The P version (6:19–20) tells how God ordered Noah to take *one pair* of every species onto the ark, while J's instruction (7:2–3) is to take *seven pairs* of clean animals and one pair of unclean animals.

For Review Answers (page 38)

1. Original Holiness means that humans were created to share in God's own life; Original Justice means that human beings would not have to suffer pain or death.
2. Original Sin is the first act of turning from God by our first parents, and it's the fallen state of human nature into which all of humankind is born.
3. Sin is separation/alienation, the abuse of the freedom God gives to us so that we can love God and one another. It is also sometimes called "missing the mark."
4. Adam and Eve's sin was a personal sin because it was a free choice made by a historical couple.
5. Satan tempted the first couple in the form of a serpent, promising them that if they ate of the tree they would be like God.
6. Harmony with and between themselves was lost. The harmony with the rest of creation was shattered. They had a knowledge of shame or guilt and realized they were naked.
7. All humans inherit a fallen human nature (propensity to sin), are deprived of Original Holiness and Justice, and are destined to die.
8. Concupiscence is the inclination to sin.
9. The Protoevangelium ("first Gospel") is God's promise to send a savior to restore, renew, and reconcile all creation.
10. Mary the mother of Jesus and the followers of her Son.

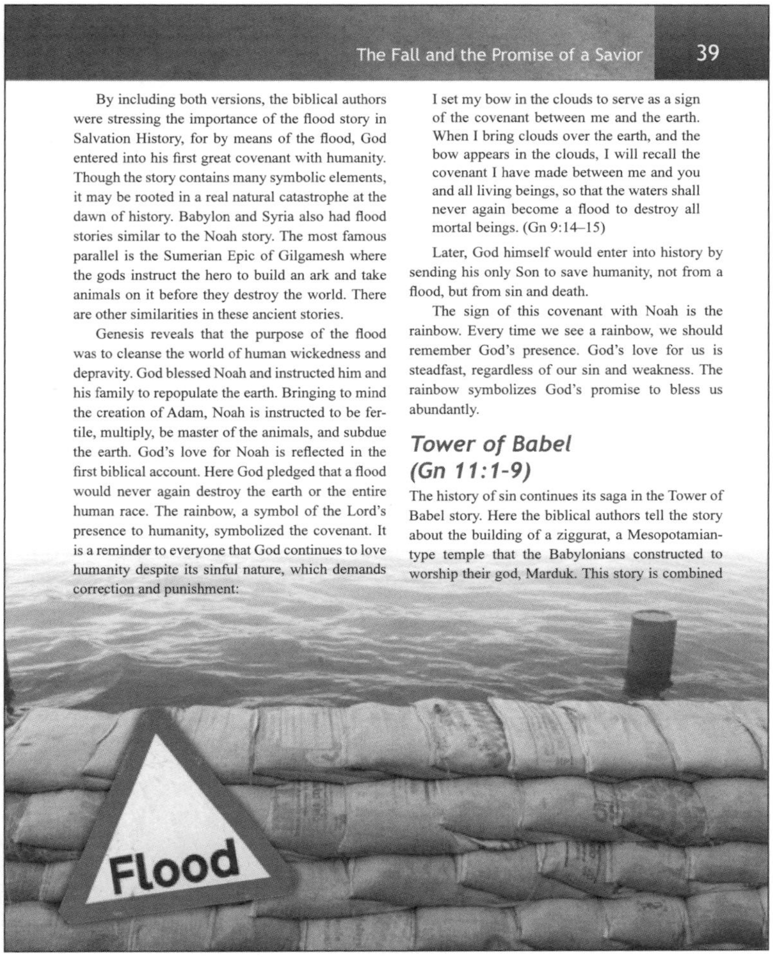

By including both versions, the biblical authors were stressing the importance of the flood story in Salvation History, for by means of the flood, God entered into his first great covenant with humanity. Though the story contains many symbolic elements, it may be rooted in a real natural catastrophe at the dawn of history. Babylon and Syria also had flood stories similar to the Noah story. The most famous parallel is the Sumerian Epic of Gilgamesh where the gods instruct the hero to build an ark and take animals on it before they destroy the world. There are other similarities in these ancient stories.

Genesis reveals that the purpose of the flood was to cleanse the world of human wickedness and depravity. God blessed Noah and instructed him and his family to repopulate the earth. Bringing to mind the creation of Adam, Noah is instructed to be fertile, multiply, be master of the animals, and subdue the earth. God's love for Noah is reflected in the first biblical account. Here God pledged that a flood would never again destroy the earth or the entire human race. The rainbow, a symbol of the Lord's presence to humanity, symbolized the covenant. It is a reminder to everyone that God continues to love humanity despite its sinful nature, which demands correction and punishment:

> I set my bow in the clouds to serve as a sign of the covenant between me and the earth. When I bring clouds over the earth, and the bow appears in the clouds, I will recall the covenant I have made between me and you and all living beings, so that the waters shall never again become a flood to destroy all mortal beings. (Gn 9:14–15)

Later, God himself would enter into history by sending his only Son to save humanity, not from a flood, but from sin and death.

The sign of this covenant with Noah is the rainbow. Every time we see a rainbow, we should remember God's presence. God's love for us is steadfast, regardless of our sin and weakness. The rainbow symbolizes God's promise to bless us abundantly.

Tower of Babel (Gn 11:1-9)

The history of sin continues its saga in the Tower of Babel story. Here the biblical authors tell the story about the building of a ziggurat, a Mesopotamian-type temple that the Babylonians constructed to worship their god, Marduk. This story is combined

Lesson 3 Objectives

The students will:

- examine the stories in Genesis that speak to the spread of sin.
- recognize that God will not be mocked.
- appreciate that God's justice is tempered by divine mercy.
- recognize how humans are related to the angels.

Lesson 3 Preview

The Scripture stories of Cain and Abel, the Flood, and the Tower of Babel are powerful reflections of the human condition as the ancients saw them: family discord, rampant sinfulness, oppression and division among peoples and classes of peoples. Recognizing these evils, the human authors drew on these stories to point out how the evils were the result of sin and to reveal God's response.

title for the message of Genesis 3:15?" (*God promises a savior who will destroy sin and its consequences.*)

- Remind the students that the true state of humankind is not the state of Original Sin but the state of Original Holiness and Justice. To help return us to that state, however, would take someone who was true man *and* true God. Call on a student to read 1 Corinthians 15:45, 47–49. Point out how St. Paul declares that Jesus, by his Life, Death, and Resurrection (Paschal Mystery), is the new man (the New Adam) come to free us from the death-dealing consequences of the Fall. Tell the students that we attain this freedom by undergoing a new birth, rising to a new and abundant life in Christ.
- Before dismissing the students, have them look at the feature "Origins of Names, Types of Sins" on page 36. Tell the students to complete both pieces of the assignment as part of their homework.

Chapter 2: The Fall and the Promise of a Savior—Lesson 3

Bell Ringers

- Ask the students to offer their responses to the ten For Review questions on page 38 (answers are on page 52 of this text). Be sure to allow the students to ask any other questions they may have.
- Review the effects of Original Sin by having students present their "Consequences Collages" to the class.
- Call on different students to share what they discovered in the activity "Origins of Names, Types of Sins" on page 36. What did they discover about the meaning of the names "Adam" and "Eve," as well as the meaning of their own names? Call on other students to share what types of sins the prophets Isaiah, Jeremiah, and Hosea criticized.
- Have the students share the lists of dos and don'ts they came up with for Internet use aimed at ending cyberbullying (from the feature "Damaging Effects of Original Sin" on page 37). Consider putting together a comprehensive list and sharing it with others in your school as well as with the parents and families of your students.
- In preparation for this lesson, have the students create a KWL Chart. Instruct them to fold a sheet of paper as if they were folding a letter in order to divide the paper into three equal sections. Direct them to label the three sections "What I KNOW," "What I WANT to know," and "What I LEARNED." Instruct the

students to write in the first section everything they know about the Genesis stories of Cain and Abel, Noah and the Great Flood, and the Tower of Babel. Then ask the students to write down everything they want to know about these stories in the second section. Tell them they will fill in the third section later.

Teaching Approaches

God Remains Faithful in Times of Sin (pages 38-41)

- Make the following points about the biblical account of Cain and Abel:
    - It reflects the historical ill will of Hebrew for Canaanite as well as the age-old conflict between farmer and herdsman over land. Cain is a settled farmer like the Canaanites. Abel is a herdsman like the nomadic Hebrews when they came into Canaan.
    - While God accepts Abel's offering, Cain's is rejected (Gn 4:3–4).
    - God warns Cain not to be resentful lest he become mastered by evil (Gn 4:5–6).
    - Cain murders his brother (Gn 4:8).
    - Cain lies to God and insolently denies any responsibility for his brother (Gn 4:9).
    - Having destroyed his relationship with both humankind and God, Cain is symbolically alienated even from the earth itself (Gn 4:10–12).
    - God, however, while punishing Cain, did not abandon him. He placed a mark on Cain to protect him from being killed (Gn 4:13–15).
- Read the account of Noah and the Great Flood. Ask the students:
    - Why did God send the flood? (*To cleanse the world of human wickedness and to repopulate the earth. See Genesis 9:1.*)
    - Why are there repetitions and differences in the biblical account? (*It is composed of both the Yahwist and the Priestly version.*)
    - What is the covenant God makes and with whom does God make it? (*The covenant God makes is never to destroy the earth by water; he makes this covenant with Noah, his descendants, and all creation. See Genesis 9:10–11.*)
    - What is the sign of the covenant? (*The rainbow—a sign not only of God's promise to Noah, but of God's continuing love and protection of us all.*)

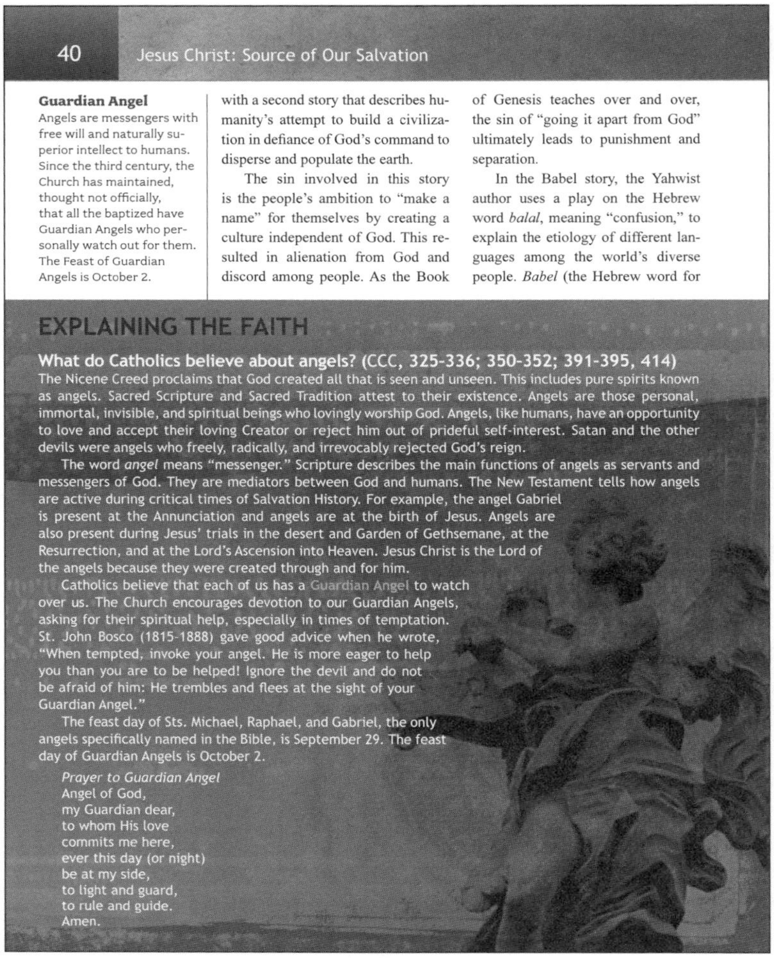
40 Jesus Christ: Source of Our Salvation

Guardian Angel
Angels are messengers with free will and naturally superior intellect to humans. Since the third century, the Church has maintained, thought not officially, that all the baptized have Guardian Angels who personally watch out for them. The Feast of Guardian Angels is October 2.

with a second story that describes humanity's attempt to build a civilization in defiance of God's command to disperse and populate the earth.

The sin involved in this story is the people's ambition to "make a name" for themselves by creating a culture independent of God. This resulted in alienation from God and discord among people. As the Book of Genesis teaches over and over, the sin of "going it apart from God" ultimately leads to punishment and separation.

In the Babel story, the Yahwist author uses a play on the Hebrew word *balal*, meaning "confusion," to explain the etiology of different languages among the world's diverse people. *Babel* (the Hebrew word for

EXPLAINING THE FAITH

What do Catholics believe about angels? (CCC, 325-336; 350-352; 391-395, 414)
The Nicene Creed proclaims that God created all that is seen and unseen. This includes pure spirits known as angels. Sacred Scripture and Sacred Tradition attest to their existence. Angels are those personal, immortal, invisible, and spiritual beings who lovingly worship God. Angels, like humans, have an opportunity to love and accept their loving Creator or reject him out of prideful self-interest. Satan and the other devils were angels who freely, radically, and irrevocably rejected God's reign.

The word *angel* means "messenger." Scripture describes the main functions of angels as servants and messengers of God. They are mediators between God and humans. The New Testament tells how angels are active during critical times of Salvation History. For example, the angel Gabriel is present at the Annunciation and angels are at the birth of Jesus. Angels are also present during Jesus' trials in the desert and Garden of Gethsemane, at the Resurrection, and at the Lord's Ascension into Heaven. Jesus Christ is the Lord of the angels because they were created through and for him.

Catholics believe that each of us has a Guardian Angel to watch over us. The Church encourages devotion to our Guardian Angels, asking for their spiritual help, especially in times of temptation. St. John Bosco (1815-1888) gave good advice when he wrote, "When tempted, invoke your angel. He is more eager to help you than you are to be helped! Ignore the devil and do not be afraid of him: He trembles and flees at the sight of your Guardian Angel."

The feast day of Sts. Michael, Raphael, and Gabriel, the only angels specifically named in the Bible, is September 29. The feast day of Guardian Angels is October 2.

Prayer to Guardian Angel
Angel of God,
my Guardian dear,
to whom His love
commits me here,
ever this day (or night)
be at my side,
to light and guard,
to rule and guide.
Amen.

Lesson 3 Homework

1. Tell the students to write their responses to the four For Review questions on page 41.
2. Call attention to the For Reflection feature and read aloud. Tell the students to be ready to share their symbol at their next session.
3. Direct the students to read "Covenants in the Old Testament" (pages 41–46) in preparation for their next lesson.
4. Once again, remind the students to continue to work on their chosen Ongoing Assignments (page 52).

Background Information

Guardian Angels

> From its beginning until death, human life is surrounded by their [angels'] watchful care and intercession. Beside each believer stands an angel as protector and shepherd leading him to life.
>
> ***Catechism of the Catholic Church*, 336**

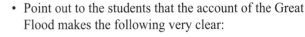

Babylon) is the place where human pride caused the Lord to confuse the speech of the world. Defying God brings about indescribable consequences such as difficulty in human communication and cooperation.

However, with all of God's punishments comes some good. The people scattered around the earth, which was one of God's commands. Eventually, after Jesus' Resurrection, various pilgrims gathered in Jerusalem on Pentecost Sunday. Even though all spoke different languages, they understood Peter's proclamation of the Gospel of Jesus Christ (see Acts 2:5–13). The coming of the Holy Spirit, who guides Christ's Body, the Church, unites all people in Jesus, the Son of God.

The Babel story ends Genesis's treatment of prehistory. As we will see in the covenants to come, God does not abandon humanity. The genealogy given after the Babel story begins with Noah's son, Shem, and ends with the patriarch Abraham. Through Abraham and his descendants, God forms a Chosen People and blesses all generations to the end of time.

For Review

1. What is a main lesson of the Cain and Abel story? What is the "mark of Cain"?
2. How did the biblical authors understand the purpose of the Flood?
3. What covenant did the Lord make with Noah? What is its sign?
4. Why were the people punished for building the Tower of Babel?

For Reflection

A rainbow is a symbol of God's abiding presence and love. What symbol is a sign of God's love and presence in your life? Explain this symbol or depict it graphically.

Covenants in the Old Testament

The covenant between God and Noah was the first Old Testament covenant. It is described from prehistory. Three other major covenants are part of the historical record of God's Chosen People. The Hebrew word for covenant is *berith*. In the ancient world, covenants between persons were solemn agreements to do, or refrain from doing, something. In some covenants, for example, the superior party (like a monarch) would unconditionally promise to do something without imposing conditions on the people. A typical covenant involved a statement of the terms of the covenant, an oath by which each party promised to observe the terms of the agreement, and a formal ratification involving some external ritual. In biblical covenants between men, God is the witness to the agreement. An example of this is the pact made between Laban and Jacob (Gn 31:44, 50).

As witnessed in the covenant with Noah, Sacred Scripture reveals that God entered into solemn covenants with humans. Biblical covenants were so important that the concept of covenant is central to Sacred Scripture. The word *testament* is a synonym for covenant. Thus, the Hebrew Scriptures are termed the Old Testament while we name the Christian Scriptures, the New Testament. The covenants in Scripture had two sacred parts: the promise made and the conditions attached to the promise.

The three other major Old Testament covenants are:

- *The Covenant with Abraham*, where God blessed Abram's family, promising to give them the land of Canaan and making them a blessing to the nations (Gn 15:18).
- *The Covenant with Moses on Mt. Sinai*, where God selected Israel as his Chosen People (Ex 19:5, 6).

For Review Answers (page 41)

1. The main lesson of the Cain and Abel story is that while sin deserves punishment, God remains merciful. The mark of Cain is God's seal/promise of protection against vengeance.
2. To cleanse the land of human wickedness and repopulate the earth. Also, the purpose seemed to be to establish a covenant between Noah and his descendants.
3. God promised never to destroy the earth by water. The sign of the covenant is the rainbow.
4. They wanted to make names for themselves by creating a culture independent of God.

For Enrichment

One of the most lasting messages from the story of Cain and Abel is the question, "Am I my brother's keeper?" Have the students read the New Testament account of the Good Samaritan (Lk 10:25–37). Discuss the similarities between these two stories; then have the students journal about the people in their lives—people that they could be making a greater effort to help.

- Point out to the students that the account of the Great Flood makes the following very clear:
  - If people choose to abuse the freedom God gives, they bring ruin upon themselves.
  - Living a moral life (like Noah) is worth it.
  - The universe is under humankind's stewardship, not its control.
  - Although God shows his justice with the flood, he shows greater mercy with his covenant.
- Before moving on, discuss with the students what implications the story of the Great Flood has on today's most pressing environmental problems, for example, global warming, greenhouse gas emissions, carbon footprints, etc.
- Call attention to the text section "Tower of Babel" (page 39). Help the students recognize that the main purpose of this story is that we should not put our faith in human triumphs, be they big towers or big bank accounts. Also, point out that the story reveals how human sin continues to cause alienation/separation. Communication breaks down when people no longer recognize or respect their common humanity.
- Draw attention to the text's mention of the Pentecost event (page 41). Have the students read Acts 2:1–13. Explain that on Pentecost, Babel was *reversed.* This passage in Acts ends with some confusion about what the Pentecost event meant. Instruct the students to continue the dialogue by writing a response to the closing questions in their notes. Remind the students to use what they know about the Tower of Babel story to interpret the event. Ask some students to share their responses.
- Ask the students to return to their KWL chart. Now direct them to compete the third section "What I LEARNED." Ask students to share some of the things they learned.
- Have the students look at the Explaining the Faith feature on angels (page 40). Note that the word "angel" means "messenger" and that angels are pure spirits. Perhaps our picturing angels as winged speaks to their living up to their messenger status. Call attention to the names of the angels mentioned in the Bible:
  - Michael (meaning "who is like God") is seen as the angel who defeated Satan and thus as a defender of the Church.
  - Raphael (meaning "God has healed") appears chiefly in the Book of Tobit and is responsible for Tobit being cured of blindness.

- Gabriel (meaning "man of God") is the chief messenger of divine mysteries and is best known for his appearance to Mary announcing the birth of Jesus.

Note, too, how all the angels' names end in "el," one of the ancient Hebrew names for God, and thus demonstrate their connection to the deity.

- Ask the students to read Psalm 91:11–12 (made so familiar by Michael Joncas's rendition of the psalm, "On Eagles' Wings") and then Matthew 18:10. Tell the students that these words of psalmist and Savior offer Old and New Testament bases for the Church's teaching on guardian angels.
- Conclude this session by reminding the students that every time we gather for Eucharist, we are joining the worship offered by the angels. That is why the priest invites us to join the choir of angels in their song of praise: "Holy, holy, holy . . ." Finally, have a student lead the class in praying the "Prayer to Guardian Angel" found on page 40.

Chapter 2: The Fall and the Promise of a Savior—Lesson 4

Bell Ringers

- Ask the students to offer their responses to the For Review questions on page 41 (answers are on page 55 of this text). Be sure to allow the students to ask any other questions they may have.
- Invite the students to share their symbol of God's love and presence in their life. If possible, display the symbols or their descriptions in the classroom.
- Briefly review the stories of Cain and Abel, the Flood, and the Tower of Babel. Call on different students to summarize each of the stories. Afterward, conclude by reminding the students that each story deals with the implications of the sinful arrogance of humankind: the events are like the ripple effect of Original Sin.
- Introduce this session by writing the following on the board: **I meant what I said, and I said what I meant. An elephant's faithful, one hundred percent**. Ask if anyone knows who said this. In case no one is familiar with the saying, tell the students it's the mantra of the elephant Horton from the children's book *Horton Hatches the Egg* by Dr. Seuss. Horton makes a promise to care for an egg and despite numerous hardships—derision by the other jungle animals, exposure to the elements, capture by hunters, a horrible sea voyage, and finally confinement in

42 Jesus Christ: Source of Our Salvation

New Covenant
The climax of Salvation History, the coming of Jesus Christ, the fullness of God's Revelation.

Gentiles
A term that means "non-Jews."

- *The Covenant with David*, where God promised that the Messiah and Savior would come from David's dynasty (2 Sm 23:5).

The Old Testament prophet, Jeremiah, foretold a **New Covenant** (Jer 31:31–34). This covenant would be written in the hearts of humankind and, as promised by the prophet Isaiah, would center in a person (Is 42:6; 49:8).

Jesus Christ is the New Covenant between God and his people. His covenant is sealed in his blood; his sacrifice is what saves and redeems us.

Covenant with Abraham (CCC, 59-61)

Abram was a nomadic herder who was born around four thousand years ago in Ur, in what is today present-day southern Iraq. God called him to journey to Shechem in the land of Canaan. God promised that he would give the new land to Abram and his progeny:

> "I will make of you a great nation,
> and I will bless you;
> I will make your name great
> so that you will be a blessing.
> I will bless those who bless you
> and curse those who curse you.
> All the communities of the earth
> shall find blessing in you." (Gn 12:2–3)

God eventually changed Abram's name to Abraham, which meant "father of a multitude of nations."

Abraham heard God's call, believed it, and obeyed. Hearing, believing, and obeying God comprise the elements of the virtue of faith. Abraham is often referred to as "father of faith," not only for Christians and Jews, but for Muslims as well. He dramatically prefigured the humble Virgin Mary who heard God's call that she was to be the Mother of the Redeemer. She heard, believed, and obeyed God's will by saying, "Behold, I am the handmaid of the Lord. May it be done to me according to your word" (Lk 1:38). Through her child, Jesus Christ, all people of the earth are indeed blessed.

Genesis 12–22 records six different times God appeared to Abraham to make or reinforce his promises. The covenant God made with Abraham extended to his descendants—blessing humanity through the patriarchs: Isaac (son of Abraham and Sarah) and Jacob (son of Isaac and Rebekah). Jacob would become Israel, which became the name of a great nation. One of Israel's sons—Judah—would be given the scepter as ruler, and Jesus, the Messiah, would come from Judah's line. Jesus' mission was to save and renew all humanity, both Jews and **Gentiles**:

> The people descended from Abraham would be the trustee of the promise made to the patriarchs, the chosen people, called to prepare for that day when God would gather all his children into the unity of

Lesson 4 Objectives

The students will:

- understand the meaning of covenant.
- appreciate the meaning and impact of God's covenants with Abraham, Moses, and David.
- create a prayer of praise and thanks.
- recognize how Christ is connected to the Old Testament covenants.

Lesson 4 Preview

In this lesson the students investigate the covenants God made with Israel. The notion of God as covenanter was absolutely revolutionary. While other religions had gods involved in human affairs, that involvement was never in real time. Israel's God intervenes in historical time. This God wants the people of Israel to be his people and is so determined to have them that he gets involved.

the Church. They would be the root on to which the Gentiles would be grafted, once they came to believe. (*CCC*, 60)

Among the provisions of the covenant with Abraham are these:

- a great nation would descend from him (Israel)
- Abraham and his family would be given a land (Canaan)
- Abraham would be blessed and his name would be revered
- the entire earth would ultimately be blessed through him
- Abraham and his wife Sarah would parent a child even though both were old (Gn 15:1–4; 17:16–21)

God also told Abraham that his descendants would be held as slaves in a foreign land (Gn15:13–14), something that transpired when the Israelites were captive in Egypt.

The sign of the covenant was that boy babies should be circumcised on the eighth day after birth. "That shall be the mark of the covenant between you and me" (Gn 17:11).

Genesis reveals that "Abram put his faith in the Lord, who credited it to him as an act of righteousness" (Gn 15:6). In the Sacrament of Baptism, through the power of the Holy Spirit, we become members of Christ's Body, the Church. Our membership and participation in the Church is an extension of the covenant God made with Abraham. Christ's saving Death on the cross has justified us before God, bringing about righteousness:

> Justification is conferred in Baptism, the sacrament of faith. It conforms us to the righteousness of God, who makes us inwardly just by the power of his mercy. Its purpose is the glory of God and of Christ, and the gift of eternal life. . . . (*CCC*, 1992)

The remaining chapters of Genesis relate the story of the patriarchs and matriarchs, that is, the fathers and mothers of our faith, including stories about Isaac and his wife Rebekah, Jacob (Israel) and his wives Leah and Rachel, and Jacob's sons, most notably Joseph. Betrayed by his brothers, Joseph won favor with the pharaoh and was an instrument of his brothers' salvation by finding them a home in Egypt during a time of famine. The Book of Exodus tells how a new Egyptian king enslaved the Israelites for fear that they might side with his enemies and leave the country. The Egyptians "dreaded the Israelites and reduced them to cruel slavery, making life bitter for them with hard work" (Ex 1:12–13). This experience of slavery led God to carve a path that would lead the Israelites to freedom and eventually a return to the Promised Land of Canaan.

Covenant with Moses (CCC, 62-63)

After two hundred years of suffering under the Egyptians, God appointed Moses to lead the Israelites out of slavery. This event is known as the Exodus (from a Greek word for "departure") from Egypt. The pharaoh's stubbornness required God to send ten plagues to force him to let the Israelites depart Egypt. However, the pharaoh regretted his decision and he pursued the departing Israelites. God thwarted his efforts by miraculously allowing the Israelites safe passage through the Red Sea and destroyed the pursuing Egyptian army.

Then began the Israelites' forty-year sojourn in the Sinai desert, a journey that brings to mind Abraham's trek to Canaan, the land promised by God. By means of the Exodus and his instructions to them while in the desert, God formed Israel as his people:

> He established with them the covenant of Mount Sinai and, through Moses, gave them his law so that they would recognize him and serve him as the one living and true God, the provident Father and just judge, and so that they would look for the promised Savior. (*CCC*, 62)

Lesson 4 Homework

1. Tell the students to write their responses to the twelve For Review questions on page 46.
2. Call attention to the For Reflection feature on page 46. Tell the students to journal their responses.
3. Have the students read "God Remains Faithful to His Promises" (pages 46–50) in preparation for their next lesson.
4. Tell the students to begin wrapping up work on their chosen Ongoing Assignments (pages 52–53).

a traveling circus—Horton is true to his word. Horton keeps his promise, no matter what. You may also read the story to the class or view online the classic Warner Bros.' cartoon version of the story.

- Discuss promise making and promise keeping. Ask:
    - What promises are worth keeping?
    - Is it important for people to keep promises? Why or why not?
    - Is there ever a good reason not to keep a promise? (*Encourage students to explain their thoughts.*)
    - Has anyone broken a promise to you? If so, how did that affect you?
    - Can you tell of a time it was difficult to keep a promise?

  Consider making a list of different types of promises on the board and asking students if they can see any similar patterns (or differences) between the types.
- Finally, invite the students to suggest the kinds of promises they think should never be broken. Help the class come to the conclusion that no promise should be broken unless it is not possible to do otherwise.

Teaching Approaches

Covenants in the Old Testament (pages 41-46)

- Write the word **covenant** on the board. Tell the students that it is one of the most theologically important words in all of Scripture. Ask the students to describe what they believe a covenant is—as the term is used in the Bible. Accept all reasonable replies. Help the students come to a consensus on the meaning of covenant in the Bible, for example: *A covenant is a binding promise between God and humankind in which God pledges enduring love and asks for faithful love in return.*
- Note the word "promise" in the definition of covenant. Tell the students that when we read the Pentateuch, we find God making promise after promise. Ask, "What promises of God did we encounter in our last lesson?" (The Protoevangelium [Gn 3:15] and the promise made to Noah [Gn 9:9–17].) Go on to note the three other major covenants detailed in this chapter: with Abraham, with Moses on Sinai, and with King David.
- Help the students investigate the Abramic covenant by having them read the following passages from Genesis:

- Genesis 12:2–3—Abram's initial call and God's threefold promise of blessing: (1) I will make you a great nation, (2) I will bless you, and (3) I will make your name great.
- Genesis 15:5–21—The actual covenant itself; God promises to give Abraham many descendants and the land of Canaan.
- Genesis 17:1–11—The reiteration of the covenant and the introduction of its sign (circumcision).
- Genesis 17:15–16—The promise of a son to Abraham and Sarah.

- Call attention to how God's covenant not only blessed Abraham with the promise of land, eminence, and uncountable descendants, but also promised that Abraham would himself be a blessing so that "all the communities of the earth shall find blessing in [him]" (Gn 12:3).
- Ask the students why Abraham is referred to as "father of faith." Note how Abraham perfectly embodies the three key elements of the virtue of faith (hearing, believing, and obeying). Remind the students that Abraham's faith was tested mightily; have the students read that "test" in Genesis 22:1–19. Afterward, ask:
    - What blessing did God bestow upon Abraham because of his faith?
    - How do we today share in the blessing promised to Abraham?
- Take a moment to discuss that if Abraham is our father in faith, surely Mary is our mother in faith. Like Abraham, she heard, believed, and unflinchingly obeyed God's word to her, even though that word seemed impossible and scandalous—a virgin pregnant with child. Mary trusted in the promises God had made "to our fathers, to Abraham and to his descendants forever" (Lk 1:54–55). Ask, "What prayer do we pray that shows how we consider Mary as especially blessed by God?" (*Hail Mary*)
- Instruct the students to create a chain-of-events flowchart depicting the events leading up to the establishment of the covenant with Moses and the Israelites. (The chart should resemble this: *Israelites suffer under the Egyptians.* → *Moses is appointed leader.* → *Ten plagues occur.* → *Israelites depart (Exodus).* → *Israelites pass through the Red Sea.* → *Israelites wander the desert for forty years.* → *God makes a covenant with the Israelites.*)
- Have the students reread the description of the Sinai covenant as expressed in the Book of Deuteronomy

44 Jesus Christ: Source of Our Salvation

The covenant God made with the Israelites is stated simply in the Book of Deuteronomy:

> For you are a people sacred to the Lord, your God; he has chosen you from all the nations on the face of the earth to be a people peculiarly his own. It was not because you are the largest of all nations that the Lord set his heart on you and chose you, for you are really the smallest of all nations. It was because the Lord loved you and because of his fidelity to the oath he had sworn to your fathers, that he brought you out with his strong hand from the place of slavery, and ransomed you from the hand of Pharaoh, king of Egypt. Understand, then, that the Lord, your God, is God indeed, the faithful God who keeps his merciful covenant down to the thousandth generation toward those who love him and keep his commandments. (Dt 7:6–9)

The events of the Exodus proved again that God was faithful to his promises to Abraham: he preserved them as a people, freed them, and promised a future Savior. In the covenant with Moses, known as the Sinai Covenant, the Lord entered into a personal union with them, revealing his special love and mercy. In return, the Israelites "shall therefore carefully observe the commandments, the statutes and the decrees which I enjoin on you today" (Dt 7:11). These are known as the Law of Moses, the Torah, or simply the Law.

The **Decalogue** summarizes the Law. It expresses what humans know in their hearts, and deduce by reason, to be right or wrong. This is known as the **natural law**, the principles of morality, of right living, that extend to the human race in all places and at all times. As the revealed expression of the natural law, the Ten Commandments are unchangeable and permanent throughout history. They correspond to basic human drives and needs:

- preservation of life ("Do not kill")
- the development of individuals and communities ("Worship God alone, honor his name, and keep holy the Lord's Day"; "Honor your father and mother"; "Do not steal"; "Do not bear false witness"; "Do not covet your neighbor's goods")
- sharing life with others ("Do not commit adultery" and "Do not covet your neighbor's wife")

By worshipping the Lord alone as the true God, and by living a life conformed to the Ten Commandments, the Chosen People were to be a beacon of God's revelation to the whole world. This understanding has helped to define the Church's relationship to the Jewish people through today. As the *Catechism of the Catholic Church* teaches, the "Jewish faith, unlike other non-Christian religions, is already a response to God's revelation in the Old Testament" (*CCC*, 839). However, a study of the Old Testament also reveals how the people would turn their backs on God. They fell into **idolatry** by worshipping false gods. The Israelites' neglect of the Law deserved punishment, and, at times, throughout their history, God did punish them: "I

For Enrichment

The Plight of Immigrants

The first question in this lesson's For Reflection section (page 46) asks the students to connect the immigrant plight of Abraham with that of immigrants today. Invite students to learn about the non-profit Catholic Legal Immigration Network, Inc. (CLINIC), established by the United States Conference of Catholic Bishops, by visiting www.cliniclegal.org.

will be your God and you shall be my people" (Jer 7:23 [see also, Ez 11:20 and Hos 2:25]).

Covenant with David

The First and Second Books of Samuel contain stories about some of the most prominent people in the Old Testament: among them Samuel, the prophet; Saul, Israel's first king; and David, Israel's greatest king. This era followed the period of the **Judges**, tribal chieftains who helped defend Israel against its enemies, settle disputes, and call Israel back to God.

Although 1 and 2 Samuel are among the historical books, history is reported from a theological perspective. The writers saw the Lord's hand in choosing David as king and in making Jerusalem the religious capital of the nation. The key promise of God's covenant with David was that Israel would be a royal dynasty, a promise that led to the belief of a Messiah (God's "anointed one"), who would save the Chosen People from their enemies. Jesus is the Christ, the Messiah, the Son of David. He is the King of Peace who came to save both Jews and all mankind. Nathan tells David:

> The Lord also reveals to you that he will establish a house for you. And when your time comes and you rest with your ancestors, I will raise up your heir after you, sprung from your loins, and I will make his kingdom firm. It is he who shall build a house for my name. And I will make his royal throne firm forever. I will be a father to him, and he shall be a son to me. (2 Sm 7:11–12)

To this good news, David replied:

> Great are you, Lord God! There is none like you and there is no God but you, just as we have heard it told. . . . You have established for yourself your people Israel as yours forever, and you, Lord, have become their God. . . . Your name will be forever great, when men say, "The Lord of hosts is God of Israel," and the house of your servant David stands firm before you. (2 Sm 7:22, 24, 26)

The Davidic covenant specified in more detail the covenants God had made with Abraham and Moses. God not only blessed Abraham and his descendants but he formed a people from them, gave them the Law to guide them, and asked them to worship him in truth and love. God further promised that the future Messiah, the Savior of all humanity, would descend from the house of King David. For their part, the Chosen People were to live the Law as a beacon to the nations of the one true, saving God. Despite the infidelities of the people and even kings like David, God always remained faithful to his promises. In his own good time, he sent his Son to be born of the Blessed Virgin Mary. Jesus—a name that means "Savior"—is the Redeemer of all humanity. David's expression of joy and praise is a right one: "Great are you, Lord God! There is none like you."

Decalogue
Literally, "ten words," it describes the Ten Commandments given by God to Moses on Sinai.

natural law
God's plan for human living that is written in the very way he created things. Binding on all people at all times, it is the light of understanding that God puts in us so we can discover what is good and what is evil.

idolatry
Worshipping something or someone other than the true God.

Judges
In ancient Israel, those who acted as temporary military leaders, as well as arbiters of disputes within and between tribes. The judges were also expected to remind people of their responsibilities to God.

For Enrichment

What if God Had Texted the Decalogue

For a bit of fun, share the following rendition of the Ten Commandments with the students.

1. no1 b4 me. srsly.
2. no omg's
3. no wrk on w/end (sat 4 now; sun l8r)
4. pos ok - ur m&d r cool
5. dnt kill ppl
6. :-X only w/ m8
7. dnt steal
8. dnt lie re: bf + myob.
9. dnt ogle ur bf's m8.
10. dnt ogle ur bf's stuf.

ttyl, JHWH.

ps.
M, pls rite on tabs & giv 2 ppl.

Source: www.mcsweeneys.net/2009/6/3quatro.html

(page 44 in the text). Afterward, emphasize the following:

- Once again—as in creation—God has made the first move. The creating, compassionate God has permanently and definitively committed himself to a people irrevocably—"down to the thousandth generation" (Dt 7:9), that is, forever.
- The Decalogue (Ten Commandments/Torah/Law) is not evidence of a legalistic relationship with God but rather the necessary code of practice for people who now belong to God and want to know how to live lives pleasing to him.

- Take a moment to point out the basic human drives and needs (on page 44) to which the Ten Commandments respond. Explain that because the Ten Commandments deal with universal precepts, they have formed—and remain—the basis upon which the morality of cultures all over the world have been and are judged. Using the list of the Ten Commandments in the *Catholic Handbook for Faith* (page 279), have students categorize each commandment number under one of the three basic needs described in the student text.
- Ask a student to read the definition of "idolatry" in the text. Explain to the students that the Israelites constantly struggled with idolatry throughout their history. Direct students to read Exodus 32. Ask:
  - Why did the Israelites create the golden calf?
  - Despite his wrath, why did God relent on his punishment?
  - Why do you think Moses was so angry?
- Move on to the text section "Covenant with David" (pages 45–46). Have the students tell what they already know about this remarkable individual.
- Make sure the students understand that while David was a very human king who often let his passions get the better of him, he was also a very devout king. God established a covenant with David, a royal dynasty that would lead to the coming of the Messiah. Have the students look up and read Isaiah 11:1–10. Note that Jesse was David's father. Explain to students that this is where the Advent tradition of creating a Jesse Tree finds its source.
- Call attention to the final paragraph in this text section (page 45). Note how well the text sums up the history of God's covenants with the Chosen People. Then show the students how to use the information in this paragraph to create a prayer of thanks called a *dayenu*,

pronounced die-on-oo, which means "it would have been enough." (*Note*: Students of this series of books on Jesus will be familiar with this prayer form.) Tell the students that a dayenu prayer expresses a joyful acknowledgement of and response to God's generous love, and recognizes God's intimate relationship with us. It focuses the praying person on God's cumulative blessings. Explain that each stanza of the prayer proclaims a divine blessing to which those praying respond: "Dayenu! It would have been enough." The following stanza in the prayer always adds to the blessing announced in the preceding stanza. The total effect of the prayer is a burgeoning recitation of praise.

- Get the students started on the prayer by offering the following:

  If you, O God, had blessed Abraham and descendents but had not formed them into a people . . . Dayenu! It would have been enough.
  If you, O God had formed the descendents into a people, but had not rescued them from Egypt . . . Dayenu! It would have been enough.

- Work with the students to help them fashion the prayer. Suggest they use a formula like the following to conclude the prayer: *But as it is, O covenanting*

For Review

1. Describe provisions of the covenant God made with Abraham.
2. Why is Abraham the "father of faith"?
3. How is Mary a perfect model of faith?
4. What was the sign of the covenant with Abraham?
5. What was the Exodus?
6. What is the summary of the Torah?
7. What is the natural law?
8. What are the three basic human needs or drives addressed by the Decalogue?
9. Why did the people make the golden calf? Why did Moses break the stone tablets (read Exodus 32)?
10. Who were the judges in the Old Testament?
11. Who was Israel's first king?
12. Summarize the Davidic covenant.

For Reflection

- How can you connect Abraham's plight as an immigrant to the experience of immigrants in the world today?
- How do you feel connected to the covenants of the Old Testament?

God Remains Faithful to His Promises

In many ways, the kingship of David was a golden period in the monarchy of Israel. He had united the kingdom with Jerusalem as its capital. For a time, he brought peace, culture, and prosperity to the land.

David, though, was a flawed figure. A notable example is how he had an affair with Bathsheba, the married wife of one of his soldiers. He then contrived to have her husband killed after she had become pregnant with David's child. When confronted by the prophet Nathan, David repented (2 Sm 11–12). However, his future reign was beset with various rebellions.

A Divided Kingdom and Captivity

David's son Solomon succeeded his father as king. Known for his wisdom, he built the Temple in Jerusalem, a center of worship and pilgrimage for the Chosen People. Unfortunately, more idolatry followed, and under Solomon's sons the kingdom divided into two: the northern kingdom of Israel, consisting of ten tribes and centered in Samaria; and the southern kingdom of Judah, consisting of the tribes of Benjamin and Judah and centered in Jerusalem.

The northern kingdom fell to Assyria in 722 BC, and the southern kingdom was overrun by Babylonia in 587 BC. During the time of political turmoil and religious backsliding, prophets in both the north and the south reminded people of God's covenant. They proclaimed the need for the Chosen People to worship the one true God in fidelity and truth and to live according to the Law, especially by looking out for the needs of the poor and powerless. As the vehicles to share God's Word, prophets were often unpopular because they challenged corrupt rulers and the status quo. They felt impelled by God to preach his message—worship the one true God and repent sinfulness. To this essential message, later prophets added reassuring words that, despite present appearances, God would never abandon his promises to them.

For Review Answers (page 46)

1. Abraham and his family would be given land; a great nation would descend from him; Abraham himself would be blessed and his name revered; all the earth would be blessed through him; he and Sarah would have a son in their old age, and they would have many descendants.
2. Abraham is the father of faith because he heard, believed, and unflinchingly obeyed God's call.
3. Mary heard, believed, and obeyed God's will as Abraham did, trusting that God would fulfill his promises.
4. Male circumcision.
5. The Exodus was Israel's escape ("departure") from slavery in Egypt—*the* liberating event for the Hebrew people.
6. The Decalogue.
7. Natural law is the principles of morality, of right living, that extend to the human race in all places and at all times.
8. Preservation of life, the development of individuals and communities, and sharing life with others.
9. They built the golden calf because they doubted God and Moses. Moses broke the tablets because he was angry about the Israelites' unfaithfulness.
10. The judges were tribal chieftains who served mainly as military leaders for Israel, settled disputes, and called the people back to God.
11. Saul.
12. The Messiah would come from David's line.

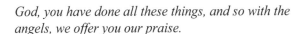

Prophets Preach Repentance and Hope

An example of a prophet who preached to the northern kingdom was Amos. Around 750 BC, he proclaimed that true worship of God required concrete deeds manifested to the weak and poor. He also chided the Israelites on their many sins: genocide, cruelty, anger, sexual excess, violence, pride, and the like. He warned that unless people repented, the nation would be destroyed. Amos offered timeless advice:

> Hate evil and love good
> and let justice prevail at the gate.
> (Am 5:15)

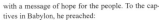

The prophet Jeremiah echoed the theme of repentance. He preached at the time of Babylonia's assault on the southern kingdom. He used props in dramatic scenes to try to get the attention of the people. For example, he shattered a jug in front of the elders and priests to serve as a warning that God would destroy those who had abandoned him. Another time, he walked through the streets of Jerusalem with a wooden yoke on his shoulders to emphasize to the people that only by submitting to Babylon could the kingdom of Judah be spared destruction. Jeremiah also balanced his dire warnings with a message of hope for the people. To the captives in Babylon, he preached:

> The days are coming, says the Lord, when I will make a new covenant with the house of Israel and the house of Judah. It will not be like the covenant I made with their fathers. . . . I will place my law within them, and write it upon their hearts; I will be their God, and they shall be my people. No longer will they have need to teach their friends and kinsmen how to know the Lord. All, from least to greatest, shall know me, says the Lord, for I will forgive their evildoing and remember their sin no more. (Jer 31:31, 33–34)

This passage is hopeful because it reminded the Chosen People that God will take the initiative by giving them new hearts so that they will be obedient to the Lord. Knowledge of God will be internal and personal. It will no longer only be written on tablets of stone or in law books. Rather, God will touch a person's heart so that the Lord may live within.

Christians understand in Jeremiah's words a prophecy of the New Covenant established by Jesus Christ. The Savior's life, Death, and Resurrection inaugurated a covenant of God's grace that heals and conquers sin. It is a covenant of new life and the outpouring of the Holy Spirit who guides us from within.

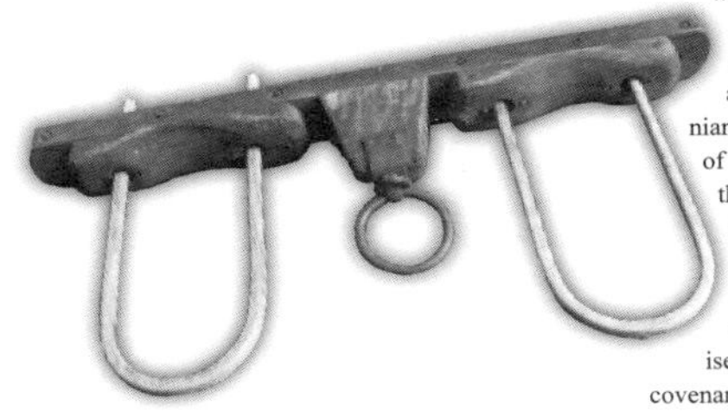

Another prophet who preached both repentance and hope was Ezekiel. For example, before Jerusalem fell to the Babylonians, Ezekiel had strongly censured the People of God for their sinful conduct and warned them of imminent destruction. However, after the fall of Jerusalem, the once highly critical Ezekiel offered a demoralized and defeated nation a message of hope. As recorded in Ezekiel 33–39, the prophet promised that a new shepherd king would make a covenant of peace with the people. He also predicted a time when God would restore the nation. He

Lesson 5 Objectives

The students will:

- discover the message and appreciate the role of the biblical prophets.
- write their own prophetic message for today's world.
- investigate the Servant Songs of Deutero-Isaiah.
- recognize how Christ is the fulfillment to the Old Testament prophecies.

Lesson 5 Preview

This lesson examines the messages and purposes of some of the Bible's greatest prophets, examining them in light of their meaning and import for Israel and their fulfillment in Jesus. The students investigate the Servant Songs of Isaiah to discover how Christians see in them a prophecy of the mission of Jesus and his suffering—his Paschal Mystery—on our behalf.

God, you have done all these things, and so with the angels, we offer you our praise.

- Write out the stanzas on the board. Assign different stanzas to different students or groups of students to read. All are to join in the response: "Dayenu! It would have been enough."
- If you wish, tell the students that when the ancient Israelites prayed the dayenu, they often danced to express their joy. In keeping with this spirit, suggest to the students that they use gestures to accompany the dayenu response:
  - At the word "*Dayenu!*" they might raise their arms above their heads.
  - On the phrase "*It would have been enough*," they could extend their raised arms outward.

  If you choose to use gestures, take a moment to practice them.
- Pray the dayenu. Conclude by singing a familiar version of the "Holy, Holy. Holy."

Chapter 2: The Fall and the Promise of a Savior—Lesson 5

Bell Ringers

- Ask the students to offer their responses to the twelve For Review questions on page 46 (answers are on page 60 of this text). Be sure to allow the students to ask any other questions they may have.
- To sum up the previous material on covenants tell the students that by choosing to relate to humankind by means of covenants, God always played the part of the suitor. Never once did God say, "You will!" Rather, God always asked, "Will you?" Even more, God continued to ask even when humanity continually reneged on its "we wills."
- Ask students to list in their notes where the coming of Jesus was foretold in the Pentateuch. (*Protoevangelium and the Davidic Covenant*)

Teaching Approaches

God Remains Faithful to His Promises (pages 46-50)

- Begin this session by displaying—if possible—a map of the two ancient Hebrew kingdoms, Israel and Judah. Explain to the students that the division took place after King Solomon's death. The ten tribes of the North (Israel) felt they were being taxed more than

the two Southern tribes (Judah). The Northern tribes met with Solomon's son and successor, Rehoboam, to ask for relief, but he refused their request and responded by raising the taxes. Refer the students to 1 Kings 12:1–17, 20–21, which gives an account of the division.

- Go on to say that while Jerusalem remained the center of worship in the Southern Kingdom (Judah), Samaria became the North's worship center. Later, when Assyria captured Israel (the Northern Kingdom) the majority of the people were taken away (the lost tribes). A few of the Israelites remained and intermarried with the Assyrians, eventually becoming the people who were known in Jesus' time as Samaritans, thus the antagonism over race and true worship between Jews and Samaritans (see John 4:1–42).
- Introduce the role of the prophets by telling the students that but for a very few exceptions, the rulers who followed Solomon were weak and pretty pitiful. They treated their own people like slaves, made alliances with pagan nations, introduced false gods, and turned away from the God who had delivered them from slavery.
- Write the words ***nabiim*** and ***prophetes*** on the board. Tell the students that the former is the Hebrew term for "prophet" and the latter is the Greek term. Explain that our English comes from the Greek word, which, in turn, is from *pro* ("before" or "for") and *phemi* ("to speak"). Thus, a prophet is someone who "speaks before" in the sense of proclaiming; or someone who "speaks for" (in the name of) another, for example, God. The Hebrew word *nabiim* similarly means "mouthpiece."
- Go on to stress that the biblical prophets were not oracles or fortunetellers. Rather, they were leaders who called the people back to God. They spoke for God to the people, reminding them of the covenant, sometimes with words of warning and repentance, at other times with words of comfort and hope.
- Call attention to the text section "Prophets Preach Repentance and Hope" (pages 47–48). Remind the students that this section deals with four great biblical prophets; one prophesied to the people of Israel (the North), the other three to the people of Judah (the South).
- Tell the students that while Amos was a prophet to the Northern Kingdom, he was actually from Judah in the south. Amos has been called the first prophet of social justice. He recognized the plight of the poor and

48 Jesus Christ: Source of Our Salvation

told of a prophetic dream he had where he stood in a field of dry bones:

> These bones are the whole house of Israel. They have been saying, "Our bones are dried up, our hope is lost, and we are cut off. . . ." Thus says the Lord God: O my people, I will open your graves and have you rise from them, and bring you back to the land of Israel. Then you shall know that I am the Lord, when I open your graves and have you rise from them, O my people! I will put my spirit in you that you may live, and I will settle you upon your land; thus you shall know that I am the Lord. I have promised, and I will do it, says the Lord. (Ez 37:11–14)

Ezekiel's vision prophesied that the people would return to the Promised Land. Their despair will be turned to hope. God will bring them back to life!

Coming of the Messiah

The Book of Isaiah actually consists of three main parts, probably composed by three different authors. Each prophesized about the future of God's People and the coming of a Messiah. Chapters 1–39 come from the original prophet, Isaiah of Jerusalem, who preached during the time of the collapse of the northern kingdom and the moral breakdown of the southern kingdom. His ministry spanned the period from 742 to 700 BC. He preached a powerful message of repentance to a sinful nation, criticizing idolatry, empty sacrifice, human pride, and cruelty to the poor. He also prophesied that God would give a sign: "The virgin shall be with child, and bear a son, and shall name him Immanuel" (Is 7:14). The child who will be born is a son upon whom God will rule:

> They name him Wonder-Counselor,
> God-Hero,
> Father-Forever, Prince of Peace.
> His dominion is vast and forever peaceful.
> (Is 9:5–6)

Christians see in Isaiah's prophecy of Immanuel (a name meaning "God is with us") a reference to the promised Messiah, the Son of God, Jesus of Nazareth.

Isaiah 40–55, sometimes called Deutero-Isaiah or Second Isaiah, is generally attributed to an anonymous poet. It may have been written around 550 BC during the Babylonian exile. The author foretold to the captive people that Babylonia was on the verge of collapse. In fact, he was correct. Cyrus of Persia defeated the Babylonians and in 538 BC permitted exiles to return home. At this time a remnant of the Jewish people returned to Jerusalem and, under leaders like Ezra and Nehemiah, rebuilt and rededicated the Temple (516 BC).

Deutero-Isaiah had many consoling words for his people. The prophet proclaimed that God is coming to save his people and that his love is enduring, like that of a mother for her baby:

> Can a mother forget her infant,
> be without tenderness for the child of her womb?
> Even should she forget you
> I will never forget you.
> See, upon the palms of my hands I have
> written your name. (Is 49:15–16a)

Besides the message of consolation, hope, and deliverance, Deutero-Isaiah also teaches that God is the one, all-powerful, creator God. Everything that exists comes from, depends on, and is subject to God: "I am the first and I am the last; there is no God but me" (Is 44:6). "I am the Lord, there is no other" (Is 45:6b).

The prophet reminds the Israelites that God called them to serve as a light to attract other nations to the worship of the one true God. As God used Cyrus of Persia to do his work, so the Lord's love for the Israelites should illuminate the way for other nations.

> I will make you a light to the nations,
> that my salvation may reach the ends of the earth. (Is 49:6)

Lesson 5 Homework

1. Ask the students to write out their answers to the nine For Review questions on page 50.
2. Direct the students to complete the second For Reflection activity (page 50) and to hand it in at their next section. (*Note*: this will be important for the chapter test.)
3. Tell the students to be ready to hand in their Ongoing Assignments at their next session.
4. Have the students read through the Chapter Quick View section on pages 51–53 and to review the chapter's Main Ideas. Tell the students to write out any questions they may have and bring them to the next session.

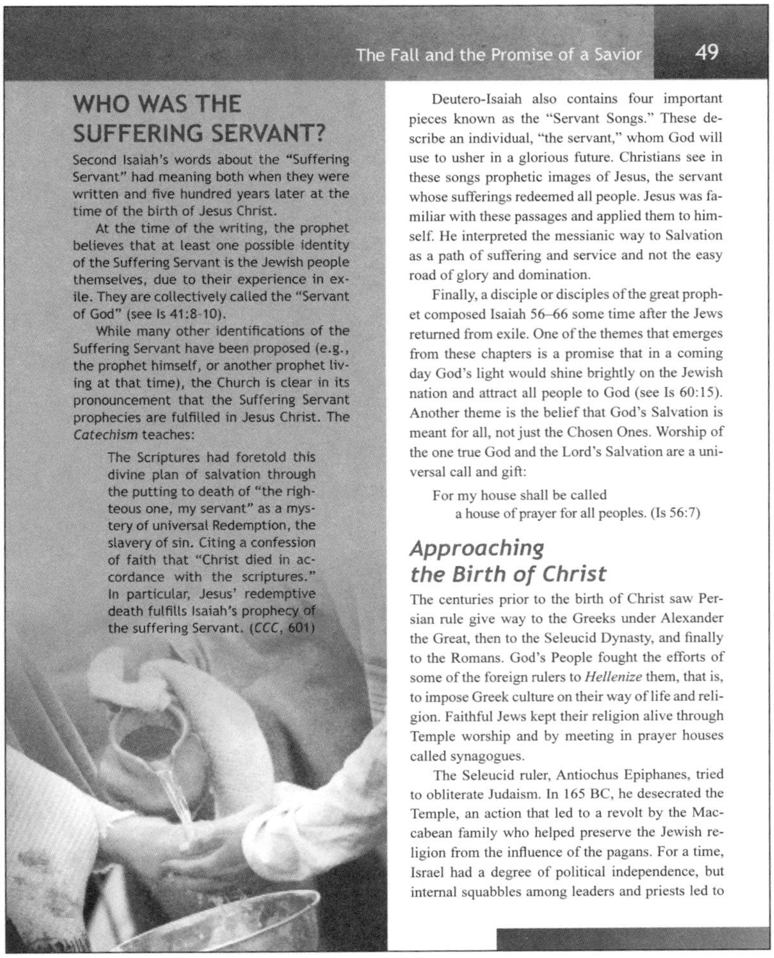

WHO WAS THE SUFFERING SERVANT?

Second Isaiah's words about the "Suffering Servant" had meaning both when they were written and five hundred years later at the time of the birth of Jesus Christ.

At the time of the writing, the prophet believes that at least one possible identity of the Suffering Servant is the Jewish people themselves, due to their experience in exile. They are collectively called the "Servant of God" (see Is 41:8–10).

While many other identifications of the Suffering Servant have been proposed (e.g., the prophet himself, or another prophet living at that time), the Church is clear in its pronouncement that the Suffering Servant prophecies are fulfilled in Jesus Christ. The *Catechism* teaches:

> The Scriptures had foretold this divine plan of salvation through the putting to death of "the righteous one, my servant" as a mystery of universal Redemption, the slavery of sin. Citing a confession of faith that "Christ died in accordance with the scriptures." In particular, Jesus' redemptive death fulfills Isaiah's prophecy of the suffering Servant. (*CCC*, 601)

Deutero-Isaiah also contains four important pieces known as the "Servant Songs." These describe an individual, "the servant," whom God will use to usher in a glorious future. Christians see in these songs prophetic images of Jesus, the servant whose sufferings redeemed all people. Jesus was familiar with these passages and applied them to himself. He interpreted the messianic way to Salvation as a path of suffering and service and not the easy road of glory and domination.

Finally, a disciple or disciples of the great prophet composed Isaiah 56–66 some time after the Jews returned from exile. One of the themes that emerges from these chapters is a promise that in a coming day God's light would shine brightly on the Jewish nation and attract all people to God (see Is 60:15). Another theme is the belief that God's Salvation is meant for all, not just the Chosen Ones. Worship of the one true God and the Lord's Salvation are a universal call and gift:

> For my house shall be called
> a house of prayer for all peoples. (Is 56:7)

Approaching the Birth of Christ

The centuries prior to the birth of Christ saw Persian rule give way to the Greeks under Alexander the Great, then to the Seleucid Dynasty, and finally to the Romans. God's People fought the efforts of some of the foreign rulers to *Hellenize* them, that is, to impose Greek culture on their way of life and religion. Faithful Jews kept their religion alive through Temple worship and by meeting in prayer houses called synagogues.

The Seleucid ruler, Antiochus Epiphanes, tried to obliterate Judaism. In 165 BC, he desecrated the Temple, an action that led to a revolt by the Maccabean family who helped preserve the Jewish religion from the influence of the pagans. For a time, Israel had a degree of political independence, but internal squabbles among leaders and priests led to

disenfranchised and so spoke out forcefully against the way Israel was treating them.

- Distribute copies of Chapter 2, Handout 2, "Prophetic Voices." Have the students look up the listed passages from the Book of Amos and then write their answers to the questions. Share responses, noting Amos's option for the poor as well as his distaste for phony religiosity—substituting religious formalities for living and acting justly.
- Call attention to the "timeless advice" from Amos on page 47 (Am 5:15). Tell the students that the messages of the prophets—like this one from Amos—still ring true because genuine prophetic messages tend to be universal. They speak not only to the prophet's original audience, but also to audiences throughout the ages.
- Move on to the prophet Jeremiah. Have the students read Jeremiah 13:20 as listed on Handout 2 and then respond to the accompanying question. *Note*: The "men from the north" were the Babylonians set to invade Judah. Tell the students that despite Jeremiah's persistence, the people did not listen. In 597 BC, the Babylonians invaded, Jerusalem fell, and the people were carried off into exile.
- Note all which was lost to the Hebrew people:
    - The capital city Jerusalem was in ruins.
    - The Temple was in ashes.
    - The entire nation was in chains.

  Help the students better appreciate the depth of this tragedy by asking them how they would feel if:

    - Washington, DC, had been destroyed.
    - All the churches were demolished or shuttered.
    - Every US citizen was forced to live outside the United States as a refugee.

  Invite the students to write their responses in their journals.
- Tell the students that it was to a heartbroken people that Jeremiah spoke words of compassion and hope. Have the students reread the passage from Jeremiah 31:31, 33–4 (on page 47). Point out that God is promising to establish a *radically new and different* kind of covenant with the people. The prophecy declares that this covenant will unite Israel and Judah, reconciling the once divided kingdoms. Also, it imposes no direct concerns about new laws in this new covenant, nor does it annul any of the laws or principles of the previous covenants. The problems of the past were due to the people—not God—breaking covenants. No new

laws are needed for this new covenant, simply new hearts—a sentiment echoed in Ezekiel 36:25–27.

- Move on to the Prophet Ezekiel. Tell the students that like Jeremiah, Ezekiel began his prophesying by trying to shock his listeners into abandoning their sinful ways. Have the students read the passage from the Book of Ezekiel referenced on Handout 2 and complete the writing activity. Afterward, call on volunteers to share their words of warning.
- Explain that Ezekiel went into exile with the people. There, in Babylon, Ezekiel changed his prophetic tune to one of consolation. Have the students read and respond to the passages from Ezekiel and John on Handout 2. Afterward, as the students share responses, suggest that in this case, Ezekiel wrote prophecies about the Messiah
- Have the students read the passage from Ezekiel 37 on page 48. Note how God promises to *in-spirit* the people—reminiscent of the *in-spiring* breath of God in Genesis 2:7. Then, if possible, play a recording of the spiritual "Dry Bones." Ask the students why this passage and song would speak so powerfully to an oppressed people.
- Invite the students to think of a person or group or a situation that may need a prophetic voice—either of warning ("Turn away from . . . and turn to . . .") and/or of comfort ("This is how all will be well . . ."). If you wish, brainstorm a list on the board. For example:

the formation of sects. In 63 BC, the Romans imposed their rule on Israel. They appointed Herod the Great, a half-Jew, to govern. Herod was a great builder and was responsible for the reconstruction of the Temple. But he was also a cruel and vindictive ruler who governed with an iron hand. It was shortly before his death, in 4 BC, that the Prince of Peace, Jesus Christ, was born. All the prophecies concerning the Messiah would come true. In him, God's covenant with the Jews and all humanity would reach its perfect fulfillment in his Passion, Death, and Resurrection. Chapter 3 focuses on the events around Christ's birth and discusses how his life fulfilled the Old Testament prophecies.

For Review

1. Explain King David's central role in Salvation History.
2. When did the northern kingdom fall to the Assyrians? When did the southern kingdom fall to the Babylonians?
3. Who were the prophets? What was their essential message?
4. Summarize the prophetic message of Amos.
5. What did Jeremiah preach about the new covenant?
6. What was the meaning of Ezekiel's dry bones vision?
7. What important Messianic prophecy does Isaiah of Jerusalem make in Isaiah 7:14?
8. What is the meaning of the title *Immanuel*?
9. How do the Servant Songs apply to Jesus Christ?

For Reflection

- Prayerfully read Isaiah 52:13-53:12. Note three ways this passage applies to Jesus Christ.
- Read and briefly describe the following Old Testament passages referring to the coming of the Messiah: Psalm 22:19, 35:11, 41:9; Isaiah 11:2, 35:56; Hosea 11:1; Micah 5:2; Zechariah 9:9, 11:12-13; Malachi 3:1.

For Review Answers (page 50)

1. Answers may vary but should reflect an understanding that David was the greatest of Israel's kings and that God's covenant with David would lead to the coming of the Messiah.
2. The Northern Kingdom fell to Assyria in 722 BC. The Southern Kingdom fell to Babylon in 587 BC.
3. The prophets were messengers who spoke for God. Their essential message was "repent and return to God." To this, the prophets added assurances that no matter what, God would never abandon his covenant with them.
4. Hate evil, love good, act with justice.
5. Jeremiah prophesied that the new covenant would be written on the people's hearts, and thus knowledge of God would be internal and personal.
6. Ezekiel's vision spoke of re-creation (in-spiration) and a return to the Promised Land.
7. The birth of a son to a virgin.
8. Immanuel means God-with-us.
9. Answers will vary but should evidence an understanding that Jesus, who was without sin, suffered a redemptive death for God's people.

The Fall and the Promise of a Savior 51

Chapter 2 Quick View

Main Ideas

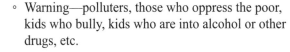

- At creation, Adam and Eve were gifted with Original Holiness and Original Justice. (p. 32)
- Among the effects of Original Sin were the loss of Original Holiness and Original Justice. (p. 32)
- The Fall of Adam and Eve is told using figurative language, though there was a real historical event that was behind the occasion of the Original Sin. (pp. 32–33)
- Temptation lead to the Original Sin; Adam and Eve sinned by preferring themselves to God. (p. 33)
- Because of Original Sin, humans have inherited a fallen human nature, are deprived of Original Holiness and Original Justice, and are subject to death. (pp. 34–35)
- Original Sin weakened human nature, but it did not totally corrupt it. (p. 35)
- The Protoevangelium, recorded in Genesis 3:15, announces God's plan for a future Messiah and Redeemer and a final victory over sin and death. (pp. 35–36)
- It is Christ's Death that is the source of our Salvation. (p. 36)
- Sin spread exponentially after the Original Sin, and occasions of sin in the Old Testament include those connected to Cain and Abel, the Great Flood, and the Tower of Babel. (pp. 38–39)
- God formed covenants with his people in the Old Testament. The first covenant was with Noah. Covenants between God and the Chosen People were those with Abraham, Moses, and David. (pp. 38–41)
- The Covenant with Abraham promised land to Abraham and his progeny. (pp. 42–43)
- The Covenant with Moses formed the Chosen People and gave them a Law, summarized in the Ten Commandments. (pp. 43–44)
- The Davidic Covenant specified in more detail that a Messiah, the Savior of all humanity, would be a descendant of King David. (pp. 45–46)
- The prophets of the Old Testament preached repentance and hope. (pp. 47–48)
- The Book of Isaiah prophesizes about the future of God's People and the coming of the Messiah. (pp. 48–50)

Terms, People, Places

Complete each sentence by choosing the correct answer from the list of terms below. You will not use all of the terms.

Decalogue
Gentiles
Guardian Angel
idolatry
Judges
Natural Law
New Adam
New Covenant
Original Sin
Protoevangelium
Satan

1. The full meaning of _______________ is only revealed in the Death and Resurrection of Jesus Christ.
2. Time and again the Chosen People would turn their backs on God and fall into the sin of _______________ by worshipping false Gods.
3. The _______________ were tribal chieftains who helped defend Israel against its enemies, settle disputes, and call Israel back to God.
4. Jesus' mission was to save all humanity, including the _______________.
5. Your _______________ is meant to watch over you and help to shield you from temptation.

Terms, People, Places Answers (pages 51-52)

1. Original Sin
2. Idolatry
3. Judges
4. Gentiles
5. Guardian Angel
6. Natural Law
7. Decalogue
8. Protoevangelium
9. New Adam
10. Satan

    - Warning—polluters, those who oppress the poor, kids who bully, kids who are into alcohol or other drugs, etc.
    - Comfort—the homeless, the sick or elderly, the depressed or suicidal, kids who feel left out, etc.

  Call attention to the heading "My Prophetic Voice" on Handout 2. Have the students use their prophetic voice by addressing one of the listed people/groups/situations as did one of the ancient prophets. Allow time for writing. Afterward, encourage students to share their responses.

- Move on to the text section "Coming of the Messiah" (pages 48–49). Distribute copies of Chapter 2, Handout 3, "Isaiah x 3." Use the outline on the handout to summarize the material in the text. Be sure to have the students use their Bibles to look up and read all the referenced passages from Isaiah that are not printed in the text itself, especially all four of the Servant Songs from Third Isaiah.
- Have the students turn to the feature "Who Was the Suffering Servant?" (page 49). Tell the students that Christians interpret the Servant Songs as referring to Jesus. Explain that while some may disagree with this interpretation—opting instead to regard all of Israel itself as the "servant"— the notion of an innocent suffering vicariously for the guilty is found in these songs and nowhere else in all of Hebrew thought. Although Israel might suffer for its own sins, it never does so for the sins of others. That is why the earliest followers of Jesus identified the Servant as Jesus.
- Call attention to the heading "The Golden Passional" on Handout 3. Read the directions to the students and then have them complete the activity on their own. Afterward, share reflections. Note similar and different insights. (*Note*: This activity is the same as the first activity of this lesson's For Reflection section on page 50.)
- Call attention to "Approaching the Birth of Christ" on page 49. Tell the students that after the Jews' return from Babylon, they remained a subjugated people for the next 600 years, first under the Persians, later under the Greeks (the Ptolemies and then the Seleucids), and then the Romans. During this long period, the people began looking more and more for the coming of a promised savior to rescue them from their subjugation. Explain that while the efforts of the Maccabees gave Israel a brief hiatus of freedom, Israel was soon under the rule of the Roman Empire. God's people longed for a Messiah—and one was on the way.

Chapter 2: The Fall and the Promise of a Savior—Review Lesson

Bell Ringers

- Discuss the students' responses to the second For Reflection activity from the previous lesson (page 50).
- Review the previous lesson by inviting the students to share responses to the nine questions in the For Review section on page 50.
- Collect the students' Ongoing Assignments for Chapter 2 (pages 52–53). Allow time for those who chose #1 or #2 (creating PowerPoint presentations) to make their presentations to the class.

Teaching Approaches

Chapter Quick View (pages 51-53)

- Call attention to Terms, People, Places on pages 51–52. Use the section as a vocabulary study tool. Have the students complete the matching exercise (answers are on page 65 of this text).
- Use the Main Ideas section to review key points. Go through the ideas with the class, having the students refer back to the chapter pages listed in the text.
- Continue the review by going over some or all of the For Review questions from the chapter. If you wish, use a game format such as "Bluff." Divide the class into two teams. Each team will have the opportunity to answer each question. The teacher will read the question to the team and each player must stand if he/she would like to attempt to answer the question. The teacher will call on a student randomly to answer the question and if the question is answered correctly, the team will be awarded the number of points equal to the number of players standing. Students may choose to "bluff" by standing to earn their team more points even if they do not know the answer. Feel free to add additional questions or invite students to create more questions related to the chapter test.
- Take some time to go over any material the students may have overlooked in their review or that you feel needs more attention. Allow time for the students to ask any questions they may have.
- As time allows, invite various students who handed in written Ongoing Assignments to share their reports with the group.

6. The ______________ is principles of morality that extend to the human race in all places and at all times.
7. The ______________ summarizes the Law.
8. Literally, the ______________ is translated as the "first gospel."
9. By becoming obedient even to Death on a cross, Jesus fulfilled his role as the ______________.
10. The fallen angel who tempted Adam and Eve is known as ______________.

Primary Source Quotations

Sin and Evil

The whole of man's history has been the story of our combat with the powers of evil, stretching, so our Lord tells us, from the very dawn of history until the last day. Finding himself in the midst of the battlefield man has to struggle to do what is right, and it is at great cost to himself, and aided by God's grace, that he succeeds in achieving his own inner integrity.

—*Gaudium et Spes*, 37

God did not make death, nor does he rejoice in the destruction of the living.

—Wisdom 1:13

I do not trust myself as long as I am in this body of death. . . . The hostile flesh always draws me toward death, that is toward enticements unlawful to indulge in.

—St. Patrick

To sin is human, but to persist in sin is devilish.

—St. Catherine of Siena

Reserve some time to pray before the Blessed Sacrament for people in your family who have gone before you to eternal rest. Pray for them by name.

Ongoing Assignments

As you cover the material in this chapter, choose and complete at least three of these assignments.

1. Prepare a PowerPoint presentation with a collection of various depictions of the creation and the fall.
2. Prepare a PowerPoint presentation on how Satan has been portrayed in Christian art.
3. Prepare a report on the seven capital sins. Use practical examples to show how the capital sins have a detrimental effect on your life.
4. Prepare a report on the three angels mentioned in the Bible: Gabriel, Michael, and Raphael. Reproduce a photo of how one of them has been depicted in art or on holy cards.
5. Report on the "hierarchy of the angels."
6. Examine some Old Testament covenants by reading the selected passages. Answer the questions that accompany each passage.
   1 Samuel 18:1–5
   - Who are the subjects of the covenant?
   - Why was it made?
   - What was the sign of the agreement?

   Ezra 10:1–5
   - What was the agreement made?
   - How was it made?

   Hebrews 9:11–22
   - Who is the mediator of the covenant?
   - What brings about forgiveness?
7. Report on the efforts of some scholars to search for the location of Noah's ark.
8. Read the following passages in Genesis where God appears to Moses. Note what God promises in each particular passage: 12:1–3; 12:7; 13:14–18; 15:4–5, 13–18; 17:1–8.
9. Report on one of the Old Testament matriarchs of the faith—Sarah, Rebekah, Rachel, and Leah—and their relationship to Mary.

Chapter 2 Quick View

Review Lesson Objectives

The students will:

- review Chapter 2 in preparation for the chapter test.
- join in prayer together.

Review Lesson Homework

1. Complete any unfinished Ongoing Assignments.
2. Reread Chapter 2.
3. Study for the Chapter 2 Test.

10. After reading a description of the Ark of the Covenant, do one of the following:
    - Draw a sketch of its probable appearance.
    - Report on what happened to it, including some modern theories.
11. Read Isaiah 40–44. Transcribe in your journal at least five verses that speak of God's mercy and tenderness to the Chosen People.

Prayer

Pope Leo XIII introduced the following Prayer to St. Michael the Archangel to be recited at the end of Mass. Though it is no longer recited as part of the Eucharistic liturgy, later popes encourage us to recite it frequently. Pope John Paul II urged us to pray it "to obtain help in the battle against forces of darkness and against the spirit of this world."

Prayer to St. Michael the Archangel
St. Michael the Archangel,
defend us in battle.
Be our protection against the wickedness and snares of the devil.
May God rebuke him, we humbly pray;
and do Thou, O Prince of the Heavenly Host—
by the Power of God—
cast into Hell, Satan and all the evil spirits,
who roam throughout the world seeking the ruin of souls.
Amen.

- *Reflection*: What is a "snare" that is tempting you to be less than the beautiful child of God you are called to be?
- *Resolution*: During the coming two weeks, recite this prayer each time you are tempted to sin.

Chapter 2 Quick View

Test Lesson Homework

1. Read the following text section of Chapter 3: "Jesus: Our Hope and Salvation" (page 56).
2. Examine the Chapter 3 Ongoing Assignments on page 79.
3. Have the students write a paragraph describing a person who has made a real difference in their life and describing just what that difference is and what it means to them.

- Provide some quiet time for the students to study on their own.

Prayer Service

- Gather the students, with their books, in a circle around a lighted candle. Call attention to the Reflection question on page 53 ("What is a 'snare' that is tempting you to be less than the beautiful child of God you are called to be?") Read it aloud; then allow some time for reflection.
- While the students reflect, consider playing a song of repentance and reconciliation such as "Healer of Our Every Ill" (Haugen, GIA).
- Lead the students in praying the "Prayer to St. Michael the Archangel" on page 53.
- Point out the Resolution on page 53. Encourage the students to make use of the prayer to St. Michael when feeling "ensnared."

Chapter 2 Test Lesson

Teaching Approaches

- Allow sufficient time for the students to work on the Chapter 2 Test (starting on page 291 of the TWE and also online at www.avemariapress.com). Collect tests as the students finish.

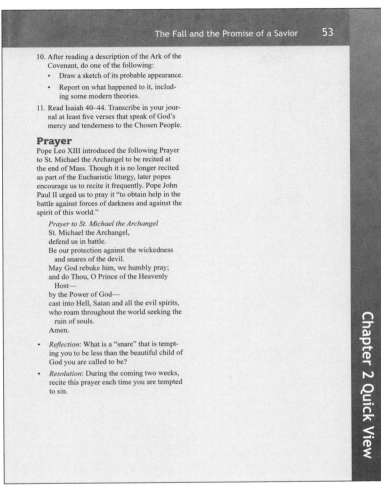

Chapter 2 Test Answers

Part 1: True or False. (3 points each)

1. F
2. T
3. F
4. T
5. T

Part 2: Fill in the Blanks. (3 points each)

1. idolatry
2. Abraham
3. myth
4. covenant
5. Concupiscence
6. Pentecost
7. Jeremiah
8. Holiness
9. rainbow
10. Tower of Babel
11. judges
12. Decalogue
13. Protoevangelium
14. Justice
15. Ezekiel
16. Isaiah
17. Cain
18. Amos

Part 3: Brief Answers. (3 points each)

1. Michael, Raphael, and Gabriel
2. Adam and Eve ate from the Tree of Knowledge so they could be like God.
3. Natural law is the principles of morality, of right living, that extend to the human race in all places and at all times.
4. The consequences of Original Sin include: the loss of Original Holiness and Original Justice, alienation from God and others, weakened human nature, concupiscence, ignorance, pain in childbearing, suffering, and death.
5. The three basic human drives and needs are preservation of life, the development of individuals and communities, and sharing life with others.
6. Answers will vary, but the students should be able to describe a biblical prophet as someone who spoke for God by calling the wayward people back to God, reminding them of the covenant, sometimes with words of warning and repentance, at other times with words of comfort and hope.
7. Answers will vary but should reflect the following: Abraham and his family would be given land and many descendants; a great nation would descend from him; Abraham himself would be blessed and his name revered; all the earth would be blessed through him; he and Sarah would have a son in their old age.

Part 4: Essay. (10 points)
Examples of Jesus fulfilling the Old Testament include the Protoevangelium, the Tower of Babel (fulfilled at Pentecost), the Davidic Covenant, Jeremiah's prophecies of the New Covenant, and Isaiah's prophecies of the Messiah and Suffering Servant.

Chapter 3: The Coming of the Messiah

Introduction

O come, O come, Emmanuel,
And ransom captive Israel,
That mourns in lonely exile here
Until the Son of God appear.
This is the anthem of eons of ache, years of yearning, lifetimes of longing.

Rejoice! Rejoice!
Emmanuel shall come to you, O Israel.
This is the paean of promise, the rejoicing refrain.

Chapter 3 set the stage for the advent of the Promised One. In this chapter, the music swells, the curtain rises, and the Messiah steps into the spotlight. In the chapter's first lesson, the students recognize the meaning and power of the virtue of hope, the virtue that had long sustained the Hebrew people over their years of wandering and waiting for the fulfillment of the covenant—the coming of Emmanuel. The students discover that God keeps his promises and fulfills his covenants in Jesus—he who comes to satisfy our hopes.

The students review their understanding of the Gospels as testaments of faith that do far more than present the record of a long-ago historical figure. Rather, they put us in touch with Jesus the Christ, present in our lives. Even more, they invite us to place our faith in him and challenge us to follow his way. Examining the origins of Jesus presented in the Gospels helps the students root Jesus in a time, a place, and a people. The students discover how each evangelist had a different perspective on Jesus' coming.

Mark, writing for an audience of persecuted Gentile-Christians, begins his Gospel by declaring that Jesus is the fulfillment of Isaiah's prophecies and one in whom God is "well pleased." Matthew, writing for an audience of Jewish-Christians, takes pains to reveal Jesus' links with the giants of the Hebrew faith—Abraham, Moses, David. Matthew's account of Jesus' birth, the magi, Herod's cruelty, and the Holy Family's forced flight into Egypt reveal that Jesus is a Messiah who would be on the side of the outcast, the refugee, the homeless, and the persecuted, since he began life as one of them.

Luke wrote his Gospel for poor Gentile-Christians. Describing Jesus' origins, Luke makes it clear that Jesus himself was the child of poor parents, born in poor surroundings, and revealed to shepherds—the poorest of the poor. From Luke the students also learn that Jesus' circumcision makes him part of God's people; his presentation acknowledges that he is "consecrated" to God, is a true "son of God"; and his adventure in the Temple at the tender age of twelve declares that already he was beginning to understand and exercise the mission for which he was sent.

The prologue to John's Gospel deals neither with prophecy nor with infancy. It deals, rather, with infinity, describing Jesus as the eternal Word, present at the beginning of all things, whispered throughout the ages, and now spoken again so clearly and so definitively in a language we best understand—the language of a person, God in the flesh. This is the meaning of Incarnation— God not only with us, among us, and for us, but *one of us*—astounding Good News!

The students discover that every aspect of the life and person of Jesus-one-of-us is revelatory of the Father's great love for us. That love is clearly stated at Jesus' baptism where God acknowledges him as his only Son. That love is tested by the tempter,

Chapter Objectives

To help the students:

- reflect on the meaning of the virtue of hope.
- recognize that Jesus is our hope fulfilled.
- examine Jesus' origins as presented in the Gospels.
- investigate the infancy narratives in the Gospels of Matthew and Luke.
- examine the Prologue of John's Gospel, especially as it regards the Incarnation.
- appreciate the purpose of the Incarnation.
- discover theological truths revealed at Jesus' baptism.
- understand the meaning of and Jesus' response to his being tempted.
- appreciate that Jesus came announcing and inviting us into the Kingdom of God.

whom Jesus rebukes and banishes, thus demonstrating his commitment to his Father's will and serving as an example to us to follow in resisting the temptations that may come our way.

The chapter concludes by introducing the students to Jesus' central message: the advent of the Kingdom of God. Jesus ushers in the Kingdom by his unique, shocking, and authoritative teaching, by gathering the disciples, and by his wonderful deeds beginning with the wedding feast at Cana.

Advance Preparations

Prepare or have on hand:

For Lesson 1

- Corrected copies of the Chapter 2 Test
- Bibles
- Copies of Chapter 3, Handout 1, "Hope"
- A recording either of the hymn "Only in God" by John Foley and the St. Louis Jesuits, or of the song "Only Hope" by the rock group Switchfoot (optional)
- Copies of Chapter 3, Handout 2, "An Act of Hope"

For Lesson 2

- Bibles
- Strips of construction paper and markers
- Copies of Chapter 3, Handout 3, "The Gospels"

For Lesson 3

- Bibles
- Copies of the music—and/or a recording of and player for—Mary's "Magnificat" (e.g., "My Soul Proclaims" by Marty Haugen; "Magnificat" by David Haas; or "Magnificat" by Michael Joncas)
- A player and a recording of the "Benedictus" (e.g., "Hallelujah, Hallelu" by Michael Mahler; "Gospel Canticle" by James Quinn, S.J.; or "Blest Be the God of Israel" by Marty Haugen)
- Copies of Chapter 3, Handout 4, "The House of Christmas"

For Lesson 4

- Bibles
- Copies of Chapter 3, Handout 5, "What Are the Gospels?"

For Lesson 5

- Bibles

For the Chapter 3 Review Lesson

- Equipment necessary for students to make PowerPoint presentations
- Candle and matches
- A recording of meditative music and a player

For the Chapter 3 Test Lesson

- Copies of the Chapter 3 Test (starting on page 291 of the TWE and also online at www.avemariapress.com)

Chapter 3 Handouts

- Handout 1, Hope—The students examine the meaning and purpose of hope.
- Handout 2, An Act of Hope—The students pray St. Augustine's Act of Hope.
- Handout 3, The Gospels—The students identify how each Gospel begins and also identify some of the unique elements in the Gospel according to Matthew.
- Handout 4, The House of Christmas—The students read and analyze a poem.
- Handout 5, What Are the Gospels?—The students recall that the Gospels are proclamations of Good News, encounters with Jesus himself, and challenges to us to believe.

Chapter 3: The Coming of the Messiah—Lesson 1

Bell Ringers

- Distribute the corrected Chapter 2 Test. Go over the test with the students, using it as a means to review the previous chapter. Address any remaining questions or concerns the students may have.
- Invite the students to share the paragraphs they wrote about a person who has made a real difference in their life. Make sure the students indicate *how* the person has made a difference, *what* the difference is, and what the difference *means* to them.
- Afterward, ask the students to offer examples of the difference Jesus has made in the life of the world. List responses on the board. For example, as mentioned in the text, Jesus and his life are the objects of more books—as well as songs, works of art, and poetry—than any other person or event in history. Also, we actually mark time based on Jesus' coming: BC and AD. Note that although BC may stand for "before Christ," AD actually stands for the Latin *anno domini,* which means "in the year of the Lord" not "after death."
- Finally, have the students share one difference that knowing Jesus has made in *their* life. How would their lives be different if Jesus had never existed? Encourage them to be specific. Invite them to write about this topic in their journals.

Teaching Approaches

Jesus: Our Hope and Salvation (page 56)

- Introduce this lesson by distributing copies of Chapter 3, Handout 1, "Hope." Read through the opening quotation from Victor Hugo. Invite the students to conjecture what the great French writer meant by the words.
- Go on to read the opening paragraph on the handout. Then have the students read the psalm aloud together. Afterward, direct them to respond to the two follow-up questions on the handout. (*Look for the students to mention the three major covenants—Noah, Abraham, David—covered in the last lesson, as well as the Protoevangelium; and to evidence an understanding that the Hebrews' greatest hope was that God would send a Messiah.*)

Jesus: Our Hope and Salvation

A college president once remarked to his student body that the world contains three kinds of people: the few who make things happen; the many who watch things happen; and the vast majority of people who are clueless about what is happening. He went on to point out that the world desperately needs more people who "make things happen."

Jesus Christ is definitely someone who made things happen. Born over two thousand years ago in a land far removed from the center of power, he changed history forever. Through his Life, Passion, Death, and Resurrection, he has won eternal Salvation for humanity. Because of this, Jesus is the most important Person to walk the face of the earth. Do an Internet search of the name Jesus, and you will find upwards of 259 million references! Search Amazon.com for books written about him, and you will find more than 275,000 at recent count!

Even nonbelievers recognize his importance. For example, the British author H. G. Wells (1866–1946) wrote, "I am a historian. I am not a believer. But I must confess as a historian that this penniless preacher from Nazareth is irrevocably the very center of history. Jesus Christ is easily the most dominant figure in all history."

Put more succinctly, Jesus is our hope and our Salvation. He is our guide and our mentor. St. Thomas Aquinas said it well, "If, then, you are looking for the way by which you should go, take Christ, because he himself is the way."

For Reflection

Describe someone you know who "makes things happen" in the name of Jesus Christ.

Gospel Portraits of Christ's Origins

St. Paul wrote in his letter to the Galatians: "But when the fullness of time had come, God sent his Son, born of a woman, born under the law, to ransom those under the law, so that we might receive adoption" (Gal 4:4–5). The coming of Jesus Christ, the Son of God who is Lord, is the Gospel, the good news of our Salvation. After centuries of preparation in the Old Testament, God himself came to his people, thus fulfilling the promises he made to Abraham and his descendants.

Son of a Jewish mother, Jesus was born in Bethlehem sometime around 4–6 BC at the time of King Herod the Great and during the reign of the Roman emperor, Caesar Augustus. Jesus' family returned to Nazareth, a small town in the northern province of Galilee. There he learned the trade of carpentry from his foster father, Joseph. After his baptism as an adult, he embarked on a preaching and healing ministry. Eventually, he ran into resistance from the authorities. Thus, he was crucified under the Roman procurator Pontius Pilate during the reign of the emperor Tiberius, either in the year AD 30 or 33.

Death is not the final chapter in the life of Jesus. Rather, his Resurrection is the "crowning truth of our faith in Christ" (*CCC*, 638). It confirms all of his works and teachings and proves his divinity. Along with the Passion and Death of Jesus, his Resurrection constitutes the Paschal Mystery of our Salvation. Through his Death, Jesus Christ frees us from sin; by his Resurrection, he opens us to a new life.

After appearances to his disciples over forty days, Jesus ascended into Heaven where he is seated at the right hand of the Father. With God the Father, he sent the Holy Spirit to guide his followers. We, like the first disciples, confess that Jesus is "Lord," a title that indicates our belief in his divine sovereignty. The Holy Spirit enables us to proclaim our

Lesson 1 Objectives

The students will:

- review Chapter 2.
- reflect on stories of people who have made a difference in their lives.
- discuss how Jesus has made a difference in the life of the world and in their own lives.
- summarize and reflect on the meaning of hope.
- describe how hope urges them to achieve the "impossible" and make a difference.
- evaluate how they allow the Lord to be the source of their life.
- pray an Act of Hope.

Lesson 1 Preview

This lesson begins with the students' investigation into the life and ministry of Jesus. It is set in a context of hope and begins by helping the students recognize how Jesus was not only the fulfillment of the messianic hopes of the Hebrews but remains our hope and Salvation today.

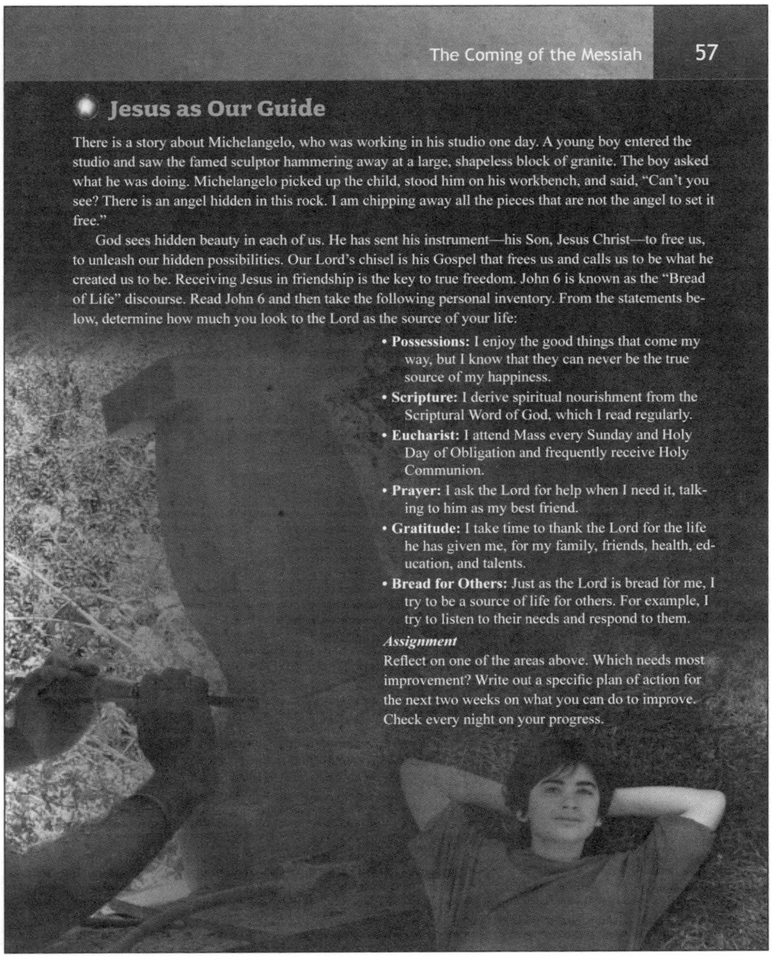
The Coming of the Messiah 57

Jesus as Our Guide

There is a story about Michelangelo, who was working in his studio one day. A young boy entered the studio and saw the famed sculptor hammering away at a large, shapeless block of granite. The boy asked what he was doing. Michelangelo picked up the child, stood him on his workbench, and said, "Can't you see? There is an angel hidden in this rock. I am chipping away all the pieces that are not the angel to set it free."

God sees hidden beauty in each of us. He has sent his instrument—his Son, Jesus Christ—to free us, to unleash our hidden possibilities. Our Lord's chisel is his Gospel that frees us and calls us to be what he created us to be. Receiving Jesus in friendship is the key to true freedom. John 6 is known as the "Bread of Life" discourse. Read John 6 and then take the following personal inventory. From the statements below, determine how much you look to the Lord as the source of your life:

- **Possessions:** I enjoy the good things that come my way, but I know that they can never be the true source of my happiness.
- **Scripture:** I derive spiritual nourishment from the Scriptural Word of God, which I read regularly.
- **Eucharist:** I attend Mass every Sunday and Holy Day of Obligation and frequently receive Holy Communion.
- **Prayer:** I ask the Lord for help when I need it, talking to him as my best friend.
- **Gratitude:** I take time to thank the Lord for the life he has given me, for my family, friends, health, education, and talents.
- **Bread for Others:** Just as the Lord is bread for me, I try to be a source of life for others. For example, I try to listen to their needs and respond to them.

Assignment

Reflect on one of the areas above. Which needs most improvement? Write out a specific plan of action for the next two weeks on what you can do to improve. Check every night on your progress.

Lesson 1 Homework

1. Have the students turn to the Ongoing Assignments on page 79. Point out that they are to choose any three of the listed assignments to complete prior to the conclusion of this chapter.
2. In preparation for their next lesson, tell the students to read "Gospel Portraits of Christ's Origins," "Four Gospel Portraits of Jesus," and "The Infancy Narratives in Matthew's Gospel (Mt 1–2)" (pages 56–61).

Background Information

" . . . Christ Jesus our hope" (1 Tm 1:1)

> . . . the mystery hidden from ages and from generations past . . . has been manifested to his holy ones, to whom God chose to make known the riches of the glory of this mystery among the Gentiles; it is Christ in you, the hope for glory.
>
> **Colossians 1:26-27**

- Play a recording either of the hymn "Only in God" by John Foley and the St. Louis Jesuits, or the song "Only Hope" by the rock group Switchfoot (also covered by Mandy Moore). If you are unable to obtain a recording of either piece of music, share the following lyrics from one or both:
  - From "Only in God"

    Only in God will my soul be at rest
    From him comes my hope of salvation.
    He alone is my rock of safety,
    My strength, my glory, my God.

  - From "Only Hope"

    Sing to me the song of the stars,
    Of your galaxy dancing and laughing and laughing again.
    When it feels like my dreams are so far,
    Sing to me of the plans that you have for me over again.
    So I lay my head back down.
    And I lift my hands and pray
    To be only yours, I pray, to be only yours
    I know now, you're my only hope.

  - Allow the students to share how the song(s) makes them feel. Then, discuss the notion and virtue of hope. Point out that hope is not wishful or magical thinking. Rather, it is the sure belief that God will act on our behalf. Call attention to the quotation from St. Augustine on the handout. Ask the students to discuss why St. Augustine would make such a suggestion.
- Point out the last paragraph in this text section on page 56, which begins "Put more succinctly . . ." Note that Jesus is our hope fulfilled. Even more, through his Passion, Death, and Resurrection, he has saved us, reshaped the future, and given us the promise of life forever with him and the Father—something worth hoping for indeed.
- Have the students look at the final section of Handout 1. Read aloud the heading: *"Hope sees the invisible, feels the intangible, and achieves the impossible. Hope is a passion for the impossible."* Direct the students to respond in writing to the two follow-up questions. Tell them they can use the back of the handout on which to respond. Afterward, have the students share in small groups their "impossible" hopes and their plans to fulfill them.
- After the sharing, go over the activity "Jesus as Our Guide" with the students. Allow time for them to read John 6, respond to the six statements, and then write out an improvement plan in their journals. Suggest

that students create a table with three sections with the following headings: (1) where I struggle the most, (2) my goal for improvement, and (3) how I plan to change. Provide an example of your own personal improvement plan to model the activity.

- Distribute copies of Chapter 3, Handout 2, "An Act of Hope." Encourage the students to pray this prayer each day as they implement their plan of action over the next weeks. Remind the students that, should they falter along the way, not to give up. Rather, have hope.
- Conclude the lesson by praying together the Act of Hope on the handout.

Chapter 3: The Coming of the Messiah—Lesson 2

Bell Ringers

- Use questions like the ones that follow to lead a discussion reviewing previous learning about the Gospels. If your students have never investigated the Gospels in previous courses, the questions can still serve as an introduction to the origins of Jesus as presented in the Gospels. You may also consider breaking students into groups to complete the questions.

infancy narratives
Stories in the Gospels of Matthew and Luke about the early life of Jesus.

Son of God
In the Old Testament, a title used for angels, kings, and others who had an intimate relationship with God. In the New Testament, through his actions and teachings, the title reveals the divinity of Jesus as the only Son of God.

Emmanuel
A name for Jesus that means "God is with us." Quoting Isaiah 7:14, Matthew uses Emmanuel to show that God's promise of deliverance is fulfilled in the birth of Jesus.

Son of David
A title for Jesus that indicates his ancestry can be traced to King David, as foretold in Scripture.

faith in the divinity of the Lord Jesus, to live Christ-like lives, and to spread the Gospel message of Salvation in Jesus Christ to the rest of the world.

Four Gospel Portraits of Jesus

The four Gospels are our primary source of knowledge about the birth, Life, Death, and Resurrection of Jesus Christ. They are the heart of the New Testament. Drawing on the testimony of eyewitnesses, they recount the saving deeds of our Lord. It is from them we learn that Jesus is the only Son of God, that he is the Lord God, our Savior, and the Messiah.

Each of the four Gospels begins the story of Jesus in a different way. The Gospel of Mark, the first Gospel written around the year AD 70, does not mention the birth of Jesus or any facts about his childhood or family life. Rather, Mark's Gospel begins by referring to a prophecy from Isaiah about a messenger coming to prepare the way of the Messiah. This messenger is John the Baptist, a distant relative of Jesus. John the Baptist preached that "One mightier than I is coming after me. I am not worthy to stoop and loosen the thongs of his sandals. I have baptized you with water; he will baptize you with the holy Spirit" (Mk 1:7–8). The opening of Mark's Gospel bridges the promises of the Old Testament with the commissioning of Jesus at his baptism in the Jordan River: "And a voice came from the heavens, 'You are my beloved Son, with you I am well pleased'" (Mk 1:11).

In contrast to how Mark's Gospel begins with an adult Jesus, the Gospel of John, written between AD 90 and 100, begins before the creation of the world:

> In the beginning was the Word,
> and the Word was with
> God,
> and the Word was God.
> (Jn 1:1)

This verse hearkens back to the opening verse of the book of Genesis and the account of creation. The prologue in John's Gospel teaches that the Word of *God* is God and that "all things came to be through him, and without him nothing came to be" (Jn 1:3). Jesus is clearly divine, the Son of God, who took on human flesh to accomplish our Salvation.

The Gospel of Matthew (written around AD 80–85) and the Gospel of Luke (written around AD 85), both begin their Gospels with **infancy narratives**. Yet there are differences between the two. For example, Matthew reports Mary and Joseph living in Bethlehem at the time of Jesus' birth. He tells the story of the magi, Herod's killing of the baby boys, and the Holy Family's flight to Egypt. Matthew's Gospel also describes how Joseph returned with his family to Nazareth out of fear of the brutality of Herod's son, Archelaus, who was ruling in Judea at the time.

In contrast, Luke reports how Mary and Joseph were already living in Nazareth when they came to

For Enrichment

Making a Difference

Read and discuss the following. Note that C. S. Lewis's book was a work of apologetics, meaning he was making logical arguments in defense of Christianity. In his famous book *Mere Christianity*, C. S. Lewis makes this statement:

> A man who was merely a man and said the sort of things Jesus said would not be a great moral teacher. He would either be a lunatic—on a level with the man who says he is a poached egg—or else he would be the Devil of Hell. You must make your choice. Either this man was, and is, the Son of God; or else a madman or something worse. You can shut him up for a fool, you can spit at him and kill him as a demon; or you can fall at his feet and call him Lord and God.

A Personal Difference

Many people would like to accept Jesus as only a great teacher or philosopher. One might say he was simply a good teacher of what all religions have in common at a very basic level. If we take Jesus Christ out of Christianity, however, there would be nothing left. Christianity is not just a philosophy of life, not an ethical standard, not a regiment of obedience to religious ritual. Christianity is based on a vital relationship with a *person*—Jesus Christ, the risen, living Savior and Lord.

Bethlehem to register for a Roman census. It was during this journey to Bethlehem that Jesus was born in a manger. After performing required religious duties in Jerusalem, the Holy Family peacefully returned to Nazareth.

The infancy narratives of Matthew and Luke have differences, but they also agree on several different points:

- Both Matthew and Luke use the infancy stories to highlight Jesus' identity.
- An angel foretold Jesus' birth in both accounts.
- Jesus is conceived by the action of the Holy Spirit. Thus, he is the **Son of God**. He is **Emmanuel**, "God is with us."
- He was born of the Virgin Mary, as was prophesied.
- Joseph, Jesus' foster father, was his legal father. Joseph was of the House of David; therefore, Jesus was truly a **Son of David**, as was promised.
- Jesus was born in Bethlehem, as prophesied in Micah 5:1.

The next sections provide an overview of the infancy narratives of Matthew and Luke and the prologue of John's Gospel.

The Infancy Narratives in Matthew's Gospel (Mt 1-2)

Matthew wrote his Gospel for a predominantly Jewish-Christian audience. One of his major concerns was to show how Jesus fulfilled God's promises to the Jews. His infancy stories accomplish this aim.

Genealogy (Mt 1:1-17)

The genealogy in Matthew links Jesus' ancestry to Abraham, the father of the Jews, and to King David, from whose dynasty the promised Messiah would come. This is meant to tell the reader how Jesus is the fulfillment of the Jewish hopes.

There are other lessons to be gleaned from the genealogy. For example, in his list of patriarchs (from Abraham to David), Matthew includes cheaters and liars (Jacob and Judah). This reminds us how Jesus himself associated with sinners in his adult life. Matthew also mentions several women in his genealogy with questionable backgrounds. He lists Tamar (Gn 38) who had children by her father-in-law, Judah; Rahab, a prostitute in Jericho who helped Jewish spies (Jo 2); Ruth, a Moabite woman who made the God of her mother-in-law her own; and Bathsheba (2 Sm 11), Solomon's mother with whom David had earlier committed adultery.

By including sinners in the genealogy, Matthew is making the point of the marvelous way that God accomplishes his plan of Salvation. Later in the Gospel, John the Baptist would identify Jesus as God's Chosen One who would separate sinners from the just, as a farmer separates wheat and chaff

Lesson 2 Objectives

The students will:

- review previous learning about "gospel" and the Gospels.
- recall the dates of Jesus' birth and death.
- make connections between Matthew's infancy narratives and the Old Testament.

Lesson 2 Preview

In this lesson, the students review past learning about the Gospels. They will study the differences among the openings of each Gospel. They will also make connections between the Gospels and the Old Testament.

- What does the word "gospel" mean? (*good news—from the Greek word* evangelion) (*Note*: Take a moment to remind the students that *Gospel* refers to [1] Jesus himself, [2] the message of Salvation Jesus proclaimed, and [3] the written records of the Good News God accomplished in Jesus as recorded by different authors, each with his own focus.)
- How many written Gospels are in the New Testament? (*four*)
- What are the names of the four Gospels? (*Mark, Matthew, Luke, and John*)
- Are the Gospels biographies of Jesus? (*No. They are* testaments of faith *about the early Christians' experiences of Jesus—Son of God, Christ-Savior, Lord, and Suffering Servant. They do more than tell us about some long-gone historical figure. They put us in touch with Christ, present in our lives—right here, right now—and invite us to place our faith in him.*)
- Which Gospels are called "synoptic"? (*Mark, Matthew, and Luke*) Why? (*They have many parallels.*)
- What does "synoptic" mean? (*seeing/looking together*)
- Which Gospel was written first? (*Mark*)
- Which Gospel was written last? (*John*)
- Which Gospel is the most theologically developed? (*John*)
- Which Gospel goes the furthest in portraying Jesus as friend of the poor, the powerless, and the sinful? (*Luke*)
- Which Gospel is the most polished? (*Luke*)
- Which Gospel is the shortest? (*Mark*)

- Before moving on, remind the students that the Jesus portrayed in the Gospels is the only Jesus we have, and that Jesus is the Jesus of faith. This means if we don't have faith in Jesus, then the Gospels will mean little or nothing to us. The Good News found in them is "good" and meaningful only for the faithful.

Teaching Approaches

Gospel Portraits of Christ's Origins (pages 56-61)

- Write the following Latin phrase on the board: ***Veni, vidi, vici***. See whether any of the students recognize it

and/or know what it means. Explain that this famous phrase is the speech—in its entirety—delivered to the Roman Senate by Julius Caesar in 47 BC, describing the military outcome of his encounter with the forces of Pharnaces II of Pontus. It translates as "I came, I saw, I conquered." Short, sweet, and succinct, its grammatical form is termed a *tricolon.*

- Distribute strips of construction paper and markers. Have the students reread the three final paragraphs of the text section "Gospel Portraits of Christ's Origins" on pages 56 and 58 to come up with a three-word summary (short, sweet, succinct) that describes the life of Jesus. Have them print their tricolon on the strip. Post them in the classroom for all to view.
- Point out that while we can sum up Jesus' life among us, the Gospels are not simple summaries. However, like a tricolon, the Gospels perform a three-part function (*list on the board*):
    - **They announce the good news of Jesus.**
    - **They provide an encounter with Jesus.**
    - **They challenge us to believe in Jesus.**
- Go on to tell the students that each Gospel has its origin in a specific place, is directed at a specific first-century audience, portrays a specific dimension of Jesus, and begins in its own unique way.

Epiphany
The feast that celebrates the mystery of Christ's manifestation as Savior of the world.

with a winnowing fan (see Matthew 3:12). From his very origins, Jesus is the Suffering Servant "who silently allows himself to be led to the slaughter and who bears the sin of the multitudes, and also the Paschal Lamb, the symbol of Israel's redemption at the first Passover" (*CCC*, 608).

Birth of Jesus (Mt 1:18-25*)*

Jesus' birth is the result of divine action, the power of the Holy Spirit. He is both divine and human. Moreover, Isaiah prophesied his divine birth:

> "Behold, the virgin shall be with child and bear a son, and they shall call him Emmanuel," which means "God is with us." (Mt 1:23)

This is the first of five Old Testament prophecies that Matthew quotes in his infancy narratives. As mentioned, Matthew 2:6 cites the prophet Micah's prediction saying that the Messiah is to be born in Bethlehem. Also, Matthew 2:15 refers to Hosea's prophecy about being called out of Egypt; Matthew 2:18 recalls Jeremiah 31:15 and Rachel's weeping over her exiled descendants, a reference to Herod's slaughter of the infants; and Matthew 2:23 connects the town of Nazareth to prophetic statements in the Old Testament.

Joseph plays a key role in Matthew's genealogy. A descendant of David, he accepts the angel's message that Mary conceived by God's power. Joseph, a righteous man, takes Jesus as his own son, making him legally a Son of David. Finally, Joseph gives his child the name Jesus. This is a most appropriate name because in Hebrew *Jesus* means "God saves." In the Person of the Son of God, God redeems us from sin.

Matthew's Jewish-Christian audience would have been familiar with the Old Testament patriarch Joseph, the son of Jacob. He was a famous interpreter of dreams who saved his family from famine in Egypt. Jesus' foster father, another Joseph, serves as an important link in the story of Salvation History. St. Joseph receives God's revelation about Jesus' origins in a dream and saves his family by taking them to Egypt.

Visit of the Magi (Mt 2:1-12)

The magi were visitors from the East, perhaps astrologers, who are meant to represent the Lord's willingness to accept Gentiles among those who worship him. They brought royal gifts of gold, frankincense, and myrrh. This scene at the beginning of Matthew's Gospel also foreshadows the end of the Gospel when the Risen Lord commands the Apostles to preach the Gospel to all nations, including the Gentiles (Mt 28:19). The visit of the magi "means that pagans can discover Jesus and worship him as the Son of God and Savior of the world only by turning toward the Jews and receiving from them the messianic promise as contained in the Old Testament" (*CCC*, 528). The Feast of the **Epiphany** celebrates the time when Jesus is manifested as the Messiah, the Son of God, and Savior of the world.

Chapter 3, Handout 3, "The Gospels" Answers

The Gospels: The students should be able to arrive at conclusions similar to the following:

- Mark—A Prophecy Fulfilled
- John—Creation Redux
- Matthew—An Infancy Narrative
- Luke—An Infancy Narrative

Unique Elements in Matthew:

- Jesus' genealogy in Matthew moves from past to present.
- Matthew presents Jesus as a descendant of Abraham and David.
- Matthew traces Jesus' genealogy through his human parent Joseph.
- An angel appears to Joseph (twice!).
- Joseph gives Jesus his name; it means "God saves."
- According to Matthew, what's lighting up the night sky? The Star of Bethlehem.
- In Matthew, the first to visit the child Jesus are the magi.
- To escape the murderous wrath of Herod, an angel warns Joseph to take Mary and Jesus off into Egypt.
- Matthew compares Jesus to Moses.

Flight into Egypt and Massacre of the Infants (Mt 2:13-18)

Matthew presents Jesus as the new Moses, the new Lawgiver. God used Moses to lead his people to freedom and to give the Law to the people on Mt. Sinai. God's Son, Jesus Christ, is the true liberator, the Savior who gives the New Law to his disciples in the Sermon on the Mount (Mt 5–7). Jesus' narrow escape from death as an infant at the hands of cruel leaders symbolizes Jesus' own future.

The incident in which Jesus escapes from the powers of evil brings to mind Moses' own narrow brush with death as an infant when a cruel pharaoh wanted to kill him (Ex 1–2). Herod's slaughter and the Holy Family's flight into Egypt reveal that from the beginning of Jesus' life, the forces of darkness were opposed to him—the "light of the world."

Jesus' "whole life was lived under the sign of persecution" (*CCC*, 530). No independent historical record reports King Herod's ordering such an atrocity at the time of Jesus' birth. However, it was very much in character for him to have done such a deed. Intensely jealous of his own power and authority, Herod did in fact kill some of his own children for fear that they would usurp his throne.

Investigating Jesus' Ancestry

1. Read Luke's version of Jesus' genealogy in Luke 3:23-38. Note at least two differences between it and Matthew's account (Mt 1:1-17).
2. Read and report on the story of one of these women mentioned in Matthew's version of Jesus' genealogy:

- Tamar–Genesis 38
- Rahab–Joshua 2
- Bathsheba–2 Samuel 11

Return to Nazareth (Mt 2:19-23)

At the Exodus, God delivered the Chosen People from Egypt. "Jesus' departure from Egypt recalls the exodus and presents him as the definitive liberator of God's people" (*CCC*, 530). As commanded by the angel, Joseph settles his family in the small town of Nazareth in Galilee, a northern province in the Holy Land that pious Jews considered to be contaminated by Gentile influence. It is from this territory that Matthew records Jesus embarking on his mission of proclaiming God's Kingdom.

The Infancy Narratives in Luke's Gospel (Lk 1-2)

Luke was a skilled writer and careful historian. Luke also wrote the Acts of the Apostles as a "part two" of his Gospel. He dedicated both of them to Theophilus, a name meaning "beloved of God." This person might have been a prominent Christian convert or Luke's patron. Some suggest the name might even be a symbol for any Christian who will read or hear Luke's Gospel.

Luke 1:1–14, the prologue to the Gospel, reveals that others had previously written about Jesus and that Luke is checking with eyewitnesses to write his own orderly account. Like Matthew's Gospel, one of Luke's likely sources was the Gospel of Mark. Luke and Matthew also drew on a common source of sayings called "Q" (from the German word *Quelle*, meaning "source"). This material represents both written and oral traditions. In addition, Luke had a source unique to him (often designated "L"), while Matthew had a source unique to him (often designated "M").

Luke and Matthew, writing in the same decade, probably did not know of each other's effort. This helps explain why they have different stories about the events surrounding Jesus' birth.

- Distribute copies of Chapter 3, Handout 3, "The Gospels." Note the place of origin, audience, and dimension of Jesus portrayed by each Gospel. Then, based on their reading, have the students complete the fifth column by writing in how the Gospel begins (answers are on page 76 of this text).

Ask:

- To which prophet and prophecy does Mark's opening refer? (*Isaiah 40:3—"A voice cries out: In the desert prepare the way of the Lord! Make straight in the wasteland a highway for our God!"*)
- To which Bible passage does John 1:1 point? (*Genesis 1:1*)

- Go on to refer the students to pages 58–59 in their text and note some of the differences between Matthew's and Luke's infancy narratives listed there.
- Direct the students to read (or reread) chapters 1 and 2 of Matthew's Gospel. Afterward, have the students draw on their Scripture reading as well as the material in the text (pages 59–61) to respond to the questions on Handout 3 under the heading "Unique Elements in Matthew" (answers are on page 76 of this text).
- Expand on Matthew's presenting Jesus as the new Moses. Point out on the handout that Matthew portrayed Jesus as a *teaching* Messiah and that he was writing for Jewish-Christians. Matthew's audience, therefore, had deep Jewish roots which made them concerned both with Jesus' links to Abraham and David and with the ways in which Jesus' origins,

Lesson 2 Homework

1. Tell the students to write out their answers to numbers one to twelve of the For Review questions on page 67.
2. Assign the first activity in the feature "Investigating Jesus' Ancestry" (page 61).
3. Ask the students to prepare, as well as they are able, their own genealogy. Have them try to go back at least three generations on either their paternal or maternal side or on both. Suggest that they enter into discussions with their parents and grandparents about their genealogy. Invite them to explore online tools at www.ancestry.com and www.geni.com to create their family trees.
4. In preparation for their next lesson, tell the students to read "The Infancy Narratives in Luke's Gospel (Lk 1–2)" as well as "The Incarnation in the Prologue to John's Gospel (Jn 1:1–18)" on pages 61–67.

For Enrichment

Display a copy of Donald Jackson's illumination, "The Genealogy of Christ," from *The Saint John's Bible*. You can find an online version at www.loc.gov/exhibits/stjohnsbible/stjohns-exhibit.html.

life, and teachings meshed with those of the great Law-giver and teacher Moses. Matthew linked Jesus to all three major Old Testament covenant figures (Abraham, Moses, and David). Ask the students to skim through the section "The Infancy Narrative in Matthew's Gospel (Mt 1–2)" and list the connections between the Gospels and the Old Testament. List these connections on the board when they are finished.

- Call attention to the quotation from the *Catechism of the Catholic Church* (*CCC,* 530) in the first sentence of the final paragraph of the text section "Flight into Egypt and Massacre of the Innocents" on page 61: ("Jesus' 'whole life was lived under the sign of persecution.'") Note how from his birth, Jesus was living under a death sentence. Forced to flee, he became a refugee. No wonder he would forever remain on the side of the outcast, the homeless, and the persecuted. He began life as one of them.
- Have the students turn to the feature "Investigating Jesus' Ancestry" on page 61. Call attention to the second activity. Divide the students into three small groups and assign each group to one of the women listed. Tell the students that they may create a skit, or offer a panel interview, or even create a song about their assigned figure. Allow ample time for the students to read the Scripture, to devise, and then to prepare their presentations.

Announcement of John the Baptist's Birth (Lk 1:5-25)

Luke masterfully interweaves the announcement and births of Jesus and his cousin John the Baptist. Yet, in his narrative, Luke clearly shows that Jesus is the Messiah, not John. It is Jesus whose origins are divine.

John the Baptist's parents were Zechariah and Elizabeth, an older, childless couple. When Zechariah was in Jerusalem for his annual two-week duty as a priest, the angel Gabriel told him that his wife would conceive a child and that he was to name the child John. Zechariah was struck speechless for expressing doubt at the angel's revelation and asking for proof. He would later regain his speech when asked what his child should be named (Lk 1:64).

John the Baptist was a bridge person between the Old Testament and the New Testament. He was a New Elijah, announcing the coming of the promised Messiah. He was the immediate precursor and forerunner of Christ, the one to "prepare the way." John first recognized the coming of the Messiah when he leaped in his mother's womb when in the presence of the Blessed Mother who was pregnant with the Savior (Lk 1:44).

Announcement of the Birth of Jesus (Lk 1:26-38)

Six months after announcing the birth of John the Baptist, the angel Gabriel appeared to Mary, a virgin who was engaged to Joseph of the house of David. The angel greeted Mary with the words "Hail, favored one! The Lord is with you" (Lk 1:28). When informed that she was to conceive a child, a child who would be great, the Son of the Most High, Mary told the angel that she had not had sexual relations. The angel then told Mary she would conceive Jesus by the power of the Holy Spirit. With great humility and faith, Mary believed the angel and said, "Behold, I am the handmaid of the Lord. May it be done to me according to your word" (Lk 1:38). This event is known as the **Annunciation**.

Mary's yes to the angel's announcement thus began the time of the fulfillment of God's promises and preparations. She, a humble daughter of Israel, was the instrument God used to bring Christ into the world. The mission of many Old Testament holy women prepared the way for Mary. For example, Eve, despite her disobedience, was promised that a descendant would conquer Satan. Sarah conceived her child Isaac in old age. And God chose other powerless women to advance his salvific work: Hannah, Deborah, Ruth, Judith, Esther, and many others.

Mary, the Blessed Mother, is above them all. She cooperated with God's plan, even knowing that her yes might bring her ridicule and condemnation. God singled out Mary among women and gave her the graces necessary to cooperate with his plan. For example, Mary was conceived without Original Sin by virtue of the merits of her son, Jesus Christ, the Savior of the human race. This is known as the **Immaculate Conception**. This freedom from the effects of Original Sin and any personal sin, a total gift from God to his chosen one, enabled Mary to

Chapter 3: The Coming of the Messiah—Lesson 3

Lesson 3 Objectives

The students will:

- illustrate the infancy narratives in the Gospel of Luke.
- identify similarities and differences in the infancy narratives.
- summarize what the Prologue of John's Gospel teaches about the Incarnation.
- describe the purpose of the Incarnation.

Lesson 3 Preview

In preparation for this lesson, carefully read over the beginnings of all four Gospels, paying particular attention to the infancy narratives in Matthew and Luke and the Prologue to John's Gospel. Your preparation can help the students appreciate the power and meaning of Jesus' coming among us. Likewise, make sure the students read these accounts for themselves at some point during the lesson. Consider allowing two class periods to cover the material in this lesson.

Bell Ringers

- Begin this session by having the students share their personal genealogy. Point out how the genealogies not only reveal who our ancestors are, but also our roots in cultures, countries, professions, and religions.
- Ask the students to offer their responses to the first twelve For Review questions on page 67 (answers are on page 82 of this text). Be sure to allow the students to ask any other questions they may have.

Teaching Approaches

The Infancy Narratives in Luke's Gospel (Lk 1-2) (pages 61-65)

- Introduce the Gospel of Luke by asking the students to recall where and for whom Luke wrote, as well as how he portrayed Jesus. (*Luke wrote from Greece;*

give the free assent of her faith to the announcement of her becoming truly the Mother of God.

Mary Visits Elizabeth (Lk 1:39-56)

Mary's compassionate concern for her aged relative prompted her to visit Elizabeth in a town in the province of Judah. After being greeted by Mary, Elizabeth immediately recognized the miracle of God's love that had taken place. With a heart bursting with joy, Elizabeth acknowledged that Mary is indeed the Mother of God:

> "Most blessed are you among women, and blessed is the fruit of your womb. And how does this happen to me, that the mother of my Lord should come to me?" (Lk 1:42–43)

Mary's response to Elizabeth is the famous canticle, the **Magnificat**. Her words echo those of Hannah, the mother of the prophet Samuel, who recited them after his birth due to God's intervention. In humility, Mary praises God as the source of blessedness. She praises his mercy for reversing normal human expectations, for raising up the lowly and overthrowing prideful and powerful people:

> The hungry he has filled with good things;
> the rich he has sent away empty. (Lk 1:53)

Birth of John the Baptist (Lk 1:57-80)

When Zechariah is given his speech back at the time of his son's birth, the Holy Spirit inspired him to sing God's praises in a prayer known as the *Benedictus*. In it, Zechariah praises God for remembering the promises he made to David for the Salvation of the Jews. In the last part of the prayer, Zechariah speaks to his newborn son:

> And you, child, will be called prophet of the Most High,
> for you will go before the Lord to prepare his ways,
> to give his people knowledge of salvation
> through the forgiveness of sins. (Lk 1:76–77)

Birth of Jesus (Lk 2:1-20)

Bethlehem, the birthplace of David and Jesus, is about six miles south of Jerusalem. Because it was his ancestral home, Joseph took the expectant Mary there to enroll in a census. Jesus was born in a manger because of the lack of suitable lodgings; he was also wrapped in swaddling clothes. While Jesus' clothing emphasizes his humility and poverty, it might also suggest his royalty since Solomon, David's son, was wrapped in swaddling clothes (Wis 7:4–5).

The expression "first-born son" is a legal designation for a child who had special rights under the Law of Moses. It does not mean that Mary had other children.

The first people to visit Jesus are poor shepherds who were considered not respectable by the standards of pious Jews. The angels announce to them the coming of the Savior who is both Messiah and Lord. He will bring "peace to those on whom his favor rests" (Lk 2:14).

Annunciation
The announcement of the birth of Jesus that takes place when the angel Gabriel tells Mary that God has chosen her to be the Mother of the Lord.

Immaculate Conception
The belief that Mary was conceived without Original Sin. The Feast of the Immaculate Conception is on December 8.

Magnificat
The Latin title for the Canticle of Mary in Luke 1:46–55 that begins *Magnificat anima me Dominum* ("My soul proclaims the greatness of the Lord").

Background Information

The Immaculate Conception is an often misunderstood teaching of the Catholic Church. Most people assume that it refers to Jesus' birth despite that fact that Jesus was never actually conceived in sexual intercourse like normal humans. Mary's birth was a normal human birth in every way except that she was born "full of grace," without the stain of Original Sin. Although this did not become officially proclaimed as Catholic dogma until 1854, Mary's special place in the economy of Salvation has been proclaimed by the Church for many years. As the "New Eve" it was important that she undo Eve's mistake and join her Son, the "New Adam," in restoring Original Holiness and Original Justice.

his audience was poor and disenfranchised Gentile-Christians; and he presented Jesus as a merciful, saving Messiah.) Point out that since Luke's audience was non-Jewish as well, they would not be as concerned as was Matthew's audience with the fulfillment of Jewish prophecy.

- Go on to tell the students that although Luke was not concerned with linking Jesus to Old Testament prophets, he does begin his Gospel by describing a prophet who would serve as a link between the Old and New Testaments: John the Baptist.
- Direct the students' attention to "Announcement of John the Baptist's Birth" on page 62. Ask students to make connections between the story of Zechariah and Elizabeth and the Old Testament story of Abraham and Sarah (Gn 18–21).
- Have the students turn to the text section "Announcement of the Birth of Jesus (Lk 1:26–38)." Ask the students to recall to whom the angel appeared in the Gospel of Matthew. (*Joseph*) Note that Luke reveals that it was Mary who was visited by the angel Gabriel during what we call the Annunciation. Emphasize that the virgin birth assures both the divinity and humanity of Jesus. God graced Mary so that she could be totally responsive and faithful to the divine will. God sought Mary's consent, and her "yes" joins the created to the Creator in the works of completing and fulfilling God's creation and God's promise in the Protoevangelium (Gn 3:15). Her response to the angel Gabriel is in direct opposition to Eve's response to the fallen angel Satan. For this reason Mary has been historically called the "New Eve" just as Jesus is referred to as the "New Adam." Likewise, her "yes" is the response to God for all who have preceded her and for all who will follow her. Mary's response embodies the fullness of Israel's trust and reliance on God. Even more, through Mary, the *particular* Salvation story of the Hebrew nation becomes a *universal* story in which *all people* (i.e., Gentiles) share.
- Note Gabriel's greeting to Mary. It is the basis for the first part of the Hail Mary.
- Have the students sing (or play a recording of) Mary's "Magnificat" (e.g., "My Soul Proclaims" by Marty Haugen; "Magnificat" by David Haas; "Magnificat" by Michael Joncas). Tell the students that Mary's prayer not only echoes sentiments in the Old Testament (for example, 1 Sm 2:1, 8), it foreshadows the Kingdom her son will establish, a Kingdom where the mighty will be lowered, the poor lifted, the hungry filled with good things (Lk 1:53).

- Note Elizabeth's response to Mary's greeting. It is the basis for the second part of the Hail Mary.
- Write the Latin word **benedictus** on the board, explaining that it means "blessed" and is the first word of the Canticle of Zechariah. Tell the students that if they have ever joined in their parish's celebration of Morning Prayer (Lauds), they will have prayed this powerful canticle of thanks.
- Have the students read the prayer in Luke 1:68–79 or listen to a recording (e.g., "Hallelujah, Hallelu" by Michael Mahler; "Gospel Canticle" by James Quinn, S.J.; "Blest Be the God of Israel," by Marty Haugen). Afterward, point out the prayer's two sections:
    - Verses 68–75 give thanks that the Messiah—the fulfillment of the covenants and the prophets—has come.
    - In verses 76–79, Zachariah addresses his newborn son, foretelling that John is to be a great prophet like Isaiah (Is 40:3), preparing the way of the Lord, the Most High.
- Go on to discuss the birth of Jesus as recorded in Luke. Ask students to list in their notes some of the elements in the story that are unique to Luke; that is, elements not found in Matthew. After the students complete the assignment, list their responses on the board. Look for examples like the following:
    - journey from Nazareth to Bethlehem because of a Roman census
    - birth in a manger and mention of swaddling clothes
    - appearance of choirs of angels
    - first sighting of the newborn by shepherds
- Point out that since shepherds had to be with their flocks, they could not follow religious prescriptions regarding keeping Sabbath, Temple worship, and ritual purity. To some extent shepherds were considered outcasts. It is significant that Luke singles them out to be the first to hear the good news of the birth of the Messiah and Lord. From birth, Jesus was aligned with the marginalized and the poor.
- Afterward, point out that our traditional celebration of the Christmas story mixes the two narratives—for example, showing magi (only in Matthew) and shepherds (only in Luke) together at the manger.
- Go on to invite the students to share the differences they found (in their homework assignment) between Luke's genealogy (Lk 3:23–38) and Matthew's. List

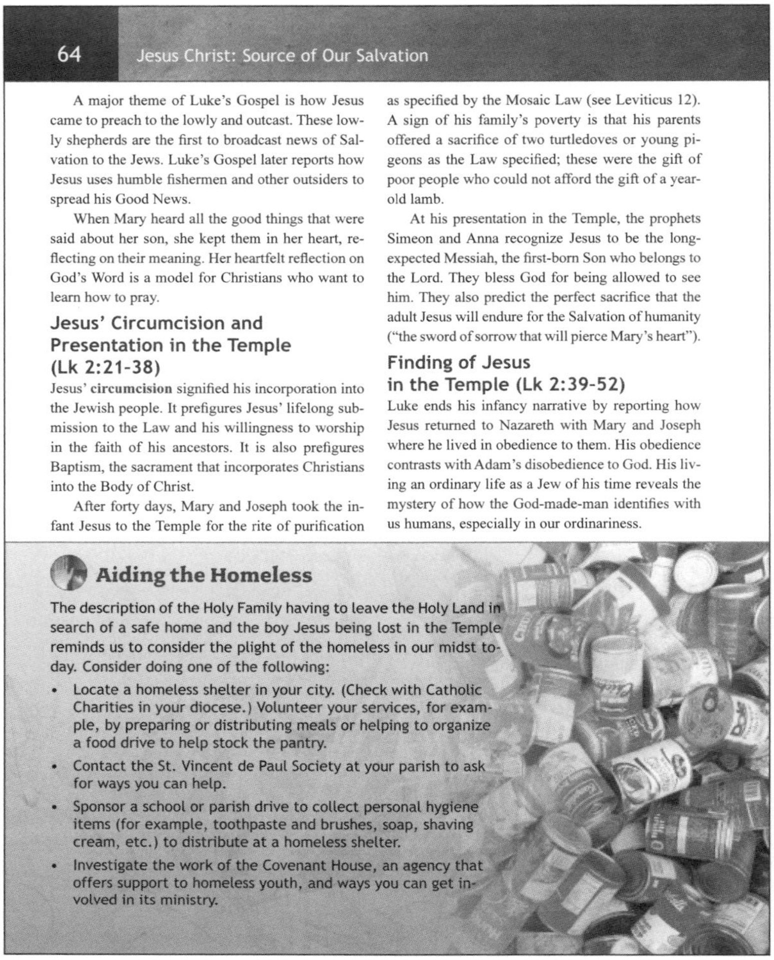
64 Jesus Christ: Source of Our Salvation

A major theme of Luke's Gospel is how Jesus came to preach to the lowly and outcast. These lowly shepherds are the first to broadcast news of Salvation to the Jews. Luke's Gospel later reports how Jesus uses humble fishermen and other outsiders to spread his Good News.

When Mary heard all the good things that were said about her son, she kept them in her heart, reflecting on their meaning. Her heartfelt reflection on God's Word is a model for Christians who want to learn how to pray.

Jesus' Circumcision and Presentation in the Temple (Lk 2:21-38)

Jesus' **circumcision** signified his incorporation into the Jewish people. It prefigures Jesus' lifelong submission to the Law and his willingness to worship in the faith of his ancestors. It is also prefigures Baptism, the sacrament that incorporates Christians into the Body of Christ.

After forty days, Mary and Joseph took the infant Jesus to the Temple for the rite of purification as specified by the Mosaic Law (see Leviticus 12). A sign of his family's poverty is that his parents offered a sacrifice of two turtledoves or young pigeons as the Law specified; these were the gift of poor people who could not afford the gift of a year-old lamb.

At his presentation in the Temple, the prophets Simeon and Anna recognize Jesus to be the long-expected Messiah, the first-born Son who belongs to the Lord. They bless God for being allowed to see him. They also predict the perfect sacrifice that the adult Jesus will endure for the Salvation of humanity ("the sword of sorrow that will pierce Mary's heart").

Finding of Jesus in the Temple (Lk 2:39-52)

Luke ends his infancy narrative by reporting how Jesus returned to Nazareth with Mary and Joseph where he lived in obedience to them. His obedience contrasts with Adam's disobedience to God. His living an ordinary life as a Jew of his time reveals the mystery of how the God-made-man identifies with us humans, especially in our ordinariness.

Aiding the Homeless

The description of the Holy Family having to leave the Holy Land in search of a safe home and the boy Jesus being lost in the Temple reminds us to consider the plight of the homeless in our midst today. Consider doing one of the following:

- Locate a homeless shelter in your city. (Check with Catholic Charities in your diocese.) Volunteer your services, for example, by preparing or distributing meals or helping to organize a food drive to help stock the pantry.
- Contact the St. Vincent de Paul Society at your parish to ask for ways you can help.
- Sponsor a school or parish drive to collect personal hygiene items (for example, toothpaste and brushes, soap, shaving cream, etc.) to distribute at a homeless shelter.
- Investigate the work of the Covenant House, an agency that offers support to homeless youth, and ways you can get involved in its ministry.

For Enrichment

A New "Look" at the Infancy Narratives

The book *The Nativity*, illustrated by Julie Vivas, provides dynamic, offbeat, deglamorized, and absolutely delightful watercolor illustrations that add new life to the familiar Christmas story. (*Note*: The book combines Luke and Matthew.) This is a great book for children, and an even better one for grown-ups. Written in 1986, it should still be available from Harcourt Brace & Co.

The Joyful Mysteries of the Rosary

Each day of the week has a particular set of mysteries attached to praying the rosary: on Mondays and Saturdays, the Joyful Mysteries; on Tuesdays and Fridays, the Sorrowful Mysteries; on Wednesdays and Sundays, the Glorious Mysteries; and on Thursdays, the Luminous Mysteries. In review and reflection on the infancy narratives, meditate on the Joyful Mysteries of the Rosary: the Annunciation, the Visitation, the Birth of Jesus, the Presentation of Jesus in the Temple, and the Finding of Jesus in the Temple.

When Jesus was twelve years old, he went to the Temple in Jerusalem with his parents for the Passover feast. When he was found missing on the caravan home, his distraught parents eventually found Jesus astounding the teachers in the Temple by his brilliant response to their questions. This prefigured the future day when he would again confound the learned scribes and rabbis, some of whom would plot his death.

When questioned by Mary as to why he remained in the city, Jesus replied, "Did you not know that I must be in my Father's house?" (Lk 2:49). Mary and Joseph did not fully understand the meaning of Jesus' words, but again Mary kept his words in her heart, prayerfully reflecting on their significance.

Luke's focus on both Temple and Jerusalem is another way his Gospel bridges the Old Testament with the New Testament. It is in the Temple that Simeon proclaims that Jesus would be the Savior for Jews and Gentiles alike. As a twelve-year-old, Jesus instructs the learned men in the Temple, and then, as an adult, he teaches in the Temple (Lk 19:47). And after Jesus' Resurrection, the disciples continue to worship there (Lk 24:53; Acts 3:1). Throughout his Gospel, Luke highlights Jesus' journey to Jerusalem, the holy city that "kills its prophets." It is in Jerusalem where Jesus' Passion, Death, and Resurrection accomplish our Salvation. And in this same city on Pentecost Sunday, the Holy Spirit descends on the Apostles and sends them to the ends of the world to proclaim Jesus as Lord and Savior.

The Incarnation in the Prologue to John's Gospel (Jn 1:1-18)

Matthew and Luke begin their Gospels with the birth of Christ. John, on the other hand, starts his Gospel from before the beginning of the world. He brilliantly retells the Genesis story about creation by clearly showing how creation came about through the Word of God:

> All things came to be through him,
> and without him nothing came to be. (Jn 1:3)

The Word of God *is* God (Jn 1:1) and

> What came to be through him was life,
> and this life was the light of the human race.
> (Jn 1:3–4)

John's Gospel then offers the earth-shaking truth: this very Word of God became man in the Person of Jesus Christ. This is known as the **Incarnation**. John chose this word to emphasize that at the appointed time, the only Son of the Father, the eternal Word, assumed our human nature—both body (flesh) and soul—and became man in order to accomplish our Salvation in that same human nature.

The Incarnation is a **dogma** of our faith. Its source is in Divine Revelation; we know it to be true because God revealed it to us:

circumcision
A sign of incorporation into Judaism. Jesus is circumcised on the eighth day after his birth as a sign of his submission to the Law.

Incarnation
The dogma that God's eternal Son assumed a human nature and became man in Jesus Christ to save us from our sins. The term literally means "taking on human flesh."

dogma
A central truth of Revelation that Catholics are obliged to believe.

Lesson 3 Homework

1. Tell the students to write out their answers to numbers thirteen to twenty-one of the For Review questions on pages 67–68.
2. Have them journal their response to the first For Reflection activity on page 68. For the second and third activity, tell the students to write about them separately and to be ready to hand them in at their next session.
3. Direct the students to read the text section "Learning from the Life of Christ" (pages 68–74) in preparation for their next session.
4. Remind the students to continue working on their chosen Ongoing Assignments.

Extending the Lesson

Show the students a video representation of the infancy narratives such as *Jesus of Nazareth* (1977) or *Ben Hur* (1959). Instruct the students to keep track of which Gospel each scene was taken from: Matthew, Luke, or both. After you show the clips of the movies, discuss why so many people assume that the Gospels all agree about the events of Jesus birth.

on the board. See to it that the students mention that in contrast to Matthew, Luke:

- presents Jesus lineage moving from present to past;
- stresses that Jesus is a descendant of Adam and of God;
- traces the genealogy through Mary;
- has Mary play a central role.

- Direct the students to turn to the feature Explaining the Faith on page 66. Note the two reasons offered for celebrating Jesus' birth on December 25: (1) to counter a pagan feast, and (2) to mark a nine-month passage from the traditional date of the Annunciation. Tell the students that some scholars would place the birth during the spring, since Luke says that shepherds were "living in the fields and keeping the night watch over their flock" (Lk 2:8). Normally, shepherds would not remain out all night with their sheep except during lambing season, which takes place in the spring; hence, the theory that Jesus—the Lamb of God—was born in springtime.
- Move on to the text section "Jesus' Circumcision and Presentation in the Temple (Lk 2:21–38)." Ask,
    - What is the significance of Jesus' circumcision? (*It signaled that he was part of the Chosen People and shared in the promises of the Abramic covenant.*)
    - What did Jesus' presentation in the Temple signify? (*That he was consecrated to God.*)
- Explain that the presentation ceremony recalled how God spared the firstborn of Israel on the night of the first Passover. The purification was for the mother (see Lv 12). It removed the burden of being "unclean" (due to the flow of blood at birth) and welcomed her back into the Temple assembly.
- Have the students read Luke 2:25–35. Discuss: "How does Simeon's prophecy speak to the meaning of the name of Jesus?" (*Remember, "Jesus" means "God saves"; Jesus will suffer and die to* save *his people.*) Which people does Simeon propose will experience Salvation? *(the Gentiles)* What does this say about Luke's audience? *(They were Gentiles.)*
- Have the students look again at Luke 2:29–32. Explain that these four verses make up the third canticle in Luke's infancy narrative—"The Canticle of Simeon," also know by its Latin title "Nunc Dimittis." Just as the "Benedictus" and the "Magnificat" are the Church's Gospel canticles of Morning Prayer and

Evening Prayer respectively, "Nunc Dimittis" is its Gospel canticle of Night Prayer.

- Ask a student to give an account in his or her own words of the finding of Jesus in the Temple. Ask the students what they feel is important about this story's inclusion in the Gospel. For example, Jesus was beginning to understand his mission.
- In order to review the events of Luke's infancy narratives, instruct students to illustrate the key events of Luke 1–2 in their notes by creating a comic strip. You may also ask them to create a similar comic strip for the infancy narrative of Matthew to compare the two versions.
- Distribute copies of Chapter 3, Handout 4, "The House of Christmas." Have the students read the poem by G. K. Chesterton silently on their own. Then have different students read it aloud, stanza by stanza. Invite the students to share their reactions to the poem.
    - What do they think it says?
    - How does it make them feel?
    - What does it challenge them to do?
    - Which Gospel's infancy narrative does this connect to and why?
- Finally, go over the suggestions for reaching out to the homeless in the feature "Aiding the Homeless" on page 64. Challenge the students to choose a specific

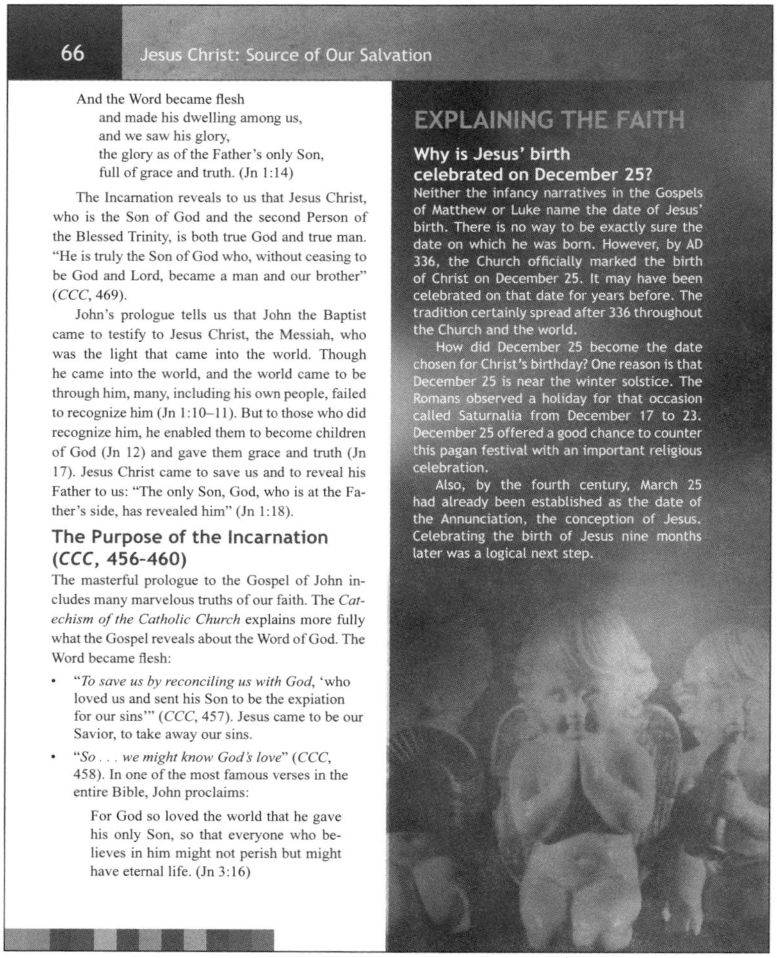

66 Jesus Christ: Source of Our Salvation

And the Word became flesh
and made his dwelling among us,
and we saw his glory,
the glory as of the Father's only Son,
full of grace and truth. (Jn 1:14)

The Incarnation reveals to us that Jesus Christ, who is the Son of God and the second Person of the Blessed Trinity, is both true God and true man. "He is truly the Son of God who, without ceasing to be God and Lord, became a man and our brother" (*CCC*, 469).

John's prologue tells us that John the Baptist came to testify to Jesus Christ, the Messiah, who was the light that came into the world. Though he came into the world, and the world came to be through him, many, including his own people, failed to recognize him (Jn 1:10–11). But to those who did recognize him, he enabled them to become children of God (Jn 12) and gave them grace and truth (Jn 17). Jesus Christ came to save us and to reveal his Father to us: "The only Son, God, who is at the Father's side, has revealed him" (Jn 1:18).

The Purpose of the Incarnation (*CCC*, 456-460)

The masterful prologue to the Gospel of John includes many marvelous truths of our faith. The *Catechism of the Catholic Church* explains more fully what the Gospel reveals about the Word of God. The Word became flesh:

- "*To save us by reconciling us with God*, 'who loved us and sent his Son to be the expiation for our sins'" (*CCC*, 457). Jesus came to be our Savior, to take away our sins.
- "*So . . . we might know God's love*" (*CCC*, 458). In one of the most famous verses in the entire Bible, John proclaims:

> For God so loved the world that he gave his only Son, so that everyone who believes in him might not perish but might have eternal life. (Jn 3:16)

EXPLAINING THE FAITH

Why is Jesus' birth celebrated on December 25?

Neither the infancy narratives in the Gospels of Matthew or Luke name the date of Jesus' birth. There is no way to be exactly sure the date on which he was born. However, by AD 336, the Church officially marked the birth of Christ on December 25. It may have been celebrated on that date for years before. The tradition certainly spread after 336 throughout the Church and the world.

How did December 25 become the date chosen for Christ's birthday? One reason is that December 25 is near the winter solstice. The Romans observed a holiday for that occasion called Saturnalia from December 17 to 23. December 25 offered a good chance to counter this pagan festival with an important religious celebration.

Also, by the fourth century, March 25 had already been established as the date of the Annunciation, the conception of Jesus. Celebrating the birth of Jesus nine months later was a logical next step.

For Review Answers (pages 67-68)

1. 4 BC.
2. The Resurrection.
3. The four Gospels.
4. Mark AD 70; Matthew AD 80–85; Luke AD 85; John AD 90–100.
5. Mark begins with a reference to a prophecy from Isaiah regarding a messenger sent to prepare the Messiah's way. John begins by referring back to the creation and the Divine Word of God (Jesus) at work from the beginning.
6. Answers may vary a bit but should include items listed on page 59 of the student text.
7. Answers will vary and may include: Isaiah (virgin bearing a son, Emmanuel); Micah (Bethlehem); Hosea (the Messiah being called out of Egypt); Jeremiah 31:15 (prophetic statements concerning Nazareth).
8. Answers should include Jesus' connection with Abraham, the father of Jews; David, from whom the Messiah was to come; cheaters and liars; and several women.
9. Both the Joseph of the Old Testament and Joseph of the New received messages in dreams and saved their families in Egypt.
10. God saves.
11. Jesus is the new Moses because he is the new lawgiver: Moses on Mount Sinai and Jesus in the Sermon on the Mount. Both also had close calls with death; both were forced to flee for their lives.

This verse has been called the "Gospel in miniature," since it tells us that our God is a God of love. God shows this love by sending us his Son to save us. If we believe in him, we will not perish. But he will give us eternal life! Indeed this is good news—truly great news!

- "*To be our model of holiness*" (*CCC*, 459). By taking on flesh, Jesus, the Second Person of the Blessed Trinity, gives us the opportunity to imitate and become more like him, God who is all holy. Again, John's Gospel gives us an important saying of Jesus: "I am the way and the truth and the life. No one comes to the Father except through me" (Jn 14:6). By Jesus' life, Death, and Resurrection, he has shown us the very meaning of what love is. And he instructs us to imitate him:

  > Love one another as I love you. No one has greater love than this, to lay down one's life for one's friends. You are my friends if you do what I command you. (Jn 15:12–14)

- *To make us "partakers of the divine nature"* (*CCC*, 460). Christ became man to adopt us into the divine family by the power of the Holy Spirit. St. Athanasius expressed it this way: "For the Son of God became man so that we might become God."

Finally, recall the Protoevangelium where God promised that a descendant of Adam and Eve will crush the head of the serpent, that is, destroy the power of Satan.

> I will put enmity between you and the woman, and between your offspring and hers; He will strike at your head, while you strike at his heel. (Gn 3:15)

On two occasions in John's Gospel, Jesus addresses his mother as "Woman," a reference to the Protoevangelium (see Jn 2:1–5 and 19:26). He is the offspring of the Woman who is the new Eve—Mary. It is he who came to destroy the power of the devil. The Paschal Mystery of his Death and Resurrection accomplished this very thing: "Indeed, the Son of God was revealed to destroy the works of the devil" (1 Jn 3:8).

For Review

1. When was Jesus likely born?
2. What is "the crowning truth of our faith in Christ"?
3. What is the primary source of our knowledge about Jesus Christ?
4. Give the approximate dates for the writing of the four Gospels.
5. Contrast the beginnings of Mark's and John's Gospels.
6. List elements that the infancy narratives in Matthew and Luke have in common.
7. Discuss how three Old Testament prophecies are fulfilled in Matthew's infancy narrative.
8. Discuss two things that Jesus' genealogy in Matthew's Gospel reveals about him.
9. How is St. Joseph like the Old Testament patriarch of the same name?
10. What is the meaning of the name Jesus?
11. How is Jesus the New Moses?
12. What Old Testament event is recalled in the Holy Family's return to Nazareth from Egypt?
13. What sources did Luke use in the writing of his Gospel?
14. Identify Theophilus.
15. What can we learn from Mary's response to Gabriel's announcement that she was to be the Mother of God?
16. What is evidence that Jesus was born in humility and poverty?
17. What is the meaning of Jesus' circumcision and Presentation in the Temple?

way they as a class can effectively make a difference for those who—like Jesus—have found themselves without a home. Suggest that they support existing organizations like the local homeless shelter, St. Vincent de Paul Society, or Covenant House.

The Incarnation in the Prologue to John's Gospel (John 1:1-18) (pages 65-67)

- Sum up the key points of this section by explaining that John recognizes Jesus as the creating word of God (the Divine Logos). As in the first creation story, when God speaks, creation happens. John stresses that Jesus is that creating Word who is truly one of us and also truly God.
- Have the students note the points the *Catechism of the Catholic Church* makes about the purpose of the Incarnation:
  - to reconcile us to God
  - to reveal God's love for us
  - to model holiness
  - to grant us a share in God's life
- Invite the students to use a mnemonic device such as an acronym to remember these four purposes of the Incarnation. You might suggest: RLHD (**R**econcile,

For Review Answers (pages 67-68) continued

12. The Exodus.
13. In writing his Gospel, Luke drew on Mark, on Q (*Quelle*), and on a source called "L."
14. Theophilus means "beloved of God." He may have been a Christian convert or Luke's patron, but could have been a symbolic name for anyone reading the Gospel.
15. Answers will vary but should speak to humility, faith, obedience.
16. He was born in a stable; he was wrapped as an infant in swaddling; shepherds were the first to see him; his parents offered turtledoves at his circumcision (the offering of a poor person).
17. Jesus' circumcision signified his incorporation into the Jewish people and prefigures submission to the Law and Jewish worship (also prefigures Baptism); the presentation was an acknowledgement of his consecration to God (recalling the first Passover).
18. Both were prophets who recognized Jesus as the Messiah during his presentation at the Temple. Simeon also foresaw Jesus' mission.
19. It prefigured the future when he would confound the religious authorities with his teaching, and it showed that he was beginning to recognize his mission, which would be accomplished in Jerusalem.
20. The Word was a creating word.
21. God became man to reconcile us with God, that we might know God's love, to model holiness, and to make us partakers in the Divine nature.

Love, **H**oliness, and **D**ivine nature) and a phrase such as "I **R**eally **L**ove **HD** TV" to remember the letters.

Chapter 3: The Coming of the Messiah—Lesson 4

Bell Ringers

- Ask the students to offer their responses to the twenty-one For Review questions on pages 67–68 (answers are on pages 82–83 of this text). Be sure to allow the students to ask any other questions they may have.
- Invite volunteers to share the personality sketches they wrote in their journals about their ancestors.
- Collect the students' essays on the second and third activities from For Reflection on page 68.

Teaching Approaches

Learning from the Life of Christ (pages 68-74)

- Remind the students that in their second lesson they recalled that the Gospels are not biographies of Jesus but *testaments of faith* about the experience of Jesus. As such, they do not simply tell us about some long-gone historical figure. Rather they are proclamations of good news, the good news that Jesus Christ himself *is* good news. Stress that when we read or listen to the Gospels, they put us in contact with the person of Jesus Christ, challenge us to believe in him, and exhort us to live out that belief.
- Distribute copies of Chapter 3, Handout 5, "What Are the Gospels?" Give the students a moment to look them over. Then have them complete both parts of the Scripture activity. Afterward, call on different students to share their responses.
- Point out that Jesus came to reveal the Father, and *every* aspect of his life does just that. Write the following bullet points on the board and use them to sum up how Christ's life is a mystery of Redemption (see page 69):
  - **his Incarnation—enriches us**
  - **his obedience—atones for us**
  - **his preaching—purifies us**
  - **his healing & exorcising—fulfills prophecies for us**
  - **his Cross & Resurrection—justifies us**

68 Jesus Christ: Source of Our Salvation

18. Identify Simeon and Anna.
19. What is the significance of Jesus' experience at the Temple at age twelve?
20. According to the prologue of John's Gospel, what role did the Word of God play in creation?
21. Discuss at least three reasons for God becoming man in Jesus Christ.

For Reflection

- Write a short personality sketch about any two of your ancestors. Comment on how you might be like them.
- What do you think Jesus might have been like as a teenager? Include some insights on how he might be like *you*. Mention some other qualities he would have that might set him apart from his peers.
- What do each of the elements of John 3:16 mean to you?

Learning from the Life of Christ (*CCC*, 512-518)

Modern biographies seem to treat every imaginable aspect of a person's life story. The Gospels are not like that. For example, the Gospels do not tell us what Jesus looked like—how tall he was, the color of his hair or eyes, a description of his face or his smile, the length of his hair. Furthermore, the Gospels reveal little about Jesus' hidden life, that is, the years from his birth until he came on to the public scene at his baptism. Except for this one incident when Jesus was twelve years old, all the Gospels focus on Jesus' public ministry, which began when he was around thirty years of age.

Even though the public ministry of Jesus forms the primary focus of the Gospels, there are even events in his life in those years that are not treated: "But these are written that you may [come to] believe that Jesus is the Messiah, the Son of God, and that through this belief you may have life in his name" (Jn 20:31).

The Evangelists' belief in Jesus moved them to want to share their faith with others. Knowing who Jesus is as the Son of God and Savior of the world, they saw and were able to help others see how the mystery of Salvation takes place in every aspect of Jesus' life. "His deeds, miracles, and words all revealed that 'in him the whole fullness of deity dwells bodily'(Col 2:9)" (*CCC*, 215). Jesus' humanity pointed to the invisible mystery of who he is as God's Son and the reason he came—to redeem us.

Therefore, every aspect of Christ's earthly life—his words and deeds, silences and sufferings, his way of being and speaking—is a Revelation of the Father. As God the Father instructed Peter, James, and John on the mountain at the time of Jesus' Transfiguration, "This is my chosen Son; listen to him" (Lk 9:35). Or as Jesus told Philip at the Last Supper, "Whoever has seen me has seen the Father"

Lesson 4 Objectives

The students will:

- describe how and why all the elements of Jesus' life reveal God's love and our Redemption.
- draw conclusions about what the Kingdom of God will be like based on the way John the Baptist preached and lived.
- summarize the theological truths revealed at Jesus' baptism.
- summarize the meaning of the temptations of Jesus and make connections between them and the Old Testament.

The Coming of the Messiah 69

(Jn 14:9). Because Jesus is God's Revelation, *everything* about Christ's life reported in the Gospels has profound meaning. From the smallest detail to the most awe-inspiring miracles, we learn about God's great love revealed to us in his Son, Jesus Christ.

The *Catechism of the Catholic Church* reiterates that Christ's whole life is a mystery of Redemption. Although Christ redeems us above all else through his sacrifice of blood on the cross, the mystery of Redemption takes place throughout our Lord's entire life. For example,

- in his Incarnation through which by becoming poor he enriches us with his poverty;
- in his hidden life we learn how his obedience to his parents atones for our disobedience;
- in his preaching he tells us of the ways of God and purifies our consciences;
- in curing the sick and driving out demons, he fulfilled the prophecy of Isaiah who said about the Messiah: "He took away our infirmities and bore our diseases" (Mt 8:17 quoting Is 53:4);
- through his Cross and Resurrection he justifies us (*CCC*, 517).

Every aspect of Christ's life: his words, his deeds, his sufferings had one purpose: to restore humanity to the original vocation that God had for us—intimacy with God as his children. The next sections address some of the mysteries of the early part of Christ's ministry—his baptism and temptations in the desert—to learn how they help reveal the mystery of Salvation. Chapter 4 presents some of the saving actions and words of Jesus during the rest of his public life up to the time of his arrest.

The Baptism of Jesus (Mk 1:2-11; Mt 3:1-17; Lk 3:1-20; Jn 1:19-34)

Jesus' baptism is linked to the figure of John the Baptist, a relative of Jesus. John the Baptist was also a prophet and a precursor of Jesus, the Messiah. John the Baptist came on the scene around AD 28 (the fifteenth year of the reign of the emperor, Tiberius, see Lk 3:1) to preach a message of repentance in preparation for God's judgment on a sinful humanity. John instructed his hearers to share with the poor; he told tax collectors to be fair in their dealings; he challenged soldiers to be gentle and content with their salaries. And he warned sinners of God's coming judgment, calling on them to repent and be baptized as a sign of their turning away from sin.

The Gospels compare John the Baptist to the Old Testament prophet, Elijah. Like Elijah, John wore a garment of camel skin and a leather belt and ate grasshoppers and wild honey for food. Jesus himself identified John the Baptist as the new Elijah, the one prophesied to usher in the Messianic age (Mt 11:14). John the Baptist attracted many followers. They asked him if he was the Messiah. John's response was, "I am baptizing you with water, but one mightier than I is coming. I am not worthy to loosen the thongs of his sandals. He will baptize you with the holy Spirit and fire" (Lk 3:16). This someone, of course, was Jesus Christ, the true Messiah.

John the Baptist was a forceful, charismatic person. Many people came from all over Palestine to hear his message. John baptized in the Jordan River, a symbol of Jewish freedom and the point of entry into the Promised Land after forty years of wandering and suffering in the Sinai desert after the Exodus. Through baptism in the Jordan, John's followers showed that they were willing to walk the path of their ancestors in the faith. They were willing to turn from self-centered sinfulness to hear once again and obey God's word. John's baptism was a public sign of repentance in preparation for the coming of the Messiah.

Jesus himself heard of John's preaching and traveled from Galilee to the Judean wilderness to hear John for himself and to be baptized by him. By doing so, he took on the identity of his people. By submitting to John's baptism, Jesus permitted himself to be numbered among sinners, identifying with

- Before moving on, stress that Jesus' mission was to restore humanity to the Original Holiness and Justice—to intimacy with God.
- Write the following quotation from the *Catechism of the Catholic Church* on the board: **"Christ's whole life is a mystery of Redemption" (*CCC*, 517).** Note the definition of "Redemption" in the text (page 296). Then underline the word **mystery** on the board. Remind the students that "mystery" is not the incomprehensible. Mystery cannot be explained away, but it can be explored.
- Direct the students' attention to the feature, "Faithful Disciple: St. John the Baptist" on page 71. Direct the students to look at the picture of John the Baptist on page 71. Tell them the iconic picture is meant to remind them that John lived in poverty, he was humble, and he did not think of himself. Then, ask:
    - How does his appearance reveal this statement from Jesus about him: "I tell you, among those born of women, no one is greater than John; yet the least in the kingdom of God is greater than he" (Lk 7:28)?
    - What does John's message and lifestyle tell us about the Kingdom of God? (*The least are the greatest in the Kingdom of God.*)

Lesson 4 Preview

This lesson has the students investigating the accounts of Jesus' baptism and temptation in the desert, events that set the stage for his announcing the advent of God's Kingdom. These biblical stories provide a foundation for the students' deeper study of the mysteries of our Redemption. (*Note:* The feature "True Values" on page 72 will not be used in this lesson, but will be employed in Lesson 5.)

Lesson 4 Homework

1. Tell the students to write their responses to the seven For Review questions on page 73.
2. Call attention to the For Reflection feature on pages 73–74. Have the students complete it as a journal activity.
3. Have the students read "The Beginning of Jesus' Ministry" (pages 74–77) in preparation for their next lesson.
4. Tell the students to begin wrapping up work on their chosen Ongoing Assignments (page 79).

- If the students have not yet read all four Gospel accounts of Jesus' baptism, allow time for them do so now (see references on page 69). Afterward, use questions to discuss the mystery of Jesus' baptism:
  - To what sort of baptism was John calling people? (*repentance*)
  - To which Old Testament prophet do the Gospels compare John? Why? (*Elijah. He was the prophet who was to usher in the age of the Messiah*)
  - What is the significance of John performing baptisms in the Jordan River? (*The Jordan was a symbol of Jewish freedom, the waters the ancient Hebrews passed through to the Promised Land; baptism in the Jordan shows that the baptizers were willing to do as their ancestors did, namely, to heed and live out the Word of God.*)
  - Since Jesus had nothing to repent, why did he choose to be baptized by John? (*In order to identify with us and to accept his role as Suffering Servant in obedience to the will of the Father.*)
- Call on different students to name the three phenomena that occur in the accounts of Jesus' baptism: (1) the heavens opened, (2) the Holy Spirit appeared as a dove, and (3) the voice of God was heard. Ask the students what deeper or symbolic

us in our spiritual need. Above all else, the mystery of Jesus' baptism displays his humility. From the beginning of his mission of preaching and healing, the Lord accepted the role of God's Suffering Servant.

In one form or another, all four Gospels include the following phenomena that took place at Jesus' baptism:

- *The sky opens*, thus revealing that God has come to meet his people through his Son, Jesus Christ. Our Lord's mission is about to begin.
- *A dove descends from the sky.* The dove signifies the coming of the Holy Spirit. It is a symbol of joy, innocence, freedom, power, and peace. In this new era, the presence of the Holy Spirit will be with Jesus as he launches his public ministry.
- *A voice proclaims, "You are my beloved Son"* (Mk 1:11). Thus two Old Testament prophecies are fulfilled. Psalm 2:7 promised the coming of the anointed-king, the Messiah; and the prophet Isaiah told about the Servant who will suffer on our behalf:

  I will proclaim the decree of the Lord,
  who said to me, "You are my son;
  today I am your father." (Ps 2:7)

  Here is my servant whom I uphold,
  my chosen one with whom I am pleased,

  Upon whom I have put my spirit;
  he shall bring forth justice to the nations.
  (Is 42:1)

  Yet it was our infirmities that he bore,
  our sufferings that he endured. (Is 53:4)

The baptism of Jesus reveals the following important theological truths by:

- showing Jesus' perfect submission to his Father's will,
- foreshadowing Jesus' death for the remission of our sins, and
- serving as a model for our own baptism.

Christ's baptism reveals his identity and his mission. He is about his Father's work of Salvation, which is accomplished by the power of the Holy Spirit. His baptism also foreshadows Christian Baptism, which is done in the name of the Father, and the Son, and the Holy Spirit. Our own Baptism enables us to participate in our Lord's work of healing and reconciliation. The Sacrament of Baptism also joins us to the Catholic Church by plunging us into the waters with Christ so that we may rise with him, be reborn in the Holy Spirit, and be adopted into God's family.

The Temptations of Jesus (Mt 4:1-11)

The three Synoptic Gospels—Matthew, Mark, and Luke—all report that Jesus retreated to the Judean wilderness after his baptism and before embarking on his public ministry. As Mark's Gospel states, "At once the Spirit drove him out into the desert, and he remained in the desert for forty days, tempted by Satan. He was among wild beasts, and the angels ministered to him" (Mk 1:12–13). Matthew and Luke fill in the details of Mark's brief statement by telling us Satan tempted Jesus three times. The three temptations of Jesus recall the temptations of the Chosen People when they wandered in the desert for forty years. By undergoing a similar three-fold test, Jesus Christ was able to bring the history of his people to a perfect conclusion.

First Temptation

Satan first tempts Jesus to turn stones into loaves of bread. This brings to mind the Chosen People's desire to turn back to the safety of slavery in Egypt because they were hungry while wandering in the desert. Though free, they longed for security and safety. In Jesus' case, his hunger would not turn him away from doing God's will. He did not have a divided heart. His steadfastness in pursuing his mission was rooted in "every word that comes forth from the mouth of God" (Mt 4:1).

For Enrichment

The Desert Fathers

Many Christians have followed in the footsteps of John the Baptist and Jesus' temptation in the desert by living an ascetic life dedicated to God. Some of the most well known ascetics in the history of the Church are the Desert Fathers. The Desert Fathers were hermits living in Egypt around the third century. They were sought after for their wisdom. Many of their teachings are recorded in what are called *The Sayings of the Desert Fathers*. Invite students to research some of these sayings by visiting http://orthodoxwiki.org/Sayings_of_the_Desert_Fathers.

ST. JOHN THE BAPTIST

Faithful Disciple

St. John the Baptist, the forerunner of Jesus and his relative, lived an **ascetic** life and preached in the Jordan region that Israel's judgment was at hand. He stripped the message of his Jewish ancestors to the basics, proclaiming a baptism for the repentance of sins. He offered his followers a baptism in water that was intended as a symbol of the washing away of their sins. When Jesus arrived at the banks of the river for baptism, John humbled himself and acknowledged Jesus as the Messiah. Jesus counted John as the last and among the greatest of the prophets. Though most of John's followers became disciples of Jesus, some continued independently. Disciples of John are cited in Acts of the Apostles 19:1–4, as Paul ministered in Ephesus.

What were the origins of John's ministry? At the time of Christ there were several branches of Judaism that were apart from the Sadducees and Pharisees, two branches mentioned often in the Gospels. The Dead Sea Scrolls, for example, helped to shed information on an apocalyptic group known as the Essenes, who believed that God would usher in his Kingdom through a dramatic, even catastrophic event. The Essenes withdrew from life to the Qumran area near the northwest shore of the Dead Sea. As celibates who did not marry, they shared goods in common and tried to be ritually pure by frequent washings throughout the day. There is a possibility that John the Baptist was part of the Essene community or another similar group of Judaism.

ascetic
A form of strict self-denial as a means of spiritual discipline. Christian ascetics imitate Christ's life of self-sacrifice in order to live the Gospel more faithfully.

For certain, John the Baptist understood his role in relationship to Christ. When he saw Jesus coming toward him at the river John said,

> Behold, the Lamb of God, who takes away the sin of the world. He is the one of whom I said, "A man is coming after me who ranks ahead of me because he existed before me." I did not know him, but the reason why I came baptizing with water was that he might be made known to Israel. (Jn 1:30)

John had already told his disciples that he would be "unworthy to untie" Jesus' sandal straps. The respect between John and Jesus was mutual. Jesus said of him: "Among those born of women there has been none greater than John the Baptist; yet the least in the kingdom is greater than he" (Mt 11:11).

Herod Antipas had John arrested and imprisoned at Machaerus Fortress on the Dead Sea when John spoke against Herod's adulterous marriage. John was beheaded at the request of Salome, the daughter of Herodias, Herod's wife.

The Feast Day of St. John the Baptist is June 24. The feast of his beheading is on August 29.

meaning they see in these happenings. Help them recognize the presence of the *Trinity*:

- The FATHER: The heavens opening speaks to God's coming among us to create a new era, a new age.
- The SON: The voice declares that Jesus is God's Son, the Messiah (the "anointed"), and the Servant who suffers on our behalf.
- The HOLY SPIRIT: The dove recalls the image of the Holy Spirit at the dawn of creation; thus, the dove speaks both to a new creation and to the Holy Spirit's presence with Jesus.

- Finally, note how Jesus' baptism also (1) reveals Jesus' obedience to God, (2) prefigures his role as a Suffering Servant who comes to remit sins, and (3) models our own Baptism. Ask students to draw conclusions about the meaning of Christian Baptism based on these messages.
- Before dealing with the temptations of Jesus, refer the students to the feature "Faithful Disciple: St. John the Baptist" (page 71). Note the Baptist's origin, prophetic role, and the respect Jesus had for him. Finally, point out that like all the prophets before him, John spoke truth to power; that is what got him killed.

Extending the Lesson

Evil Personified

- Invite the students to think of an evil they recognize as real because they have experienced it either personally or vicariously. To avoid any embarrassing personal disclosure, suggest experiences centered on **greed, envy**, or **hatred**. List these three evils on the board and have the students add to the list. Eliminate any evil that is too global—that is, beyond immediate personal experience—such as world hunger.
- Select an evil from the list. Begin to personify it by asking questions like the following:
  - If (name of evil) were in the form of a living being and it walked into this classroom, what would it look like?
  - What characteristics would it possess?
  - What color would it be?
  - If it could speak, how might it sound?
  - What might it say?
- Repeat the above for other evils on the list.
- Discuss what happens in people's lives when they encounter these evils.

- Call on a volunteer to read the account of Jesus' temptation in the desert (Mt 4:1–11). Afterward, ask:
    - In the first temptation, what does the tempter try to persuade Jesus to trust in? (*Instant bread—that is, instant gratification, the easy fix.*)
    - In the second temptation, what does the tempter try to persuade Jesus to do? (*To put God to the test by creating a situation that would* compel *God to rescue him.*)
    - In the third temptation, with what does the devil tempt Jesus? (*Instant worldly fame and power*)
- Summarize Jesus' responses:
    - First temptation: only in God can we find complete gratification.
    - Second temptation: we cannot force God's hand.
    - Third temptation: only God provides true gratification, fulfillment, and future.

  Stress how each of Jesus' responses was an affirmation of his willingness and his resolve to undertake and complete the mission for which the Father had sent him, namely, our Redemption.
- Draw a diagram on the board with the three temptations on the left side and arrows pointing to empty circles on the right side. Label the right side "Old Testament Connections" and instruct students to use their books to find the Old Testament stories that are connected to each temptation of Christ. After the students have completed the assignment, review it as a class.

Second Temptation

Next, Satan challenges Jesus to throw himself down from the Temple's pinnacle, thus endangering his life. Here Jesus is tempted to preserve himself from destruction, to test God's love for him while pursuing his mission. At the heart of Jesus' temptation is whether he would continue to love God even at the risk of death. Would he stay faithful to his mission despite suffering and pain that will come his way? Jesus' faithful answer to the devil was, "You shall not put the Lord, your God, to the test" (Mt 4:7). Trust in God's love, despite obstacles, will be the hallmark of Jesus' ministry.

Third Temptation

The third temptation is to power and wealth. The devil offers Jesus the kingdoms of the world if he will worship him. Jesus rejects the easy, pleasurable, popular way. He is committed to be faithful to God at all times. Only God is worthy of our worship. Jesus rebukes Satan by saying, "The Lord, your God, shall you worship and him alone shall you serve" (Mt 4:10).

Jesus' temptations in the desert prefigure certain temptations he would face in his public ministry. His heart was undivided in preaching the Gospel, despite the temptation to settle down and live a life of leisure. He was willing to offer his life for all humans rather than to flee from suffering and a cruel death. He put his Father's will above everything as he lived a life of poverty and rejected every effort to make him a worldly king.

Jesus undoubtedly related his temptations to his disciples, telling them that they would also be tempted. Temptation is not a sin but a trial or a test. Temptation forces us to respond, to show what we will do in a given situation. In his letter to the Galatians, St. Paul warns us to be watchful and avoid temptations. In the Lord's Prayer, Jesus instructs us to ask God that we not be led into temptation. The reason is simple, "The spirit is willing but the flesh is weak" (Mk 14:38).

However, the truth is that as Christ's followers, we *will* be tempted. We will be asked to take the easy way out, to seek pleasure rather than to do God's will. Society will tempt us to worship money or power or prestige or sex outside of marriage rather than to serve God and obey his Law. We will be tempted to look out for ourselves first and neglect the needs of the ones we love or the weak and helpless in our midst.

We can turn to Jesus when we are tempted because he can identify with us. Jesus, our Suffering Servant, has conquered Satan, the tempter, for us and for our Salvation. The Letter to the Hebrews reminds us,

True Values

By resisting Satan's temptations, Jesus revealed his true values. Examine how well you share two of his values by reading the Scripture quotations below and responding to the questions.

1. *Every person is sacred.* Jesus stayed true to his mission. He offered his life for every human being. He teaches that God cares about everything (Mt 10:29-31). Our loving God does not want a single person to be lost (Mt 18:10-14).
    - How do you treat others when you meet them—more as strangers or as brothers and sisters in Christ?
2. *Know what is important.* Jesus came to do God's will. Nothing would deter him (Lk 9:62 and Mt 6:19-24).
    - Rate your commitment to do God's will on a scale of 1 to 10, with 10 being "most committed." Explain your rating.

For we do not have a high priest who is unable to sympathize with our weaknesses, but one who has similarly been tested in every way, yet without sin. So let us confidently approach the throne of grace to receive mercy and to find grace for timely help. (Hb 4:15–16)

Jesus' fidelity to the Father in the desert contrasts with the Chosen People who gave into sensuality in the desert and worshipped false gods in the form of statues. Jesus is the New Israel. He is also the New Adam. Unlike our first parents, he ignored the enticements of the devil. Decisively conquering Satan, Jesus' victory in the desert foreshadowed the ultimate victory he won through the Paschal Mystery of his Passion, Death, and Resurrection.

Jesus faced temptation and set his ministry on the path of gentle, compassionate service of others. Jesus kept on the path of truth and love and invites his friends to believe in him and walk with him. His way of love and obedience to God is tough and demanding. It contrasts with Satan's easy enticements, but it is the only way to proceed in truth and righteousness.

For Review

1. What was the main criterion the Evangelists used in including certain details of Christ's life in the writing of their Gospels?
2. Why is everything in the life of Christ significant?
3. What is significant about John the Baptist baptizing in the Jordan River?
4. What were the three events that took place at Jesus' baptism? What did each mean?
5. What theological truths are revealed at Jesus' baptism?
6. What happens when Christians receive the sacrament of Baptism?
7. How do Jesus' temptations reveal him as the New Israel and the New Adam?

For Reflection

- Jesus asked "Who do the crowds say that I am? (Lk 9:19)." Why do you believe they may have made this identification?

- Write the following on the board: **It is human to be tempted; it is inhuman to sin**. Invite the students' comments. Make sure they understand that temptation is not sinful, only giving in to temptation is sinful. Tell the students that Jesus' willingness and resolve to resist temptation was not due to his being fully God but to his being fully *human*. Jesus, the New Adam, showed us what God created human beings to be: sinless, holy, and just. Jesus came to restore Original Holiness and Original Justice.
- Draw the students' attention to the feature "True Values" on page 72. Take a few moments to discuss the temptations teenagers face today—temptations to instant gratification, to power (e.g., "lording" it over others), to worship something other than God (e.g., fame, money, prestige). Then, go on to discuss ways to help resist such temptations (e.g., praying, avoiding "tempting" situations, reading Scripture, having a good friend to talk to, fasting, having an open relationship with parents, etc.). Encourage the students to take note of these "helps" and try to incorporate them into their lives.

For Review Answers (page 73)

1. To help readers come to believe.
2. It all reveals the Father.
3. The Jordan River was a symbol of Jewish freedom; passing through these waters showed that those being baptized were willing to follow the path of their ancestors in faith and obey God's will for them.
4. (1) The heavens open—God has come among us in the person and mission of Jesus; (2) A dove descends—The Holy Spirit is with Jesus; (3) A voice from Heaven—fulfills the prophecies regarding the coming of the Messiah and declares Jesus' Divine Sonship.
5. Jesus' baptism reveals the following theological truths: (1) It shows Jesus' submission to the will of the Father; (2) It foreshadows Jesus' Passion and Death; (3) It serves as a model for our Baptism.
6. Our Baptism empowers us to share in Jesus' healing and reconciling mission as well to become part of the Catholic Church through rebirth in the Holy Spirit. Like Jesus, we become beloved sons and daughters of the Father.
7. Jesus' resistance is in contrast to the desert actions of the Israelites who gave into temptation, thus making him the New Israel. Likewise, unlike our first parents, Jesus ignored the enticements of the devil and did not try to play God; thus, he is the New Adam.

Chapter 3: The Coming of the Messiah—Lesson 5

Bell Ringers

- Ask the students to offer their responses to the seven For Review questions on page 73 (answers are on page 89 of this text). Be sure to allow the students to ask any other questions they may have.
- Continue the review of the previous session by asking the students to respond to the following questions:
  - What did Jesus' baptism by John reveal? (*It revealed that Jesus was obedient to God's will; it foreshadowed his Death for the forgiveness of sin; and it served as a model for our own Baptism.*)
  - Why do you think the Gospel writers wanted us to know that Jesus suffered temptation? (*Jesus' suffering temptation shows us that he identifies with us in our trials. It also shows us that, like Jesus, we can resist the lure of sinfulness—that it's the human thing to do.*)
- Before moving on into today's topics, write the word **value** on the board. Then offer the following definition: *a belief that we choose to act on.*
- Direct the students to turn to the feature "True Values" on page 72. Have the students work with a partner to complete the activity. Circulate as the students share.
- Afterward, introduce today's lesson by telling the students that the coming of the Kingdom of God was Jesus' number one value.

Teaching Approaches

The Beginning of Jesus' Ministry (pages 74-77)

- Call attention to the quotation from Matthew 1:14–15 on page 74. Ask one of the students to read it aloud. Call attention to the definition of *Kingdom of God* in the text. Tell the students that this is the *central* proclamation of the Gospel.
- Go on to explain that the Kingdom of God is not a place but the advancement of God's loving power into all areas of life where it has not been previously recognized. The coming of the Kingdom of God signals the ultimate power of God and the ultimate freedom of human beings—freedom from oppression, injustice, poverty, and fear.

74 Jesus Christ: Source of Our Salvation

- Think of temptation in the terms of this formula:

  temptation = desire + opportunity
  For example, when taking a test, you want to do well (the desire) and you sit next to a smart classmate (opportunity). The temptation to cheat from your classmate is not a sin, but it can turn into sin if you follow this formula:

  sin = desire + opportunity + action
  Analyze three common temptations to sin that have troubled you in the past. Write out your temptations as in the formula above. Discuss one way you can resist each of the temptations you diagrammed.

The Beginning of Jesus' Ministry (*CCC*, 541-546; 567)

Both Mark 1:14–20 and Matthew 4:12–25 report that Jesus began to preach after John the Baptist was arrested. His preaching took place in Galilee, and its theme is summarized in this simple verse: "This is the time of fulfillment. The kingdom of God is at hand. Repent, and believe in the gospel" (Mk 1:14–15). This chapter concludes with a brief treatment of how the Gospels report the beginning of Jesus' public ministry. Chapter 4 will then review the major themes of Jesus' preaching ministry, discuss his miracles, and explain why the authorities plotted his Death.

Coming of God's Kingdom

The central theme in Jesus' preaching is simply the coming of the **Kingdom of God.** This important expression refers to God's rule or reign, "of righteousness, peace, and joy in the holy Spirit" (Rom 14:17). Jesus is the principal agent of the Kingdom. He ushers in the Kingdom with his words and deeds, and by sending out his disciples to call people to himself. The Paschal Mystery of the Lord's Death and Resurrection accomplishes once and for all the coming of God's Kingdom. Today, the Kingdom remains in our midst in the Eucharist. And the Holy Spirit forms God's people into the Church, in which the Kingdom of God is mysteriously present. It will be fully established at the Second Coming of Jesus Christ who will hand it over to his Father.

As Chapter 4 points out in more detail, Jesus demonstrated in word (including in his parables) and in deed (including his miracles) that the Kingdom of God is that of a loving, merciful Father who embraces everyone, including poor people and sinners. God's Kingdom is a free gift that we cannot earn. However, to gain entrance into the Kingdom, we must repent of our sins, believe in Jesus Christ, and respond to others in love by imitating the Lord himself and following the inspirations of the Holy Spirit.

From the very start of his ministry he chose Apostles—Simon (Peter) and his brother Andrew and two other brothers, James and John, the sons of a man named Zebedee to preach God's Kingdom. Jesus would form these men to carry on his work after his Ascension into Heaven. He would build his Church on them and give them and their successors—the Holy Father and the bishops—the authority to forgive sins in his name, to teach in matters of doctrine, and to guide God's People in morality and Christian living. The Church Jesus would later found is the Body of Christ and the Temple of the Holy Spirit. It is the seed and beginning of God's Kingdom.

Teaching with Authority

Luke reports that Jesus began his public life by teaching in the synagogues of Galilee. At the beginning of his ministry, Jesus went to his own **synagogue** in Nazareth. He did one of the Sabbath readings, the one from Isaiah 61:1ff, which prophesied the coming of the Messiah:

Lesson 5 Objectives

The students will:

- describe the meaning of the Kingdom of God.
- recognize that Jesus taught with unique authority.
- summarize the meaning and importance of Jesus' first "sign" at the wedding at Cana.

Lesson 5 Preview

This lesson introduces the students to Jesus' public ministry. The students discover that Jesus came to proclaim and reveal the Kingdom of God. They learn that he was a one-of-a-kind teacher whose methods were unique and challenging. Finally, with the wedding feast at Cana, they get a first taste of Jesus' miraculous actions performed to reveal the coming of the Messianic age.

"The Spirit of the Lord is upon me
because he has anointed me to bring glad tidings to the poor.
He has sent me to proclaim liberty to captives
and recovery of sight to the blind,
to let the oppressed go free,
and to proclaim a year acceptable to the Lord." (Lk 4:18–19 quoting Is 61 ff.)

At first, his townsfolk marveled at Jesus' dramatic reading of this famous prophecy. However, when he applied it to himself by saying that he was the fulfillment of the passage, the people became irate. They wondered aloud how could the Messiah be so ordinary, the son of a neighbor, the carpenter Joseph. Jesus remarked that a prophet is honored everywhere but in his own hometown. So incensed were the people, they tried to lead him to a cliff and throw him off. This passage foreshadows the rest of Jesus' public life: At first, people accept him. However, later, Christ is rejected and killed in Jerusalem.

Call of Disciples

Coming immediately after the prologue, John 1:19–2:12 also presents deep theological insight into the Person of Jesus. John the Baptist is named as a primary witness to Jesus' identity: "Behold, the Lamb of God, who takes away the sin of the world" (Jn 1:29). John's Gospel also reveals that some

Kingdom of God
The reign of God proclaimed by Jesus and begun in his Life, Death, and Resurrection. It refers to the process of God's reconciling and renewing all things through his Son and his will being done on earth as it is in Heaven. The process has begun with Jesus in the Church and will be perfectly completed at the end of time.

synagogue
A meeting place for study and prayer.

Lesson 5 Homework

1. Ask the students to write their responses to the six For Review questions on page 77.
2. Tell the students to be ready to hand in their Ongoing Assignments at their next session.
3. Have the students read through the Chapter Quick View section on pages 78–80 and to review the chapter's Main Ideas. Tell the students to write out any questions they may have and bring them to the next session.

- Note the following points about the Kingdom of God. If you wish, list them on the board.
    - It refers to the process of God's reconciling and renewing all things through his Son and his will being done on earth as it is in Heaven.
    - Jesus brought it about through his words, deeds, and sending out disciples.
    - The Paschal Mystery proclaimed the coming of the Kingdom.
    - The Kingdom is present in the Eucharist and in the Church (the People of God).
    - The Kingdom is the free gift of a loving and compassionate God.
    - While we cannot "earn" our way into the Kingdom, entrance requires repentance, faith, self-denial, and loving/caring for others (i.e., a life of service).
- Have the students read Luke 4:16–30 in their Bibles. Afterward, explain that when Jesus applies this prophecy from Isaiah to himself, he is, in effect, claiming to be the Messiah. He is beginning his mission by asserting that he is no backwater carpenter, but a teacher of overwhelming authority. Not only that, he is not basing his teaching on the authority of another—as other teachers/rabbis have always done—but on *himself*. He is proclaiming, "Hey! The Kingdom of God is here, *in* me!"
- Tell the students that, put simply, Jesus is challenging his listeners to decide whether he is lunatic or Lord. Ask: "What do Jesus' fellow Nazareans choose?" (*lunatic*)
- Direct attention to the text section "Call of Disciples" on pages 75–76. Ask,
    - What choice did Andrew, Simon Peter, Philip, and the sardonic Nathanael make? Lunatic or Lord?
    - What do you think it was about Jesus that enabled the first disciples to drop everything and become his followers?
- Ask the students to turn to For Reflection on page 77. Invite students to share how they had misjudged someone based on a superficial reason, but then had occasion to alter that judgment later on.
- Move on to note how John calls the miracles that reveal who Jesus is, "signs." In fact, John's Gospel is sometimes called the "Book of Signs." List on the board the following references to the seven signs found in John's Gospel:

- **John 2:1–12**
- **John 4:43–54**
- **John 5:1–15**
- **John 6:5–15, 25–40**
- **John 6:16–21**
- **John 9:1–9**
- **John 11:1–44**

- Have the students look up each passage to discover the action that shows who Jesus is.
    - John 2:1–12—*He provides wine to save a wedding feast from disaster.*
    - John 4:43–54—*He heals a sick child.*
    - John 5:1–15—*He cures a crippled man by helping him into a healing pool of water.*
    - John 6:5–15, 25–40—*He feeds 5,000 people with only five loaves and two fish.*
    - John 6:16–21—*He rescues his disciples from a storm at sea.*
    - John 9:1–9—*He heals a man born blind.*
    - John 11:1–44—*He raises a friend (Lazarus) from the dead.*
- Tell the students to read John 2:1–12 in their Bibles. Go on to discuss the Scripture passage by asking:
    - What human problems do Jesus and Mary encounter at Cana?
    - What sign does Jesus give? What does this show us about who Jesus is and why he has come?
    - What does the steward mean when he says, "You have kept the good wine until now"?

of Jesus' earliest disciples were originally followers of John the Baptist. Andrew and another disciple heard John call Jesus the "Lamb of God." When Andrew's brother Simon went to see Jesus, the Lord changed his name to Cephas, which means Peter.

When Jesus returned to Galilee, he met Philip and asked him to be a disciple. Philip joyfully told his friend, Nathanael, that Jesus, the son of Joseph, from Nazareth, was the promised Messiah. Nathanael sarcastically responded, "Can anything good come from Nazareth?" He, like many of his contemporaries, did not expect God to come to them through an ordinary carpenter from a small, insignificant place like Nazareth.

When Jesus met Nathanael and told him that he had seen him sitting under a fig tree, Nathanael was startled but inspired to proclaim, "Rabbi, you are the Son of God; you are the King of Israel" (Jn 1:49). The Lord said,

> Do you believe because I told you that I saw you under the fig tree? You will see greater things than this. . . .You will see the sky opened and the angels of God ascending and descending on the Son of Man. (Jn 1:50–51)

Wedding at Cana

John's Gospel is organized around seven "signs" or miracles that reveal who Jesus is. The first took place at a wedding feast in Cana, before Jesus began his public preaching. Mary, Jesus' mother, informed him the hosts had run out of wine. Mary was likely sensitive to the virtue of hospitality and the great shame that would befall the hosts if they were unable to provide refreshment for their guests.

Mary displayed here simple and confident faith that Jesus would help the host family, even though he told his mother that his time to manifest himself openly had not yet come. "My hour has not yet come" refers to Jesus' Passion, Death, Resurrection, and Glorification when his real glory would be

manifested. The sign he would perform at Cana, the changing of water to wine, like all the other signs in John's Gospel, point to the Paschal Mystery, the climax of his heavenly mission of surrendering his life so that all humanity might gain eternal life (Jn 3:16).

In this first sign, there are clear references to three sacraments. Jesus' attendance at a wedding feast shows that he was in touch with ordinary people and enjoyed a good celebration. But this celebration is a wedding, which celebrates human love and new life. The Lord's attendance at this wedding blesses marriage as a sacrament of divine love. The Sacrament of Matrimony signifies the union of Christ and the Church and it gives spouses the grace to love each other with the love Christ has for the Church. The miracle Christ performed at Cana involved transforming jugs of water. The water in them was used for cleansing oneself before eating the meal. They symbolize the waters of the sacrament of Baptism, the purifying waters that cleanse us of sin and bring us new life in Christ. Finally, wine—which, at the Last Supper, Jesus changes into his own blood—points to the Eucharist. It brings spiritual life, that is, communion with Jesus, our Lord and Savior.

John's first sign also reveals a caring Jesus, who has power over nature. It also shows the influence of his mother who intercedes on behalf of others. His loving response to his mother's request shows that he is in touch with people and is willing to act with authority as the situation demands.

For Review

1. Define Kingdom of God.
2. What did Jesus proclaim in the synagogue in Nazareth? Why did people reject him?
3. Explain three ways the prophecy of Isaiah quoted in Luke 4:18-19 applies to Jesus Christ.
4. Summarize John the Baptist's testimony about Jesus.
5. What does Jesus tell Nathanael that he will witness? What does it mean?
6. What is the meaning of the miracle at Cana?

For Reflection

At first, Nathanael misjudged Jesus. When was a time when you made a false judgment about someone because of some external detail? Comment on how you were able to come to a proper judgment about the person.

- Remind the students that a sign is something that points to something else. Explain that abundant food and plentiful wine are signs of God's presence and blessing. Write the following Old Testament passages on the board: **Amos 9:13; Jeremiah 31:12; Hosea 14:7**. Call on different students to read each one aloud. Note how such abundance is emblematic of the Messianic age.
- Explain that John wants us to understand that the over-abundant wine Jesus provides at Cana reveals that Jesus is the Messiah who gathers the human race in joy and abundance. Emphasize that Jesus' first sign transformed what might have been a distressing and divisive event into a joyous and bonding celebration. This sign tells us that Jesus came to transform the way humans live from discord to harmony, from sadness to joy.
- Finally, point out that our sacraments are signs. Remind the students that the actions of the sacraments continue Jesus' actions. Ask: "To which sacraments does this first sign of Jesus refer?" (*Marriage, Baptism, Eucharist*)

For Review Answers (page 77)

1. The Kingdom of God refers to the process of God renewing and reconciling all things though Christ.
2. Jesus said he was the fulfillment of Isaiah's prophecy of the coming of the Messiah. His fellow townsfolk found it impossible to believe that someone from their hometown could be the Messiah, so they thought Jesus was a blasphemer and lunatic.
3. Answers will vary but could include reference to the Spirit, anointing, service to the poor, curing of the blind, and freedom from sin.
4. John the Baptist calls Jesus the "Lamb of God," referring to the Paschal Lamb whose blood was shed to save the people. This is precisely what the Messiah would do by dying on the Cross.
5. Jesus tells Nathanael that he will see the sky open up and angels descending and ascending. This refers to the coming of the Kingdom of God.
6. Cana declares that Jesus is the Messiah who comes to unite and bring great joy to all people. It was also a precursor to three sacraments: Baptism, Eucharist, and Matrimony.

Chapter 3: The Coming of the Messiah—Review Lesson

Bell Ringers

- Review the previous lesson by inviting the students to share responses to the six questions in the For Review section on page 77.
- Collect the students' Ongoing Assignments for Chapter 3. Allow time for those who chose #2 (creating a PowerPoint presentation) to make their presentations to the class.

Teaching Approaches

Chapter Quick View (pages 78-80)

- Call attention to Terms, People, Places on page 78. Use the questions in this section to help the students review key elements of the unit.
- Divide the class into groups of three or four. Direct the groups to work together to go over again the chapter's For Review sections by taking turns to ask one another the questions. If possible create additional questions to help prepare the students for the test. Encourage the students to try to answer without checking their journals or notes. Circulate to offer assistance should questions of difficulties arise.
- Invite anyone who had questions after going over the Chapter 3 Main Ideas section on page 78 to ask them now. Invite other class members to offer answers. Clarify any remaining confusion.
- Check vocabulary by asking the students to find a partner and then quiz one another on the terms.
- Allow some quiet time for the students to study on their own. If students have more questions, invite them to approach you privately while their classmates study.

Prayer Service

- Gather the students, in a circle around a lighted a candle. Have meditative music playing.
- Ask different students to prayerfully read each of the four Primary Source Quotations (from page 78). Pause for silence between each reading.
- Then lead the students in the centering prayer activity on page 79.
- Call attention to Reflection and Resolution on page 80.

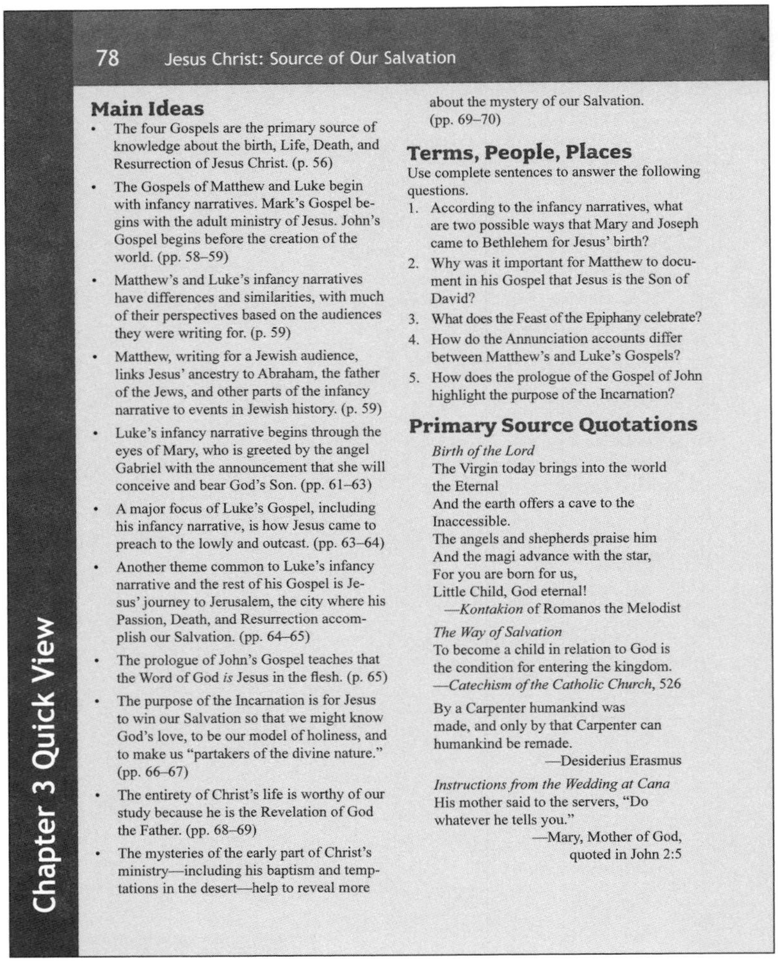
78 Jesus Christ: Source of Our Salvation

Chapter 3 Quick View

Main Ideas

- The four Gospels are the primary source of knowledge about the birth, Life, Death, and Resurrection of Jesus Christ. (p. 56)
- The Gospels of Matthew and Luke begin with infancy narratives. Mark's Gospel begins with the adult ministry of Jesus. John's Gospel begins before the creation of the world. (pp. 58–59)
- Matthew's and Luke's infancy narratives have differences and similarities, with much of their perspectives based on the audiences they were writing for. (p. 59)
- Matthew, writing for a Jewish audience, links Jesus' ancestry to Abraham, the father of the Jews, and other parts of the infancy narrative to events in Jewish history. (p. 59)
- Luke's infancy narrative begins through the eyes of Mary, who is greeted by the angel Gabriel with the announcement that she will conceive and bear God's Son. (pp. 61–63)
- A major focus of Luke's Gospel, including his infancy narrative, is how Jesus came to preach to the lowly and outcast. (pp. 63–64)
- Another theme common to Luke's infancy narrative and the rest of his Gospel is Jesus' journey to Jerusalem, the city where his Passion, Death, and Resurrection accomplish our Salvation. (pp. 64–65)
- The prologue of John's Gospel teaches that the Word of God *is* Jesus in the flesh. (p. 65)
- The purpose of the Incarnation is for Jesus to win our Salvation so that we might know God's love, to be our model of holiness, and to make us "partakers of the divine nature." (pp. 66–67)
- The entirety of Christ's life is worthy of our study because he is the Revelation of God the Father. (pp. 68–69)
- The mysteries of the early part of Christ's ministry—including his baptism and temptations in the desert—help to reveal more about the mystery of our Salvation. (pp. 69–70)

Terms, People, Places

Use complete sentences to answer the following questions.

1. According to the infancy narratives, what are two possible ways that Mary and Joseph came to Bethlehem for Jesus' birth?
2. Why was it important for Matthew to document in his Gospel that Jesus is the Son of David?
3. What does the Feast of the Epiphany celebrate?
4. How do the Annunciation accounts differ between Matthew's and Luke's Gospels?
5. How does the prologue of the Gospel of John highlight the purpose of the Incarnation?

Primary Source Quotations

Birth of the Lord
The Virgin today brings into the world
the Eternal
And the earth offers a cave to the
Inaccessible.
The angels and shepherds praise him
And the magi advance with the star,
For you are born for us,
Little Child, God eternal!
—*Kontakion* of Romanos the Melodist

The Way of Salvation
To become a child in relation to God is the condition for entering the kingdom.
—*Catechism of the Catholic Church*, 526

By a Carpenter humankind was made, and only by that Carpenter can humankind be remade.
—Desiderius Erasmus

Instructions from the Wedding at Cana
His mother said to the servers, "Do whatever he tells you."
—Mary, Mother of God, quoted in John 2:5

Review Lesson Objectives

The students will:

- review Chapter 3 in preparation for the chapter test.
- join in prayer together.

Review Lesson Homework

1. Complete any unfinished Ongoing Assignments.
2. Reread Chapter 3.
3. Study for the Chapter 3 Test.

Read Simeon's prophecy about Jesus' destiny (Lk 2:34–35). Discuss how this prophecy would eventually be fulfilled.

Ongoing Assignments

As you cover the material in this chapter, choose and complete at least three of these assignments.

1. Research ten quotations about Jesus spoken by famous people. Reproduce them in an attractive format and present them to the class.
2. Create a PowerPoint presentation on some aspect of one of these biblical places mentioned in the Bible.
   - Bethlehem
   - Capernaum
   - Nazareth
   - Cana
3. Write a report on what Josephus, the Jewish historian, said about the death of John the Baptist.
4. Write a commentary on the essay "Jerusalem at the Time of Jesus" (St. Anthony Messenger Press) by Fr. Jerome Murphy-O'Connor.
5. Report on some aspect of daily life in the time of Jesus.
6. Where did Jesus travel in the early years of his ministry? Research the issue and draw a map that depicts the footsteps of Jesus.
7. Prepare a report on scientific theories that attempt to explain the star of Bethlehem at the time of Jesus' birth.
8. Read the following passages from John's Gospel. Make a list of what Jesus reveals about himself. John 6:35, 41, 48–51; 8:12; 9:5; 10:7, 9; 10:11, 14; 11:25; 14:6; 15:1, 5.
9. Report on Jewish wedding customs at the time of Jesus.
10. Report on the death of John the Baptist by reading Mark 6:17–29 and Matthew 14:3–12. Who did Herod think Jesus was (Mt 14:1–2; Mk 6:16)? Include with your report a classical painting that depicts John the Baptist's death.
11. Research and report on information about the National Shrine of the Immaculate Conception. Include a sample of some Marian prayers. Name and explain your favorite prayers.

Prayer

When Mary heard the news that she was to be the Mother of God, she prayed the following prayer, the Magnificat. This prayer teaches the true meaning of humility and doing God's will. Pray it with confidence and faith in God's goodness.

Magnificat
My soul proclaims the greatness of
the Lord,
My spirit rejoices in God my Savior,
for he has looked with favor on his
lowly servant.
From this day all generations will
call me blessed:
the Almighty has done great things
for me,
and holy is his Name.
He has mercy on those who fear him
in every generation.
He has shown the strength of
his arm,
he has scattered the proud in
their conceit.
He has cast down the mighty from
their throne,
and has lifted up the lowly.
He has filled the hungry with
good things,
and the rich he has sent away empty.
He has come to the help of his
servant Israel
for he has remembered his promise
of mercy,
the promise he made to our fathers,
to Abraham and his children forever.
Glory to the Father and to the Son
and to the Holy Spirit,

Test Lesson Homework

1. Read the following text section of Chapter 4: "What Is Really Important" on pages 84–85.
2. Examine the Chapter 4 Ongoing Assignments on pages 106–107.

Chapter 3 Test Lesson

Teaching Approaches

- Allow sufficient time for the students to work on the Chapter 3 Test (starting on page 291 of the TWE and also online at www.avemariapress.com). Collect tests as the students finish.

as it was in the beginning, is now,
and will be forever. Amen.

- *Reflection*: Jesus has exalted you, too. You are great in his eyes.
- *Resolution*: Think of one thing you can do for Jesus this week to thank him for the gift of his friendship. Be sure to follow through on your promise.

Chapter 3 Quick View

Chapter 3 Test Answers

Part 1: True or False. (2 points each)

1. T	4. T	7. F	10. F	13. F	16. T	19. T	22. T	25. F
2. F	5. F	8. T	11. T	14. F	17. T	20. T	23. T	26. F
3. F	6. T	9. F	12. F	15. T	18. F	21. T	24. T	

Part 2: Matching. (2 points each)

1. C 2. E 3. A 4. B 5. D

Part 3: Fill in the Blanks. (2 points each)

1. John
2. Mark
3. ascetic

Part 4: Short Answers. (3 points each)

1. God became man to reconcile us with God, that we might know God's love, to model holiness, and to make us partakers in the Divine Nature.
2. The baptism of Jesus (1) revealed Jesus' perfect submission to his Father's will, (2) foreshadowed Jesus' Death for the remission of our sins, and (3) models our own Baptism.

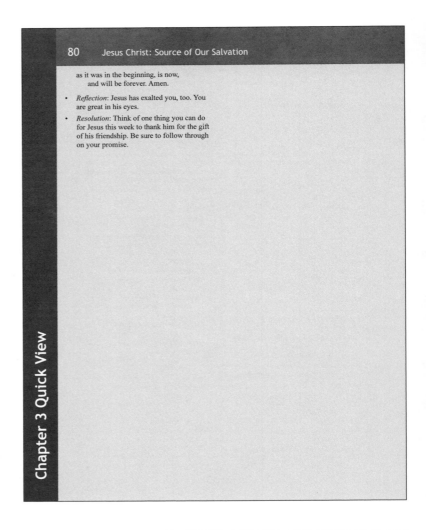

Chapter 3 Test Answers continued

3. Jesus was tempted (1) with bread, (2) to test God, and (3) with fame and power.
4. Baptism, the Eucharist, and Matrimony were referenced in Jesus' miracle at the wedding feast at Cana.

Part 5: Essays. (10 points each)

1. Students should describe the infancy narratives of Matthew and Luke (including their major differences), the preaching of John the Baptist in Mark, and the reference to the creation story in the Gospel of John.
2. Students may make connections between the infancy narratives; the figures of John the Baptist, Mary, Zechariah and Elizabeth, or Joseph; Jesus' baptism; or the temptation of Jesus.

Chapter 4: The Ministry and Message of Jesus Christ

Introduction

You are cordially invited
into God's Kingdom.
Répondez s'il vous plait!

Another name for this chapter could be "You're Invited." In this chapter the students discover Jesus scouring the countryside for partygoers, welcoming one and all into the Kingdom of God. Such generous and unqualified hospitality is both comforting and disconcerting. To know that God is a hospitable host who welcomes us despite our faults and frailties is a comfort. We find that God very attractive. To know that same God also welcomes those who are our enemies, however, is confusing and, often, distressing.

Most of us expect the obvious. We live according to standards of fairness and reciprocity, with a bit of charity thrown in here and there. When someone cuts us off on the freeway for example, we are often less concerned with the person's safety or the safety of others than we are that the "offender" gets caught. After all, we figure, what's fair is fair. We want the punishment to fit the crime—at least when someone else is committing it—and when it does not, we cry foul. We find it difficult to believe in true graciousness. We look with suspicion on such gratuity. It's disquieting and humbling to be loved in such an unqualified manner.

But that was precisely Jesus' manner. He came announcing the Kingdom of God, a God who loves us—a revelation much easier to say than to accept. In his parables and his miracles, Jesus continually extended the invitation to God's Kingdom. He extended it particularly to those whom the world considered outsiders, unclean, and beyond the reach of God's benevolence. Jesus made it abundantly clear that whenever we turn to one another in love, and especially to those we may deem unlovable, we are accepting God's invitation. Whenever we turn away from others, the least among us, we are rejecting not only the Kingdom's invitation but the one who extends the invitation as well.

In this chapter the students see how Jesus used parables to paint a picture of the Kingdom of God and to challenge his listeners to accept it. Jesus draws no conclusions in his parables. Rather, his parables ask questions by giving a complete twist to the listeners' expectations. Also, because parables are open-ended, they are perfect vehicles for describing the Kingdom of God, which is both present and yet to come. The students' study of Jesus' parables reveals that God is a determined and lavish gift-giver who never turns away, who cannot be provoked, who reaches out to welcome all people, and whose great concern is that one and all receive and accept the invitation to the Kingdom.

The chapter also leads the students to appreciate how Jesus' miracles were signs that the Kingdom of God had come. The students examine the types and purpose of Jesus' miraculous acts. They discover that each was a manifestation of the power of God's Kingdom that created harmony and wholeness—physical, psychological, and spiritual wholeness. Jesus' miracles demonstrated that even when human beings have exhausted all possibilities in their struggles with sickness, with the forces of nature, with personal sinfulness, and even with death, God's power is not exhausted, and God's power will prevail.

Finally, the students look at the miracles of the Transfiguration and the Eucharist. The former not only offers a glimpse of Jesus in the fullness of his divinity, but also sheds new light on the meaning of suffering, demonstrating that it can lead to life. In the Eucharist, Jesus offers himself to us so that we might have that

Chapter Objectives

To help the students:

- redefine their understanding of "success."
- examine the meaning and characteristics of the Kingdom of God.
- examine Jesus' Sermon on the Plain, especially his Beatitudes.
- discuss the purpose, meanings, and types of parables.
- appreciate how parables are glimpses into the Kingdom of God.
- discover and examine the types and purposes of Jesus' miracles.
- recognize that miracles are signs of the power of God's Kingdom.
- discover what Jesus' Transfiguration reveals.
- understand how and why Jesus instituted the Eucharist.

life and have it to the full. Through the Eucharist, Jesus' suffering and sacrifice make our sacrifice holy, join it to his, and offer it to the Father. In the Eucharist, we become Kingdom people, people who respond with a resounding "Yes!" to the Kingdom's invitation and who are challenged and gifted to extend that invitation to others.

Advance Preparations

Prepare or have on hand:

For Lesson 1

- Corrected copies of the Chapter 3 Test
- Bibles
- Copies of Chapter 4, Handout 1, "The Measure of Success"

For Lesson 2

- Bibles
- Copies of Chapter 4, Handout 2, "Definitely Different Viewpoints"
- Access to a computer and printer

For Lesson 3

- Bibles
- Bible commentaries and/or access to computers and online biblical commentaries
- Copies of Chapter 4, Handout 3, "I See Myself . . ."
- A sample letter as described in Chapter 4, Handout 3 (optional)

For Lesson 4

- Bibles
- Copies of Chapter 4, Handout 4, "Works, Wonders, and Signs"

For Lesson 5

- Bibles

For the Chapter 4 Review Lesson

- Equipment necessary for students to make PowerPoint presentations
- Candle and matches
- A recording of meditative music and a player
- Copies or a recording of a reconciliation hymn such as "Healer of Our Every Ill" by Marty Haugen (GIA)

For the Chapter 4 Test Lesson

- Copies of the Chapter 4 Test (starting on page 291 of the TWE and also online at www.avemariapress.com)

Chapter 4 Handouts

- Handout 1, The Measure of Success—The students describe their understanding of success and successful people.
- Handout 2, Definitely Different Viewpoints—The students experience how things differ depending on their point of view.
- Handout 3, I See Myself . . .—The students describe how they see themselves and how they believe God sees them.
- Handout 4, Works, Wonders, and Signs—The students discover how Jesus' miracles all point to something more than meets the eye and what the miracles have power over.

Chapter 4: The Ministry and Message of Jesus Christ—Lesson 1

Bell Ringers

- Distribute the corrected Chapter 3 Test. Go over the test with the students, using it as a means to review the previous chapter. Address any remaining questions or concerns the students may have.
- Introduce this lesson by distributing copies of Chapter 4, Handout 1, "The Measure of Success." Have the students complete the activities on their own. Then lead the students in a discussion to decide on a class definition of "success."
- Tell the students that you will recite a list of facts about a person's life and you want them to be honest in evaluating whether each statement is a "success" or a "failure." Explain that if they believe a statement indicates a success, give a thumbs-up; if a failure, a thumbs-down.
    - His mother got pregnant before she was married.
    - He spent the first years of his life as a refugee.
    - As an adult he hung out with society's outcasts.
    - He scandalized many and really upset religious leaders.
    - Political leaders saw him as a crazy peasant.
    - One of his closest friends sold him out for money.
    - His right-hand man turned traitor.
    - He did time in jail and was given the death penalty.
    - He died owning nothing but the clothes on his back, and even those were taken from him.
    - He was buried in a borrowed tomb.

  First, ask the students if they know who this person is, then revisit the class definition of success. Ask the students to critique their definition based on this description of the life of Christ.
- Suggest to the students that our understanding of success is determined by our values. Help the students recall (from Chapter 3, Lesson 5) what a value is—*a belief that we choose to act on.* Tell the students that values are what we believe in most strongly. They reflect our deepest needs and wants. They are beliefs that are precious to us and for which we are willing to make sacrifices. Have the students create a list of their

What Is Really Important

William Randolph Hearst, the early-twentieth-century newspaper tycoon, was fabulously wealthy and a famed patron of the arts. One day he found a description of a piece of art that he greatly desired to purchase for his collection. He sent an art dealer to Europe to find it and secure it for his collection. After months of tedious inquiries, the art dealer reported to Hearst that he had located the desired object. "Where is it?" inquired the tycoon. "In your own warehouse," the dealer replied. It was still in a crate with many other priceless treasures that Hearst had purchased over the years. The wealthy newspaper publisher had been looking for a treasure that was already in his possession.

The danger of too much wealth is that it can blind us to the treasures we already have. Jesus' wise teachings often warn against amassing worldly possessions and ignoring our spiritual well-being. For example, in the parable of the rich fool (Lk 12:16–21), Jesus told about a farmer who had a great harvest and so planned to tear down his old barns and build new ones to hold the grain for future years. The farmer's plan was to live off of his good fortune and "rest, eat, drink, and be merry" (Lk 12:19). But the man was foolish. He thought *he* was in control of his future; he ignored the truth that God is in charge of our lives. Everything God gives to us is a gift of his goodness; it is not something we earn or deserve. And God can call us to himself at any time. This is exactly what happened to the rich man who died the very night he was making plans about how to handle his newfound wealth.

NOTING THE GOSPEL OF LUKE

This chapter will highlight some important teachings of Jesus, especially as they appear in the Gospel of Luke. As you begin Chapter 4, read Luke 4:31–21:38. Make note in your journal of the following:

- the most *challenging* verse for you
- the verse that *encourages* you the most
- your *favorite* verse
- the most *informative* verse
- the most *difficult* verse to understand
- your favorite *parable*
- the *miracle* of Jesus that most impresses you

When you finish making these notes, go back over the list and explain why you chose the verses you did.

Lesson 1 Objectives

The students will:

- review Chapter 3.
- define success.
- develop a list of their most important values.
- appreciate the dangers of being outwardly religious and having too much wealth.
- discover Jesus' greatest value.
- recognize what is crucial to being "successful."

Lesson 1 Preview

This lesson prepares the students to better appreciate the ministry of Jesus and the Good News he came to proclaim. It strives to help the students focus on what is really important in our lives as followers of Christ.

Jesus' message is that we should grow rich in the sight of God. This is what is important: "For where your treasure is, there also will your heart be" (Lk 12:34). Our society often preaches the message that wealthy people are more successful and more important than poor people, but this is not the case. Jesus clearly teaches that "one's life does not consist of possessions" (Lk 12:15). He came to tell us that God loves all of us and that our focus in life should not be on what we have but who we are as God's beloved children.

This chapter reviews other important teachings of Jesus and unique elements of his ministry, including: the announcement of God's Kingdom, his use of parables and miracles to help us to witness the Kingdom, and his gift of Eucharist as a pledge of love.

For Reflection

What do you think are dangers in accumulating too much wealth?

Jesus Announces the Kingdom of God (*CCC*, 541-545)

In the Old Testament, God's kingly rule referred to his justice and judgment over the Israelites. After the Babylonian Exile and the oppressive rule of the Persians, Greeks, and Romans, the Jews looked to God's kingship as taking place in the future with some great event in which God would deliver his

Paradox in Jesus' Teaching

A paradox is a statement that, at first glance, seems self-contradictory, but in reality expresses a possible truth. Several of Jesus' teachings are thought-provoking paradoxes that contain important truths. Reflect on the following teachings of Jesus. Then respond to the questions given.

> "For whoever wishes to save his life will lose it, but whoever loses his life for my sake will save it" (Lk 9:24).
> "For the one who is least among all of you is the one who is the greatest" (Lk 9:48).
> "Some are last who will be first, and some are first who will be last" (Lk 13:30).
> "For everyone who exalts himself will be humbled, but the one who humbles himself will be exalted" (Lk 14:11).

- What do you think Jesus meant by each of these sayings? Do they fit the definition of paradox?
- Research the context for each of these verses. To whom is Jesus speaking? How might his teaching apply to all his followers?
- Choose one of the teachings above. In your own life, how have you observed it to be true?

Lesson 1 Homework

1. Assign the activity outlined in the feature "Noting the Gospel of Luke" (page 84).
2. Have the students turn to Ongoing Assignments on pages 106–107. Point out that they are to choose any three of the listed assignments to complete prior to the conclusion of this chapter.
3. In preparation for their next lesson, tell the students to read "Jesus Announces the Kingdom of God" (pages 85–90).

greatest values. Ask if they think they would consider themselves to be living up to the definition of "success" that the class created or if they feel they have been successful in acting on their greatest values.

- Go on to ask the students if they have ever played the board game *Monopoly*. Then ask, "On what underlying value do you think the game is based?" (*Whoever gets the most stuff—money, property, hotels, houses—wins.*) Note that in our culture, the acquisition of money and stuff is heavily touted as a value—as something that is really important—and as *the* measure of success.

Teaching Approaches

What Is Really Important (pages 84-85)

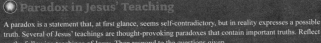

- Call on a student to tell the story of William Randolph Hearst. Ask:
  - What value did Hearst's quest for the art piece reveal?
  - What did his not realizing that he already possessed the art piece say about Hearst's values?
- Go on to tell the students that Jesus said that he pitied two groups of people. To discover these two groups, have them look up and read the following passages in Matthew's Gospel:
  - Matthew 23:23 (*Those with empty piety*)
  - Matthew 19:23–24 (*Those with too much money*)
- Explain that Jesus recognized that both groups felt *no sense of need*. Lacking a sense of need, people had no hold on grace as the oxygen of enterprise.
  - Those who saw themselves as pious and righteous felt little need for any kind of repentance.
  - Those who were wealthy saw little need to be grateful.
- Call attention to the question in the section For Reflection on page 85. Have the students discuss the dangers of amassing too much wealth.
- Afterward, stress that while Jesus did not see poverty as a virtue, and, indeed, made it abundantly clear that it is an evil to be remedied, he recognized a greater danger in poverty's opposite. He saw that people with too much money, like people with too much piety, are too easily seduced to reckon Salvation as something that is purchased.
- Have the students look up and read John 10:10b ("I came so that they might have life and have it more

abundantly"). Tell the students that Jesus wanted us to recognize that *what was really important—what our greatest value should be—was possessing life with God*, life that could not be dimmed or defeated by death. Emphasize that Jesus' mission and ministry were dedicated to helping us succeed in possessing that "abundant life."

- Tell the students to turn to the Primary Source Quotations section of this chapter on pages 105–106. Call attention to the quotation from Bl. Julian of Norwich. Read it aloud. Note that the human longing for God and the divine longing for humankind both coincide with Jesus' mission of bringing us abundant life.
- Have the students turn to "Paradox in Jesus' Teaching" on page 85. Go over the directions. Allow time for the students to complete the activity. Afterward, share findings.

People. For example, the Book of Daniel tells of a cosmic battle led by the Archangel Michael, a great tribulation, and the vindication of the righteous in the resurrection to eternal life. Other Jewish writings spoke of God bringing a new Heaven and a new earth ruled by justice, peace, and goodness. Some thought that God would send a Messiah, an anointed one, to usher in the Kingdom.

Jesus *is* the Messiah. He is God's only Son, Emmanuel—"God-with-us." He is the one who announced the coming of God's Kingdom, God's reign of peace, justice, truth, and goodness. He asked people to prepare for God's rule by turning from their sins and believing in the Gospel. Jesus not only announced the coming of the Kingdom of God, but he inaugurated it in his own person. As God's Son, Jesus Christ gathers all human beings into the family of God. His preaching and the signs he performed invite all people to gather around him. Especially in the Paschal Mystery of his Death and Resurrection, Jesus accomplished the coming of the Kingdom. Jesus announced the Kingdom of God from the beginning of his public ministry. In Galilee, Jesus preached, "This is the time of fulfillment. The kingdom of God is at hand. Repent, and believe in the gospel" (Mk 1:15).

Jesus' contemporaries understood the expression "Kingdom of God" to be a time in the future when God would show his power, pass judgment, and establish his divine rule over all of creation. At that time, every creature would recognize the one true God—the God who revealed himself to the Chosen People. When this future day would come, that is, when God's Kingdom is fully established, God's will would be accomplished on earth just as it is in Heaven.

The Kingdom of God has many unique characteristics, explained in the sections that follow.

The Kingdom Has a Present and Future Dimension

Matthew 13 contains a number of short parables where Jesus teaches about the "Kingdom of Heaven." Writing for a Jewish-Christian audience, Matthew used the expression "Kingdom of Heaven" rather than "Kingdom of God." He did this as a sign of reverence because Jews typically avoided saying the holy name of God. The parables in Matthew 13 (for example, the parables of the mustard seed and the yeast in Matthew 13:31–33) also point out that the Kingdom has both a present and future dimension. The Kingdom begins small, for example, in the preaching of Jesus, but it will bring about great results. The small mustard seed will grow into a large bush; the yeast will cause the dough to rise.

For Enrichment

Why are . . . poor people more ready to share their goods than rich people? The answer is easy: the poor have little to lose; the rich have more to lose and they are more attached to their possessions. Poverty provides a deeper motivation for understanding your neighbors, welcoming others and attending to those who are suffering. I would go so far as to say that poverty helps you understand what happiness is, what serenity is in life.

—Piero Gheddo

The world would become better off if people tried to become better.
And people would become better if they stopped trying to become better off.

—Peter Maurin

God does not create poverty. We do, because we do not share.

—Bl. Mother Teresa of Calcutta

Be careful, gentlemen, lest you set off planning to do good, but end up doing well.

—Msgr. J. J. O'Sullivan

The Ministry and Message of Jesus Christ 87

The Kingdom is present now, but it will flourish in the future.

Additionally, Matthew 13 reveals in the parables of the hidden treasure and the pearl of great price (Mt 13:44–46) that the Kingdom is extremely valuable; it requires our total commitment. The coming of the Kingdom also indicates that God will separate the good from the bad and reward the faithful and punish evildoers. This is the theme of the parable of the wheat and weeds (Mt 13:24–30, 36–43) and the fishing net (Mt 13:47–50).

The Kingdom Is Meant for All, Especially the Poor

God's Kingdom is open to everyone. Although it is first announced to the Chosen People, Christ invites all people to enter the Kingdom. The parable of the sower (Mt 13:1–9, 18–23) teaches that we must hear Jesus' words, take them to heart, and put them into practice. The Kingdom does not take root in some people because of their lack of understanding and being tempted by the devil; others are superficial, easily giving up on Jesus' Word when tempted by trials or persecutions; still others do not let the Word take root in them because of worldly concerns and the lure of wealth. But for those who hear Jesus' Word and properly understand it, the results will be amazing.

Although the Kingdom is open to everyone, Jesus announces it in a special way to the poor and the lowly. The Beatitudes in Luke's Gospel begin this way:

> Blessed are you who are poor,
> for the kingdom of God is yours.
> Blessed are you who are now hungry,
> for you will be satisfied.
> Blessed are you who are now weeping,
> for you will laugh. (Lk 6:20–21)

Jesus himself shared the life of the poor, from his humble birth to his Death on the cross, stripped of his clothes. He knew hunger and thirst. He had no possessions. "Foxes have dens and birds of the sky have nests, but the Son of Man has nowhere to rest his head" (Mt 8:20).

Jesus taught that we must respond to the needs of the poor by feeding the hungry, giving drink to the thirsty, welcoming the stranger, clothing the naked, caring for the sick, visiting the imprisoned (Mt 25:31–46). These are the conditions that he set for us to enter his Father's Kingdom at the time of judgment. In the parable of the great feast, Jesus says, "Blessed is the one who will dine in the kingdom of God" (Lk 14:15). A special invitation is extended to "the poor and the crippled, the blind and the lame" (Lk 14:21), that is, those whom society ignores—the helpless ones, the overlooked, the lost and powerless. God's Kingdom is open to them.

The Kingdom Is Open to Sinners

"Christ Jesus came into the world to save sinners" (1 Tm 1:15). He preached and ministered to sinners, including Levi and Zacchaeus. Levi and Zacchaeus were tax collectors or, in other words, public sinners in the eyes of the Jews because of their alignment with the Romans.

The Gospel of Luke describes how Levi gave a great banquet for Jesus at his house. The Pharisees and scribes thought that if you ate with sinners you showed approval of them. They scrupulously avoided table fellowship with tax collectors and sinners, fearing that they would be contaminated by their immorality. When they grumbled to Jesus' disciples about his association with sinners, Jesus said, "Those who are healthy do not need a physician, but the sick do. I have not come to call the righteous to repentance but sinners" (Lk 5:31–32).

Luke gives another example of a tax collector who followed Jesus—Zacchaeus (Lk 19:1–10). Jesus stayed at the house of Zacchaeus, again evoking the criticism of observers. But Zacchaeus won the praise of Jesus because he did what Jesus required—repented of his sins. To prove that he really did turn

Lesson 2 Objectives

The students will:

- summarize Jesus' key teachings about the Kingdom of God.
- describe how the Kingdom of God is in both the present and the future.
- appreciate that all are welcome in the Kingdom of God, especially the poor and sinners.
- investigate Jesus' Sermon on the Plain.
- appreciate that the Beatitudes are guidelines for Kingdom living.
- summarize the Beatitudes.
- examine and create a plan to combat prejudice.

Lesson 2 Preview

In this lesson the students consider the attributes of the Kingdom of God. They refresh their understanding of the radical nature of Jesus' teaching and study how they are called to live as Kingdom people.

Chapter 4: The Ministry and Message of Jesus Christ—Lesson 2

Bell Ringers

- Have the students share with a partner the results of their Scripture study from the feature "Noting the Gospel of Luke" (page 84). Have the students note whether they have chosen some of the same verses as their partner.
- Invite the students to write about or draw what they picture the Kingdom of God will be like. After giving them time to complete this activity, discuss and list on the board some common descriptions.

Teaching Approaches

Jesus Announces the Kingdom of God (pages 85-90)

- List on the board or in a PowerPoint lecture the following points about Jesus' key teachings about the Kingdom of God described in the *Catechism of the Catholic Church* (*CCC*, 541–546):
    - **The coming of the Kingdom of God was accomplished through the Paschal Mystery (*CCC*, 542).**
    - **The Kingdom of God is beginning in the Church (*CCC*, 541).**
    - **Everyone is called to enter the Kingdom of God (*CCC*, 543).**
    - **The Kingdom of God belongs to the poor and lowly (*CCC*, 544).**
    - **Jesus invites sinners into the Kingdom of God (*CCC*, 545).**
    - **To gain the Kingdom of God, one must give everything (*CCC*, 546).**
- Before moving on, take a moment to point out that while Mark and Luke use the term "Kingdom of God," Matthew does not. Ask: "What term does Matthew use instead of 'Kingdom of God' and why?" (*Kingdom of Heaven; so as not to offend his Jewish audience by using the name "God"*)
- Assign each student one of the following parables. Provide them with the following instructions: "Read the passage thoroughly. What do you think each person or thing represents? Which of the messages about

the Kingdom in the *Catechism of the Catholic Church* does this parable support?"

- Mustard Seed (Mt 13:31–32)
- Yeast in Dough (Mt 13:33)
- Wheat and Weeds (Mt 13:36–43)
- Treasure in the Field (Mt 13:44)
- The Pearl (Mt 13:45–46)
- The Net Filled with Fish (Mt 13:47–48)
- New and Old Treasures (Mt 13:51–53)

Discuss the parable of the sower (Mt 13:1–9, 18–30) as an example for the students to follow. Read the parable as a class (Mt 13:3–9); then read Jesus' explanation of the parable (Mt 13:18–23). Ask students to identify which of the messages from the *Catechism of the Catholic Church* the parable supports. Explain that this parable reveals that everyone is called to enter the Kingdom of God (*CCC*, 543), the Kingdom belongs to the poor and lowly (*CCC*, 544), and to gain the Kingdom, one must give everything (*CCC*, 546). Once the students have finished their assignments, have them join other students who were assigned the same parable to check their interpretations. Then, using responses from each group, record the name of each parable next to the corresponding messages from the *Catechism of the Catholic Church* on the board or projector.

- Next, set the stage for investigating Jesus' Sermon on the Plain. Explain the following: Jesus has gathered a large number of disciples. He then goes up a mountain to pray all night, after which he chooses twelve disciples to be his Apostles. He descends the mountain to meet the rest of his disciples and numerous curious onlookers. There, on a level plain, Jesus delivers his sermon—a sermon directed at his disciples, who, Jesus knows, will be persecuted because they are his followers.
- Distribute copies of Chapter 4, Handout 2, "Definitely Different Viewpoints." Invite the students to tell you what they see in each one. After the students respond, note that what we think we are looking at can immediately change, simply by shifting our point of view, that is, by focusing on the negative or the void space. What we perceive to be a young woman becomes an older woman; a vase becomes two profiles; an inkblot becomes the face of Jesus; an elephant with four legs becomes one with five. Or vice versa. Pictures like these topple our assumptions. Jesus did the same with his Beatitudes.

88 Jesus Christ: Source of Our Salvation

Beatitudes
Beatitude means "supreme happiness." The eight Beatitudes preached by Jesus in the Sermon on the Mount respond to our natural desire for happiness.

prejudice
An unsubstantiated or preformed judgment about an individual or group.

from a life of sin, Zacchaeus told the Lord that he gave away half of his possessions to the poor and repaid four times over anyone he had defrauded of money. Jesus assured the reformed sinner that he was saved, "For the Son of Man has come to seek and to save what was lost" (Lk 19:10).

By his association with sinners and his care for their welfare, Jesus showed forth God's mercy, a sign of the coming of the Kingdom.

The Beatitudes Model the Kingdom

Because a new age has dawned and God's reign is here, Jesus expects his followers to live in such a way that they will attract others to God's Kingdom. The **Beatitudes** preached in the Sermon on the Mount (Mt 5–7) instruct his followers on how to live to be able to enter the Kingdom of God (Mt 5:20). In Luke's Gospel, the Beatitudes are presented in the Sermon on the Plain (Lk 6:17–49), about a third of the length of the Sermon on the Mount. Luke's Beatitudes correspond to the first, fourth, second, and eighth of Matthew's Beatitudes, but with some differences. The fourth Beatitude in Luke is essential because it shows that Jesus' disciples have identified with the Lord, who has suffered rejection:

> Blessed are you when people hate you,
> and when they exclude and insult you,
> and denounce your name as evil
> on account of the Son of Man. (Lk 6:22)

The Beatitudes teach that wealth can blind us to the truth that God is the source of all gifts, which we should share with others. Jesus compares wealthy and well-fed people to false prophets who spoke flattering words to get people to think highly of them. What Jesus requires of us is to love, even our enemies:

> But to you who hear I say, love your enemies, do good to those who hate you, bless those who curse you, pray for those who mistreat you. (Lk 6:27)

The Kingdom of God requires high standards. Not only must we live by the Golden Rule—"Do to others as you would have them do to you" (Lk 6:31)—but we must do even more. We must imitate God himself by being kind to ungrateful and wicked people. As Jesus teaches, we must "Be merciful, just as [also] your Father is merciful" (Lk 6:36). Imitating the Father requires that we not judge or condemn others. Rather, we must be generous. We must give without counting the cost because God himself is so generous. He will shower his blessings on us, his children:

> Give and gifts will be given to you; a good measure, packed together, shaken down, and overflowing, will be poured into your lap. For the measure with which you measure will in return be measured out to you. (Lk 6:38)

Like a good tree bearing good fruit (see Lk 6:43–45), disciples will bring about good results only if they listen to the words of Jesus and make them

Lesson 2 Homework

1. Tell the students to write out their answers to the For Review questions on page 89.
2. Have them journal their response to the For Reflection activity on page 90.
3. Direct the students to read the text section "Jesus Teaches About the Kingdom of God in Parables" (pages 90–95) in preparation for their next session.
4. Remind the students to continue working on their chosen Ongoing Assignments.

come alive in their lives. Words are not enough: "Why do you call me, 'Lord, Lord,' but not do what I command?" (Lk 6:46). A person who comes to Jesus, listens to his words, and acts on them is like a person who builds his house on a foundation of rock so as to withstand the floods of a river. The foundation of a Christian life, of working for God's Kingdom, requires both listening and action, hearing Jesus and obeying him.

For Review

1. What two things did Jesus ask people to do when he announced the coming of the Kingdom of God?
2. How do the parables of the mustard seed and yeast (Mt 13:31-33) stress both the present and future dimensions of the Kingdom of God?
3. What is the meaning of the parable of the wheat and weeds (Mt 13:24-30, 36-43)?
4. According to the parable of the sower (Mt 13:1-9, 18-23), name two situations that keep people from entering the Kingdom of God.
5. Identify Levi and Zacchaeus. Why did Jesus associate with tax collectors?
6. List three things from the Sermon on the Plain (Lk 6:17-49) that the Lord requires of his followers.

Examining Prejudice

When Jesus said to "stop judging and you will not be judged" (Lk 6:37), he was talking about the prejudicial judgments that people make about others, that is, judgments made with insufficient evidence. Prejudice diminishes people and results in behaviors like talking against people, avoidance, discrimination, and even violence.

Examine the prejudices that might be exhibited in your school toward the following groups of people. Discuss any stereotypes ("oversimplified generalizations about persons or groups without regard for individual differences") attached to this group. (For example, "All rich people are selfish.") Then devise a concrete plan of action that you and your classmates can take to combat the prejudice directed toward one or more of the groups you discussed.

- overweight girls
- overweight boys
- a particular ethnic group
- a particular racial group
- non-Catholic students
- star athletes
- elderly teachers
- add to this list

For more information on the topic, review the booklet, *101 Ways to Combat Prejudice*, a joint project of Barnes and Noble and the Anti-Defamation League, for some ideas on how to fight prejudice.

- Tell the students that Jesus recognized that we make assumptions about God's nature and preferences based on how we view the world and the people in it. Over the centuries, people had established categories for things good and things bad, distinguishing virtue from vice, good from evil, light from darkness, clean from unclean, blessing from curse. All things "good" were considered pure, whole, new, healthy, strong—obviously loved by God. All things "bad" were considered fouled, broken, old, diseased, and weak—obviously displeasing to God. Jesus gave us something different to consider.
- Call on one of the students to read aloud Luke 6:20–26. Afterward, note how Jesus confounds conventional thinking. Surely the question running through the minds of Jesus' listeners is, "How can the poor, the hungry, or the sorrowing be blessed?" Jesus is proposing paradoxes again and insisting that in the world of God's blessings the marginalized have the center stage.
- Divide the class into four small groups. Assign one Beatitude and its corresponding woe to each group. Have the groups list ways in which they see their peers honoring the Beatitude—that is, reaching out to the poor, feeding the hungry, comforting the sorrowful, dealing with prejudice/persecution. Then ask the teens to list ways their peers are *not* honoring the Beatitude. Finally, ask the students to list specific

For Review Answers (page 89)

1. Repent and believe the Good News (Gospel).
2. Answers will vary but should evidence an understanding that like the seed or yeast in dough, the Kingdom is now present, but it will flourish in the future when the seed sprouts and blossoms and when the yeast expands the dough.
3. God will separate the good from the bad and will reward the faithful and punish the evildoers.
4. Answers may contain any two of the following: lack of understanding; temptation of the devil; giving in to trials and persecution; lure of wealth; or other worldly concerns.
5. Both were tax collectors. They were hated individuals because they worked for the Romans and, since they were paid on commission, routinely skimmed money from their tax collections. Jesus wanted to let outsiders in, to offer sinners the opportunity to repent, and to make it clear that repentant sinners were welcome in the Kingdom of God.
6. Jesus requires his followers to love even their enemies; follow the Golden Rule; imitate God; and listen to the words of Jesus and make them come alive in their hearts.

ways teens can live out the Beatitude today. (*Note:* If necessary, remind the class that they are not to list the actions of specific individuals.)

- Ask each group to choose a spokesperson to share lists with the class. While the groups are sharing, invite dialog about the issues that are raised.
- Conclude by emphasizing that our vision of reality, about power and weakness, wealth and poverty, blessing and woe, is not the vision of God's Kingdom.
- Point out the text section "The Kingdom Is Open to Sinners" (page 87). Tell the students that by his association with—especially his celebrating with—perceived sinners like Levi and Zacchaeus, Jesus was establishing a new community (Kingdom) of justice and compassion and revealing God's love and mercy at work.
- Ask the students to read Luke 6:27–36. Then call attention to the first sentence of the third paragraph of the text section "The Beatitudes Model the Kingdom" (page 88): "The Kingdom of God requires high standards." Then ask the students to name the Golden Rule. (*Do unto others as you would have them do unto you.*) Stress how in the Kingdom of God living by the Golden Rule is not enough. Jesus is calling us to a generosity beyond reciprocity. Kingdom living demands we go *beyond* the Golden Rule to love even our enemies—and who are these enemies? They are those mentioned in Luke's fourth Beatitude: the people who hate, exclude, insult, and denounce us (Lk 6:22).
- Have the students read Luke 6:38. Explain that Jesus is telling us that Kingdom people are people of love-in-action and that the measure of love given us will be determined by the measure of our active love for others. Then ask:
    - What measure did Jesus use to measure love? (*Accept all reasonable replies and then refer the students to John 15:13: "No one has greater love than this, to lay down one's life for one's friends."*)
    - What measure will be used to measure our love? (*Accept all reasonable replies and then refer the students to Matthew 25:40: "Amen, I say to you, whatever you did for one of these least brothers of mine, you did for me."*)
- Call attention to the feature "Examining Prejudice" (page 89). Allow the students time to talk about how they stereotype others or have prejudice toward individuals or groups. Stress that such judgmental actions

For Reflection

Think about three different people, for example, a sibling, a classmate, a parent, a teacher, or a teammate. For each person, write a few sentences on how you would like them to treat *you*. Then, in light of what you wrote, list a specific thing you can do for each of the persons you wrote about.

Jesus Teaches about the Kingdom of God in Parables (*CCC*, 546)

In teaching about the Kingdom of God, Jesus often told stories to reveal what the Kingdom was like. He drew from images that were familiar to his audience, including illustrations from farming, fishing, and everyday life. Jesus told stories in the form of a **parable**. In general, a parable is an analogy where one reality is compared to something that is better known. Jesus' parables teach about some aspect of the Kingdom of God. Jesus wanted his hearers to think about what living in the Kingdom requires of us right now and how cooperating with God's reign looks to a glorious future of eternal life with our loving Father.

parable
A favorite teaching device of Jesus in which he told a short story with a striking, memorable comparison that taught a religious message, usually about some aspect of God's Kingdom.

The subject of Jesus' parables ranged from fishing and farming to wedding celebrations and joyful meals celebrated with friends. He talked about planting seeds, baking bread, and winemaking. His stories involved characters like an unjust judge, good servants, a wayward son, a persistent widow, a good shepherd, and a loving father. The elements in his stories include ordinary objects like lost coins, weeds, bread, and withered trees.

Jesus' parables are important for many reasons:

1. *They convey the heart of his message.* To learn from them is to learn much about the major theme of his preaching about the Kingdom of God.
2. *They show that Jesus was an outstanding teacher.* Parables like the Good Samaritan and the Prodigal Son are among the most famous stories ever told. They are easy to remember and therefore easily bring to mind important points in Jesus' teaching.
3. *They give us a good idea of how Jesus was able to defend himself against opponents.* For example, when questioned why his disciples do not fast the way the disciples of John the Baptist or the Pharisees did, Jesus compared himself to a bridegroom at a wedding. Because he is present, it is a time for celebration. He also told why it is unwise to sew new cloth on old cloth and pour new wine in old wineskins (Lk 5:33–39). The point of these parables is that the Gospel is new and revolutionary. The

For Enrichment

Read and discuss the following:

The Radical Kingdom

This doctrine of the Kingdom of Heaven (God), which was the main teaching of Jesus and which plays so small a part in the Christian creeds, is surely one of the most revolutionary doctrines that ever stirred and changed human thought.

—H. G. Wells

The New Racism

Many times the new face of racism is the computer printout, the graph of profits and losses, the pink slip, the nameless statistic. Today's racism flourishes in the triumph of private concern over public responsibility, individual success over social commitment and personal fulfillment over authentic compassion.

—US Catholic Bishops, *Brothers and Sisters to Us*

are not actions of Kingdom people. Remind the students that Jesus never asks us to be judges; rather, he calls us to be witnesses to the Good News. Even God does not judge anyone in this life. Neither should we.

- Provide access to a computer and printer to download the booklet from the Anti-Defamation League mentioned in the text (page 89). Then, drawing on ideas from the booklet, help the students develop a way to end prejudice toward one or more of the groups they identified.

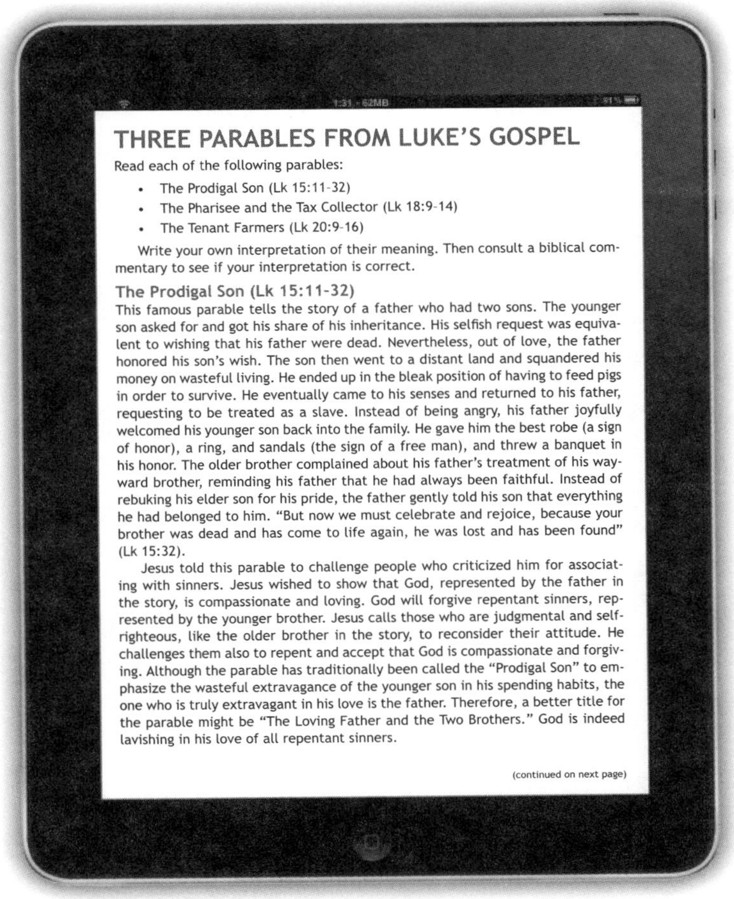

THREE PARABLES FROM LUKE'S GOSPEL

Read each of the following parables:

- The Prodigal Son (Lk 15:11-32)
- The Pharisee and the Tax Collector (Lk 18:9-14)
- The Tenant Farmers (Lk 20:9-16)

Write your own interpretation of their meaning. Then consult a biblical commentary to see if your interpretation is correct.

The Prodigal Son (Lk 15:11-32)

This famous parable tells the story of a father who had two sons. The younger son asked for and got his share of his inheritance. His selfish request was equivalent to wishing that his father were dead. Nevertheless, out of love, the father honored his son's wish. The son then went to a distant land and squandered his money on wasteful living. He ended up in the bleak position of having to feed pigs in order to survive. He eventually came to his senses and returned to his father, requesting to be treated as a slave. Instead of being angry, his father joyfully welcomed his younger son back into the family. He gave him the best robe (a sign of honor), a ring, and sandals (the sign of a free man), and threw a banquet in his honor. The older brother complained about his father's treatment of his wayward brother, reminding his father that he had always been faithful. Instead of rebuking his elder son for his pride, the father gently told his son that everything he had belonged to him. "But now we must celebrate and rejoice, because your brother was dead and has come to life again, he was lost and has been found" (Lk 15:32).

Jesus told this parable to challenge people who criticized him for associating with sinners. Jesus wished to show that God, represented by the father in the story, is compassionate and loving. God will forgive repentant sinners, represented by the younger brother. Jesus calls those who are judgmental and self-righteous, like the older brother in the story, to reconsider their attitude. He challenges them also to repent and accept that God is compassionate and forgiving. Although the parable has traditionally been called the "Prodigal Son" to emphasize the wasteful extravagance of the younger son in his spending habits, the one who is truly extravagant in his love is the father. Therefore, a better title for the parable might be "The Loving Father and the Two Brothers." God is indeed lavishing in his love of all repentant sinners.

(continued on next page)

Chapter 4: The Ministry and Message of Jesus Christ—Lesson 3

Lesson 3 Objectives

The students will:

- summarize the purpose, meanings, and types of parables.
- recognize that Jesus employed parables to give us clues to the Kingdom of God.
- summarize the six primary messages of Jesus' parables.
- analyze three parables.
- appreciate that they are valuable, loved by God, and invited into the Kingdom.

Lesson 3 Preview

In this lesson the students discover how Jesus used parables to invite us unconditionally into the joy of the Kingdom of God. (*Note:* Please take note of the letter writing activity [Chapter 4, Handout 3, "I See Myself . . ."]. Decide whether to write a sample letter yourself.)

Bell Ringers

- Ask the students to offer their responses to the six For Review questions on page 89 (answers are on page 105 of this text). Be sure to allow the students to ask any other questions they may have.
- Invite the students to mention their favorite of Jesus' parables and to explain why.

Teaching Approaches

Jesus Teaches About the Kingdom of God in Parables (pages 90-95)

- Write the word **parable** on the board. Explain that the word derives from a Greek term meaning "comparison." Point out the following about parables:
    - In contrast to fables that arise from fantasy (e.g., Aesop's the tortoise and the hare, or the fox and the grapes), parables generally come from familiar everyday life.
    - A parable's meaning is at the same time simple and profound. Parables demonstrate a lesson to be learned or a quality to be garnered in a timeless, universal way.
- Call attention to page 90 and the three reasons why Jesus' parables are so important. Go over the list with the students. Point out that Jesus used parables to reveal truth in an attention-grabbing, out-of-the-ordinary way to give us clues to the Kingdom of God.
- Continue with the text "The Message of the Parables" (pages 93–95). Note the six types of messages we can garner from parables, and list them on the board:
    - **Salvation is here!**

- **The Kingdom of God is a pure gift.**
- **God loves sinners.**
- **The Good News about the Kingdom of God requires an urgent response.**
- **The Good News of God's Kingdom demands repentance.**
- **Following Jesus may bring suffering.**

- Have students fold a piece of notebook paper in thirds as though they were folding a letter, then have them fold it in half again in order to create six boxes. Have the students title each box with one of the six messages from page 93. Direct the students to reread the textbook description of the message and then write it in their own words. Then, using the brief description of each message and the chart on page 94, have the students write down the names of the parables that reveal each message in the appropriate box. You may consider dividing the students into groups to accomplish this activity.
- Finally, summarize Jesus' use of parables by explaining that all of them are invitations to become part of the Kingdom of God. We respond to those invitations by uniting ourselves with Jesus himself. And as Matthew 25 makes clear, the way we do this is by loving others, by recognizing that no one is excluded from the Kingdom, and by understanding that if *we* exclude anyone—for whatever reason—we are excluding Jesus himself.
- Allow time for the students to complete the Scripture activity described in the feature "Three Parables from Luke's Gospel" (page 91). Have Bible commentaries available and/or provide access to online biblical commentaries, for example, www.bcbsr.com/survey/jpbl.html or www.rc.net/wcc/readings/parables.htm. Likewise, refer the students to the commentaries on these three parables in the text (pages 91–92).
- Afterward, call on different students to share their interpretation of one of the parables. Ask questions like the following about each parable:
  - How does your interpretation differ from that of the biblical commentaries in the textbook or provided in class?
  - Does this parable reveal a theological truth? Explain.
  - Does the parable suggest a way to behave or an attitude to possess? Explain.

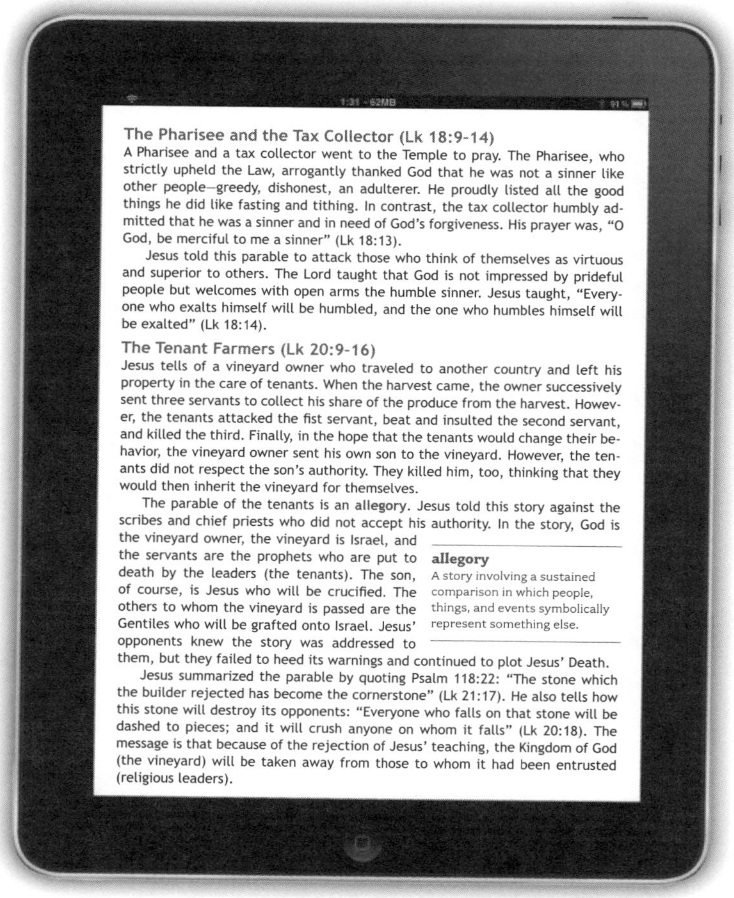

The Pharisee and the Tax Collector (Lk 18:9-14)
A Pharisee and a tax collector went to the Temple to pray. The Pharisee, who strictly upheld the Law, arrogantly thanked God that he was not a sinner like other people—greedy, dishonest, an adulterer. He proudly listed all the good things he did like fasting and tithing. In contrast, the tax collector humbly admitted that he was a sinner and in need of God's forgiveness. His prayer was, "O God, be merciful to me a sinner" (Lk 18:13).

Jesus told this parable to attack those who think of themselves as virtuous and superior to others. The Lord taught that God is not impressed by prideful people but welcomes with open arms the humble sinner. Jesus taught, "Everyone who exalts himself will be humbled, and the one who humbles himself will be exalted" (Lk 18:14).

The Tenant Farmers (Lk 20:9-16)
Jesus tells of a vineyard owner who traveled to another country and left his property in the care of tenants. When the harvest came, the owner successively sent three servants to collect his share of the produce from the harvest. However, the tenants attacked the fist servant, beat and insulted the second servant, and killed the third. Finally, in the hope that the tenants would change their behavior, the vineyard owner sent his own son to the vineyard. However, the tenants did not respect the son's authority. They killed him, too, thinking that they would then inherit the vineyard for themselves.

The parable of the tenants is an **allegory**. Jesus told this story against the scribes and chief priests who did not accept his authority. In the story, God is the vineyard owner, the vineyard is Israel, and the servants are the prophets who are put to death by the leaders (the tenants). The son, of course, is Jesus who will be crucified. The others to whom the vineyard is passed are the Gentiles who will be grafted onto Israel. Jesus' opponents knew the story was addressed to them, but they failed to heed its warnings and continued to plot Jesus' Death.

allegory
A story involving a sustained comparison in which people, things, and events symbolically represent something else.

Jesus summarized the parable by quoting Psalm 118:22: "The stone which the builder rejected has become the cornerstone" (Lk 21:17). He also tells how this stone will destroy its opponents: "Everyone who falls on that stone will be dashed to pieces; and it will crush anyone on whom it falls" (Lk 20:18). The message is that because of the rejection of Jesus' teaching, the Kingdom of God (the vineyard) will be taken away from those to whom it had been entrusted (religious leaders).

Lesson 3 Homework

1. Ask the students to complete the For Reflection activity (page 95) and to be ready to share their paragraphs at their next session.
2. Direct the students to write out their answers to the five For Review questions on pages 93–95.
3. Tell the students to read the text section "Jesus' Miracles: Signs of the Kingdom of God" (pages 95–100) in preparation for their next session.
4. Encourage the students to continue working on their chosen Ongoing Assignments.

Kingdom of God is an entirely new way of believing and living.

The Message of the Parables

The Gospels remind us that Jesus "taught them at length in parables" (Mk 4:2). Listed on the next page are the parables of Jesus recorded in the Gospels of Mathew, Mark, and Luke.

The forty-one parables contain the heart of the Good News. A short summary of the primary messages of the parables (with references) follows:

- *Salvation is here!* Jesus ushers in the Kingdom of God just as spring brings leaves to the fig tree (Mt 24:32–35). Like a mustard seed, the Kingdom begins small but will grow (Mk 4:30–32). God makes it grow by his own design (Mk 4:26–29) and eventually it will reach a great harvest (Lk 8:5–8).
- *The Kingdom of God is a pure gift.* Jesus invites everyone into the Kingdom, even people we might consider unworthy (Lk 14:15–24). The heavenly banquet is for everyone (Mt 22:1–14). God is like a vineyard owner who freely dispenses his gifts, far beyond what one has earned (Mt 20:1–16). For our part, we are servants who can only joyfully and gratefully accept God's love (Lk 17:7–10).
- *God loves sinners.* The essence of the Good News is God's love for sinners. He is the Good Shepherd who seeks out the lost sheep (Lk 15:3–7) or the woman who searches frantically for her lost coin and rejoices when she finds it (Lk 15:8–10). He is the merciful father who welcomes back the lost son and deals gently with another son who harshly judges his brother (Lk 15:11–32). God's joy over the returned sinner is great. He only asks in return that we forgive others as we have been forgiven (Mt 18:23–35).
- *The Good News about the Kingdom of God requires an urgent response.* The time for decision is now. We must be ever watchful for God's return (Lk 12:35–40). The Bridegroom (Jesus) can come at any time (Mt 25:1–13). Some people will refuse to respond to him, like tenants in a vineyard who refuse to give the owner his proper share (Mt 21:33–46). They will complain like little children who are acting like spoilsports (Lk 7:29–35). In the end, they will be judged. Wheat will be separated from the weeds (Mt 13:24–30), and bad fish will be tossed out of the net (Mt 13:47–50). If the Kingdom is found, one must be wily like a crafty businessman in order to gain it (Lk 14:25–35). It is like finding a pearl or a hidden treasure; one must give all to gain it (Mt 13:44–46).
- *The Good News of God's Kingdom demands repentance.* Having accepted the gift of the Kingdom, we must be prepared for the feast (Mt 22:1–14). We must be faithful (Mt 21:28–32). We must ask for God's forgiveness, as did the sinful tax collector (Lk 18:9–14). We must forgive others (Mt 5:25–26) and pray without ceasing, like the friend begging for bread at midnight (Lk 11:5–8) or the woman badgering the unjust judge (Lk 18:1–8). Above all else, we must love everyone, even our enemies, following the example of the Good Samaritan (Lk 10:25–37). Finally, Jesus' followers must put the goods of this world into proper perspective; for example, money is a means to Heaven, not an end in itself (Lk 12:13–21; 16:1–12).
- *Following Jesus may bring suffering.* Those who suffer for Jesus will be rewarded while those who take advantage of others will be punished (Lk 16:19–31). If we respond to the "least of these," we respond to Jesus and will enter into the fullness of God's Kingdom for eternity (Mt 25:31–46).

For Review

1. What is a parable?
2. What is the general message of Jesus' parables?
3. What is the meaning of the parable of the Prodigal Son?

(continued on page 95)

   - Does the parable present its message in an attention-grabbing, out-of-the-ordinary way? Describe how it turns conventional expectations upside down.
   - Speaking personally, what is the most important truth about God and/or God's Kingdom that this parable helped you discover?
   - What does the parable help you discover about yourself?

- Invite the students to imagine that God, like the father in the story of the Prodigal Son, is throwing a party. Ask:
   - Whom would God invite to the party?
   - Whom would God exclude?
   - How do you think guests would feel when they received an invitation?
   - What sort of party would God have?
- Tell the students to read (again) the parable of the feast in Luke 14:15–24. Afterward, ask:
   - Why doesn't the host of the party simply call it off when the first guests do not show up?
   - What does the fact that the host sent out his servants tell you about the host?
   - Do people seem free to choose whether or not to attend the party?

For Review Answers (pages 93-95)

1. A parable is a short story with a striking, memorable comparison that Jesus used to reveal a religious truth about some aspect of the Kingdom of God.
2. Answers will vary but should show an understanding that every parable is an invitation to become part of the Kingdom of God.
3. God is a compassionate, loving, non-judgmental father whose love cannot be earned or depleted.
4. To reject the notion that the outwardly religious are superior to other people and to show that God welcomes the humble sinner. (*Note:* Both the tax collector and the Pharisee were spiritually bereft. It was only the sinful tax collector, however, who recognized his spiritual poverty. At the end of his rope, he understood that only God could save him. Unlike the rich Pharisee, the tax collector was so "poor" he didn't even have pride to swallow.)
5. Answers should evidence understanding that the vineyard owner is God, the tenants are the religious leaders of Israel, the servants are God's prophets, and the son is Jesus himself.

Extending the Lesson

Invite the students to work in small groups and then to present one of Jesus' parables in a modern setting. They may simply rewrite the parable, or they could choose to present it as a song, a poem, a rap, a skit, etc.

- What do you think Jesus is saying about this party-throwing God?
- What does the parable tell you about the sort of interest God takes in his guests?
- If you attended the party, what do you think God might say to you?

Record the students' responses to the final question above on the board. If the students do not suggest positive statements about themselves, encourage them to think carefully about the God whom Jesus revealed in his parables.

- Distribute copies of Chapter 4, Handout 3, "I See Myself . . ." On the first half of the handout, have the students write thank-you letters to themselves—thank-you letters for you being you—and to follow only one rule when writing: *you only write good and positive things about yourself. You may not write anything negative*. Provide time for them to compose their letters. (*Note:* If, prior to class, you chose to write a letter about yourself, read it to get the students started.)
- When the students finish their letters, point out the second part of the handout, "And God Sees Me. . . " Have the students think about how they would answer the question: "What might God believe about me?" Then tell the students to complete the statement by drawing on the good qualities they listed in their thank-you letter to themselves.
- Afterward, encourage sharing, either with a partner or with the whole class.

Parable	Matthew	Mark	Luke
A Lamp Under a Bushel	5:15–17	4:21–22	8:16–18
New Cloth on Old Garments	9:16	2:21	5:36
New Wine in Old Wine Skins	9:17	2:22	5:37
The Sower	13:3–23	4:2–20	8:4–15
The Mustard Seed	13:31–32	4:30–32	13:18–19
Yeast	13:33		
The Tenant Farmers	21:33–45	12:1–12	20:9–19
The Budding Fig Tree	24:32–35	13:28–32	21:29–33
A House Built on a Rock	7:24–27		6:47–49
Wayward Children	11:16–19		7:31–35
Leaven	13:33		13:20–21
Lost Sheep	18:12–14		15:3–7
A Treasure Hidden in a Field	13:44		
A Pearl of Great Value	13:45–46		
Dragnet	13:47–50		
The Unmerciful Servant	18:23–25		
Laborers in the Vineyard	20:1–16		
A Father and Two Sons	21:28–32		
The Marriage Feast for the King's Son	22:1–14		
The Wise and Foolish Maidens	25:1–13		
The Servants and Their Talents	25:14–30		
Separating Sheep from Goats	25:31–46		
A Seed Growing Silently		4:26–29	
The Doorkeeper on Watch		13:34–37	
Two Debtors			7:41–43
The Good Samaritan			10:25–37
A Friend at Midnight			11:5–10
The Rich Fool			12:16–21
Watchful Servants			12:35–38
The Wise Steward	24:45–51		12:42–48
The Barren Fig Tree			13:6–9
Dinner Guests			14:16–24
A Lost Coin			15:8–10
The Prodigal Son			15:11–32
The Dishonest Steward			16:1–13
The Rich Man and Lazarus			16:19–31
Useless Servants			17:7–10
The Persistent Widow			18:1–8
The Pharisee and the Tax Collector			18:9–14
Ten Pounds			19:11–27

4. Why did Jesus tell the parable of the Pharisee and the tax collector (Lk 18:9-14)?
5. Explain how the parable of the Tenant Farmers (Lk 20:9-16) is an allegory that applies to Jesus himself.

For Reflection

The basic message of the parable of the Good Samaritan (Lk 10:25-37) is that we need to love our neighbors, which includes our enemies. But this parable has a richer meaning as well. For example, St. Augustine saw this parable as an allegory and interpreted it this way:

Jerusalem	=	Heaven
Jericho	=	the world
robbers	=	Satan and the bad angels
wounded man	=	Adam
priest	=	the Law (Torah)
Levite	=	prophets
Samaritan	=	Jesus
the inn	=	the Church
Samaritan's return	=	Jesus' return at the end of time

Using the allegorical elements from St. Augustine, write a paragraph explaining what the parable means.

Jesus' Miracles: Signs of the Kingdom of God (*CCC*, 547-550)

Jesus' miracles were signs that the Messianic age had dawned. They attest that the Father had sent him. They also invite people to believe in him. And Jesus responds to their faith by granting what they ask. Miracles, therefore, can strengthen faith in Jesus as God's Son, doing his work. Miracles are defined as observable events that the laws of nature cannot explain. They happen as the result of God's action. Scripture calls Jesus' miracles "works, wonders, and signs," which accompany his words. They reveal that the Kingdom of God was present in his very person. They prove that he is the promised Messiah, the Son of God.

However, the marvelous signs Jesus performed did not automatically cause people to believe. His opponents could not deny that he healed people and performed other miracles. But they questioned the source of his power; sometimes they even said that it came from Satan. For example, this happened when he drove a demon out of a mute person who was then able to speak. Some attributed this to the power of Satan; others wanted a clear sign from Heaven. But Jesus knew that their charge was absurd. His miracles always resulted in a great good, revealing the defeat of evil and God's power over Satan. Jesus challenged his critics by saying:

> Every kingdom divided against itself will be laid to waste and house will fall against house. And if Satan is divided against himself, how will his kingdom stand? (Lk 11:17–18)

Jesus clearly showed how his works and signs point to the coming of God's Kingdom. He asked his critics to consider the truth of following: "But if it is by the finger of God that [I] drive out demons, then the kingdom of God has come upon you" (Lk 11:20). Jesus' miracles were clear signs of the coming of the Kingdom of God.

Jesus performed miracles to free people from earthly problems and the evils of hunger, injustice, illness, and even death. However, Jesus' mission was not to abolish all human sufferings here on earth, but to free us from the worst slavery, that of sin. Furthermore, Jesus' exorcisms (see below) offered freedom from the power of demons. They prefigured the victory of his Paschal Mystery, which

Lesson 4 Objectives

The students will:

- describe the four types and purposes of Jesus' miracles.
- understand how all miracles are signs of the power of God's Kingdom.
- categorize Jesus' miracles into four types of miracles.
- interpret some of Jesus' miracles.

Lesson 4 Preview

Miracles are powerful signs of God's presence and action on our behalf. In this lesson the students discover how Jesus' miracles brought healing, wholeness, inclusion, and reconciliation—all portents of Jesus' approaching victory over sin and death.

Chapter 4: The Ministry and Message of Jesus Christ—Lesson 4

Bell Ringers

- Ask the students to offer their responses to the five For Review questions on pages 93–95 (answers are on page 109 of this text). Be sure to allow the students to ask any other questions they may have.
- Invite the students to share their paragraphs regarding allegory from the For Reflection exercise on page 95. Note similarities and differences in the students' interpretations.
- Whether or not the students have studied *Jesus Christ: God's Revelation to the World* and *Jesus Christ: His Mission and Ministry*, take a moment to set the stage for their understanding Jesus' miracles. Present the following information in your own words:

> In the world of Jesus' time most ordinary people felt that they were powerless in the face of the many forces that threatened human life and freedom: political injustice, widespread disease, evil forces, rampant superstition, sinfulness, and death. Even nature itself posed constant powerful threats to livelihood and well-being.
>
> In the face of this collective powerlessness, Jesus' miracles served as acts of power and control, which demonstrated the spread of God's influence into areas of life that hitherto had seemed to be the province only of evil and off limits, so to speak, to the divine. Jesus' miracles were signs that the Kingdom of God had arrived, and the reign of Satan was on the downswing. They spoke the human hope for re-creation and they were signs of God's abiding love for all creation.

Teaching Approaches

Jesus' Miracles: Signs of the Kingdom of God (pages 95-100)

- Use the board to tell/remind the students that the word for **miracle** in the Synoptic Gospels is *dynamis* ("act of power"). In John's Gospel it is *ergon* ("work") and/or *semion* ("sign"). Note that Jesus' miracles, then, are powerful acts or works that have a meaning *beyond* what can be experienced by the senses (i.e., they are signs of something more).

- Distribute copies of Chapter 4, Handout 4, "Works, Wonders, and Signs." Tell the students that the numbered elements summarize the material in the text and delineate what Jesus' miracles do. Go through each with the students, noting how each element also points to something *more*: (1) the Kingdom of God, (2) the divine mission, (3) an invitation to faith, and (4) the Paschal Mystery.
- Call attention to the types of Jesus' miracles listed on the handout. Ask the students to draw on their reading of the text and to offer examples of each type.

96 Jesus Christ: Source of Our Salvation

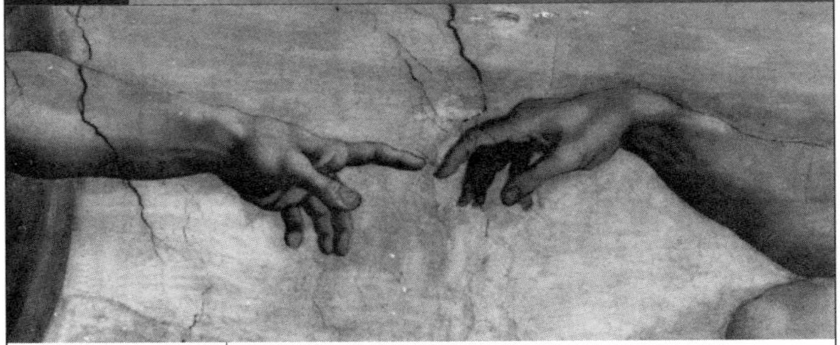

blasphemy
Any thought, word, or act that expresses hatred or contempt for Christ, God, the Church, saints, or holy things.

would abolish the power of Satan, defeat sin and death, and win for us eternal life with God.

Kinds of Miracles

Jesus performed various signs, all of which pointed to the coming of the Kingdom of God in Christ's very life. The four examples discussed below are from the Gospel of Luke.

Physical Healings

Physical healings demonstrate Jesus' power over sin and reveal that the coming of God's Kingdom brings wholeness and true happiness. They also reveal who Jesus is.

In Luke's Gospel, there are a variety of healings. For example, Jesus healed Simon Peter's mother-in-law. He also healed a leper who approached him with faith, "Lord, if you wish, you can make me clean" (Lk 5:12). Jesus stretched out his hand and touched the leper and cured him.

Jesus also responded to the faith of a Gentile—a centurion—who pleaded with Jesus to cure his slave (Lk 7:1–10). Jesus was amazed at the man's faith and granted his wish.

On another occasion, Jesus cured a blind beggar who shouted at him as he walked by: "Jesus, son of David, have pity on me!" (Lk 18:38). Jesus then asked the man, "'What do you want me to do for you?' He replied, 'Lord, please let me see'" (Lk 18:41). Jesus granted the blind man his wish. The man immediately followed Jesus and praised God. This miracle teaches how Jesus wants us to approach him and to ask him directly for what we need. He responds to our faith.

Another time, Jesus cured a man with a withered hand on the Sabbath (Lk 6:6–11). Some of the religious leaders thought that healing on the Sabbath was forbidden by the Law, but Jesus asked them, "Is it lawful to do good on the Sabbath rather than to do evil, to save life rather than to

Chapter 4, Handout 4, "Works, Wonders, and Signs" Answers

- Physical Healings—power over *illness and sin*
- Exorcisms—power over *Satan and evil*
- Nature Miracles—power over *nature*
- Raisings from Death—power over *life and death*

Lesson 4 Homework

1. Direct the students to write out their answers to the For Review questions on pages 98–100.
2. Tell the students to read the text section "Two Great Miracles of Jesus" (pages 100–104) to prepare for their next session.
3. Tell the students to begin wrapping up work on their chosen Ongoing Assignments.

destroy it?" (Lk 6:9). Jesus healed the man, thus proving that he is Lord of the Sabbath while teaching that the Son of God came to do good works.

In Luke 5:17–26 one of Jesus' healings revealed his identity as God's Son. A paralyzed man was lowered through the roof tiles into the crowded room where Jesus was teaching. After Jesus saw the faith of those who helped their friend, he said, "As for you, your sins are forgiven" (Lk 5:20). This outraged some scribes and Pharisees who were present. They believed Jesus committed the sin of **blasphemy** because only God could forgive sins. However, to demonstrate that he had the authority to forgive sin and that he was indeed the Son of God, Jesus ordered the paralyzed man to rise, pick up his stretcher, and go home. The man did so, which astonished the onlookers. They were awestruck as they began to glorify God and say, "We have seen incredible things today" (Lk 5:26).

Exorcisms

Exorcisms are the expulsion of evil spirits from a person. Jesus performed them to establish his power over Satan and the demons who war against God's purposes and tempt humans to do evil.

One of the exorcisms recorded in Luke takes place in a synagogue in Capernaum (Lk 4:31–37). After driving a demon out of a man, Jesus' action caused amazement, "What is there about his word? For with authority and power he commands the unclean spirits and they come out" (Lk 4:36).

When Jesus encountered the Gerasene demoniac in Luke 8:26–39, the demons recognized Jesus as the Son of God and feared him. Jesus sent the demons into a herd of pigs, an unclean animal for the Jews. The pigs rushed down the steep cliff and were drowned in the sea. When the people learned how the man was cured, they were afraid to be in the presence of one so mighty. Therefore, they asked Jesus to leave their territory. The man whom Jesus freed from the demons wished to follow him, but Jesus told him to return to his own home to recount how God delivered him.

Nature Miracles

Nature miracles attest to Jesus' power over the forces of nature, since all creation came about through him. As John's Gospel puts it, "In the beginning was the Word . . . and the Word was God. All things came to be through him, and without him nothing came to be" (Jn 1:1, 3).

Among the nature miracles is Jesus' calming of the storm at sea in Luke 8:22–25. As God's Son, Jesus has power over creation. When he demonstrates this power, even his disciples ask the question, "Who then is this, who commands even the winds and the sea, and they obey him?" (Lk 8:25).

Another dramatic nature miracle is the multiplication of the loaves and fishes (Lk 9:10–17), a miracle recorded in all four Gospels. The miracle recalled God's feeding the Chosen People in the desert. It also continues to remind Church leaders to feed God's people with Gospel and the Holy Eucharist. In fact, the wording of Luke 9:16—"Then taking the five loaves and the two fish, and looking up to heaven, he said the blessing over them, broke them, and gave them to the disciples to set before the crowd"—brings to mind the Last Supper and Jesus' institution of the Eucharist, the sacrament of Holy Communion with the Lord who gives eternal life.

Raisings from the Dead

Jesus' raising people from the dead bears witness that he has mastery over life and death.

The three raisings from the dead recorded in the Gospels include Jesus' raising of his friend Lazarus in John 11:1–44, the raising of the synagogue leader's daughter reported in all the Synoptic Gospels, and the raising of the son of the widow of Nain in Luke 7:11–17. These examples foreshadow Jesus' own Resurrection. They are clear signs that God is in our midst, that the Messiah has come, a time when Isaiah prophesied:

- Go on to remind the students that every miracle is a sign of the power of the Kingdom of God. Have the students fill in the blanks indicating what Jesus has power over. Then review their work as a class (answers are on page 112 of this text).
- Then, have students cite two examples of each type of miracle using their textbook or Bibles. Review their work and write some of these examples on the board.
- Have the students turn to page 98 in the text and the list of the six things Jesus' miracles accomplish. Go through the list with the students. Encourage questions.

For Enrichment

Miracles Today

On a quiet Friday at the start of this month, Pope Benedict XVI made it official: the healing of a Marshfield man's chronic back pain was a miracle, attributable to the intervention of John Henry Newman, an English cardinal who has been dead since 1890.

The Marshfield man is Jack Sullivan, a magistrate at Plymouth District Court and a deacon at a Pembroke parish, who had suffered crippling back pain that was relieved, twice, after he prayed for Newman's help. After an exhaustive review of Sullivan's medical history, the Vatican determined that his recovery could not be explained by medicine and appears to be permanent.

The miracle is the first to be attributed to Newman, an influential religious thinker and writer who is currently a candidate for sainthood.

—Michael Paulson
July 12, 2009

- Before moving on, write the following phrase on the board: **Jesus' miracles were unique**. Point out the following about the uniqueness of Jesus' miracles:
  - Jesus refused any compensation for his astounding works.
  - Jesus used no elaborate ritual or ceremony of any kind when working a miracle; he simply operated under *his own* authority only.
  - Jesus' miraculous power was vast, extending over all areas of life's brokenness: illness, possession, the forces of nature, evil and sin, and even death itself.
  - Jesus never worked a miracle for its own sake, and he rebuked those who asked him to do so (e.g., Mt 16:1–4).

The blind regain their sight, the lame walk, lepers are cleansed, the deaf hear, the dead are raised, the poor have the good news proclaimed to them. (Lk 7:22)

In the miracle of the raising of the son of the widow Nain, Jesus reveals his great compassion: "He was moved to pity for her" (Lk 7:13). As a widow, she was powerless; her dead son was her only means of support. Jesus' heart went out to her. He touched the coffin and ordered the dead youth to get up. The youth obeyed and began to speak. This miracle brings to mind the Old Testament prophet Elijah who also performed an act of mercy for a mother whose son stopped breathing (see 1 Kings 17:17–24). The power of God exhibited in Jesus, his Son, at first made the people afraid. But soon, they began to glorify God. They recognized what had taken place: "A great prophet has arisen in our midst. . . . God has visited his people" (Lk 7:16).

In total, Jesus' miracles accomplish many things:

- They show that God's power has broken into human history through the coming of his Son.
- They show that Jesus Christ has dominion over Satan and the forces of darkness and evil. God's Kingdom is here; Satan's reign is ending.
- They reveal that because he is God, he has the power to forgive sins.
- Therefore, they reveal his identity as God's only Son, the Savior and the Messiah.
- As signs of God's Kingdom that has broken into human history, the miracles demonstrate in a remarkable way God's love and compassion for us.
- They lead people to put their faith in him, helping them recognize who he is: Emmanuel—"God-with-us."

For Review

1. What was the purpose of Jesus' miracles?
2. Name the four kinds of miracles Jesus performed.
3. Why did Jesus' opponents think he committed blasphemy?

(continued on page 100)

EXPLAINING THE FAITH

Do miracles happen today?

God continues his work through the ages. Church history is full of examples of God's miraculous intervention in the lives of people. This is true even today. For example, it is possible to view the incorrupt bodies of some saints (their bodies were not mummified at death). Science cannot explain this phenomenon. At Fatima, Portugal, where Mary appeared in 1917, more than seventy thousand people saw the sun "dance" and appear to plummet to earth. At Lourdes, France, where Mary appeared to St. Bernadette Soubirous in 1858 more than seven thousand people have reported cures in the years since to the Medical Bureau at Lourdes. An objective commission of scientists and medical personnel examined the cures and led the bureau to declare that sixty-seven cases should be officially acknowledged as miraculous.

Many miracles are attributed to saints. Holy persons like St. Pio of Pietrelcina bore the stigmata (wounds of Christ) and cured many people during his lifetime, including curing a lady of blindness. Incredibly, the woman had no pupils, and yet she was able to see. The Church conducts a very thorough procedure to determine if a candidate for canonization has worked a miracle. A doctor, whose job it is to determine if these medical wonders attributed to saints are really miracles, calls them "fantastic, incredible, and well-documented."

Modern skeptics, influenced by the belief that it is impossible for God to intervene in the natural world, claim that miracles do not happen. But this opinion does not square with the facts. For those who believe in the Good News of Jesus Christ, we know that the world is full of grace. Wonders do take place.

For Review Answers (pages 98-100)

1. Answers should evidence an understanding that the purpose of Jesus' miracles was to announce the presence of the Kingdom of God
2. Jesus performed physical healings, exorcisms, nature miracles, and he raised people from the dead.
3. Because he claimed a power reserved to God—the power to forgive sin.
4. He healed a paralyzed man.
5. Students may reply with any or all of the six "accomplishments" listed on page 98 of the text.

Extending the Lesson

Have the students compose an online newspaper or website about Jesus' miracles. Suggest they include the following: news stories about when, what, and where Jesus performed miracles; map of the region; interviews with people who responded to Jesus with faith; interviews or guest columns by representatives of different groups who witnessed a miracle—Romans, Pharisees, Sadducees, the poor, and the Apostles. Encourage the students to find and import illustrations of people presented in the newspaper or to use modern photos.

Interpreting Jesus' Miracles

Here is a list of some key miracles of Jesus'. Write a report that summarizes the miracles listed in boldface type. Follow these directions:

1. Read all of the versions of each miracle listed in **boldface** type.
2. Note what has taken place on the surface level; for example, Jesus cures a man's blindness.
3. Decide to which of the four categories of miracle listed above this particular one belongs.
4. Then interpret the deeper meaning of the miracle. How does it show God's *power*? What *significance* does it have? For example, in the case of the blind man, you might say that God's power makes people see the true light. Or you might conclude that faith in Jesus enabled him to see God working through his Son who enables us to walk in the light.
5. Share your conclusions with your classmates.

Miracle	Mt	Mk	Lk	Jn
Changing Water into Wine				2:1–11
Healing of the Nobleman's Son				4:46–54
Disciples Catch Fish			5:1–11	
Stilling of the Storm	8:23–27	4:35–41	8:22–25	
Demoniacs of Gerasene	8:28–34	5:1–20	8:26–39	
Raising Jairus's Daughter	**9:18–26**	**5:21–43**	**8:40–56**	
Healing the Woman with a Hemorrhage	9:20–22	5:24–34	8:43–48	
Healing of the Two Blind Men	9:27–31			
Healing of Possessed Mute	9:32–34			
Healing of the Paralytic	9:1–8	2:1–12	5:17–26	
Cleansing of the Leper	8:1–4	1:40–45	5:12–16	
Healing the Centurion's Servant	8:5–13		7:1–10	
Demoniac at Capernaum		**1:23–27**	**4:33–36**	
Healing of Simon's Mother-in-Law	8:14–15	1:29–31	4:38–39	
Raising of the Widow's Son			7:11–17	
Healing at the Pool of Bethesda				5:1–15
Healing of the Blind and Deaf Mute	12:22			
Feeding of the Five Thousand	**14:15–21**	**6:34–44**	**9:12–17**	**6:5–14**
Walking on Water	14:22–23	6:45–52		6:14–21
Healing the Man Born Blind				**9:1–41**
Healing the Man with a Withered Hand	12:9–13	3:1–5	6:6–11	
Healing the Woman on the Sabbath			13:10–17	
Healing the Man with Dropsy			14:1–6	
Cleansing the Ten Lepers			17:11–19	
Healing the Syrophoenician Woman	15:21–28	7:24–30		
Healing the Deaf and Dumb Man		7:31–37		
Healing of the Suffering	15:29–31			
Feeding the Four Thousand	15:32–39	8:1–9		
Healing the Blind Man at Bethesda		8:22–26		
Healing of the Lunatic Child	17:14–21	9:14–29	9:37–42	
Finding the Coin in the Fish's Mouth	17:24–27			
Raising of Lazarus				11:1–54
Healing the Two Blind Men	20:29–34	10:46–52	18:35–43	
Cursing the Barren Fig Tree	21:18–22	11:12–24		
Healing of Malchus's Ear			22:49–51	
Second Miraculous Catch of Fish				21:1–14

- Direct attention to the feature "Interpreting Jesus Miracles" (page 99). Review the directions with the group. Assign each of the remaining miracles to individual students to categorize and interpret. Post large papers around the room labeled with the four types of miracles (or write each type of miracle on the board with space underneath). Invite the students to write the name of their miracle on the appropriate paper (or under the appropriate type of miracle on the board).
- Tell the students to look at the feature For Reflection on page 100. Have them write their notes in the spaces provided on Handout 4. Afterward, if you wish, invite sharing.
- Before dismissing the students, have them look at the feature Explaining the Faith on page 98. Invite the students to share any other modern miracles they know about. Consider sharing some of the material in the For Enrichment section below.

For Enrichment

More about Miracles

Miracles are not contrary to nature, but only contrary to what we know about nature.

—**St. Augustine**

I think miracles exist in part as gifts and in part as clues that there is something beyond the flat world we see.

—**Peggy Noonan**

Miracles are a retelling in small letters of the very same story which is written across the whole world in letters too large for some of us to see.

—**C. S. Lewis**

Miracles happen everyday; change your perception of what a miracle is and you'll see them all around you.

—**Jon Bon Jovi**

Chapter 4: The Ministry and Message of Jesus Christ—Lesson 5

Bell Ringers

- Ask the students to offer their responses to the five For Review questions on pages 98–100 (answers are on page 114 of this text). Be sure to allow the students to ask any other questions they may have.
- Invite the students to share their paragraphs regarding allegory from the For Reflection exercise on page 95. Note similarities and differences in the students' essays.

Teaching Approaches

Two Great Miracles of Jesus (pages 100-104)

- Write the word **Transfiguration** on the board and invite the students to offer definitions. Then tell the class that in Greek the word is *metamorpho*, a verb made up of two other Greek words: *meta*, meaning "to change," and *morphe*, meaning "form." Thus, the term means "to change into another form." At the same time, the term also means to change the outside to match the inside. In the case of the Transfiguration of Jesus, then, it means to change the outward form (Jesus' human nature) to mirror the inward reality (Jesus' divine nature). At the Transfiguration, the glory of God incarnate in the Son was displayed. It was a genuine epiphany, a clear revelation of the divine.
- Ask a student to read aloud Matthew 17:1–9. Afterward, remind the students that this event follows on the heels of Peter's profession of faith in Jesus as Messiah (Lk 9:18–20). Then ask the following:
    - What essentially took place at the Transfiguration? (*Jesus revealed his divinity and his approaching Passion, Death, and Resurrection.*)
    - Who were Moses and Elijah? What does the presence of Moses and Elijah tell us about Jesus? (*Moses represents the Law, Elijah the prophets. Jesus is the fulfillment of both the Law [the new Moses] and the prophets.*)
    - Where else have we encountered a revelation where God the Father proclaimed from a cloud that Jesus was his Son? (*At Jesus' baptism—Mt 3:7; Mk 1:11; Lk 3:22*)

100 Jesus Christ: Source of Our Salvation

4. How did Jesus show through a miracle that he had the power to forgive sin?
5. What do Jesus' miracles accomplish?

For Reflection

Jesus put to the blind man this question: "What do you want me to do for you?" Name one thing you need in your life right now. Write a note addressed to Jesus telling him what you think he can do for you. Then write another note telling Jesus what you think *you can do for him*.

Two Great Miracles of Jesus

At the end of 2002, Pope John Paul II declared that the next calendar year would be the Year of the Rosary. At the same time, the Pope introduced another set of mysteries in addition to the Joyful, Sorrowful, and Glorious mysteries that have been part of praying the Rosary since the sixteenth century.

The new set of mysteries are known as the Mysteries of Light. They are made up of these mysteries: the Baptism of the Lord, the Wedding at Cana, Jesus' Proclamation of the Kingdom of God, the Transfiguration of the Lord, and the Institution of the Eucharist.

The text has previously detailed Christ's Baptism, his first miracle at Cana, and his initiation of the Kingdom of God. The next sections focus on Christ's Transfiguration and the Eucharist.

Transfiguration of Jesus (CCC, 551-556; 568)

One of the most dramatic and important miracles in the life of Jesus is his **Transfiguration.** It was witnessed by three of his Apostles and took place after Peter's confession of Jesus as the Messiah (Lk 9:18–21). The event unfolds this way: Jesus went off to pray by himself; the Apostles were with him. On this occasion, he asked them what the crowds of people were saying about him. The answers varied. Some, perhaps even Herod Antipas, thought Jesus was John the Baptist come back to life (see Lk 9:7); others thought he was Elijah; still others believed him to be a great prophet. Although the people thought highly of Jesus, and considered him a mouthpiece for God, none of them believed that he was the Messiah.

What Jesus really wanted was for his Apostles to answer the same question: "But who do you say that I am?" (Lk 9:19). Peter, speaking on behalf of the Apostles, acknowledged the great truth: Jesus is "The Messiah of God" (Lk 9:20). Matthew's Gospel reports Peter's confession this way: "You are the Messiah, Son of the living God" (Mt 16:16).

After witnessing Jesus' miracles and hearing him teach, the Apostles grew to know him as more than

Lesson 5 Objectives

The students will:

- describe the meaning of Transfiguration.
- describe what Jesus' Transfiguration reveals about him and his mission.
- summarize how and why Jesus instituted the Eucharist.

Lesson 5 Preview

The Transfiguration and Eucharist speak volumes about Jesus and his mission. As you present the material on the Eucharist, however, keep in mind that Eucharist is far more than a *thing*; it is an activity. In fact, it's not an "it" at all. The Eucharist is, rather, a whole way of being together. Eucharist is communion, involving real people, one with another and together with God. Be careful, then, not to speak of Eucharist as a private commodity or personal treasure. There's no such thing as solitary Eucharist separated from communal relationship.

just a healer and an inspired teacher. They came to know him as the Messiah, as God himself who had come to announce the Kingdom and save humanity. Though the Apostles may have had a correct glimpse of Jesus' true identity, it was not until after the Resurrection and Ascension of Jesus, and the coming of the Holy Spirit, that they fully began to understand the impact of their words. For example, immediately after Peter's confession of faith, Jesus predicted that he would suffer and die. But Peter could not believe that the Messiah would have to endure this pain and Death, and so he took Jesus aside and began to argue with him, "God forbid, Lord! No such thing shall ever happen to you" (Mt 16:22). Jesus in turn rebuked Peter for judging not by God's standards of the Messiah as Suffering Servant but by the standards of human beings (see Mt 16:23).

Eight days after Peter's confession of faith, and Jesus' first prediction that he would suffer and be killed by the leaders, yet rise on the third day, Jesus gave Peter, James, and John a glimpse of his divine glory, of his true identity as God's beloved Son. He took them on a high mountain where his face "shone like the sun and his clothes became as white as light" (Mt 17:2). Through this manifestation, known as the Transfiguration, Jesus was giving his Apostles a foretaste of God's Kingdom.

In his book on Jesus of Nazareth, Pope Benedict XVI observed that the Transfiguration happened while Jesus was praying. At the Transfiguration, Jesus' being was suffused with the light of God. "In his oneness with the Father, Jesus is himself "light from light."

Two Old Testament figures—Moses and Elijah—also appear at Jesus' Transfiguration. This brings to mind how the Law (given to Israel through Moses) and the Prophets (Elijah was a great prophet) had announced the sufferings of the coming Messiah. The Transfiguration also reveals all Three Persons of the Blessed Trinity: the Father (in the voice), the Son, and the Holy Spirit (in the shining cloud).

In the Transfiguration, Jesus momentarily reveals his divine glory, thus confirming the faith of Peter. But he also reveals that he must die in Jerusalem in order to enter into his glory. He instructed Peter, James, and John not to report this vision until after the Resurrection. They were to withhold news of this remarkable event "until the Son of Man has been raised from the dead" (Mt 17:9). Though he was the Son of God, Jesus came not as an earthly king. He came to preach the Good News of God's love. This preaching led him to Jerusalem and his own Death at the hands of the authorities.

Institution of the Eucharist (CCC, 611, 1337-1344)

In the Eucharist, Christ shares the gift of himself. When we open ourselves to accepting this gift, we are nourished by the **Real Presence** of God in our lives. Luke 22:1–38 is a source

Transfiguration
The mystery from Christ's life in which God's glory shone through and transformed Jesus' physical appearance while he was in the company of the Old Testament prophets Moses and Elijah. Peter, James, and John witnessed this event.

Real Presence
The presence of Jesus Christ in the consecrated species of bread and wine.

- Why do you think Jesus told the three Apostles not to tell anyone what they had seen until he had risen from the dead?

- Emphasize that the Transfiguration confirmed beyond a doubt that Jesus was not just another rabbi or wonder-worker or rabble rouser, but the named "Son" of the divine Lord. Ask, "What was the ramification of this experience for the Apostles?" Accept all reasonable replies. Then help the students appreciate that the Apostles were now faced with abandoning any notion that Jesus was simply announcing the coming of the Messiah. They were forced to accept that not only was he *the* Messiah but a *suffering* Messiah to boot (see Matthew 16:21), and that if they were to "listen to him" (Mt 17:5) and share in his glory, they must share in his suffering as well. Point out that the Apostles' challenge is ours as well. (*Note:* See the quotation from Pope John Paul II, "The Consecrated Life," in the For Enrichment section on page 120 of this text.)
- On index cards or half-sheets of paper, check the students' understanding of the Transfiguration by asking them to write down how the Apostles would respond to Jesus' question, "Who do you say that I am?" after the Transfiguration. As they read Luke's account of the Last Supper, check to make sure the students have written that the Apostles would answer that Jesus was the Messiah, Son of God, fulfillment of the Law and the prophets, and/or the Suffering Servant.

Lesson 5 Homework

1. Tell the students to write out their answers to the For Review questions on pages 103–104.
2. Call attention to the For Reflection feature on page 104. Have the students conduct the interviews and be ready to hand in their written reflection when you take the chapter test. Tell them to complete the second Reflection activity as a journal activity.
3. Tell the students to be ready to hand in their work on their chosen Ongoing Assignments at their next session.
4. Have the students read through the Chapter Quick View section on pages 105–107 and to review the chapter's Main Ideas. Tell the students to write out any questions they may have and bring them to the next session.

Extending the Lesson

The Luminous Mysteries of the Rosary

In a letter commemorating the twenty-fifth year of his Pontificate in 2002, Pope John Paul II proposed an additional set of five new mysteries of the Rosary, which he called Luminous Mysteries or the Mysteries of Light. As a review of chapters three and four, invite students to pray the Rosary in deep meditation on the Luminous Mysteries: the Baptism of the Lord, the Wedding at Cana, the Proclamation of the Kingdom of God, the Transfiguration, and the Institution of the Eucharist.

- Call attention to the text section "Institution of the Eucharist" on page 101. Have the students read Luke's account of the Last Supper (Lk 22:1–20).
- Point out that Luke sets the institution of the Eucharist in the context of a Passover meal. Ask the students why this setting is important and why the Passover was so important to the Jewish people.
- Write the word **Passover** on the board. Invite the students to silently come up to the front of the room to write a word or phrase that describes something they know about the Passover. Afterward, review what the students have written and add any important information they may have missed.
- Make sure the students understand that the Passover was (and remains) a memorial of Israel's deliverance from death to life. By celebrating the Passover, Jews recognize that God's past saving activity on their behalf continues to be present for them. The Passover is not so much people's remembering what God has done as it is a celebration of *God remembering* his people. And when God remembers, something is effected on behalf of his people.
- Go on to tell the students that when Jesus celebrated this ancient meal at the Last Supper with his Apostles, they recognized that their eating and drinking was a sharing here and now in the Passover sacrifice. But then Jesus did something radically new. He identified

that details the institution of the Eucharist beginning with Jesus' entrance to Jerusalem.

In reading Luke's Gospel from start to finish, it is easy to notice how the travel narrative centers on Jerusalem. This city becomes Jesus' destination "for it is impossible that a prophet should die outside of Jerusalem" (Lk 13:33). Jesus entered Jerusalem for the final time on the back of a colt to fulfill the prophecy of Zechariah who predicted the Savior would come as a humble king. As he approached the city, Jesus wept over it, foreseeing the day when the Romans would destroy the Temple in the Jewish Revolt (AD 66–70). He then entered the Temple area and drove out those who were selling things, reminding people that God's house should be a house of prayer, not a den of thieves (Lk 19:46).

During the following days, Jesus returned to the Temple to teach. He defended his authority to teach when questioned by the chief priests, scribes, and elders. In doing so, he told the parable of the tenant farmers (Lk 20:9–19) and fended off questions about the paying of taxes and the nature of the Resurrection. Jesus warned about the hypocrisy of the scribes and told how a poor widow's two small coins were more pleasing to God than the contributions of wealthy people who gave in order to be noticed by others. Jesus also taught about the destruction of the Temple, signs of the end of the world, and the coming of the Son of Man—the Resurrected Lord who will judge everyone. Jesus encouraged his disciples to watch and to pray, to always be ready for the arrival of the Son of Man.

Jesus taught these themes during the day and returned to the Mount of Olives every evening. The common people liked hearing him, but the leaders were at the same time plotting his death. Satan tempted Judas, one of the Apostles, to contact the chief priests and Temple guards to discuss a way to hand Jesus over to them. They offered him money to do so at a time when crowds of people would not be around Jesus.

The narrative turns to the preparations Jesus made with his Apostles to celebrate a Passover meal with them. Originally, the Jewish feasts of the Unleavened Bread and the Passover were celebrated separately but were soon joined to recall God's deliverance of Israel from Egypt. Passover came on the first of the seven days of Unleavened Bread. The disciples did as Jesus told them by finding a man with a jar of water who would lead them to the guest room where Jesus would celebrate the Last Supper with his Apostles.

The Synoptic Gospels report that Jesus' Last Supper was a Passover meal. In John's Gospel, the supper takes place the night before; Jesus died at the exact moment that the Passover lamb was sacrificed. John's Gospel is the only one to report that Jesus washed the feet of his disciples as a sign that they should serve one another. Jesus also gave his followers the great command to love:

Background Information

The Different Modes of Christ's Presence

Christ is always present in his Church, especially in her liturgical celebrations. He is present in the sacrifice of the Mass, not only in the person of his minister . . . (but) above all under the species of the Eucharist. By his power he is present in the sacraments, so that when a man baptizes it is really Christ himself who baptizes. He is present in his word, since it is he himself who speaks when the holy scriptures are read in the Church. He is present, lastly, when the Church prays and sings, for he promised: "Where two or three are gathered together in my name, there am I in the midst of them" (Mt 18:20).

—Pope Paul VI, *Constitution on the Sacred Liturgy*, 7

In order that they should achieve a deeper understanding of the mystery of the Eucharist, the faithful should be instructed in the principal ways in which the Lord is present to his Church in liturgical celebrations.

He is always present in a body of the faithful gathered in his name (see Mt 18:20). He is present, too, in his Word, for it is he who speaks when the Scriptures are read in the Church.

In the sacrifice of the Eucharist he is present both in the person of the minister, "the same now offering through the ministry of the priest who formerly offered himself on the cross," and above all under the species of the Eucharist. For in this sacrament Christ is present in a unique way, whole and entire, God and man, substantially and permanently. This presence of Christ under the species "is called 'real' not in an exclusive sense, as if the other kinds of presence were not real, but par excellence."

—Sacred Congregation of Rites, *Instruction on the Worship of the Eucharistic Ministry*, 9

> This is my commandment: love one another as I love you. No one has greater love than this, to lay down one's life for one's friends. . . . This I command you: love one another. (Jn 15:12–13, 17)

Jesus understood that his hour had come and that he was to return to his Father. But he did not abandon his disciples. He left them a pledge of his love, so that he would never depart from his own, and to make them sharers in his Passover. Therefore, he instituted the Eucharist as a memorial of his Death and Resurrection. He also commanded his Apostles to celebrate the Eucharist until he returned once again. Jesus chose the Passover feast to fulfill what he proclaimed at Capernaum. He gave his disciples his Body and his Blood in the form of bread and wine.

> When the hour came, he took his place at table with the apostles. He said to them, "I have eagerly desired to eat this Passover with you before I suffer, for, I tell you, I shall not eat it [again] until there is fulfillment in the kingdom of God." Then he took a cup, gave thanks, and said, "Take this and share it among yourselves; for I tell you [that] from this time on I shall not drink of the fruit of the vine until the kingdom of God comes." Then he took the bread, said the blessing, broke it, and gave it to them, saying, "This is my body, which will be given for you; do this in memory of me." And likewise the cup after they had eaten, saying, "This cup is the new covenant in my blood, which will be shed for you." (Lk 22:14–20)

The *Catechism of the Catholic Church* explains the significance of what Jesus did at the Last Supper:

> By celebrating the Last Supper with his apostles in the course of the Passover meal, Jesus gave the Jewish Passover its definitive meaning. Jesus' passing over to his father by his death and Resurrection, the new Passover, is anticipated in the Supper and celebrated in the Eucharist, which fulfills the Jewish Passover and anticipates the final Passover of the Church in the glory of the kingdom. (*CCC*, 1340)

Jesus commanded his followers to celebrate the Eucharist in memory of him—his Life, Death, Resurrection, and his intercession for us before the Father. From her very beginnings, the Church has faithfully celebrated the Eucharist, especially by doing so on Sunday, the day of the Lord's Resurrection. Catholics recognize in the Holy Eucharist the very center of the Church's life in Christ. It both celebrates and creates the Church, allowing Jesus Christ to live in and transform us.

After the Supper was over, Jesus led his disciples to the Mount of Olives where his Passion would begin and the Paschal Mystery would unfold. The Paschal Mystery of Jesus' Death and Resurrection rescued humanity from sin and death. This is the message that the Gospels want us to hear: Jesus, the Christ, is the Son of God. He has died for your sins and risen from the dead! Everything has changed now. God's Kingdom is here. Believe the Good News of your Salvation. Repent of your sins. Be baptized. Allow the Lord Jesus and the Holy Spirit into your lives and be guided by them.

For Review

1. What were some common opinions of who Jesus was that were held by some of his contemporaries?
2. What did Peter confess about Jesus' identity?
3. What was the Transfiguration of Jesus?
4. Who appeared with Jesus at the Transfiguration?
5. How were all three Persons of the Blessed Trinity present at the Transfiguration?

himself with the bread and wine. He identified himself as the *new* Passover sacrifice. What Jesus did with the bread and wine—broken, poured out, and shared—reveals the meaning of his Death on the Cross.

- Revisit the students' words or phrases about the Passover on the board. Ask them to identify how Jesus fulfills each of these words or phrases in his Paschal sacrifice.
- Call attention to the final words in Luke 22:19: "Do this in memory of me." These words of Jesus assure us that when we gather to break the bread and share the cup, Christ will be truly present. Whenever we eat the broken bread and drink the wine poured out, we share in the very Body and Blood of Christ and in his saving Death and Resurrection. (See *CCC*, 1409.)
- Tell the students that the account of the institution of the Eucharist occurs in all three Synoptic Gospels. John's is the only Gospel that does not record Jesus breaking bread and sharing wine at the Last Supper. Instead, John tells us about Jesus as the Bread of Life right after his account of the multiplication of the loaves and fishes. The crowds wanted more loaves and fishes. Jesus had other food in mind. Direct the students to read John 6:35, 48–56. Then ask:

For Review Answers (pages 103-104)

1. Some thought he was John the Baptist come back to life, others Elijah, still others a prophet, but not *the* Messiah.
2. He declared that Jesus was the Messiah, God's Son.
3. The Transfiguration was an epiphany event in which the glory of God was revealed through the Son.
4. Moses and Elijah.
5. The Father in the voice, Jesus in the flesh, the Holy Spirit in the bright cloud.
6. Jerusalem was Jesus' destination because as a prophet, Jesus knew he must go there to die.
7. Answers should show an understanding that Jesus chose to transform the Passover meal into the new Passover, to become our Passover Lamb, and to leave us a memorial of his Death and Resurrection.
8. He instituted the Eucharist by identifying himself with the broken bread and the wine poured out and shared. He gave us the Eucharist to remember him, to enable us to share in his sacrifice on the Cross and his rising to new life.
9. The Eucharist both creates and celebrates the Church, allowing Jesus to dwell in us and transform us.

  - What sort of food did Jesus want to give the people? (*himself*)
  - What did Jesus claim for himself? (*that he was sent by God and that he is the Bread of Life*)
  - What does Jesus promise for those who accept his Body and Blood? (*eternal life*)

- Go on to remind the students that John's inclusion of Jesus' washing his followers' feet (Jn 13:1–15) is a clear reminder of what the Eucharist demands—a life of loving service, a willingness to be broken like bread and poured out like wine for others.
- Use the following questions to spark discussion about the Eucharist:
  - How do you experience the presence of Jesus?
  - How is your relationship strengthened by taking part in the Eucharist?
  - What can you do to enrich your celebration of the Eucharist?
  - What can you do to enrich others' celebration of the Eucharist?
- Write the following (from the *Constitution on the Church*, 11) on the board: "**The Eucharist is the source and summit of the whole Christian life**." Have the students draw on their reading and experience to write a paragraph explaining what they feel the statement means for them. Afterward, have the students share in small groups.

6. In Luke's Gospel, why does Jerusalem play a central role for Jesus' ministry?
7. What is the significance of Jesus celebrating a Passover meal with his Apostles?
8. How did Jesus institute the Eucharist? Why did he do so?
9. Why is the Eucharist the center of the Church's life?

For Reflection

- Interview three people to see who they think Jesus is. Then write a reflection comparing and contrasting their views with your own.
- Because Jesus is present in the Blessed Sacrament, he deserves reverence. How do you show reverence to our Lord in the Blessed Sacrament? List ways "irreverence" is shown to people in your school, in your neighborhood, in our society.

For Enrichment

The Transfiguration: Heavenly Bodies

At his Transfiguration Christ showed his disciples the splendor of his beauty, to which he will shape and color those who are his: "He will change our lowly body to conform with his glorified body" (Phil 3:21).

—St. Thomas Aquinas

The Transfiguration: Prepping for the Passion

The Transfiguration is not only the revelation of Christ's glory but also a preparation for facing Christ's Cross. It involves both "going up the mountain" and "coming down the mountain." The disciples who have enjoyed this intimacy with the Master, surrounded by the splendor of the Trinitarian life, are immediately brought back to daily reality, where they see Jesus only, in the lowliness of his human nature. And we are invited to return to the valley, to share with him the toil of God's plan and to set off courageously on the way of the Cross.

—Pope John Paul II, *The Consecrated Life*, 14

Main Ideas

- The focus of our love should not be on what we have but who we are as God's beloved children. (pp. 84–85)
- Jesus announced the coming of God's Kingdom, a Kingdom of peace, justice, truth, and goodness. (pp. 85–86)
- The Kingdom of God begins small but grows on to flourish in the future. (p. 86)
- Jesus announces the Kingdom of God in a special way to the poor and lowly. (p. 87)
- God's mercy to sinners is a characteristic of the Kingdom of God. (p. 87)
- The Beatitudes instruct us on how to live in and be a part of God's Kingdom. (p. 88)
- Jesus' parables teach about God's Kingdom; they convey the heart of Jesus' message, show that he was an outstanding teacher, and give an idea of how he was able to defend himself against his opponents. (p. 90)
- The parables also teach that Salvation is here, that the Kingdom is a gift of pure love, that God loves sinners, that the Kingdom requires an urgent response and also repentance, and that it may also require suffering. (p. 93)
- The miracles of Jesus are other signs of the Kingdom; they reveal the Kingdom's presence in the life of Christ. (p. 95)
- Jesus performed different kinds of miracles, including: physical healings, exorcisms, nature miracles, and raisings from the dead. (pp. 96–98)
- Two great miracles that are part of the Mysteries of Light of the Rosary are the Transfiguration of Jesus and the Institution of the Last Supper. (pp. 100–101)

Terms, People, Places

Use a vocabulary word from the list below to help rewrite the following sentences to make them true.

allegory
Beatitudes
blasphemy
parables
prejudice
Real Presence
Transfiguration

1. At the Sermon on the Mount, Jesus appeared to Peter, James, and John, and God's glory shone through and transformed his appearance.
2. The word *racism* comes from a Latin word that we can translate as "prejudge."
3. Jesus taught that those who wish to embrace God's Kingdom must live according to the laws set out by the nation's authority.
4. Jesus is truly with us in the consecrated species of bread and wine at Mass, a mystery described as liturgy.
5. A key to understanding Jesus' parables involves realizing that they often contain metaphor.
6. The crime that Jesus was accused of and that led to his death was sorcery.
7. To teach the people in creative and interesting ways and to help them remember what he taught, Jesus addressed them with short, concise statements that took the form of dogma.

Primary Source Quotations

The Kingdom of God
Just as the life of Jesus, in his obedience and dedication to the Father, is a living parable of the "God with us," in the same way the concrete commitment of consecrated persons to God and brothers becomes an eloquent sign of

Chapter 4 Quick View

Review Lesson Objectives

The students will:

- review Chapter 4 in preparation for the chapter test.
- join in prayer together.

Terms, People, Places Answers (page 105)

1. ~~Sermon on the Mount~~ / **Transfiguration**
2. ~~*racism*~~ / **prejudice**
3. ~~nation's~~ / **Beatitudes'**
4. ~~*liturgy*~~ / **Real Presence**
5. ~~miracles~~ / **parables**
6. ~~sorcery~~ / **blasphemy**
7. ~~dogma~~ / **allegory**

Chapter 4: The Ministry and Message of Jesus Christ—Review Lesson

Bell Ringers

- Review the previous lesson by inviting the students to share responses to the nine questions in the For Review section on pages 103–104.
- Collect the students' Ongoing Assignments for Chapter 4 (pages 106–107). Allow time for those who chose #5 and/or #9 (creating a photo presentation) to make their presentations to the class.

Teaching Approaches

Chapter Quick View (pages 105-107)

- Call attention to Terms, People, Places on page 105. Have the students rewrite the sentences as directed. Use the corrected statements in this section to help the students review key elements of the unit (answers are on page 121 of this text).
- Use the Main Ideas section to review key points. Go through the ideas with the class, having the students refer back to the chapter pages listed in the text.
- Continue the review by going over some or all of the For Review questions from the chapter. Consider using a simple game format. Divide the class into teams. Call on a representative from a team to answer a question. If the representative has difficulty, allow him or her to get help from the team. Award five points for an individual's correct response, two points if the person needed help. Clarify any confusion.
- Take some time to go over any material the students may have overlooked in their review or that you feel needs more attention. Allow time for the students to ask any questions they may have.
- As time allows, invite various students who handed in written Ongoing Assignment number 3 to share it with the class.
- Be sure to provide some quiet time for the students to study on their own. If students have more questions, invite them to approach you privately while their classmates study.

Prayer Service

- Gather the students without their texts, in a circle around a lighted a candle. Have meditative music playing.
- Have a Bible at the ready with Luke 7:36–50 marked. Lead the students through the meditative prayer found on page 107. Include the Reflection and Resolution on page 107 as part of the prayer experience.
- If you wish, conclude with a song of reconciliation, such as "Healer of Our Every Ill" by Marty Haugen (GIA).

Chapter 4 Quick View

the presence of the Kingdom of God for the world of today.

—Pope Benedict XVI

If there be a true way that leads to the everlasting Kingdom, it is most certainly of suffering, patiently endured.

—St. Colette

Thy Kingdom Come

It may even be . . . that the Kingdom of God means Christ himself, whom we daily desire to come, and whose coming we wish to be manifested quickly to us.

—St. Cyprian

Only a pure soul can boldly say: "Thy kingdom come." One who has heard Paul say, "Let not sin therefore reign in your mortal bodies," and has purified himself in action, thought, and word will say to God: "Thy kingdom come!"

—St. Cyril of Jerusalem

Our natural will is to have God, and the good will of God is to have us, and we may never cease willing or longing for him until we have him in the fullness of joy. [Christ] will never have full bliss in us until we have our full bliss in him.

—Bl. Julian of Norwich

In Matthew 13:44–50, Jesus offers several short parables describing what "the Kingdom of God is like." Take some time to write at least three statements beginning with "The Kingdom of God is like . . ."

Ongoing Assignments

As you cover the material in this chapter, choose and complete at least three of these assignments.

1. Read and write a summary of one of the following articles by Fr. Daniel Harrington, S.J. (both from St. Anthony Messenger Press):
   - "The Truth About Jesus and Women"
   - "Miracles: Signs of God's Presence"
2. Select several passages from your reading of the Gospel of Luke. Make a poster with the passages accompanied by your own illustrations or popular clipart. Display your poster board in the classroom.
3. The film *Jesus*, sponsored by the Campus Crusade for Christ, is based on the Gospel of Luke. Watch the film. Write a review of the acting, storyline, authenticity with the Gospel, and potential appeal to your peers.
4. Research the origins of the disputes between the Jews and Samaritans in Jesus' time. Write a report that summarizes your findings.
5. Choose a favorite parable. Then create a PowerPoint presentation or printed booklet targeted for a third-grader that includes both the words of the parable and illustrations that you find to depict the parable's scenes.
6. With several classmates, prepare and enact a mime presentation on one of the parables.
7. Choose a parable from Luke's Gospel not covered in this chapter. Research three commentaries to discover what the parable means. Write a one-page report summarizing your findings and using appropriate footnotes. Conclude the paper with your own interpretation of the parable.
8. Read the following parables. Write your answers to the questions in your journal.

   A Friend at Midnight (Lk 11:5–10)
   - What is the meaning of this parable?
   - Rewrite the parable in a modern setting. Be sure to make the same point as Jesus did.

   The Rich Man and Lazarus (Lk 16:19–31)
   - Does Jesus condemn wealth by means of this parable? Explain your response.
   - What is it that Jesus wants us to do with the "riches" we have been given?
9. Take some digital photos of some scenes in nature. Choose several as the basis of a short parable that teaches a truth about the Kingdom of God. Be sure the message is consistent with the message that Jesus

Review Lesson Homework

1. Complete any unfinished Ongoing Assignments.
2. Reread Chapter 4.
3. Study for the Chapter 4 Test.

himself preached. Using your parable and digital photos, create a PowerPoint presentation to share with your classmates.

Prayer

A great way to pray with the Gospels is by using meditative prayer. Meditation is a searching form of prayer. It helps the mind to understand the "why and how of the Christian life" (*CCC*, 2705) and to respond to what Christ is asking of us. Besides the Gospels and the rest of Sacred Scripture, holy icons, liturgical texts of the day or season, writings of the Church Fathers, and other works of spirituality are among the sources of meditative prayer.

Try this simple meditation with Luke 7:36–50. Use the following steps to help you to engage in meditative prayer.

1. *Calm down.* Find a restful prayer position. Breathe slowly and deeply. Let the cares of the day drain from you.
2. *Enter into the presence of the Lord.* Feel the warmth of his love all around you. Imagine Jesus next to you assuring you of his love. Look at his features: his clothing, the length and color of his hair, his complexion, his smile, his eyes. Feel him putting his arm around you.
3. *Read the Gospel passage (Lk 7:36–50).* Put yourself and Jesus into the passage. For example, make yourself a character in the story. Use all your senses—sight, smell, touch, taste, hearing. Listen carefully to the words of the passage. Pause often and let them sink in. But let your imagination flow with the picture.
4. *Reflect.* Return to the present. Ask the Lord to show you what the passage might be saying to you in your life right now.
5. *Conclude.* Thank the Lord for the time he spent with you. Make a resolution from your prayer time and try to put it into practice.

- *Reflection*: How are you lead into sin? Are you willing to take your sins to Jesus and hear his message of love, forgiveness, and peace?
- *Resolution*: Examine your conscience this week on those actions and attitudes that are keeping you from being a more loving person. To experience the Lord's forgiveness, resolve to celebrate the Sacrament of Penance at the earliest possible time.

Chapter 4 Quick View

Test Lesson Homework

1. Read the following text section of Chapter 5: "So Another Might Live" (pages 110–111).
2. Examine the Chapter 5 Ongoing Assignments on page 130.

Chapter 4 Test Lesson

Teaching Approaches

- Collect the students' completed interviews and reflection from the previous lesson's For Reflection feature (see page 104).
- Allow sufficient time for the students to work on the Chapter 4 Test (starting on page 291 of the TWE and also online at www.avemariapress.com). Collect tests as the students finish.

Chapter 4 Test Answers

Part 1: Fill in the Blanks. (2 points each)

1 & 2. mustard; yeast 3. wheat 4 & 5. Mount; Plain 6 & 7. Sanhedrin; Rome 8 & 9. repentance; belief

10. Beatitudes 11. Golden Rule. 12. comparison 13 & 14. Levi; Zacchaeus 15. Jesus 16. Transfiguration

17. Miracles 18. Trinity 19. Passover 20 & 21. bread; wine 22. Samaritan 23. Jerusalem 24. prejudice

Part 2: True or False. (2 points each)

1. T 2. F 3. T 4. F 5. T 6. T 7. F 8. F 9. T 10. F 11. F 12. F

Part 3: Essays. (points vary)

1. Answers could include the description of the Kingdom of God, found in the *Catechism of the Catholic Church* (*CCC*, 541–546), or the six messages of Jesus' parables described in the student text on page 93. **(6 points)**
2. Answers should include living the Golden Rule, being kind to the ungrateful and wicked, being merciful, and giving without counting the cost. **(2 points)**
3. Students should respond with examples of miracles connected to physical healings, exorcisms, nature miracles, or raisings from the dead. **(8 points)**
4. Answers could include connections between the Israelites' passing over from slavery to freedom, and Christians passing over from slavery to sin to freedom from sin; the sacrificial lamb for the Lamb of God, and the Passover meal with unleavened bread and the Last Supper. **(2 points)**

Part 4: Interpreting a Parable. (10 points)

Students should be given up to ten points for making connections between the lost coin and sinners, between the woman and God/Christ, between the neighbors and the angels. Students should also show that this parable explains that everyone is called to enter the Kingdom of God (*CCC*, 543), that Jesus invites sinners into the Kingdom of God (*CCC*, 545), that Salvation is here, and that God loves sinners.

Chapter 5: The Passion and Death of Jesus Christ

Introduction

If, then, you are looking for the way by which you should go, take Christ, because he himself is the way.

—St. Thomas Aquinas

Death is a fact of life. No one can avoid it. It has also been said that death is the wage of sin. Some paycheck! Death is so stark, bleak, and inexorable that it has a unique authority over our emotions. Like love, we do not really understand it. Like love, it is something we can't ignore. There is no anesthetic against grief's pain, no medicine to prolong life beyond a given span. We live our lives between the poles of love and death. For it is love that makes for increase and love that longs for immortality—for something that lasts and defies even dissolution and death. Only love has the courage to believe in its eternity.

This chapter is all about love and death. Following in the footsteps of Jesus, the students walk the way of love, the Way of the Cross. They recall that throughout his ministry, Jesus revealed a God who is love without limit. If God is love without limit, Jesus the God-man must demonstrate it. He did this by suffering and Death—the Cross. The students discover that had Jesus not suffered and died, he would not have been one of us—like us in all ways except sin. He showed us that sin was no conqueror and death no finale. He revealed death to be the culmination of a life of loving and the passage to Resurrection and, ultimately, to life forever with God.

In their study of the passion narratives, the students confront the harsh reality of the Cross. The passion narratives reveal that Jesus' Passion and Death were brought on by the sin of all people. Pilate and the Jewish leaders may have given Christ the sentence, but Christ died because of the sins of the world. He paid a debt he did not owe because we owed a debt we could not pay.

This chapter is an invitation for students to delve deep into the mystery of Christ's Passion and Death. Within this great story of sacrificial love is an invitation to take up our own cross and follow Jesus. Salvation history comes to a climax with the Paschal Mystery. It is the greatest story ever told and hearing it again anew is an opportunity for repentance.

Advance Preparations

Prepare or have on hand:

For Lesson 1

- Corrected copies of the Chapter 4 Test
- Bibles
- Index cards

For Lesson 2

- Bibles
- Index cards, six per student
- Copies of Chapter 5, Handout 1, "Jesus on Trial"

For Lesson 3

- Bibles
- Copies of Chapter 5, Handout 2, "Elements of the Passions"
- Copies of Chapter 5, Handout 3, "Jesus' Way of the Cross"

Chapter Objectives

To help the students:

- discover and discuss the meaning of sacrifice.
- appreciate the sacrifice of St. Maximilian Kolbe and identify other people who have sacrificed for others.
- investigate the scriptural bases for Jesus' Passion.
- discover the theological meaning of Jesus' Death and who bears the ultimate responsibility for it.
- appreciate that Old Testament prophecies are fulfilled in the Passion of Christ.
- investigate key elements of the Passion.
- reflect on Mary's role in Jesus' Passion and Death.
- discuss ways to take up the Cross of Christ.

For Lesson 4

- Bibles
- A player and a recording of Mozart's "Ave Verum Corpus" (optional)
- Copies of—or a player and a recording of—a Passion/ Palm Sunday hymn such as "All Glory, Laud, and Honor" (optional)

For Lesson 5

- Bibles
- A player and a recording of the hymn "Were You There?" (optional)
- Copies of Chapter 5, Handout 4, "The Memorare"
- Have available a player and a recording of the aria "Komm, süßes Kreuz" ("Come, Sweet Cross"), *St. Matthew's Passion* by J. S. Bach (optional)

For the Chapter 5 Review Lesson

- Equipment necessary for students to make PowerPoint presentations
- Cross or crucifix
- A recording of meditative music and a player
- Copies of—or a player and a recording of—a hymn such as "Behold the Wood" by Dan Schutte or "In the Cross of Christ" by Marty Haugen (optional)

For the Chapter 5 Test Lesson

- Copies of the Chapter 5 Test (starting on page 291 of the TWE and also online at www.avemariapress.com)

Chapter 5 Handouts

- Handout 1, Jesus on Trial—The students develop arguments and possible witnesses in defense or prosecution of Jesus of Nazareth.
- Handout 2, Elements of the Passions—The students study core elements of each of the passion narratives.
- Handout 3, Jesus' Way of the Cross—The students trace the steps of Jesus from the Last Supper to the burial tomb.
- Handout 4, The Memorare—The students learn and offer a prayer to Mary.

Chapter 5: The Passion and Death of Jesus Christ—Lesson 1

Bell Ringers

- Distribute the corrected Chapter 4 Test. Go over the test with the students, using it as a means to review the previous chapter. Address any remaining questions or concerns the students may have.
- Introduce this lesson by brainstorming the word **sacrifice**. List ideas on the board. Likewise, discuss the following quotation from Mohandas Karamchand Gandhi: "Sacrifice which causes sorrow to the doer of the sacrifice is no sacrifice. Real sacrifice lightens the mind of the doer and gives him a sense of peace and joy."
- Go on to help the students come to appreciate that "sacrifice" does not, therefore, mean undertaking some onerous duty or giving up something in order to become more holy. Rather, sacrifice—true sacrifice—is always an act of self-giving love aimed at demonstrating and strengthening a loving relationship. Offer the following examples:
    - Parents who give up an evening out on their own in order to use the money saved to pay their child's sports fee at school or to use the time to work at a Loaves and Fishes site are demonstrating the loving relationship they have with their child or the poor. They are making a sacrifice.
    - Teenagers who choose to care for a younger sister or brother when they could be attending an event with their friends are remembering the relationship they have or want to have with their sibling and are doing something to strengthen it. They are making a sacrifice.
- Emphasize that making a sacrifice builds, strengthens, and restores relationships. That is why *every* sacrifice—no matter how large, no matter how small—is doing what is *saving* and *holy*.
- Write the following definition on the board: **Sacrifice = An Act of Self-Giving Love**. Then ask:
    - How has someone performed an act of self-giving love for you? What did he or she sacrifice for your sake?
    - Have you ever performed an act of self-giving love for another? What was your motivation for doing so?

110 Jesus Christ: Source of Our Salvation

So Another Might Live

The humility and sacrifice of Jesus Christ has inspired many people through the centuries to live and die for him. One such person was Maximilian Kolbe, a Polish Franciscan priest who was arrested and accused by the Nazis of publishing materials in opposition to them. Also, during the Nazi persecutions in World War II, his friary helped hide and shelter thousands of Jews and Poles. The Gestapo sent him to the infamous death camp at Auschwitz in 1941. There he was assigned to a special work crew that included other priests and that was supervised by vicious guards.

In July 1941, an Auschwitz prisoner tried to escape. As punishment, the camp's commander paraded all the prisoners into the blazing sun and selected ten of them to be executed. One of the men selected to die was Francis Gajowniczek who cried out, "My wife, my children, I shall never see them again!"

Fr. Maximilian stepped out of line and asked the commander to choose him to die since he did not have a family. The commander obliged since he did not care who died, just that ten men be executed to serve as a warning for any future attempts at escape. The commander did ask Fr. Maximilian why he would volunteer for execution. Maximilian replied simply, "Because I am a Catholic priest." Fr. Maximilian suffered two weeks of starvation, all the while ministering to and comforting the other men who were condemned with him. He was the last to die, on August 14, 1941, after the guards injected him with carbolic acid to bring about instant death.

In 1982, Pope John Paul II canonized Fr. Maximilian as a "martyr of charity." His feast day is August 14.

St. Maximilian Kolbe surrendered his life so that a man might live. His inspiration for doing so was his Lord and Savior, Jesus Christ. Philippians 2:5–11 (partially quoted on page 108) tells us of the humility of Jesus Christ. Jesus, God's only Son,

Fullness in Following Christ

St. Jerome said "One is rich enough who is poor with Christ." Sometimes, as in the life of St. Maximilian Kolbe, the person who aligns himself or herself with Christ is called to the gift of **martyrdom**. Take some time to brainstorm the names of people (famous or not so famous) you believe have found fullness of life by following Jesus. Don't get stuck only on "churchy-types." Think of friends, relatives, neighbors, teachers, and acquaintances who reflect a spirit of having found fullness of life in Jesus Christ. Make a list of five to ten names and then answer the questions that follow:

- What is a wise quotation about faith in Jesus or life in general you have heard someone on your list say?
- How has someone on your list incorporated sacrifice into his or her life, that is, giving up some pleasures in order to develop the self-discipline of following Jesus?
- What have you learned from anyone on your list about how you should treat others, including your enemies?
- Who on your list do you think would be willing to give up his or her life for another? Explain why you chose that person.
- Is there anyone you would be willing to die for? Describe a possible scenario when you might be willing to be a martyr.

Lesson 1 Objectives

The students will:

- review Chapter 4.
- discuss the meaning of sacrifice.
- describe the sacrifice of St. Maximilian Kolbe.
- identify people who have made sacrifices for the sake of others.

Lesson 1 Preview

This lesson readies the students to delve into the great sacrifice of Jesus made on the Cross. They grow in their understanding of what true sacrifice is and means. They examine their own willingness to do as Jesus did, that is, to sacrifice for others.

became man and lived with us. He so loved us that he gave up his life for us. He came to save the last, the lost, and the least, dying so that our sins may be forgiven and we might have eternal life. The Letter to the Philippians continues by saying that because of Jesus' actions

> . . . God greatly exalted him
> and bestowed on him the name
> that is above every name,
> that at the name of Jesus every knee should bend,
> of those in heaven and on earth and under
> the earth,
> and every tongue confess that
> Jesus Christ is Lord,
> to the glory of God the Father.
> (Phil 2:9–11)

Jesus Christ is Lord—our eternal friend and Savior. St. Maximilian Kolbe died so that one man might live. Jesus Christ died so that all people might have eternal life.

For Reflection

Who is someone or what is something you could be compelled to give up your life for?

Christ's Redemptive Death (*CCC*, 595–623)

Jesus Christ's redemptive Death on the cross and his Resurrection is the high point of human history. It was not the result of chance but part of the mystery of God's saving plan of Salvation, promised to humanity immediately after the Original Sin of Adam and Eve. Sacred Scripture itself had foretold God's plan of Salvation through the death of a Suffering Servant prophesied in Isaiah 53. Also, St. Paul professed that "Christ died for our sins in accordance with the scriptures" (1 Cor 15:3). After his Resurrection, when he appeared to

martyrdom
The word *martyr* means "witness." Martyrdom applies to a person who bears witness to the truth of his or her faith even unto death. Jesus died the death of a faithful martyr. St. Stephan is recognized as the first Christian martyr.

Reading the Passion

Read the Passion narrative in the Gospel of John, chapters 18–19. To summarize the reading, write one or two key Scripture passages for each of these events.

- Jesus Is Arrested
- Peter's Denials
- Trial before Pilate
- Crucifixion of Jesus
- Taking Jesus Down from the Cross
- Burial of Jesus

Lesson 1 Homework

1. Assign the activity outlined in the feature "Reading the Passion" (page 111).
2. Have the students turn to Ongoing Assignments on page 130. Point out that they are to choose any three of the listed assignments to complete prior to the conclusion of this chapter.
3. In preparation for their next lesson, tell the students to read "Christ's Redemptive Death" (pages 111–116).

Teaching Approaches

So Another Might Live (pages 110–111)

- If possible, have the students watch one of the numerous videos (many are free and available online) about the life and martyrdom of St. Maximilian Kolbe. If viewing a video is not feasible, simply call on different students to draw on their reading and to tell in their own words the sacrifice made by this modern-day saint.
- Afterward, have the students turn to "Desire of the Martyrs" in this chapter's Primary Source Quotations section on pages 129–130. Read aloud the quotation from St. Catherine of Siena. Go on to point out that Maximilian Kolbe's choice for martyrdom was not some super-human act, but a very human one, an act of self-giving love, a true sacrifice.
- Call attention to the For Reflection feature on page 111. Invite the students to give the question some serious thought and then to write on a slip of paper or index card the name of someone or something for which they would give up their life. Then have the students share what they wrote with a partner expressing why they chose this person or thing, and what they expect other students to choose. Discuss the responses as a class and decide what types of things teenagers would give their life in self-sacrifice. Have them post their index cards in their lockers or at home in their rooms.
- Have the students turn to the opening activity "Fullness in Following Christ" on page 110. Read over the directions with the class. Then allow time for the students to make their lists of people who have found fullness of life in Jesus and to write their responses to the activity's five questions. Afterward, invite the students to share their responses with a partner or in small groups.

Chapter 5: The Passion and Death of Jesus Christ—Lesson 2

Bell Ringers

- Give each student six index cards. Divide a bulletin board or whiteboard into six sections. Label each section with the core events of Jesus' Passion (from John's Gospel) as detailed in the feature "Reading the Passion" on page 111. Let each event serve as the heading of a separate column:
  - Jesus Is Arrested
  - Peter's Denials
  - Trial Before Pilate
  - Crucifixion of Jesus
  - Taking Jesus Down from the Cross
  - Burial of Jesus

  Have the students share a passage they discovered about each event by writing it on the index card and then affixing it beneath the proper event heading.
- Once all the passages are posted, invite the students to place themselves in a spirit of prayer. Call on different students to read each column aloud. Note how even if the passages are out of order or if there are repetitions, the power of the Passion shines through.
- Before moving on, take a moment to brainstorm the word "passion." Besides its connotations of suffering, the term also speaks to fervor, zeal, delight, or ardor. Suggest to the students that as they delve deeper into Jesus' Passion, to pay attention to how it reveals God's ardor for us.

Teaching Approaches

Christ's Redemptive Death (pages 111-116)

- Remind the students of Paul's words: "Christ died for our sins in accordance with the scriptures" (1 Cor 15:3). Review the importance of Isaiah's prophecy of the Suffering Servant. Reread Isaiah 53 and ask the students to explain why Christ had to suffer. What will result from his suffering? Why was it necessary for Jesus to suffer on the Cross?
- Call attention to "Theological Meaning of the Death of Jesus" (page 112). Point out the results of Jesus'

112 Jesus Christ: Source of Our Salvation

his disciples on the road to Emmaus, and then later to the Apostles, Jesus showed them how his Death and Resurrection were recorded in Scripture:

> He said to them, "These are my words that I spoke to you while I was still with you, that everything written about me in the law of Moses and in the prophets and psalms must be fulfilled." Then he opened their minds to understand the scriptures. And he said to them, "Thus it is written that the Messiah would suffer and rise from the dead on the third day and that repentance, for the forgiveness of sins, would be preached in his name to all the nations, beginning from Jerusalem. You are witnesses of these things." (Lk 24:44–48)

"God proves his love for us in that while we were still sinners Christ died for us" (Rom 5:8). The sins of humans, following Original Sin, result in the punishment of death. But God did not abandon humankind. He sent his own Son to redeem us from our sins. Jesus embraced his Father's plan of Salvation from the first moment of his Incarnation. Jesus said, "My food is to do the will of the one who sent me and to finish his work" (Jn 4:34). As John the Baptist testified, Jesus was the Lamb of God, the Suffering Servant who bore the sins of the people and the Paschal Lamb, the symbol of Israel's Redemption at the first Passover.

Theological Meaning of the Death of Jesus

By his Passion and Death, Jesus showed us the depth of God's love, which desires the Salvation of all people. His sacrifice redeemed us, took away our sins, and restored us to communion with God. Christ's sacrifice is unique. It is a gift from the Father who handed his Son over to sinners to reconcile us with himself. "At the same time it is the offering of the Son of God made man, who in freedom and love offered his life to his Father through the Holy Spirit in reparation for our disobedience" (*CCC*, 614).

Jesus chose to be crucified to prove beyond doubt his immense love for us. In obedience to the Father, according to God's plan, Jesus' Death on the cross won our Salvation, bestowing on us, through the Holy Spirit, God's own abundant life. In his unique and definitive sacrifice, Christ took our sins to the cross and, like a New Adam, *represented* us to the Father. By substituting for each human being, Jesus took on our guilt and died a death we deserve. His motive was simply his desire to buy our freedom with his very Person and his eternal love. In his suffering and Death, Jesus' humanity became the free and perfect instrument of divine love, a self-surrendering gift of love on our behalf. It opened eternal life to us, a supreme gift that we sinners do not deserve. Jesus shows us God with a human face. His sacrifice on the cross is the perfect example of love. He gave all that we might have eternal life.

Lesson 2 Objectives

The students will:

- reflect on the key events of Jesus' Passion.
- define the meaning of "passion."
- summarize the scriptural bases for Jesus' Passion.
- describe the theological meaning of Jesus' Death.
- describe why Pilate, the Jewish religious leaders, and all sinners are to blame for executing Jesus.
- decide who is ultimately responsible for the Death of Jesus.

Lesson 2 Preview

This lesson helps the students better understand the reasons for Christ's Death on the Cross. Consider drawing on material from the Background Information below to enhance your presentation of the lesson's major themes.

Who Is Responsible for Jesus' Death?

With the eyes of faith, and instructed by the Magisterium, we can understand how Jesus' Death was part of God's plan of Salvation. What is more difficult to understand is why certain people living in Jesus' time conspired to put him to death. The sections below examine some of the historical reasons that led to Jesus' Death.

Crucified under Pontius Pilate

Jesus died by crucifixion, a punishment the Romans used mainly for slaves and revolutionaries. Crucifixion was one of history's most brutal forms of capital punishment. It was meant to torture and shame the condemned man and serve as a warning to those who witnessed it not to commit the same crime. The variations of crucifixion included nailing or tying the extremities to the cross, stretching the arms on the crossbeam, and impaling the genitals. The traditional image of Jesus with his feet and wrists nailed to the cross is also historically plausible. In contrast, the Jewish method of capital punishment was by stoning. This is what some tried to do to the woman caught in adultery (Jn 8:1–11). It was the way St. Stephen, the first Christian martyr, was put to death (Acts 7:54–60).

Specifically, the Roman charge against Jesus was that he was "the King of the Jews." This crime was written on the official inscription posted on the cross on which Jesus hung. Pontius Pilate, governor or prefect of Judea, in the year AD 30 condemned Jesus to death after hearing charges against him and examining him in a hearing. The Synoptic Gospels report that Pilate offered the crowd a choice of releasing Barabbas (a bandit or insurrectionist) or Jesus. The chief priests incited the crowd to ask for Barabbas, so Pilate caved in to their demands and had Jesus scourged and crucified. John 18:28–40 also tells of a hearing before Pilate. In this Gospel as well, Pilate disregarded the truth and had Jesus executed.

Ironically, Jesus truly was the King of the Jews, the Messiah whom the Jews were awaiting. However, Jesus' rule was not one of political or military power but one of humble service. Both Pilate and the Jewish leaders who opposed Jesus viewed him as a threat to Roman authority and the relatively peaceful relations the Jewish authorities had with Roman occupation forces. So Pilate dealt with Jesus the way Romans dealt with all potential revolutionaries—by executing him. Significantly, Jesus died with two other men who were also seen as threats, men described as "bandits" or "rebels."

Ultimately, then, the one person responsible for Jesus' Death was Pontius Pilate, the Roman prefect of Judea, Samaria, and Idumea from AD 26 to 36. With the cooperation of some religious authorities in Jerusalem, Pilate sentenced Jesus of Nazareth to death, probably in April of AD 30. The Jewish writer Philo described Pilate as "corrupt, violent, abusive and cruel." The Gospels suggest that Pilate thought Jesus was probably innocent of the charge brought against him. However, he violated his conscience and did the politically expedient thing by having Jesus executed.

The Role of Jewish Officials in Jesus' Death

Jesus was a popular teacher who rubbed some of the Jewish officials of his day in the wrong way. Furthermore, though he was not a trained rabbi, he spoke with authority on points of the Law. And people listened to him.

Among the Jewish officials who were upset by Jesus were the Pharisees, a strict Jewish sect that tried to perfectly follow the requirements of the Mosaic Law. On many occasions they felt that Jesus disregarded the Mosaic Law. Jesus responded: "Do not think I have come to abolish the law of the prophets. I have not come to abolish but fulfill" (Mt 5:17). Jesus was a new lawgiver. He got to the root

Lesson 2 Homework

1. Tell the students to write out their answers to the For Review questions on page 116.
2. Direct the students to read the text section "Overview of the Passion Narratives" (pages 116–119) in preparation for their next session.
3. Remind the students to continue working on their chosen Ongoing Assignments.

suffering on our behalf: (1) Redemption, (2) reconciliation, and (3) restoration.

- To explain that no one other than God himself can fulfill this promise, read aloud the following from Psalm 49:8–10, 16:

> One cannot redeem oneself, pay to God
> a ransom. Too high the price to redeem a
> life; one would never have enough to stay
> alive forever and never see the pit. . . .
> But God will redeem my life, will take me
> from the power of Sheol.

- Stress that deliverance must come from God. Human beings are not capable of self-redemption. Just as the first move in the act of creation belonged to God, so does the first move in Redemption/re-creation.
- Explain to the students that describing Christ's sacrifice as a ransom paid for sinners has always been a popular analogy used by the Church. This terminology, taken from Psalm 49:7 and placed in the context of Philippians 2:5–11, became popular in the feudal society of the Middle Ages. Feudal lords kept peasants in debt to the point of slavery. Only a lord could discuss the debt with another landlord. So Christ, "though he was in the form of God," took the "form of a slave" and paid a ransom for the debt of sin. "The Son of Man did not come to be served, but to serve, and to give his life as a ransom for many." (Mt 20:28; Mk 10:45)
- Write the following question on the board: **Who killed Jesus?**
- Begin by calling on the students to describe Pontius Pilate and his role in the Death of Jesus. Help the students recognize that Pilate focuses on Jesus' political identity. He accuses Jesus of claiming to be king of the Jews. Jesus does not deny his kingship (Mk 15:2; Mt 27:11; Lk 23:3), but he does deny that his reign is of the present order of things. Discuss what motive Pilate would have to sentence Jesus to death despite finding no fault in him.
- Discuss the role of the Jewish religious leaders in Jesus' Death. Ask:
  - Why was Jesus so upsetting to the Pharisees and scribes?
  - Why did some accuse Jesus of being in line with the devil?
  - Why was Jesus' "attack" on the Temple so upsetting? (*Note*: Jesus' attack on the Temple was an attack not only on the sellers and moneychangers but also on the Temple priesthood whose prestige

and income were tied to the Temple and the Temple tax.)

- What charge did the Sanhedrin bring against Jesus?

- Draw attention to "All People Bear Responsibility for Jesus' Death," pages 115–116. Read from the *Catechism of the Catholic Church* the following quotation from St. Francis of Assisi:

> We must regard as guilty all those who continue to relapse into their sins. Since our sins made the Lord Christ suffer the torment of the cross, those who plunge themselves into disorders and crimes crucify the Son of God anew in their hearts (for he is in them) and hold him up to contempt. And it can be seen that our crime in this case is greater in us than in the Jews. As for them, according to the witness of the Apostle, "None of the rulers of this age understood this; for if they had, they would not have crucified the Lord of glory." We, however, profess to know him. And when we deny him by our deeds, we in some way seem to lay violent hands on him. Nor did demons crucify him; it is you who have crucified him and crucify him still, when you delight in your vices and sins. (*CCC*, 598)

anti-Semitism
Unfounded prejudice against the Jewish people.

Sanhedrin
The seventy-one-member supreme legislative and judicial body of the Jewish people. Many of its members were Sadducees.

of what the Law required. For example, whereas the Law forbid killing, Jesus said that we should avoid anger because it leads to murder. He agreed that we should not commit adultery, as the Law commanded, "but I say to you whoever looks at a woman with lust has already committed adultery with her in his heart" (Mt 5:28). Jesus also taught on certain ritual purity and dietary laws, declaring that all foods are "clean" and it is "what comes out of a person, that is what defiles" (Mk 7:20). Moreover, Jesus criticized the Pharisees who followed certain customs to avoid responsibility for paying lip service to what God really requires, such as taking care of their parents (Mk 7:8–15).

Also, Jesus associated with sinners, tax collectors, and prostitutes—activities which scandalized the Pharisees and scribes. Jesus defended himself by sharing the parable of the lost or prodigal son (Lk 15:11–32), justifying his behavior by showing that he and his Father are compassionate like the loving father in the parable. To make such a claim—to do what only God could do, to forgive sin—was considered blasphemy and a crime punishable by stoning to death under Jewish Law. In John 8:31–59 Jesus even explicitly claimed to be God when he said, "Amen, Amen, I say to you, before Abraham came to be, I AM." The people immediately recognized that Jesus was claiming to be God ("I AM" is the translation for the Hebrew word for God, *Yahweh*), so they picked up stones to throw at him.

Some religious leaders thought that Jesus was possessed by Satan. Certain exorcisms and other miracles Jesus performed led some of his opponents to question the source of Jesus' power. Since they could not accept that he was the Messiah, a friend of sinners, and one who violated some of their customs and challenged their authority, they concluded that his power must come from Satan. Jesus answered:

> I am not possessed; I honor my Father, but you dishonor me. I do not seek my own glory; there is one who seeks it and he is the one who judges. (Jn 8:49–50)

A tipping point in the judgment of Jesus came shortly before his Passion when he predicted that the temple of his body would be destroyed and

Background Information

Did the Father demand the death of the Son?

In the Old Testament, sin might be called the opposite of the idea of God. God is strength, and God's whole action tends only to give strength and life. Sin, however, always produces a state of weakness, which is the forerunner of death. God initiates the relationship between himself and humanity; sin is a failure on the part of humanity to communicate and keep open the relationship with God. Wherever sin rears its ugly head, it destroys communion with God and delivers the sinner either to himself, herself, or to evil forces. Thus, if humans sin, and "there is no man who does not sin" (1 Kgs 8:26), then they stand in need of Redemption. Who can redeem humankind? Not humans themselves (see Psalm 49:8–10), for to do so, humans would have to bring a ransom to God, and no human being is so worthy. Atonement of sin, therefore, must come from God.

The Old Testament reveals that every means humanity used for reconciliation with God was put at their disposal by God. In God's great love, God desired to save all of humanity. God's plan was to raise human beings to have a share in his divine life and glory. In the Old Testament, God gave his people many means to forgiveness (e.g., Leviticus 16—the Day of Atonement, Yom Kippur), and yet none was adequate enough to join humanity to God. Thus, God had to complete the plan himself by sending his Son into the world as a human being. Jesus, God-with-us, set about joining humankind to God—a mission of atonement.

rebuilt in three days (see Jn 2:14–23). Certain witnesses who heard this teaching interpreted Jesus' prediction as an attack on the Jerusalem Temple, even claiming that he was involved in revolutionary activity. Again, the actual evidence did not merit such a belief. Jesus had always honored the Temple. He was presented there forty days after his birth and taught in it at the age of twelve. In addition, Jesus traveled to the Temple in Jerusalem to celebrate the Passover feast. In his public life, he taught in the Temple precincts during certain Jewish feasts, even on one occasion removing the moneychangers stationed there. Quoting Scripture, he said, "My house shall be a house of prayer, but you have made it a den of thieves" (Mk 19:46).

The chief priest, Joseph Caiaphas, and members of the Jewish ruling body, the **Sanhedrin**, had an economic and religious interest in the Temple. They feared a rebellion. They wanted the peaceful status quo that kept them in power and did not want any excuse for the Romans to clamp down a rebellion with repressive measures. So they brought the charge of insurrection to Pilate. Coupled with it was what to many of them was outrageous and blasphemous—Jesus' claim to be the "Messiah, the son of the Blessed One" (see Mk 14:61). This led Caiaphas to say, "[I]t is better for you that one man should die instead of the people, so that the whole nation may not perish" (Jn 11:50).

In summary, there were many reasons certain Jewish officials wanted Jesus removed. His association with sinners, his exorcisms, his teachings on dietary and ritual purity laws, his teaching with unique authority, his claims to be the Messiah, his forgiving of sin, and his claim to be Lord of the Sabbath were all factors that led religious leaders like the chief priest and members of the Sanhedrin to turn Jesus over to Pilate for execution.

All People Bear Responsibility for Jesus' Death

A tragic historical reality has been to blame the Jewish people as a whole for the death of Jesus. The complex trial of Jesus shows that only a few Jewish officials were in cohort with Pilate, who ultimately put Jesus to death. The real authors and instruments of Jesus' crucifixion are sinners, that is, each of us. We believers crucify Jesus every time we betray him through our sins. It is for our sins that Jesus died.

Jesus freely offered his life to liberate us from our sins and bestow eternal life on us. He underwent the excruciating torments of the most painful form of death devised by human beings out of his immense love for us.

Today, blaming the Jews as a people for Jesus' death—a form of **anti-Semitism**—is contrary to the love of Christ. The Second Vatican Council teaches:

> [W]hat happened in His passion cannot be charged against all the Jews, without distinction, then alive, nor against the Jews of today. . . . [T]he Jews should not be presented as rejected or accursed by God, as if this followed from the Holy Scriptures. . . .
>
> Furthermore, in her rejection of every persecution against any man, the Church . . . decries hatred, persecutions, displays of anti-Semitism, directed against Jews at any time and by anyone.
>
> Besides, as the Church has always held and holds now, Christ underwent His passion and death freely, because of the sins of men and out of infinite love, in order that all may reach Salvation. . . .
>
> We cannot truly call on God, the Father of all, if we refuse to treat in a brotherly way any man, created as he is in the image of God. Man's relation to God the Father and his relation to men his brothers are so linked together that Scripture says: "He who

- Ask one of the students to read the definition of anti-Semitism. Share a brief summary of this history of the Jewish people since the coming of Christ and the destruction of the Temple in AD 70. Highlight the harsh treatment of the Jews by Christians during the Crusades, the Inquisition, and even the Holocaust of World War II. Note that Vatican II hoped to eliminate the anti-Semitic view that the Jewish people were to blame for the crucifixion of Christ.
- Divide the class into two groups. Call attention to the feature "Jesus on Trial," page 116. Assign one group to be Jesus' prosecution, the other his defense. Distribute Chapter 5, Handout 1, "Jesus on Trial" and instruct students to individually write down arguments for both sides of the case. Then, invite them to write down why Pilate, the Sanhedrin, and all sinners wished to crucify Jesus.
- Have the students join the rest of their group to prepare a "case" against or for Jesus' conviction. Ask them to make a list of witnesses that they would call to support their case. Direct the groups to assign each member a role in the trial: lawyers or witnesses. Allow ample time for the groups to prepare for the trial by completing the handout.

Background Information continued

To speak about atonement in first-century Judea, we must do so in *sacrificial* terms. Those were the terms Jesus used, because they were the only terms readily understandable to his Jewish contemporaries. To understand the meaning of Jesus' Death, then, we must look to the reason Jesus himself gave: "This is my blood of the covenant, which will be shed on behalf of many for the forgiveness of sins" (Mt 26:28), a reason echoed and reinforced in 1 John 2:2; 4:10; Hebrews 9:11–10:18; Romans 3:21–26. Jesus *poured out his blood* "for the forgiveness of sin," thus linking his actions to the acts of atonement in the Old Testament. Jesus *chose* to atone (expiate) "for sin" in a *sacrificial manner.* His sacrifice—his suffering and Death—were not precipitated by a bloodthirsty and rancorous deity but by a sinful humanity.

Jesus did not elect himself a hero. Nor did the Father demand a martyr. Jesus' Paschal Mystery was an act of overwhelming love for God the Father and for all humankind. Jesus gave his life in perfect freedom in order to do the Father's will: to lead humankind past sin, through death, and to life forever with God: "I lay down my life in order to take it up again. No one takes it from me, but I lay it down on my own. I have power to lay it down, and power to take it up again. This command I have received from my Father" (Jn 10:17–18). So, did the Father demand the death of the Son? No. Our sin demanded it. And that demand was met by a holy saving act of self-giving love, God's own self-sacrifice.

- The format of the trial should proceed as follows: opening arguments, prosecution witnesses called to testify (with opposing questions from defense), defense witnesses called to testify (with opposing questions from the prosecution), and closing arguments. The teacher will act as the judge and jury. Be sure to discuss the trial, the arguments, and the decision with the students after the activity is completed.
- Conclude by playing a recording of the hymn "What Wondrous Love Is This?" Afterward, put the following equation on the board: **1 Cross + 3 Nails = 4given**. Point out that both the hymn and the aphorism remind us that Jesus died for *our* sins. Indeed Jesus makes this clear, declaring that his blood will be shed "for the forgiveness of sins" (Mt 26:28).

does not love does not know God (1 John 4:8)." (*Declaration on the Relationship of the Church to Non-Christian Religions*, No. 4–5)

For Review

1. Why did Jesus die?
2. What was the method of capital punishment used by the Romans? What was the method of capital punishment used by the Jews during Jesus' time?
3. Why did Pontius Pilate crucify Jesus?
4. Name three factors that led some Jewish opponents of Jesus to conspire against him.
5. Why is it wrong to blame the Jewish people for the death of Jesus Christ?
6. How are all people implicated in the death of Jesus?

Jesus on Trial

Develop a prosecution and defense as if you were putting Jesus on trial in a court of law. To prepare for either side of the case, read the following passages:

- Arrest of Jesus (Mk 14:43-52)
- Jesus before the Sanhedrin (Mk 14:53-62)
- Jesus before Pilate (Mk 15:1-15; Jn 18:28-38; Lk 23:1-5)

The prosecution argument must build a case against Jesus. Possible accusations might include the threat to tear down the Temple, blasphemy, claiming to be king, misleading the people on the payment of taxes (Lk 23:2), instigating riots. Draw additional "evidence" from the Gospels, such as violation of Sabbath laws and disturbing the peace.

Your defense response will examine the charges and then answer them one by one by citing appropriate Scripture passages.

You may wish to work on this exercise with a partner. Each of you will take a different side in the case. Then argue the case in front of a teacher or your classmates.

For Reflection

Write a short reflection that discusses the following proposition: "To be anti-Semitic is to be anti-Christian."

Overview of the Passion Narratives

The Paschal Mystery of Christ's Passion, Death, and Resurrection is the heart of the Gospel. These events are commemorated in a special way liturgically during Holy Week when the Church celebrates the Paschal Mystery of God's love for his people. The Sacrament of Baptism initiates us into the Paschal Mystery. The Eucharist represents (makes present) the Paschal Mystery and allows us to enter into it. In the Gospels, the **passion narratives** detail the events of Christ's Passion, Death, and Resurrection.

The Passion narratives were probably the oldest stories about Jesus proclaimed by the early Church. They were formed and added very quickly to the liturgy. They included many references to Old Testament prophecies that alluded to the death of the Messiah. For example, Mark's account of Jesus' crucifixion includes the following references to Old Testament prophecies:

- the offer of wine (Ps 69)
- the division of Jesus' garments (Ps 22)

For Review Answers (page 116)

1. Jesus chose to die to prove his love; by his Death he redeemed us, reconciled us, and restored us to communion with God.
2. Crucifixion. Stoning.
3. He was cruel and, persuaded by the large crowd led by the Sanhedrin, he had Jesus executed in the same way he would have executed any revolutionary.
4. Jesus' association with sinners; his exorcisms; his teachings on the Law; his unique authority; his Messianic claims; his claim to be able to forgive sins; his calling himself Lord of the Sabbath; and his prophecy of the Temple being destroyed.
5. Blaming the Jews today for the Death of Jesus is a form of anti-Semitism. Such prejudicial and uncharitable behavior is contrary to the love Christ preached and showed by his Death.
6. Jesus died because of human sinfulness. We are all guilty of sin, which affects Christ himself. When we sin we crucify Christ in our hearts.

The Passion and Death of Jesus Christ 117

- the presence of two robbers (Is 63)
- the reactions of the mockers (Ps 22; Wis 2)
- the darkness (Am 8)
- Jesus' final prayer (Ps 22)
- the offer of vinegar (Ps 69)
- the loud cry of Jesus (Ps 31)
- the tearing of the Temple veil (Ex 26)

Different Points of Emphasis in the Passion Narratives

The Evangelists agree on the essential details in the passion narratives but wrote from unique perspectives with different points of emphasis. Each of the Paschal narratives includes the following common elements:

- the arrest
- questioning by the high priest
- the trials before the Sanhedrin and Pontius Pilate
- the condemnation
- the crucifixion
- the death
- the burial

The Evangelists shaped the events of Christ's Passion in order to emphasize certain theological points. The Gospels of Matthew and Mark stress elements of abandonment but also vindication at the end. Some elements of abandonment include Judas betraying Jesus, the three disciples falling asleep during Jesus' agony, and Peter's denial. Also, when Jesus

is arrested, everyone flees; even the young man lurking on the outskirts runs away and loses his garment (see Mk 14:51). The Jewish and Roman authorities harshly judge Jesus, and he is sentenced to death. Even then, Jesus is mocked by the soldiers and crowds. Vindication comes immediately after Jesus breathes his last breath: the veil in the Temple is torn in two, indicating that a New Covenant is in force and that a new age has dawned. A Roman centurion—ironically a Gentile—confesses Jesus' identity: "Truly this man was the Son of God!" (Mk 15:39).

Luke's Gospel presents the disciples in a more favorable light; for example, they fall asleep only once, not three times, and only then because they are sorrowful at Jesus' impending fate. Luke emphasizes Jesus' compassion through the whole ordeal. Jesus heals the slave's ear in

passion narratives
The name for the four separate accounts of the Passion of Christ. The passion narratives of the Synoptic Gospels follow a general literary and thematic plan. The passion narrative of John's Gospel provides an independent version.

Lesson 3 Objectives

The students will:

- make connections between the Old Testament prophecies and the Passion of Christ.
- investigate key elements of the Passion.
- compare and contrast the passion narratives of the Gospels.
- label a map of Jerusalem with the events of Jesus' Passion and Death.

Lesson 3 Preview

This lesson leads the students along the pathway to the Cross. The passion narratives recount more than the story of Jesus' last three days. They serve as the highpoint of the Good News. Be sure to allow ample time for the students to read and reflect on these important Gospel passages.

Chapter 5: The Passion and Death of Jesus Christ—Lesson 3

Bell Ringer

- Ask the students to offer their responses to the six For Review questions on page 116 (answers are on page 134 of this text). Encourage the students to ask any other questions they may have.

Teaching Approaches

Overview of the Passion Narratives (pages 116-119)

- Introduce this lesson on the passion narratives by listing on the board the following Gospel references to the narratives:
  - **Matthew 26:14–27:66**
  - **Mark 14:1–15:47**
  - **Luke 22:14–23:56**
  - **John 18:1–19:42**
- Call attention to the text which says that these narratives were probably the earliest and clearly the most important stories about Jesus proclaimed by the Church. In fact, when the Church chose which books would be included in the New Testament canon, the presence of the passion narrative was always essential. Stress that they remain crucial to our liturgy and life today. Remind the students that we hear one of the synoptic passion narratives proclaimed on Passion/Palm Sunday each year (Matthew: Year A, Mark: Year B, Luke: Year C). The Passion according to John is proclaimed on Good Friday every year.
- Assign one of the Gospels to each student. Ask them to read the crucifixion account of their Gospel (Mt 27, Mk 15, Lk 23, Jn 19) and then write the verse that applies to each of the references to the Old Testament prophecies. Note that not all the Gospels will include all of the prophecies. Afterward, point out in the text (pages 116–117) that Mark included numerous references to Old Testament prophecies. Have the students use their Bibles to find and then write out the particular verse(s) that speak to the prophecies. Afterward, have the students share their findings:
  - *the offer of wine—Psalm 69:21–22 (Mt 27:34; Mk 15:23)*
  - *the division of Jesus' garments—Psalm 22:19 (Mt 27:35; Mk 22:24; Lk 23:34; Jn 19:24)*

  - *the presence of two robbers—Isaiah 53:12 (Mt 27:38; Mk 15:27; Lk 23:33; Jn 19:18)*
  - *the reactions of the mockers—Psalm 22:8–9 and Wisdom 2:16–19 (Mt 27:39–43; Mk 15:29–32; Lk 23:35–36)*
  - *the darkness—Amos 8:9 (Mt 27:25; Mk 15:33; Lk 23:44)*
  - *Jesus' final prayer—Psalm 22:2–3 (Mt 27:46; Mk 34)*
  - *the offer of vinegar—Psalm 31:21–22 (Mt 27:48; Mk 15:36; Lk 23:36; Jn 19:29–30)*
  - *the loud cry of Jesus—Psalm 31:6 (Mt 27:50; Mk 15:27; Lk 23:46)*
  - *the tearing of the Temple veil—Exodus 26:31 (Mt 27:51; Mk 15:38; Lk 23:45)*
- After the students have completed the assignment, match them up with students who focused on one of the three other Gospels. Invite them to discuss which Gospels included all of the prophecies, which Gospel left the most out, and why certain Gospels did not include certain prophecies. Afterward, discuss these questions as a class.
- Distribute copies of Chapter 5, Handout 2, "Elements of the Passions." Use the text section "Different Points of Emphasis in the Passion Narratives" (pages 117–119) to fill in the spaces connected to the headings Matthew and Mark, Luke, John, and Common to All Narratives. Answer should include:

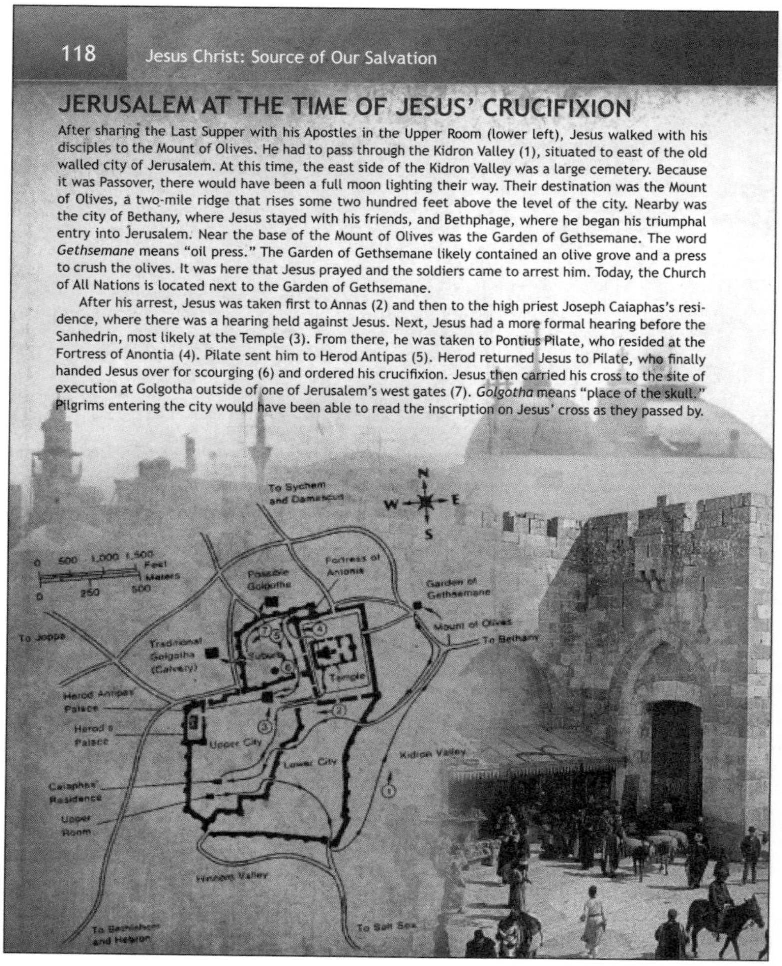

118 Jesus Christ: Source of Our Salvation

JERUSALEM AT THE TIME OF JESUS' CRUCIFIXION

After sharing the Last Supper with his Apostles in the Upper Room (lower left), Jesus walked with his disciples to the Mount of Olives. He had to pass through the Kidron Valley (1), situated to east of the old walled city of Jerusalem. At this time, the east side of the Kidron Valley was a large cemetery. Because it was Passover, there would have been a full moon lighting their way. Their destination was the Mount of Olives, a two-mile ridge that rises some two hundred feet above the level of the city. Nearby was the city of Bethany, where Jesus stayed with his friends, and Bethphage, where he began his triumphal entry into Jerusalem. Near the base of the Mount of Olives was the Garden of Gethsemane. The word *Gethsemane* means "oil press." The Garden of Gethsemane likely contained an olive grove and a press to crush the olives. It was here that Jesus prayed and the soldiers came to arrest him. Today, the Church of All Nations is located next to the Garden of Gethsemane.

After his arrest, Jesus was taken first to Annas (2) and then to the high priest Joseph Caiaphas's residence, where there was a hearing held against Jesus. Next, Jesus had a more formal hearing before the Sanhedrin, most likely at the Temple (3). From there, he was taken to Pontius Pilate, who resided at the Fortress of Anontia (4). Pilate sent him to Herod Antipas (5). Herod returned Jesus to Pilate, who finally handed Jesus over for scourging (6) and ordered his crucifixion. Jesus then carried his cross to the site of execution at Golgotha outside of one of Jerusalem's west gates (7). *Golgotha* means "place of the skull." Pilgrims entering the city would have been able to read the inscription on Jesus' cross as they passed by.

Lesson 3 Homework

1. Tell the students to write out their responses to the three For Review questions on page 119.
2. Tell the students to read the first part of the section "Tracing the Events of Our Salvation," pages 119–121 (through the section "The Last Supper").

For Review Answers (page 119)

1. Answers should include: the offer of wine, the division of Jesus' garments, the presence of two robbers, the reactions of the mockers, the darkness, Jesus' final prayer, the offer of vinegar, the loud cry of Jesus, and the tearing of the Temple veil.
2. Mark and Matthew focus on abandonment and vindication; Luke focuses on the compassion of Christ, and John focuses on Jesus' control over the events.
3. Itineraries should include: (1) the Mount of Olives and the Garden of Gethsemane, (2) Joseph Caiaphas's residence, (3) the Temple, (4) Fortress of Antonia, (5) to Herod Antipas, (6) back to Pilate, scourging, the carrying of the cross, and then (7) Golgotha.

the Garden; he comforts the women while carrying his cross on the way to Calvary; he promises that the Good Thief will be with him in Paradise; and he forgives his executioners while hanging on the cross. His last words are a faith-filled cry, "Father, into your hands I commend my spirit" (Lk 24:46).

The passion narrative in John 18–19 describes Jesus in control of the events. For example, he freely enters into the Passion: "I lay down my life in order to take it up again. No one takes it from me, but I lay it down on my own. I have power to lay it down, and power to take it up again" (Jn 10:17–18). At the time of his arrest, when asked if he is Jesus of Nazareth, he answered: "I AM," the divine name, which caused the soldiers to fall to the ground. When Peter wishes to defend him, Jesus tells him to put his sword away and indicates that what is happening is part of God's plan: "Shall I not drink the cup that the Father gave me?" (Jn 18:11). In John's Gospel, during the interrogation, Pilate, not Jesus, is put on the defensive. Jesus counters Pilate's threat by saying, "You would have no power over me if it had not been given to you from above" (Jn 19:11). On the way to Calvary, Jesus carries his own cross, with no help from Simon of Cyrene. From the cross, Jesus looks to the future by entrusting his mother to the Beloved Disciple. His last words are, "It is finished" (Jn 19:30), indicating that the work he came to do, his Father's will, the prophesies made in the Old Testament, and our Salvation have now been accomplished.

For Review

1. List five Old Testament prophecies that are fulfilled in Jesus' Passion narratives.
2. Describe the different theological emphases in the passion narratives of Mark, Matthew, Luke, and John.
3. Trace the itinerary of Jesus from the Last Supper to the time of his crucifixion.

For Reflection

- Which Gospel portrait of the Passion do you most identify with? Why?
- Imagine you were with Jesus in the Garden of Gethsemane. Give an honest assessment of how you would have responded to the situation.

Tracing the Events of Our Salvation

The events of our Salvation are part of God's eternal plan. Jesus said, "the Son of Man did not come to be served but to serve and give his life as ransom for many" (Mk 10:34). He also said:

> I am the good shepherd. A good shepherd lays down his life for his sheep. . . . No one takes [my life] from me, but I lay it down on my own. I have power to lay it down, and power to take it up again. This command I received from my Father. (Jn 10:11, 18)

How did these events unfold? The account in Matthew 26–27 (drawn in good part from Mark's Gospel) provides a detailed account.

Jesus Enters Jerusalem (Mt 21:1-13)

Recall that Jesus enters Jerusalem during the week before Passover, the feast that celebrates God's deliverance of the Israelites from slavery into freedom. When Jesus and his disciples reach the small villages of Bethphage and Bethany, near the Mount of Olives, he tells two of his disciples where to find a colt and they go off to retrieve it. Jesus rides into Jerusalem on the colt, thus fulfilling a prophecy of Zechariah 9:9. The crowds greet Jesus as a prophet. They spread out their cloaks as a sign of respect for

Lesson 4 Objectives

The students will:

- list the events leading up to the Passion and Death.
- describe significance of each event leading up to Jesus' Passion.
- identify misunderstandings they had about the events leading up to the Passion and Death of Jesus Christ.

Lesson 4 Preview

The final section of this chapter describes in detail the significance of each event during the last days of Jesus' life from his entry into Jerusalem to his burial. This lesson will focus on the events leading up to Christ's Passion and Death and Jesus' parting lessons to the disciples at Jerusalem.

- *Common to All Narratives*: Jesus' arrest, questioning by the high priest, trials before the Sanhedrin and Pilate, condemnation, crucifixion, Death, and burial.
- *Matthew and Mark*: elements of abandonment (Judas' betrayal, Apostles' sleeping, Peter's triple denial, the disciples' desertion, the unjust judgment, and the mocking) and vindication (torn Temple curtain, and the Centurion's divinity declaration).
- *Luke*: disciples fall asleep only once, and Jesus' compassion (healing of the servant's ear, comforting the women of Jerusalem, promising paradise to the good thief, forgiving the executioners, and the faith-filled final cry).
- *John*: Jesus in control of the events (Jesus' power over his destiny, declaration of divinity ["I AM"], refusing a violent defense, carrying his own cross, guaranteeing the future by making arrangements for his mother, and the claim of completion, "It is finished").

- Refer the students to the map feature "Jerusalem at the Time of Jesus' Crucifixion" on page 118. As you go through the key elements, point out where they took place on the map. Distribute Chapter 5, Handout 3, "Jesus' Way of the Cross." Have the students label the key places on the handout using the map on page 118 of the student text. Afterward, have students check their answers with a partner.

Chapter 5: The Passion and Death of Jesus Christ—Lesson 4

Bell Ringers

- Ask the students to offer their responses to the three For Review questions on page 119 (answers are on page 136 of this text). Encourage the students to ask any other questions they may have.
- Give the students three minutes to write every event they can remember from Jesus' entry into Jerusalem to his burial. Challenge the students to write as quickly and as much as possible. After the time is up, have the students get into groups of three or four and combine their answers. Finally, combine all of the lists of events into one master list for the class. Refer back to this periodically in comparison to the actual details of the Passion and Death.

Teaching Approaches

Tracing the Events of our Salvation (pages 119-121)

- Call on a volunteer to read aloud Matthew 21:1–13. Then have another student read Zechariah 9:9, while the rest of the class follows along in their Bibles. Ask the students to explain why Jesus would ride into the city on a colt. Afterward, you may wish to have the students sing—or play a recording of—a Passion/Palm Sunday hymn such as "All Glory, Laud, and Honor."
- Write the following on the board: **Hosanna in the highest**! Ask the students if they know what the word "hosanna" means. It means "come, save" or "save us now." This cry of the people is like a prayer and the answer to that prayer is Jesus. Ask the students to recall the meaning of the name "Jesus" ("God saves"). Point out that the two words have very similar meaning in Hebrew. Remind students that we sing "Hosanna" just before the consecration of the bread and wine just as the people sang "Hosanna" to welcome Jesus into Jerusalem before he celebrated the Last Supper.
- Note that Jesus driving out the moneychangers demonstrated his authority over Israel's religious practices and, as they saw in the previous lesson, it also spoke to his challenging the old and corrupt sacrificial system, abolishing all sacrifice but the one he was about to make.
- Ask another student to read Matthew 26:1–5, as the rest of the class follows along in their Bibles. Point out that the conspirators—all from the ranks of the spiritual elite, Sadducees, Pharisees, and scribes—were reacting to Jesus' attacks on their arrogance not, as they claimed, on their religion. Remind the students that Jesus himself said he did not come to overthrow the Law. Nevertheless, these leaders recognized that Jesus was challenging them and their authority. Have the students read Matthew 21:45–46.
- Call on a volunteer to read Matthew 26:6–13 and have the class follow along. Note the dual purpose of the anointing: (1) to point to Jesus' being anointed after death, and (2) to affirm his identity as the Messiah, the Anointed One, the Christ. Remind the students that "Christ" is not Jesus' last name, but a title that means "Anointed One."
- Have the students read Matthew 26:14–16 and John 22:3–6. Afterward, discuss Judas's actions. Discuss what the students feel drove Judas to betray Jesus: avarice or Satan's temptation?
- Ask a volunteer to read Matthew's account of the Last Supper (Mt 26:17–35). Ask the students to share what they think is significant about this event based

120 Jesus Christ: Source of Our Salvation

high priest
In Jewish history, the priest in charge of the Temple worship. The high priest shared in the general priestly duties, however, he was the only one allowed to enter the holy of holies, and only then on the Day of Atonement. He was a descendent of Aaron.

him and wave palm branches as they enthusiastically shout:

> Hosanna to the Son of David;
> blessed is he who comes
> in the name of the Lord;
> hosanna in the highest.
> (Mt 21:9)

Jesus enters the Temple area and drives out the moneychangers. He quotes to them the Scriptural passage, "My house shall be a house of prayer, but you are making it a den of thieves" (Mt 21:13). The incident is unusual because the business conducted at the Temple was religious in nature. Jesus' charge that the Temple had become a den of thieves showed that he had authority over the religious practices of Israel, a fact that enrages the religious leaders.

Conspiracy against Jesus (Mt 26:1-5)

The leaders conspire against Jesus while he teaches in the Temple. They want to do so in such a way that the crowds will not come to his defense and cause an uprising. However, the plan to not arrest Jesus "during the festival that there may not be a riot among the people" (Mt 26:5) failed. He was actually arrested on the night of Nisan 14, the Preparation Day of the Passover, and put to death the next day. Joseph Caiaphas, the **high priest**, is quoted in John 11:50 saying that it was better for Jesus to die than for the whole nation to perish. Other groups, for example, the Pharisees and Herodians (see Mk 12:13–17) also oppose Jesus. They question things like the source of his teaching authority, his views on beliefs like the resurrection of the dead, and whether it is lawful to pay taxes to Rome or not. They are also upset by Jesus' criticism of their hypocrisy, for example, when he told them, "You pay tithes of mint and dill and cumin, and have neglected the weightier things of the law: judgment and mercy and fidelity" (Mt 23:23). Jesus also upset the Sadducees, an aristocratic class that cooperated with Roman rule. They saw Jesus as a threat to the civil order and a danger to their position of leadership: "If we leave him alone, all will believe in him, and the Romans will come and take away both our land and our nation" (Jn 11:48).

Anointing at Bethany (Mt 26:6-13)

In Mark and Matthew's Gospel, an anonymous woman anoints Jesus' head with expensive oil at Bethany. (John's Gospel identifies the woman as Mary, the sister of Lazarus.) Some people (identified as Judas in John's Gospel) complain about the waste, observing that the costly ointment could have been sold for alms for the poor. But Jesus commends the woman's generous action because it foreshadows the anointing of his body after his Death. Anointing a body for burial was considered of higher merit than giving money to the poor, a task that could always be done. Proper burial of the dead was considered an essential condition for sharing in the Resurrection. Recall also that *Christ*

Lesson 4 Homework

1. Tell the students to write out their answers to the first three questions in the For Review section on pages 127–128.
2. Direct the students to read the rest of the section "Tracing the Events of Our Salvation" (pages 121–128) in preparation for their next session.
3. Remind the students to begin wrapping up work on their chosen Ongoing Assignments.

The Passion and Death of Jesus Christ 121

means, "anointed one." This woman of simple faith recognizes Jesus' true identity and mission when so many others do not.

Judas's Betrayal (Mt 26:14-16)

Judas Iscariot betrays Jesus for thirty pieces of silver. His motive of avarice fits John's description of Judas as the one who kept the money purse of the Apostles and who stole from it (Jn 12:6). Judas is willing to "hand him over," the same Greek verb used to describe how Jesus is handed over to Death. The Gospels of Luke and John mention that Satan influences Judas to betray his friend (Jn 22:3–6).

The Last Supper (Mt 26:17-35)

Jesus carefully plans the Passover meal by instructing his disciples to meet a man in whose house he will celebrate with his disciples. Jesus' planning of the Passover meal shows that he is in control of the events. The sacrifice he will make on our behalf is truly free since love is only love if it is freely given.

At the meal, Jesus foretells his betrayal. The Apostles are confused and deny that they would ever betray their master. But when Judas asks, "Surely it is not I, Rabbi?" Jesus answers, "You have said so" (Mt 26:25). The emphasis in Jesus' response is on the pronoun *you* to imply that Jesus would have answered if the question had not been asked.

Jesus then celebrates a Passover meal with his Apostles where he took bread, blessed it, broke it, and gave to his disciples saying, "Take and eat; this is my body" (Mt 26:26). In a similar way he took a cup, gave thanks, and gave it to his disciples saying, "Drink from it all, of you, for this is my blood of the covenant, which will be shed on behalf of many for the forgiveness of sin" (Mt 26:27–28). With these words, Jesus instituted the Eucharist, a celebration of Jesus' Passover from death to new life and the gift of himself to all believers under the forms of bread and wine. Jesus' Passion, Death, and Resurrection is God's new covenant with us, his way of delivering his people. The Eucharist that Christ instituted at the Last Supper is the memorial of his sacrifice. The Apostles (and their successors) will serve as the priests of the New Covenant, calling to mind what Jesus has accomplished for us and commanding us to pour ourselves out in service to others in imitation of him.

After the meal, Jesus and the Apostles make their way to the Mount of Olives where Jesus prays in great sorrow, just as King David did after his trusted son Absalom had betrayed him. On the way, Jesus predicts that the disciples will flee during the coming trials. But he also reassures them that after his Resurrection, he will go before them to Galilee where he—the Good Shepherd—will re-gather his flock. Jesus then predicts that Peter will deny him three times, though Peter proclaims, "Even though I should have to die with you, I will not deny you" (Mt 26:35).

The Agony in the Garden and the Arrest of Jesus (Mt 26:36-56)

Jesus' sorrow at his impending Death reveals a natural human response. From the depths of his soul, Jesus prays that the cup of impending death, which also involves his battle with Satan and sin, be taken from him. But he also prays the perfect prayer that not his will, but his Father's be done: "My Father, if it is possible, let this cup pass from me; yet, not as I will, but as you will" (Mt 26:39).

Jesus courageously accepts his destiny and does not flee from it. The Apostles are overcome with grief and cannot stay awake to comfort Jesus during his time of trial. Three times he needs to tell them to stay awake to prepare for the coming test. He warns them, "The spirit is willing, but the flesh is weak" (Mt 26:41). Their threefold failure to heed his plea

Lesson 5 Objectives

The students will:

- describe the key elements of Matthew's Passion with regard to Jesus' crucifixion, Death, and burial.
- write a prayer in reflection on the Passion and Death of Christ.
- reflect on the role of Mary.
- discuss ways to join themselves to the Cross of Christ.
- write an account of the Passion and Death from the perspective of one of the witnesses.

on previous chapters, and write the responses on the board. Review the connection Jesus makes between his sacrifice and the Paschal sacrifice of the Old Covenant.

- Point out that Jesus shared many meals with his friends and followers. He recognized that more passed between people than food. He even used the image of a banquet to stand as the greatest symbol of the Kingdom. Jesus gave more than bread and wine; he gave himself totally. He gave what we all seek, a larger life. Its price would be a death, but a death freely given and therefore holy and saving.
- Before moving on, consider playing play a recording of Mozart's "Ave Verum Corpus." (*Note*: Many versions are available on the Internet, e.g., on YouTube.) Tell the students this ancient hymn speaks to Jesus' sacrifice and real presence for us in the Eucharist. If you wish, post the Latin words and English translation on the board:

  Ave, verum corpus
  Hail, true body
  natum de Maria Virgine,
  born of the Virgin Mary,
  Vere passum immolatum
  Who truly suffered, sacrificed
  in Cruce pro homine,
  on the Cross for man,
  Cujus latus perforatum
  Whose pierced side overflowed
  unda (aqua) fluxit (et) sanguine,
  with water and blood,
  Esto nobis praegustatum
  Be for us a foretaste
  in mortis examine.
  in the test of death.

- To solidify the students' understanding of the events in this chapter, invite them to create an illustrated children's book depicting the events leading up to the Passion and Death of Christ. Have them fold blank sheets of printer paper in half to create these books. Each page should include the title of the event (Jesus' Entry into Jerusalem, Jesus Drives the Moneychangers Out of the Temple, Jesus Teaches in the Temple, the Anointing at Bethany, Judas's Betrayal, and the Last Supper), a picture of the event, and a short sentence that describes the significance of the event. Make sure students do not describe the picture in the sentence, but describe the *significance* of the event.

Chapter 5: The Passion and Death of Jesus Christ—Lesson 5

Bell Ringers

- Ask the students to offer their responses to the first three For Review questions on pages 127–128 (answers are on page 145 of this text). Encourage the students to ask any other questions they may have.
- To ready the students for this lesson, consider playing a recording of the hymn "Were You There?" Have them imagine that they were witnesses of the crucifixion. Invite them to journal about what they imagine.

Teaching Approaches

Tracing the Events of our Salvation (pages 121-128)

- This section of the text is full of many details about the Passion and Death of Christ. You may invite students to create a chart in their notes with three columns: Event, Summary of the Event, and Significance of the Event. Give students the opportunity to complete this chart as you progress through the lesson. Give them the opportunity to refer to their textbooks to complete the chart.
- Ask a volunteer to read Matthew 26:36–56. Point out the words of Jesus' prayer in the garden. Ask, "Of what other prayer of Jesus does this one remind you?" (*The Our Father/Lord's Prayer: ". . . thy will be done"*)
- Go on to tell the students that Jesus knows what is about to happen to him. Like it would affect any of us, it frightens him; and in his humanness, he wishes to avoid it. Nevertheless, his love for the Father and for us allows him to humble himself for our sakes and to do the will of his Father.
- Invite a student to read Mark 15:53–64. Explain to the students that it was illegal for the Sanhedrin to hold a trial at night that sought the death penalty, illegal to hold a trial during a religious festival (Passover), and illegal to have a trial without someone speaking on behalf of the accused. Ask the students to find the three accusations that the Sanhedrin made against Jesus. (*He claimed to destroy the Temple; he claimed to be the Messiah; and he committed blasphemy.*)

foreshadows Peter's threefold denial that is soon to come.

Sadly, one of Jesus' closest followers, Judas Iscariot, leads an armed crowd sent from the chief priest and elders of the people to arrest Jesus. Judas betrays Jesus with a kiss, and he does so under the cover of dark, the realm of Satan. A disciple of Jesus (identified as Peter in John's Gospel) draws his sword and cuts off the ear of the high priest's servant (named Malchus in John's Gospel). Jesus warns his disciple, "Put your sword back into its sheath, for all who take the sword will perish by the sword" (Mt 26:52). Jesus also reprimands the crowd that came to arrest him for using weapons. Jesus always taught openly and always taught peace. Even here in the Garden Jesus is consistent in refusing to conform to the expectation of many who believe the Messiah

would be a political, military leader who would use force against the Romans.

As he had predicted, all his disciples abandon Jesus at the time of his arrest.

Jesus before the Sanhedrin and Peter's Denial (Mt 26:57-27:10)

John 13 provides further detail that Jesus had a hearing before the former high priest Annas as well as the current high priest Joseph Caiaphas, and a session in front of the Sanhedrin. The exact sequence of events is not totally clear. However, Matthew's Gospel tells us that there was a night trial before Caiaphas at which were present scribes, elders, priests, and members of the Sanhedrin, the seventy-one-member official judicial and legislative body of the Jewish people. At this hearing, they try to obtain false evidence in order to pronounce a death penalty against him. They bring in false witnesses, two of whom claim that Jesus said he would destroy the Temple. Finally, Caiaphas asks Jesus if he is the Messiah, the Son of God. Jesus affirms he is and then says,

> From now on you will see "the Son of Man seated at the right hand of the Power" and "coming on the clouds of heaven." (Mt 26:64)

Jesus' proclamation outrages the religious leaders. The high priest tears his robes and accuses Jesus of committing the sin of blasphemy (that is, insulting God). Under Jewish law, blasphemy was punishable by death. Others (apparently the members of the Sanhedrin itself) in an act of total disrespect, spit on Jesus, strike, slap, and mock him, saying, "Prophesy for us, Messiah: who is it that struck you?" (Mt 26:68).

Meanwhile, Peter is out in the courtyard and is recognized by a maid as a friend of Jesus. Peter who had confessed Jesus to be the Messiah now betrays his friend and Master. As Jesus predicted,

Lesson 5 Preview

Be sure to read over the Scripture passages listed in the text as well as those cited in this lesson plan. With regard to Jesus' suffering, help the students realize that the important point is not that Jesus suffered more than anyone else, but that he suffered *like* anyone else. More than that, his suffering was profound and voluntary and the climax of a life and a Gospel of love. In other words, Jesus did not have to die in order to appease an angry and affronted God. Jesus died to identify with us and to conquer sin and death, not to appease a bloodthirsty God.

three times Peter denies knowing him. When the cock crows, Peter remembers Jesus' prediction. He immediately repents of his grave sin and weeps bitterly. His repentance and sorrow at his betrayal is in stark contrast to Judas who, once he realized his sin, despairs and commits suicide (Mt 27:5). Peter ends up bravely proclaiming his Lord after the Resurrection and, according to tradition, is crucified himself in an inverted position under one of Nero's persecutions. Peter's repentance and sorrow serve as a model to all sinners who have turned against Jesus through their sins. Christ will always accept us back as his friend if we repent and accept his forgiveness.

Under the Roman laws of occupation in effect in AD 30, only the Roman prefect had the right to inflict the death penalty for crimes of a nonreligious nature. Pilate would have scoffed at the Sanhedrin's religious charge of blasphemy. However, accusing Jesus of trying to usurp the emperor was seditious and a capital offense. This is the charge the Jewish authorities took to Pontius Pilate, hoping that he would pronounce the death penalty.

Jesus before Pilate (Mt 27:11-31)

The Jewish historian Josephus, writing in an independent source apart from Scripture, portrays Pontius Pilate as arrogant and cruel. He tells how Pilate once unleashed his soldiers, dressed as civilians, to beat Jewish citizens who were protesting Pilate's use of the Temple treasury to build an aqueduct. According to Josephus, toward the end of Pilate's ten-year rule (26–36), he inflicted violence on a Samaritan religious procession, an act that got him dismissed from his post and sent into exile.

Corroborating this evidence, all the Gospels portray Pilate as cynical. He knows that Jesus is innocent, yet he fails to follow his conscience. Matthew records Pilate's wife's warning to her husband not to execute Jesus. Luke's Gospel testifies that Pilate sends Jesus to Herod Antipas, the tetrarch of Galilee, who was in Jerusalem for the Passover celebration. When Jesus refuses to perform a sign, Herod mocks Jesus and his soldiers abuse him and send him back to Pilate.

Pilate then schemes to escape his responsibility by involving a Passover custom of freeing a prisoner of the citizens' choosing. Mark's and John's Gospels also mention this custom; Luke's original manuscript does not. There is no mention of this custom anywhere else apart from Scripture. Pilate thinks the crowd might call for Jesus to be released, but they choose Barabbas instead, a criminal who in fact is responsible for inciting riots. Jesus accepts Pilate's charge that he is King of the Jews, but does not answer the inquiries of the priests and elders. Pilate caves into the crowd's cry "Let him be crucified" when they ask him what he should do

Lesson 5 Homework

1. Tell the students to write out their answers to questions number four to eight in the For Review section on pages 127–128.
2. Remind the students to be ready to hand in their work on their chosen Ongoing Assignments at their next session.
3. Have the students read through the Chapter Quick View section on pages 129–131 and to review the chapter's Main Ideas. Tell the students to write out any questions they may have and bring them to the next session.

- Have a student read aloud Matthew 26:57–68 and 27:1–10. After the reading, ask: Why did the Sanhedrin, which accused Jesus of *blasphemy*, bring the charge of *sedition* to Pilate instead? (*Pilate would care little about a charge of blasphemy against a deity he didn't believe in, but he would worry about an anti-Roman political act such as sedition.*)
- Move on to have a student read aloud Matthew 27:11–31. Afterward, invite the students to speculate about what sort of person Pilate was. Ask them if Pilate is culpable in Jesus' Death. Could he have simply released Jesus? (*Note:* Draw on the material in the Background Information section below to expand the students' understanding of Pontius Pilate.)
- Note that scourging was part of the sentence of crucifixion. It was employed to weaken the condemned and to sap his or her strength, thus bringing a quicker death on the cross. The crowning with thorns and mocking by the soldier, however, are not. The meaning of this cruel episode is found in the soldiers' mocking acclamation, "Hail, king of the Jews!" (Mt 27:29) which ends the "trial" scenes. Thus, first the Sanhedrin, then Pilate, and now the Roman soldiers all reject Jesus' claim to be the Messiah, the Christ. Ironically, their mode of rejection proclaims his true identity—king of the Jews and Gentiles alike.
- Have different students read passages from Matthew 27:32–56. Afterward, draw on the text and the Gospel itself to make the following points:
    - Cyrene is a city in Northern Africa (modern day Libya). Simon of Cyrene was probably a Diaspora Jew who had traveled to Jerusalem to celebrate Passover. Perhaps Simon is a poignant reminder of Jesus' words: "Whoever wishes to come after me must deny himself, take up his cross, and follow me" (Mt 16:24).
    - Remind the students that the "wine flavored with gall" (Mt 27:34) is reminiscent of Psalm 69:21–22. Ask one of the students to look up the verses and read them aloud.

- Read aloud the following from Matthew 27:35a ("After they had crucified him . . ."). Ask the students if they notice anything odd about the brief passage. Go on to note that the Gospel presents the moment of crucifixion rather quickly, even off-handedly. In fact, unlike some cinematic renderings of the Passion, *none of the Gospels* dwells on the gory details of Jesus' sufferings. Why? Because the goal of the Gospels is not to drum up sympathy for Jesus, but to emphasize the *meaning* of his suffering. The statements of those who mock Jesus, the scriptural allusions, and Jesus' own words reveal the *significance* of what is happening.
- Tell the students that by Roman law, soldiers had the right to the garments of an executed criminal. The Gospel here alludes to Psalm 22:18b–19: "They stare at me and gloat; they divide my garments among them; for my clothing they cast lots."

with Jesus. Pilate pronounces Jesus guilty of sedition, has Jesus scourged, and hands him over for crucifixion.

Pilate's soldiers mock Jesus, strip him, and dress him in a scarlet military cloak. They crown him with thorns and put a reed in his right hand. Kneeling before him, they mock him, calling him "King of the Jews." All the while they treat him as an object to be scorned. They spit on him in utter contempt and lead him off to the site of crucifixion.

Crucifixion and Death of Jesus Christ (Mt 27:32-56)

The beatings so weakened Jesus that a passerby, Simon of Cyrene, is pressed into carrying the horizontal crossbeam. (The vertical beam was fixed in the ground at the site of crucifixion—Golgotha—a small, elevated hill that resembled a skull.)

When Jesus arrives at Golgotha, he refuses to drink the wine mixed with gall—a slight narcotic meant to ease the pain of the condemned men. As mentioned, crucifixion was one of humanity's worst forms of torture ever invented. While it is possible that Jesus' wrists and feet were nailed to a cross in an elongated plus sign, as traditionally pictured, it is also possible that the cross was in the form of the letter **"T"**. Whether the cross had a support for his feet, or a little seat for his buttocks, is unknown. The purpose of the supports was to allow the person to breathe and thus prolong the agony. Whatever the mode of crucifixion, it resulted in a horrible death, usually by dehydration, loss of blood, shock, and respiratory arrest. (The emperor Constantine finally banned crucifixion as a form of capital punishment in the fourth century.)

After stripping Jesus and nailing him to the cross, the soldiers cast lots to divide his garments. Jesus is crucified between two bandits, called by Matthew "revolutionaries," thus showing the indignity that befell the innocent Jesus. Both men taunt Jesus. (Luke's Gospel, however, reports that one of these bandits rebukes his fellow criminal and asks Jesus to remember him when he enters his Kingdom. Jesus assures him that he will be in Paradise with him that very day.) An inscription written in Hebrew, Greek, and Latin ironically advertises Jesus' crime—"King of the Jews." Passersby, priests, scribes, and elders mock him and challenge him to rescue himself. We can only imagine the indignities heaped on Jesus. Yet, he resists any temptation to strike his tormenters and save himself. He is faithful to his Father to the very end.

Darkness descended on the land from noon until three in the afternoon, the time of Jesus' death. His last words are "My God, my God, why have you forsaken me?" (Jesus' address to his Father as "God" symbolizes his utter agony as a human being who cries out to his God for help.) Observers mistakenly think that Jesus is calling on the prophet Elijah for help, again displaying their continued misunderstanding of Jesus. They fail to recognize that Jesus is reciting the first lines of Psalm 22 in Arabic: *"Eli, Eli, lema sabachthani."* This heartfelt Psalm ends with joyful confidence that God will indeed rescue the petitioner out of his terrible fate. Soon thereafter Jesus lets out a loud cry and gives up his spirit. At the moment of his death, the veil in

Extending the Lesson

Have a photo or miniature replica of Michelangelo's *Pietà* for the students to examine. Explain that this statue is probably the most classic portrait of the love between Jesus and Mary. Then using the statue as a starting point, lead the students in a prayerful reflection on Mary. Ask the students to look at Mary's face. What do you see? Not anger, not anguish, not even sorrow. Mary's is an expression of peace, the peace of someone who sees that even this awful death has not fouled the plan of Salvation, that her son has not died in vain, that good and God will prevail. As she has always done, she *believes*. Note the emphasis on "believe." Linguists translate the word as "believe-into" to show movement and commitment, a word which historians tell us meant much more in Jesus' day than today. Today we hear the word as intellectual assent, an act of the mind. Then it was understood as an act of the heart—which spoke for the whole person—and it was commitment, solidarity, and loyalty *no matter what*.

For Enrichment

If possible, have the students listen to one of the most beautiful arias ever written: "Erbarme dich" from *St. Matthew's Passion* by J. S. Bach. Versions are available at most libraries as well as downloadable recordings from the Internet. This gorgeous, heartfelt aria brilliantly renders the pathos in Peter's repentance. The translation from the German is as follows:

> Have mercy, my God,
> for the sake of my tears!
> See here, before you
> heart and eyes weep bitterly.
> Have mercy, my God.

MARY, THE MOTHER OF GOD

Faithful Disciple

Mary, a young Jewish girl living in or around Nazareth near the beginning of the first century AD, was born to play a crucial role in Salvation History. At that time, an angel appeared to her with a message that most would find unbelievable: "Behold, you will conceive in your womb and bear a son, and you shall name him Jesus" (Lk 1:30). This news was immense, for Mary was a virgin and engaged to Joseph but unmarried at the time she conceived her Son. Jesus was conceived solely by the power of the Holy Spirit, fulfilling the prophecy of Isaiah: "Behold, a virgin shall conceive and bear a son" (Is 7:14). Mary's virginity was perpetual throughout her life. The Church holds that Jesus is Mary's only son, but her spiritual motherhood extends to all.

Mary gave birth to Jesus, and she and Joseph raised him in a loving, prayer-filled home. They taught and cared for him. When Jesus came on the public scene, Mary continued to witness to and support him, even as he experienced his arrest, suffering, and Death on the cross. In addition, she was the first and foremost disciple who prayed with the Apostles in the Upper Room awaiting the descent of the Holy Spirit on Pentecost Sunday. Without a doubt, Mary was the most faithful witness to Jesus. She obeyed God's will; she fully cooperated with Jesus' work of Salvation; she generously responded to the graces of the Holy Spirit. All of these qualities make her the perfect model of Christian faith and love.

Because of her example, the Church honors Mary with many titles, all of which tell us something about what we believe about her. Mary is Our Lady, the Immaculate Conception, the Blessed Mother, the Mother of the Church, Ever Virgin, the Queen of Heaven and Earth. Mary continues to plead with us before her Son. This is why the Church prays to Mary using these titles: Advocate, Helper, Benefactress, and Mediatrix.

Of all the titles of Mary, the most significant is that she is the Mother of God. She is our Mother, too, the loving Mother who fully cooperated with the Holy Spirit to bring Christ into the world.

- Draw particular attention to the taunt, "He trusted in God; let him deliver him now if he wants him. For he said, 'I am the Son of God.'" Note how these words echo those of the Tempter in Matthew 4:3, 6: "If you are the Son of God . . ." In an ironic twist, those who once accused Jesus of being a pawn of Satan (Mt 9:34) are now themselves acting as Satan's mouthpieces. They are offering a final temptation, one that Jesus resists. They are seeking a "sign," when Jesus had clearly stated that the only sign to be given would be the "sign of Jonah" (see Matthew 12:38; 16:1), which prefigured Jesus' Death and Resurrection.

- Have the students turn to the feature "INRI" on page 126. Go through the meaning of INRI with the class, explaining that the letter "J" was rendered in Latin as "I." Then ask a student to read aloud Matthew 27:37: "And they placed over his head the written charge against him: This is Jesus, the King of the Jews." Note the words "This is." Here Matthew is making a formal declaration of Jesus' identity. The placard, intended as a form of derision of a crucified Jewish insurgent, becomes a proclamation of Gospel truth. It declares that this impaled man is, by the fact of his giving of his life, worthy of the name "Jesus." He is the one who "will save his people from their sins" (Mt 1:21). By his sacrifice (his act of self-giving love) this Jesus is, in fact, enthroned as the messianic liberator of God's people.

Background Information

Pontius Pilate

Pontius Pilate was the Roman governor or procurator of Judea from AD 26 to 36, covering the whole of the active ministry both of John the Baptist and of Jesus. His official residence was in Caesarea, which lay on the coast of the Mediterranean Sea and was both the military and civil capital of Judea. Pilate commanded a garrison of about 3,000 soldiers. Pilate and his troops would venture to Jerusalem only at festival times, when the city was full of visitors and there was greater danger of disturbances. Pilate, therefore, was in Jerusalem during the days of Passover when Jesus was arrested. We know little of the man except that he had slight concern for the Jews and their sensibilities. Even Roman historians didn't think much of him. According to the historian Philo of Alexandria, Pilate was corrupt and brutal. Philo wrote that Pilate's tenure was associated with "briberies, insults, robberies, outrages, wanton injustices, constantly repeated executions without trial, and ceaseless, savage ferocity and grievous cruelty" (*On the Embassy of Gaius Caiaphas*).

As high priest and chief religious authority in the land, Joseph Caiaphas (son-in-law to Anna, the high priest emeritus) had many important responsibilities, including performing religious rituals, controlling the Temple treasury, managing the Temple police and other personnel, and—central to the Passion accounts—serving as president of the Sanhedrin, the Jewish council and court that considered the case of Jesus. The high priest also served as a sort of liaison between Roman authority and the Jewish population. High priests, drawn from the Sadducee aristocracy, received their appointment from Rome since the time of Herod the Great; and Rome, in turn, relied on the high priests to keep the Jewish populace in line.

- Have the students look up and read the following Scripture references: Matthew 27:55–56; Mark 15:40–41; Luke 24:10; John 19:25–27. Afterward, ask the students "What do the Gospels have in common?" (*All four Gospels report that all but one of Jesus' disciples who remained with him at the foot of the Cross were women.*) Invite the students to discuss what courage it would take to stand by Jesus at the crucifixion. (*Note:* Interestingly, as we shall see, all four Gospels also report that after his Resurrection, Jesus appeared first to women and commissioned them to go proclaim his Resurrection to his male followers.)
- Direct attention to the feature "You Are There" on page 127. Allow time for the students to compose their prayers. Explain that they will use the prayers later in this session and at their next meeting as well.
- Have the students look at the feature "Faithful Disciple: Mary, the Mother of God" on page 125. Ask:
    - Since Mary was able to stand at the Cross while others fled, what gave her that strength?
    - What does Mary's example teach us about dealing with sufferings that may come our way?

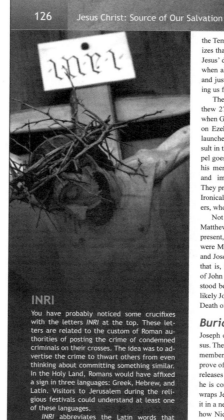

INRI

You have probably noticed some crucifixes with the letters *INRI* at the top. These letters are related to the custom of Roman authorities of posting the crime of condemned criminals on their crosses. The idea was to advertise the crime to thwart others from even thinking about committing something similar. In the Holy Land, Romans would have affixed a sign in three languages: Greek, Hebrew, and Latin. Visitors to Jerusalem during the religious festivals could understand at least one of these languages.

INRI abbreviates the Latin words that would have been posted: *Iesus Nazarenus Rex Judeorum*, which translates to "Jesus of Nazareth, King of the Jews."

the Temple's sanctuary is split in two. This symbolizes that the days of the Old Covenant have ended. Jesus' death initiates the New Covenant, a new age when all people can worship God directly, in truth and justice. Jesus has removed the barrier separating us from God.

The Gospel describes certain signs in Matthew 27:51b–53 that were supposed to take place when God's Kingdom came in its fullness. Drawing on Ezekiel 37, Matthew shows how Jesus' Death launches a new stage in history, a stage that will result in the resurrection of the dead. Matthew's Gospel goes on to report how the Roman centurion and his men greatly feared the events they witnessed and immediately understood their significance. They proclaimed, "Truly, this was the Son of God!" Ironically, it is Gentiles, not Jesus' closest followers, who recognize Jesus' true identity.

Not everyone abandons Jesus at his crucifixion. Matthew's Gospel states that many women were present, looking on from a distance. Among them were Mary Magdalene; Mary, the mother of James and Joseph; and the mother of the sons of Zebedee, that is, the Apostles James and John. The Gospel of John also tells us that Mary, the Blessed Mother, stood beneath the cross with the Beloved Disciple, likely John. All these disciples were witnesses to the Death of Jesus.

Burial of Jesus (Mt 27:57-66)

Joseph of Arimathea was a wealthy disciple of Jesus. The Gospels of Mark and Luke identify him as a member of the Sanhedrin but as one who did not approve of the council's condemnation of Jesus. Pilate releases Jesus' body to Joseph of Arimathea because he is completely certain that Jesus is dead. Joseph wraps Jesus' body in a clean linen cloth and places it in a new tomb in the rock. (John's Gospel reports how Nicodemus assists Joseph in anointing Jesus' body with a hundred pounds of spices, an anointing worthy of a king). This takes place hurriedly late on Friday afternoon since the Sabbath begins

For Enrichment

Marian Web Resources

Tell the students that the University of Dayton's Mary webpage—http://campus.udayton.edu/mary—has a wealth of resources about the Mother of Our Lord.

The Sorrowful Mysteries of the Rosary

In review and reflection on the passion narratives, have your students pray and meditate on the Sorrowful Mysteries of the Rosary: the Agony in the Garden, the Scourging at the Pillar, the Crowning of Thorns, the Carrying of the Cross, and the Crucifixion.

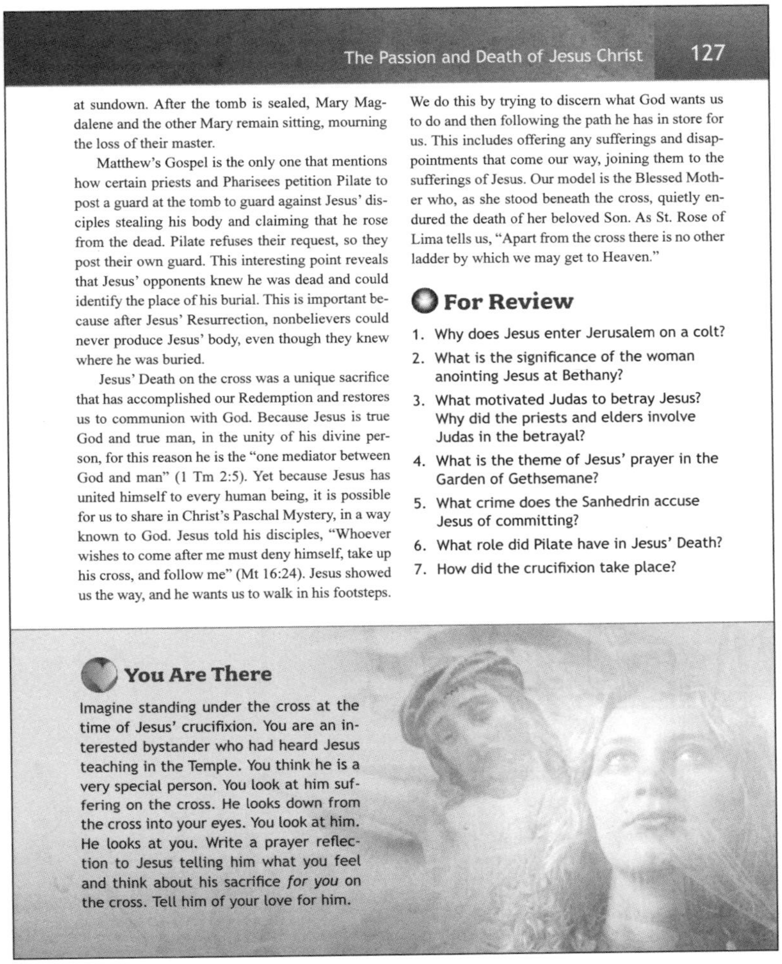

The Passion and Death of Jesus Christ 127

at sundown. After the tomb is sealed, Mary Magdalene and the other Mary remain sitting, mourning the loss of their master.

Matthew's Gospel is the only one that mentions how certain priests and Pharisees petition Pilate to post a guard at the tomb to guard against Jesus' disciples stealing his body and claiming that he rose from the dead. Pilate refuses their request, so they post their own guard. This interesting point reveals that Jesus' opponents knew he was dead and could identify the place of his burial. This is important because after Jesus' Resurrection, nonbelievers could never produce Jesus' body, even though they knew where he was buried.

Jesus' Death on the cross was a unique sacrifice that has accomplished our Redemption and restores us to communion with God. Because Jesus is true God and true man, in the unity of his divine person, for this reason he is the "one mediator between God and man" (1 Tm 2:5). Yet because Jesus has united himself to every human being, it is possible for us to share in Christ's Paschal Mystery, in a way known to God. Jesus told his disciples, "Whoever wishes to come after me must deny himself, take up his cross, and follow me" (Mt 16:24). Jesus showed us the way, and he wants us to walk in his footsteps. We do this by trying to discern what God wants us to do and then following the path he has in store for us. This includes offering any sufferings and disappointments that come our way, joining them to the sufferings of Jesus. Our model is the Blessed Mother who, as she stood beneath the cross, quietly endured the death of her beloved Son. As St. Rose of Lima tells us, "Apart from the cross there is no other ladder by which we may get to Heaven."

For Review

1. Why does Jesus enter Jerusalem on a colt?
2. What is the significance of the woman anointing Jesus at Bethany?
3. What motivated Judas to betray Jesus? Why did the priests and elders involve Judas in the betrayal?
4. What is the theme of Jesus' prayer in the Garden of Gethsemane?
5. What crime does the Sanhedrin accuse Jesus of committing?
6. What role did Pilate have in Jesus' Death?
7. How did the crucifixion take place?

You Are There

Imagine standing under the cross at the time of Jesus' crucifixion. You are an interested bystander who had heard Jesus teaching in the Temple. You think he is a very special person. You look at him suffering on the cross. He looks down from the cross into your eyes. You look at him. He looks at you. Write a prayer reflection to Jesus telling him what you feel and think about his sacrifice *for you* on the cross. Tell him of your love for him.

- Distribute copies of Chapter 5, Handout 4, "The Memorare." Explain that this prayer to Mary is one the students may use when they feel overwhelmed by suffering or fearful in their faith. Assure them that Mary, the Mother of God, will intercede for them.
- Direct attention back to the text section "Burial of Jesus (Mt 27:57–66)." Ask a student to read the indicated verses from Matthew aloud. Point out that this simple account relates the fulfillment of two prophecies: Isaiah 53:8b–9a ("When he was cut off from the land of the living, and smitten for the sin of his people, a grave was assigned him among the wicked and a burial place with evildoers") and, as we've just seen, Matthew 12:40 ("Just as Jonah was in the belly of the whale three days and three nights, so will the Son of Man be in the heart of the earth three days and three nights").

For Review Answers (pages 127-128)

1. To fulfill the prophecy of Zechariah 9:9.
2. It foreshadows the anointing of his body for burial and it speaks to his being the Christ, the "Anointed One."
3. Judas may have been motivated by avarice, or he may have been disappointed in the type of Messiah Jesus was. The Gospels of Luke and John speak of Judas being tempted by the devil to betray Jesus. The religious leaders involved Judas because they needed an insider to deliver up Jesus.
4. Jesus' prayer in the garden was one of humble willingness to accept and follow God's will for him.
5. Blasphemy and sedition.
6. Pilate was the agent of capital punishment. Without his say-so, Jesus could not legally have been put to death.
7. Answers will vary a bit, so accept all reasonable replies that give detailed accounts of the crucifixion.
8. Joseph of Arimathea with the aid of Nicodemus buried Jesus. The religious leaders posted a guard at the tomb because they feared Jesus' followers would steal his body so as to fake a resurrection.

- Have the students turn to "Unique and Definitive Sacrifice" in this chapter's Primary Source Quotations section on page 129–130. Read the quotation from the *Catechism of the Catholic Church*, which points out the twofold nature of Jesus' sacrifice. Then direct attention to the feature Explaining the Faith on page 128. Remind the students that they have already seen that Jesus' sacrifice on the Cross was not offered to appease an angry God. Rather, it was the profound and voluntary conclusion of a life of self-giving love.
- Ask the students to turn once again to this chapter's Primary Source Quotations section on page 129–130. Have one of the students read aloud the quotation "Suffering for the Lord" by St. Alphonsus Liguori. Then tell the students to look at For Reflection on page 128. Discuss what it means for them today to shoulder the cross and follow Jesus. Call attention to the quotation from St. Rose of Lima on page 127 of the text: "Apart from the cross there is no other ladder by which we may get to Heaven."
- As a final review of this section, invite the students to utilize their artistic abilities once again by creating a revised version of the Stations of the Cross. Using their notes, have them draw and describe the events of Jesus' Passion and Death. Invite them to write a short prayer for each event that others might use in a meditation on the Paschal Mystery.
- Conclude the lesson by inviting one or two students to share the prayer they wrote earlier. Tell the students to hang on to their prayers for use in their next lesson. Finally, pray together the *Memorare* from Chapter 5, Handout 4.

8. Who buried Jesus? Why is a guard posted at his tomb?

For Reflection

What does it mean to pick up your cross and follow Jesus?

EXPLAINING THE FAITH

Why would God the Father allow Jesus, his only begotten Son, to suffer and die?

Simply put, God the Father permitted the suffering and Death of Jesus Christ, his only begotten Son, because of his immense love for us humans (see *CCC*, 599-609). God's love invites us to live eternally with him in Heaven. Through his Passion and Death, we learn from Jesus about the depth of the Father's love that helps overcome evil, sin, and death.

It is because of the sin of Adam and Eve that all of us are born with a wounded human nature. Original Sin deprives us of Original Holiness and Original Justice; has wounded the natural powers proper to human nature; subjects us to ignorance, suffering, and death; and inclines us to sin (*CCC*, 405). Because of Original Sin and our fallen state, the life of Christ's grace did not live in us. As a result, we could not live with God in eternity without first being redeemed.

Jesus' suffering and Death was a supreme sacrifice that destroyed once and for all the power of sin and restored our friendship with God. Out of love for his Father and all human beings, whom his Father wants to save, Jesus freely accepted his Passion and Death. The *Catechism of the Catholic Church* puts it this way:

> By giving up his own Son for our sins, God manifests that his plan for us is one of benevolent love, prior to any merit on our part: "In this is love, not that we loved God but that he loved us and sent his Son to be the expiation for our sins" (1 Jn 4:10, 4:19). God "shows his love for us in that while we were yet sinners Christ died for us" (Rom 5:8). (*CCC*, 604)

One final point: When we reflect on the terrible sufferings and Death Jesus endured on our behalf, we begin to understand the seriousness and gravity of sin and its horrible consequences. Jesus' Paschal Mystery of his Passion, Death, and Resurrection have destroyed the worst effect of sin—death—by opening the gates of Heaven to us and promising us a participation in his Resurrection and a life of eternal joy with the Blessed Trinity. The Father allowed his Son to make this sacrifice simply out of his and his Son's immense love for each one of us—none of whom he wants lost.

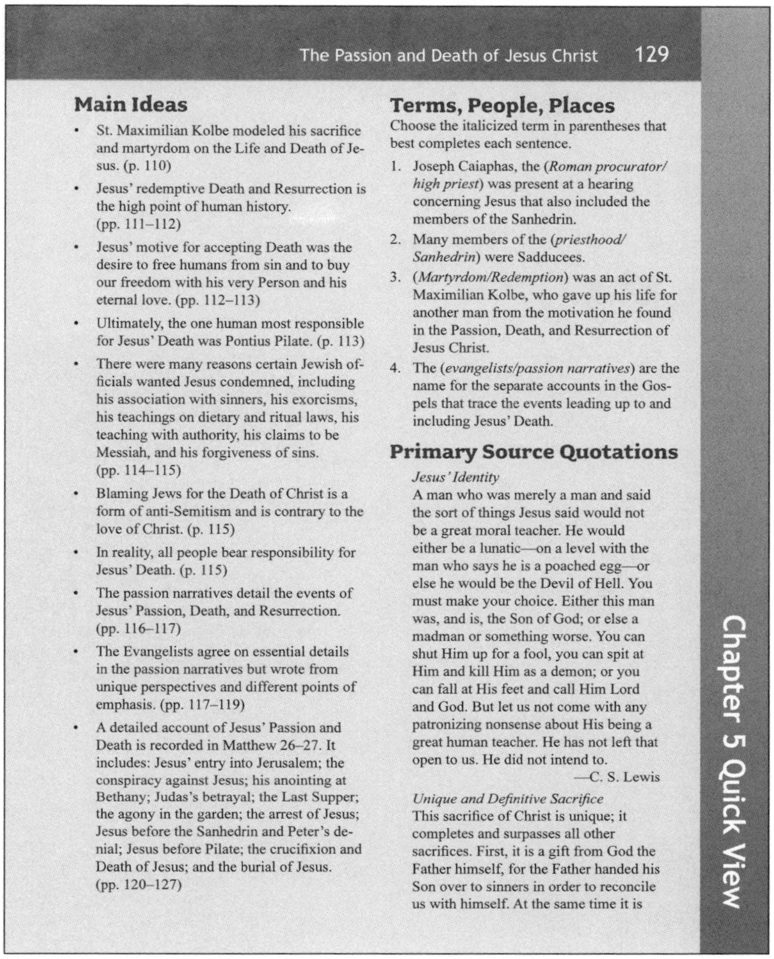

The Passion and Death of Jesus Christ 129

Main Ideas

- St. Maximilian Kolbe modeled his sacrifice and martyrdom on the Life and Death of Jesus. (p. 110)
- Jesus' redemptive Death and Resurrection is the high point of human history. (pp. 111–112)
- Jesus' motive for accepting Death was the desire to free humans from sin and to buy our freedom with his very Person and his eternal love. (pp. 112–113)
- Ultimately, the one human most responsible for Jesus' Death was Pontius Pilate. (p. 113)
- There were many reasons certain Jewish officials wanted Jesus condemned, including his association with sinners, his exorcisms, his teachings on dietary and ritual laws, his teaching with authority, his claims to be Messiah, and his forgiveness of sins. (pp. 114–115)
- Blaming Jews for the Death of Christ is a form of anti-Semitism and is contrary to the love of Christ. (p. 115)
- In reality, all people bear responsibility for Jesus' Death. (p. 115)
- The passion narratives detail the events of Jesus' Passion, Death, and Resurrection. (pp. 116–117)
- The Evangelists agree on essential details in the passion narratives but wrote from unique perspectives and different points of emphasis. (pp. 117–119)
- A detailed account of Jesus' Passion and Death is recorded in Matthew 26–27. It includes: Jesus' entry into Jerusalem; the conspiracy against Jesus; his anointing at Bethany; Judas's betrayal; the Last Supper; the agony in the garden; the arrest of Jesus; Jesus before the Sanhedrin and Peter's denial; Jesus before Pilate; the crucifixion and Death of Jesus; and the burial of Jesus. (pp. 120–127)

Terms, People, Places

Choose the italicized term in parentheses that best completes each sentence.

1. Joseph Caiaphas, the (*Roman procurator/high priest*) was present at a hearing concerning Jesus that also included the members of the Sanhedrin.
2. Many members of the (*priesthood/Sanhedrin*) were Sadducees.
3. (*Martyrdom/Redemption*) was an act of St. Maximilian Kolbe, who gave up his life for another man from the motivation he found in the Passion, Death, and Resurrection of Jesus Christ.
4. The (*evangelists/passion narratives*) are the name for the separate accounts in the Gospels that trace the events leading up to and including Jesus' Death.

Primary Source Quotations

Jesus' Identity

A man who was merely a man and said the sort of things Jesus said would not be a great moral teacher. He would either be a lunatic—on a level with the man who says he is a poached egg—or else he would be the Devil of Hell. You must make your choice. Either this man was, and is, the Son of God; or else a madman or something worse. You can shut Him up for a fool, you can spit at Him and kill Him as a demon; or you can fall at His feet and call Him Lord and God. But let us not come with any patronizing nonsense about His being a great human teacher. He has not left that open to us. He did not intend to.

—C. S. Lewis

Unique and Definitive Sacrifice

This sacrifice of Christ is unique; it completes and surpasses all other sacrifices. First, it is a gift from God the Father himself, for the Father handed his Son over to sinners in order to reconcile us with himself. At the same time it is

Chapter 5 Quick View

Review Lesson Objectives

The students will:

- review Chapter 5 in preparation for the chapter test.
- join in prayer together.

Terms, People, Places Answers (page 129)

1. high priest
2. Sanhedrin
3. Martyrdom
4. passion narratives

Chapter 5: The Passion and Death of Jesus Christ—Review Lesson

Bell Ringers

- Ask the students to offer their responses to the For Review questions on pages 127–128 (answers are on page 145 of this text). Encourage the students to ask any other questions they may have.
- Collect the students' Ongoing Assignments for Chapter 5 (page 130). Allow time for those who chose #1 or #3 (creating PowerPoint presentations) to make their presentations to the class.

Teaching Approaches

Chapter Quick View (pages 129-131)

- Call attention to Terms, People, Places on page 129. Use the section as a vocabulary study tool. Have the students complete the exercise (answers are on page 147 of this text).
- Divide the class into small groups of three or four. Direct the groups to work together to go over the chapter's For Review sections by taking turns asking one another the questions. Encourage the students to try to answer without checking their journals or notes. Circulate to offer assistance should further questions or difficulties arise.
- Invite anyone who had questions after going over the Chapter 5 Main Ideas section on page 129 to ask them now. Invite other class members to offer answers. Clarify any remaining confusion.
- Check vocabulary by asking the students to find a partner and then to quiz one another on the terms.
- Allow some quiet time for the students to study on their own. If students have more questions, invite them to approach you privately while their classmates study.

Prayer Service

- Gather the students in a circle around a cross or crucifix. Have meditative music playing.
- Lead the students on a guided meditation on the seven last words of Christ. Use the material on pages 130–131 of the text as your guide.
- End the meditation by reading aloud the quotation from C. S. Lewis on page 129 in the Primary Source Quotations section of this chapter.
- Invite volunteers to offer the prayers they wrote in the previous lesson.
- Afterward, sing or listen to a recording of a hymn such as "Behold the Wood" by Dan Schutte or "In the Cross of Christ" by Marty Haugen.
- Finally, conclude the prayer and the lesson by inviting the students to mark themselves with the sign of Christians, the sign of the Passion, the Sign of the Cross.

Chapter 5 Quick View

the offering of the Son of God made man, who in freedom and love offered his life to his Father through the Holy Spirit in reparation for our disobedience.
—*Catechism of the Catholic Church*, 614

Desire of the Martyrs
The martyrs desired death, not to fly labor, but to attain their goal. And why do they not fear death, from which man naturally shrinks? Because they had vanquished the natural love of their own bodies by divine and supernatural love.
—St. Catherine of Siena

Suffering for the Lord
Say always, "My beloved and despised Redeemer, how sweet it is to suffer for you." If you embrace all things in life as coming from the hands of God, and even embrace death to fulfill his holy will, assuredly you will die a saint.
—St. Alphonsus Liguori

Think again about Christ's Passion and Death. Make a list of fifteen things that you had not previously thought of that could have happened on Good Friday.

Ongoing Assignments

As you cover the material in this chapter, choose and complete at least three of these assignments.

1. Dedicate a time to pray the Stations of the Cross.
   Write a summary paper that tells when, where, how, and with whom you prayed the stations. *Optional*: Make a PowerPoint presentation of your own Stations of the Cross. Write your own reflections and download images to accompany your prayers.
2. Research and write a report on the Shroud of Turin, what many believe to be the burial cloth of Christ.
3. Create a PowerPoint presentation that describes the geography, history, and religious nature of the Mount of Olives.
4. Investigate and write a report on crucifixion as it was used as the death penalty in the ancient world.
5. Research meditations the saints have written on the Passion of Jesus. Then write your own meditation on Jesus' Passion.
6. Write a script dialogue that retells the Passion story from the point of view of Peter or the Blessed Mother.
7. In an artistic representation, design a crucifix made up of a collage of photos that depict the sufferings of the world—past and present—that Christ redeemed by his Death on the Cross. Share a short oral report that explains your work.
8. Prepare an illustrated talk on the symbolism of several different types of Christian crosses.
9. Write a three- to five-page report on the life of St. Maximilian Kolbe.

Prayer

Throughout the ages, Christians have memorized and meditated on the "Seven Last Words of Jesus," that is, the seven last things Christ said from the cross. These words reveal his values and tell us about his suffering for us.

1. *"Father, forgive them, they know not what they do" (Lk 23:34).*
   - Who has trouble understanding me? How can I help them to know and love the real me?
2. *"Amen, I say to you, today you will be with me in Paradise" (Lk 23:43).*
   - Do I comfort others when they are hurt or lonely?
3. *"Woman, behold, your son. . . . Behold, your mother" (Jn 19:26–27).*
   - What good things have I done for my mother of late? How do I make her proud of me?
4. *"My God, my God, why have you forsaken me?" (Mt 27:46).*
   - Do I have faith that God will be there for me when the going gets tough?

Review Lesson Homework

1. Complete any unfinished Ongoing Assignments.
2. Reread Chapter 5.
3. Study for the Chapter 5 Test.

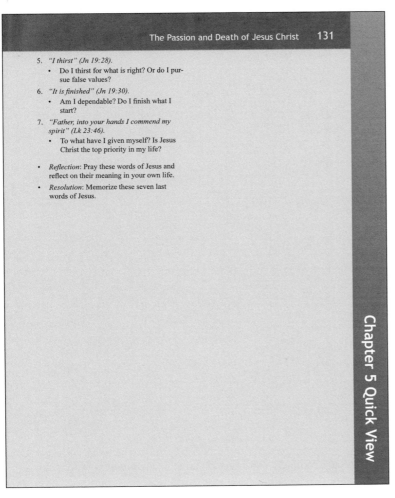

5. *"I thirst" (Jn 19:28).*
   - Do I thirst for what is right? Or do I pursue false values?
6. *"It is finished" (Jn 19:30).*
   - Am I dependable? Do I finish what I start?
7. *"Father, into your hands I commend my spirit" (Lk 23:46).*
   - To what have I given myself? Is Jesus Christ the top priority in my life?

- *Reflection*: Pray these words of Jesus and reflect on their meaning in your own life.
- *Resolution*: Memorize these seven last words of Jesus.

Test Lesson Homework

1. Read the following text sections of Chapter 6: "The Fog Lifted" (pages 134–135) and "Redemption Accomplished and Promise Fulfilled" (pages 135–138).
2. Examine the Chapter 6 Ongoing Assignments on pages 155–156.

Chapter 5 Test Lesson

Teaching Approaches

- Allow sufficient time for the students to work on the Chapter 5 Test (starting on page 291 of the TWE and also online at www.avemariapress.com). Collect tests as the students finish.

Chapter 5 Test Answers

Part 1: True or False. (**2 points each**)

1. T 2. T 3. T 4. F 5. T 6. T 7. F 8. F 9. T 10. F 11. T 12. T 13. T

14. T 15. F 16. T 17. F 18. F 19. T 20. T 21. T 22. T 23. T 24. F 25. T 26. T

Part 2. Fill in the Blanks. (**2 points each**)

1. colt
2. Caiaphas
3. Passover
4. Gethsemane
5. Golgotha
6. Simon
7. Joseph
8. Jesus of Nazareth, King of the Jews
9. Sanhedrin
10. martyr
11. Holy of Holies
12. anti-Semitism

Part 3: Brief Answers.

1. Students may choose to write about Pilate, the Jewish leaders, or all sinners. Award one point for the person/group and one point for an acceptable reason for them to be blamed. **(4 points)**
2. Students may choose any of the connections between the Old Testament and the passion narratives found on pages 116–117. Award one point for an accurate connection and one point for the description of the connection. **(6 points)**
3. Answers may include Jesus' arrest, questioning by the high priest, trials before the Sanhedrin and Pilate, condemnation, crucifixion, Death, and burial. Each response should be worth one point. **(4 points)**
4. Students should describe events in Matthew/Mark that focus on abandonment and vindication; in Luke, compassion; and in John, control. Each response should be worth one point. **(6 points)**
5. Answer may include **(4 points)**:
   - out of love for all human beings so that we can be with him in Heaven
   - to reveal the depths of the Father's love for humanity
   - because we were in need of Redemption
   - to destroy the power of sin
   - to show the gravity and seriousness of sin

Chapter 6: The Resurrection of Jesus Christ

Introduction

> *Blessed be the God and Father of our Lord Jesus Christ, who in his great mercy gave us a new birth to a living hope through the resurrection of Jesus Christ from the dead, to an inheritance that is imperishable, undefiled, and unfading, kept in heaven for you.*
>
> —1 Peter 1:3-4

Empty! No body there. We know it, believe it. But the body is here now—we believe it with the faith that is the "evidence of things not seen" (Heb 11:1). We recall Jesus' promise, "I am with you always, until the end of the age" (Mt 28:20), and we believe. He who was made flesh, who suffered and died is now risen and alive. This is our conviction about the risen, ascended, and glorified Lord who is not seen now, but who is to be revealed. We know it, believe it.

This chapter examines the meaning of the Resurrection. The Resurrection is the pivotal moment not only for those of us who call ourselves Christians, but for all people, for all time. It proclaims that sin's chokehold is broken, that death's dominion is destroyed. The students examine the Resurrection in each of the Gospel accounts. They study the empty tomb, the appearances of the Risen Lord, and the testimony of those whom he encountered. The students recognize that while each Gospel shines its own light on the Resurrection, highlighting different facets, all the Gospels reveal the same incandescent news: "The Lord is risen! He is risen, indeed!" The Father has vindicated Jesus, just as Jesus said he would.

The chapter speaks to the criticisms of those who would deny the Resurrection and even offers rebuttals to the objections of its truthfulness. The great *proof* we possess is the Easter faith of the disciples—the same disciples who three days previous had lost all faith, all hope. The chapter helps the students recognize the Resurrection's message: God has brought about the Kingdom in and through the suffering and Death of Jesus his Son!

As the students progress through this chapter, they begin to understand and appreciate that the Resurrection proves all that Jesus did and said regarding God's Kingdom and, at the same time, promises that each and every one of us who believes will become its citizens. Nothing will stop us—not sin, not death. Like Jesus, we will rise again. Such is the meaning of the Resurrection.

Advance Preparations

Prepare or have on hand:

For Lesson 1

- Corrected copies of the Chapter 5 Test
- Bibles
- Copies of Chapter 6, Handout 1, "Eureka!"

For Lesson 2

- Bibles
- Equipment necessary for students to make PowerPoint presentations or large post boards
- A player and a recording of the hymn "In the Breaking of the Bread" by Bob Hurd and Michael Downey (optional)

For Lesson 3

- Bibles
- Copies of Chapter 6, Handout 2, "Resurrection Reflections"

Chapter Objectives

To help the students:

- recognize that the historical and transcendent event of the Resurrection is the quintessential element of our faith.
- discover the meaning and message of the *kerygma.*
- analyze the Resurrection accounts in the Synoptic Gospels.
- analyze the Resurrection account in the Gospel of John.
- recognize similarities and differences in all the Gospel Resurrection accounts.
- appreciate how we encounter the Risen Lord in the sacraments of the Church.
- understand what the Ascension, Assumption, and Pentecost mean for the Church.

- Copies of old picture magazines and other art materials
- A soft ball that can be thrown inside a classroom

For Lesson 4

- Bibles
- Copies of old picture magazines and other art materials
- Copies of Chapter 6, Handout 3, "Resurrection Consequences—The 4 Cs"
- Copies of Chapter 6, Handout 4, "On the Feast of Pentecost"

For the Chapter 6 Review Lesson

- Equipment necessary for students to make PowerPoint presentations
- Cross or crucifix
- A recording of meditative music and a player
- Copies of—or a player and a recording of—a hymn such as "Send Us Your Spirit," by David Haas or "Send Down the Fire" by Marty Haugen (optional)

For the Chapter 6 Test Lesson

- Copies of the Chapter 6 Test (starting on page 291 of the TWE and also online at www.avemariapress.com)

Chapter 6 Handouts

- Handout 1, Eureka!—The students solve visual puzzles.
- Handout 2, Resurrection Reflections—The students fashion creative responses to poems about the Resurrection.
- Handout 3, Resurrection Consequences—The 4 Cs—The students discover the results of the Resurrection.
- Handout 4, On the Feast of Pentecost—The students examine and pray the Opening Prayer for the Feast of Pentecost.

Chapter 6: The Resurrection of Jesus Christ—Lesson 1

Bell Ringers

- Distribute the corrected Chapter 5 Test. Go over the test with the students, using it as a means to review the previous chapter. Address any remaining questions or concerns the students may have.
- Ask the students if they have ever experienced a "eureka moment," that is, a moment when a problem or process with which they've struggled suddenly became clear. Allow the students to offer examples.
- Distribute copies of Chapter 6, Handout 1, "Eureka!" Tell the students that the handout has ten puzzles—some visual, some verbal—that may, at first, seem unclear. However, once they solve one ("Eureka!"), solving the others should be easier. Give the students some time to finish the puzzles. You may motivate the students to complete the puzzles with a prize (candy, pens, pencils, etc.) for the first person to complete all of the puzzles.
- Go over the answers as a class (answers are on page 155 of this text).

Teaching Approaches

The Fog Lifted (pages 134–135)

- Tell the students that sometimes a eureka moment is like the fog lifting, allowing us to see clearly. Call on the students to tell the story of the Duke of Wellington's eureka/fog-lifting experience.
- Afterward, explain that sometimes a eureka moment can offer such a powerful jolt of clarity; it makes everything fall into place. It enlightens us and even changes our lives. Stress that the Resurrection experience was just such a moment for Jesus' disciples. It was a moment that not only affirmed their faith and affected their lives, but also altered the future of all humankind.
- Ask the students to define the term *kerygma* from their textbook. Point out that the core of the Christian message—the *kerygma*—was faith in the risen Christ. The Apostles not only preached a Christ crucified, but a Christ raised from the dead. Today that same message is at the core of our beliefs.

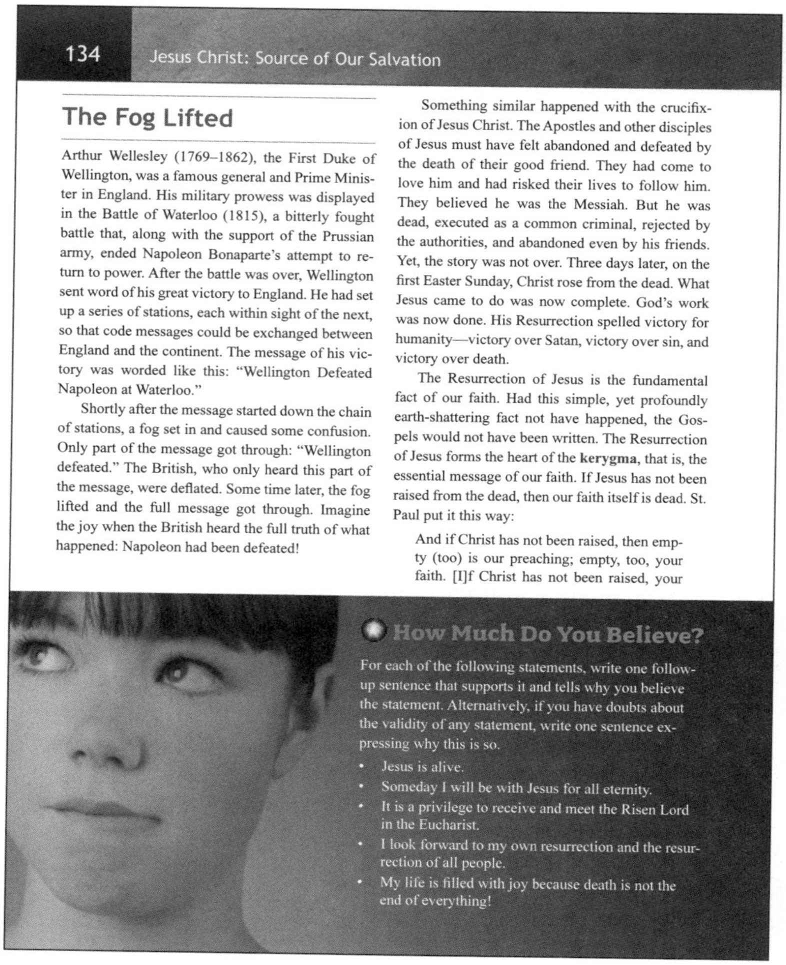

134 Jesus Christ: Source of Our Salvation

The Fog Lifted

Arthur Wellesley (1769–1862), the First Duke of Wellington, was a famous general and Prime Minister in England. His military prowess was displayed in the Battle of Waterloo (1815), a bitterly fought battle that, along with the support of the Prussian army, ended Napoleon Bonaparte's attempt to return to power. After the battle was over, Wellington sent word of his great victory to England. He had set up a series of stations, each within sight of the next, so that code messages could be exchanged between England and the continent. The message of his victory was worded like this: "Wellington Defeated Napoleon at Waterloo."

Shortly after the message started down the chain of stations, a fog set in and caused some confusion. Only part of the message got through: "Wellington defeated." The British, who only heard this part of the message, were deflated. Some time later, the fog lifted and the full message got through. Imagine the joy when the British heard the full truth of what happened: Napoleon had been defeated!

Something similar happened with the crucifixion of Jesus Christ. The Apostles and other disciples of Jesus must have felt abandoned and defeated by the death of their good friend. They had come to love him and had risked their lives to follow him. They believed he was the Messiah. But he was dead, executed as a common criminal, rejected by the authorities, and abandoned even by his friends. Yet, the story was not over. Three days later, on the first Easter Sunday, Christ rose from the dead. What Jesus came to do was now complete. God's work was now done. His Resurrection spelled victory for humanity—victory over Satan, victory over sin, and victory over death.

The Resurrection of Jesus is the fundamental fact of our faith. Had this simple, yet profoundly earth-shattering fact not have happened, the Gospels would not have been written. The Resurrection of Jesus forms the heart of the **kerygma**, that is, the essential message of our faith. If Jesus has not been raised from the dead, then our faith itself is dead. St. Paul put it this way:

> And if Christ has not been raised, then empty (too) is our preaching; empty, too, your faith. [I]f Christ has not been raised, your

How Much Do You Believe?

For each of the following statements, write one follow-up sentence that supports it and tells why you believe the statement. Alternatively, if you have doubts about the validity of any statement, write one sentence expressing why this is so.

- Jesus is alive.
- Someday I will be with Jesus for all eternity.
- It is a privilege to receive and meet the Risen Lord in the Eucharist.
- I look forward to my own resurrection and the resurrection of all people.
- My life is filled with joy because death is not the end of everything!

Lesson 1 Objectives

The students will:

- review Chapter 5.
- recognize that the Resurrection is the fundamental element of our faith.
- define *kerygma*.
- summarize the main points of the *kerygma* preached by the early Church.
- describe the evidence that Jesus' Resurrection was a historical event.
- describe why the Resurrection is considered to be a transcendent event.

Lesson 1 Preview

The previous chapter focused on the Cross and Death of the Lord. This chapter turns attention to the Resurrection, the crowning truth of our faith. The students begin to understand that far from being the experience of one man (Jesus), the Resurrection is the legacy of all who believe.

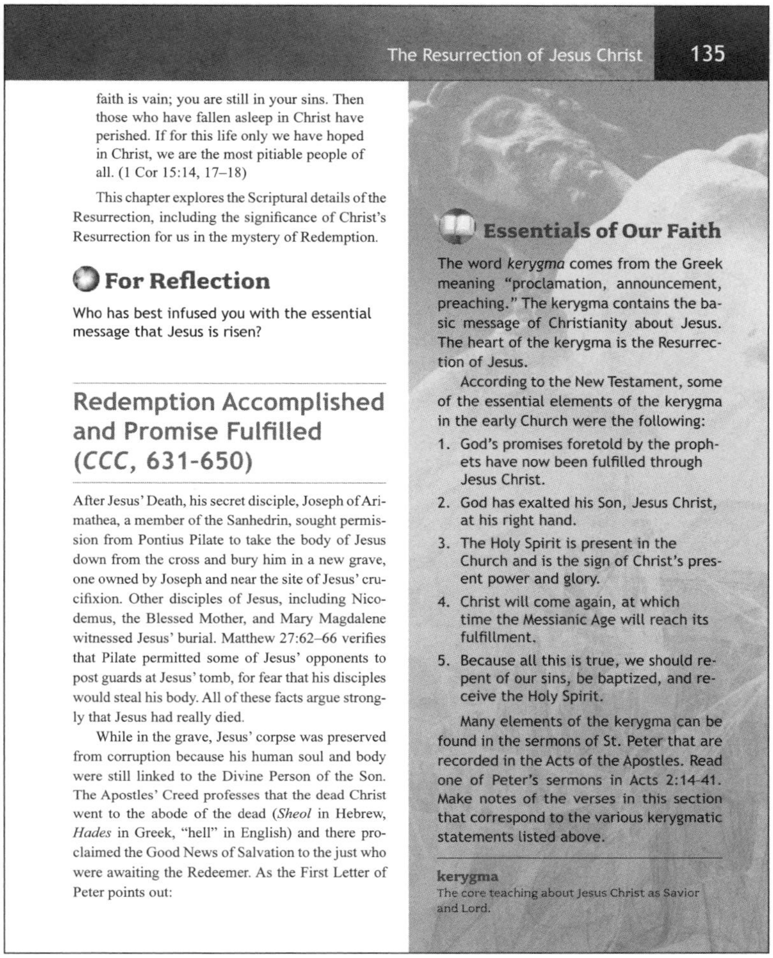

faith is vain; you are still in your sins. Then those who have fallen asleep in Christ have perished. If for this life only we have hoped in Christ, we are the most pitiable people of all. (1 Cor 15:14, 17–18)

This chapter explores the Scriptural details of the Resurrection, including the significance of Christ's Resurrection for us in the mystery of Redemption.

For Reflection

Who has best infused you with the essential message that Jesus is risen?

Redemption Accomplished and Promise Fulfilled (*CCC*, 631–650)

After Jesus' Death, his secret disciple, Joseph of Arimathea, a member of the Sanhedrin, sought permission from Pontius Pilate to take the body of Jesus down from the cross and bury him in a new grave, one owned by Joseph and near the site of Jesus' crucifixion. Other disciples of Jesus, including Nicodemus, the Blessed Mother, and Mary Magdalene witnessed Jesus' burial. Matthew 27:62–66 verifies that Pilate permitted some of Jesus' opponents to post guards at Jesus' tomb, for fear that his disciples would steal his body. All of these facts argue strongly that Jesus had really died.

While in the grave, Jesus' corpse was preserved from corruption because his human soul and body were still linked to the Divine Person of the Son. The Apostles' Creed professes that the dead Christ went to the abode of the dead (*Sheol* in Hebrew, *Hades* in Greek, "hell" in English) and there proclaimed the Good News of Salvation to the just who were awaiting the Redeemer. As the First Letter of Peter points out:

Essentials of Our Faith

The word *kerygma* comes from the Greek meaning "proclamation, announcement, preaching." The kerygma contains the basic message of Christianity about Jesus. The heart of the kerygma is the Resurrection of Jesus.

According to the New Testament, some of the essential elements of the kerygma in the early Church were the following:

1. God's promises foretold by the prophets have now been fulfilled through Jesus Christ.
2. God has exalted his Son, Jesus Christ, at his right hand.
3. The Holy Spirit is present in the Church and is the sign of Christ's present power and glory.
4. Christ will come again, at which time the Messianic Age will reach its fulfillment.
5. Because all this is true, we should repent of our sins, be baptized, and receive the Holy Spirit.

Many elements of the kerygma can be found in the sermons of St. Peter that are recorded in the Acts of the Apostles. Read one of Peter's sermons in Acts 2:14-41. Make notes of the verses in this section that correspond to the various kerygmatic statements listed above.

kerygma
The core teaching about Jesus Christ as Savior and Lord.

Chapter 6, Handout 1, "Eureka!" Answers

1. sleep with the fishes
2. square dance
3. wise crack
4. a New York State of mind
5. Australia (Down Under)
6. a ten-foot pole
7. a stitch in time
8. *base*ball
9. a bird in the hand is worth two in the bush
10. Beethoven's Fifth

- Have the students turn to "Essentials of Our Faith" on page 135. Call attention to the term *kerygma*. Explain that it means "proclaiming/sharing the Good News" and that it is the first element of the fourfold mission Jesus left his followers. List on the board:
    - **Share the Message—*kerygma***
    - **Live in Community—*koinonia***
    - **Serve Others—*diakonia***
    - **Worship the Lord—*leitourgia***
- Go through the main points of the *kerygma* (page 135). Then allow time for the students to read one or more of the kerygmatic sermons of St. Peter (Acts 2:14–41), noting where the sermon corresponds to the elements of the *kerygma* listed in the text. Afterward, allow time for sharing.
- Call attention to the activity "How Much Do You Believe?" on page 134. Explain to the students that there are no wrong answers here, and that doubt is often simply faith seeking greater faith. Have the students write their answers on a separate sheet of paper.
- When the students finish writing, tell them that they need not put their names on the papers, but do collect them. Then, invite the students to share some of the responses or questions. Take time to discuss each with the class. Remind them that doubt is not rejection, only faith seeking understanding.

Redemption Accomplished and Promise Fulfilled (pages 135-138)

- Call on different students to recall and relate the events that took place after Jesus' body was removed from the Cross—from the Preparation Day (Friday) through the Sabbath (Saturday).
- Call attention to the second paragraph of the above text section, the paragraph beginning, "While in the grave . . ." Point out how the earliest Christian creed (the Apostles' Creed) declares that after his burial, Jesus "descended to the dead/into hell." Invite the students to recall the sort of God Jesus came to reveal. He is God who is "Abba"; who is good; who cares about humankind with fidelity and passion; and who is a God of prodigal acceptance, infinite love, overwhelming concern, and complete forgiveness.
- Explain that the Paschal Mystery is completed by the Resurrection. The latter declares that the only life that can be relied upon to endure comes in and through death. In fact, new life in Christ is so powerfully real and good precisely because the threat of death is so

powerfully real and threatening. Life and death exist forever in a fateful dance that forces us to decide which one we will choose to align with our faith.

- Write the following question on the board: **Did the Resurrection really happen?** Have the students draw on their reading to respond. List evidence of the Resurrection on the board. For example:
  - Jesus' fearful disciples seemed to abandon Jesus at his Death but boldly proclaimed his rising afterward.
  - The tomb is empty.
  - Jesus appears to Mary Magdalene, the Apostles, doubting Thomas, the disciples on their way to Emmaus, to the 500, and to Saul/Paul. Direct the students to read 1 Corinthians 15:3–8, which gives us the first report (prior to any of the Gospel accounts) of Jesus' post-Resurrection appearances.
- Go on to tell the students that the empty tomb and the multiple appearances together with the paradigm shift in Jesus' followers declare that Jesus truly rose from the dead.
- Remind the students that the disciples had abandoned Jesus. Jesus' arrest, crucifixion, and Death had shaken them to the core. Fearful and hidden away in a locked room, the last thing they expected was the Resurrection. Even when it was first announced to them, they refused to believe. Yet, once Jesus appeared, this cowardly band was transformed into a courageous company of evangelists, not only ready to stand up and live like Jesus but to lie down and die for him as well.

Paschal Lamb
In Jewish history, the Paschal Lamb was what the Israelites were commanded to eat as part of the Passover celebration. Jesus is the new Paschal Lamb because he shed his blood for the Redemption of the world.

grace
A free and unearned favor from God, infused into our souls at Baptism, that adopts us into God's family and helps us to live as his children.

soul
The innermost or spiritual part of a person. The soul is the subject of human consciousness and freedom. Body and soul together form one human nature. The soul does not die with the body. It is eternal and will be reunited with the body in the final resurrection.

Last Judgment
Jesus Christ's judgment of the living and the dead on the last day when he comes to fully establish God's Kingdom.

> For this is why the gospel was preached even to the dead that, though condemned in the flesh in human estimation, they might live in the spirit in the estimation of God. (1 Pt 4:6)

Jesus' mercy and love for sinners extends to all people, opening the gates of Heaven for all the good and just people who lived before the Son of God came to earth. Then, on Easter Sunday, the most important event in Salvation History took place.

The Resurrection and the Paschal Mystery

The Paschal Mystery refers to Christ's Death *and* Resurrection. They are inseparable. It is called a *mystery* in the sense that the Salvation won by Jesus Christ is a visible sign of the invisible action that God accomplished on our behalf. *Paschal* refers to the Passover, Christ's passing through death to new life. He is the **Paschal Lamb** whose Death leads to his Resurrection and Salvation for all humanity. When we participate in Christ's Paschal Mystery, we die to sin's power over us, and the influence of Satan. We also receive **grace** in this life and eternal life with the Blessed Trinity in Heaven. Jesus' Death and Resurrection have defeated sin. What this means is that our **souls** will survive physical death and our bodies will rise again at the **Last Judgment**.

The Resurrection was a Historical Event

The disciples were not expecting Jesus' Resurrection. In fact, they were heartbroken, saddened, and afraid after his crucifixion. They were in hiding in Jerusalem, fearful that they too might be arrested and executed. Yet, verifiable evidence indicates that the Resurrection of Jesus was a real, historical event that took place in a definite place at a definite time and totally changed the frightened disciples into zealous preachers of the Gospel of Jesus Christ.

The empty tomb—reported in each Gospel—is one of the signs that Jesus rose from the dead. Neither Jesus' friends nor his enemies ever claimed to have found Jesus' body. No one ever proved that his corpse was stolen. The empty tomb does not of itself prove faith. In fact, some disciples were skeptical, simply refusing to believe when told the tomb was empty. Even seeing it empty for themselves did not cause all of them to believe that Jesus had actually risen from the dead. Nevertheless, the empty tomb is a concrete historical marker, a sign that points toward belief that the Father brought his Son back to life, as had been prophesied by Jesus himself.

More definitive are the reports that Jesus was *actually seen* by various people: Mary Magdalene, who embraced Jesus' feet; doubting Thomas, who saw Jesus' wounds and proclaimed, "My Lord and My God" (Jn 20:28); the Apostles in the Upper

Lesson 1 Homework

1. Assign the six For Review questions on page 137. Likewise, have the students write out their answers to the two For Reflection questions on page 138.
2. Ask the students to turn to Ongoing Assignments on pages 155–156. Have them choose three of the listed assignments to complete prior to the conclusion of this chapter. Tell the students the assignments are due on the day they gather for their chapter review.
3. To prepare for their next lesson, have the students read "The Resurrection Accounts in the Four Gospels," up to but not including the text section "The Resurrection in John 20–21" (pages 138–143).

Room; two disciples, who walked with Jesus on the road to Emmaus and recognized him in the breaking of the bread. As 1 Corinthians 15:38 states, the Risen Lord appeared to more than five hundred people at one place, many of whom were still alive when St. Paul was writing his Letter to the Corinthians in the 50s. Finally, St. Paul himself claims to have seen the Risen Jesus, now ascended to Heaven, on the road to Damascus. This encounter changed Paul from a fierce persecutor of Christians into a great missionary who preached the Gospel of Jesus Christ far and wide.

The Resurrection as a Transcendent Event

All of these facts reveal that the Resurrection was a real, verifiable historical event. Yet the Resurrection of Jesus is also a *transcendent* event, that is, one that goes beyond history and our own understanding of space and time. The Resurrection can be described as transcendent because no Gospel account reports anyone seeing how it physically happened. No one actually saw how Jesus' earthly body transformed into a risen or glorified body. It is true that Jesus' glorified body could be seen and touched by others. Jesus could even share a meal with his disciples. (Jesus did these things to prove to his disciples that they were not seeing a ghost. Ghosts do not eat meals with their living friends.) However, Jesus' Resurrection and his glorified body go beyond his earthly body and historical events. In his Resurrection, Jesus was fully restored to life: "In his risen body he passes from the state of death to another life beyond time and space" (*CCC*, 646).

Jesus' glorified body had certain qualities that transcend ordinary life. For example, unlike Lazarus, whom Jesus raised and who did die again, Jesus' glorified body would never again die. His resurrected body is both immortal and eternal, possessing supernatural qualities. Jesus' resurrected body could appear wherever he wished, whenever he wished. For example, Jesus materialized in the Upper Room by passing through a closed door. He has a real body, but it is glorified, belonging to Heaven. The Holy Spirit transformed Jesus' body, giving it "the glorious state of Lordship" (*CCC*, 648). In sum, Jesus' human body was gloriously transfigured, filled with the Holy Spirit, into an incorrupt, glorious, immortal body "seated at the right hand of the Father."

For Review

1. Define *kerygma*.
2. Summarize the main points of the kerygma preached in the early Church.
3. Why did Jesus' body not decay in the tomb?
4. What does it mean to say that Jesus "descended into hell"?
5. Cite evidence that Jesus' Resurrection is a historical event.
6. What does it mean to say that the Resurrection is also a transcendent event?

- Have the students turn to the text section "The Resurrection as a Transcendent Event" (page 137). Once again, point out that the Resurrection is part of the Paschal Mystery: *Paschal* because of the connection with the Passover from death into life, and *Mystery* because it forever exceeds our ability to fully explain or comprehend it. Tell the students that "transcendent" means "beyond comprehension."
- Remind the students that Jesus did not come back from death like Lazarus (see John 11:39–44). Rather, he *went through death* to a new life that was unbounded by time and space, a passage that paved the way for us to follow him.
- Tell the students that Jesus' body affected time and space (e.g., could be touched and required nourishment); it was also outside both (e.g., was not immediately recognized, could appear in a locked room).
- Have the students draw and label what they know about Jesus' risen body from the Resurrection accounts. Students' drawings should include artistic representations of Jesus' glorified body, which can be seen and touched, has the ability to share a meal, is ghost-like, and includes the wounds caused by his torture and crucifixion.

For Review Answers (page 137)

1. *Kerygma* is a term meaning "proclamation, announcement, or preaching." It refers to the core teaching about Jesus Christ as Savior and Lord.
2. Answers should reflect a knowledge of the five essential elements of the *kerygma* as described on page 135 of the text.
3. Jesus' body did not decay because both his body and soul were linked to his divine person.
4. This means that Jesus announced the saving Good News to those who had died prior to his coming and his Paschal Mystery.
5. The students should be able to mention the paradigm shift of the disciples, empty tomb, no physical evidence of Jesus' body, and a number of his post-Resurrection appearances.
6. The Resurrection is a transcendent event because it goes beyond (transcends) history and our understanding of time and space. No one actually witnessed the transformation of Jesus' body into a glorified body.

Chapter 6: The Resurrection of Jesus Christ—Lesson 2

Bell Ringers

- Call on different students to offer their responses to the six For Review questions on page 137 (answers are on page 157 of this text).
- Continue the review by asking the following:
  - Jesus' resurrected body was not a real body. Agree or disagree? Why?
  - Give two reasons to believe the Resurrection was a historical event.
  - Why is the Resurrection considered to be a transcendent event?
- Introduce this lesson by reviewing the tradition about where and for whom the Synoptic Gospels were written, as well as how each portrayed Jesus as Messiah. Before listing the following on the board, however, see whether the students can recall what they learned in Chapter 3.

Author	*Written At*	*Audience*	*Jesus Portrayed As*
Matthew	**Antioch**	**Jewish Christians**	**Teaching Messiah**
Mark	**Rome**	**Persecuted Gentiles**	**Suffering Messiah**
Luke	**Greece**	**Poor Gentile-Christians**	**Merciful Messiah**

- If you wish, you may also have the students recall who the Gospels are named after and when they were likely to have been written:
  - Mark (also called John-Mark): a disciple of Peter —AD 67–73
  - Matthew: a Jewish scribe—AD 80s
  - Luke: a Gentile-Christian (perhaps a physician and friend of St. Paul)—AD 75–90
- Finally, remind the students that Mark's was the first written Gospel and that Matthew and Luke drew upon Mark as well as Q or *Quelle*, meaning "source"

138 Jesus Christ: Source of Our Salvation

For Reflection

- How is your life different because Jesus is risen?
- What is more important to you: historical or transcendent evidence of Jesus' Resurrection? Explain.

The Resurrection Accounts in the Four Gospels

The Resurrection accounts in the four Gospels can be outlined by the main events in the chart on page 139. The next sections examine Scriptural evidence on the Resurrection of Jesus from all four Gospel accounts. Prior to reading each section, make sure to first read the Gospel citation that is suggested.

The Resurrection in Matthew 28

Women at the Empty Tomb (Mt 28:1-8)

Mary Magdalene and her companion know exactly where Jesus is buried. When they get to his grave, they meet an angel who had rolled back the stone in front of the tomb. The angel tells the women not to be afraid because Jesus, the crucified one, has been raised from the dead. The angel asks the women to inspect the empty tomb and then to report to the disciples that Jesus is raised from the dead and that the disciples should go to Galilee to meet him.

Jesus Appears to the Women (Mt 28:9-1)

The women, both afraid yet filled with joy, report to the disciples what they discovered. Along the way, Jesus appears to them. They embrace Jesus' feet and pay him homage. The Risen Lord then tells the women to instruct the Apostles to leave Jerusalem, the place where he was rejected, and go to Galilee where he will meet them.

The Report of the Guards (Mt 28:11-15)

Only Matthew's Gospel tells us why the Pharisees and chief priests posted guards at Jesus' tomb; it was due to their fear that Jesus' body would be stolen. When the guards report what actually happened, they are bribed to say that Jesus' disciples stole his body from the tomb. Jesus' foes do not actually doubt that Jesus died and was buried, but they do not believe he was raised from the dead. Therefore, they circulate the story that "His disciples came by night and stole him while we were asleep" (Mt 28:13).

Jesus Appears to the Eleven before His Ascension (Mt 28:16-20)

In Matthew's Gospel, both the mountain and Galilee are important places where Jesus revealed himself

Lesson 2 Objectives

The students will:

- review the authorship, audience, and purpose of the Synoptic Gospels.
- compare and contrast the Synoptic Gospel accounts of the Resurrection.
- explain why the Gospel of Mark probably ends at Mark 16:8.

Lesson 2 Preview

This lesson begins a gospel-by-gospel examination of the Resurrection accounts. As you present the material, be sure to use the chart on page 139 of the text that compares the accounts. Rely on the words of the Gospels themselves. Consider spacing the material over more than one class period.

The Resurrection of Jesus Christ 139

Event	Matthew	Mark	Luke	John
Some women find Jesus' tomb empty	28:1–8	16:1–8	24:1–11	20:1–2, 11–13
Peter and the Beloved Disciple run to the tomb	*	*	24:12 (only Peter)	20:2–10
Jesus appears to the women	28:9–10	16:9–11	*	20:14–18
Guards report to the authorities	28:11–15	*	*	*
Jesus and the two disciples on the road to Emmaus	*	16:12–13	24:13–35	*
Jesus appears to the disciples on Sunday evening	*	*	24:36–43	*
Jesus appears to Thomas and the disciples	*	*	*	20:24–29
Jesus appears to the Eleven at the table	*	16:14–18	*	*
Jesus appears to the Eleven before his Ascension—giving the Great Commission	28:16–20	*	*	*
Jesus' last words before the Ascension	*	16:19–20	24:44–53	*
Jesus appears to his disciples at the Sea of Tiberias	*	*	*	21:1–23

to his disciples. For example, Jesus began his public ministry in Galilee after the arrest of John the Baptist. He taught the Sermon on the Mount with authority on a mountain. At the Transfiguration, he revealed his glory to Peter, James, and John on the mountain.

After the suicide of Judas Iscariot, there are now eleven Apostles left, all of whom initially doubt that Jesus has been raised. However, like the women, they quickly worship Jesus once they see him.

The very last verses of Matthew's Gospel contain the commissioning of Jesus' disciples (Mt 28:16–20). Jesus says that his heavenly Father has given him supreme power in Heaven and on earth. All authority on earth and in Heaven is his. Therefore, Jesus is sending the Eleven out to all nations of

(probably a collection of Jesus' sayings), and on separate, independent sources in writing their Gospels.

Teaching Approaches

The Resurrection Accounts in the Four Gospels (pages 138-143)

- Divide the class into three groups (or six groups) and assign each group one of the Synoptic Gospels. Have the students read the Gospel account of the Resurrection together. Then, have them work together to create summaries of the events as they are portrayed in their Gospel to present to the class. Students may consider creating PowerPoint presentations, poster boards, timelines, or short plays.
- Invite each group to present their summaries to the class. While the groups are presenting, have the students in the audience list the differences they notice between their Gospel and the Gospels of the other presentations.
- Before looking at each Gospel account in detail, discuss the presentations and the major differences they noticed. Create a list with the class of the things that were in all of the accounts. Then, create a list including the parts of the accounts that are not found in all of the Synoptic Gospels.
- Have the students reread Matthew 28 in its entirety. Drawing on the Gospel and the material in the text, use questions like the following to discuss Matthew's Resurrection account:
  - Who are the original witnesses to the empty tomb in Matthew's account? (*Mary Magdalene and another Mary*)
  - Do they go to the tomb filled with faith and expecting a resurrection? (*No. They go to "see the tomb" [Matthew 28:1].*)
  - How is the "huge stone" (Mt 27:60), which had been "secured . . . by fixing a seal to the stone and setting the guard" (Mt 27:66), moved aside? (*By an earthquake, similar to the earthquake mentioned in Matthew 27:52*)
  - Does Jesus burst forth from the tomb? (*No, the Resurrection has already taken place, while the tomb was sealed. The tomb is empty. Note that in Matthew, as in the other Gospels, we do not actually have a "Resurrection account" in the strict sense, but a "post-Resurrection account." Remind the students that this is one of the reasons why the Resurrection was a transcendent event.*)

- What does the angel commission the two women to do? (*To announce the good news to the Apostles—to be the first evangelists*)
- How do they respond? (*They set off to do as they were told, only to encounter the Risen Lord, who repeats the same commission.*)
- Where does the angel and later Jesus himself tell the women to announce the news of the Resurrection? (*Galilee*) Take a moment to explain that Galilee has special meaning for Matthew, who has Jesus beginning his ministry in Galilee, which he calls "Galilee of the Gentiles" (Mt 4:15–16). For Matthew, Galilee is the gateway to the non-Jewish world. The command to go to Galilee is to spread the light of Divine Revelation to all the nations, not just Israel.
- Who else witnessed what the two women witnessed? (*the guards*)
- How did they respond? (*They reported to the elders, who bribed them to say that Jesus' disciples had stolen Jesus' body.*)

- Note how both the women and the guards have witnessed the same thing. Both are commanded to speak about the event. Both are to report more than what was (originally) seen. For the women, the events at the empty tomb happened because Jesus has been raised. For the guards, the events at the empty tomb happened because they fell asleep and the disciples stole the body. Matthew wants us to realize that it is the elders who are perpetrating a hoax, not those announcing the Resurrection.
- Remind the students that if the Gospel writers had simply invented the Resurrection stories, they surely would have provided witnesses other than women, whose testimony was not recognized as valid or trustworthy in the ancient world.
- Have a student read aloud Matthew 28:16–17. Note how the disciples "saw" and "worshiped" Jesus, but still "doubted." This is undoubtedly reported correctly, because it would seem counterproductive for Matthew to include it if it had not been a key part of the testimony that was passed to him. Stress that here the Gospel recognizes that doubt is a normal part of faith development.
- Ask another student to read Jesus' "Great Commission" in Matthew 28:18–20. Have the students write this passage in their journals and have them write the ways they can live it out in their own

140 Jesus Christ: Source of Our Salvation

discipleship
The life of following Jesus Christ. The word *disciple* comes from a Latin word that means "learner."

the world, not just the Jews, to make them disciples. They are to preach the Gospel, teach Jesus' commandments, and baptize in the name of the Father, and of the Son, and of the Holy Spirit. Finally, Jesus promises that he will remain with the Church until the final coming of God's Kingdom at the end of time. The Risen Jesus Christ is truly Emmanuel, God-with-us, who will guide and protect his followers until the end of time. On this hope-filled promise of the Risen Lord himself, the Gospel of Matthew ends.

The Resurrection in Mark 16

Women at the Tomb (Mk 16:1-8)

Mary Magdalene; Mary, the mother of James; and Salome go to the tomb to anoint Jesus' body, since there had not been time to do so before the Sabbath began after Jesus' Death late Friday afternoon. (According to John's Gospel, Jesus' corpse had already been anointed, but Mark assumes that the preparations had not been completed.) The women are concerned about who will roll back the large round slab that fits into the groove at the entrance to Jesus' tomb. Apparently, the women did not consider who would do this before they set out for Jesus' tomb. However, when they get there, the task is already done. A young man (an angel) clothed in white greets them. The women are "utterly amazed." The young man tells them that Jesus of Nazareth has been raised. After inspecting the empty tomb, the women are instructed to tell Peter and the disciples to go meet

Lesson 2 Homework

1. To prepare for their next lesson, have the students read the remainder of the text section "The Resurrection Accounts in the Four Gospels," beginning with "The Resurrection in John 20–21" (pages 143–149).
2. Continue working on their chosen Ongoing Assignments.

The Resurrection of Jesus Christ 141

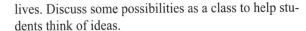

Jesus in Galilee where they will see him, as Jesus himself told them. "Then they went out and fled from the tomb seized with trembling and bewilderment. They said nothing to anyone, for they were afraid" (Mk 16:8).

The abrupt conclusion in Mark 16:8 causes some to believe that the original ending of Mark's Gospel may have been lost. However, that the women disobey Jesus' instructions and say nothing is consistent with the rest of Mark's Gospel where his disciples continually misunderstood Jesus. But consider the brilliance of the Evangelist Mark. He wants us to step into the story and to do what the women failed to do through chapter 16, verse 8. He challenges us to spread the Good News—without fear or confusion—that Jesus of Nazareth is risen from the dead. This is the task of all believers: to be bearers of the Gospel, to tell the world of the Salvation won for us by the Death and Resurrection of Jesus Christ. Mark wrote his Gospel to show us the example of Jesus who endured all so that we may have eternal life. It is now our task to carry on his work, the work of **discipleship**.

The Longer Ending of Mark's Gospel (Mk 16:9-20)

The vocabulary and style of Mark 16:9–20 indicate that Mark's Gospel was likely composed by someone other than Mark. The Church has traditionally accepted it as part of the canon and it was defined as such at the Council of Trent. It was likely added by the Church in the second century, perhaps not believing that Mark intended to end the Gospel the way he did—with astonished women who were too afraid to spread the news about Jesus' Resurrection. Notice how similar they are to the stories from some of the other Gospels, especially Luke, from which they were probably taken. The scenes that appear in the Longer Ending are:

- *Mary Magdalene (16:9–11).* Jesus appears to Mary Magdalene "out of whom he had driven seven demons." When she told the Apostles that she had seen the Risen Jesus, they did not believe her. Note the similarity between the Risen Jesus and Mary Magdalene in this passage compared to John 20:11–18.
- *Two disciples on the road (16:12–13).* Jesus appears to two disciples on a country road. The disciples report what they saw to the others, but once again they are not believed. Note the similarity in this meeting to Jesus' appearance on the road to Emmaus (Lk 24:13–35).
- *Jesus appears to the Eleven (16:14–18).* Similar to the commissioning of the disciples in Matthew 28:1–10, Jesus appears to the Apostles at a meal. Jesus rebukes them for not believing the reports of others who had seen him. He then instructs them to go to into the whole world and proclaim the Gospel. Jesus also tells them that the disciples will be able to perform exorcisms, speak in tongues, handle deadly serpents and drink poisons without harm, and heal the sick in his name.
- *The Ascension of Jesus (16:19–20).* The last two verses of Mark's longer ending parallel the report of Jesus' Ascension in Luke 24:50–53. The Gospel tells how the Apostles boldly preached the Gospel everywhere and how the Lord worked with and through them by confirming their preaching with signs.

The Shorter Ending

The so-called "shorter ending" placed in brackets after Mark 16:20 was found immediately after Mark 16:8 and before the Longer Ending in fourth- to ninth-century Greek manuscripts, as well as in one Latin manuscript. The shorter ending tells how the women did indeed report to Peter and the other Apostles. It also gives Jesus' commission to preach the Good News of Salvation from east to west. The Church may have thought the Gospel ended at Mark 16:8 because either Mark wrote a longer ending but it was lost, or something happened to Mark before he was able to complete his Gospel. This may have also been the motive for the Church to tack on the new endings. Nevertheless, there is good reason to

Background Information

Emmaus and the Mystagogia

Luke's account of the disciples on the road to Emmaus functions as a kind of prototype for a method of teaching or catechesis in the Catechumenate by using the ancient process known as Mystagogy (the "Study of the Mysteries"). The time of Mystagogy has generally been reserved for the fifty days of Easter. Its purpose is to help those newly baptized at the Vigil of Easter to explore the sacraments; to connect the experience of the sacraments to their personal experience, the experience of the faith community, and the Church's teaching; and to shape and identify ministry in their daily life. The Mystagogy helps the newly baptized figure out how to live out their Baptism in their day-to-day lives.

lives. Discuss some possibilities as a class to help students think of ideas.

- Sum up Matthew by telling the students that faith in the Resurrection does not arise so much on the basis of evidence, of which the soldiers and elders had plenty, but on the basis of the following (list on the board):
  - **the experience of the presence of the Risen Lord**
  - **the testimony of those to whom he appeared**
  - **the Risen Lord's continuing presence among his followers**
- Have the students reread Mark 16:1–8. Afterward, point out that Mark contains no description whatsoever of any Resurrection appearance. Rather, Mark's account is little more than a repetition of the earliest *kerygma* proclamation (1 Cor 15:3–8) placed within the story of the empty tomb.
- Remind the students that throughout his Gospel, Mark stresses that each of us must decide for ourselves who Jesus is: "Who do you say that I am?" (Mk 8:29). Also, Mark stresses that decision is to be a decision of faith, not of empirical knowledge. The question for us from Mark is, "Will we have faith without exact evidence?" Or will we be like the Pharisees and Jesus' own disciples, demanding Heaven-sent signs and wonders (Mk 8:11–12) to lead us to believe?
- Point out that the longer ending (Mk 16:9–20), added by a later editor, drew upon material from Matthew and Luke, especially Luke. Mark's original ending, however, challenges his readers to base belief in the Resurrection only on the evidence of Jesus' pre-Resurrection preaching and on the declaration of the young man (angel) at the empty tomb. Ask, "Would that 'evidence' be enough for you to believe?"
- Take a moment to address the notion of fear regarding the Resurrection. Point out the following:
  - Mark mentions the women's fear (Mk 16:8).
  - Matthew has both the angel and Jesus tell the two Marys not to be afraid (Mt 28:5, 10).
  - Luke says that the women who went to the tomb were "terrified" (Lk 24:5), and when Jesus appeared to the Apostles, they, too, were "startled and terrified" (Lk 24:37).
  - Even John's Gospel reports that the Apostles were frightened (Jn 20:19). He attributes their fear to that of the Jewish leaders.

- Suggest that all of us *fear* Resurrection. Why? Because it asks for a dying, a dying to comfort, to sameness, and to the status quo. Belief in the Resurrection is the faith of the fearless, and most of us are afraid. Fear is the great opponent of faith. Faith in the Resurrection means repentance, reconciliation, renewal. These are all fearful tasks and the demands of Resurrection. Ask the students to answer the following questions in their journals:
    - What is it about the Resurrection that frightens you?
    - How can you accept the challenge to do what the women in Mark were initially too frightened to do?
- Move on to the Gospel of Luke. Direct the students to reread Luke 24:1–53. Afterward, remind the students again that Luke's main audience was composed of poor and disenfranchised Gentile-Christians. Likewise, Luke is likely the only Gentile Gospel writer. Also, Luke's first great theme is *rejoicing*, which is made genuine by Luke's second theme, s*alvation is for all people*.
- Use the chart on page 139 to compare Luke to Matthew and Mark, noting how like his fellow Synoptic writers, Luke begins by describing the visit of women to Jesus' tomb. However, the angels (plural in Luke), rather than directing the women to tell the disciples to go to Galilee, direct them to remember what Jesus told them while in Galilee, namely, that he was to suffer, die, and rise again (Lk 24:7). Once the women remember, they go to share this Good News with others.
- Take a moment to point out that Luke places all Jesus' post-Resurrection appearances, even the Ascension, in and around Jerusalem, not Galilee. For Luke, Galilee was the place where Jesus began his work, but Jerusalem is the place where the Apostles will begin their work.
- Invite the students to tell the Emmaus story—unique to Luke—in their own words. As the students share, outline the account's key points on the board:
    - **The dejected disciples do not recognize Jesus nor expect to see him alive.**
    - **They share with this "stranger" their dashed messianic hopes.**
    - **Jesus says they are foolish, not because they don't recognize him, but because they did not have faith in the words of the prophets concerning the Messiah.**

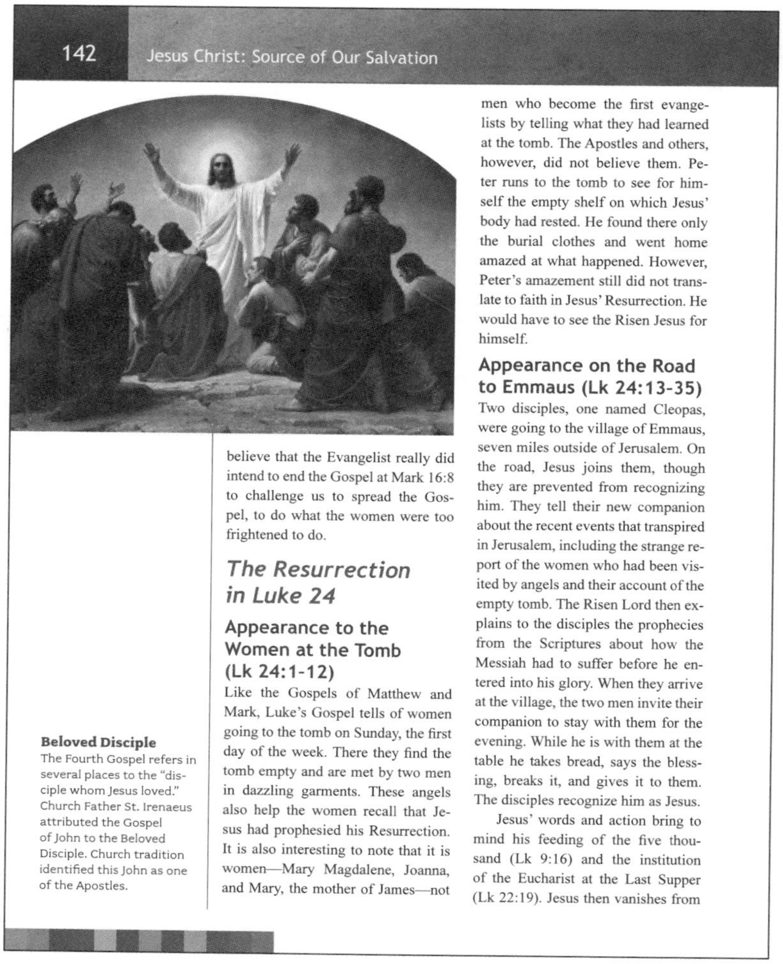

142 Jesus Christ: Source of Our Salvation

believe that the Evangelist really did intend to end the Gospel at Mark 16:8 to challenge us to spread the Gospel, to do what the women were too frightened to do.

The Resurrection in Luke 24

Appearance to the Women at the Tomb (Lk 24:1-12)

Like the Gospels of Matthew and Mark, Luke's Gospel tells of women going to the tomb on Sunday, the first day of the week. There they find the tomb empty and are met by two men in dazzling garments. These angels also help the women recall that Jesus had prophesied his Resurrection. It is also interesting to note that it is women—Mary Magdalene, Joanna, and Mary, the mother of James—not men who become the first evangelists by telling what they had learned at the tomb. The Apostles and others, however, did not believe them. Peter runs to the tomb to see for himself the empty shelf on which Jesus' body had rested. He found there only the burial clothes and went home amazed at what happened. However, Peter's amazement still did not translate to faith in Jesus' Resurrection. He would have to see the Risen Jesus for himself.

Appearance on the Road to Emmaus (Lk 24:13-35)

Two disciples, one named Cleopas, were going to the village of Emmaus, seven miles outside of Jerusalem. On the road, Jesus joins them, though they are prevented from recognizing him. They tell their new companion about the recent events that transpired in Jerusalem, including the strange report of the women who had been visited by angels and their account of the empty tomb. The Risen Lord then explains to the disciples the prophecies from the Scriptures about how the Messiah had to suffer before he entered into his glory. When they arrive at the village, the two men invite their companion to stay with them for the evening. While he is with them at the table he takes bread, says the blessing, breaks it, and gives it to them. The disciples recognize him as Jesus.

Jesus' words and action bring to mind his feeding of the five thousand (Lk 9:16) and the institution of the Eucharist at the Last Supper (Lk 22:19). Jesus then vanishes from

Beloved Disciple
The Fourth Gospel refers in several places to the "disciple whom Jesus loved." Church Father St. Irenaeus attributed the Gospel of John to the Beloved Disciple. Church tradition identified this John as one of the Apostles.

their sight. The disciples are filled with love and understand what Jesus had been saying to them on the road. Their hearts were burning within them because the Lord had visited them. They immediately return to Jerusalem to tell the Eleven what they had experienced. But they also learn that Jesus had already appeared to Peter, "The Lord has truly been raised and has appeared to Simon!" (Lk 24:34). Neither Luke nor any other Gospel elaborates on this special appearance to Peter, but it is important because Peter is the one Jesus appointed to be leader of the Apostles, the one on whom he established the Church.

This Emmaus story includes rich themes that Luke developed in his Gospel, including those of journey, faith correlated to seeing, and hospitality to the stranger. Luke closes this vignette by reminding us that Jesus was made known "in the breaking of the bread." This is a reference to the Eucharist, the event in which we both hear the Word of God proclaimed in the readings and receive the Lord in Holy Communion. Even though Catholics of later generations do not "see" Jesus in visions as did the early disciples after the Resurrection, we can experience the living Lord in Sacred Scripture, his Holy Word, and in the Seven Sacraments, especially the Eucharist.

Jesus Appears to the Disciples in Jerusalem (Lk 24:36-49)

Immediately after the disciples from Emmaus report what they have experienced, Jesus appears in their midst and greets them: "Peace be with you" (24:36). The disciples are startled, thinking they are seeing a ghost. But Jesus assures them he is not a ghost, showing them his wounded hands and feet, inviting them to touch him, and eating a piece of baked fish. We learn here that there is a continuity between the body of the historical Jesus and the Resurrected Lord. He is recognizable as the same Person.

The Lord then opens his disciples' minds to understand what the Scriptures had foretold: the suffering of the Messiah and his Resurrection on the third day. He tells the Apostles that they were witnesses to all that he had done and that their task has only begun because he and the Father are going to send the Holy Spirit to empower them to go forth from Jerusalem to the ends of the world to proclaim the Gospel.

The Ascension (Lk 24:50-53)

Jesus' final appearance to his disciples is near Bethany, where the Lord raises his hands, blesses them, and is taken up to Heaven. The Acts of the Apostles, also written by Luke, describes this taking place after Jesus appears to his disciples for forty days (Acts 1:3). Overwhelmed, the disciples worship Jesus, return to Jerusalem joy-filled, and go to the Temple to praise God as they await Jesus' sending of the Holy Spirit. Luke's Gospel ends where it began—in the Temple in Jerusalem. From there, the Apostles will take the Good News of Salvation to the ends of the earth.

The Resurrection in John 20-21

The Empty Tomb (Jn 20:1-10)

All the Gospels agree that Mary Magdalene went to the tomb on the first day of the week, in the morning. Only in John's Gospel does Mary go and report the empty tomb to Peter and the "other disciple whom Jesus loved." She thinks someone has taken Jesus' body. Peter and the **Beloved Disciple** run to the tomb to see for themselves. The Beloved Disciple arrives first and sees the discarded burial garments. However, he allows Peter to enter the tomb first to see the burial clothes. The Beloved Disciple then goes in, and with only minimal proof of Jesus' Resurrection (the discarded burial clothes), he believes.

- **So Jesus taught them the meaning of the Scriptures.**
- **The disciples show genuine hospitality to the stranger, inviting him to share a meal with them.**
- **At the meal, they recognize Jesus in the breaking of the bread (Lk 24:35).**
- **After Jesus removes himself, the disciples realize the importance of what he had done in revealing the Scriptures to them (Lk 24:32).**
- **They return to share with the disciples, their story and the Good News of Jesus risen.**

- Point out the themes in the Emmaus story that have been developed throughout Luke's Gospel (see pages 142–143): journeying, faith related to seeing, hospitality, and joy. Note, too, how the Emmaus story speaks to the meaning of the Eucharist for us and how, like the disciples on that road long ago, we continue to recognize Jesus in the Scriptures proclaimed, the bread broken and shared, and the hospitality joyfully celebrated at every Eucharist.
- Before moving on, consider singing or playing a recording of the hymn "In the Breaking of the Bread" by Bob Hurd and Michael Downey or another song about the Eucharist.
- Move on by calling attention to the text section "Jesus Appears to the Disciples in Jerusalem" (page 143). Ask the students to point out some of the details that Luke includes to demonstrate that Jesus was real, alive, and resurrected (e.g., invites his followers to touch him and asks for something to eat).
- Go on to point out that Jesus then goes back to the basics, teaching his disciples what the Scriptures revealed about him. Finally, Jesus commissions them to witness to the truth that he is the Messiah, and to preach repentance and the forgiveness of sins with the help of the Holy Spirit (Lk 24:39).
- Tell the students that Luke is the only Gospel writer to describe the Ascension. Point out how Luke ends by placing the followers back in Jerusalem, in the Temple, and note the mood—"great joy" (Lk 24:52).
- Before concluding this lesson, have the students turn to the feature "Living the Corporal Works of Mercy" on page 146. Read aloud the introductions. Then, tell the students, in addition to resolving as individuals to do one of the listed actions, to discuss which of the actions they are willing to undertake as a class. Once the students decide on a "corporal work" to do, help them plan how to carry out their decision.

Chapter 6: The Resurrection of Jesus Christ—Lesson 3

Bell Ringers

- As you did for the Synoptic Gospels in the previous lesson, introduce this lesson by reviewing the tradition about John the Evangelist. List the following on the board.
  - **Author: John the Apostle (the Beloved Disciple)**
  - **Written: in Ephesus around AD 90**
  - **Audience: Jewish and Gentile Christians**
  - **Presents: Jesus as a life-giving, life-fulfilling Messiah**
- If the students have studied *Jesus Christ: His Mission and Ministry*, see if they can recall the structure/outline of John's Gospel. If not, simply list the following on the board:
  1. **Prologue (1:1–18)**
  2. **The Book of Signs (1:19–12:50)**
  3. **The Book of Glory (13:1–20:31)**
  4. **Epilogue: Resurrection Appearances in Galilee (21:1–25, written by a disciple of St. John)**

  Explain that in today's lesson they will be investigating the final section of the Book of Glory as well as the Epilogue.

Teaching Approaches

The Resurrection Accounts in the Four Gospels, continued (pages 143-149)

- Call attention to the subsection "The Empty Tomb (Jn 20:1–10)" on page 143. Have the students reread John 20:1–10. Ask, "What seems odd about the account compared to the ones in the Synoptic Gospels?" (*No earthquake, no angels, no frightened guards, etc.*)
- Go on to ask:
  - Like the authors of the Synoptics, John places Mary Magdalene at the empty tomb first, but what is different about John's account? (*Only John reports that Mary returned to tell Peter and the Beloved Disciple what she had witnessed.*)
  - How much proof does it take for the Beloved Disciple to believe Jesus had risen? (*only the*

144 Jesus Christ: Source of Our Salvation

The Lord Appears to Mary Magdalene (Jn 20:11-18)

Mary stays at the tomb after Peter and the Beloved Disciple depart. She is weeping. But then she looks into the tomb and sees two angels. When questioned why she is weeping, Mary says, "They have taken my Lord, and I don't know where they have laid him" (Jn 20:13). After saying this, she turns and sees Jesus, at first thinking he is the gardener. It seems that even the friends of Jesus have some difficulty recognizing him. He is the same, but different. However, when Jesus addresses Mary by name, she recognizes Jesus and calls him "Rabbouni" (Teacher). Her recognition of Jesus' voice recalls a theme in John's Gospel where Jesus says that the sheep will recognize the voice of the Good Shepherd. Mary then tries to hold Jesus, but the Lord tells her not to cling to him because he has not yet ascended to his Father. The Lord instructs Mary to go and tell the brothers that she has seen Jesus and to deliver this message: "I am going to my Father and your Father, to my God and your God" (Jn 20:17).

Jesus Appears to the Twelve (Jn 20:19-23)

On Sunday evening, Jesus appears in the room where the Apostles are staying. He mysteriously appears in their midst even though the doors are locked. The Apostles are hiding in fear of the authorities. Jesus wishes them peace, shows them his wounds, and commissions them to continue his work. In John's Gospel, it is here on Easter Sunday that Jesus gives his disciples the gift of the Holy Spirit and the authority to forgive sins in his name through the Sacraments of Baptism and Penance and to announce God's Salvation through the forgiveness of sins in the name of his Son, the Lord Jesus Christ.

The Lord Appears to Thomas (Jn 20:24-29)

The Apostle Thomas was not present when Jesus appeared to the others, so he did not believe in the Resurrection. A week later, the Lord once again appears behind the locked doors, offers peace to his disciples, and invites Thomas to put his fingers in his wounds so that he will believe. Thomas cries out a great act of faith, "My Lord and my God!" (Jn 20:28). Jesus says to the doubting Thomas, and to all Christians, "Blessed are those who have not seen and have believed" (Jn 20:29). These verses lead to what many scholars think is the original ending of the Gospel of John (20:30–31) where the Evangelist says that Jesus performed many other signs not recorded in the Gospel. But the ones that have been recorded were done for one purpose—that we "may come to believe that Jesus is the Messiah, the Son of God, and that through this belief you may have life in his name" (Jn 20:31). Thomas proclaims what every Christian must proclaim: Jesus is Lord. Jesus is God.

Appearance by the Sea (Jn 21:1-14)

John 21 is labeled as an "epilogue" to the Gospel. There are many parts of this chapter that are similar to other writings of John, and others that suggest the Greek style present in Luke. It treats some issues that were of concern to the original community for whom the Gospel of John was written, especially the relationship between Peter and the Beloved Disciple. The first appearance recounted in this section takes place at the Sea of Tiberias in Galilee. This particular story gives us the impression that this was the Lord's first appearance to the disciples because they have gone back to their occupation as fishermen. It parallels somewhat the traditions of Mark and Matthew who say Jesus appeared to his disciples in Galilee.

In the same account, the men have been out all night, but have caught nothing. However, it is now daylight, and Jesus stands on the shore. He instructs his disciples to cast their net out the right side of the boat. They obey him, and their catch is so great (153 large fish) that they cannot pull it in to the boat.

Lesson 3 Objectives

The students will:

- recall the authorship, audience, and purpose of the Gospel of John.
- examine the Resurrection account in the Gospel of John.
- compare and contrast the Resurrection account in the Gospel of John and the Synoptic Gospels.
- debate the historical reality of Jesus' Resurrection from the dead.

Lesson 3 Preview

This lesson concludes the gospel-by-gospel examination of the Resurrection accounts by delving into the Gospel of John. As in the previous lesson, be sure to use the chart on page 139 of the text that compares the accounts and relies on the words of the Gospel itself.

The Resurrection of Jesus Christ 145

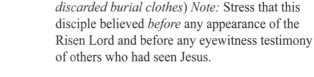

The Beloved Disciple is the first to recognize Jesus. He tells Peter, who then impetuously jumps into the water and runs to the shore. When all the disciples arrive with the catch, Jesus cooks breakfast, providing them with fish and bread. He does so on a charcoal fire, which brings to mind the fire that was burning in the courtyard when Peter denied knowing Jesus. Once again, it is the Lord who serves his disciples. Somewhat mysteriously, they do not ask who Jesus is because they recognize that he is the Lord.

The meaning of this particular story is striking. It talks about a large catch of fish, symbolizing that the Apostles, with Peter as the rock, will be fishers of people, bringing the whole world to Christ. Further, the Apostles recognize Jesus in the course of a meal as the host who provides them with the fish and bread. This is remindful of the Eucharist where believers recognize and receive the Lord.

Dialogue between the Risen Lord and Peter (Jn 21:15-25)

After breakfast, the scene turns to an interchange between Jesus and Peter. Jesus asks, "Simon, son of John, do you love me more than these?" The most intimate Greek word for love, *agape*, is used in this passage by Jesus. When Peter responds to Jesus, "Yes, Lord, you know that I love you," the Gospel records the word for love as the Greek *phile*, meaning love for a friend. Jesus, again repeats, "Agape, Simon?" Peter responds "Phile." At the third question Jesus says, "Simon, son of John, Phile?" One meaning of this exchange is that Jesus will accept whatever level of love and commitment Peter (and we) can give.

Peter's threefold "yes" to Jesus reverses his betrayal in the courtyard. The Lord establishes Peter as the leader of the Church by telling Peter to feed his sheep. Thus, Peter is the pastor (or shepherd) who is to guide the Church, to be its leader, to serve others in love. Jesus had previously taught on the role of the Good Shepherd, one who is willing to lay down his life for his flock. This is what Jesus himself did for the sake of our Salvation. It is also what all good pastors must be willing to do for their flock and what our Lord said would happen to Peter, who himself was crucified under one of the persecutions of the emperor Nero.

Peter then asks the Lord what would happen to the Beloved Disciple. Some in the community for which the Gospel was written might have misinterpreted Jesus, thinking that the Beloved Disciple would not die before the Lord would return again. The scene takes on a different significance, however, if the Beloved Disciple, who was the probable eyewitness source for the Gospel of John, had already died at the time chapter 21 was written. The death of the Apostles and those of their generation caused problems in the early Church because of a belief that Jesus was to have returned first. Ultimately,

Lesson 3 Homework

1. Tell the students to write out their answers to the eleven For Review questions on pages 147 and 149.
2. Direct the students to read "Our Participation in Christ's Resurrection" (pages 149–151) and "The Ascension and Glorification of Jesus Christ" (pages 152–153) in preparation for their next lesson.
3. Distribute copies of Chapter 6, Handout 2, "Resurrection Reflections." Tell the students that the two poems on the handout speak to the meaning of the Resurrection *for us*. Direct the students to choose one of the poems and create a response. Explain that their response may be a poem of their own, a song, a brief essay, a letter addressed to Jesus, an artwork (painting, sculpture, collage, etc.), a song or rap, or even a text message. Tell the students that this response will be due when they gather for the review lesson on this chapter.
4. Remind the students to begin wrapping up work on their chosen Ongoing Assignments (pages 155–156).

discarded burial clothes) *Note:* Stress that this disciple believed *before* any appearance of the Risen Lord and before any eyewitness testimony of others who had seen Jesus.

- Call on a volunteer to read aloud John 20:11–18. Point out how John stresses that it is *personal encounter* with Jesus that summons faith. Likewise, note that Mary recognizes Jesus only when he *speaks* to her. Tell the students that we, too, can recognize Jesus and can be assured of his presence in his proclaimed Word (Gospel), especially as proclaimed in the celebration of the Eucharist. Then ask, "What in the account points to Jesus' bodily presence?" (*Jesus saying to Mary, "Stop holding on to me" [Jn 20:17].*) Finally, point out that once again, it is a woman whom Jesus sends to be the first witness to the Resurrection.
- Refer the students to the text section "Jesus Appears to the Twelve" (page 144). Direct the students to note the mood in the Upper Room (fear) and then Jesus' gift (peace). Stress that Jesus' greeting and gift of peace reestablishes relationship with his followers, a relationship that death had severed. *Jesus' gift banishes fear and leads to faith.*
- Point out that Jesus goes on to commission the Apostles to share that peace with others and to help others reestablish their broken relationships with God by offering them forgiveness for sins.
- Ask a student to read the account of doubting Thomas in John 20:24–29. Afterward, ask:
    - Does Thomas actually touch Jesus? (*No, it was the sight of Jesus and his offer to allow Thomas to reach out and touch him that enabled Thomas to believe.*)
    - Why do we owe Thomas and his doubt a debt of gratitude? (*Thomas's demands demonstrated that the only Jesus worthy of belief was the same Jesus who lived, suffered, and died on the Cross; Thomas was unwilling to believe in a hallucination or a ghost.*)
    - Given the manner in which Jesus responded to doubting Thomas, how do you think he might respond to us when we have our doubts?
- Point out to the students that when Jesus says to Thomas, "Have you come to believe because you have seen me? Blessed are those who have not seen and have believed" (Jn 20:29), he is not giving the Apostle a dressing-down. Rather, he is offering a blessing to those who believe in the Resurrection without having any physical proof. This is meant to

be a compliment to the readers of John's Gospel who have not seen Jesus.

- Call attention to the For Reflection feature on page 149. Give the students time to write about the scene in the Upper Room. Have them describe their feelings and how they expect they might change due to their encounter with the resurrected Lord. Afterward, invite volunteers to share their responses.
- Before moving on, note that Thomas made the only genuine response possible to the fact of Resurrection, the *response of faith*: "My Lord and my God!" (Jn 20:28).
- Ask the students to recall why the epilogue was added by a later disciple of John the Evangelist. (*To resolve issues like the relationship between Peter and the Beloved Disciple*)
- Move on to the accounts of Jesus' appearance by the sea and of his dialogue with Peter (Jn 21:1–25). Explain that the point of both accounts is addressing the need to spread the Good News of the Resurrection.
    - Just as the net is filled with every fish, so should every person be gathered into the fold.
    - Just as Jesus feeds his disciple, so must his disciples feed others.
    - Just as Jesus shepherded his flock with love, so must Peter lovingly care for them. (*Note:* The threefold questioning of Peter's love parallels his threefold denial. Here, Jesus is making sure Peter is *the* shepherd worthy to lead the flock.)
- Invite the students to list in their notes the differences in the Resurrection account of the Gospel of John compared to the Synoptic accounts. Then, as a class, discuss the differences and list them on the board.
- Go over the key elements of the text section "Summary of the Four Gospel Accounts" (pages 146–147) with the students. Again, use the chart on page 139 of the text to point out similarities. Stress that although there are some variances, due to the evangelists' different audiences and different sources, the Gospels agree on the following major points:
    - a Sunday rising
    - women were first at the tomb
    - an empty tomb
    - messengers send the women to proclaim the Resurrection

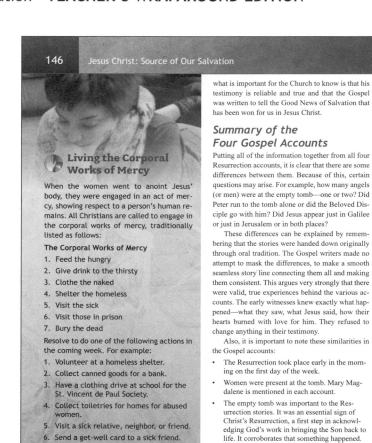

146 Jesus Christ: Source of Our Salvation

Living the Corporal Works of Mercy

When the women went to anoint Jesus' body, they were engaged in an act of mercy, showing respect to a person's human remains. All Christians are called to engage in the corporal works of mercy, traditionally listed as follows:

The Corporal Works of Mercy

1. Feed the hungry
2. Give drink to the thirsty
3. Clothe the naked
4. Shelter the homeless
5. Visit the sick
6. Visit those in prison
7. Bury the dead

Resolve to do one of the following actions in the coming week. For example:

1. Volunteer at a homeless shelter.
2. Collect canned goods for a bank.
3. Have a clothing drive at school for the St. Vincent de Paul Society.
4. Collect toiletries for homes for abused women.
5. Visit a sick relative, neighbor, or friend.
6. Send a get-well card to a sick friend.
7. Collect magazines to distribute to patients in the hospital.
8. Visit a neighbor who has recently experienced the death of a loved one.

what is important for the Church to know is that his testimony is reliable and true and that the Gospel was written to tell the Good News of Salvation that has been won for us in Jesus Christ.

Summary of the Four Gospel Accounts

Putting all of the information together from all four Resurrection accounts, it is clear that there are some differences between them. Because of this, certain questions may arise. For example, how many angels (or men) were at the empty tomb—one or two? Did Peter run to the tomb alone or did the Beloved Disciple go with him? Did Jesus appear just in Galilee or just in Jerusalem or in both places?

These differences can be explained by remembering that the stories were handed down originally through oral tradition. The Gospel writers made no attempt to mask the differences, to make a smooth seamless story line connecting them all and making them consistent. This argues very strongly that there were valid, true experiences behind the various accounts. The early witnesses knew exactly what happened—what they saw, what Jesus said, how their hearts burned with love for him. They refused to change anything in their testimony.

Also, it is important to note these similarities in the Gospel accounts:

- The Resurrection took place early in the morning on the first day of the week.
- Women were present at the tomb. Mary Magdalene is mentioned in each account.
- The empty tomb was important to the Resurrection stories. It was an essential sign of Christ's Resurrection, a first step in acknowledging God's work in bringing the Son back to life. It corroborates that something happened. The enemies of the early Christians were never able to produce Jesus' corpse, though they probably tried to do so.

- There were "messengers" at the tomb. The women were instructed to tell the disciples what they had witnessed.
- Jesus appeared to his disciples. Note the different people mentioned who encountered the Risen Jesus: Mary Magdalene, Peter and the other Apostles (with and without Thomas), two disciples on the road to Emmaus, and seven disciples by the sea of Tiberias. These appearances convinced a group of frightened men and women that the crucified Jesus was alive, that he was Lord, that he was God's Son. So life-changing were these appearances that, along with the coming of the Holy Spirit, they transformed Jesus' disciples from frightened, confused, and disappointed followers into bold, courageous witnesses who willingly lived and died proclaiming, "Jesus Christ is Lord."

Note several aspects of Jesus' appearances. Jesus appeared only to his disciples. Sometimes they were slow to recognize him. Why? First, they were not expecting the Lord to come back to life. And second, Jesus appeared in his glorified body, one recognizable to the disciples yet shining with the glory of God's life. The Gospel accounts also insist that Jesus was not a ghost. Luke, for example, reports that the resurrected Jesus ate fish, while John reports that Jesus ate breakfast with his disciples. Furthermore, Jesus asks Thomas to touch his wounds. The resurrected Jesus is not a ghost; but neither is he a corpse that is breathing again. He is alive in a transformed, glorified body that still has an aspect of "bodiliness" to it. He is the same but different.

For Review

1. What is the significance of the empty tomb?
2. Explain why Mark 16:8 may be the place where the Evangelist concluded his Gospel.
3. Who are the first evangelists of the Resurrection of Jesus in Luke's Gospel?
4. When do the disciples on the road to Emmaus recognize Jesus?
5. Where do Catholics meet the Risen Lord in the Sunday liturgy?
6. What typical greeting did the Risen Lord give to his disciples when he appeared to them?
7. Who is a model of faith in the Resurrection narratives in John's Gospel?

(continued on page 149)

Who Is Jesus to Me?

While she was recovering in the hospital in Rome in 1983, Blessed Mother Teresa wrote down these thoughts and feelings about who Jesus was to her. Write your own series of statements of who Jesus is to *you*, perhaps in a similar style. Select two or three photos to help illustrate your reflections. Use these reflections as a prayer of thanksgiving to Jesus:

Jesus is the Word Made Flesh.
Jesus is the Victim offered for our sins on the Cross.
Jesus is the Word—to be spoken.
Jesus is the Truth—to be told.
Jesus is the Way—to be walked.
Jesus is the Light—to be lit.
Jesus is the Life—to be lived.
Jesus is the Love—to be loved.
Jesus is the Hungry—to be fed.
Jesus is the Homeless—to be taken in.
Jesus is the Lonely—to be loved.
Jesus is the Unwanted—to be wanted.
Jesus is the Little One—to embrace him.
Jesus is the Old—to be served.
Jesus is my God.
Jesus is my only Love.
Jesus is my Everything.

- numerous post-Resurrection appearances of Jesus whose body, while glorified, was a body of flesh and blood.

- Call attention to Explaining the Faith on pages 148–149. Divide the class into two groups. Assign one side of the argument to each group. Have the students work individually to read and study the arguments to prepare for a debate. Challenge the students to think of additional arguments and evidence to use during the debate. Invite the students to join the rest of their group, discuss the strongest arguments, and choose one person to present an opening argument. Have the students from both sides turn their desks toward one another and get out a soft ball to use for the debate. Present the rules of the debate: (1) students may only speak when holding the ball; (2) the ball will alternate sides after each person speaks; (3) students must gently toss the ball to the opposing side or lose the opportunity to speak. Award points to each team according to the quality and relevance of each statement. The team with the most points at the end of a designated amount of time will win.
- Have the students turn to Primary Source Quotations on page 155. Call on different students to read aloud the three "Eyewitness Testimony" quotations from the Gospels, as well as the quotation "From the Easter Proclamation." Point out that those people who

For Review Answers (pages 147, 149)

1. The empty tomb is strong evidence that Jesus' dead body, which had been laid there and guarded by Jesus' foes, was no longer to be found.
2. Mark may have concluded his Gospel at 16:8 in order to stress the astonishment at Jesus' Resurrection as well as to challenge his readers (including us) to step into the story and do what the frightened women could not, namely, to spread the news that Jesus is risen.
3. The women: Mary Magdalene, Joanna, and Mary, the mother of James.
4. In the breaking of the bread.
5. In the Gospel proclaimed and in the sharing of the Eucharist (Communion).
6. "Peace."
7. The Beloved Disciple.
8. Jesus' body is both tangible and able to enter a room without passing through a door.
9. So that the reader might come to faith in Jesus as the Messiah, the Son of God, and, therefore, have life.
10. Discrepancies show that the Gospel writers were not working together to make all the accounts agree with one another. The discrepancies reflect different witnesses and their recollections.
11. The students may list any of the points of agreement in the Resurrection narratives: (1) the Resurrection took place on the first day of the week, (2) women were first at the tomb, (3) the tomb was empty, (4) messengers sent the women to proclaim the Resurrection, and (5) there were numerous post-Resurrection appearances of Jesus whose body, while glorified, was a body of flesh and blood.

witnessed Jesus alive and risen from the dead were so convinced of the veracity of their claims that many devoted their lives to proclaiming what they had seen, and some died for it. That faith was founded on the interlocking evidence of:

- the empty tomb
- the numerous appearances of Jesus
- confidence in the witness of others

- Conclude the discussion by emphasizing that the Resurrection does not so much vindicate Jesus, proving that he is divine, as it vindicates the Kingdom of God Jesus came to establish. While Calvary is always *then*, Resurrection is always *now*. The great miracle of Resurrection is not that one man rose from the dead, but that because of that rising, all of us will rise. In other words, the Resurrection signals not only Jesus' glorification but also ours in the Kingdom of God. Tell the students that in their next lesson, they will look at the ways we share in the Resurrection.
- Call attention to the feature "Who Is Jesus to Me?" on page 147. Have copies of old picture magazines and other art materials available. Provide ample time for the students to begin working on the assignment in class. (*Note:* You may also have the students complete their work at home or the beginning of the next class session.)

EXPLAINING THE FAITH

How can we respond to those who deny that Jesus rose from the dead?

We live in a skeptical age where it becomes rote to deny the possibilities of grace and goodness. There have always been people who doubted that Christ rose from the dead, even among his first disciples. To counteract those who doubt, Scripture testifies to these facts about the Resurrection of Jesus.

1. *Jesus actually did die by being crucified on a cross by Pontius Pilate.* The reality of his death was reported by the Jewish historian, Josephus, and the Roman historian, Tacitus. Even the Jewish Talmud reports that Jesus was crucified. The fact of his death is as certain as any death reported in the ancient world.

2. *The Apostles and other disciples of Jesus were convinced that he rose from the dead.* In fact, after the Resurrection, the disciples changed from frightened men hiding from the authorities to brave missionaries who suffered martyrdom for spreading the Gospel. Their testimony of the Risen Jesus is supported by other early Church writers, for example, by St. Clement of Rome, the fourth pope. Clement personally knew some of the Apostles. In a letter to the church at Corinth, composed at the end of the first century, he wrote:

> Now, the Gospel was given to the Apostles for us by the Lord Jesus Christ; and Jesus the Christ was sent from God. That is to say, Christ received His commission from God, and the Apostles theirs from Christ. The order of these two events was in accordance with the will of God. So thereafter, when the Apostles had been given their instructions, and all their doubts had been set at rest by the resurrection of our Lord Jesus Christ from the dead, they set out in the full assurance of the holy Spirit to proclaim the coming of God's kingdom.

3. *St. Paul saw the Risen Lord.* Saul of Tarsus was a fierce opponent of the early Christians and played an instrumental role in persecuting them. He was even involved in the death of St. Stephen, the first martyr. On his way to Damascus to persecute Christians, Saul had a vision of the Risen Christ that totally changed his life. He went from a fierce opponent of Christians to a zealous missionary who sacrificed his life for the truth of the Gospel.

4. *Jesus' tomb was empty.* The empty tomb was substantiated by several witnesses, including Jesus' enemies.

Arguments against Christ's Resurrection

Given the bedrock facts, there are still those who do not believe in the incidents around Jesus' Death, and especially his Resurrection. Note some of the following alternative theories that have been proposed:

1. *The Gospel writers fabricated the Resurrection stories.* If this is true, then they did not do a very good job. For one thing, all of the Gospel accounts say that Mary Magdalene had a prominent role in testifying to the empty tomb. Furthermore, John's Gospel singles her out as being the first person to whom Jesus appeared. If Jesus' followers were going to make something up during the first century in either the Roman or Jewish cultures, a woman wouldn't be named because her testimony would not hold up in court. Second, the Gospel writers did not attempt to smooth out the discrepancies in the various accounts. If they were going to make something up, it would have made more sense to change various elements so that there would be total harmony in the accounts. They did not.

2. *There is nothing unique about Christianity. The Resurrection accounts simply copy other religious myths, for example, the spring fertility rites.* In stark contrast to the mythological stories associated with pagan religions, Christianity was founded by Jesus of Nazareth, a real, historical person. He was actually born, lived with a family in a historical place, and died a Death that was publicly recorded, even by his enemies.

3. *The Apostles stole Jesus' body or had it moved.* This theory begets several questions that begin with "how" or "why." For example, How were they—simple fishermen—able to overpower the Roman guards? And why would they steal or move his body? Additionally, what did they gain from it? Remember

For Enrichment

Resurrection—Spoken in the Language of God

> Doctrines are translations into our concepts and ideas of that which God has already expressed in language more adequate, namely the actual incarnation, crucifixion, and resurrection.
>
> —C. S. Lewis

All or Nothing

> It is, of course, impossible to exaggerate the importance of the historicity of what is commonly known as the Resurrection. If, after all his claims and promises, Christ had died and merely lived on as a fragrant memory, he would only be revered as an extremely good but profoundly mistaken man. His claims to be God, his claims to be himself the very principle of life, would be mere self-delusion. His authoritative pronouncements on the nature of God and Man and Life would be at once suspect. Why should he be right about the lesser things, if he was proved to be completely wrong in the greater?
>
> —J. B. Phillips

Talmud
A collection of rabbinical teachings collected after the destruction of the Jerusalem Temple in AD 70.

they were afraid when Jesus was killed and went into hiding. Would they really have been willing to die for such a lie and cover-up? The only thing the Apostles gained was the loss of their lives.

4. *His friends so much wanted to see Jesus alive that they imagined or hallucinated that they saw him.* Hallucinations are an individual, subjective experience. There is no such thing as mass hallucination.

5. *Paul was delusional. He felt guilt for persecuting the Christians and only imagined he saw the Risen Lord.* Those who were with Paul said they heard a voice and saw a bright light, though they themselves did not see Jesus.

6. *The Resurrection stories are merely symbolic ways of saying that Jesus' spirit lives on.* If true, the Apostles could have simply said, "Our teacher's spirit lives on." They had the vocabulary to do so.

7. *Resurrection is scientifically impossible.* Science cannot explain many things, including the creation of the universe. The Resurrection of Jesus is only impossible if our human existence is impossible. But it is not. Consider the words of the famous philosopher and mathematician, Blaise Pascal:

> What reason have they [atheists] for saying that we cannot rise from the dead? What is more difficult, to be born or to rise again; that what has never been should be, or that what has been should be again? Is it more difficult to come into existence than to return to it?

For Reflection
What for you is the strongest argument for the fact that Jesus really did rise from the dead?

8. Describe two qualities of Jesus' resurrected body.
9. According to the original ending (Jn 20:30-31), why did John write his Gospel?
10. How do the discrepancies in the Resurrection narratives actually argue for their historical value?
11. List four similarities in all the Resurrection narratives.

For Reflection

Imagine you were one of the Apostles in the room when Jesus appeared in your midst. Describe the scene: your feelings, what Jesus said to you, how he looked, etc. Explain how you think your life might change as a result of this encounter.

Our Participation in Christ's Resurrection (*CCC*, 651-655)

Jesus' Resurrection is the essential fact of Salvation History, the bedrock of our faith, the heart of the Good News. As St. Paul observed, "If Christ has not been raised, then empty [too] is our preaching; empty, too, your faith" (1 Cor 15:14). The following points summarize the meaning and saving significance of Christ's Resurrection:

- *The Resurrection confirms all Christ's works and teaching.* It proves Jesus' claims to be God's Son. It fulfills the Old Testament promises and those of Jesus himself made during his earthly life. Jesus referred to himself by the Hebrew name for God—Yahweh: "When you lift up the Son of Man, then you will realize that I AM" (Jn 8:28). Therefore, the Resurrection offers proof for the divinity of Jesus.

Lesson 4 Objectives

The students will:

- summarize the meaning and significance of the Resurrection.
- appreciate how they encounter the Risen Lord in the sacraments of the Church.
- describe the message of the Ascension and the Assumption.
- describe the effects of Pentecost on the Apostles.

Lesson 4 Preview

In this lesson, the students wrap up their study of the way Christians participate in the mystery of the Resurrection.

Chapter 6: The Resurrection of Jesus Christ—Lesson 4

Bell Ringers

- Ask the students to offer their responses to the eleven For Review questions on pages 147 and 149 (answers are on page 167 of this text). Be sure to allow the students to ask any other questions they may have.
- If necessary, allow additional time for the students to complete their work on the feature "Who Is Jesus to Me?" (page 147). Be sure to have copies of old picture magazines and other art materials available. Afterward, have the students share their completed work in small groups or with a partner.
- Introduce this lesson by reminding the students that Jesus did not suffer, die, and rise for his sake but for ours. Stress that the primary effect of Resurrection was and is to reestablish the relationship between God and humankind whose relationship had been severed by sin, and among humans whose relationships had been severed by death.

Teaching Approaches

Our Participation in Christ's Resurrection (pages 149-151)

- Call attention to the quotation from 1 Corinthians on page 149. Make certain the students understand that belief in the Resurrection of Jesus is a primary *necessity* of Christianity.
- Distribute copies of Chapter 6, Handout 3, "Resurrection Consequences—The 4 Cs." For each "C", have the students look up and write out the relevant Scripture passage(s) listed on the handout. Then, drawing on the material in the text (pages 149–150), use the handout to help the students better understand the significance of the Resurrection. Suggest that the students commit the 4 Cs to memory.

- Move on to discuss how we encounter the Risen Lord today. Begin by asking a student to look up and read aloud Matthew 18:20 ("where two or three are gathered together in my name, there am I in the midst of them"). Explain that the relationship that the Resurrection reestablished between humankind and God is meaningful for Christians primarily in the context of the faith community (the Church), which the Risen Lord established.
- Write the word **liturgy** on the board. Point out that the seven sacraments and the way they are celebrated make up the liturgy. Explain that the word means "work of the people," and that this first and most important *work* of the Church (the People of God) is to *make present* the mystery of Redemption here and now. This is especially the case in the sacrament of the Eucharist.
- List the seven sacraments on the board. Point to each one and ask for a show of hands as to how many students have celebrated it. Most should have celebrated Baptism, Confirmation, Eucharist, and Penance. Some may also have celebrated Anointing of the Sick. Go through each sacrament, using the material in the text to describe how we "make present" and encounter the Risen Lord in each. Pay particular attention to the sacrament of the Eucharist.

- *The Resurrection, following Christ's sacrifice on the cross, accomplished our Salvation.* By vanquishing death, Jesus conquered the most evil effect of sin. Thus, he is victorious over sin, has opened Heaven's gates, and has won our Redemption.
- *The Resurrection gives us new life, justifies us in God's grace, and adopts us into the divine family.* We become, through the gift of God's grace and love, brothers and sisters to Jesus Christ. We share in his life. The Gospel of John states: "For God so loved the world that he gave his only Son, so that everyone who believes in him might not perish but might have eternal life" (Jn 3:16). The Resurrection allows Jesus to live in us; thus, we already share "eternal life," the life of the Lord who abides in us.
- *Through the power of the Holy Spirit, Christians participate in the Life, suffering, Death, and Resurrection of Jesus.* By accepting Jesus into our lives and allowing his love to dominate our journey on earth, the Risen Lord promises that we will rise again with him to eternal life in Heaven.

The Resurrection of Jesus gives new meaning to our lives. Death does not have the last word. Superabundant, eternal life with Jesus in community with the Father and the Holy Spirit and all others who love the Lord is our ultimate destiny.

Meeting the Risen Lord

Not limited by space and time, the Risen Lord lives and reigns forever. He lives in his Body, the Church. As members of the Body of Christ, we can find Jesus in the Church, in our brothers and sisters in Christ. Recall that Jesus said that whatever we do to each other, especially the least in our midst, we do to him (Mt 25:40).

Catholics participate in the mystery of his Redemption through the sacramental life of the Church. Christ instituted the Seven Sacraments as powerful

Lesson 4 Homework

1. Have the students write out their answers to the three For Review questions on page 151 and the four For Review questions on page 153.
2. Tell the students to be ready to hand in their Ongoing Assignments at their next session.
3. Have the students read the Chapter Quick View section on pages 154–156 and review the chapter's Main Ideas. Tell the students to write out any questions they may have and bring them to the next session.

signs of his presence and love. For example, by the power of the Holy Spirit, the Lord comes to us at Baptism, forming us into his own image and initiating us into the Church. In the Sacrament of Confirmation, the Holy Spirit strengthens us with spiritual gifts to live Christ-like lives. In the Sacrament of Penance, we experience the Lord's forgiveness, just as the countless people did who met him during his earthly life. He welcomes us back into the family the way the loving father did in the parable of the Prodigal Son. In the Sacrament of the Anointing of the Sick, we experience the healing touch of the Lord in the stressful times of illness. And in the Sacraments of Holy Orders and Matrimony, Christ comes to us to help us live loving lives of service and help build up the People of God.

In a most special way, Jesus Christ is alive in the Holy Eucharist, which is "the heart and summit of the Christian life, for in it Christ associates his Church and all her members with his sacrifice of praise and thanksgiving offered once for all on the cross to his Father" (*CCC*, 1407). The Eucharist contains our Paschal sacrifice, who is Christ himself. By his sacrifice he pours out the graces of Salvation on the Church. Additionally:

> At the heart of the Eucharistic celebration are the bread and wine that, by the words of Christ and the invocation of the Holy Spirit, become Christ's Body and Blood. (*CCC*, 1333)

When we worthily receive the Lord under the forms of bread and wine, the Risen Jesus joins us. In Holy Communion, we become united with our Lord and Savior. We receive Christ to become Christ for one another and, in a special way, the least in our midst: poor people, victims of discrimination, the powerless, the suffering, the lonely.

The word *Eucharist* means "thanksgiving." In this holy sacrament it is indeed right and just to give thanks to God for the gift of his Son, for the Salvation he has won for us, for his defeat of sin and death, and for the eternal life he bestows on us. In this sacrament, we praise the Lord and recognize his presence to us in Holy Scripture, in the assembled Church, in the priest who represents us before God, and most especially in the consecrated bread and wine that we receive as the most precious gift Christ has left us: himself. The graces or effects of receiving Holy Communion are many, including:

- a more intimate union with Jesus Christ;
- separation from sin by wiping away venial sin and strength to combat mortal sin;
- greater unity with other members of Christ's body, the Church;
- better ability to see Christ in the poor whom we must serve;
- a commitment to work for unity among all Christians. (*CCC*, 1391–1401)

In the Eucharist, the Lord comes to us and he is present in our midst, though in a hidden way. The Eucharist anticipates the Savior's Second Coming. On that day we shall see God as he is. Each Mass carries on the work of Redemption because it provides what we need for eternal life—the Lord Jesus himself who makes it possible for us to live forever with him, the Father, and the Holy Spirit in Heaven.

For Review

1. What has Christ's Resurrection accomplished for us?
2. How can we meet Christ in each of the sacraments?
3. List four benefits of receiving Christ in Holy Communion.

For Reflection

When was a time that you felt especially close to the Lord in the Sacrament of the Holy Eucharist?

- Write the following from the *Catechism of the Catholic Church* on the board:

> **The Eucharist is the memorial of Christ's Passover, that is, of the work of salvation accomplished by the life, death, and resurrection of Christ, a work made present by the liturgical action. (*CCC*, 1409)**

- Go on to note the five effects of receiving the Eucharist as presented in the text (page 151). Discuss with the students any personal experience you might have had with any of the effects of receiving the Eucharist in your own life. Then, invite the students to share their experience with the Eucharist.
- Conclude by emphasizing that the Eucharist is our way of "getting one foot in Heaven," so to speak. Write the following from the *Catechism of the Catholic Church* on the board, and encourage the students to copy it in their journals:

> **By the Eucharistic celebration we already unite ourselves with the heavenly liturgy and anticipate eternal life, when God will be all in all. (*CCC*, 1326)**

- Before moving on, have the students share with a partner their response to the For Reflection question on page 151.

For Review Answers (page 151)

1. The students should be able to recount the "4 Cs" of the Resurrection (see Chapter 6, Handout 3) and the corresponding bullet points from the student text.
2. We meet Christ in the sacraments in the following ways: in Baptism, as he forms us into his Church; in Confirmation, by strengthening us with the gifts of the Holy Spirit; in Penance, with the Lord's forgiveness; in the Anointing of the Sick, with the Lord's healing; in Holy Orders and Matrimony, with help in living lives of loving service; in the Eucharist, with the Body and Blood of the Lord himself.
3. Students may list any of the following: a more intimate union with Christ; the forgiveness of venial sin and strength against mortal sin; greater unity with other members of the Church; keener ability to recognize Christ in the poor whom we must serve; and a commitment to work for Christian unity.

The Ascension and Glorification of Jesus Christ (pages 152-153)

- Have the students read the account of the Ascension as recorded in Acts 1:1–12. Note the image of the "cloud" (a reference to God's presence) and of the "two men dressed in white" (Acts 1:9–10). Ask the students "Where else have we seen reference to two white-garbed figures in Luke?" (*At the Transfiguration [Lk 9:28–31] and at the empty tomb [Lk 24:1–8]*)
- Stress to the students that just as the Resurrection reveals that we *are not* destined for death, the Ascension reveals that we *are* destined for Heaven.
- Have the students turn to "On to Eternity" in the Primary Source Quotations section of this chapter (page 155). Call on different students to read aloud the quotations by Blessed Julian of Norwich and St. Elizabeth Seton. Note that both quotations speak to homesickness, to a longing for a homecoming to Heaven.
- Call attention back to the Assumption of Mary as described in the text (page 152). Point out that the Church holds that since Mary, the Mother of God, was preserved from all sin, it would impossible for her to suffer the corruption of the body that all people experience after death. Thus, she was taken "home" to Heaven, body and soul, to be reunited in full communion with her son.

The Ascension and Glorification of Jesus Christ (*CCC*, 659-667)

It is important to remember that though the focus of Chapter 6 has been on the Resurrection of Jesus Christ, the Resurrection should be considered as part of the Paschal Mystery, the saving action of Christ that includes Jesus' Death (Good Friday), his descent to the dead (Holy Saturday), and his glorification. Jesus' glorification consists of the Resurrection (Easter Sunday), his Ascension into Heaven (forty days after Easter), and Pentecost, when the Father and Son send the Holy Spirit to the Church (fifty days after Easter).

The **Ascension** of Jesus refers to the time when Jesus stopped appearing to the disciples in visible form and his glorified body took its rightful place in Heaven as equal to the Father. Jesus' body was glorified at the moment of his Resurrection, as proved by the supernatural qualities it manifested. But during his appearances to his disciples, which lasted forty days, his glory remained hidden under the appearance of ordinary humanity. His "final apparition ends with the irreversible entry of his humanity into divine glory, symbolized by the cloud and by heaven, where he is seated from that time forward at God's right hand" (*CCC*, 659).

The Ascension indicates a difference between the way the glory of the Risen Christ was revealed and that of "Christ exalted to his Father's right hand" (*CCC*, 660). "Being seated at the right hand" means that Christ now glorifies the Father as the Incarnate Son of God, that he continually intercedes for us with the Father, prays for us, and prepares a place for us with him in Heaven. This is the beginning of the Kingdom of God, one that will have no end.

The Ascension of Jesus reminds us that our rightful home is Heaven; we live in the hope that we may one day follow him there. Our model is the Blessed Mother, the one who stayed with the Apostles in the Upper Room after the Death of her son, praying constantly for the coming of the Holy Spirit. When her earthly life was over, she was taken up body and soul into heavenly glory where the Lord exalted her and made her Queen of Heaven. This is known as the **Assumption** of the Blessed Virgin. Her Assumption "is a singular participation in her Son's Resurrection and an anticipation of the resurrection of other Christians" (*CCC*, 966). She is our Blessed Mother and serves as our model because she obeyed God's will, cooperated with her Son's redemptive work, and was open to the work of the Holy Spirit in her life. She is our model both in faith and in charity—our Advocate, Helper, Benefactress, and Mediatrix.

Though Jesus Christ has entered the sanctuary of Heaven once and for all, he has not abandoned us. He constantly prays for us to the Father. Moreover, he promised to be with us forever (Mt 28:20). Further, before his Death on Good Friday, Jesus promised that he would send the Holy Spirit: "I will ask the Father, and he will give you another Advocate to be with you always, the Spirit of truth" (Jn 14:16). Jesus fulfilled his promise by sending the Holy Spirit to his Church on **Pentecost** Sunday.

On Pentecost Sunday, the Holy Spirit descended on the Apostles and gave them the power and courage to preach with conviction the Good News that

For Enrichment

The Glorious Mysteries of the Rosary

In review and reflection on the Resurrection accounts, have your students pray and meditate on the Glorious Mysteries of the Rosary: the Resurrection, the Ascension, the Descent of the Holy Spirit (Pentecost), the Assumption of Mary, and the Crowning of Mary as the Queen of Heaven and Earth.

Faith and the Resurrection

> We proclaim Christ crucified, a stumbling block to Jews and foolishness to Gentiles
>
> **—1 Corinthians 1:23**

In the earliest days of the Church, it was the Cross—the ignominious Death of Jesus—that was a scandal to many, an obstacle to faith. Today, it seems that the Resurrection has become faith's main impediment. Why? Today, we demand *proof*, and no one can *prove* the Resurrection in a scientific, empirical sense. We trust the scientific methodology, which is built on repeatable empirical evidence. Not only has the Resurrection never been repeated by anyone, neither was the initial event witnessed by anyone. The scientific mind finds that a major stumbling block to the truth or the "proof" of the Resurrection. The early Church, however, never made any attempt to prove the Resurrection by worldly tests, scientific or otherwise. Rather, the Church simply proclaimed it to be true, because they believed the eyewitness testimony of those who had encountered the Risen Lord. The key to faith in the Resurrection, then, was to accept the proclamation of the Good News when it was proclaimed by believers. That key remains the same today.

Jesus Christ rose from the dead and is Lord of the universe. Peter, the one who was so afraid of being associated with his Master and thus denied him three times, became a bold and courageous witness for Jesus Christ. Inspired by the Holy Spirit, he preached to the Jewish people who had come to Jerusalem for the Pentecost feast. He reviewed with them the history of Salvation and recounted the life of Jesus Christ, proclaiming his Death and Resurrection. The crowds were amazed at his preaching and that of the other Apostles; people understood them even though many did not speak their language. So filled with the power of the Holy Spirit were Peter and the Apostles, some thought they were drunk, yet it was still early in the morning!

Three thousand people converted to Jesus Christ on Pentecost. They were baptized and received the Holy Spirit. The Holy Spirit enabled the Apostles to understand more clearly the full significance of Jesus. They now knew that he was truly the Lord, the Savior, the Son of God who is true God. The Holy Spirit was also fully revealed. The Third Person of the Blessed Trinity, the Holy Spirit, continues to live in the Church, the Body of Christ. The Church is the Temple of the Holy Spirit, the soul of the Mystical Body, the source of the Church's life. He bestows on its members divine life, the power of love, and adoption into the divine family. By joining us to the Risen Lord Jesus Christ, he makes it possible for us to inherit eternal life and join our Lord in his heavenly Kingdom.

The Good News of Christ's Resurrection is that death is not our final chapter. We do not cease to exist. We do not come back as reincarnated beings. We do not exist as mere spirits. No, Christ's Paschal Mystery—his Passion, Death, Resurrection, and glorious Ascension—offers us the opportunity for Salvation and Redemption. While remaining aware that our choices in this life may instead merit after death a time of purification (Purgatory) or even eternal separation from God (Hell), we do look forward in confidence to our own resurrection, when God will call us to himself and reunite our souls to a glorified body and bestow on us a life of eternal happiness with our loving God, our family and friends, and all those who love God.

For Review

1. What does the Ascension of Jesus remind us of?
2. What does it mean to say that Jesus sits at the right hand of the Father?
3. What is the Assumption of Mary?
4. How were Peter and the Apostles changed on Pentecost?

For Reflection

- What do you look forward to in Heaven?
- How is Mary a model in your own life?

Ascension
Jesus' passage from humanity into divine glory in God's heavenly domain forty days after his Resurrection. It is from this domain that Jesus will come again.

Assumption
The Church dogma that teaches that the Blessed Mother, because of her unique role in her son's Resurrection, was taken directly to Heaven when her earthly life was over. The Feast of the Assumption is on August 15 and is a holy day of obligation.

Pentecost
The day when the Holy Spirit descended on the Apostles and gave them the power to preach with conviction the message that Jesus is risen and Lord of the universe.

- Remind the students that as *our* Mother, Mary is already in the presence of Jesus her Son. We can rely on her to keep him informed of our needs.
- Before moving on, discuss the two For Reflection questions on page 153.
- Write the word **Pentecost** on the board. Explain that the Greek word *pentekostē* means "fiftieth day." Explain that on the feast of Pentecost—*fifty* days after Passover and the day of the Resurrection—the promised Spirit came upon the fearful Apostles, transforming them into fiery-tongued witnesses to the Good News of the Resurrection.
- Ask a volunteer to read aloud the account of the Pentecost event in Acts 2:1–4. Afterward, distribute copies of Chapter 6, Handout 4, "On the Feast of Pentecost." Give the students a moment to read the prayer silently. Then go on to explain that the Holy Spirit comes to create and enliven the Church. Without the Spirit, the Church would not be, nor would the Resurrection be proclaimed. For it is the Spirit who alone empowers us to witness and proclaim, "Jesus is Lord."
- Conclude the lesson by praying the prayer together.

For Review Answers (page 153)

1. The Ascension reminds us that Heaven is our home.
2. This means that Jesus glorifies the Father as the incarnate Son, and constantly intercedes with the Father on our behalf.
3. The taking up into Heaven of Mary, the Mother of Jesus, body and soul, after her death.
4. These frightened followers were inspired to become bold witnesses of the Good News and understood more clearly the full significance of Jesus' Resurrection.

Chapter 6: The Resurrection of Jesus Christ—Review Lesson

Bell Ringers

- Ask the students to offer their responses to the three For Review questions on page 151 (answers are on page 171 of this text) and the four For Review questions on page 153 (answers are on page 173 of this text). Encourage the students to ask any other questions they may have.
- Collect the students' Ongoing Assignments for Chapter 6 (pages 175–176). Allow time for those who chose #2 (creating a PowerPoint presentation) to make their presentations to the class.

Teaching Approaches

Chapter Quick View (pages 154-156)

- Call attention to Terms, People, Places on pages 154–155. Have the students complete the eleven sentences. Check responses (answers are on page 174 of this text).
- Divide the students into pairs. Have partners use the chapter's For Review questions to quiz one another. If a partner answers correctly, he or she gets a point. Give the students 15–20 minutes to work together on this exercise. Ask partners to share scores with the class.
- Invite anyone who had questions after going over the Chapter 6 Quick View section on pages 154–156 to ask them now. Invite other class members to offer answers. Clarify any remaining confusion.
- Allow some quiet time for the students to study on their own. If students have more questions, invite them to approach you privately while their classmates study.

154 Jesus Christ: Source of Our Salvation

Chapter 6 Quick View

Main Ideas

- The Resurrection of Christ forms the heart of the kerygma, the essential message of our faith. (pp. 134–135)
- Christ's Resurrection is part of the Paschal Mystery. (p. 136)
- The Resurrection was also a historical event with verifiable facts reported by Jesus' disciples and his enemies. (pp. 136–137)
- The Resurrection is a transcendent event because it goes beyond the realm of history and our own understanding of space and time; there are no reports of how it physically happened. (p. 137)
- Though the Risen Jesus was recognizable, his glorified body transcended ordinary life. (p. 137)
- The four Gospels report both differences and similarities in the Resurrection accounts. (pp. 138–139)
- Matthew's Gospel concludes with the great commissioning of the disciples to the ends of the earth. (p. 140)
- Mark's Gospel may end abruptly as a challenge for us to carry on the work of discipleship. (pp. 141–142)
- The Emmaus story is unique to Luke's Gospel; it describes how the disciples eventually recognized Jesus in the breaking of the bread. (pp. 142–143)
- One of the incidents unique to John's Gospel is the Apostle Thomas first doubting the Resurrection and then later identifying Jesus as "My Lord and God." (p. 144)
- That the Gospel writers made no attempt to mask the differences between the accounts actually argues that there were true, valid, experiences behind each of them. (pp. 146–147)
- There were also several similarities in the four Gospel accounts: the Resurrection took place on Sunday morning; there were women present; the tomb was empty; there were "messengers" at the tomb; and there were several appearances to the disciples. (pp. 146–147)
- Several verifiable facts help us to respond to those who are skeptical about the validity of the Resurrection. (pp. 148–149)
- The Resurrection of Jesus gives new meaning to our life in several ways. (pp. 149–150)
- In the Seven Sacraments, especially the Holy Eucharist, we participate in the Passion, Death, *and* Resurrection of Jesus in a tangible way. (pp. 150–151)
- The Ascension of Jesus to Heaven and the coming of the Holy Spirit on Pentecost are continuations of the Resurrection accounts. (pp. 152–153)

Terms, People, Places

Complete each sentence by choosing the correct answer from the list of terms below.

Ascension
Assumption
Beloved Disciple
discipleship
grace
kerygma
Last Judgment
Paschal Lamb
Pentecost
soul
Talmud

1. Jesus is the ____________ whose Death leads to his Resurrection and Salvation for all humanity.
2. The ____________ can be considered an "independent" source that reported that Jesus was crucified.
3. The ____________ is the time when God's Kingdom will be fully established.

Review Lesson Objectives

The students will:

- review Chapter 6 in preparation for the chapter test.
- join in prayer together.

Terms, People, Places Answers (pages 154-155)

1. Paschal Lamb
2. Talmud
3. Last Judgment
4. Pentecost
5. *kerygma*
6. soul
7. Assumption
8. Beloved Disciple
9. Ascension
10. grace
11. discipleship

4. Jesus fulfilled his promise to send the Holy Spirit on ____________ Sunday.
5. ____________ is a term that describes the essential message of our faith.
6. The ____________ is the innermost part of a person.
7. The feast of the ____________ is celebrated on August 15.
8. The Gospel of John is attributed to the ____________.
9. Jesus' passage from humanity into divine glory occurred at the ____________.
10. When we participate in Christ's Paschal mystery we receive ____________ in this life and eternal life with the Blessed Trinity in Heaven.
11. A message of the short ending of Mark's Gospel is that it is now our task to carry on Jesus' work through ____________.

Primary Source Quotations

Eyewitness Testimony

Do not be afraid! I know that you are seeking Jesus the crucified. He is not here, for he has been raised just as he said. Come and see the place where he lay.

—Matthew 28:6

Why do you seek the living one among the dead?

—Luke 24:5

The Lord has truly been raised and has appeared to Simon!

—Luke 24:34

From the Easter Proclamation

Rejoice, heavenly powers! Sing, choirs of angels!
Exult, all creation around God's throne!
Jesus Christ, our King, is risen!
Sound the trumpet of salvation.

—The *Exsultet*

On to Eternity

My understanding was lifted up into Heaven, where I saw our Lord like a lord in his own house who has called his valued servants and friends to a solemn feast.

—Bl. Julian of Norwich

Eternity, eternity, when shall I come to You at last? . . . in eternity where we will love with a glance of the soul.

—St. Elizabeth Seton

Write fifteen words that come to mind when you think about the life to come in Heaven.

Ongoing Assignments

As you cover the material in this chapter, choose and complete at least three of these assignments.

1. Imagine that you were present at the time of the Resurrection of Jesus. Write a short essay explaining what happened as if you were writing for a contemporary who does not believe.
2. Create a PowerPoint presentation on how the Resurrection of Jesus has been depicted in art through the ages. Include at least five images. Single out the one that best illustrates one of the Gospel passages and prepare an explanation for why you believe this is so.
3. Imagine you were one of the guards at Jesus' tomb. Write a letter of explanation to the Roman governor as to what happened to the missing body you were guarding.
4. Interview five practicing Catholics about Jesus' Resurrection. Ask them how essential to their Christian faith is the fact that Jesus rose from the dead. Write a report summarizing your findings.
5. Prepare a one-page report on Mary Magdalene. Illustrate it with an image from a famous piece of art downloaded from the Internet.

Chapter 6 Quick View

Review Lesson Homework

1. Complete any unfinished Ongoing Assignments.
2. Reread Chapter 6.
3. Study for the Chapter 6 Test.

Prayer Service

1. Gather the students around a cross or crucifix. Invite them to share their responses that they created to the poems on Chapter 6, Handout 2, "Resurrection Reflections."
2. After the sharing, lead the students in the prayer to the Holy Spirit on page 156.
3. Point out the Reflection and Resolution sections on page 156.
4. Conclude with a hymn to the Holy Spirit, e.g., "Send Us Your Spirit" by David Haas or "Send Down the Fire" by Marty Haugen or another song related to the Resurrection, Ascension, or Pentecost.

Chapter 6 Test Lesson

Teaching Approaches

- Allow sufficient time for the students to work on the Chapter 6 Test (starting on page 291 of the TWE and also online at www.avemariapress.com). Collect tests as the students finish.

Test Lesson Homework

1. Read the following text section of Chapter 7: "The Wonders of Our Salvation" (pages 160–161).
2. Examine the Chapter 7 Ongoing Assignments on pages 181–182.

Chapter 6 Quick View

6. Visit a Catholic cemetery. Find symbols on tombstones that display belief in life after death. Take photos of these symbols and create a slide presentation to share with your classmates.
7. Imagine you were one of the disciples who met the Risen Lord on the way to Emmaus. Write a dialogue between you and Jesus concerning what you discussed along the way.
8. Find graphics to illustrate several images of the Holy Spirit (examples: wind, fire, dove). Explain the imagery and select an appropriate quotation from Acts 3 to accompany the images.
9. Report on the Jewish feast of Weeks/Pentecost.
10. After reading Peter's kerygmatic sermon in Acts 2:14–39, create an outline for a talk you might deliver to a youth group on retreat. Emphasize the person of Jesus and what the teens should do in response to him.
11. Read what Luke records in the Acts of the Apostles about Paul's conversion: Acts 9:1–19; 22:1–22; 26:9–24. Compare Luke's reporting to what Paul himself wrote in Galatians 1:11–24. Then briefly summarize what happened.
12. Use Luke 24:50–53, Acts 1:6–12, and Mark 16:19 to help you write a short essay describing the Ascension.

Prayer

God the Father and God the Son sent the Holy Spirit to be with the Church and to help Christians live Christ-like lives. Pray the following Prayer to the Holy Spirit:

Prayer to the Holy Spirit
Lord our God, you call us out of darkness
into light,
out of self-deception into truth,
out of death into life.
Send us your Holy Spirit
to open our ears to your call.
Fill our hearts with courage
to be true followers of your Son.
We ask this through Christ our Lord. Amen.

- *Reflection*: Who or what is calling you to respond to the Lord in your life? Are you open to the call?
- *Resolution*: The Spirit is the source of courage and perseverance. During the coming weeks, ask the Holy Spirit to give you the courage to do what you know is right.

Chapter 6 Test Answers

Part 1: True or False. (2 points each)

1. T 2. T 3. T 4. F 5. F 6. T 7. T 8. F 9. T 10. F 11. T 12. F 13. T
14. T 15. T 16. T 17. T 18. T 19. F 20. T 21. F 22. F 23. T 24. F 25. F 26. F

Part 2: Fill in the Blanks. (2 points each)

1. kerygma 2. Lamb 3. Talmud 4. Eucharist 5. John 6. Ascension
7. Assumption 8. disciple 9. Judgment 10. soul

Part 3: Six "3s" (3 points each)

1. Student may include: the appearance to Mary Magdalene, the appearance of Jesus to the disciples on the road to Emmaus, the commissioning of the disciples, and the Ascension.
2. The Resurrection confirms all Christ's works and teachings; completes our Salvation; confers new life, justification, and adoption; and creates new life within us.
3. Answers will vary; students may name any three of the sacraments. For example, we meet Christ in the sacraments: in Baptism as he forms us into his Church; in Confirmation—the strengthening gifts of the Holy Spirit; in Penance—the Lord's forgiveness; in the Anointing of the Sick—healing; in Holy Orders and Matrimony—help in living lives of loving service; in the Eucharist—the Body and Blood of the Lord himself.

The Resurrection of Jesus Christ 157

Chapter 6 Quick View

Chapter 6 Test Answers continued

4. Answer should include the empty tomb, no physical evidence of Jesus' body, and the number of post-Resurrection appearances.
5. Jesus' body was a glorified body, not recognizable to many; it maintained his wounds; he was ghost-like and able to walk through walls.
6. Answers may include:
    - a more intimate union with Jesus Christ
    - separation from sin by wiping away venial sin and giving strength to combat mortal sin
    - greater unity with other members of the Church
    - better ability to see Christ in the poor
    - a commitment to work for unity among all Christians

Part 4: Essay. (10 points)

1. See the arguments on pages 148–149 of the student text for correct responses.

Chapter 7: Redemption through the Paschal Mystery

Introduction

Having been tenant long to a rich lord,
Not thriving, I resolvèd to be bold,
And make a suit unto him, to afford
A new small-rented lease, and cancel th' old.

In heaven at his manor I him sought;
They told me there that he was lately gone
About some land, which he had dearly bought
Long since on earth, to take possessiòn.

I straight returned, and knowing his great birth,
Sought him accordingly in great resorts;
In cities, theaters, gardens, parks, and courts;
At length I heard a ragged noise and mirth

Of thieves and murderers; there I him espied,
Who straight, Your suit is granted, said, and died.

—George Herbert

In the poem "Redemption," the poet George Herbert uses the imagery of a tenant and landlord to portray how God graciously redeemed us through Christ's Paschal Mystery. All the ancient covenants are ratified, all promises fulfilled, all "suits," as the poet would have it, are granted. Even more, the Paschal Mystery breaks through the great barriers that stand between humankind and God—the barriers of sin and death—and clears our way to eternal happiness with the God who has created us for and calls us to himself.

This chapter leads the students to reflect on the God who has so wonderfully created the universe and all things in it. They recall how Jesus became one of us in the Incarnation and fulfilled the covenants. They appreciate the Good News of the Kingdom by re-committing themselves to the principles of Kingdom living, recognizing that Kingdom living calls for repentance and conversion. They uncover how the Paschal Mystery accomplishes our Redemption and how we celebrate that mystery in the sacraments, especially the Eucharist. Finally, they investigate the last things and the culmination in the fulfillment of God's Kingdom.

While most of the chapter reinforces what the students have already discovered about creation, covenants, the Incarnation, the Good News of God's Kingdom, and the Paschal Mystery of Christ, it also presents new material on the last things. As you present that material, be aware that death, judgment, Heaven, and hell are not "easy listening" topics for anyone, even for young people who tend to envision death, etc., as faraway events. In particular, the whole idea of "judgment" seems to cause a knot in the stomach. It is important, therefore, to help the students realize that judgment is more about vindication than retribution, and that it is the final step on our journey to life forever with God. In fact, when it comes to judgment, the verdict is ours. We are the ones passing judgment on ourselves, according to the choices we have made and the lives we have lived. Jesus, the gentle and compassionate judge, simply imposes the verdict we have already reached. Help the students recognize that just as the loving

Chapter Objectives

To help the students:

- discover the wonders of creation, Jesus, and themselves.
- understand that all creation reveals the goodness of the Creator.
- recall God's covenants with the Israelites.
- appreciate that the Incarnation is the fulfillment of all God's promises and the means to our Salvation.
- appreciate the call for repentance and conversion.
- understand that the sacraments, especially the Eucharist, celebrate our friendship with Jesus.
- investigate death, judgment, the Resurrection and the last things.
- compare and contrast the states of Heaven, hell, and Purgatory.

God, unchangeable in purpose, nevertheless chose to suffer with us in Christ and redeem us through the Paschal Mystery, so will this same God, when we press our "suit" at death, grant us everlasting life.

Advance Preparations

Prepare or have on hand:

For Lesson 1

- Corrected copies of the Chapter 6 Test
- Access to a computer(s) with an Internet connection

For Lesson 2

- Bibles

For Lesson 3

- Bibles
- Copies of Chapter 7, Handout 1, "The Eucharist—A Meal of Friendship"

For Lesson 4

- Bibles
- A recording of the song "We Remember" by Marty Haugen and a player (optional)

For Lesson 5

- Bibles
- Copies of Chapter 7, Handout 2, "Death—Then What?"
- A variety of art materials
- A recording of "The Battle Hymn of the Republic" or "Soon and Very Soon" and a player (optional)

For the Chapter 7 Review Lesson

- Equipment necessary for students to make PowerPoint presentations
- Candle and matches
- Copies of Chapter 7, Handout 3, "Prayer for a Happy Death"

For the Chapter 7 Test Lesson

- Copies of the Chapter 7 Test (starting on page 291 of the TWE and also online at www.avemariapress.com)

Chapter 7 Handouts

- Handout 1, The Eucharist—A Meal of Friendship—The students will describe how the Eucharist strengthens our friendship with Jesus and the Church.
- Handout 2, Death—Then What?—They examine what happens after death and at the Parousia.
- Handout 3, Prayer for a Happy Death—The students receive a prayer to pray for a happy death.

Chapter 7: Redemption through the Paschal Mystery—Lesson 1

Bell Ringers

- Distribute the corrected Chapter 6 Test. Go over the test with the students, using it as a means to review the previous chapter. Address any remaining questions or concerns the students may have.
- Write the word **wonder** on the board. Brainstorm its meaning as a *noun*. Help the students recognize the following connotations:
  - something strange and surprising; a cause of surprise, astonishment, or appreciation
  - the emotion excited by what is strange and surprising; a feeling of surprised or puzzled interest, sometimes tinged with admiration
  - a miraculous deed or event; a remarkable phenomenon
- Invite the students to name someone or something they consider a "wonder" or to share an experience—of a thing or a person or an event—that filled them with wonder.

Teaching Approaches

The Wonders of Our Salvation (pages 160-161)

- Go through the list of the seven wonders of the ancient world as listed in the text (page 160). If you have a computer available, have the students view illustrations of the seven wonders on a website such as www.crystalinks.com/seven.html.
- Move on to the "new wonders" of the world. Explain that in addition to the statue of Christ the Redeemer, the Swiss poll listed the Coliseum in Rome, India's Taj Mahal, the Great Wall of China, Jordan's ancient city of Petra, the Incan ruins of Machu Picchu in Peru, and the ancient Mayan city of Chichén Itzá, in Mexico. Share pictures of these wonders on a website such as www.time.com/time/photogallery/0,29307,1639775,00.html.

160 Jesus Christ: Source of Our Salvation

The Wonders of Our Salvation

Classical authors once listed the "seven wonders of the world," which represented the greatest architectural, technological, and artistic achievements of ancient civilizations. The seven wonders of the ancient world were:

1. the Great Pyramid at Giza (still standing)
2. the Hanging Gardens of Babylon (destroyed by an earthquake after the first century AD)
3. the Temple of Artemis at Ephesus (burnt down in fourth century BC, rebuilt by Alexander the Great, destroyed again by the Goths in AD 409)
4. the Statue of Zeus at Olympia (destroyed by fire or earthquake in fifth–sixth century AD)
5. the Mausoleum at Halicarnassus (damaged by an earthquake and disassembled by Crusaders in 1494)
6. the Colossus of Rhodes (toppled by earthquake in third century BC)
7. the Pharos Lighthouse of Alexandria (destroyed by earthquakes in fourteenth century AD)

Ever since this classic list of ancient wonders was constructed, people have been making lists of even more wonders, that is, natural or man-made works that evoke "awe, astonishment, or admiration." For example, the Great Wall of China appears on a list of the "Seven Wonders of the Medieval Mind" while the Grand Canyon and Victoria Falls make a list of the "Seven Natural Wonders of the World." Interestingly, in 2007, a Swiss-based nonprofit group sponsored an online and telephone poll to choose the new wonders of the world. Its organizers claim that over one hundred million votes were cast, the largest poll taken in human history.

From a Christian's point of view, one of the most interesting "wonders" to make the final list of seven is the famous statue of Jesus named "Christ the Redeemer" (*Cristo Redentor*) that stands 130 feet high on Corcovado mountain overlooking the city of Rio de Janeiro in Brazil. This massive and beautiful statue is an icon both for its city and country, of which the majority of its inhabitants are Roman Catholic. The size and location of the statue are well intentioned: to dramatically point to Jesus Christ, our Redeemer, who has made it possible for us to inherit eternal life.

This chapter reminds us of the "wonders" of Salvation History that are essential to our lives as those redeemed by the Life, Death, Resurrection, and Ascension of Jesus Christ. Among those wonders are the Seven Sacraments. This chapter highlights how the sacraments make present the Paschal Mystery

Lesson 1 Objectives

The students will:

- review Chapter 6.
- describe some wonders of the world, of Jesus, and of themselves.

Lesson 1 Preview

This lesson begins a chapter devoted to the wonders of our Redemption. In this first lesson, the students investigate the wonders of our natural world and then move on to what fills them with wonder about themselves and about Jesus.

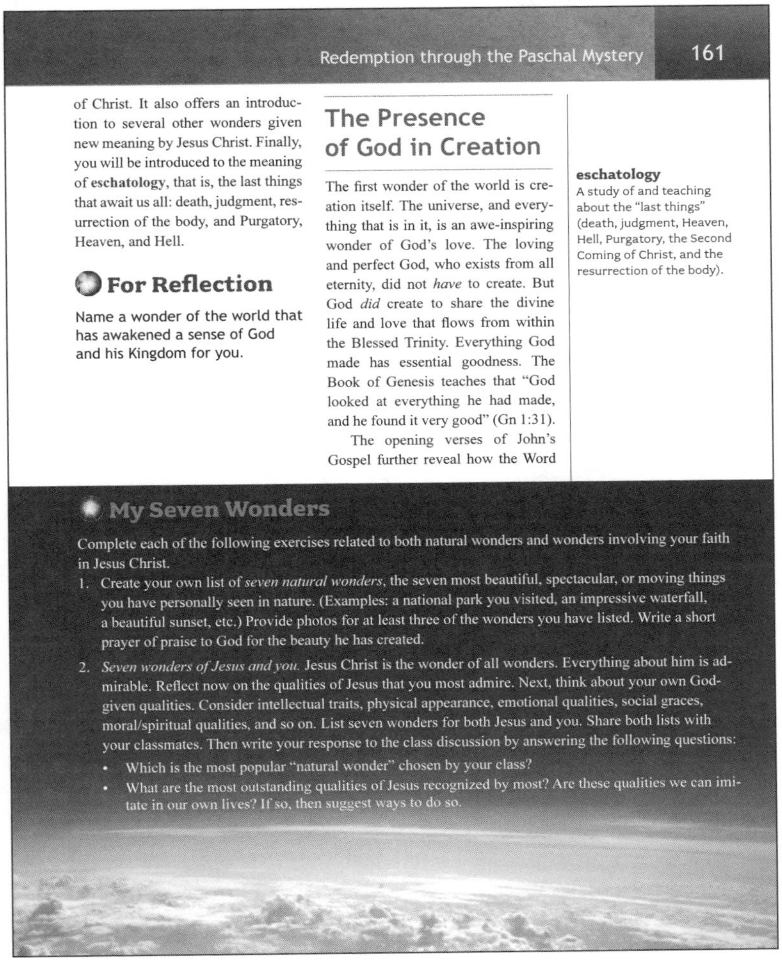

of Christ. It also offers an introduction to several other wonders given new meaning by Jesus Christ. Finally, you will be introduced to the meaning of **eschatology**, that is, the last things that await us all: death, judgment, resurrection of the body, and Purgatory, Heaven, and Hell.

For Reflection

Name a wonder of the world that has awakened a sense of God and his Kingdom for you.

The Presence of God in Creation

The first wonder of the world is creation itself. The universe, and everything that is in it, is an awe-inspiring wonder of God's love. The loving and perfect God, who exists from all eternity, did not *have* to create. But God *did* create to share the divine life and love that flows from within the Blessed Trinity. Everything God made has essential goodness. The Book of Genesis teaches that "God looked at everything he had made, and he found it very good" (Gn 1:31).

The opening verses of John's Gospel further reveal how the Word

eschatology
A study of and teaching about the "last things" (death, judgment, Heaven, Hell, Purgatory, the Second Coming of Christ, and the resurrection of the body).

My Seven Wonders

Complete each of the following exercises related to both natural wonders and wonders involving your faith in Jesus Christ.

1. Create your own list of *seven natural wonders*, the seven most beautiful, spectacular, or moving things you have personally seen in nature. (Examples: a national park you visited, an impressive waterfall, a beautiful sunset, etc.) Provide photos for at least three of the wonders you have listed. Write a short prayer of praise to God for the beauty he has created.
2. *Seven wonders of Jesus and you.* Jesus Christ is the wonder of all wonders. Everything about him is admirable. Reflect now on the qualities of Jesus that you most admire. Next, think about your own God-given qualities. Consider intellectual traits, physical appearance, emotional qualities, social graces, moral/spiritual qualities, and so on. List seven wonders for both Jesus and you. Share both lists with your classmates. Then write your response to the class discussion by answering the following questions:
   - Which is the most popular "natural wonder" chosen by your class?
   - What are the most outstanding qualities of Jesus recognized by most? Are these qualities we can imitate in our own lives? If so, then suggest ways to do so.

- Finally, summarize that this chapter will investigate the "wonders" of our Salvation, including the seven sacraments and the last things.
- Call attention to the opening activity, "My Seven Wonders" on page 161. Allow time for the students to complete the listing for the first exercise, explaining that they can find photos for the wonders they list and write their prayers as a homework assignment. Invite the students to share their lists.
- Proceed to the second exercise by listing the qualities of Jesus they most admire and their own best qualities. Share the lists as a class. Finally, respond to the activity's two discussion questions.

Lesson 1 Homework

1. Ask the students to turn to Ongoing Assignments on pages 181–182. Have them choose three of the listed assignments to complete prior to the conclusion of this chapter. Tell the students the assignments are due on the day they gather for their chapter review.
2. To prepare for their next lesson, have the students read "The Presence of God in Creation" (pages 161–165).
3. Remind the students to complete the first exercise of the activity, "My Seven Wonders" by finding photos/illustrations to accompany at least three of the items on their list *and* by composing a prayer of praise.

Chapter 7: Redemption through the Paschal Mystery—Lesson 2

Bell Ringers

- Have the students share the photos/illustrations they found to accompany the first exercise of the activity "My Seven Wonders" (page 161). If you wish, post the photos/illustrations in the classroom.
- Collect the students' prayers of praise. Choose one at random and read it aloud to introduce this session. (*Note:* Continue drawing on the prayers to begin and end each of the remaining lessons in this chapter.)

Teaching Approaches

The Presence of God in Creation (pages 161-165)

- Call attention to the quotation from Genesis 1:31. Emphasize that all things that are, come from the hand of a God who is compassionate and good. Thus, all creation is likewise good, no strings attached. Each created thing manifests God's glory—God's own goodness and love.
- Next, call attention to the passage from John's Prologue (Jn 1:1–4) on page 162. Note how the passage speaks to infinity, describing Jesus as the eternal Word, present at the creation of all things.
- Point out the examples of the many ways creation reveals God's love (see page 162). Help the students recall how, in the opening activity of Chapter 1, Lesson 1, they found and shared photos representing the goodness of creation. Likewise, they wrote explanations of how the pictures made them feel. Invite them to name ways creation continues to reveal God's compassionate love to them and how that revelation makes them feel.
- Call on a student to read aloud Genesis 1:26–30. Emphasize that God did not spend his creativity and labor of love so that earth would languish on its own. Rather, God created humankind, crowning us with "glory and honor" (Ps 8:6), so that we might share in the Divine's creative action and image forth God in our care for the rest of creation.
- Have a student read aloud the passage from Isaiah 49:15–16 (see page 163). Ask:
  - What does this passage say about God's care and concern for humankind?

of God was involved in the creation of the world. Christ, the Son of God, participated in creation:

> In the beginning was the Word,
> and the Word was with God,
> and the Word was God.
> He was in the beginning with God.
> All things came to be through him,
> and without him nothing came to be.
> What came to be through him was life,
> and this life was the light of the human race. (Jn 1:1–4)

Creation reveals God's love in profound ways and encourages us to take notice. Consider the following:

- a glorious sunset over an ocean horizon;
- a vast, starlit sky on a cold winter night;
- majestic mountains covered with scented pines reaching to the clouds;
- a gentle rain that quenches the thirst of a parched field;
- an animal world filled with amazing creatures that enrich our diverse ecosystem: birds warbling their songs as they take flight; lions stalking their prey; porpoises dancing on waves; insects humming their songs.

The natural world asks us to take notice of God's power, intelligence, goodness, and love. And down through the ages, the vast majority of people have done just that: acknowledged a superior spiritual being—God—who has created and now keeps in existence the material world around us.

The masterpiece of God's creation is human beings. People are at the summit of God's creation. Human beings are made in God's own image and

Lesson 2 Objectives

The students will:

- understand that all creation reveals the goodness of the Creator.
- recall the events (the promises God made in his covenants) that were fulfilled in the Incarnation.
- describe the key lessons God teaches us about human dignity and worth through the Incarnation.
- recognize that the sacraments celebrate the presence of the incarnate Lord.

Lesson 2 Preview

This lesson reviews and also sheds new light on how God has revealed his care and love for us through creation, covenants, and the coming of the Messiah. Consider having the students look back to Chapter 2 as they go through this lesson.

likeness, capable of thinking, of making choices, of loving. We are a complex creature, a unity of matter and spirit, who can study the world and discover the Divine Artisan who crafted it. We know that we did not come into existence by our own efforts but that an infinitely generous and loving God gave us life and a beautiful world in which to live. Furthermore, this loving God makes it possible for us to respond to and share in God's own life and love. So marvelous and special is the human creature that the psalmist wrote:

> When I see your heavens, the work of your fingers,
> the moon and stars which you set in place—
> What are humans that you are mindful of them,
> mere mortals that you care for them?
> Yet you have made them little less than a god,
> crowned them with glory and honor.
> You have given them rule over the works of your hands,
> put all things at their feet. . . .
> O Lord, our Lord,
> how awesome is your name through all the earth! (Ps 8:4–7, 10)

The psalmist helps us see that each of us is a special creature of God, one he crowned with "glory and honor." Each of us is a true wonder of God's creation, a special, one-of-a-kind daughter or son, each endowed with unique gifts and talents. Our very existence is a special sign of God's love, a love that is beyond human comprehension. The prophet Isaiah tells us that God is always thinking of us. Each of us is special in his eyes:

> Can a mother forget her infant,
> be without tenderness for the child of her womb?
> Even should she forget,
> I will never forget you.
> See, upon the palms of my hands I have written your name. (Is 49:15–16)

Creation points to God's existence and tells us of his love. The Sacrament of Baptism celebrates the marvels of God's creation. It symbolizes and brings about our *re*-creation and *re*-birth into the Church. Baptism proclaims God's presence and activity in the world and brings true life, companionship, and a share in God's own life to the Church.

The Incarnation

> And the Word became flesh
> and made his dwelling among us,
> and we saw his glory,
> the glory as of the Father's only son
> full of grace and truth. (Jn 1:14)

This verse from the Gospel of John highlights the key event in God's creation and the history of the world: the Incarnation of Jesus Christ, the Second Person of the Blessed Trinity. By becoming flesh in the Person of Jesus Christ, God accomplished the work of our Salvation. We can never totally appreciate what God has done for us in becoming one of us. In an act of supreme humility, the Son of God became human in order to save us, conquer sin, and bring us into eternal life. The Incarnation of the Son of God is an essential truth of our faith: Jesus Christ is God-made-man, Emmanuel, "God-with-us."

Recall that the Incarnation was the fulfillment of a series of promises God made to human beings after the Original Sin of Adam and Eve. Though Adam and Eve lost their friendship with God through their sinful disobedience, God never abandoned them. Salvation History records the gradual unfolding of God's plan to save all people through his Son Jesus Christ. God's Revelation, or self-communication to humanity, led to his promise to a man of faith—Abraham—that he would fashion a people from his family, a people from whom would come the Messiah.

An important chapter in Salvation History was God's freeing the Israelites from slavery in Egypt during the time of the Exodus. He sustained them in the desert and, after forty years, delivered them into

- What response can we give for such care and concern?

- Write the word **Incarnation** on the board and ask the students to recall its meaning. Read aloud the passage from John 1:14 (on page 163). Stress how John says that the Incarnation is the fulfillment of God's promise, a promise whispered throughout the ages, and now spoken again so clearly and so definitely in a language we best understand—the language of a person, God not only with us, among us, and for us, but *one of us*.
- Write the following phrase on the board: **God is a God of Promises.** Then write the word **covenant** on the board. Remind the students that "covenant" is one of the most theologically important words in all of Scripture. Then ask them to recall the definition of covenant they agreed on in Chapter 2, viz., *A covenant is a binding promise between God and humankind in which God pledges enduring love and asks for faithful love in return.*
- Call on different students to recall and describe the divine covenants they have already studied (see Chapter 2):
  - the Protoevangelium (*first Gospel*): Gn 3:15—God's promise to send a Savior who will destroy sin and its consequences

Lesson 2 Homework

1. Tell the students to write their responses to the four For Review questions on pages 164–165.
2. Direct the students to read the sections "Good News: The Kingdom of God Is at Hand" (pages 165–166) and "Forgiveness of Sins" (pages 166–169) in preparation for their next lesson.
3. Encourage the students to be working on their chosen Ongoing Assignments (pages 181–182).

For Enrichment

Incarnation—A Shocking Reality

If New Testament Christianity is to reappear today with its power and joy and courage, [we] must recapture the basic conviction that this is a visited planet. It is not enough to express formal belief in the "Incarnation" or in the "Divinity of Christ," the staggering truth must be accepted afresh—that in this vast, mysterious universe, of which we are an almost infinitesimal part, the great Mystery, whom we call God, has visited our planet in person. It is from this conviction that there springs unconquerable certainty and unquenchable faith and hope. It is not enough to believe theoretically that Jesus was both God and man; not enough to admire, respect, and even worship him; it is not even enough to try to follow him. The reason for the insufficiency of these things is that the modern intelligent mind, which has had its horizons widened in dozens of different ways, has got to be shocked afresh by the audacious central fact—that, as a sober matter of history, God became one of us.

—J. B. Phillips, *New Testament Christianity*

- the Covenant with Noah: Gn 9:10–11—God's promise never again to destroy the earth by water (sign = rainbow)
- the Covenant with Abraham: Gn 12:2–3—God's threefold promise of blessing: I will make you a great nation; I will bless you; I will make your name great (sign = circumcision—see Genesis 17:1–11)
- The Covenant with Moses/Sinai Covenant: Dt 7:6–9—God promises to reveal his special love and mercy to Israel (sign = the Decalogue/Ten Commandments)
- The Covenant with David: 2 Sm 7:11–12—God promises that the Messiah will spring from David's line (see Isaiah 11:1–10)

• Go on to remind the students that it was God whom the Israelites continually ignored or reneged on the covenants. Even so, God did not abandon his people. Rather, God sent prophets to call them back to encourage them to honor the covenants they had made. Invite the students to recall some of the prophets' messages by reviewing the following passages:

- Amos 5:12–15 (a cry for justice)
- Jeremiah 31:31–34 (a pledge of a new and very personal covenant with God)
- Ezekiel 37:11–14 (a re-creation)
- Isaiah 53:1–12 (the coming of a servant whose suffering promises to save all humankind)

Conclude by noting that the prophets spoke a message from God that rebuked but also reconciled, cautioned but also consoled.

• Point to the word **Incarnation**, which you wrote earlier on the board. Tell the students that the doctrine of the Incarnation expresses the conviction of Christians that the covenanting God has made himself known fully, specifically, and personally, by taking our

a land flowing with milk and honey. Using Moses as his prophet and spokesman, Yahweh entered into a covenant with the people, a solemn agreement that made them his Chosen People. For their part, the Israelites were to witness to the one true God and to live the Law, that is, a life worthy of their vocation as God's people. In return, God promised everlasting love and protection.

In the Old Testament, which is the written record of Divine Revelation, we learn how time and again the Chosen People repeatedly ignored the covenant. Though their actions led to a divided kingdom, then the destruction of the northern kingdom and the enslavement of the southern kingdom, God never abandoned his People. Through their sufferings, captivity by foreign powers, and oppression by pagan leaders, God remained with them. He sent prophets to warn them to be faithful, to comfort them in their sorrows, and to recall God's promises to be with them always.

Finally, in the fullness of time, Jesus of Nazareth was born in Bethlehem, as prophesied. As a child, he grew in wisdom, age, and grace before God and man. Around the age of thirty, he was baptized by a distant relative, John the Baptist, and after John's arrest began his own preaching and healing ministry. He gathered twelve Apostles to assist him in his work and to carry it on after his time on earth was complete.

The Incarnation of the Son of God teaches us many important truths:

- By becoming a human being, God teaches that all human beings have tremendous dignity. He shows us that we can be godlike, that we are not insignificant "nothings" in the cosmic scheme of things. Rather, each of us is valuable in God's eyes, a brother and sister to the Son of God.
- The Incarnation gives worth to *all* of creation. Everything connected to human life is valuable. The food we eat, the clothes we wear, the games we play, the jokes we enjoy, the work we do, the rest we seek are all important to God. Jesus shared our life. He was born and died. He laughed and cried. He worked. He was tempted. He was like us in everything but sin.
- God shares both our personal joy and suffering. What concerns us matters to the Lord. What is important and has meaning for us concerns Jesus, God made man, who took on our life and shares every aspect of it. We should never forget his words:

> Come to me, all you who labor and are burdened, and I will give you rest. Take my yoke upon you and learn from me, for I am meek and humble of heart; and you will find rest for your selves. For my yoke is easy, and my burden light. (Mt 11:28–30)

The Seven Sacraments help us celebrate the wonder of the Incarnation. The Lord continues to come to us in the special moments of our lives. For example, God comes to us at birth (in Baptism) and in illness and death (Anointing of the Sick). The Holy Spirit strengthens us as we grow and gives us courage to live authentically (Confirmation). The Lord feeds us at the banquet table of his Eucharist. He forgives us when we sin and are guilt-ridden (Penance). He sustains us in the vocation of marriage (Matrimony) or as a special minister to God's people (Holy Orders). In the Seven Sacraments, ordinary objects and actions—bread and wine, water and oil, human touch—become instruments of God's grace.

For Review

1. How does creation reveal God's love?
2. Why is the Incarnation a wonder of God's love?
3. What does Jesus' Incarnation teach us about human dignity and worth?
4. How do the Seven Sacraments meet us in the special moments of our lives?

For Review Answers (pages 164-165)

1. God has always revealed himself to us through the "normal," the physical, the temporal, the mundane things of this life. We have always been able to know about God by looking at what God has created, for all creation reflects the goodness of its Creator.
2. The Incarnation is the manifestation of God's love for us *in the flesh.*
3. The Incarnation shows us how valuable we are to God. Human beings are, indeed, god-like, images of the Divine, and sisters and brothers of the Son of God himself.
4. Each sacrament is a means of grace, allowing us to experience the presence of Christ at all the various moments of our life: birth (Baptism), death (Anointing of the Sick), growth (Confirmation), eating (Eucharist), forgiveness of sin (Penance), marriage (Matrimony), and special ministry (Holy Orders).

Redemption through the Paschal Mystery 165

For Reflection

Jesus preached against being anxious. He said: "Do not worry about tomorrow; tomorrow will take care of itself" (Mt 6:34). What are your five most common worries? What might be an antidote to worrying about these concerns that you have?

Good News: The Kingdom of God Is at Hand

The Gospel or Good News itself is another wonder or truth that flows from God. The structure around which the Good News was preached is Christ's ushering in of the Kingdom of God. Jesus proclaimed with authority that God's effective rule over people was drawing near. Jesus himself is the principal agent of this rule, or Kingdom. Preaching in his own town of Nazareth, Jesus claimed that he fulfilled the prophecy from Isaiah about the coming of the Messiah; he himself is the Promised One:

> The Spirit of the Lord is upon me,
> because he has anointed me
> to bring glad tidings to the poor.
> He has sent me to proclaim liberty to captives
> and recovery of sight to the blind,
> to let the oppressed go free,
> and to proclaim a year acceptable to the Lord. (Lk 4:18–19)

In his parables and other teachings, Jesus revealed the true nature of God: a loving Abba, a gentle father who cares deeply for his children and will do anything to nourish, teach, welcome, and save them. Jesus' public life began the process of healing the world through peace, justice, and love. Through him, the Father is drawing all men, women, and children to him. Salvation is taking place *right now*—through Jesus.

The miracles of Jesus were signs that God's Kingdom has broken into human history. These mighty works demonstrated the power of God's presence and love through Jesus. When Jesus announced the advent of God's Kingdom, he called his listeners to both repentance and faith. Mark's Gospel sums up Jesus' preaching: "This is the time of fulfillment. The kingdom of God is at hand. Repent, and believe in the gospel" (Mk 1:15). Repentance means a change of mind, a turning from sin so one can be open to Jesus and his message. We must believe that Jesus is the way, the truth, and the life (Jn 14:6); the bread of life (Jn 6:51); and the one who brings us everlasting life: "I am the resurrection and the life; whoever believes in me, even if he dies, will live, and everyone who lives and believes in me will never die" (Jn 11:25–26).

For Enrichment

Incarnation—The Essential Truth

The central idea of the Christian religion, the idea which cannot be doubted or minimized without sacrificing the essential truth of Christianity, is that God, who had always through his messengers and prophets communicated his word to man, at last, as the climax of his grace, sent his only Son into the world. The Divine Nature, which is omnipresent and eternal, free from the human limitations of space and time, materialized itself in human form upon the earth, voluntarily subjecting itself to those limitations and yet continuing to be divine.

—William M. Ramsay,
Pictures of the Apostolic Church

human nature unto himself, by coming among us as a particular human being, without in any way ceasing to be the eternal and infinite God. Then go through the truths of the Incarnation as listed in the text.

- Have the students create a timeline or flowchart on a blank sheet of paper that depicts the major events that were fulfilled in the Incarnation. Direct them to visually represent each of the covenants, their rejection by the Israelites, and the arrival of the prophets. Finally, have them depict the significant events of Jesus' life that fulfilled the Old Testament including the Incarnation and the Paschal Mystery.
- Sum up by explaining that the Incarnation teaches us that while the created order has always contained within it a window into the agency and genius of the Creator, in God's self-revelation in the man Jesus we see *God himself.* By becoming a human like us, God took upon himself our human nature, and in so doing he purified our humanity and made it possible for us to become one with God. Review the bullet points on page 164 that describe the lessons God teaches about human dignity and worth through the Incarnation. Ask students to reflect on these truths in their journals.
- Call attention to the final paragraph of this section, which deals with how the sacraments help us celebrate the Incarnation. Point out that the concept of the Incarnation is critical to the functioning of the *means* of grace. In other words, it is precisely because God became a human in Jesus Christ that we can come to know God and receive God's gifts of love and life. We can now experience his presence through Scripture, prayer, and, in particular, the sacraments.
- Explain to the students that Jesus, in and through his Incarnation, is *the sacrament* of all sacraments. Thus, far from being mere lifeless reminders of that which they signify, each sacrament, by virtue of its conveying the presence of Jesus, becomes what it represents. The sacraments reveal the presence of the incarnate Lord in the special moments of our lives.
- Invite the students to look at the For Reflection activity on page 165 and to make a list of their five most common worries. Afterward, have the students share in small groups and discuss some possible comforts to those worries.
- Conclude class with one of the prayers of praise that the students wrote.

Chapter 7: Redemption through the Paschal Mystery—Lesson 3

Bell Ringers

- Begin class with one of the students' prayers of praise. Then call on different students to offer their responses to the four For Review questions on pages 164–165 (answers are on page 184 of this text).
- Begin this lesson by making sure the students understand the meaning of "Gospel." If necessary, remind them that the Gospel is not a "once upon a time" story of long ago. The Gospel is Good *News*, because it is a call to pay attention *today*. The Gospel declares not only that Jesus brings Good News, but also that he is himself Good News. The Gospel does not invite us to read about Jesus and appreciate him. Rather, the Gospel calls us to pay attention, to believe, and to follow him.

Teaching Approaches

Good News: The Kingdom of God Is at Hand (pages 165-166)

- Invite the students to recall the meaning of the term "Kingdom of God," which they discovered in Chapter 3. (*The Kingdom of God is the reign of God proclaimed by Jesus and begun in his Life, Death, and Resurrection [Paschal Mystery]. It refers to the process of God's reconciling and renewing all things through his Son, and God's will being done on earth as it is in Heaven.*) Remind the students that the Kingdom of God signals both the ultimate power of God and the ultimate freedom of human beings—freedom from oppression, injustice, poverty, and fear.
- Call on a student to read aloud the passage from Luke 4:18–19. Note that in applying Isaiah's prophecy to himself, Jesus is declaring that the Kingdom of God is present through him.
- Invite the students to recall how Jesus' neighbors greeted this Good News. (*They thought him a lunatic and tried to toss him off a cliff.*)
- Briefly note that Jesus taught, told parables, and even worked miracles, all in order to broadcast the Good News of the Kingdom. Direct the students to search their Bibles for a specific example of how Jesus broadcast the Good News of the Kingdom of God. Have them behave like a reporter and write a news story to describe the event. Make sure the students can

Liturgy of the Word
An essential part of the celebration of the Sacrament of the Holy Eucharist that draws on readings from the Old and New Testaments and features a reading from one of the Gospels and a homily that is an exhortation to accept these readings as the Word of God.

Jesus wants all of his followers to be open to God's Kingdom in their lives. Openness to God's Kingdom requires faith, that is, a wholehearted acceptance of and commitment to Jesus, his message, and his example. Jesus calls people to *conversion*, that is, turning our hearts and minds away from sin. This means we must give up whatever is keeping us from God—fighting and complaining, senseless competition where we try to best others, making gods out of pleasure or sex or material possessions, ignoring others and their needs, and so forth. Service, peace, harmony, and loving God above everything and our neighbor as ourselves—these are the necessary virtues for God's Kingdom to reign in our hearts.

The Seven Sacraments celebrate the Good News. They are sacred signs of God's reign and they help bring it about. They increase our faith and help us continue to embrace Jesus and the Gospel. For example, at Mass, we hear the Kingdom proclaimed in the **Liturgy of the Word**. We receive Jesus in Holy Communion so that we can allow him, with the help of the Holy Spirit, to live in us and move us out to love and serve the world.

For Review

1. What does Jesus preach about the Kingdom of God?
2. What is the connection between the Kingdom of God and the Person of Jesus?
3. What does it mean to repent?
4. How does the Eucharist celebrate God's Kingdom?

For Reflection

What is evidence that God's Kingdom is alive in your family, school, parish, and community?

Forgiveness of Sins (*CCC*, 1691-1698)

Some of the most powerful words Jesus spoke during his public life were to a paralyzed man: "Child, your sins are forgiven" (Mk 2:5). These words summarize an essential part of Jesus' mission—the forgiveness of sins. Jesus preached repentance—turning from sin and embracing God's Kingdom. Moreover, he makes it possible

Conversion of Heart, Body, and Soul

Read the following miracle accounts. Summarize how each illustrates the theme of conversion.

- Water into wine (Jn 2:1-11)
- Canaanite woman (Mt 15:21-28)
- Woman with hemorrhage (Lk 8:43-48)
- Blind Bartimaeus (Mk 10:46-52)

Lesson 3 Objectives

The students will:

- understand that the Gospel is another God-given wonder.
- recall how Jesus showed the coming of the Kingdom of God.
- appreciate the call and the need for repentance and conversion and recognize how the sacraments celebrate both.
- understand that we are friends of Jesus.
- recognize the challenges of forgiving others.
- make connections between Jesus' message of forgiveness and friendship and the sacraments.

Lesson 3 Preview

This lesson sheds light on three other God-given wonders: the Good News of the Kingdom of God, the forgiveness of sins, and our friendship with Jesus.

for us to do what he commands—he forgives our sins.

Sin is destructive. It alienates us from God, other people, and ourselves. It riddles us with guilt. It demeans and depersonalizes. Sin is evil, all-pervasive, and its effects are all around us. Ultimately, sin leads to death. Forgiveness, then, is a true marvel of God's graciousness.

Jesus, whose name means "Yahweh saves," brings Salvation. He came to forgive sin and free all people from its powerful grip. He announced forgiveness and embodied God's loving forgiveness by welcoming the worst of sinners.

Through the forgiveness of sin, Jesus reveals the profound love of his heavenly Father. Recall that when Jesus forgave the paralytic, the scribes accused him of blasphemy because only God can forgive sin. But Jesus—God's own Son—indeed had power to both forgive sin and make a paralyzed man walk:

> "But that you may know that the Son of Man has authority to forgive sins on earth"—he said to the paralytic, "I say to you, rise, pick up your mat, and go home." He rose, picked up his mat at once, and went away in the sight of everyone. They were all astounded and glorified God, saying, "We have never seen anything like this." (Mk 2:10–12)

Jesus demonstrated by his ongoing example the astonishing truth that God loves and forgives sinners. Jesus proved this by associating with those who did not keep the Law, tax collectors, prostitutes, and other outcasts. He also taught about forgiveness, including especially the parable of the Prodigal Son, which challenged his enemies with the truth of God's immense, unfathomable love for sinners. Like the father in the parable, Jesus and his Father will welcome back anyone who repents of sin.

Forgiveness is central to Jesus' message. He wants us—his friends and followers—to imitate him. In the Lord's Prayer, Jesus instructs us to pray, "Forgive us our debts, *as* we forgive our debtors"

(Mt 6:12). Our forgiveness of others should have no bounds. For example, when Peter asked how many times we should forgive, Jesus said "seventy-seven times" (Mt 18:22), a symbolic number meaning an infinite number of times. We are called to be forgiving.

The most powerful example of God's forgiving love occurs at Jesus' crucifixion. In the midst of his horrific pain, Jesus said: "Father, forgive them, they know not what they do" (Lk 23:34). Even at his Death, Jesus prays to his Father to forgive us. And his Father listens!

All of the sacraments help us celebrate and make real God's compassion for us. The *Catechism of the Catholic Church* teaches:

> By the sacraments of rebirth, Christians have become "children of God," "partakers of the divine nature." Coming to see in the faith their new dignity, Christians are called to lead henceforth a life "worthy of the gospel of Christ." They are made capable of doing

explain the importance of the event for the coming of the Kingdom of God.

- Afterward, sum up by emphasizing to the students that the Kingdom of God is the active presence of divine love, justice, truth, and Salvation working in the world through Jesus Christ. The key component of the Kingdom message is that God is a loving parent—an Abba, a father, a daddy—who loves each and every one of us and seeks to draw all people to him.
- Draw attention to the quotation from Mark 1:15 (page 165). Have a student read it aloud. Ask the students, "What are the two prerequisites for belonging to God's Kingdom?" (*repentance and belief*) Point out that to repent means to *change one's mind*. With the coming of God's Kingdom, all things are different. Repentance here means believing in Jesus and then living justly and lovingly.
- Write the word **conversion** on the board. Brainstorm synonyms and list them on the board as well. Make sure that repentance and penance are included in the list as synonyms. See if the students can agree on a definition close to the following: "Conversion means a radical reorientation of one's life away from sin and evil, toward God."
- Call attention to the feature "Conversion of Heart, Body, and Soul" on page 166. Have the students work with a partner to look up, read, and summarize the

Lesson 3 Homework

1. Tell the students to write out their answers to the four For Review questions on page 166 and the five For Review questions on page 169.
2. Direct the students to read the text section "The Paschal Mystery Wins Our Redemption" (pages 169–171) in preparation for their next session.
3. Remind the students to continue working on their chosen Ongoing Assignments.

For Review Answers (page 166)

1. Jesus preaches that the Kingdom of God is at hand and that he is the principal agent of the Kingdom.
2. Jesus is the principal agent of the Kingdom of God; Salvation takes place through Jesus.
3. To repent means to change one's mind and turn from sin, to be open to Jesus and his message.
4. When we receive Jesus in Holy Communion, we allow him to live in us and take us out to love and serve the world.

four miracle accounts. Call on different partners to explain how they feel an account illustrates the theme of conversion. Afterward, point out the necessary virtues for belonging to God's Kingdom: *service, peace, harmony, loving God above all, and loving our neighbor as self* (see page 166).

- Use the four For Review questions on page 166 to discuss the meaning and message of the Kingdom of God.

Forgiveness of Sins (pages 166–169)

- Ask the students to think back to Chapter 2 and to recall how they discovered that sin is that which separate or alienates us from God, one another, ourselves, and all of creation.
- Note that sin is not something that happens to us; it is something we do. Note, too, that the result of sin is death. To conquer death, then, Jesus also had to conquer sin.
- Write the word **forgiveness** on the board. Tell the students that the whole of Christianity turns on this word. It is not turning a blind eye. It is complete restoration, total medicine, amazing new wine. It restores the future. It is the force that crushes fear. Jesus spent his entire ministry revealing the forgiving God.
- Go on to stress that God *has* to be forgiving, because sin is too large and too lethal for us overcome on our own. That is why Jesus said, "Without me you can do nothing" (Jn 15:5).
- Tell the students that Jesus did, however, offer an antidote to sin. Have the students read Luke 7:36–50. Ask, "What is the opposite of sin in this passage?" (*faith*) Faith in God's compassionate love and a commitment to forgiving other and to doing loving service is the way we turn from sin. That is why we celebrate the sacraments, each a celebration of faith, each a celebration of reconciliation. Ask:
    - What sort of reconciliation happens in the Sacrament of Baptism?
    - What sort of reconciliation happens in the Sacrament of Penance?
- Have the students turn to the feature "The Challenge of Forgiveness" on page 168. Read the directions. Suggest the students do their rating on a scale of 1 to 5, with 1 being the least difficult, and 5 the most difficult. Allow ample time for the students to write their explanations. For privacy's sake, however, warn them not to name names as they cite specific incidents. Afterward, encourage sharing in small groups or with partners.

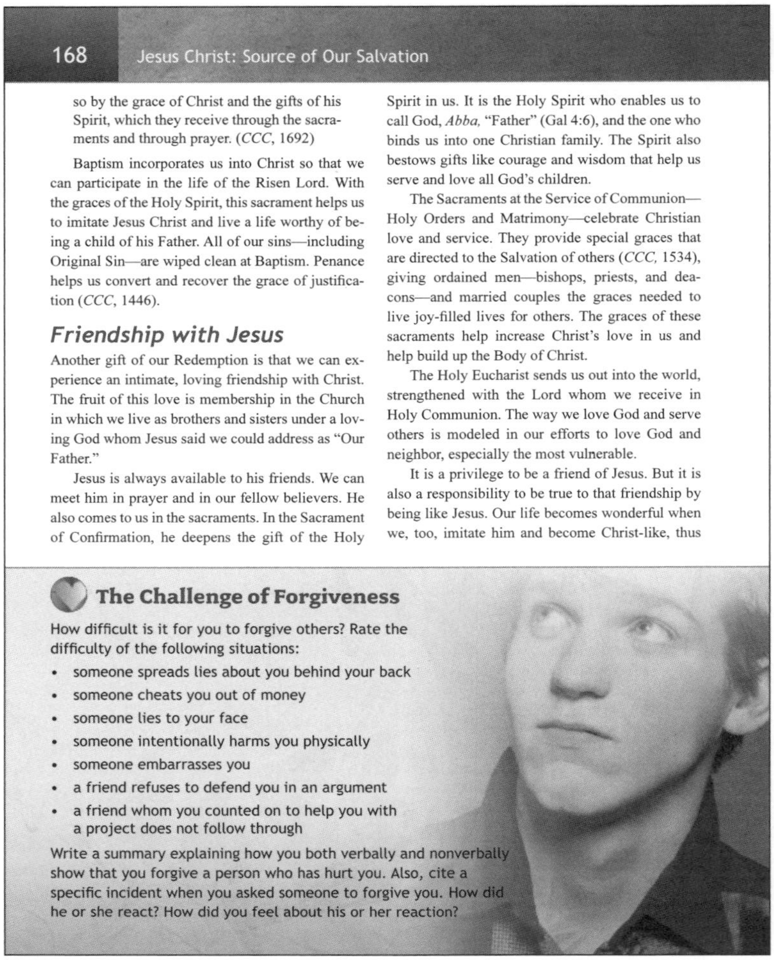

168 Jesus Christ: Source of Our Salvation

> so by the grace of Christ and the gifts of his Spirit, which they receive through the sacraments and through prayer. (*CCC*, 1692)

Baptism incorporates us into Christ so that we can participate in the life of the Risen Lord. With the graces of the Holy Spirit, this sacrament helps us to imitate Jesus Christ and live a life worthy of being a child of his Father. All of our sins—including Original Sin—are wiped clean at Baptism. Penance helps us convert and recover the grace of justification (*CCC*, 1446).

Friendship with Jesus

Another gift of our Redemption is that we can experience an intimate, loving friendship with Christ. The fruit of this love is membership in the Church in which we live as brothers and sisters under a loving God whom Jesus said we could address as "Our Father."

Jesus is always available to his friends. We can meet him in prayer and in our fellow believers. He also comes to us in the sacraments. In the Sacrament of Confirmation, he deepens the gift of the Holy Spirit in us. It is the Holy Spirit who enables us to call God, *Abba*, "Father" (Gal 4:6), and the one who binds us into one Christian family. The Spirit also bestows gifts like courage and wisdom that help us serve and love all God's children.

The Sacraments at the Service of Communion—Holy Orders and Matrimony—celebrate Christian love and service. They provide special graces that are directed to the Salvation of others (*CCC*, 1534), giving ordained men—bishops, priests, and deacons—and married couples the graces needed to live joy-filled lives for others. The graces of these sacraments help increase Christ's love in us and help build up the Body of Christ.

The Holy Eucharist sends us out into the world, strengthened with the Lord whom we receive in Holy Communion. The way we love God and serve others is modeled in our efforts to love God and neighbor, especially the most vulnerable.

It is a privilege to be a friend of Jesus. But it is also a responsibility to be true to that friendship by being like Jesus. Our life becomes wonderful when we, too, imitate him and become Christ-like, thus

The Challenge of Forgiveness

How difficult is it for you to forgive others? Rate the difficulty of the following situations:

- someone spreads lies about you behind your back
- someone cheats you out of money
- someone lies to your face
- someone intentionally harms you physically
- someone embarrasses you
- a friend refuses to defend you in an argument
- a friend whom you counted on to help you with a project does not follow through

Write a summary explaining how you both verbally and nonverbally show that you forgive a person who has hurt you. Also, cite a specific incident when you asked someone to forgive you. How did he or she react? How did you feel about his or her reaction?

For Review Answers (page 169)

1. Sin separates us from God, others, creation, and self; it brings guilt, anxiety, and leads to death.
2. Answers will vary a bit (e.g., Jesus continually extended forgiveness, associated with the outcast, taught us that we will receive forgiveness in the same measure as we forgive, called us to forgive unremittingly, forgave his executioners while he was on the Cross; etc.).
3. As Jesus' followers, we are to image his forgiving love; also, we will be forgiven in the same measure as we forgive (viz., the Lord's Prayer).
4. Baptism incorporates us into Christ and helps us to imitate Christ. Penance helps us to convert and recover the grace that was lost in sin.
5. Matrimony and Holy Orders.

attracting others to him. This is our vocation as his followers . . . and friends.

For Review

1. What are the effects of sin?
2. Give evidence that forgiveness is central to Jesus' mission.
3. Why must Jesus' followers forgive others?
4. Discuss how the sacraments of Baptism and Penance celebrate Christ's forgiveness.
5. Which are the sacraments in the Service of Communion?

For Reflection

- What is required of a friend of Jesus?
- When was a time you called on Jesus to share either an experience of joy or suffering?

The Paschal Mystery Wins Our Redemption

Christ's work of Redemption, whereby "dying he restored our death, and rising he restored our life," is accomplished principally by the Paschal Mystery, his Passion, Death, Resurrection, and Ascension into Heaven. The Paschal Mystery is celebrated and made present in the liturgy of the Church, and its saving effects are communicated in the sacraments, especially the Eucharist. Christ's own work in the liturgy is sacramental. Now seated at the right hand of the Father, Christ pours out the blessings of the Holy Spirit through the sacraments of the Church. His Body, which is the Church, dispenses the gift of Salvation. Through the liturgy, we are able to participate, as a foretaste, in the heavenly liturgy.

Also, through the sacraments, we receive the Lord's help and strength to live the Paschal Mystery in our own lives. The sacraments also proclaim the Good News of a future resurrected life in eternity.

The Holy Eucharist in a special way commemorates the Paschal Mystery by celebrating Jesus' sacrifice and Resurrection and his exalted place at the Father's right hand. The Eucharist also helps us participate in the Paschal Mystery by giving us the Lord himself in Holy Communion. It is the Risen Lord himself, in the Holy Spirit, who enables us to love by reaching out to our brothers and sisters. Finally, the Eucharistic liturgy looks to the time when we will gather in a heavenly banquet to celebrate God's goodness and love.

Jesus calls all of us to live the Paschal Mystery in our daily lives by dying to sin and selfishness and by reaching out in love to others. The Holy Spirit is God's gift to us, helping us to better imitate the Lord in this life while preparing to live in communion with the Blessed Trinity, the angels, saints, and our faithful friends and relatives in eternity. The Spirit guides us to

- live the Beatitudes and the Christian and human virtues,
- recognize sin in our lives and turn from it, and
- put into practice Christ's command to love both God and neighbor as part of the Church community which is the Body of Christ.

The Gift of the Holy Spirit

Blessed Mother Teresa said, "The most terrible poverty is loneliness, and the feeling of being unloved." And the poet John Milton remarked, "Loneliness is the first thing which God's eye named not good." It is truly a marvel of God's love that Jesus did not leave us alone. At the Last Supper, he made this promise to his friends:

- Move on by asking the students to think about their closest friends and the many different things they do with them. Then ask them to describe in their journals what they feel are the four most important things they do with their friends. Invite the students to share their responses. Note those that speak to the following:
  - being together, hanging out, or gathering together
  - sharing stories, jokes, secrets, or just conversing, texting, or twittering
  - eating or celebrating together
  - working together on a shared goal/project, e.g., winning a sports game, serving at a homeless shelter, etc.
- Go on to have the students read John 15:15. Ask:
  - Do you believe Jesus' words? That is, do you believe Jesus really thinks of *you* as a friend? Why or why not?
  - Do you think of *Jesus* as a friend? Why or why not?
  - Discuss the two questions in the For Reflection section on page 169.
- Call attention to the lists of things the students do with their friends. Ask, "Do you think these are things you can do with Jesus? Explain."
- Point out that when we celebrate the sacraments, we are celebrating our friendship with Jesus. Explain:

For Enrichment

To Pardon

Let us pardon those who have wronged us. For that which others scarcely accomplish—I mean the blotting out of their own sins by means of fasting and lamentations, and prayers, and sackcloth and ashes—this it is possible for us easily to effect without sackcloth and ashes and fasting, if only we blot out anger from our heart, and with sincerity forgive those who have wronged us.

—**St. John Chrysostom**

Forgiving the Inexcusable

To excuse what can really produce good excuses is not Christian charity; it is only fairness. To be a Christian means to forgive the inexcusable, because God has forgiven the inexcusable in you. This is hard. It is perhaps not so hard to forgive a single injury. But to forgive the incessant provocations of daily life—to keep on forgiving the bossy mother-in-law, the bullying husband, the nagging wife, the selfish daughter, the deceitful son—how can we do it? Only, I think, by remembering where we stand, by meaning our words when we say in our prayers each night, "Forgive us our trespasses as we forgive those who trespass against us." We are offered forgiveness on no other terms. To refuse it means to refuse God's mercy for ourselves. There is no hint of exceptions and God means what he says.

—**C. S. Lewis**

- In Baptism, we are marked with the Sign of the Cross; named "Christians," friends of Jesus; and are reborn as brothers and sisters of the Lord.
- In Confirmation, we share the gift of Jesus, God's own Spirit, who enables us to call God "Father."
- In Penance and Anointing of the Sick, Jesus reaches out to us as a forgiving, reconciling, and healing friend.
- In Holy Orders and Matrimony, Jesus grants us the grace to act as a friend to others and welcome others into the circle of Jesus' friends.
- And most especially in the Eucharist:
  - We *gather* together as friends of the Lord, marking ourselves again with the Sign of his Cross.
  - We *share stories* of our faith and the Gospel's Good News; likewise, we share our wants and needs, confident in our friendship with Jesus and his Father.
  - We *eat* the friendship meal Jesus left us, receiving him into our very selves as friend.
  - We *promise* to obey the command of Jesus by going forth to call others into God's friendship. And we keep our promise, because that is what friends do.

- Distribute Chapter 7, Handout 1, "The Eucharist—A Meal of Friendship." Have the students complete the activity on the sheet. Afterward, encourage sharing. Discuss ways the parish or school could improve its celebration of the Eucharist to better image a meal of friendship. Consider sharing ideas with the pastor/liturgy director.
- Close class with one of the students' prayers of praise.

Chapter 7: Redemption through the Paschal Mystery—Lesson 4

Bell Ringers

- Begin class with one of the prayers of praise the students composed.
- Ask the students to offer their responses to the four For Review questions on page 166 (answers are on page 187 of this text) and the five For Review questions on page 169 (answers are on page 188 of this

> If you ask anything of me in my name, I will do it. If you love me, you will keep my commandments. And I will ask the Father, and he will give you another Advocate to be with you always, the Spirit of truth, which the world cannot accept, because it neither sees nor knows it. But you know it, because it remains with you, and will be in you. I will not leave you orphans; I will come to you. (Jn 14:14–18)

The Father and the Son kept this promise when they sent the Holy Spirit on Pentecost. God's love comes to us through the Holy Spirit who is poured into our hearts (*CCC*, 733). The mission of Christ and the Holy Spirit is brought to completion in the Church. It is Christ, as head, who pours out the Holy Spirit on the Church, building, animating, and sanctifying us, her members, to live out our baptismal calling. The Church does not have a new mission apart from the mission of Christ and the Holy Spirit. Rather, the Church spreads the mystery of the communion of the Holy Trinity.

> By virtue of our Baptism, the first sacrament of the faith, the Holy Spirit in the Church communicates to us, intimately and personally, the life that originates in the Father and is offered to us in the Son. (*CCC*, 683)

The Holy Spirit is the first to awaken faith in us and to communicate to us new life. He binds us into one family and showers us with countless gifts that help us live fully with dignity and worth. Allowing the gift of the Holy Spirit to work in us brings forth much spiritual fruit, which are defined as follows:

> The fruits of the Spirit are perfections that the Holy Spirit forms in us as the first fruits of eternal glory. The tradition of the Church lists twelve of them: "charity, joy, peace, patience, kindness, goodness, generosity, gentleness, faithfulness, modesty, self-control, chastity." (*CCC*, 1832, see also Gal 5:22–23)

When the fruits of the Spirit are enacted in our lives, the outcome is that we are able to be more like Christ.

The Holy Spirit is present in all the sacraments. At Baptism we are initiated into the life of the Holy Spirit. At Confirmation, the Spirit's gifts are strengthened in us. The Sacrament of the Anointing of the Sick asks the healing power of the Holy Spirit to touch those who are ill and suffering. In the Sacrament of Holy Orders, the Spirit empowers a man to serve the Church in a special way, especially in proclaiming the Gospel, celebrating the Eucharist, and extending Christ's forgiving love.

The poet Gerard Manley Hopkins wrote, "The world is charged with the grandeur of God." This faith-filled exclamation declares that God's grace, love, and presence fill up the entire universe. Hopkins looked at creation and saw God's loving touch everywhere. When we reflect on the mysteries of our faith—God's wonderful creation, Jesus and his message about God's Kingdom, forgiveness, love, the Paschal Mystery, and the gift of the Holy Spirit —we too stand in awe at the incredible grandeur

Lesson 4 Objectives

The students will:

- review the meaning of the Paschal Mystery and appreciate that by its graces our Redemption was gained.
- make connections between the Eucharist and the Paschal Mystery.
- understand that the Holy Spirit is God's gift of self, dwelling within us and guiding us to glory.
- describe the fruits of the Spirit.

Lesson 4 Preview

This lesson continues the ongoing investigation of the wonders God has granted us so that we might live forever with him in glory. The students review the meaning and power of the Paschal Mystery and see how we celebrate it in the Eucharist. They grow in their awareness of the gift of the Holy Spirit within them and learn to appreciate and practice the fruits of the Spirit in their lives as followers of the Risen Lord.

and goodness of God's love. These gifts of our faith help us to reflect on the eternal life to which our loving God calls us.

For Review

1. How is the Paschal Mystery made present?
2. What is the greatest and first gift God gives to us? How do we receive it?
3. What are the "fruits" of the Holy Spirit?
4. Name two examples of how the sacraments celebrate the gift of the Holy Spirit.

For Reflection

Love is the greatest gift of the Holy Spirit (see 1 Corinthians 13:1-31). Share examples of how you have put each of the following qualities of love into practice both at school and among your family and friends: patience, kindness, unpretentiousness, good manners, amiableness.

The Last Things: Christian Death and the Resurrection of the Body (*CCC*, 1002-1003; 1005-1014; 1016-1019)

One day, all of us will face death, defined as the separation of the eternal soul from the body. The Church teaches about the last things—death, resurrection of the body, particular judgment, the Last or General Judgment, Heaven, Purgatory, and Hell. The study of these last things is called eschatology.

Consider the last words of St. Robert Francis Bellarmine (1542–1621), an Italian Jesuit cardinal, archbishop, and Doctor of the Church, whose written works responded brilliantly to the Protestant reformers. As he lay dying of a fever, he recited the Apostles' Creed. His very last words were: "I believe . . . in the resurrection of the body and the life everlasting. Amen." What a fitting end to a life dedicated to Jesus Christ and his Church. St. Robert Bellarmine believed the truth of what Jesus taught, "I am the resurrection and the life; whoever believes in me, even if he dies, will live, and everyone who lives and believes in me will never die" (Jn 11:25–26).

God did not originally intend for us to die. Scripture reveals that death is a price we pay for sin. Because of Adam's sin, humanity was infected with death: "Therefore, just as through one person sin entered the world, and through sin, death, and thus death came to all, inasmuch as all sinned" (Rom 5:12). Jesus Christ has rescued us from our natural fate. He has conquered death.

Also, Jesus showed us how to accept our inevitable deaths. In the Garden of Gethsemane, anxious about his own impending death, Jesus prayed, "Abba, Father, all things are possible to you. Take this cup away from me, but not what I will but what you will" (Mk 14:36). Jesus' words describe his final act of total self-giving to the Father. In faith we imitate him and say, "Father, into your hands I commend my spirit" (Lk 23:46).

Our fervent hope as Christians is that we will rise on the last day with Christ in all his glory. Our Baptism has already united us with the Risen Lord; in a mysterious way we already participate in his heavenly life. The Eucharist helps nourish us with Christ's heavenly life; we are already members of his body. We must always to be ready to live each day as though it were our last so that we can die in union with the Lord. As he lay dying, Pope Clement XI (1649–1721) advised his nephew, a cardinal, about what is really important in life: "See how all the honors of the world come to an end. Only that is great which is great in God's sight. Make it your endeavor to be a saint." Pause and take up the exercise

text). Be sure to allow the students to ask any other questions they may have.

- Introduce this session by writing **Paschal Mystery** on the board. Invite students to come to the board and write words, phrases, and definitions that they associate with the Paschal Mystery. Afterward, take a moment to review the meaning of the terms "paschal" and "mystery."
- Begin by explaining that the term "paschal" comes from a Hebrew root, meaning *to pass through, to pass over, to exempt, or to spare.* It specifically refers to the Exodus event where, while slaying the firstborn of Egypt, God's angel of death "passed over" the ancient Hebrews' homes that were marked with the blood of a lamb. "Paschal" is also the name of the sacrificial offering (a lamb) that was made in the Temple during Jesus' time to commemorate the Passover.
- Go on to explain that Christians believe that just as God "passed over" the Jews in Egypt and just as the Jews "passed through" the waters of the Red Sea to freedom, Jesus—our paschal lamb—"passed through" death to the freedom of new life, not only for himself, but for all humanity.
- Discuss the meaning of "mystery." Help the students recall that "mystery" does not refer to something to be solved, like a problem. Rather, a mystery is a truth to be explored. Note that the more we know about a

Lesson 4 Homework

1. Have the students write out their answers to the four For Review questions on page 171.
2. Tell the students to continue their work on their chosen Ongoing Activities.
3. Have the students read "The Last Things: Christian Death and the Resurrection of the Body" (pages 171–175) and "More about Eternal Life" (pages 175–179) in preparation for their next session.

For Review Answers (page 171)

1. The Paschal Mystery is made present in the celebration of the liturgy of the Church, in particular, in the celebration of the Eucharist.
2. The Holy Spirit. We first receive the Spirit in the Sacrament of Baptism.
3. They are perfections that the Holy Spirit forms in us as the first fruits of eternal glory. They are charity, joy, peace, patience, kindness, goodness, generosity, gentleness, faithfulness, modesty, self-control, and chastity.
4. Answers will vary. For example: Baptism initiates us into the life of the Spirit. In Confirmation, the Spirit's gifts are strengthened in us. In the Sacrament of Anointing of the Sick, the healing power of the Spirit touches the sick person. Holy Orders ordains a man with the Spirit to serve the Church as its minister.

problem, the smaller it becomes. The more we know about mystery, however, the larger it becomes. Ask for or offer some examples of mystery: the universe, beauty, love, another person, our own personality. Emphasize that this does not mean that mystery is unintelligible. Quite the contrary, mystery is comprehensible, but it is also inexhaustible. The more we become involved in mystery, the deeper the mystery becomes.

Teaching Approaches

The Paschal Mystery Wins Our Redemption (pages 169–171)

- Have the students read John 12:24. Point out that these words of Jesus best explain what the Paschal Mystery means. Namely, the path to the fullness of life demands letting go of the present life, and that letting go requires a "dying" and a "rising." That is precisely what Jesus did for our sake; and that mystery is what we celebrate every time we gather for Eucharist.
- Have the students sing or play a recording of "We Remember" by Marty Haugen. Pay particular attention to the refrain:

  We remember how you loved us to your
  death,
  and still we celebrate, for you are with us
  here;
  and we believe that we will see you when
  you come in your glory, Lord.
  We remember, we celebrate, we believe.

- Note how the song so beautifully sums up the threefold manner in which the Eucharist celebrates the Paschal Mystery—*commemoration, participation, anticipation*:
  - First, it *commemorates* Jesus' sacrifice on the Cross; our remembering both fulfills Jesus' command "Do this in memory of me" and makes present his saving actions on our behalf.
  - Second, it enables us to *participate* in the Paschal Mystery by our sharing the meal Jesus left us, the bread and wine that *is* Jesus present for us.
  - Third, it *anticipates* the heavenly banquet where all the faithful will gather in celebration of God's compassionate love.
- Finally, point out that the Paschal Mystery calls each of us to die every day in little ways, and all these little deaths are paschal moments leading us deeper and deeper into the Paschal Mystery of Christ. Invite the

yourself. Imagine that you only have one day left to live. Would you not try to live like a saint, loving God above everything and loving your neighbor as yourself? If we imitate Jesus in the way we live, then we need not fear death. If he is our friend in this life, he will not forget us in eternity.

Resurrection of the Body after Death (CCC, 988–1001; 1004; 1015–1017)

God created human beings with bodies of flesh. The term *flesh* refers to humans in our state of weakness and mortality. God's Son took on a human body (flesh) in order to redeem it. Furthermore, the "resurrection of the flesh" completes the creation and Redemption of the human body. It means that not only will our immortal souls live on after death, but our mortal bodies will also come to life. These interlocking truths of the resurrection of our bodies and the gift of everlasting life are fundamental Christian beliefs, based on our faith in the Lord's own Resurrection.

How will this occur? At death, our souls will separate from our human bodies, which we know do corrupt. We believe that immediately after death, God will judge us in a particular judgment that refers our lives to Christ. We will receive either entrance into Heaven—immediately or through a purification—or immediate damnation. At the Second Coming, by the power of his own Resurrection, the most Blessed Trinity will raise our bodies in a way that goes beyond our imagination and understanding. Our resurrected bodies will be made incorrupt, and they will rejoin our souls. God will raise all people, both good and evil, from the dead on the last day. In talking about that day, Jesus said,

> Do not be amazed at this, because the hour is coming in which all who are in the tombs will hear his voice and will come out, those who have done good deeds to the resurrection of life, but those who have done wicked deeds to the resurrection of condemnation. (Jn 5:29)

In a miracle of God's love, he will make our bodies incorruptible when they reunite with our souls.

The most important quality of our resurrected bodies will be immortality; we will never die again. In 1 Corinthians 15, St. Paul lists certain qualities of our resurrected bodies, including immortality. Our resurrected bodies will be imperishable, glorious, powerful, and spiritual. We will never feel pain, and our bodies will shine brightly, reflecting the glory of the **Beatific Vision**, that is, "seeing God face to face" in heaven. Material creation will not hinder us; for example, we will be able to move about easily and swiftly. Finally, our spirits will control our glorified bodies.

We also believe that God will transform *all* material creation in Christ, creating a suitable environment where our resurrected, glorified bodies will thrive for eternity.

Beatific Vision
Seeing God "face to face" in Heaven; it is the source of our eternal happiness and final union with the Triune God for all eternity.

particular judgment
The individual's judgment immediately after death, when Christ will rule on one's eternal destiny to be spent in Heaven (after purification in Purgatory, if needed) or in Hell.

Purgatory
The state of purification that takes place after death for those who need to be made clean and holy before meeting the all-holy God in Heaven.

Parousia
The Second Coming of Christ when the Lord will judge the living and the dead.

For Enrichment

The Holy Spirit

> The Holy Spirit is . . . born from Love and is of Love, all its treasures are of love, and if we are to believe our Gospels it is received by love and love only. I am aware that to talk of love vaguely like this is not much help. I know how difficult it is to die to pride and self-concern, to the cowardice of a spiritual apathy that dare not face itself for what it fears to know. I know how difficult it is to remember, and to act as though we knew, that only forgiveness has a Resurrection, resentment has not—all those things that are the great and tormenting enemies to Love and its gracious freedoms.
>
> —Florence Allshorn

Belief in the Holy Spirit

> Every time we say, "I believe in the Holy Spirit," we mean that we believe that there is a living God able and willing to enter human personality, and change it.
>
> —J. B. Phillips

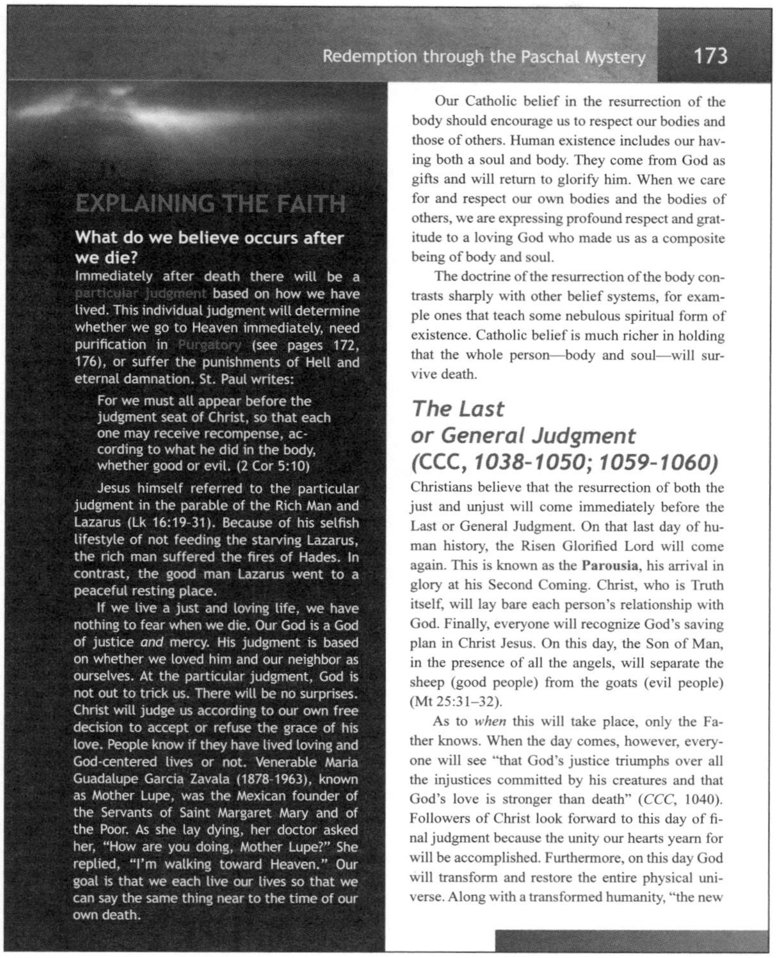

Redemption through the Paschal Mystery 173

EXPLAINING THE FAITH

What do we believe occurs after we die?

Immediately after death there will be a particular judgment based on how we have lived. This individual judgment will determine whether we go to Heaven immediately, need purification in Purgatory (see pages 172, 176), or suffer the punishments of Hell and eternal damnation. St. Paul writes:

> For we must all appear before the judgment seat of Christ, so that each one may receive recompense, according to what he did in the body, whether good or evil. (2 Cor 5:10)

Jesus himself referred to the particular judgment in the parable of the Rich Man and Lazarus (Lk 16:19-31). Because of his selfish lifestyle of not feeding the starving Lazarus, the rich man suffered the fires of Hades. In contrast, the good man Lazarus went to a peaceful resting place.

If we live a just and loving life, we have nothing to fear when we die. Our God is a God of justice *and* mercy. His judgment is based on whether we loved him and our neighbor as ourselves. At the particular judgment, God is not out to trick us. There will be no surprises. Christ will judge us according to our own free decision to accept or refuse the grace of his love. People know if they have lived loving and God-centered lives or not. Venerable Maria Guadalupe Garcia Zavala (1878-1963), known as Mother Lupe, was the Mexican founder of the Servants of Saint Margaret Mary and of the Poor. As she lay dying, her doctor asked her, "How are you doing, Mother Lupe?" She replied, "I'm walking toward Heaven." Our goal is that we each live our lives so that we can say the same thing near to the time of our own death.

Our Catholic belief in the resurrection of the body should encourage us to respect our bodies and those of others. Human existence includes our having both a soul and body. They come from God as gifts and will return to glorify him. When we care for and respect our own bodies and the bodies of others, we are expressing profound respect and gratitude to a loving God who made us as a composite being of body and soul.

The doctrine of the resurrection of the body contrasts sharply with other belief systems, for example ones that teach some nebulous spiritual form of existence. Catholic belief is much richer in holding that the whole person—body and soul—will survive death.

The Last or General Judgment (CCC, 1038-1050; 1059-1060)

Christians believe that the resurrection of both the just and unjust will come immediately before the Last or General Judgment. On that last day of human history, the Risen Glorified Lord will come again. This is known as the **Parousia**, his arrival in glory at his Second Coming. Christ, who is Truth itself, will lay bare each person's relationship with God. Finally, everyone will recognize God's saving plan in Christ Jesus. On this day, the Son of Man, in the presence of all the angels, will separate the sheep (good people) from the goats (evil people) (Mt 25:31–32).

As to *when* this will take place, only the Father knows. When the day comes, however, everyone will see "that God's justice triumphs over all the injustices committed by his creatures and that God's love is stronger than death" (*CCC*, 1040). Followers of Christ look forward to this day of final judgment because the unity our hearts yearn for will be accomplished. Furthermore, on this day God will transform and restore the entire physical universe. Along with a transformed humanity, "the new

students to name ways they die and rise; for example, letting go of bad habits and sinful behaviors such as selfishness; facing grief, alienation, pain, anxiety, doubt and fear about the future, or loneliness. Invite the students to write about these experiences in their journals.

- Write the following on the board: **You are not alone**. Explain that we don't have to face the paschal elements of life on our own. Assure the students that in Baptism and Confirmation, the Holy Spirit comes into our hearts and remains there forever. Thus, in all our daily dying, the Holy Spirit is with us to help us rise again.
- Call attention to the text section "The Gift of the Holy Spirit" (page 169–171). Ask one of the students to read aloud the words of Blessed Mother Teresa and the poet John Milton. Point out that loneliness taken to its most extreme has another name: hell. Hell is total loneliness—the complete turning *to* self and *away from* God. Emphasize that it is the Holy Spirit dwelling within us who assures us that we are not alone. It is the Spirit who encourages and strengthens us to remain in communion with God.
- Have the students open their Bibles to Matthew 7:17–20. Call on a volunteer to read the passage aloud. Invite the students to notice that Jesus is telling us that we will be known by the way we act—by our "fruits."
- Write the phrase **Fruits of the Spirit** on the board. Note the list on page 170 of the text. Write the fruits of the Spirit on the board. Explain that these "fruits" are actually good habits or virtues which Jesus himself possessed. When we work to develop these virtues, we're working to become more like Christ. Finally, tell the students that each person possesses the Spirit's fruits differently, and each fruit has a different shape in each person. Nevertheless, all these fruits will show themselves in us as we grow closer to Christ.
- Use questions like the following to discuss the fruits of the Spirit:
    - Is there someone you admire who displays one or more of the fruits of the Spirit? Share what you admire. Describe how the quality(ies) helps (help) others.
    - How do people you know value the fruits of the Spirit?
- Continue the discussion by drawing on the For Reflection feature on page 171. Have the students read the passage from 1 Corinthians. Then, have them

share how they have put love into action as described in the feature.

- After the discussion, give the students a writing assignment. Have them write which of the fruits of the Spirit are most crucial to them and then describe which fruit they reckon will take the most courage on their part to live out. Allow time for writing. Afterward, in small groups or as an entire class, have them share what they wrote.
- Before moving on, explain that we can be sure that the Spirit is at work wherever we see evidence of these fruits.
- Call attention to the text paragraph that begins "The Holy Spirit is present in all the sacraments" (page 170). Note how the Spirit comes to us in special ways in the Sacraments of Baptism, Confirmation, and Holy Orders.
- Finally, note how the concluding paragraph of this text section beautifully sums up the entire chapter thus far; it mentions the wonders of creation, the gift of Jesus, the Good News of the Kingdom, God's compassionate forgiveness and overwhelming love, the saving Paschal Mystery, and the gift of the powerful and indwelling Holy Spirit.
- Conclude the session with one of the students' prayers of praise.

heavens and new earth" will share in Christ Jesus' own glory. Since we do not know the exact hour of Christ's return and our final judgment, we should always be ready.

Today we have a glimpse of our future life because Christ has already initiated the Kingdom of God on earth. The Church "is the Reign of Christ already present in mystery" (*Lumen Gentium* 3, quoted in *CCC*, 763). Despite the sinful forces at work in the world to undermine God's saving love, his loving grace in the Church is very much alive to help attract people to the Triune God. The Holy Spirit gives Catholics the power and the mission of cooperating with Christ's work of freeing people from the bondage of sin. The Spirit strengthens us with virtues like fortitude to work tirelessly as peacemakers. We can work for justice by helping people attain their God-given rights. We also cooperate in Christ's plan when we promote human solidarity and respect the dignity of every human being. In a special way, we promote the Kingdom of God when we extend mercy to the weak, poor, and defenseless.

The Holy Spirit also gifts us with the virtue of hope. Hope helps us look forward to the glorious day of Christ's Second Coming. It helps us pray the prayer that ends the very last book of the Bible: "Amen! Come, Lord Jesus! The grace of the Lord Jesus be with you all" (Rv 22:20–21). In his encyclical *Spe Salvi* (Saved in Hope), Pope Benedict XVI described the hope we have in eternal life when we will join with Christ forever. He wrote about eternity this way:

> The term "eternal life" is intended to give a name to this known "unknown." . . . It would be like plunging into the ocean of infinite love, a moment in which time—the before and after—no longer exists. We can only attempt to grasp the idea that such a moment is life in the full sense, a plunging ever anew into the vastness of being, in which we are simply overwhelmed with joy. This is how Jesus expresses it in Saint John's Gospel:

Reflection: RIP

RIP is an abbreviation for the short Latin prayer, *Requiescat in pace*, "May he/she rest in peace."

Perhaps you have also seen a print of a medieval painting with a monk at his desk. A skull sits on his desk. The monk is contemplating the skull and what it represents. The artist may also have added the words, *Sic transit loria mundi*, "Thus passes the glory of the world." The skull reminds us that we have only a brief time to make our mark. Time speeds quickly by. What the world holds important may not be so in God's eyes.

Let these Latin phrases help you reflect on your own life. What would you like to do with your life? Write an obituary notice for yourself that would appear in a daily newspaper. Include things like:

- Your name and age
- Cause of death
- Occupation
- Loved ones left behind
- Major accomplishments
- Unfinished tasks
- Epitaph on gravestone

In your journal, write an entry that describes five personal qualities that you could offer to Jesus at your particular judgment that show how you have lived a Christian life. Write a detailed plan explaining how you will implement practice of these qualities in the next two weeks.

Chapter 7: Redemption through the Paschal Mystery—Lesson 5

Bell Ringers

- Once again, begin class with one of the students' prayers of praise.
- Call on different students to offer their responses to the four For Review questions on page 171 (answers are on page 191 of this text).
- On the board, write the sentence, **In this world, nothing is certain but death and taxes**. Ask the students if they know to whom this quotation is attributed (*Benjamin Franklin*). Then ask them to describe what they think it means.
- Afterward, point out that while some of us may avoid taxes, none of us will avoid death. Everything that lives on earth must die. Have the students look up and read Ecclesiastes 3:1–2. Afterward, ask, "Given

Lesson 5 Objectives

The students will:

- share fears about death.
- write their obituary.
- describe what will happen immediately after death.
- compare and contrast particular judgment and the General Judgment.
- compare and contrast the states of Heaven, hell, and Purgatory.
- appreciate that eschatology deals with the fulfillment of the Kingdom of God.

"I will see you again and your hearts will rejoice, and no one will take your joy from you" (16:22). We must think along these lines if we want to understand the object of Christian hope, to understand what it is that our faith, our being with Christ, leads us to expect." (*Spe Salvi*, 12)

The joy and happiness that God has in store for us is indeed something for which to hope and pray.

For Review

1. Why is death a part of the human experience?
2. How does Jesus' example of dying help us at the time of our own deaths?
3. What do Catholics believe about the resurrection of the body?
4. Define *Beatific Vision*.
5. What is the particular judgment?
6. Define *Parousia*.
7. What will happen at the Second Coming of Christ?

For Reflection

- How do you imagine an incorruptible heavenly body?
- Describe a situation when you feel you have been judged fairly.

More about Eternal Life (*CCC*, 1023-1037; 1052-1058)

Our eternal life will begin immediately after death and the particular judgment. The particular judgment will be confirmed in the final judgment at the end of time when Christ will come again and raise our bodies, those who have lived a life of love and merit eternal reward (in Heaven) as well as those who have died separated from God and deserve punishment (in Hell). The reward of Heaven is eternal life spent in union with God and all those who share in God's life. Hell is eternal separation from God.

The existence of Heaven and Hell show very seriously the reality of human freedom. If we use our freedom properly, then we will choose our own eternal destiny—a joyous life with our loving, Triune God. On the other hand, if we choose freely to model ourselves into heartless, unloving, selfish people, then God will respect our decision. When we choose self over God, then it is we who have chosen Hell. Our loving God respects our freedom and will give us what we want. More significantly,

Lesson 5 Preview

This lesson involves the students in something that puzzles us all, faces us all, and frightens almost all of us: death and the last things. Be aware of the students' fears and misconceptions as they approach these topics. As you present this material, keep the students focused on the compassion and mercy Jesus has for them and on their living the life Jesus has called them to live—the life of love. The "last things" should not be a cause of fear or guilt but a cause of rejoicing for the follower of Christ. After all, we ardently wait for the coming of the Kingdom—a Kingdom that will be fulfilled only on the last day. Since this lesson covers a large amount of material and since you will want to leave enough time for the students to discuss and ask questions about it, consider presenting the lesson over two or more class periods.

death's inevitability, why is it that we so strongly resist it?" Accept all replies.

- Call attention to the text section Primary Source Quotations (page 181), and have volunteers read aloud the quotations on death from 1 Timothy and St. Ambrose. Then ask the students what they fear most about death:
    - your own death?
    - the death of loved ones?
    - the prospect of death?
    - the fact of death?
    - the process of dying?
    - what happens after death?
- Suggest that perhaps our resistance to the prospect of death is God-given. Help the students understand that Christians believe that we have an innate desire for life, life unfettered by death, life beyond death, life forever in the presence of God. Remind the students that this was God's will for us from the beginning.
- Direct attention to the feature "Reflection: RIP" on page 174. Have the students think about their life and then write about it by creating an obituary.
- When the students finish writing, share and post the obituaries in the classroom.

Teaching Approaches

The Last Things: Christian Death and the Resurrection of the Body (pages 171-175) *and* More about Eternal Life (pages 175-179)

- Write the term **eschatology** on the board. Explain that it means "the study of the last things." Tell the students that our understanding of the last things—of what comes *after* death—developed slowly over time. Our concepts are a combination of our deepening understanding of physical reality, as well as of God and of God's justice and mercy. (*Note:* For more on eschatology, see articles in Background Information below.)
- Call attention to the quotation from John 11:25–26 on page 171 of the text. Then write the following sentence on the board: **In our faith, two things are certain: first, Jesus is risen; second, like him, we will rise again**. Remind the students that in his Resurrection, Jesus did not *come back from death* like his friend Lazarus. Rather, Jesus *went through death* to a new life that was not corralled by time or space,

and Jesus' passage paved the way for us to follow him.

- On the board write the statement, **Our spirits live on after death while our bodies stay on earth forever**. Ask the students whether this statement is true or false. (*Note*: Many students will mistakenly think that the afterlife is only a spiritual experience. Many of them will find the concept of the resurrection of the *body* very new and surprising to them.) Reassure the students that this statement is false.
- Remind the students that in the Apostles' Creed, we profess our belief in the resurrection of the body. Spend a few moments discussing what the resurrection of the body means. Begin by asking the students to recall and describe the post-Resurrection appearances of Jesus.
    - Jesus appeared as a *whole* person, *physically* present, body *and* soul, not as some disembodied spirit (e.g., Lk 24:29–30, 41–43, and Jn 20:27).
    - At the same time, material restraints did not bind Jesus. For example, he simply appeared in a locked room (Jn 20:19).
- Have the students read 1 Corinthians 15:1–8, 35–55. Explain that St. Paul first tells us that he has seen the Risen Lord; then he gives us an eyewitness account of what a resurrected body looks like. Note the qualities of the resurrected body as listed on page 172 of the text: "imperishable, glorious, powerful, and spiritual."
- Invite the students to name ways they respect and care for their bodies. Then divide the class into two groups. Have one group brainstorm ways our culture shows disrespect for our bodies; have the other group come up with examples of how our society respects and cares for our bodies.
- Remind the students that Jesus never spoke scornfully of the body. In fact, when Jesus relayed his real presence, he said, "This is my body"—the totality of his person. The resurrection of the body is not a liberation from the body, but a perfection of the body. Resurrection *completes* us as persons—soul *and* body. Make certain the students recognize that resurrection does not mean a return to everyday life. Rather, it is a breakthrough to the larger life Jesus spoke about. Like Jesus, we will not "come back" from the dead; we will "go through" it. Also, like Jesus, we will rise as total persons—soul *and* body. To rise any other way would be to deny our creation.
- Go on to read aloud the following sentence from page 172 in the text:

God generously rewards those who use freedom to choose what is right and good.

Heaven

If we die in God's friendship and grace, and are perfectly purified, we will receive the reward of a life of perfect eternal happiness in Heaven. Living with Jesus Christ forever, we will be blessed with the Beatific Vision where we will see God face to face, as he really is, contemplating his heavenly glory. Perfect life with the Most Holy Trinity, our Blessed Mother, and all the angels and saints, including our relatives and friends who have lived a God-centered life, is called **Heaven**. In Heaven, God

> will wipe every tear from their eyes, and there shall be no more death or mourning, wailing or pain, [for] the old order has passed away. (Rv 21:4)

Jesus' Death and Resurrection have opened Heaven to us. In Heaven, we will be fully incorporated into Christ. Although we will have perfect communion with him, we will both retain and find our true individual identities as his brother or sister. We will continue to fulfill God's will in Heaven and will reign with Christ Jesus forever.

The pleasures and happiness in store for us in Heaven are beyond human imagination. Scripture uses images to help describe them: wedding feast, light, life, peace, paradise, the Father's house, heavenly Jerusalem. But as it is written, the joy is really incomprehensible to us on earth: "What eye has not seen, and ear has not heard, and what has not entered the human heart, what God has prepared for those who love him" (1 Cor 2:9).

The Hall of Fame baseball great, Yogi Berra, once observed, "You've got to be careful if you don't know where you are going, because you might not get there." Another time he cautioned, "If you don't know where you are going, you'll wind up somewhere else." His amusing remarks seem a little confused, but his main point is clear: if we do not have a well-planned, positive goal in life, wrong turns can lead us to a place we do not want to be. There is no goal more worthwhile than getting to Heaven. This is why we should take to heart the advice of St. Francis de Sales who said, "Resolve henceforth to keep Heaven before your mind, to be ready to forgo everything that can hinder you or cause you to stray on your journey there." However, if we do stray, we should never forget that we are able to turn to our merciful Lord and ask for his forgiveness in order to get back on the path that leads to eternal happiness.

Purgatory

Purgatory is the name the Church gives to the final purification of those who die in God's grace and friendship but who need purification or cleansing to achieve the holiness necessary to enter Heaven.

Catholic belief in the existence of Purgatory is based on Biblical passages like 2 Maccabees 12:41–45, which encourages those who are living

For Review Answers (page 175)

1. Death is the price we pay for sin.
2. Jesus showed us that while we may resist death, we can trust in the Father's love and give ourselves into his hands.
3. Catholics believe that God will raise our bodies on the last day and they will be rejoined with our souls.
4. Beatific vision is our seeing God face-to-face in Heaven.
5. The particular judgment in an encounter with God that determines our eternal fate: hell, Heaven, or Purgatory (leading to Heaven).
6. Parousia refers to the Second Coming of Christ.
7. Our souls will be reunited with our resurrected bodies and the General Judgment will take place.

Redemption through the Paschal Mystery 177

to pray for the dead so that they may be released from their sins. In addition, Church Tradition has interpreted certain New Testament passages (see 1 Corinthians 3:15; 1 Peter 1:7) as referring to a place of a "cleansing fire" after death.

Church teaching on the **Communion of Saints**, that is, the unity in Christ of all those he has redeemed, is also related to the existence of Purgatory. The Communion of Saints includes three groups of people:

- the *pilgrim Church* (those of us who are living today on earth, also known as the "Church militant");
- the *Church suffering* (those undergoing purification in Purgatory); and
- the *Church triumphant* (the blessed in heaven).

By the power of the Holy Spirit, the Risen Lord, who is the source of all holiness, makes holy and binds the Church into a communion of the faithful. We—both the living and those who have died—are one family united in the Spirit of Jesus Christ. As a family, we can continue to show our love and concern for each other, even after death. This is why, from the first centuries, the Church has honored the dead by offering the Eucharist for them and encouraging the faithful to pray for them. In addition, the Church recommends almsgiving, indulgences, and acts of penance for the "poor souls in Purgatory."

The doctrine of Purgatory, "purification," makes sense. To embrace an all-loving God, we must be free of any imperfection in our own capacity to love. Only a pure person can enter Heaven to embrace the all-holy God. Not everyone who dies has cleansed himself or herself of his or her **venial sins** or any punishment due sins that are present at death. Although with God's help we can accomplish the process of purification while we are alive, the process of dying to attachment to sin and selfishness is long and painful.

Purgatory involves "letting go" to our sins and selfishness, a process that is both joyful and painful. Those in Purgatory are happy that the Lord has promised them Heaven. At the same time, the Church suffering need to leave behind their selfish attachments before meeting the all-holy God. Giving up what we have clung to in life (for example, the desire to dominate others) can be difficult. This painful process of "letting go and letting God" may be what the expression "cleansing fire" means. The process of purgation might be one of burning with sorrow and shame over a sinful life, and a profound wish to be united to the loving, good, and saving God. To be separated from the Lord whom they love so deeply brings suffering to our brothers and sisters in Purgatory. However, when their purgation is complete, their suffering will end as they enter into the bliss of Heaven.

Because we in the pilgrim Church are members of the Communion of Saints, we should remember to pray for those in Purgatory, especially at Mass, and to ask for their prayers as well. We can honor our relatives who

Heaven
Our final communion with the Blessed Trinity, Mary, the angels, and all the saints.

Communion of Saints
The unity of Jesus Christ with all those he has redeemed—the Church on earth, in Heaven, and in Purgatory.

venial sins
Actual sins that weaken and wound our relationship with God but do not destroy divine life in our souls.

Lesson 5 Homework

1. Direct the students to write out their answers to the seven For Review Questions on page 175 as well as the six For Review Questions on page 179.
2. Tell the students to be ready to hand in their Ongoing Assignments at their next session.
3. Tell the students to read over the Chapter Quick View section on pages 180–182 and to review the chapter's Main Ideas. Have the students write out any remaining questions they may have and bring them to the next session.

For Enrichment

Why Pray for the Dead?

As members of the Communion of Saints, Catholics regularly pray for the dead. We know that prayer is unfettered by space or time, thus the prayer we offer for the dead not only puts us in communion with the deceased but also can affect and help that person even at the moment of the person's past death experience, when he or she met God face-to-face.

We also believe that God will transform *all* material creation in Christ, creating a suitable environment where our resurrected, glorified bodies will thrive for eternity.

- Tell the students that when thinking about the "places" in which our bodies will spend eternity, it's helpful to think of them as states of being. For example, the state of being we're in now we call "life." After death, we believe we will find ourselves is a different state of being.
- Distribute copies of Chapter 7, Handout 2, "Death—Then What?" Use the outline on the handout to present the material on the last things. Begin by drawing attention to the text definition of "particular judgment" on page 172. Have the students reread the section. Then go through Jesus' stories of Lazarus and the rich man in Luke 16:19–31 and the sheep and goats in Matthew 25:31–46. Explain that these stories are the basis for our beliefs about judgment. Note, too, how there is no malice on the part of the judge in the stories. Rather, as far as the judge is concerned, the stories seem to indicate not only a delight in the choices made by Lazarus and the sheep, but also a deep sadness regarding the selfish choices of the rich man and the goats.
- Emphasize that, like the figures in Jesus' stories, we die as that which we have become—someone who is loving or someone who is unloving. That is why, as far as judgment is concerned, it is more accurate to say that we pass judgment *on ourselves*.
- Have the students complete the Scripture activity described in the feature "The Bible on Judgment" on page 179. Afterward, call on different students to share their findings regarding the feature's five questions.
    - "What is assigned to the Son by the Father?" (*judgment*) Take a moment to emphasize that it is the loving and compassionate Jesus who will be our judge.
    - "What is the basis of judgment?" (*our good/wicked deeds*)
    - "What is the downfall of Jesus' opponents?" (*their pride and acceptance of praise from one another rather than seeking praise from God*)
    - "List three things the Gentiles like to do." (*live in debauchery, entertain evil desires, and engage in drunkenness, orgies, carousing, and wanton idolatry*)

  - "List three things one should do as the end nears." (e.g., *pray, love one another, act with hospitality, serve one another, share the Good News*)

- Move on to investigate the state of Heaven by calling on different students to read aloud the quotations regarding Heaven by St. Benedict Joseph Labré and by St. Augustine (in the section Primary Source Quotations on page 181) as well as the quotation by Pope Benedict XVI on pages 174–175 of the text. Then, if possible, play a recording of "Eye Has Not Seen" by Marty Haugen (based on 1 Corinthians 2:9–10). Refer the students to the section "Heaven" on page 176 of the text and have them note how the handout describes Heaven as a state of unremitting love. Have art materials available and allow time for the students to draw their conception of Heaven based on what they have read in the book and discussed in class. Afterward, have the students share their drawings.
- Draw attention to the quotation from 1 Corinthians 2:9 on page 176. Tell the students that the reason Paul says, "Eye has not seen . . . what God has prepared for those who love him," is because love is so difficult to depict. Our faith, however, assures us that believing is seeing. That is, if we have believed in love and acted with love, we shall see God face to face and find an eternal home with him. Put simply, Heaven is home. It is where we are loved and where we love others forever.
- Call on two volunteers to read aloud the quotations on hell by Blessed Charles de Foucauld and St. Gemma Galgani (see Primary Source Quotations, page 181). Afterward, have the students turn in their texts to the section "Hell" (pages 178–179). Note how hell is chosen; it's eternal separation from God, isolation, and loneliness. It is the state of those who reject the compassion and mercy of God even at the last moment of their life. Point out that just as Heaven is the choice of the God-and-neighbor-lover, so hell is the choice of the inordinate self-lover. Hell indicates the state of those who freely and definitively separate themselves from God, the source of all life and joy. Like Heaven, hell is a choice we make in life, not a judgment by God after we die. (*Note:* See the Background Information quotes on the "last things" [pages 198, 200].)
- Have art materials available and allow time for the students to draw their conception of hell based on what they have read in the book and discussed in class. Afterward, have the students share their drawings. Discuss how the drawings of Heaven and hell

178 Jesus Christ: Source of Our Salvation

have gone before us by praying for them and offering our good works and sacrifices on their behalf. When they make it to Heaven, they will be sure to remember us before our heavenly Father.

Hell

Hell is defined as an eternal separation from God brought on by deliberate **mortal sin**. Its principal punishment is separation from our loving God who created us with the intention that we would find and seek love, life, joy, and happiness—our deepest yearnings that only God can satisfy. Sacred Tradition speaks of the "fires of Hell." These describe the loss of love, self-hatred, and the total loneliness that results from failure to love God above all others and our neighbor as ourselves for the love of God. Those in Hell grieve over their eternal punishment, suffer spiritually and physically, and give up all hope of Salvation.

God does not predestine anyone for Hell. God made us to love him. However, for those who freely choose to commit mortal sin by refusing to love God, and die without repenting of their lack of love, their own free choice will forever separate them from God.

Sacred Scripture and Sacred Tradition both affirm the existence of Hell. For example, Jesus referred several times to *Gehenna,* a Jewish term associated with Hell. One example is the parable of the sheep and goats—a judgment scene at the end of time when those who fail to love the needy are condemned to Hell. On other occasions, Jesus talked about divine judgment (Mt 13:41–42) and separation from God because of selfishness, as in the parable of Lazarus and the rich man (Lk 18:19–31).

The doctrine of Hell is related to our belief that God is a loving God who made us truly free. God respects our freedom, even if, out of pride, we choose to reject his love, grace, and mercy. God forever showers his love on us; his mercy is always there for us to embrace. However, despite God's constant love, people can be hard-hearted and stiff-necked, adamantly selfish and unloving. Humans can and do commit mortal sin. Having created us free beings, God respects our freedom, even if it results in destructive and sinful actions.

God does not send anyone to Hell; unrepentant mortal sin does. We cannot say with certitude who is in Hell because we do not know which persons have defiantly turned their backs on God. Jesus warns us not to judge others lest we be judged ourselves (see Luke 6:37). What we can and should do is pray for all sinners, including ourselves, to repent of sin and accept God's love and forgiveness.

If we try to live with love in our hearts, and perform acts of love for God and others, the existence of Hell should not frighten us. If we turn from sin as Christ calls us to do and struggle to live lives of love, then we should trust and believe that Christ

Background Information

More about Eschatology

Eschatology is that area of theology which is directly concerned with the study of "last thing(s)." The "last thing" is God, or, more precisely, the final manifestation of the reconciling, renewing, and unifying love of God. The "last things" are various moments or stages in the final manifestation process: death, particular judgment, heaven, hell, purgatory, Second Coming of Christ, resurrection of the body, general judgment, consummation of all things in the perfection of the Kingdom of God. . . . At the very least, eschatology provides a wider context for the discussion of every other theological question, for eschatology is about the Kingdom of God.

—Richard P. McBrien,
Catholicism

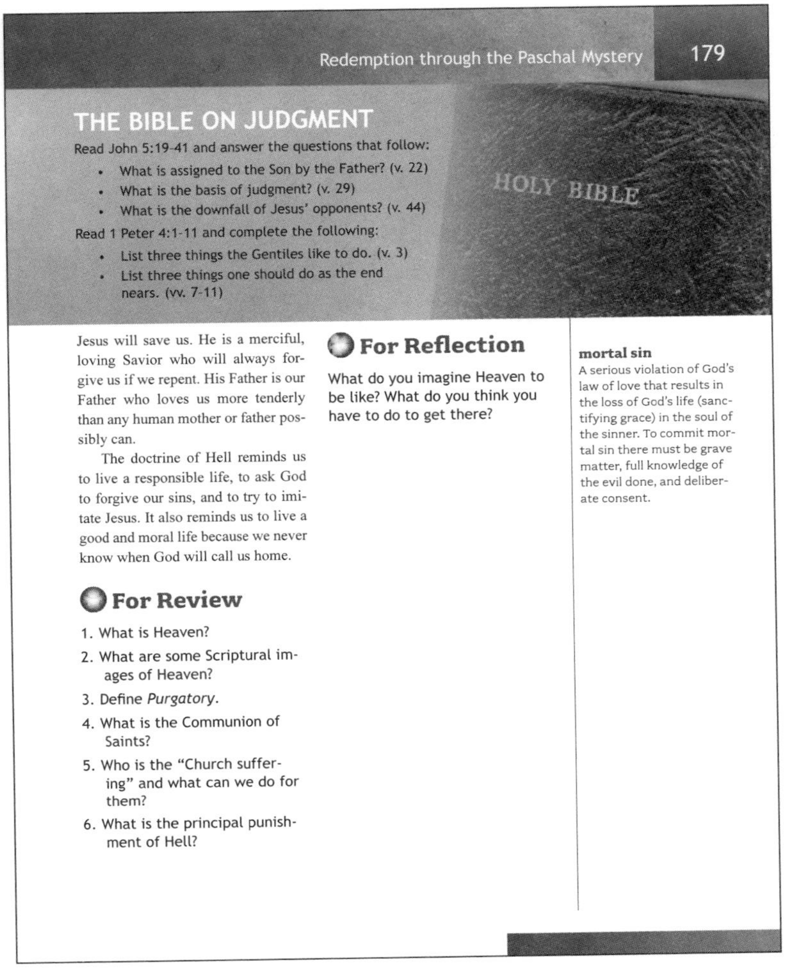

THE BIBLE ON JUDGMENT

Read John 5:19-41 and answer the questions that follow:

- What is assigned to the Son by the Father? (v. 22)
- What is the basis of judgment? (v. 29)
- What is the downfall of Jesus' opponents? (v. 44)

Read 1 Peter 4:1-11 and complete the following:

- List three things the Gentiles like to do. (v. 3)
- List three things one should do as the end nears. (vv. 7-11)

Jesus will save us. He is a merciful, loving Savior who will always forgive us if we repent. His Father is our Father who loves us more tenderly than any human mother or father possibly can.

The doctrine of Hell reminds us to live a responsible life, to ask God to forgive our sins, and to try to imitate Jesus. It also reminds us to live a good and moral life because we never know when God will call us home.

For Reflection

What do you imagine Heaven to be like? What do you think you have to do to get there?

mortal sin
A serious violation of God's law of love that results in the loss of God's life (sanctifying grace) in the soul of the sinner. To commit mortal sin there must be grave matter, full knowledge of the evil done, and deliberate consent.

For Review

1. What is Heaven?
2. What are some Scriptural images of Heaven?
3. Define *Purgatory*.
4. What is the Communion of Saints?
5. Who is the "Church suffering" and what can we do for them?
6. What is the principal punishment of Hell?

For Review Answers (page 179)

1. Heaven is life of perfect eternal happiness forever in the presence of God.
2. Scriptural images of Heaven include a wedding feast, light, peace, life, paradise, the house of the Father, the heavenly Jerusalem.
3. Purgatory is the state for those who die in God's grace and friendship, but who need purification or cleansing in order to enter Heaven.
4. The Communion of Saints is the unity in Christ of all those whom he has redeemed—it includes the living, the saints in Heaven, and the souls in Purgatory.
5. The souls in Purgatory are the "Church suffering." We can pray for them and apply indulgences to them.
6. Eternal separation from the presence of God.

compare. Make a list of differences between Heaven and hell on the board.

- Discuss the ways that people choose to live in Heaven or in hell every day. To begin, point to the displayed images of Heaven. Then refer the students to the For Reflection question on page 179 ("What do you imagine Heaven to be like? What do you think you have to do to get there?"). Tell the students to describe Heaven, not what it looks like but how it feels:
  - How do people in Heaven feel about being there?
  - How do they feel about/toward the other people who are there?
  - What feelings accompany God's presence?
- Continue the discussion by having the students join together in small groups. Have them consider what activities create those same kinds of feelings, even if only in a much weaker form. Again, have the spokesperson from each group share a summary of the group's ideas.
- Repeat the exercise with the state of hell, discussing first what it feels like to be there and then secondly what activities in the here-and-now summon those same emotions. Before moving on, have the students turn to the final paragraph in the section Primary Source Quotations on page 181. Read C. S. Lewis's quotation. Then discuss Lewis's statement regarding the road to hell.
- Move on to the topic of Purgatory. Direct the students to look at the section "Purgatory" on pages 176–178. Summarize the information in the text about this state. Give particular emphasis to the material on the Communion of Saints. Tell the students that one of the earliest images of the Church (found in the Roman catacombs) is that of a ship or boat sailing in choppy waters. Jesus is at the helm, setting its course. Above the boat, cloudlike figures representing the faithful who have died and are present with God in Heaven fill the boat's sails with zephyrs of their prayers. The deck of the boat is crowded with sturdy folk working the oars. These are the living members of the Church whose shared efforts and prayer power the craft. Below decks are sleeping figures, representing the souls of those who have died (and who are in Purgatory), and are being supported and transported by the efforts and prayers of those on deck and those above the clouds. Tell the students that this image reminds us that all of us in the Church—living and dead—are in the same boat. (*Note:* If the students have questions about prayers for the dead and/or the question of indulgences, draw on the material in the

Background Information sections below to address the issues.)

- Go on to emphasize how Purgatory is a transitional state of purification in which the imperfect person encounters the perfection of God. Note that all people in Purgatory will eventually be in Heaven. Invite the students to suggest some experiences that might be considered *purgatorial*. Ask:
  - What are some experiences, though painful, that bring us closer to God, or open our eyes to see God's action in the world?
  - How might the popular slogan "No pain, no gain" be applied to the state of Purgatory?
- Suggest that faced with the perfect God, the imperfect person would find such an encounter necessarily purging and therefore painful. In this purgatorial encounter, we quickly come to the realization that we have not chosen consistently for God and neighbor, a realization that is not only agonizing but purifying as well.
- Have the students turn back in their texts to "The Last or General Judgment" on pages 173–175. Note on the outline on Handout 2 that the Second Coming is known as the Parousia, a word meaning "presence—presence of the Lord." Remind the students that at the Second Coming, our souls and bodies will be reunited (resurrection of the body) and the Final or General Judgment will take place.
- Again have art materials available and allow time for the students to draw their conception of Purgatory based on what they have read in the book and discussed in class. Afterward, have the students share their drawings. Discuss how the drawings compare. Make a list of differences between Heaven, hell, and Purgatory on the board. You might draw a triple Venn diagram to illustrate the differences and similarities.
- Direct attention to the section For Reflection on page 175. Discuss what the students think an incorruptible body might be like, and then have them share situations where they believe they have been judged with fairness. Finally, invite them to tell what sort of emotions/feelings the General Judgment elicits in them.
- Go on to explain that the General Judgment will be a public repetition of the particular judgment. Why? So that the justice, wisdom, and mercy of God may be glorified in the presence of all creation. It is not so much the event that vindicates the good and condemns the wicked, as it is the event that vindicates and completes the Kingdom of God. The General

Chapter 7 Quick View

Main Ideas

- The Life, Death, Resurrection, and Ascension of Jesus Christ is life's greatest "wonder." (pp. 160–162)
- The sacraments make God's work present and help us to celebrate the gift of Redemption. (p. 161)
- Creation itself is the first wonder of the world; it reveals God's love for us in profound ways. (pp. 161–162)
- The masterpiece of God's creation is human beings. (pp. 162–163)
- The Incarnation of Jesus Christ was the fulfillment of God's promises and effected our Salvation. (p. 163)
- The Incarnation teaches that humans have great dignity, that all creation has worth, and that God shares in both our personal joy and suffering. (pp. 163–164)
- The Kingdom of God was ushered in with the birth of Jesus; it brings structure to the events of our Redemption. (pp. 164–166)
- An essential part of Jesus' mission was his forgiveness of sin; he calls us to forgive others, including our enemies. (pp. 166–167)
- Another gift of our Redemption is that we can experience a deep friendship with Christ. (p. 168)
- It is through the events of the Paschal Mystery that our Redemption is ultimately won. (p. 169)
- God's gift of the Holy Spirit helps us to imitate Christ; by enacting the fruits of the Spirit we become more like him. (pp. 169–170)
- The study of the last things is called eschatology. (p. 171)
- We believe in the "resurrection of the flesh," that is, that our soul will be reunited with the body after the Final Judgment. (p. 172)
- We also believe that God will transform all material creation in Christ. (p. 172)
- Immediately after death, we will experience an individual, particular judgment to determine whether we will go to Heaven, Purgatory, or Hell. (pp. 173–174)
- At the Last or General Judgment, Christ will come again, and everyone will recognize God's saving plan in Christ Jesus. (p. 175)
- The virtue of hope helps us to look forward to the glorious day of Christ's Second Coming. (pp. 175–176)
- If we die in God's friendship and grace, and are perfectly purified, we will receive the reward of eternal life in Heaven. (pp. 175–176)
- Purgatory is the name for the place that those who die in God's grace and friendship but need purification or cleansing go before entering Heaven. (pp. 176–177)
- Our belief in the Communion of Saints, including the pilgrim Church, the Church suffering, and the Church triumphant, help to support our understanding of Purgatory. (pp. 176–177)
- Hell is the eternal separation from God brought on by deliberate mortal sin and the failure to repent. (p. 177)

Terms, People, Places

On a separate piece of paper, write the following statements. Then supply the missing term from the vocabulary list.

Beatific Vision
Communion of Saints
eschatology
Liturgy of the Word
mortal sin
Parousia
particular judgment
Purgatory
venial sins

Background Information

Purgatory and the Communion of Saints

Just as in their earthly life believers are united in the one Mystical Body, so after death those who live in a state of purification experience the same ecclesial solidarity which works through prayer, prayers for suffrage and love for their other brothers and sisters in the faith. Purification is lived in the essential bond created between those who live in this world and those who enjoy eternal beatitude.

—Pope John Paul II

Hell and Damnation

Eternal damnation, therefore, is not attributed to God's initiative because in his merciful love he can only desire the salvation of the beings he created. In reality, it is the creature who closes himself to his love. Damnation consists precisely in definitive separation from God, freely chosen by the human person and confirmed with death that seals his choice forever. God's judgment ratifies this state.

—Pope John Paul II

1. ____________ These weaken our relationship with God but do not destroy divine life in our souls.
2. ____________ A goal for our lives; this is a gift that we desire for eternal life.
3. ____________ A study of the "last things."
4. ____________ This is a time when we hear the Kingdom of God proclaimed.
5. ____________ A determination will be made at this time whether we go to Heaven immediately, need purification in Purgatory, or suffer the punishments of Hell.
6. ____________ The Second Coming of Christ when the Lord will judge the living and the dead.
7. ____________ Its principal punishment is separation from our loving God.
8. ____________ Catholic belief in this is based on Biblical passages that encourage us to pray for the dead.
9. ____________ It includes three groups: the pilgrim Church, the Church suffering, and the Church triumphant.

Primary Source Quotations

On Death

For we brought nothing into the world, just as we shall not be able to take anything out of it.

—1 Timothy 6:7

To the good man to die is gain. The foolish fear death as the greatest of evils, the wise desire it as a rest after the labors and the end of ills.

—St. Ambrose

On the Brink of Hell

However wicked I may be, however great a sinner, I *must* hope that I should get to Heaven. You forbid me to despair.

—Charles de Foucauld

If I saw the gates of Hell open and I stood on the brink of the abyss, I should not despair, I should not lose my hope of mercy, because I should trust in Thee, my God.

—St. Gemma Galgani

On Heaven

God is so good and merciful that to obtain Heaven is sufficient to ask it of him in our hearts.

—St. Benedict Joseph Labré

To get to heaven, turn right and keep straight. The peace of the celestial city is the perfectly ordered and harmonious enjoyment of God, and of one another in God.

—St. Augustine, *City of God*, 426

In his novel *The Screwtape Letters*, C. S. Lewis wrote, "The safest road to Hell is the gradual one—the gentle slope, soft underfoot, without sudden turnings, without milestones, without signposts." What did Lewis mean by that statement? Is Lewis correct? Offer evidence.

Ongoing Assignments

As you cover the material in this chapter, choose and complete at least three of these assignments.

1. Research and report on any two of the so-called "wonders of the world" that you find interesting.
2. Great and impressive basilicas, churches, and abbeys belong on any list of great wonders of the Christian world. Do an illustrated slide or PowerPoint presentation on one of the following (or a similarly famous) churches or basilicas:
   - St. Peter's Basilica in Vatican City
   - Sistine Chapel in Vatican City
   - Chartres Cathedral in Chartres, France
   - St. Mark's Basilica in Venice, Italy
   - Mont Saint-Michel in Normandy, France
   - Basilica of the National Shrine of the Immaculate Conception in Washington, DC

Chapter 7 Quick View

Review Lesson Objectives

The students will:

- review Chapter 7 in preparation for the chapter test.
- join in prayer together.

Judgment is the answer to the prayer, "Thy Kingdom come; thy will be done." Discuss with the students how this General Judgment differs from the particular judgment. Make a list of differences on the board and have the students copy this list in their notes.

- Quiz the students on the differences between particular judgment and General Judgment. For example, ask:
  - Which judgment happens immediately after death?
  - Which judgment occurs during the Second Coming of Christ?
  - Which occurs at the Parousia?
  - In which judgment will we have our bodies?
- Finally, assure the students that the Second Coming and General Judgment are not a time to fear. To discover what it is a time for, have the students look up Luke 21:28 in their Bibles and write the verse in the space provided on Handout 2. (*"A time to . . . stand erect and raise your heads because your redemption is at hand."*)
- Instead of using one of the students' praise prayers, consider concluding this lesson by singing or listening to a recording that speaks to the Second Coming—e.g., "The Battle Hymn of the Republic" or "Soon and Very Soon," and by leading the students in the Lord's Prayer.

Chapter 7: Redemption through the Paschal Mystery—Review Lesson

Bell Ringers

- Ask the students to offer their responses to the seven For Review questions on page 175 (answers are on page 196 of this text) and the six For Review questions on page 179 (answers are on page 199 of this text). Be sure to encourage the students to ask any other questions they may have.
- Collect the students' Ongoing Assignments for Chapter 7 (pages 181–182). Allow time for those who chose #2 (creating a PowerPoint presentation) to make their presentations to the class.

Teaching Approaches

Chapter Quick View (pages 180-182)

- Have the students complete the fill-in-the-blanks activity on Terms, People, Places, pages 180–181. Check responses (answers are on page 202 of this text).
- Use the Main Ideas section to review key points. Go through the ideas with the class, having the students refer back to the chapter pages listed in the text.
- Continue the review by going over some or all of the For Review questions from the chapter. If you wish, use a game format. Divide the class into teams. Call on a representative from a team to answer a question. If the representative has difficulty, allow him or her to get help from the team. Award five points for an individual's correct response, two points if the person needed help.
- Take some time to go over any material the students may have overlooked in their review or that you feel needs more attention. Allow time for the students to ask any questions they may have.
- As time allows, invite various students who handed in written or visual Ongoing Assignments reports to share their information with the group.
- Provide some quiet time for the students to study on their own.

Prayer Service

- Gather the students, with their books, in a circle around a lighted candle. Either write on the board or simply read aloud the following quotation from the late Irish poet John O'Donohue's book, *Anam Cara* (Cliff Street Books: New York, 1997), 228:

> I believe that our friends among the dead really mind us and look out for us. Often there might be a big boulder of misery over your path about to fall on you, but your friends among the dead hold it back until you have passed by.

- Invite the students to tell whether they agree with this sentiment. Then have them recall what they discovered about the Communion of Saints in their previous lesson. Encourage them to explain how those in the communion support one another. Remind the students that all of us in the Communion of Saints are "in the same boat," as it were, all pulling for one another.
- Call attention to the Reflection question on page 182. Invite the students to recall the names of the deceased who rely on their prayers. Then lead the students in

---

182 Jesus Christ: Source of Our Salvation

Chapter 7 Quick View

- St. Joseph's Oratory, Montreal, Quebec, Canada

3. Read Psalm 104, which praises God for his wondrous creation. Find a picture that speaks to you of God's grandeur. Then compose your own prayer of praise to God for the wonders of creation. Create a poster of your prayer and picture.
4. Read Matthew 18:23–35. What is the point of this parable? Rewrite it in a modern-day setting. Be sure to make the same point that Jesus does in his parable.
5. Prepare a report that contrasts belief in reincarnation with the Catholic doctrine of the resurrection of the body.
6. Research and report on what one of the following religions teaches about the afterlife: Judaism, Islam, a Native American religion.
7. Read 1 Corinthians 15:35–58. Answer the following questions:
   - What analogy from agriculture does St. Paul use to describe what will happen to our bodies in the resurrection?
   - How will the resurrection take place as described in verses 50–54?
   - What is the "sting of death"?
   - Assemble Scripture quotations related to Christ's Second Coming.
8. Report on the life of a saint that Pope Benedict XVI mentions in his encyclical *Spe Salvi*: St. Josephine Bakhita. See: www.vatican.va/news_services/liturgy/saints/ns_lit_doc_20001001_giuseppina-bakhita_en.html
9. Devise a project with several other classmates to put into action two of the corporal works of mercy: visiting the sick and burying the dead. For example: (1) visit a nursing home and chat with some of the lonely patients there; (2) do chores for an elderly neighbor; (3) help serve a luncheon (through your parish's hospitality committee) for the family members and friends of a deceased parishioner after the funeral Mass and burial.
10. Read the parable of the Weeds (Mt 13:24–30, 36–43) and the parable of the Dragnet (Mt 13:47–50). Write an interpretation of each these parables. In the parable of the Weeds, identify the following symbols: the field, the sower of the wheat, the good seed, the sower of the weeds, the weeds, the harvest, the harvesters.

Prayer

Pray these prayers for the souls in Purgatory:

Prayer for the Forgotten Dead
O merciful God, take pity on those souls who have no particular friends and intercessors to recommend them to You, who either through negligence of those who are alive or through length of time, are forgotten by all. Spare them, O Lord, and remember Your own when others forget to appeal to Your mercy. Let not the souls You have created be parted from You, their Creator. Amen.

Prayer for the Faithful Departed
Eternal rest grant unto them, O Lord, and let perpetual light shine upon them. May their souls and the souls of all the faithful departed, through the mercy of God, rest in peace. Amen.

- *Reflection*: Which deceased relatives, friends, or acquaintances need your prayers?
- *Resolution*: In the upcoming weeks, offer some prayers for the souls in Purgatory.

Terms, People, Places Answers (pages 180-181)

1. venial sins
2. Beatific Vision
3. eschatology
4. Liturgy of the Word
5. particular judgment
6. Parousia
7. mortal sin
8. Purgatory
9. Communion of Saints

Review Lesson Homework

1. Complete any unfinished Ongoing Assignments.
2. Reread Chapter 7.
3. Study for the Chapter 7 Test.

Redemption through the Paschal Mystery 183

Chapter 7 Quick View

Test Lesson Homework

1. Read the following text section of Chapter 8: "The Light of Christ" (pages 186–187).
2. Examine the Chapter 8 Ongoing Assignments on page 208.

praying the "Prayer for the Faithful Departed" on page 182.

- Continue the prayer by asking the students for a show of hands of how many know the names of their great, great, great grandparents on their mother's side (most likely not many). Invite them to consider the many relatives and others who have gone before them who may stand in need of their prayers. Likewise, remind the students of the many people who die alone and forgotten. These "least ones" (Mt 25:45), too, demand our prayers.
- Lead the students in praying the "Prayer for the Forgotten Dead" on page 182. Then, conclude by praying the Hail Mary together, with perhaps a bit more emphasis on the words, "Pray for us sinners now and at the hour of our death."
- Before the students leave, distribute copies of Chapter 7, Handout 3, "Prayer for a Happy Death." Explain that the prayer is by former Philippine president Corazon C. Aquino, who died August 1, 2009. Suggest the students include this simple but profound prayer in their daily prayers.

Chapter 7 Test Lesson

Teaching Approaches

- Allow sufficient time for the students to work on the Chapter 7 Test (starting on page 291 of the TWE and also online at www.avemariapress.com). Collect tests as the students finish.

Chapter 7 Test Answers

Part 1: Fill in the Blanks. (2 points each)

1. Purgatory
2. Incarnation
3. Confirmation

4 & 5. sacrament; grace

6. Kingdom of God
7. Eschatology
8. Baptism
9. hell

10 & 11. Holy Orders; Matrimony

12 & 13. repentance; belief

14 & 15. Gehenna; Hades

16. Paschal Mystery
17. Parousia

18 & 19. Penance; Anointing of the Sick

20. Heaven
21. Beatific Vision
22. Communion of Saints

Part 2: True or False. (2 points each)

1. F 2. T 3. T 4. F 5. F 6. F 7. F 8. F 9. T 10. F 11. F 12. F 13. F 14. T 15. T

Part 3: Short Answers. (3 points each)

1. The fruits of the Holy Spirit are charity, joy, peace, patience, kindness, goodness, generosity, gentleness, faithfulness, modesty, self-control, and chastity.
2. Answers may vary a bit but should evidence the following understanding: The particular judgment takes place immediately after death. It determines whether we gain entrance into Heaven immediately, need purification in Purgatory, or must suffer the isolation of hell. The General Judgment takes place on the last day after the resurrection of all the dead; this judgment will reveal each person's eternal relationship with God and thus fulfill the Kingdom.

Part 4: After Death. (10 total points)

1. A 2. F 3. C 4. D 5. E 6. B

Part 5: Take-Home Essay. (10 points)

The seven sacraments help us to celebrate the wonder of the Incarnation and our Salvation. The Lord is present in the special moments of our lives: birth (Baptism), growth (Confirmation), meals (Eucharist), forgiveness (Penance), marriage (Matrimony), special ministry (Holy Orders), and illness and death (Anointing of the Sick). They connect us with the Paschal Mystery through participation in the Death and rising of Christ through Baptism. We experience God's forgiveness in the Sacrament of Penance and are strengthened by receiving Holy Communion. We receive the fruits of the Holy Spirit through the Sacraments of Baptism and Confirmation.

Chapter 8: Living the Paschal Mystery: A Call to Holiness

Introduction

There's no heavier burden than a great potential!

—**Linus from *Peanuts***

Linus speaks for us all, doesn't he? This is especially true when it comes to our "holiness heritage" and our vocation to saintliness. We tend to view both as prospects too prodigious, as burdens too heavy to bear. We consider holiness as wholly beyond us. We shrug off sainthood as purely for the pious. And yet, holiness is our original condition, our original blessing; and sainthood is the home of all the baptized. While ours may well be a heavy potential, it is not a burdensome one. "My yoke," says Jesus, "is easy and my burden light" (Mt 11:30).

Recognizing that our potential may be a bit daunting, this chapter helps the students recognize what it means to become holy and to claim saintliness. They learn that all holiness exists in relationship, for that is how God—Father, Son, and Spirit—is holy. They discover what virtue is, how the virtues lead us to choosing what is right and good, and what living the life of virtue is all about. In their study of the theological virtues, the students discover what it means and what it takes to be a person of faith. They begin to appreciate how hope is the confidence that God will act on our behalf. They take a deeper look at what it means to say that God is love, and begin to appreciate that since God loves us—and loves us first—we can love God and love others in return.

This same loving God even provides the gift of grace, which is the means to love. This gift is the divine spark that sets the fires of love ablaze in us, blessing us in numerous ways. It increases our faith and hope. It empowers us to draw on the inspiring Spirit and his many gifts and it helps us grow in holiness though the moral virtues. We have been endowed with other gifts as well. Human reason is the gift that makes it possible for us to discover the God-given laws of the universe and to hear God's voice in all that is. The gift of free will empowers us to choose between alternatives, to make our lives our own, and, most importantly, to choose the good for others.

The chapter also helps the students better understand that it is through our informed conscience that we choose to be saintly. The students learn ways to form their conscience as well as how to go about making a conscientious decision. Conscientious decision-making, in turn, leads us closer and closer to holiness, the dwelling place of the saints.

Advance Preparations

Prepare or have on hand:

For Lesson 1

- Corrected copies of the Chapter 7 Test
- A recording of "This Little Light of Mine" and player (optional)
- Copies of Chapter 8, Handout 1, "Saintliness"

Chapter Objectives

To help the students:

- recognize that they are called to saintliness.
- discover human virtues.
- appreciate how the cardinal virtues help us live out our Redemption.
- recognize the theological virtues, what they accomplish in us, and how they empower us.
- distinguish between and among the different types of grace.
- examine charisms, especially the gifts of the Holy Spirit.
- recognize that real love often demands suffering.
- investigate the gifts of human reason and free will.
- appreciate how the formation of a sound conscience is crucial to moral decision making.

For Lesson 2

- Bibles
- A recording of "Let Justice Roll Like a River" by Marty Haugen and player (optional)
- Copies of Chapter 8, Handout 2, "The Four Faces of Justice"
- Copies of Chapter 8, Handout 3, "Just or Unjust?"

For Lesson 3

- Bibles
- Copies of Chapter 8, Handout 4, "I Think Faith Is Like . . . "
- A recording of a hymn such as "Where Charity and Love Prevail" or "Ubi Caritas" and player (optional)
- Copies of Chapter 8, Handout 5, "Measuring Up to Love"

For Lesson 4

- Bibles
- Paper plates, markers, masking or double-sided tape
- A recording of the hymn "Amazing Grace" and of a hymn such as "We Are Many Parts" by Marty Haugen and player (optional)
- Candle and matches

For Lesson 5

- Bibles
- A recording of the Beatles' song, "All You Need Is Love" and a player (optional)

For the Chapter 8 Review Lesson

- A recording of a hymn to the Holy Spirit such as "Spirit of God" by James E. More Jr. and player (optional)

For the Chapter 8 Test Lesson

- Copies of the Chapter 8 Test (starting on page 291 of the TWE and also online at www.avemariapress.com).

Chapter 8 Handouts

- Handout 1, Saintliness—The students discover how saintliness is their birthright, vocation, task, and challenge.
- Handout 2, The Four Faces of Justice—The students discuss the four types of justice.
- Handout 3, Just or Unjust?—The students decide whether a situation is just or unjust and then evaluate how just they themselves are.
- Handout 4, I Think Faith Is Like . . . —The students choose what they think faith is like.
- Handout 5, Measuring Up to Love—The students evaluate how well they feel they are living out the virtue of charity.

Chapter 8: Living the Paschal Mystery: A Call to Holiness—Lesson 1

Bell Ringers

- Distribute the corrected Chapter 7 Test. Go over the test with the students, using it as a means to review the previous chapter. Address any remaining questions or concerns the students may have.
- Ask the students to define the word "saint." Then have them describe what saints are like and what it takes to become a saint. List their responses on the board and discuss. Create a class description of what it takes to be a saint.

Teaching Approaches

The Light of Christ (pages 186-87)

- Ask the students to raise their hands if they think they are holy or saint-like. Tell the students that most of us think we are not saint-like, because we mistakenly believe that "holy" suggests a superiority that we can never obtain. Assure them that nothing could be farther from the truth. Jesus himself said that the "last shall be first."
- Write the following quotation on the board: "**We cannot do great things on earth, only small things with great love**."—**Mother Teresa.** Ask the students to explain what they think Mother Teresa meant. Discuss the quotation as a class.
- Make sure the students appreciate that holiness is not the "more-than-human," nor is saintliness beyond their reach. Note how the text tells us that holiness is our heritage and sainthood our vocation (pages 186–187).
- Ask the students to describe how this understanding of the saints differs from their description from the beginning of class. What does it take for us to be a saint?
- Distribute copies of Chapter 8, Handout 1, "Saintliness." Have one of the students read aloud the passage from Genesis 1:27–28, 31. Point out that while canonization might be for the few, we are all called to be saints. We are all called to conform to the image of God.
- Ask another student to read the quotation from Pope John Paul II on the handout, under the subheading "Your Vocation."

The Light of Christ

A little boy was on vacation with his family, touring one of the great cathedrals in Europe. The child was fascinated with the great stained-glass windows that adorned the massive structure. He especially was awestruck by the sun streaming through the stained glass and the beautiful, rainbow colors that splashed on the floor of the cathedral. He looked up to his father and asked, "Who are all those people in the pretty window?" His dad replied, "They are the saints."

Later that night as the father was tucking his boy into bed, his son told him, "I know who the saints are."

The father smiled and said, "Do you? Who are they?" The boy replied, "They are the persons who let the light shine through."

The boy in the story was correct. Saints are indeed those who allow the light of Christ to shine through. The word *saint* comes from the Latin word, *sanctus*, which means "holy." The words *holy* and *holiness* originally referred to God. In the Old Testament, *holy* meant being separated from the ordinary, everyday world. God is holy in the sense that he is "wholly other," perfectly good, and totally and absolutely separated from evil and sin. When we speak of people, places (like a cathedral), or things (like a blessed water) as being "holy," it is because they are related to God. God is the source of all holiness because he alone is truly holy, that is, all-good and separate from all evil.

We are called by God to be holy people, that is, to be good and to be Christ-like. This is a call or **vocation**, one given to us by Jesus himself. With the help of God's grace, the presence of the Holy Spirit in our lives, and a life of self-denial and prayer, each of us can work at growing in holiness, that is, to separate ourselves from sin and evil. This is a worthy goal, one that not only makes us better people for this world but also helps us gain a place in God's

Growing in Everyday Holiness

Every day presents many ways we can let the light of Christ shine through our lives. Read through the list of situations where you have the opportunity to bring Christ to others. For each category, evaluate and briefly write how you are doing, as well as how you can improve in this area.

At Home
- I readily obey my parents without arguing.
- I am patient with my brothers and sisters.
- I volunteer to do some chores without being asked.
- I willingly spend time with my family.
- I make a point to be on time for family meals.

At School
- I am respectful of my teachers and other adults.
- I greet my classmates.
- I try to make new friends.
- I fully participate in the extracurricular activities of which I am a member.
- I resist temptations to cheat.

Other
- I carefully listen to others when they speak to me.
- I go to Mass every weekend.
- I pray every day.
- I'm careful with how I use the Internet, spending my time wisely and avoiding harmful and immoral sites.
- I share some of my wealth of talents, time, and money with others, including those who are less fortunate.

Assignment
Write a profile of the "holiest" person that you personally know. How does the light of Christ shine through this person? What might you have to do in your own life to become more like him or her?

Lesson 1 Objectives

The students will:

- review Chapter 7.
- critique the common description of a saint.
- discover that they are called to be saints.
- reflect on their personal vocations.

Lesson 1 Preview

This lesson introduces the students to their vocation to saintliness. Be sure to take some time with this concept since many young people believe that a holy person is some sort of super-holy person. They may also figure that saintliness is something beyond their abilities to attain. Holiness, however, is our birthright, and saintliness is the destiny to which God calls each and every one of us. This lesson strives to help the students recognize both these truths, and it assures them that there is plenty of help along the way.

eternal kingdom. In short, we are called to be saints, holy ones of God, who, with the help of the Holy Spirit, allow the life and light of Christ to shine through us to attract others to him and to his heavenly Father.

Don't think of saints as "perfect people" or without sin. They aren't. Also, don't think you can become a saint in one day. Becoming a saint is a lifelong task. Holiness requires perseverance, repenting of our sins when we fall, fighting temptations that come our way, and the constant help of God and the graces he sends to us. The key to growing in holiness, goodness, and freedom from sin requires staying close to Jesus Christ who meets us in his Church, in the sacraments, and in prayer. These are tasks addressed in this chapter.

For Reflection

What is your reaction to the thought that you are called to be a saint?

Living a Life of Virtue (*CCC*, 1803-1845)

The Paschal Mystery of Christ's saving actions has redeemed us. This means that the Passion, Death, Resurrection, and glorious Ascension of Jesus Christ gained for us eternal life and made us adopted children of the Triune God. We need God's grace in order to accept grace. His preparation of us for the reception of grace is already the work of grace. For our part, we are then to accept and live the grace of Redemption by

- repenting of our sins,
- believing in the Gospel of Jesus Christ, and
- living a life of holiness.

Living a virtuous life and cooperating with the graces God sends to us are two important ways to grow in holiness.

What is a **virtue**? In general, "a virtue is an habitual and firm disposition to do the good" (*CCC*, 1803). Virtues enable us to perform good acts and to give the best of ourselves, empowering us to become what God wants us to be. Practicing virtues helps us to be more like Jesus Christ. There are two major categories of virtues: the human virtues (especially the four cardinal virtues) and the theological virtues.

vocation
A word that means "call." For Catholics the primary call is to be disciples of Jesus Christ. This call, given at Baptism, requires Catholics to bring God's love to others and to share the Good News.

virtue
A firm attitude, stable disposition, and habitual disposition of our intellect and will that regulates our actions, directs our passions, and guides our conduct according to reason and faith.

Lesson 1 Homework

1. Ask the students to turn to Ongoing Assignments on page 208. Have them choose three of the listed assignments to complete prior to the conclusion of this chapter. Tell the students the assignments are due on the day they gather for their chapter review.
2. To prepare for their next lesson, have the students read "Living a Life of Virtue—Human Virtues" (pages 187–191).
3. Remind the students to complete the Assignment section of the activity "Growing in Everyday Holiness" (page 186) for their next session.

- Ask another student to read aloud the quotation from the *Dogmatic Constitution on the Church* on the handout, under the heading "Your Life-Long Task." Go on to explain that the original meaning of "saint" was "baptized." St. Paul, for example, regularly addresses his converts as saints (holy ones), for a saint is a sinner who has been converted. At the same time, St. Paul had no qualms about pointing out to his "saints" their failings (e.g., 1 Cor 4). Conversion to saintliness, it seems, is neither an automatic nor a one-time deal. Saintliness comes from a lifetime's worth of time and effort.
- Ask another student to read aloud the last quotation from Pope John Paul II on the handout, under the heading "Your Challenge." Then refer them to the question in the For Reflection feature on page 187 of the text. Have the students respond to the question in the space provided on the handout under the heading "Your Reaction." When the students finish writing, invite them to share with a partner.
- Remind the students that sainthood is our vocation, but we must choose the path we will take to get there. Mother Teresa also said, "What we are doing is just a drop in the ocean. But if that drop was not in the ocean, I think the ocean would be less because of that missing drop. I do not agree with the big way of doing things." Ask the students to take a moment to think about what small splash they will make in the ocean of life.
- Have the students think about their vocation by drawing a table with three columns. Read to them a quotation by Frederick Buechner: "Vocation is the place where your passion meets the world's great need." Have them label the three columns: My Passion, My Talents, and The World's Great Need. Give them some time to list their passions and talents, then have them write related needs of the world. Note that the list does not have to be particularly religious. Finally, challenge them to consider what actions, careers, or volunteer work they might do to connect their passion and the world's great need.
- Call attention to the feature "Growing in Everyday Holiness" on page 186. Explain that the categories listed (*At Home, At School, Other*) offer ways to meet the challenge of saintliness/holiness in our everyday lives. Direct the students to respond to the categories' statements in their journals. Explain, however, that they are to do the Assignment on separate paper as homework to be handed in at their next session.
- Consider playing some background music while the students write. As time allows, encourage, but don't demand, sharing.

Chapter 8: Living the Paschal Mystery: A Call to Holiness—Lesson 2

Bell Ringers

- Call on a number of students to share their essays on the Assignment section of the activity "Growing in Everyday Holiness" (page 186). Collect the essays.
- Write the following on the board as the headings of three columns: **Repent, Believe, Act Accordingly**. Point out that these three are the imperatives for living the grace of the Paschal Mystery, the grace of Redemption. Under "Repent," write **Of Our Sins**. Under "Believe," write **The Good News**. Under "Act Accordingly," write **With Virtue**. Stress to the students that although Salvation is pure gift, it does require repentance, faith, and virtuous living.

Teaching Approaches

Living a Life of Virtue—Human Virtues (pages 187-191)

- For this lesson and for the rest of this chapter, suggest that the students create vocabulary flash cards to help them practice memorizing the definitions. Instruct them to write the vocabulary term on one side and the definition on the other.
- Introduce the topic of virtue by telling the students that when a man asked, "How do I get to Carnegie Hall?" the great pianist Arthur Rubinstein allegedly replied, "Practice, practice, practice." The same may be said about Heaven and virtue. Practice makes perfect.
- Go on to tell the students that playing the piano like Rubenstein, or playing football like Peyton Manning, requires tackling a difficult subject and working hard at it until it becomes habit.
- Discuss how we form habits. Ask students to describe good habits they have worked to develop. Encourage them to notice how habits make it more likely that we will make a given choice—good or bad—and how they make it easier or harder for us to keep or break a resolution. Invite the students to give examples of *good* moral habits they have observed in themselves or in others their age.
- Call attention to the text section "Human Virtues" on page 188. Note now the text describes their purpose: to "help us to choose the good and then to follow the

---

188 Jesus Christ: Source of Our Salvation

cardinal virtues
The four hinge virtues that support moral living: prudence, justice, fortitude, and temperance.

vice
A bad habit, such as laziness, that inclines us to choose the evil rather than the good.

religion
The relationship between God and humans that results in a body of beliefs and a set of practices: creed, cult, and code. Religion expresses itself in worship and service to God and by extension to all people and all creation.

Human Virtues

Virtues that we are able to acquire by our own human efforts are known as human or moral virtues. The human virtues help us to choose the good and then to follow the right course of action. According to the *Catechism of the Catholic Church*:

> Human virtues are firm attitudes, stable dispositions, habitual perfections of intellect and will that govern our actions, order our passions, and guide our conduct according to reason and faith. They make possible ease, self-mastery, and joy in leading a morally good life. (*CCC*, 1804)

Effort on our part can help us acquire and strengthen the human virtues. They are also called *moral virtues* because when we perform morally good acts, virtues become good habits that help us draw closer to God and to relate to other people with Christ-like love. There are countless human virtues, including forgiveness, compassion, courage, courtesy, devotion, generosity, honesty, humility, kindness, loyalty, patience, purity, respect, and trustworthiness. However, four moral virtues play a central role in living a moral life. They are the **cardinal virtues** prudence, justice, fortitude, and temperance. The term *cardinal* comes from the Latin *cardo*, which means "hinge." These four virtues are the source of all other virtues.

How can we gain the cardinal virtues and make them part of our lives? We gain cardinal virtues through understanding their meaning and by putting them into practice through frequent repetition. However, it is not as easy as it may sound. Because humans are weakened by the effects of Original Sin and are prone to laziness, moral living is a challenge. Yet, God helps us in this struggle to live a virtuous life by sending us the Holy Spirit and giving us graces that enable us to grow in holiness. A worthy goal for all is to live a virtuous life. Living the virtues is a foundation for being more like Jesus Christ. A brief description of the four cardinal virtues follows.

Prudence

Prudence is a virtue that helps us decide responsibly. It equates with common sense and wisdom. Following the ancient Greek philosopher Aristotle, St. Thomas Aquinas defined prudence as "right reason in action." When we exercise prudence, we use our memory, foresight, imagination, and openness to learning to help our intellects discover the right course of action in every situation. Prudence helps form our conscience and the right means of achieving what is good. In short, prudence is a virtue that helps us think and judge carefully before acting so that we can make wise choices and do things well. The *Catechism* teaches that:

> With the help of this virtue we apply moral principles to particular cases without error and overcome doubts about the good to achieve and the evil to avoid. (*CCC*, 1806)

Lesson 2 Objectives

The students will:

- define virtue and vice.
- appreciate how the cardinal virtues help us live out our Redemption.
- describe the four types of justice.
- choose the best way they can put the cardinal virtues into practice.

Lesson 2 Preview

Aristotle said, "It is easy to perform a good action, but not easy to acquire a settled habit of performing such actions." This lesson aims to help students on the path of getting into the habit called virtue. As you lead the students through the material, help them avoid any tendency to see virtue as the opposite of joy. Rather, point out how the virtuous life is the only way to true enjoyment and ultimate happiness.

Consider the example of Tara, a high school student, deciding whether or not to go to a concert on a school night. Tara has an important exam the next day, which demands several hours of study. After weighing all the options, and considering that if she went to the concert, she would likely do poorly on the exam, Tara made a prudent decision to forego the pleasure of the moment for the greater good of academic success. She stayed home, studied, and got a good grade on the exam.

The opposite of a virtue is a **vice**, or a bad habit that is acquired by repeated sin in violation of the proper norms of morality. Impetuosity, or acting on the spur of the moment without thinking, is contrary to the virtue of prudence. For example, when Tim, a college freshman, is free of parental supervision, he gives in to the temptation to party and engages in binge drinking the first days he is on campus. His impetuous behavior does not consider the consequences of his snap decision, consequences that can lead to great physical and spiritual harm.

Justice

Justice consists of a person always giving his or her due to God and neighbor. Justice toward God results in the virtue of **religion** where we worship God and thank him as the source of all that is good. God is all-loving, the One who calls us into existence; he is due our love and adoration. Justice toward our neighbor requires that we respect the rights of others and work for equity in regard to persons and the common good. Catholic teaching has distinguished among four types of justice: commutative, distributive, legal, and social.

Commutative justice regulates relationships of exchange, for example, in contracts between individuals and social groups. An example of commutative justice would be if you agree to baby-sit your neighbor's child for a given wage per hour, then your neighbor is obligated to pay you the negotiated amount. This is only fair. Respect for the dignity of

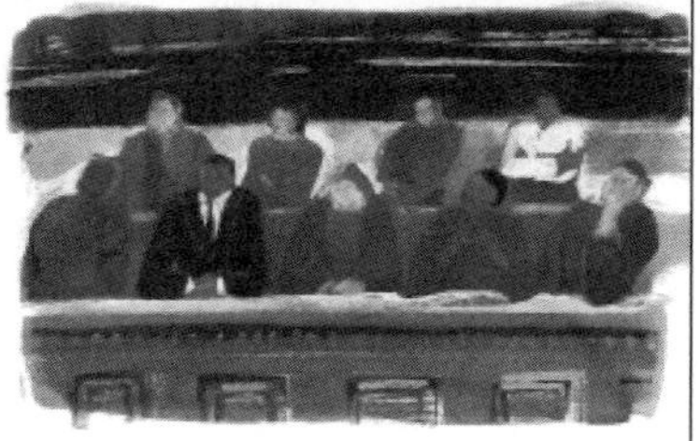

others takes place when we fulfill our obligations toward them.

Distributive justice protects and guarantees the common welfare. It seeks the fair distribution of the goods of creation. Governmental agencies are often responsible for guaranteeing distributive justice to a country's citizens, especially the most vulnerable. Laws that require citizens to pay taxes to support school systems, police forces, and health-care agencies for the poor are ways that the government and citizens support the work of distributive justice.

Legal justice governs what individuals owe society as a whole. Because we are members of a society, living with and for other people, we have the duty to contribute to the common good. Therefore, it is a work of legal justice to obey the just laws of the society in which we live—for example, paying taxes, serving on juries, and coming to the aid of our fellow citizens in times of peril.

Finally, *social justice* applies the Gospel message of Jesus Christ to the structures, systems, and laws of society in order to protect the dignity of persons and guarantee the rights of individuals. Social justice holds that each person has a right to a fair voice in the economic, political, and social institutions of the society in which he or she lives. According to one's ability, each person has a right to contribute to how society functions. Therefore, social justice is sometimes called *contributive justice*.

Lesson 2 Homework

1. Call attention to the feature "Practicing Cardinal Virtues" on page 194. Direct the students to undertake at least one of the suggested activities.
2. Assign the first five For Review questions on page 195.
3. To prepare for their next lesson, have the students read, "Living a Life of Virtue—Theological Virtues" (pages 191–196).

right course of action." Have the students underline the word "right" in their texts.

- Have the students look up and read Wisdom 8:7 in their Bibles:

  > . . . if one loves righteousness, the fruits of her (Wisdom's) works are virtues; for she teaches temperance and prudence, justice and fortitude, and nothing in life is more useful for mortals than these.

- Note the virtues mentioned in the Scripture passage. List them on the board in the following order:
  - **Prudence**
  - **Justice**
  - **Fortitude**
  - **Temperance**
- Invite the students to discuss why these virtues are important to living well. Be sure the students understand that although these virtues are not the only virtues, they are the "hinges" on which all the other virtues turn. For example, chastity is the virtue that helps humans moderate the desire for sex. Chastity, therefore, is categorized under the cardinal virtue of temperance.
- Point out how the text notes that St. Thomas calls prudence "right reason in action" (page 188). Once again, have the students underline the word "right." The emphasis is important. Explain that we cannot simply make a decision and then describe it as "prudential." Prudence requires us to distinguish between what is right and what is wrong. Prudence, therefore, is the virtue that helps us recognize what is good and what is evil in a situation.
- Go on to suggest to the students three steps to making a prudent decision:
  - Step 1: Follow the dictates of our conscience and the counsel of others.
  - Step 2: Judge correctly based on the evidence at hand.
  - Step 3: Act according to the norms of the decision made.
- If we later find that our judgment is incorrect, then we need to judge again and, perhaps, make amends for our imprudent judgment.
- Tell the students to note in particular the third step. The prudent person is one who *does* the good, as opposed to one who merely *knows* the good. For example, the imprudent person may know it is best to

cross a busy intersection at the semaphore but jay-walks anyway.

- Before moving on, note the opposite of virtue—*vice* (page 188). Point out that bad choices exercised repeatedly become habits as well; these are called vices. Invite the students to suggest vices that are the opposite of prudence, for example:
    - Thoughtlessness—failing to consider the consequences of an action.
    - Impetuosity—failing to consider all available means to an end.
    - Negligence—failing to act according to the norms of the decision made.
    - Inconstancy—repeatedly failing to act on (to do) what is right, while knowing what is right.
- If possible, introduce the virtue of justice by singing or playing a recording of "Let Justice Roll Like a River" by Marty Haugen.
- Afterward, tell the students that the word "justice" derives from the Latin word *jus*, meaning "right," a term that implies a relationship of equality. If an unjust state of affairs is "made right," we mean that a certain equality has been established/re-established. For example, if you lend someone money, it is right for you to receive back what you lent (that which is your due); likewise the person to whom you lent the money is obliged to hand over the money that is due to you. Wherever there is a "right," there is a debt of sorts, an obligation on the part of someone else to establish a relation of equality—that is, to make things *right*. Justice, then, means a *relationship of equality*. The just person habitually wills such a relationship of equality.
- Stress to the students that even though we often hear the term "justice" used in a negative sense (e.g., "she was brought to justice"), the focus of the virtue is positive. While lawful authorities may justly punish evildoers, our concern as individuals is to respect and protect the rights of others, particularly when we owe them a debt or when our actions might restrict their exercise of or deprive them of their rights.
- Distribute copies of Chapter 8, Handout 2, "The Four Faces of Justice." Use the quotations from the Church's treasury of social teaching to discuss the four types of justice mentioned in the text (pages 189–190).
    - Commutative justice—regulates relationships of reciprocity.
    - Distributive justice—champions the common good.

Justice also equates with avoiding all forms of discrimination and prejudice and justice always respects the God-given rights of other people. The person practicing this virtue looks out for the needs of the poor and powerless, those whom society tends to ignore.

Fortitude

Fortitude is another word for courage. It is a virtue that enables a person to conquer fears, even the fear of death, for a just cause. Fortitude helps us overcome fears of other people's criticisms, failure, rejection, and disappointment when we are trying to do right. The virtue of fortitude can help in resisting peer pressure, which is often the source that leads to sin.

How can you increase this virtue for your life? One way is through acts of self-denial. Being consistent in all our endeavors, especially by hard work, gives us the courage to follow through when tempted to take the easy way out. The Holy Spirit also strengthens us with the gift of fortitude so that we can live a Christian life.

The ultimate example of fortitude is martyrdom. Recall that *martyr* means "witness." Though most of us will never be called to lay down our lives for others, we do witness to our faith each time we are courageous enough to do the right thing, especially in the face of strong peer pressure. For example, it takes fortitude to stick up for a classmate who is picked on or to not cheat on a test when everyone else is doing it. Doing the right thing often takes the courage of standing alone. St. Bruno wrote,

> What shall I say of fortitude, without which neither wisdom nor justice is of any value? Fortitude is not of the body, but is a constancy of soul; with it we are conquerors in righteousness, patiently bearing all adversities, and in prosperity are not puffed up. Fortitude is never conquered, or if conquered, is not fortitude.

Temperance

Temperance is a virtue of self-control, delayed gratification, and moderation. Humans are weak and subject to sin. We live in a world where advertisements and other media tempt us to indulge all of our appetites. A common mantra today is "If it feels good, do it." But the trouble is, the pursuit of pleasure can get out of hand. When we are intemperate, the vices of greed, gluttony, and lust control us. Temperance is the "moral virtue that moderates the attraction of pleasures and provides balance in the use of created goods" (*CCC*, 1809). As humans, we have the wherewithal to temper the pleasures of food, drink, and sex in ways that God intends for our own good.

St. Thomas Aquinas distinguished three parts to practicing the virtue of temperance. *Abstinence* tempers our desires for food and other pleasure-producing substances like tobacco and drugs. *Sobriety* moderates our desires for alcoholic beverages. And

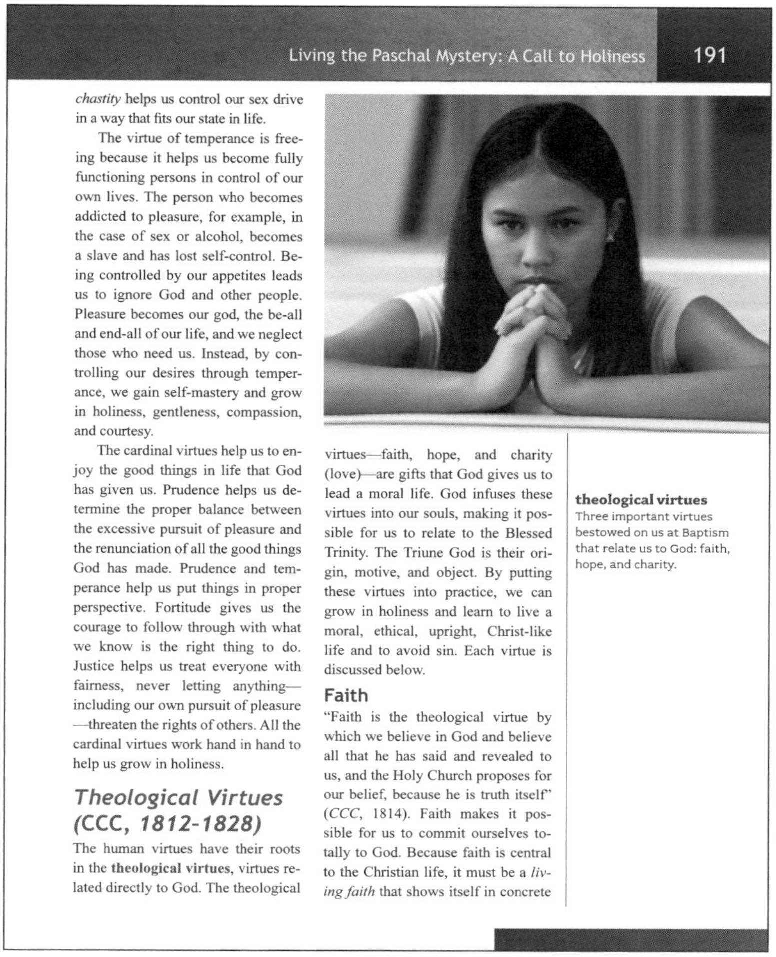

Living the Paschal Mystery: A Call to Holiness 191

chastity helps us control our sex drive in a way that fits our state in life.

The virtue of temperance is freeing because it helps us become fully functioning persons in control of our own lives. The person who becomes addicted to pleasure, for example, in the case of sex or alcohol, becomes a slave and has lost self-control. Being controlled by our appetites leads us to ignore God and other people. Pleasure becomes our god, the be-all and end-all of our life, and we neglect those who need us. Instead, by controlling our desires through temperance, we gain self-mastery and grow in holiness, gentleness, compassion, and courtesy.

The cardinal virtues help us to enjoy the good things in life that God has given us. Prudence helps us determine the proper balance between the excessive pursuit of pleasure and the renunciation of all the good things God has made. Prudence and temperance help us put things in proper perspective. Fortitude gives us the courage to follow through with what we know is the right thing to do. Justice helps us treat everyone with fairness, never letting anything—including our own pursuit of pleasure—threaten the rights of others. All the cardinal virtues work hand in hand to help us grow in holiness.

Theological Virtues (CCC, 1812-1828)

The human virtues have their roots in the **theological virtues**, virtues related directly to God. The theological virtues—faith, hope, and charity (love)—are gifts that God gives us to lead a moral life. God infuses these virtues into our souls, making it possible for us to relate to the Blessed Trinity. The Triune God is their origin, motive, and object. By putting these virtues into practice, we can grow in holiness and learn to live a moral, ethical, upright, Christ-like life and to avoid sin. Each virtue is discussed below.

Faith

"Faith is the theological virtue by which we believe in God and believe all that he has said and revealed to us, and the Holy Church proposes for our belief, because he is truth itself" (*CCC*, 1814). Faith makes it possible for us to commit ourselves totally to God. Because faith is central to the Christian life, it must be a *living faith* that shows itself in concrete

theological virtues
Three important virtues bestowed on us at Baptism that relate us to God: faith, hope, and charity.

- Legal justice—secures societal solidarity; it refers to rights and responsibilities of citizens to obey everyone else's rights and to obey laws that have been put in place to protect peace and social order.
- Social justice—seeks fair (re)distribution of resources, opportunities, and responsibilities; challenges the roots of oppression and injustice; empowers people to exercise self-determination and realize their full potential; and builds social solidarity and community capacity for collaborative action.

- Give students some time to memorize the definitions of each type of justice. Suggest that they create and study flashcards of each type of justice. For visual learners, invite them to draw a picture to remind them of the definition of the term.
- Distribute copies of Chapter 8, Handout 3, "Just or Unjust?" Have the students complete the first activity on the handout. Then, in small groups or as a class, have the students share and explain their choices. Note how justice is not a simple thing and how different people may perceive each situation differently.
- After the students share and discuss the five statements, have them complete the self-evaluation. It is not necessary to have the students share with you or others their self-evaluations. It is important, however,

For Enrichment

Invite the students to use one of the following prayers to strengthen one of the theological virtues within them, or recite these prayers before you begin each part of this lesson on the theological virtues.

Act of Faith
O, my God,
I believe that you are one God
in three divine persons,
the Father, the Son and the Holy Spirit.
I believe that your divine Son became a human being,
died for our sins, and that he will come to judge the
living and the dead.
I believe these and all the truths the holy Catholic
Church teaches,
because you have revealed them,
who can neither deceive nor be deceived.
Amen.

Act of Hope
O my God,
relying on your almighty power and infinite goodness and
promises,
I hope to obtain pardon of all my sins,
the help of your grace, and life everlasting,
through the merits of Jesus Christ, my Lord and Redeemer.
Amen.

Act of Love
O my God,
I love you above all things, with my whole heart and soul,
because you are all-good and worthy of all love.
I love my neighbor as myself for the love of you.
I forgive all who have injured me,
and ask pardon of all whom I have injured.
Amen.

to encourage them to work hard at being people of justice. Conclude by asking the students:

- What are the benefits of acting justly?
- What are the disadvantages?

- Before moving on, have the students name vices that are the antithesis of justice, for example: intolerance, prejudice, paternalism, bias, discrimination, exclusivity.
- Have the students turn to the text section "Fortitude" on page 190. Help the students recognize that fortitude is not fearlessness, but courage in spite of fear. The virtue of fortitude enables us to do the right thing even when it is difficult or frightening (e.g., resisting peer pressure). Fortitude helps us persevere, try new things, and even admit mistakes.
- Ask the students to name vices that are the direct opposite of fortitude, for example: cowardice, timidity, inconstancy.
- Go on to have the students describe what they understand "temperance" to mean. Then note the three parts of temperance as described by St. Thomas Aquinas: (1) abstinence, (2) sobriety, and (3) chastity.
- Make the following points:
  - The virtue of temperance allows us—not chemicals or things or emotions—to control our lives.
  - Temperance enables us to create a healthy balance in life between work and play, rest and exercise.
  - Temperance leads to modesty, helping us set healthy boundaries about our bodies, our privacy, and the bodies and privacy of others.
  - Overall, the temperate person is someone who is centered, in control, and at ease even when things around him or her seem out of control.
- Ask the students to name some situations where the virtue of temperance would help them stay in control. Finally, have them name vices that are the opposite of temperance, for example: gluttony, drunkenness, concupiscence, lack of self-control.
- Call attention to the final paragraph in this text section (page 191), which sums up what the cardinal virtues do for us as we strive to live out our Redemption.
- Give the students some time to create matching quizzes for the cardinal virtues. Challenge them to create at least two questions for each virtue. Afterward, have them exchange their quizzes, complete the answers, and check their answers together.

corporal works of mercy
Charitable actions that include feeding the hungry, clothing the naked, visiting the sick and the imprisoned, sheltering the homeless, and burying the dead.

spiritual works of mercy
Seven practices of Catholic charity directed toward the soul of our neighbor; based on the teaching of Christ and the Tradition of the Church from the time of the Apostles. They are: counsel the doubtful, instruct the ignorant, admonish the sinner, comfort the sorrowful, forgive injuries, bear wrongs patiently, and pray for the living and the dead.

acts: professing it, bearing witness to it, and spreading the Good News of Salvation in Jesus Christ to others, even if it leads to suffering. Faith is strengthened through practices like the following:

- *Pray*. We can ask the Lord to make our faith stronger, much like the father of the son suffering from epilepsy in Mark's Gospel: "I do believe, help my unbelief" (Mk 9:24).
- *Read Scripture*. Reading, studying, and praying with the Bible brings us closer to God and his word. The Scriptures are also proclaimed at Mass. The dismissal rite at Mass encourages us to take the Gospel out to the world and translate our faith into concrete deeds of love of and service to others.
- *Celebrate the sacraments*. The sacraments themselves celebrate the mysteries of our faith, especially the Paschal Mystery. Participation in the Sacrament of Penance can remind us of Christ's forgiving love. Receiving our Lord in Holy Communion nourishes and strengthens our belief.
- *Study your faith*. Studying and deepening our understanding of the lessons of faith is a lifelong experience. We can exercise our faith by learning more about it—in religion classes, on retreats and days of recollection, and in homilies. Catholic colleges and parishes offer courses and workshops to facilitate study. We can also study summaries of our faith like the Apostles' Creed and the Nicene Creed, learning what each phrase means.
- *Draw on the faith of friends*. Choose friends and companions who share your commitment to God and the Church. Their Christian values and virtues will help you in times of temptation. Join with peers who participate in youth group, retreats, pilgrimages, service projects, and faith rallies.
- *Put your faith into action*. Keep your faith alive by being Christ for others. An excellent way of doing this is to practice the **corporal works of mercy** and the **spiritual works of mercy**, thereby serving and loving others in imitation of Christ.

Hope

Hope is related to the virtue of faith. Because we believe that God is all-good, all-loving, all-just, and all-merciful, we trust that he controls the future and looks out for each of us. As the *Catechism* defines: "Hope is the theological virtue by which we desire the kingdom of heaven and eternal life as our happiness, placing our trust in Christ's promises and relying not on our own strength, but on the help of the grace of the Holy Spirit" (*CCC*, 1817).

We believe and hope that good does triumph over evil; that eternal life awaits us on the other side of death; and that every wrong will be righted. Christians who hope place great value in Jesus' comforting words:

> Therefore I tell you, do not worry about your life and what

you will eat, or about your body and what you will wear. For life is more than food and the body more than clothing. Notice the ravens: they do not sow or reap; they have neither storehouse nor barn, yet God feeds them. How much more important are you than birds! Can any of you by worrying add a moment to your lifespan? If even the smallest things are beyond your control, why are you anxious about the rest? Notice how the flowers grow. They do not toil or spin. But I tell you, not even Solomon in all his splendor was dressed like one of them. If God so clothes the grass in the field that grows today and is thrown into the oven tomorrow, will he not much more provide for you, O you of little faith? As for you, do not seek what you are to eat and what you are to drink, and do not worry anymore. All the nations of the world seek for these things, and your Father knows that you need them. Instead, seek his kingdom, and these other things will be given you besides. Do not be afraid any longer, little flock, for your Father is pleased to give you the kingdom. (Lk 12:22–32)

Christ's own life is a model of hope. For example, as he was suffering on the cross and dying for our Salvation, Jesus turned to his Abba in prayer and, in the midst of his agony and loneliness said, "Father, into your hands I commend my spirit" (Lk 23:46). In his encyclical *Spe Salvi* (Saved in Hope), Pope Benedict XVI offers wise advice on how to grow in the virtue of hope:

> A first essential setting for learning hope is prayer. When no one listens to me any more, God still listens to me. When I can no longer talk to anyone or call upon anyone, I can always talk to God. When there is no longer anyone to help me deal with a need or expectation that goes beyond the human capacity for hope, he can help me. When I have been plunged into complete solitude . . . ; if I pray I am never totally alone. (*Spe Salvi*, 32)

Charity

St. Thomas Aquinas stated that charity (*agape* in the Greek, *caritas* in Latin)—also translated as love—is the "mother of all virtues." "Charity is the theological virtue by which we love God above all things for his own sake, and our neighbor as ourselves for the love of God" (*CCC*, 1822). God's very nature is love; God *is* love. As God's adopted children, we are called to a holy relationship with him in the same way as expressed in the relationship among the Three Persons of our Triune God. The First Letter of John describes this goal:

> Beloved, let us love one another, because love is of God; everyone who loves is begotten by God and knows God. Whoever is without love does not know God, for God is love. In this way the love of God was revealed to us: God sent his only Son into the

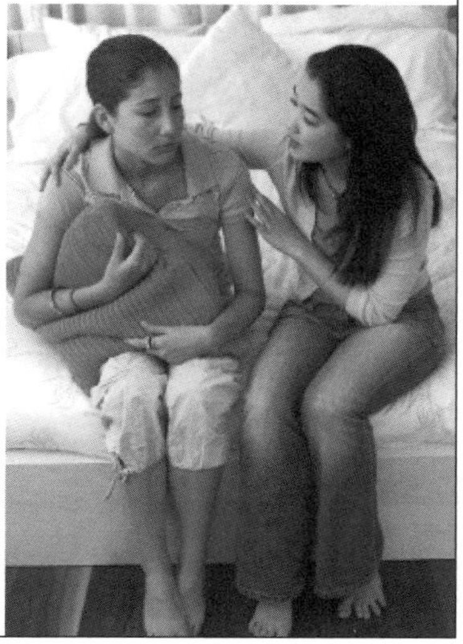

Lesson 3 Objectives

The students will:

- describe the theological virtues.
- describe how to strengthen the theological virtues in our lives.
- identify ways to live out the works of mercy in the world.

Lesson 3 Preview

This lesson guides the students farther along the path of living a life of virtue. It presents the theological virtues of faith, hope, and love as empowering forces enabling us to live as followers of Christ in this life as well as to attain eternal happiness in the next.

- To review all of the cardinal virtues, have the students get into groups of four or more. Have them create and act out scenarios in which each of the four cardinal virtues are needed. After they act out the scenarios, have them describe when each virtue was needed and how the person in the scenario lived it out.
- Conclude the session by having the students respond to the For Reflection question on page 196 ("What can you do to grow in each of the four cardinal virtues?"). Allow adequate time for discussion.

Chapter 8: Living the Paschal Mystery: A Call to Holiness—Lesson 3

Bell Ringers

- Ask the students to offer their responses to the first five For Review questions on page 195 (answers are on pages 216–217 of this text). Be sure to allow the students to ask any other questions they may have.
- Introduce this lesson by having the students read 1 Corinthians 13:13. List on the board the virtues mentioned in the passage (**Faith**, **Hope**, and **Love**). Ask:
    - What do we call these virtues? (*the theological virtues*)
    - Why "theological"? (*They are gifts from God, infused directly into our souls.*)
- Go on to explain that the theological virtues are virtues that empower us.
    - Faith empowers us to believe in God, in all God has revealed, and in what the Church teaches; faith also inspires us to share our faith with others.
    - Hope empowers us to trust that God will keep his promises and act on our behalf.
    - Love empowers us to keep the Great Commandment (love God, love neighbor as self), transforming our human love to be ever more Godlike.
- Ask students to rate the strength of each of the theological virtues in their lives from one to ten (ten being very strong). Invite them to journal about why they rated themselves this way with specific examples of their strengths or weaknesses related to each virtue.

Teaching Approaches

Living a Life of Virtue—Theological Virtues (pages 191-196)

- Introduce discussion on the virtue of faith by distributing copies of Chapter 8, Handout 4, "I Think Faith Is Like . . . " and give the students time to complete it on their own. Then, give them the opportunity to share their responses with a partner before discussing people's responses as a class. For each statement, have students who circled each "option" tell why they made the choice they did. Repeat this procedure for each statement. The point of this activity is not to define faith, but to help the students reflect on the meaning of faith in their lives.
- Like a muscle, faith needs exercise or it shrinks and may even atrophy. Note the six ways of strengthening faith as outlined on page 192—prayer, reading Scripture, celebrating the sacraments, studying the faith, drawing on the faith of others, putting faith into action. Encourage the students to draw upon all these avenues in order to strengthen and grow in their faith.
- Invite the students to artistically represent the practices that strengthen faith by creating a poster. Suggest some themes that could go along with the design: a weight-room, training equipment, a shield, building blocks, etc.

194 Jesus Christ: Source of Our Salvation

world so that we might have life through him. In this is love: not that we have loved God, but that he loved us and sent his Son as expiation for our sins.

Beloved, if God so loved us, we also must love one another. No one has ever seen God. Yet, if we love one another, God remains in us, and his love is brought to perfection in us.

This is how we know that we remain in him and he in us, that he has given us of his Spirit. Moreover, we have seen and testify that the Father sent his Son as savior of the world. Whoever acknowledges that Jesus is the Son of God, God remains in him and he in God. We have come to know and to believe in the love God has for us. God is love, and whoever remains in love remains in God and God in him. (1 Jn 4:7–16)

Christ tells us that the Law is summarized in the command to love God above all things and our neighbor as ourselves (see Mt 22:34–40). The virtue of charity enables us to follow Christ's injunction to love even our enemies. It helps us practice all the other virtues and supports "and purifies our human ability to love, raising it to the supernatural perfection of divine love" (*CCC*, 1827). In today's world, many people distort the true meaning of love, for example, by claiming that unbridled sexual passion (known as **lust**) is love. But lust is not love. The virtue of charity—true love, which has its source in God himself—is self-giving. Jesus Christ, the perfect exemplar of love, teaches by his words and deeds that charity involves:

- *Obedience*. Jesus' will was perfectly attuned to his Father's. Love means obeying Jesus' commands.
- *Reverence*. Love involves respecting and valuing the absolute goodness of God and the goodness of other people made in his image and likeness.
- *Sacrifice*. Love requires commitment, walking the extra mile, and never giving up on God, other people, or oneself. Spiritual disciplines like fasting, prayer, sharing with the poor, and the like increase love in our hearts.

Charity results in many fruits or benefits, including joy, peace, and mercy. It is generous and reciprocal. It leads to friendship and communion with

Practicing Cardinal Virtues

To build strength of character, and practice the cardinal virtues, do one of the following:

- *Prudence*: Name an important decision you are trying to make. For example, whether to begin an exclusive relationship or which college you will attend. Discuss it with a trusted adult. Write out the pros and cons of each possible course of action. Pray for the Lord's help in making your decision. After considering all your options, decide, act, and then review your decision. Write a summary of this process.
- *Justice*: Search the news for an example of an injustice that is taking place in your local community. After gathering some facts about the issue, including the teaching of the Catholic Church, write a letter to a media outlet or a government official expressing your thoughts on how to address the issue.
- *Fortitude*: Make it a practice to avoid gossip. If challenged by your peers, in a nonjudgmental way, tell them why you do not like participating in character assassination. Note in your journal how you felt when you did the right thing in this setting.
- *Temperance*: Give up dessert, snacks, or soda for two straight weeks, thus practicing the virtue of abstinence. Donate the money saved on these items to a hunger center.

For Review Answers (page 195)

1. Human virtue is virtue that we can acquire by our own efforts.
2. Answers will vary a bit, but students should be able to respond in a way similar to the following:
    - Prudence—helps us to decide responsibly and choose what is right.
    - Justice—consists of a person always giving his or her due to God and neighbor.
    - Fortitude—helps us become courageous and overcome fearfulness.
    - Temperance—helps us overcome temptation, become centered and in control of our lives.
3. Vice is a bad habit, acquired by repeated sin in violation of the proper norms of morality, that inclines us to choose evil over good.
4. Answers will vary, but students should be able to respond in a way similar to the following:
    - Commutative justice—regulates relationships of reciprocity.
    - Distributive justice—champions the common good.
    - Legal justice—secures societal solidarity; it refers to rights and responsibilities of citizens to obey everyone else's rights and to obey laws that have been put in place to protect peace and social order.
    - Social justice—seeks fair (re)distribution of resources, opportunities, and responsibilities; challenges the roots of oppression and injustice; empowers people to exercise self-determination and realize their full potential; and builds social solidarity and community capacity for collaborative action.

others. In his encyclical *Deus Caritas Est* (God Is Love), Pope Benedict XVI reminds us that Christ's love is ever-present to us. By recognizing it, we are better able to respond to it.

> God is visible in a number of ways. In the love-story recounted by the Bible, he comes towards us, he seeks to win our hearts, all the way to the Last Supper, to the piercing of his heart on the Cross, to his appearances after the Resurrection and to the great deeds by which, through the activity of the Apostles, he guided the nascent Church along its path. Nor has the Lord been absent from subsequent Church history: he encounters us ever anew, in the men and women who reflect his presence, in his word, in the sacraments, and especially in the Eucharist. In the Church's Liturgy, in her prayer, in the living community of believers, we experience the love of God, we perceive his presence and we thus learn to recognize that presence in our daily lives. He has loved us first and he continues to do so; we too, then, can respond with love. (*Deus Caritas Est,* 17)

Finally, never forget that love is the greatest virtue, the only one that survives into eternity:

> Love is patient, love is kind. It is not jealous, (love) is not pompous, it is not inflated, it is not rude, it does not seek its own interests, it is not quick-tempered, it does not brood over injury, it does not rejoice over wrongdoing but rejoices with the truth. It bears all things, believes all things, hopes all things, endures all things. . . . So faith, hope, love remain, these three; but the greatest of these is love. (1 Cor 13:4–7, 13)

For Review

1. Define *human virtue*.
2. Name the cardinal virtues. What does each do?
3. Define *vice*.
4. Distinguish among these four kinds of justice: commutative, distributive, legal, and social.
5. Give an example of a vice that is contrary to each of the cardinal virtues.
6. What does the theological virtue of faith accomplish?
7. Discuss two ways we can strengthen the virtue of faith.
8. List the corporal and spiritual works of mercy.
9. What does the theological virtue of hope enable us to do?
10. What does the theological virtue of charity enable us to do?
11. Why should Christians love?

- Have the students fold a notebook piece of paper twice to make four boxes (quadrants) on the page. Label the two boxes on the left "Spiritual Works of Mercy" and "Corporal Works of Mercy." Have the students list examples of both sets of works within the boxes. Label the right two boxes "The Spiritual/ Corporal Works in Action." Invite them to list ways they can live out each of the works of mercy in their daily lives.
- Move on to the virtue of hope. Have the students take out their journals and list everything that is causing them to worry (or typically causes them to worry). When they have finished, instruct them to write the word "HOPE" over each of the worries so that they are no longer legible. Invite a student to read the definition of hope from the *Catechism* (page 192). Explain that with the theological virtue of hope, we trust God rather than our own strength.
- Point out in the text (page 193) how, at the moment of Jesus' life when the worst seemed most certain, his cry (Lk 23:46) declared that God was still his hope. Jesus did not ask for rescue from death, and God did not provide it. However, *God did act on Jesus' behalf.* Jesus' cry of hope led to more than rescue from death. It led to Resurrection.
- Call attention to the quotation from Pope Benedict XVI on page 193, where the pope assures us that,

For Review Answers (page 195) continued

5. Answers may include thoughtlessness, impetuosity, negligence, inconstancy (prudence); intolerance, prejudice, paternalism, bias, discrimination, exclusivity (justice); cowardice, timidity, inconstancy (fortitude); and gluttony, drunkenness, concupiscence, and lack of self-control (temperance).
6. Faith allows us to commit ourselves totally to God and believe what he has said.
7. Students should name and describe any of the following: prayer, reading Scripture, celebrating the sacraments, studying the faith, drawing on the faith of others, putting faith into action.
8. *Corporal works of mercy*: feed the hungry; give drink to the thirsty; clothe the naked; visit the sick and imprisoned; shelter the homeless; bury the dead. *Spiritual works of mercy*: counsel the doubtful; instruct the ignorant; admonish the sinner; comfort the sorrowful; forgive injuries; bear wrongs patiently; pray for the living and the dead.
9. Answers should evidence the understanding that hope enables us to place our trust in God, rather than rely on our own strength.
10. Charity allows us to love God above all else for his own sake and our neighbor as ourselves.
11. Answers will vary, but should show that if Christians love, then God will remain in them and they in God; and they will receive joy, peace, and mercy.

through prayer, we can find God acting on our behalf and grow in hope. Then have the students find Romans 8:24–27 in their Bibles:

> For in hope we were saved. Now hope that sees for itself is not hope. For who hopes for what one sees? But if we hope for what we do not see, we wait with endurance. In the same way, the Spirit too comes to the aid of our weakness; for we do not know how to pray as we ought, but the Spirit itself intercedes with inexpressible groanings. And the one who searches hearts knows what is the intention of the Spirit, because it intercedes for the holy ones according to God's will.

Assure the students that hope is not easy, especially when what we hope for us is difficult to see and prove. The Spirit strengthens us with hope to trust in Christ instead of ourselves. If we want to strengthen hope, we must allow the Holy Spirit to strengthen it within us.

- Finally, to make it clear that hope is not a passive virtue, write the following quotation from St. Augustine on the board: **"Hope has two beautiful daughters: their names are anger and courage. Anger that things are the way they are. Courage to make them the way they ought to be."**
- Tell the students that like faith, hope also demands action. In fact, it spurs us to action. Explain that only the person of hope can be successful in the pursuit of justice and peace in seemingly hopeless situations, for in the face of the improbable, hope is the passion for the possible.
- Introduce the theological virtue of charity by singing or playing a recording of a hymn such as "Where Charity and Love Prevail" or "Ubi Caritas." Note how the hymns declare God's presence in love and in loving situations.
- Call attention to the definition of charity from the *Catechism*: "Charity is the theological virtue by which we love God above all things for his own sake, and our neighbor as ourselves for the love of God" (*CCC*, 1822). In other words charity is the virtue that empowers us to keep the Great Commandment (Mt 22:34–40).
- Stress to the students that the passage from 1 Corinthians makes it pretty clear that love is a *way of being* in the world. In particular, it is the way of being that Jesus demonstrated, which is why his commandment is not "love one another" *period*; but rather, "love one another" *comma* "as I have loved you."
- Distribute copies of Chapter 8, Handout 5, "Measuring Up to Love." Have the students complete

196 Jesus Christ: Source of Our Salvation

justification
The Holy Spirit's grace that cleanses us from our sins through faith in Jesus Christ and baptism. Justification makes us right with God.

charisms
Special gifts the Holy Spirit gives to individual Christians to build up the Church.

gifts of the Holy Spirit
God-given abilities that help us live a Christian life with God's help. Jesus promised these gifts through the Holy Spirit, especially the Sacrament of Confirmation. The seven gifts are wisdom, understanding, knowledge, counsel, (right judgment), fortitude (courage), piety (reverence), and fear of the Lord (wonder and awe).

fruits of the Holy Spirit
Perfections that result from living in union with the Holy Spirit.

For Reflection

What can you do to grow in each of the four cardinal virtues?

God Helps Us Grow in Holiness (*CCC*, 1996-2005; 1266)

God wants us to be holy, often a difficult task. But the Lord provides us with many helps along the way, including grace and the gift of the Holy Spirit who gives us many gifts that enable us to grow in holiness. **Justification** is a special gift of the Holy Spirit that not only frees us from sin but sanctifies us in the depth of our being.

Grace

Grace is God's "*favor*, the *free and undeserved help* that God gives us to respond to his call to become children of God, adoptive sons, partakers of the divine nature and of eternal life" (*CCC*, 1996). We cannot earn grace in any way because it is a total gift from God. The Holy Spirit infuses grace into our souls when we are baptized, making us different creatures from what we were when we were born. God's free gift of grace blesses us in many ways. Grace:

- enables us to address God as Abba
- adopts us into God's family
- enables us to share in the life of the Blessed Trinity
- makes us heirs of Heaven
- enables us to live as God's sons and daughters, in the way Jesus taught us
- unites us to our Lord and Savior, Jesus Christ
- allows the Holy Spirit to live in us

The Catholic Church has traditionally termed this grace of justification *sanctifying*, meaning, "to make holy." Because God's grace justifies us, God's own righteousness is given to us, and we are united to the Lord's Paschal Mystery. Therefore, sanctifying grace is a means to grow in holiness. Sanctifying grace

- enables us to believe and hope in God and to love him through the theological virtues (see pages 191–193);
- gives us the power to live under the influence of the Holy Spirit through the gifts he bestows on us; and

Lesson 3 Homework

1. Assign the final six For Review questions on page 195.
2. Have the students read "God Helps Us Grow in Holiness" (pages 196–199) in preparation for their next lesson.
3. Encourage the students to continue working on their chosen Ongoing Activities.

Extending the Lesson

Celebrate Hope

After presenting the material on the virtue of hope, celebrate a brief prayer service. To prepare:

- Have each student write a hope he or she has for the future.
- Have matches and a candle available.
- Ask one of the students to be the prayer leader and another to be the reader.
- Divide the rest of the class into two groups. Give each student a copy of Chapter 8, Handout 6, "Hope Prayer Service."

- allows us to grow in goodness through the moral virtues (*CCC*, 1266).

Sanctifying grace is also a *habitual* grace, a "permanent disposition to live and act in keeping with God's call" (*CCC*, 2000). We distinguish it from *actual* graces, which are God's interventions "at the beginning of conversion or in the course of sanctification" (*CCC*, 2000). Other types of grace are *sacramental* graces, which are specific gifts that come from particular sacraments; **charisms**, which are special gifts that the Holy Spirit gives to individual Christians to build up the Body of Christ, the Church; and "graces of state," which are the help God gives to particular ministries in the Church.

God never forces his grace on us. He respects our freedom. This is why we, as believers, must freely respond to the graces that God gives. He implanted in us a desire to do good and to search for truth. This inborn desire points to God himself, the only One who can satisfy the yearnings of our hearts. Thus, God has already begun the work of grace in us by preparing for and calling forth our free response. If we say yes to God's inner call, and use the gifts and helps he gives us, then our human freedom is made perfect. Our inner longing for truth and goodness is satisfied.

Gifts of the Holy Spirit

The Holy Spirit also showers on us what we need to live Christ-like lives. Another help for our growth in holiness are the **gifts of the Holy Spirit**. These gifts, given to us at Baptism and Confirmation, are qualities the Old Testament prophet Isaiah (Is 11:2–3) said would identify the Messiah. Jesus Christ himself lived each of these gifts perfectly. The traditional list of these seven gifts is given below with a brief explanation of each.

- *Wisdom* is looking at reality from God's point of view. Wisdom encourages us to pray before making decisions and to seek guidance from saints, the Church's teaching, priests, and other trusted adults. This gift helps us discover truth.
- *Understanding* involves taking the time to uncover the deeper meaning of faith and the mysteries of God's magnificent creation. We will use this gift throughout our lives to better appreciate the depth of God's love for us.
- *Knowledge* is the grace to see how God is working in our lives, especially when we are trying to judge what is right and wrong.
- *Counsel (right judgment)* helps us form our conscience in light of Church teaching. We do this by praying and by consulting others before deciding moral issues. This gift helps us act prudently.
- *Fortitude (courage)* is the strength to follow our own convictions in the face of peer pressure. It also involves the willingness to suffer for the Lord.
- *Piety (reverence)* is respect we show to the Lord through praise and worship. Respecting the dignity and worth of others is another way we express this gift.
- *Fear of the Lord (wonder and awe)* enables us to show concern about the reality of sin in our life and to avoid anything that might alienate us from God and others.

Fruits of the Holy Spirit in Your Life

The *Catechism of the Catholic Church* defines the fruits of the Holy Spirit as "perfections that the Holy Spirit forms in us as the first fruits of eternal glory" (*CCC*, 1832). Write a prayer with twelve petitions that focus on each fruit of the Holy Spirit. For example: "Lord, increase the fruit of generosity in my life. When a classmate asks for my help in preparing for an exam, help me to oblige."

Lesson 4 Objectives

The students will:

- define justification and grace.
- discover some of their individual gifts.
- distinguish between and among the different types of grace.
- identify and describe charisms, especially the seven gifts of the Holy Spirit.
- pray together.

Lesson 4 Preview

In this lesson, the students recognize how they are gifted people, inspired to share their gifts with others. Graced and blessed in that sharing, they advance along the way of holiness.

the exercise on their own. Afterward, if the students are comfortable, have them share responses with a partner or in small groups. Conclude by pointing out that none of us measures up to love perfectly. That's why God offers us help.

- Write the word **grace** on the board. For now, simply stress that God is love and that grace is God's own life and love in us. Be sure the students understand that we neither earn grace nor deserve it. It is pure gift—a gift of love. In order to become loving persons, we need God's help, his grace.
- Finally, call attention to the phrase at the bottom of Handout 5: "God does not love you because you are good. You are good because God loves you." Invite the students to meditate on this truth in their prayer over the next week.

Chapter 8: Living the Paschal Mystery: A Call to Holiness—Lesson 4

Bell Ringers

- Check over the students' responses to For Review questions 6–11 on page 195 (answers are on page 217 of this text). Be sure to allow the students to ask any other questions they may have.
- Continue to review the previous lesson by using the first two activities in the feature For Reflection on page 199 by having the students reread the quotation from *Deus Caritas Est* (on page 195), then share how they have discovered the love of God in their lives.
- Introduce this lesson by having the students discover/identify their personal gifts. Distribute paper plates and markers. Direct the students to fasten the plates to their backs with masking tape or double-sided tape. Have students circulate and write on one another's plates a gift the other has. Explain that a gift is a personal quality: e.g., kindness, sense of humor, determination. Allow about five or so minutes for this exercise.
- After they have finished, have the students remove their paper plates and read what their classmates have written about them. Point out that these are gifts *others* see in them. Ask the students to add gifts they feel they possess that others did not write down.
- Have the students turn over the plate and divide it with a horizontal line. Write the following sentences on the board, and ask the students to copy and complete them on the top part of their paper plates:

- **My favorite gift is ________________.**
- **The best gift I have to offer others is ______________.**

Finally, have the students set aside the plates for use later in the session. (*Note*: These plates will be used again in Chapter 9, Lesson 4.)

Teaching Approaches

God Helps Us Grow in Holiness (pages 196–199)

- Write the phrase **Holiness and the Gift of Grace** on the board. Then make the following points:
  - Holiness was humankind's original condition.
  - Through sin, we lost original holiness and became separated from God.
  - On our own, there is not much we can do about the separation of sin. That's why Jesus tells us, "Without me, you can do nothing" (Jn 15:5). Sin is too lethal a poison for us. Only the mercy of God can destroy sin in us.
  - We call this divine mercy *justification*—the grace of the Holy Spirit that wipes away sin through faith in Jesus and opens the door to holiness.
- Go on to note the definition of grace in the text (page 196): grace is the "free and undeserved help that God gives us to respond to his call to become children of God, adoptive sons, partakers of the divine nature and of eternal life." Point out that grace is not something we earn.
- Finally, discuss the ways God's gift of sanctifying grace blesses us (its *effects*), as well as ways it helps us grow in holiness (page 196).
- List the following types of grace on the board and have the students copy them in their notes. Then help the students define each type:
  - **Sanctifying grace**: disposes us to live like God.
  - **Actual graces**: enable us to turn from sin and to follow Jesus on the way to holiness.
  - **Sacramental graces**: flow from particular sacraments.
  - **Charisms:** gifts given to individuals to help the Church grow.
  - **Graces of state:** special helps God grants to particular ministries in the Church.

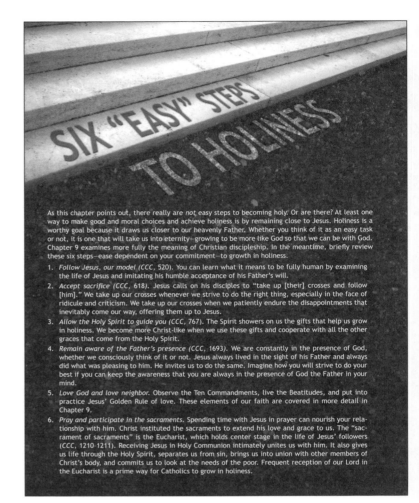

As this chapter points out, there really are *not* easy steps to becoming holy. Or are there? At least one way to make good and moral choices and achieve holiness is by remaining close to Jesus. Holiness is a worthy goal because it draws us closer to our heavenly Father. Whether you think of it as an easy task or not, it is one that will take us into eternity—growing to be more like God so that we can be with God. Chapter 9 examines more fully the meaning of Christian discipleship. In the meantime, briefly review these six steps—ease dependent on your commitment—to growth in holiness.

1. *Follow Jesus, our model (CCC,* 520). You can learn what it means to be fully human by examining the life of Jesus and imitating his humble acceptance of his Father's will.
2. *Accept sacrifice (CCC,* 618*)*. Jesus calls on his disciples to "take up [their] crosses and follow [him]." We take up our crosses whenever we strive to do the right thing, especially in the face of ridicule and criticism. We take up our crosses when we patiently endure the disappointments that inevitably come our way, offering them up to Jesus.
3. *Allow the Holy Spirit to guide you (CCC,* 767). The Spirit showers on us the gifts that help us grow in holiness. We become more Christ-like when we use these gifts and cooperate with all the other graces that come from the Holy Spirit.
4. *Remain aware of the Father's presence (CCC,* 1693*)*. We are constantly in the presence of God, whether we consciously think of it or not. Jesus always lived in the sight of his Father and always did what was pleasing to him. He invites us to do the same. Imagine how you will strive to do your best if you can keep the awareness that you are always in the presence of God the Father in your mind.
5. *Love God and love neighbor.* Observe the Ten Commandments, live the Beatitudes, and put into practice Jesus' Golden Rule of love. These elements of our faith are covered in more detail in Chapter 9.
6. *Pray and participate in the sacraments.* Spending time with Jesus in prayer can nourish your relationship with him. Christ instituted the sacraments to extend his love and grace to us. The "sacrament of sacraments" is the Eucharist, which holds center stage in the life of Jesus' followers (*CCC*, 1210-1211). Receiving Jesus in Holy Communion intimately unites us with him. It also gives us life through the Holy Spirit, separates us from sin, brings us into union with other members of Christ's body, and commits us to look at the needs of the poor. Frequent reception of our Lord in the Eucharist is a prime way for Catholics to grow in holiness.

Lesson 4 Homework

1. Assign the four For Review questions on page 199.
2. Have the students read "Essential Elements of Holiness" (pages 199–206) in preparation for their next lesson.
3. Encourage the students to begin wrapping up their chosen Ongoing Activities.
4. Have the students turn to the feature "Fruits of the Holy Spirit in Your Life" on page 197. Remind the students that they can find the list of the Fruits of the Spirit on page 170 in Chapter 7. Remind them, too, how they learned that the fruits are actually the virtues Jesus himself possessed. Thus, when we work to develop these virtues, we're working to become more like him. Assign the writing of the prayer as homework. Tell the students that their prayer will serve as part of their chapter test.
5. Assign the three-part Scripture project outlined in the feature "St. Paul on Charisms and Living a Holy Life" (page 199). Tell the students that, as with the previous assignment, this project will serve as part of their chapter test.

St. Paul on Charisms and Living a Holy Life

Complete each of the following assignments:

- Read 1 Corinthians 12 to find some of the special gifts that the Holy Spirit gave to certain members of the Church. List five of them.
- Read Ephesians 4:1-5:20, to see instructions on how to live a holy and moral life. List five positive actions that help us live holy lives and five practices that lead us away from God.
- Research the origins, main themes, year composed, and background of the First Letter to the Corinthians or the Letter to the Ephesians. Write a one-page report on your findings.

For Review

1. Define *grace*.
2. List five effects of sanctifying grace.
3. Distinguish between and among these terms: sanctifying grace, actual grace, sacramental grace, and charisms.
4. Name the gifts of the Holy Spirit.

For Reflection

- Reread the quotation of Pope Benedict XVI from his encyclical *Deus Caritas Est* (page 195). Then write and discuss how you have personally experienced the love of God in your life.
- Name a quality of love that you have experienced in your own life.
- Which gift of the Holy Spirit is most evident in your life right now? Which gift needs more work in your life?

Essential Elements of Holiness (*CCC*, 826, 1248, 2012-2014, 2028, 2045, 2813)

God the Father calls us to holiness in every aspect of our lives. He is the source of our life in Jesus Christ. In the Lord's Prayer, we petition that God's name be made holy. The way we do so is by growing in holiness ourselves. When each member of Christ's Body stays true to his or her Christian beliefs and convictions, and lives moral and holy lives, then Christ's presence in the world becomes more visible and the Father's glory and name are honored. In addition, the Body of Christ, the Church, of which Christ is the head, increases, grows, and develops, attracting others to Jesus Christ, the source of our Salvation.

As Catholics, we are able to grow in holiness as members of Christ's Body, the Church, in three general ways:

- *First*, we must practice the virtue of charity because it is the essential means to holiness. Charity is the "soul" of holiness because it "governs, shapes, and perfects all the means of sanctification" (*Lumen Gentium*, 42).
- *Second*, we must celebrate the sacraments because they help bring us into union with Jesus Christ by the power of the Holy Spirit.

For Review Answers (page 199)

1. Grace is the free and undeserved help that God gives us to respond to his call to become children of God.
2. Students may mention any of the following: calling God "Abba"; adoption into God's family; sharing in the life of the Trinity; becoming heirs of Heaven; empowering us to live as God's children as Jesus taught; union with Jesus; the indwelling of the Holy Spirit. See page 196.
3. Sanctifying grace disposes us to live like God; actual graces enable us to turn from sin and to follow Jesus on the way to holiness; sacramental graces flow from particular sacraments; charisms are gifts given to individuals to help the Church grow.
4. Wisdom, Understanding, Knowledge, Counsel, Fortitude, Piety, Fear of the Lord.

- Have the students study these terms by creating a matching quiz. For review, have them add the virtues from previous lessons to the quiz. Invite them to exchange their quizzes with a partner. After they have finished another student's quiz, have them meet and discuss their answers. Clarify any confusions about the terms if they arise.
- Take a moment to point out that as gifts, all these graces are ours to accept or reject. God gives and keeps on giving, but does not *oblige* us to accept his gifts.
- Finally, sing or play a recording of the first verse of the hymn "Amazing Grace": *Amazing grace, how sweet the sound / that saved a wretch like me. / I once was lost, but now I'm found; / was blind, but now I see.* Point out how the hymn reveals that grace is *saving gift* that grants us *purpose and direction*, and *opens our eyes to new ways of living.*
- Move on by calling attention to the text section "Gifts of the Holy Spirit" (page 197). Point out that the gifts are qualities of the Messiah who is guided by God's own Spirit. Remind the students that the Hebrew word "Messiah" ("Christ" in Greek) means "anointed." Explain that we call ourselves "Christians" because, confirmed in the Spirit, we are anointed ones too.
- Go through the list of the seven gifts of the Holy Spirit with the students. In addition to the material provided in the text (page 197), share the following with the students:
    - *Wisdom:* The word "wisdom" comes from the Greek "to see clearly." Wisdom is distinct from the other gifts in that we can see as God sees.
    - *Understanding* helps us get the point of what we believe; it also helps us accept others as they are, without judgment.
    - *Knowledge* is the gift that helps us uncover the information we need in certain situations. It is different from wisdom and understanding in that it relates specifically to the acquisition of information.
    - *Counsel (right judgment)* helps us discern the meaning of God's action in our lives and to choose the best way to respond to it. This gift helps us recognize possible consequences of our actions and so to make good decisions.
    - *Fortitude (courage)* helps us to choose and act for someone or something beyond ourselves and to follow through on our choice; as a bonus, courage also gives us hope, enabling us to trust that God will act on our behalf.

- *Piety (reverence)* is the gift that enables us both to recognize that God is the source of all life and love, and to respect all that comes from God and to respond in praise of him.
- *Fear of the Lord (wonder and awe)* has nothing to do with anxiety. Rather, this gift enables us to marvel and express our delight that the totally "other," all-powerful God is intimately one with us.

- Go on to discuss the Spirit's gifts. Begin by asking the third question in the For Reflection section on page 199: "Which gift of the Holy Spirit is most evident in your life right now? Which gift needs more work in your life?"
- Continue the discussion, using additional questions, such as:
  - Who is someone you admire who exhibits one or more of the gifts of the Holy Spirit? Explain.
  - Which of the gifts is most important to you? Why?
  - Which gift do you feel might be the most daunting to live out? The most exciting?
- After the discussion, have the students turn to the feature "Six 'Easy' Steps to Holiness" on page 198. Briefly go over the steps, assuring the students that each step will receive further explanation in ensuing chapters.
- Before concluding this lesson with prayer, take a moment to contrast the world's understanding of "gifts" with the Christian understanding. Explain that the world too often sees gifts as things we have earned that give us certain privileges (e.g., the way we treat movie stars or professional athletes). Christians, however, recognize that God has entrusted us with abilities so that we might use them to do God's will and to act as the Body of Christ in the world. To whom much is given, much is expected. Our gifts are not our own to hoard as we choose. That is why they're called "gifts." They're God-given and meant for us to share with all. Further develop this point by having the students read the parable of the talents (Mt 25:14–30).
- Gather the students for prayer around a lighted candle. Remind them that prayer is not an option for those who are gifted by God's Spirit. It is a necessity. In prayer, we respond to God's great love, and we support one another as we grow in faith and love.
- Have the students write the following prayer on the back of the paper plate where their gifts were listed at the beginning of the session:

- *Third,* Christ calls us to pick up a cross to follow him. Holiness requires effort and self-denial. It involves conversion of the heart, a turning from sin and embracing Christ's values while we reject anything that keeps us from the Lord.

These general practices do not come automatically to Catholics. The vocation to holiness, to become perfect like our heavenly Father, is a great call from God. But it is not an impossible call, because God created us with great dignity, in his image and likeness. We have been created in the divine image in and through Christ, "the image of the invisible God" (Col 1:15). Our God-given gifts of human reason, free will, conscience (and its related moral decision-making) are all essential elements of our growth in holiness. They are discussed in the following sections.

Humans Are Capable of Holiness (CCC, 1703-1706)

Humans are unique because God made us to share in his own life. We are the only creatures on earth that God willed for their own sake. God is pure Spirit, a being without physical or material qualities. He, the Supreme Being, is all-good and possesses infinite knowledge and truth. God is a Trinitarian community of perfect love: Father, Son, and Holy Spirit. By creating us in his image, God endowed humans with godlike qualities: the abilities to think, to choose, to love, and to relate to others in community. These endowments make it possible for us to share, through knowledge and love, in God's own life.

Because God made us in his image, we are spiritual beings and possess incomparable dignity, value, and worth. We are not mere *somethings.* We are *someones*—persons who can know and relate to God and to other people. From the moment of conception in our mother's womb, God destined each of us for eternal happiness.

Made in God's image and likeness, humans are created out of love, for love, and to love. This is why we can grow in holiness and enter more deeply into a relationship with our Creator.

The Gift of Human Reason

Humans participate in the light and power of the divine Spirit. Endowed with the ability to think, that is, to reason, we can understand the laws God put into his creation. We can, aided by the Holy Spirit, discover truth, goodness, and beauty. Being able to discover the truth with our intellects leads us to

Background Information

Grace and "Earn" vs. "Merit"

None of us "earns" grace. Like salvation, it is pure gift. However, we can "merit" it. For example, imagine that a wealthy landowner hires a landscaper and out of pure generosity pays the landscaper one hundred times as much as anyone else would pay. In order to receive these wages, however, the landscaper has to work faithfully. Clearly, the landscaper does not "earn" such a substantial salary. At the same time, if the landscaper performs as the landowner stipulates and expects, the landscaper certainly "merits" that salary. So it is for us when it comes to meriting grace and salvation.

Living the Paschal Mystery: A Call to Holiness 201

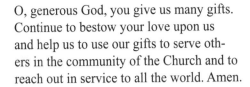

the highest norm of human life—the divine law. By means of this eternal objective, and universal law, "God orders, directs and governs the entire universe and all the ways of the human community according to a plan conceived in wisdom and love" (*Declaration on Religious Freedom*, 3). God has made us to participate in this law; humans must seek this truth.

Human reason enables us to recognize God's voice, which urges us to do good and avoid what is evil. We must follow this law, which we hear in our conscience (see below), by loving God and neighbor.

The Gift of Free Will

Free will is the capacity to choose among alternatives. Free choice helps humans make ourselves the kind of persons God calls us to be. God calls us to be holy. We can grow in holiness by making good choices and avoiding evil choices. We can also learn from our mistakes.

Free choices help us determine how our lives can be uniquely our own. Free will enables us to rise above heredity and environment. For example, free will makes it possible for a person raised by parents who exhibit racial prejudice to rise above that example and to not personally be prejudiced any longer. It gives us some control over our lives by allowing us to use our God-given talents and to cooperate freely with the many graces the Holy Spirit sends to us. Moreover, free will allows us to choose the good for other people, even at the cost of personal sacrifice. This is what love is—choosing for God above everything and for our neighbor as ourselves.

Forming a Good Conscience (CCC, 1776-1802)

Basic to living any Christian life of holiness is making moral choices. To do this we must form and then follow a good **conscience**. The Second Vatican Council described conscience as "the most secret core and sanctuary" of a person. Our conscience helps us to determine what is the Christ-like, moral, and holy thing to do. It helps us distinguish between good and evil, whether something is in accord with God's plan or not. The *Catechism of the Catholic Church* defines conscience this way:

> Conscience is a judgment of reason whereby the human person recognizes the moral quality of a concrete act that he is going to perform, is in the process of performing, or has already completed. (*CCC*, 1778)

Our conscience helps us grasp what is the moral thing to do both before we perform an action as well as while we are doing it. But it also helps us judge whether we did the right thing after we act. Therefore, our conscience calls us to be responsible, telling us to repent if we have sinned by violating it and turning from the Lord's law of love.

In the depths of our conscience, we are alone with God. He calls us

free will
The "power, rooted in reason and will . . . to perform deliberate actions on one's own responsibility" (*CCC*, 1731).

conscience
A person's most secret core and sanctuary that helps the person determine between good and evil. It moves a person at the appropriate times to make specific choices, approving those that are good and rejecting those that are evil.

Lesson 5 Objectives

The students will:

- discover that they are called to be saints.
- describe the ways Christians grow in holiness.
- apply the cardinal and theological virtues to real-life situations.
- describe the gifts of human reason and free will.
- appreciate how the formation of a sound conscience is crucial to moral decision making.
- describe the steps to forming a good conscience.
- apply the sources for making moral decisions to moral dilemmas.

Lesson 5 Preview

Made in God's image and sharing in God's grace, we are called to and capable of attaining holiness. In this lesson, the students see that human reason, free will, and conscience formation all lead to living the moral life and growth in holiness.

> O, generous God, you give us many gifts. Continue to bestow your love upon us and help us to use our gifts to serve others in the community of the Church and to reach out in service to all the world. Amen.

- Call the group to prayer, saying, "My sisters and brothers, let us gather to celebrate the giver of gifts and to rejoice in the name of the Father, and of the Son, and of the Holy Spirit. Amen."
- Invite one of the students to read 1 Corinthians 12:4–12.
- Have the students say together the prayer they wrote on the back of their paper plates.
- Conclude by singing or playing a recording of an appropriate hymn such as "We Are Many Parts" by Marty Haugen.

Chapter 8: Living the Paschal Mystery: A Call to Holiness—Lesson 5

Bell Ringers

- Review the students' responses to four For Review questions on page 199 (answers are on page 221 of this text). Be sure to allow the students to ask any other questions they may have.
- Collect the students' work on the feature "St. Paul on Charisms and Living a Holy Life" (page 199).
- Collect the students' work on the feature "Fruits of the Holy Spirit in Your Life" (page 197). If you wish, use one of the prayers to begin today's lesson.

Teaching Approaches

Essential Elements of Holiness (pages 199-206)

- Remind the students of the following quotation (from Chapter 8, Handout 1, "Saintliness") by Pope John Paul II:

> Our fundamental vocation is the vocation to holiness, that is, the perfection of charity. Holiness is the greatest testimony of the dignity conferred on a disciple of Christ and the basic charge entrusted to all the sons and daughters of the Church.

- Note that the pope says that holiness is a vocation and God does not call without giving us the means to

respond. And what are the "means"? (*Note:* If possible, surprise the students by playing a bit of the refrain of the Beatles' song, "All You Need Is Love.") Love!

- Go on to ask the students, "What does Jesus teach about love?" List their replies on the board. Read John 15:12–13 as a class and add to the list if necessary.
- Stress that growth in holiness through the practice of Christian love/charity is not about pleasure, popularity, domination, or limitless freedom. Living and loving as Jesus showed us is more about:
  - the willingness to suffer for the sake of others
  - the resolve to be disliked for standing up for what is true and good
  - the choice to be vulnerable to the cruelties of others even when they could be avoided
  - the turning away from the merely physical "goods" of this world out of a sense of justice
  - the decision to bind our fate and future—as did Jesus—with the lives of those we profess to love
- Explain that the three general ways we grow in holiness all connect to love (see pages 199–200). Tell the students that practicing the virtue of charity means *self-offering for the sake of others*. The sacraments help us enter into a loving union with Christ who instituted the sacraments to give Christians his life and love. And holiness requires that disciples take up their own crosses of self-denial for the sake of the Kingdom of God.

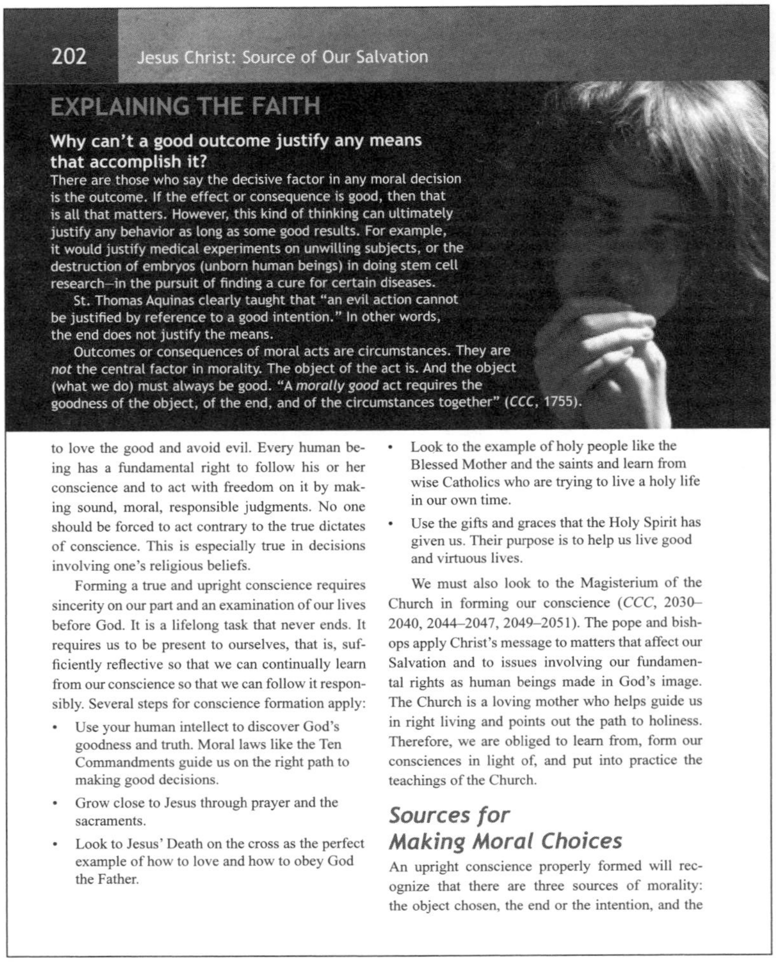

202 Jesus Christ: Source of Our Salvation

EXPLAINING THE FAITH

Why can't a good outcome justify any means that accomplish it?

There are those who say the decisive factor in any moral decision is the outcome. If the effect or consequence is good, then that is all that matters. However, this kind of thinking can ultimately justify any behavior as long as some good results. For example, it would justify medical experiments on unwilling subjects, or the destruction of embryos (unborn human beings) in doing stem cell research—in the pursuit of finding a cure for certain diseases.

St. Thomas Aquinas clearly taught that "an evil action cannot be justified by reference to a good intention." In other words, the end does not justify the means.

Outcomes or consequences of moral acts are circumstances. They are *not* the central factor in morality. The object of the act is. And the object (what we do) must always be good. "A *morally good* act requires the goodness of the object, of the end, and of the circumstances together" (*CCC*, 1755).

to love the good and avoid evil. Every human being has a fundamental right to follow his or her conscience and to act with freedom on it by making sound, moral, responsible judgments. No one should be forced to act contrary to the true dictates of conscience. This is especially true in decisions involving one's religious beliefs.

Forming a true and upright conscience requires sincerity on our part and an examination of our lives before God. It is a lifelong task that never ends. It requires us to be present to ourselves, that is, sufficiently reflective so that we can continually learn from our conscience so that we can follow it responsibly. Several steps for conscience formation apply:

- Use your human intellect to discover God's goodness and truth. Moral laws like the Ten Commandments guide us on the right path to making good decisions.
- Grow close to Jesus through prayer and the sacraments.
- Look to Jesus' Death on the cross as the perfect example of how to love and how to obey God the Father.
- Look to the example of holy people like the Blessed Mother and the saints and learn from wise Catholics who are trying to live a holy life in our own time.
- Use the gifts and graces that the Holy Spirit has given us. Their purpose is to help us live good and virtuous lives.

We must also look to the Magisterium of the Church in forming our conscience (*CCC*, 2030–2040, 2044–2047, 2049–2051). The pope and bishops apply Christ's message to matters that affect our Salvation and to issues involving our fundamental rights as human beings made in God's image. The Church is a loving mother who helps guide us in right living and points out the path to holiness. Therefore, we are obliged to learn from, form our consciences in light of, and put into practice the teachings of the Church.

Sources for Making Moral Choices

An upright conscience properly formed will recognize that there are three sources of morality: the object chosen, the end or the intention, and the

Lesson 5 Homework

1. Assign the ten For Review questions on pages 204 and 206.
2. Assign the For Reflection feature on page 206 as a journaling activity.
3. Have the students write out their responses to the fifteen statements/questions in the feature Terms, People, Places on pages 207–208.
4. Remind the students to be ready to hand in their three completed Ongoing Assignments at their next session.

circumstances surrounding an action. The *moral object* is the matter of our actions, that is, what we do. It is the most important source of morality. There are some actions that are always seriously wrong. They involve a disorder of the will and are not ordered to the good and our ultimate end, which is God. Examples of actions that are always seriously wrong are murder, adultery, child abuse, blasphemy, and perjury. Nothing can ever justify them—including a good intention or circumstances.

The *intention* of an action involves our motivation, our purpose for doing something. We must always intend good when we act, or what we propose to do is wrong. However, a good intention can never justify an intrinsically evil act. Abortion is always wrong, even if the persons involved in the procedure are doing it for what they think is a good reason like allowing a teenage girl to finish high school.

The *circumstances* are the secondary factors that surround an action, like the time, place, and method of performing the act. They can increase or reduce the evil or goodness of an act. For example, driving while under the influence of alcohol is immoral because it threatens the lives of others. It doesn't matter when or where the incident of drunk driving occurred. It doesn't matter if the person who drove under the influence was a man or woman, a twenty-year-old or a fifty-year-old. None of these circumstances can make an immoral action moral.

In short, a good conscience will recognize the necessity of all three elements of our actions to be morally good: the object (what you do) must be good, your intention must be good, and the circumstances must be good. Jesus is our best guide to forming a sensitive, loving conscience. By praying to him and the Holy Spirit, we can learn how to live a Christ-centered life. It is always good to ask, "What would Jesus do?" to help us distinguish between good and evil. And we should always measure our acts against his Golden Rule: "Do to others whatever you would have them do to you" (Mt 7:12).

Following Your Conscience (CCC, 1790-1794; 1801)

Having made a sincere effort to constantly form our conscience, we are then obliged to follow it. Guided by the Holy Spirit, we must eventually act on what our conscience tells us is the right course of action. "A human being must always obey the certain judgment of his conscience" (*CCC*, 1800).

After we have performed an action, our conscience can help us evaluate whether or not we did the right and good thing. If we were sincere, tried to learn the truth, prayed, and followed the teaching of Jesus and the Church, then we will have a clear conscience. St. Augustine said, "A good conscience is the palace of Christ; the temple of the Holy Ghost; the paradise of delight." Making good conscientious decisions helps us grow in virtue. We form good habits that assist our growth in holiness.

On the other hand, if we violate what our conscience tells us is the good to do, or the evil to avoid, then we have sinned. The Letter of James verifies this: "So for one who knows the right thing to do and does not do it, it is a sin" (Jas 4:17). Pangs of conscience that cause guilt can alert us to a bad decision. A person of integrity will heed their conscience, ask for God's forgiveness, and then reform his or her life so as not to sin again.

It is also possible for a conscience to be wrong. For example, ignorance—lacking proper information about what should be the right and good course of action—can contribute to an erroneous conscience. Emotions also can affect our conscience

- Before moving on, call attention to the feature "Suffering for Christ" on page 204. Have the students look up and read Luke 9:23–24. Tell them that Christianity is not a religion of comfort but of challenge. In calling us to follow, Jesus guarantees only the Cross. Stress, however, that the Way of the Cross is the way of love. We do not seek to suffer for suffering's sake, but for love's sake, for God's sake, and for Heaven's sake.
- Move on to point out to the students that we are able to love like this because God makes us in the divine image, because we are recipients of God's grace, and because God has given us human reason and free will.
- Write the phrase **human reason** on the board. Explain that human reason is the God-given ability to understand the laws of creation. It enables us to recognize God's voice.
- Then write the phrase **free will** on the board and ask the students to tell what they think this means. Help them recognize that the deepest meaning of "free will" is our ability to choose to cooperate with God's will and to do what is right and just.
- Go to brainstorm the term **conscience**. List replies on the board.
- Call attention to the quotation about conscience from the *Catechism of the Catholic Church* (*CCC*, 1778) on page 201. To review of the gifts of the Holy Spirit, have the students describe how each of the gifts assists the conscience in judging the moral quality of an action. Note the five steps of good conscience formation listed in the text (page 202). Then point out that the Church's Magisterium (teaching) is also a source for conscience formation and guidance along the path to holiness. Stress that without consistent conscience formation, even what we might term our "conscientious decisions" can be *wrong*, even sinful.
- Have the students work in small groups to come up with situations in which a decision of conscience is required. Direct the groups to speculate on outcome if a decision is made based on the principles of conscience formation. If you wish, offer suggestions like the following:
  - whether or not to cheat on an important test
  - whether or not to turn in a friend who is dealing drugs
  - whether or not to intervene when you see someone is a victim of prejudice
  - whether or not to contradict an authority figure when you feel he or she is in the wrong

- Give each group the opportunity to explain its situation and its "conscientious decision."
- Briefly go over the elements of morality as outlined in the text:
  - The object chosen—what we do (the moral object)
  - The intention—our motive for the action we chose
  - The circumstances of our action—the context and circumstances surrounding the chosen action
- Go through each of the elements with the students, briefly explaining each:
  - *The Moral Object*: A bad act cannot be made good by a good intention or circumstance. Some actions are always seriously wrong.
  - *The Intention*: Our intention answers the question, "Why did you do that?" Make sure the students understand that even the best of intentions cannot make an evil action good. (*Note:* Refer the students to the information in the feature Explaining the Faith on page 202.)

decisions. For example, anger or the strong craving for pleasure might cloud our thinking and judgment. At times, we are not fully at fault for not knowing the right course of action. But at other times we are fully blameworthy because we made little or no effort to find out the truth.

We must always strengthen our conscience by sincerely trying to correct it when it is wrong, by consulting with competent and wise people when we are in doubt, by learning from our mistakes and not repeating them, and by avoiding those situations that have led us to make wrong and sinful decisions in the past.

Because we are God's adopted children, he has called us to holiness. Jesus instructs us to "Be perfect, as our heavenly Father is perfect" (Mt 5:48). His call to holiness, to perfection, is meant for all of his followers, no matter who we are or what our walk in life might be. A way of being holy is to form a good conscience, put Jesus' example of love into practice, and ask for the help of the Holy Spirit. Doing these things allows us to make good and moral choices, an essential element of holiness.

For Review

1. Discuss three ways a person can grow in holiness.
2. Why are human beings capable of holiness?

(continued on page 206)

SUFFERING FOR CHRIST

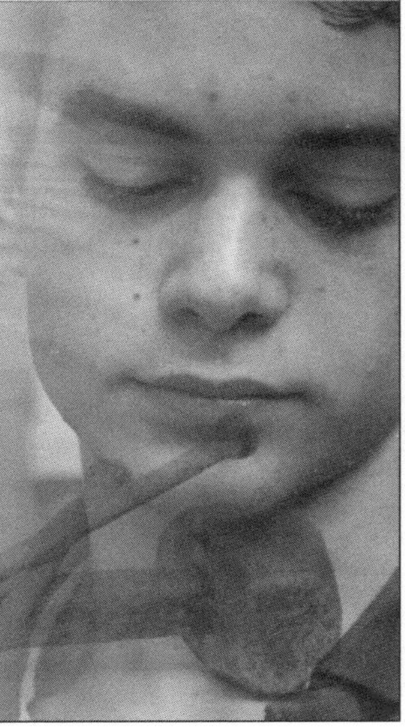

You cannot watch television without being bombarded with advertisements for various drugs that are meant to relieve suffering. We live in a world that preaches a message of ease and convenience. Some nonbelievers simply do not understand why followers of Jesus Christ are willing to make sacrifices and endure suffering, especially in witnessing to Christ and their faith.

Christians sacrifice and endure pain for many reasons. First, they are imitating Jesus Christ whose suffering and death won Salvation for us. Jesus also told his followers that they would suffer for their faith, but he promised that he would be with them in their suffering. Therefore, Christians believe Jesus is present to them when they suffer. In faith, they patiently accept suffering while always trusting that God will send them grace and the strength of the Holy Spirit's gift of fortitude to see them through the tough times.

As Jesus' disciples, we know that suffering can guide us to Heaven because it can help make up, to a certain degree, for some of the harm caused by our sins. In the midst of our suffering, we can look to the suffering, Death, Resurrection, and Ascension of Jesus Christ and know that the sufferings of this world are not absolute and final. Eternal life with God in Heaven is the reward and the result.

When suffering comes our way, we should pray to Jesus. He will strengthen us to endure the suffering and help us become more like him. If we unite our suffering to his, it can become part of the mystery of Christ's own redemptive activity, a means of purification and of Salvation for us and for others (*CCC*, 618, 1505).

For Review Answers (pages 204 and 206)

1. A person can grow in holiness by practicing the virtue of charity, by uniting with Christ in the sacraments, and by self-denial with the commitment to follow Christ even to the Cross.
2. Human beings are capable of holiness because they are "made in God's image and likeness, . . . created out of love, for love and to love."
3. Free will is the capacity to choose among alternatives.
4. Conscience is a judgment of reason whereby the human person recognizes the moral quality of an act.
5. Answers will include using human intellect, learning the moral laws, participating in the sacraments, looking to Jesus' Death, looking to the example of the saints and Mary, and using the gifts of the Holy Spirit.

continued on page 228

BL. PIER GIORGIO FRASSATI

Faithful Disciple

Termed "the man of the eight Beatitudes" by Pope John Paul II at his beatification ceremony in Rome in 1990, Bl. Pier Giorgio Frassati was a joy-filled man who lived only to age twenty-four but who remains a model for bountiful love and service today. His sister said of him: "He represented the finest in Christian youth: pure, happy, enthusiastic about everything that is good and beautiful."

Pier was born to a wealthy and politically connected family in Turin, Italy. He was an average student but a great athlete and mountain climber. His peers adored him and called him "Terror" because of the practical jokes he played. After high school, he studied mineralogy in an engineering program. He participated in Catholic groups like Apostleship of Prayer and the Company of the Most Blessed Sacrament. Both of these groups were known for helping poor people and promoting Eucharistic adoration, Marian devotion, and personal chastity.

Pier also became active in political groups—like the Young Catholic Workers, Catholic Action, and *Milites Mariae*—that ministered to poor people, fought fascism, and put into practice the Church's social teachings. He gave his money to needy people and visited the sick. It was while ministering to the sick that he contracted an acute case of polio that took his life. Bl. Pier Giorgio offers these words of advice on how to grow in holiness:

> With all the strength of my soul I urge you young people to approach the Communion table as often as you can. Feed on this bread of angels whence you will draw all the energy you need to fight inner battles. Because true happiness, dear friends, does not consist in the pleasures of the world or in earthly things, but in peace of conscience, which we have only if we are pure in heart and mind.

- *The Circumstances*: This element is concerned with the *who, where, when*, and *how* of an action. Note the example (drunk driving) given in the text. Invite the students to come up with examples of their own.

- Have the students work in small groups of three or four to create a scenario for a moral dilemma. Then have groups switch dilemmas with another group, so that no group works on its own scenario. Direct each small group to analyze the scenario in terms of the moral objective, the intention, and the circumstances and then to recommend the best possible solution to the dilemma. Allow sufficient time for the small groups to present their dilemmas and solutions. Conclude by making sure that the students understand that the goodness of an act is dependent on: *what* we do; *why* we do it; and the *circumstances* of what we do.
- Call attention to the text section "Following Your Conscience" on page 203–204. Explain that having formed our conscience, we are required to follow it and that if we neglect the good our conscience tells us to do, we sin. However, as mentioned above, it is possible to have a poorly formed conscience and thus even our "conscientious" decisions may be wrong. Ignorance and emotions may negatively affect our conscientious decision-making. Call on different students to name the ways we can strengthen our conscience:

For Enrichment

On Conscience

Labor to keep alive in your breast that little spark of celestial fire called conscience.

—George Washington

Every judgment of conscience, be it right or wrong, be it about things evil in themselves or morally indifferent, is obligatory, in such wise that he who acts against his conscience always sins.

—St. Thomas Aquinas

Cowardice asks the question, "Is it safe?" Expediency asks the question, "Is it politic?" Vanity asks the question, "Is it popular?" But, conscience asks the question, "Is it right?" And there comes a time when one must take a position that is neither safe, nor politic, nor popular, but one must take it because one's conscience tells one that it is right.

—Dr. Martin Luther King Jr.

   - Correct it when it is wrong.
   - Consult with wise people when we're in doubt.
   - Learn from mistakes.
   - Avoid occasions that lead us to sin.
- Before dismissing the students, refer them to the feature "Faithful Disciple: Bl. Pier Giorgio Frassati" (page 205). If the students have not read the story of this amazing young man, allow time for them to do so now. Suggest they pay special attention to the information Pier Frassati gives regarding "peace of conscience." Note how Pier Frassati highlights the importance of receiving the Eucharist often. Remind the students that the Eucharist, like all the sacraments, is an encounter with the person of Jesus Christ. Our celebration of the sacraments gives us grace to choose what is right and then to act.
- Have the students write in their journals about a time when they were aware they were making an important (moral) choice. Direct them to address what part praying and celebrating the sacraments (e.g., receiving Eucharist, celebrating Penance) played in the decision-making process.

3. What is free will?
4. Define *conscience*.
5. Name at least four steps that are necessary to form a good conscience.
6. Why must we always follow our conscience?
7. What is the role of the Magisterium in helping people do the right thing?
8. What are the three sources of every moral action?
9. Explain how conscience can sometimes be in error. What must we do to correct it?
10. What role does suffering have in the life of Christians?

For Reflection

- Think about a decision dealing with right and wrong that you made this past week. What were the steps you took to make your decision to act? Did you have a clear conscience after making the decision? Why or why not?
- Quaker founder William Penn contemplated the Paschal Mystery and the meaning of suffering and said: "No pain, no palm; no thorns, no throne; no gall, no glory; no cross, no crown." What does this quotation mean to you?

For Review Answers (pages 204 and 206) continued form page 226

6. We must follow our conscience because making good conscientious decisions helps us form good habits of virtue and by doing so we respond to God's call for us to be holy.
7. The role of the Magisterium is to apply Christ's message to matters that affect our Salvation and to issues involving our fundamental rights as human beings made in God's image.
8. The three sources of every moral action are the object chosen, the end or intention, and the circumstances surrounding the action.
9. Lacking proper information about right and wrong can lead to error. Emotions can also affect conscience. To correct error we must learn from our mistakes, sincerely try to correct them, and learn from others.
10. Suffering connects us to Christ and can guide us to Heaven. It can help to make up for harm caused by sin.

Living the Paschal Mystery: A Call to Holiness 207

Main Ideas

- Our call to holiness is a vocation given to us by Jesus himself. (p. 186)
- Living a virtuous life and cooperating with God's grace are two ways to grow in holiness. (p. 187)
- Human virtues are virtues we can acquire by human effort. (p. 188)
- The cardinal virtues—prudence, justice, fortitude, and temperance, are the source of the other human virtues. (pp. 188–190)
- Prudence is equated with common sense and wisdom. (p. 188)
- Justice—giving due to God and neighbor—is distinguished by four types of justice: commutative, distributive, legal, and social. (p. 189)
- Fortitude is a virtue that allows for the courage to conquer fears, even the fear of death, for a worthy cause. (p. 190)
- Temperance is distinguished by three parts: abstinence, sobriety, and chastity. (pp. 190–191)
- Sanctifying grace is the free and undeserved gift that God gives to us that blesses us in many ways and helps us to grow in holiness. (p. 196)
- Sanctifying grace is distinguished from actual graces, sacramental graces, and graces of state. (pp. 196–197)
- The seven gifts of the Holy Spirit—wisdom, understanding, knowledge, counsel (right judgment), fortitude (courage), piety (reverence), and fear of the Lord (wonder and awe) also help us to live Christ-like lives. (p. 197)
- The theological virtues—faith, hope, and charity (love)—are related directly to God. (p. 191)
- Faith makes it possible for us to commit totally to God. (pp. 191–192)
- Hope is the virtue that allows us to desire the Kingdom of Heaven and happiness in eternal life. (pp. 192–193)
- Charity, the "mother of virtues," is the only virtue that lasts into eternity; it allows us to love God for his own sake and our neighbor as ourselves for the love of God. (pp. 193–194)
- Humans are capable of holiness because God has made us to share in his own life. (pp. 199–200)
- Through the gift of human reason and aided by the Holy Spirit, we are able to uncover truth, goodness, and beauty. (p. 200)
- The gift of free will allows us the opportunity to make use of our God-given talents and to cooperate with the graces of the Holy Spirit. It allows us to make moral choices. (p. 201)
- Essential to making good moral choices is the formation of a good conscience. (p. 201)
- An upright conscience recognizes three sources for morality: the object chosen, the end or intention, and the circumstances surrounding the action. (pp. 202–203)
- Following a well-informed conscience and making a moral choice based on it is an opportunity for growth in holiness. (pp. 203–204)

Terms, People, Places

On a separate sheet of paper, write the answers to the following:

1. *Vocation*: Write a word that is synonymous with vocation.
2. *Virtue*: Name a human virtue that has helped you to lead a moral life.
3. *Cardinal Virtues*: Why are the cardinal virtues called "hinge virtues"?
4. *Vice*: Name an example of a vice.
5. *Religion*: How does religion express itself?
6. *Justification*: What is the grace of justification traditionally called?

Chapter 8 Quick View

Review Lesson Objectives

The students will:

- review Chapter 8 in preparation for the chapter test.
- join in prayer together.

Review Lesson Homework

1. Call attention to the Reflection and Resolution on page 209 and encourage the students to write their responses in their journals.
2. Reread Chapter 8.
3. Study for the Chapter 8 Test.

Chapter 8: Living the Paschal Mystery: A Call to Holiness—Review Lesson

Bell Ringers

- Consider using one of the students' prayers from the feature "Fruits of the Holy Spirit in Your Life" (page 197) to begin the session.
- Review the previous lesson by inviting the students to share responses to the ten questions in the For Review section on pages 204 and 206.
- Collect the students' Ongoing Assignments for Chapter 8. Allow time for any students who prepared skits on a cardinal virtue (Assignment # 3) to present them to the class.

Teaching Approaches

Chapter Quick View (pages 207-209)

- Call on different students to offer what they wrote in response to the statements/questions of the feature Terms, People, Places (on pages 207–208). Use the questions in this section to help the students review key elements of the unit. Answers for each question will vary.
- Divide the class into groups of three or four. Direct group members to go over the chapter's For Review sections by taking turns asking one another the questions. Encourage the students to try to answer without checking their journals or notes. Circulate to offer assistance should questions or difficulties arise.
- Have the students look over the Chapter 8 Main Ideas section on page 207. Encourage questions and invite class members to offer answers. Clarify any confusion.
- Check vocabulary by asking the students to find a partner and then quiz one another on the terms. Consider having students create and use flashcards to review the many vocabulary terms in this chapter.
- Allow some quiet time for the students to study on their own. If students have more questions, invite them to approach you privately while their classmates study.

Prayer Service

- Gather the students in a circle around a lighted candle.
- Sing or play a recording of a hymn to the Holy Spirit such as "Spirit of God" by James E. More Jr.
- Lead the students in praying "St. Augustine's Prayer to the Holy Spirit" on pages 208–209.
- Conclude by sharing a sign of peace and unity.

Chapter 8 Test Lesson

Teaching Approaches

- Assign the Chapter 8 Test (starting on page 291 of the TWE and also online at www.avemariapress.com).

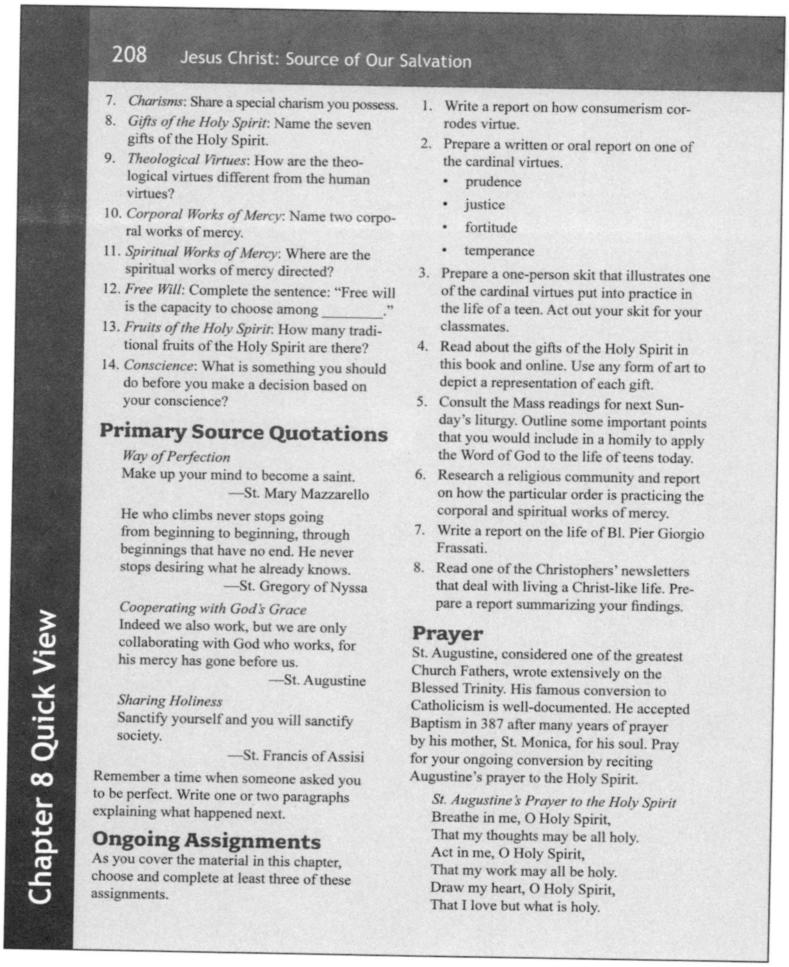

208 Jesus Christ: Source of Our Salvation

Chapter 8 Quick View

7. *Charisms*: Share a special charism you possess.
8. *Gifts of the Holy Spirit*: Name the seven gifts of the Holy Spirit.
9. *Theological Virtues*: How are the theological virtues different from the human virtues?
10. *Corporal Works of Mercy*: Name two corporal works of mercy.
11. *Spiritual Works of Mercy*: Where are the spiritual works of mercy directed?
12. *Free Will*: Complete the sentence: "Free will is the capacity to choose among ________."
13. *Fruits of the Holy Spirit*: How many traditional fruits of the Holy Spirit are there?
14. *Conscience*: What is something you should do before you make a decision based on your conscience?

Primary Source Quotations

Way of Perfection
Make up your mind to become a saint.
—St. Mary Mazzarello

He who climbs never stops going from beginning to beginning, through beginnings that have no end. He never stops desiring what he already knows.
—St. Gregory of Nyssa

Cooperating with God's Grace
Indeed we also work, but we are only collaborating with God who works, for his mercy has gone before us.
—St. Augustine

Sharing Holiness
Sanctify yourself and you will sanctify society.
—St. Francis of Assisi

Remember a time when someone asked you to be perfect. Write one or two paragraphs explaining what happened next.

Ongoing Assignments

As you cover the material in this chapter, choose and complete at least three of these assignments.

1. Write a report on how consumerism corrodes virtue.
2. Prepare a written or oral report on one of the cardinal virtues.
   - prudence
   - justice
   - fortitude
   - temperance
3. Prepare a one-person skit that illustrates one of the cardinal virtues put into practice in the life of a teen. Act out your skit for your classmates.
4. Read about the gifts of the Holy Spirit in this book and online. Use any form of art to depict a representation of each gift.
5. Consult the Mass readings for next Sunday's liturgy. Outline some important points that you would include in a homily to apply the Word of God to the life of teens today.
6. Research a religious community and report on how the particular order is practicing the corporal and spiritual works of mercy.
7. Write a report on the life of Bl. Pier Giorgio Frassati.
8. Read one of the Christophers' newsletters that deal with living a Christ-like life. Prepare a report summarizing your findings.

Prayer

St. Augustine, considered one of the greatest Church Fathers, wrote extensively on the Blessed Trinity. His famous conversion to Catholicism is well-documented. He accepted Baptism in 387 after many years of prayer by his mother, St. Monica, for his soul. Pray for your ongoing conversion by reciting Augustine's prayer to the Holy Spirit.

St. Augustine's Prayer to the Holy Spirit
Breathe in me, O Holy Spirit,
That my thoughts may be all holy.
Act in me, O Holy Spirit,
That my work may all be holy.
Draw my heart, O Holy Spirit,
That I love but what is holy.

Chapter 8 Test Answers

Part 1: True or False. (2 points each)

1. F 2. T 3. T 4. F 5. T 6. T 7. T 8. F 9. F 10. F 11. F 12. T 13. T 14. T

Part 2: Matching. (2 points each)

1. A 2. E 3. F 4. A 5. B 6. B 7. D 8. G 9. C

1. D 2. A 3. G 4. E 5. B 6. C 7. F

Part 3: Brief Answers. (points vary)

1. When it comes to forming our conscience, there are three sources of morality: (1) the object chosen—what we choose do (the moral object), (2) the intention—our motive for the action we've chosen, (3) the circumstances of our action—the context and circumstances surrounding the chosen action. **(6 points)**
2. The types of grace include:
   - Sanctifying grace—the grace of justification, makes us holy, unites us to the Lord's Paschal Mystery, and is also called habitual grace
   - Actual grace—God's interventions at the beginning of conversion or in the course of sanctification
   - Sacramental grace—specific gifts that come from particular sacraments
   - Charisms—special gifts of the Holy Spirit to help Christians build up the Body of Christ
   - Graces of state—the help God gives to particular ministries in the Church (**8 points**)

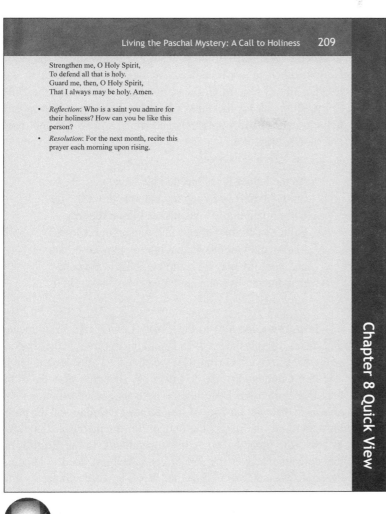

Strengthen me, O Holy Spirit,
To defend all that is holy.
Guard me, then, O Holy Spirit,
That I always may be holy. Amen.

- *Reflection*: Who is a saint you admire for their holiness? How can you be like this person?
- *Resolution*: For the next month, recite this prayer each morning upon rising.

Test Lesson Homework

1. Read the following text sections of Chapter 9: "The Fellowship of the Unashamed" (page 212) and "Discipleship Means Following Jesus and His Teachings" (pages 212–216).
2. Examine the Chapter 9 Ongoing Assignments on pages 235–236.

Chapter 8 Test Answers continued

3. The four types of justice are:
   - Commutative justice—regulates relationships of reciprocity
   - Distributive justice—champions the common good
   - Legal justice—secures societal solidarity; it refers to rights and responsibilities of citizens to obey everyone else's rights and to obey laws that have been put in place to protect peace and social order
   - Social justice—seeks fair (re)distribution of resources, opportunities, and responsibilities; challenges the roots of oppression and injustice; empowers people to exercise self-determination and realize their full potential; and builds social solidarity and community capacity for collaborative action (**8 points**)
4. The students may include any three of the following ways we may go about strengthening the virtue of faith: prayer, Scripture reading, celebrating the sacraments, studying the faith, drawing on the faith of friends, and putting faith into action. (**6 points**)
5. The students may include any three of the following steps we can employ to strengthen our conscience:
   - Correct it when it is wrong.
   - Consult with wise people when we're in doubt.
   - Learn from mistakes.
   - Avoid occasions that lead us to sin. (**6 points**)
6. The gifts of the Holy Spirit include wisdom, understanding, knowledge, counsel, fortitude, piety, and fear of the Lord. Their definitions can be found on page 197. (**6 points**)

Chapter 9: Discipleship: Following in the Footsteps of Jesus

Introduction

Will you come and follow me if I but call your name?
Will you go where you don't know and never be the same?
Will you let my love be shown?
Will you let my name be known?
Will you let my life be grown in you and you in me?

—John L. Bell, "The Summons"

The words of the hymn pose some difficult questions, and we should not offer glib answers. They summon us to follow in Jesus' footsteps as his disciples, and we had best understand what responding to that summons entails. Why? Because following Jesus is not culturally relevant—for what Jesus teaches us is different from what culture and society teaches us. Why? Jesus is calling us out of the kingdoms of this world and into the Kingdom of God. Living as citizens of that Kingdom is what a disciple is summoned to do.

This chapter helps the students learn, first of all, that a disciple of Jesus is someone who is willing to follow, to allow Jesus to take the lead, and to learn from his leadership. Disciples, then, must be pupils striving to understand the Gospel—studying it, praying over it, and obeying it. By doing so, pupils come to know not simply the words of Jesus but the Word himself. Such intimacy makes pupils friends and allows them to share a personal relationship with Jesus, a relationship which, in turn, empowers friends to become followers—to do as Jesus did and to spread the Good News to others in word and deed. All together, discipleship means living a life of love of God and of neighbor. Happily, the Holy Spirit equips us for that life of love by dwelling within us and helping us face life's pressures and trials, and so become more and more Christ-like.

Jesus tells his disciples:

> As the Father loves me, so I also love you. Remain in my love. If you keep my commandments, you will remain in my love, just as I have kept my Father's commandments and remain in his love. I have told you this so that my joy may be in you and your joy may be complete. This is my commandment: love one another as I love you. (Jn 15:9–12)

Jesus' love led him to the Cross. Loving like Jesus means that, as his disciples, we will end up living our lives in the shadow of the Cross as well. On our way, we have the Father's commands (the Ten Commandments) to guide us. Disciples also have the blessings called the Beatitudes. These unique benedictions enable us to discover the face of Jesus among us today—in the poor, the mourning, the meek, the hungering, the merciful, the clean of heart, the peacemakers, and the righteous. In the Beatitudes, the students discover the sort of discipleship needed to become evangelizers—sharers of the Good News in word and deed—and so ensure the coming of God's Kingdom.

The chapter helps the students learn that Jesus is calling them to be good stewards of the gifts God has given them. Even more, this chapter helps the students recognize that no matter their age or maturity level in the Christian life, they *do* have something to offer—something uniquely their own. Christ is calling all his

Chapter Objectives

To help the students:

- discover the sort of commitment necessary to be disciples of Jesus.
- understand that a disciple is a pupil, friend, and follower of Jesus.
- investigate the Ten Commandments as ways of following in Jesus' footsteps.
- investigate the Beatitudes as guides for living as Jesus' disciples.
- discover ways to be an evangelist.
- understand that stewardship is a requirement of the evangelist.
- investigate what stewardship entails and requires.
- discover the connection between love and forgiveness and self-denial.
- understand that love demands care for the poor and outcast.

disciples, no matter who they are, to take up their cross, love others, and spread the Good News.

The summons to discipleship is a summons to love. For love is not simply an emotion. It is a way of being in the world. For disciples this means the "way of being" that Jesus demonstrated. Remember, his command is not "love one another *period,*" but rather, "love one another *comma* as I have loved you." The love required of a disciple of Jesus is about caring for the outcast, the poor, and all those pushed to the edges of society. It entails self-sacrifice and promises no worldly prizes such as pleasure, popularity, power, or possessions. What it does promise, however, is the ability to travel in Jesus' company, to move, live, and grow in him, and, as the hymn "The Summons" so beautifully puts it, "to never be the same."

Advance Preparations

Prepare or have on hand:

For Lesson 1

- Corrected copies of the Chapter 8 Test
- A recording of the song "Day by Day," from the soundtrack of *Godspell,* and a player (optional)
- Bibles

For Lesson 2

- Bibles
- Note cards
- Chapter 9, Handout 1, "Understanding the Ten Commandments"

For Lesson 3

- Bibles
- Old newspapers, magazines, and art materials (scissors, glue, tape, markers, paper, etc.)
- A recording of a Beatitudes hymn such as "Blest Are They" by David Haas or "Beatitudes" by the Dameans (optional)

For Lesson 4

- Bibles
- Copies of Chapter 9, Handout 2, "No One Else Can Do What God Is Calling *You* to Do"
- Copies of the students' paper plates listing gifts from Chapter 8, Lesson 4

For Lesson 5

- Bibles
- Copies of Chapter 9, Handout 3, "Easy Essays"
- A copy of the Steward's Prayer (from Chapter 9, Handout 2)

For the Chapter 9 Review Lesson

- Audio-visual equipment needed to view slide show and PowerPoint presentations
- A cross or crucifix
- A recording of a discipleship themed hymn, such as "Anthem" by Tom Conry or "Take Up Your Cross" by David Haas (optional)

For the Chapter 9 Test Lesson

- Copies of the Chapter 9 Test (starting on page 291 of the TWE and also online at www.avemariapress.com)

Chapter 9 Handouts

- Handout 1, Understanding the Ten Commandments—The Students review the requirements and forbidden sins connected to each of the commandments.
- Handout 2, No One Else Can Do What God Is Calling *You* to Do—The students name how they will share their time, talent, treasure, and tradition; and they learn a stewardship prayer.
- Handout 3, Easy Essays—The students consider and discuss what is necessary to live as faithful disciples of Christ.

Chapter 9: Discipleship: Following in the Footsteps of Jesus—Lesson 1

Bell Ringers

- Distribute the students' corrected Chapter 8 Tests. Go over the test with the group, using it as a means to review the previous chapter. Address any remaining questions or concerns the students may have.
- If possible, introduce this lesson by playing a recording of the song "Day by Day" from the soundtrack of *Godspell*. Then point out the prayer by St. Richard of Chichester (see page 210 of the student text), on which the song is based. Lead the students in the prayer.
- Tell the group that this is an excellent prayer for anyone seeking or claiming to be a disciple of Jesus. Encourage them to pray it as they progress through the lessons of this chapter.

Teaching Approaches

The Fellowship of the Unashamed (page 212)

- Have the students reread the letter written by the Zimbabwe martyr. Ask them to imagine themselves in this situation. How would they react? Invite them to journal about their fears and write a letter as though they were in a similar situation.
- Read aloud the following quotation from G. K. Chesterton to the students: "Jesus promised his disciples three things—that they would be completely fearless, absurdly happy, and in constant trouble." Then call attention to the four things Jesus taught us about what it means to be his disciple on page 212. Finally, invite the students to tell how Chesterton's words apply to the martyred Zimbabwe pastor.
- Point out the For Reflection section on page 212. Encourage the students to give the question some serious thought as they proceed through this chapter.

The Fellowship of the Unashamed

The following note was found on the desk of a pastor who was martyred in Zimbabwe, where it had been said: "You'd better watch out. One dead missionary is as good as a hundred dead terrorists to us." The author is unknown, but the message is strong. He has taken to heart Jesus' core message of what it means to be his disciple: "Whoever wishes to come after me must deny himself, take up his cross and follow me" (Mk 8:3–4). The letter defines discipleship:

> I'm part of the fellowship of the unashamed. I have the Holy Spirit's power. The die has been cast. I have stepped over the line. The decision has been made—I am a disciple of his. I won't look back, let up, slow down, back away, or be still. My past is redeemed, my present makes sense, my future is secure. I'm finished and done with low living, sight walking, smooth knees, colorless dreams, tamed visions, worldly taking, cheap giving, and dwarfed goals.
>
> I no longer need preeminence, prosperity, position, promotions, plaudits, or popularity. I don't have to be right, first, tops, recognized, praised, regarded, or rewarded. I now live by faith, lean in his presence, walk with patience, am uplifted by prayer, and I labor with power.
>
> My face is set, my gait is fast, my goal is Heaven, my road is narrow, my way rough, my companions are few, my Guide reliable, my mission clear. I cannot be bought, compromised, detoured, lured away, turned back, deluded, or delayed. I will not flinch in the face of sacrifice, hesitate in the presence of the enemy, pander at the pool of popularity, or meander in the maze of mediocrity.
>
> I won't give up, shut up, let up, until I have stayed up, stored up, prayed up, paid up, preached up, for the cause of Christ. I am a disciple of Jesus. I must go till he comes, give till I drop, preach till all know, and work till he stops me. And, when he comes for his own, he will have no problem recognizing me . . . my banner will be clear!

This brave priest knew exactly what it meant to be a disciple of Jesus Christ. Each of us can only hope to attain the level of freedom and commitment he had in following his Lord and witnessing to his faith in him.

During his ministry and on his journey to Jerusalem and the saving events of the Paschal Mystery, Jesus taught what it means to be a disciple:

- A disciple must put personal desires aside to follow his Father's will.
- A disciple must accept suffering, even to the point of death.
- A disciple must serve others.
- A disciple must love others, even those who are enemies.

This chapter explores some of the practical and dramatic tasks that make up Christian discipleship.

For Reflection

"The decision has been made—I am a disciple of his." How strongly do you agree with this statement for your own life?

Discipleship Means Following Jesus and His Teachings

You may recall from an earlier course of study the following aspects of Christian discipleship. A disciple is a:

- *pupil* of Jesus, that is, one who learns from him, demonstrating an ability to grasp

Lesson 1 Objectives

The students will:

- review Chapter 8.
- discover the sort of commitment needed to be Jesus' disciple.
- rate themselves on how well they are living the Beatitudes.
- list the three senses of discipleship of Jesus: pupil, friend, and follower.
- describe the meaning of discipleship.
- appreciate what it means to obey Jesus' commands.
- identify the Twelve Apostles.

Lesson 1 Preview

In this lesson, the students discover the steps necessary to become a disciple of Jesus. They learn that Jesus trusts them and cherishes them and that he asks them to keep his commands and share the Good News with others in what they say and do.

Core Gospel Values

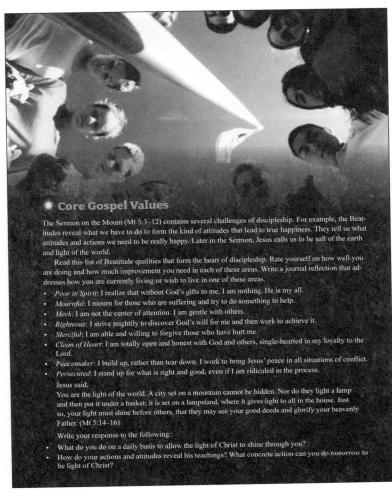

The Sermon on the Mount (Mt 5:3–12) contains several challenges of discipleship. For example, the Beatitudes reveal what we have to do to form the kind of attitudes that lead to true happiness. They tell us what attitudes and actions we need to be really happy. Later in the Sermon, Jesus calls us to be salt of the earth and light of the world.

Read this list of Beatitude qualities that form the heart of discipleship. Rate yourself on how well you are doing and how much improvement you need in each of these areas. Write a journal reflection that addresses how you are currently living or wish to live in one of these areas.

- *Poor in Spirit*: I realize that without God's gifts to me, I am nothing. He is my all.
- *Mournful*: I mourn for those who are suffering and try to do something to help.
- *Meek*: I am not the center of attention. I am gentle with others.
- *Righteous*: I strive mightily to discover God's will for me and then work to achieve it.
- *Merciful*: I am able and willing to forgive those who have hurt me.
- *Clean of Heart*: I am totally open and honest with God and others, single-hearted in my loyalty to the Lord.
- *Peacemaker*: I build up, rather than tear down. I work to bring Jesus' peace in all situations of conflict.
- *Persecuted*: I stand up for what is right and good, even if I am ridiculed in the process.

Jesus said,

You are the light of the world. A city set on a mountain cannot be hidden. Nor do they light a lamp and then put it under a basket; it is set on a lampstand, where it gives light to all in the house. Just so, your light must shine before others, that they may see your good deeds and glorify your heavenly Father. (Mt 5:14–16)

Write your response to the following:

- What do you do on a daily basis to allow the light of Christ to shine through you?
- How do your actions and attitudes reveal his teachings? What concrete action can you do *tomorrow* to be light of Christ?

Lesson 1 Homework

1. Direct the students to write out their answers to the two For Review questions on page 216.
2. Assign the For Reflection question on page 216 as a journal activity.
3. Ask the students to turn to the Ongoing Assignments on pages 235–236. Have them choose three of the listed assignments to complete prior to the conclusion of this chapter. Tell the students that the assignments are due on the day they gather for their chapter review.
4. Tell the students to read "Following Jesus' Commands—Ten Commandments" (pages 216–223) in preparation for their next lesson.

- Write the following on the board: **Beatitude = Happiness**. Explain that "beatitude" means *blessing* or *happiness*, and remind the students that the New Testament defines happiness as the coming of the Kingdom of God. Remind them, too, of the "present-but-not-yet" quality of the Kingdom of God. Tell them that Jesus gives the Beatitudes to show us what we ought to be doing in order to assure the Kingdom's advance. The Beatitudes pave the way for the people of God to usher in the coming of the God's Kingdom.
- Call attention to the opening activity "Core Gospel Values" (page 213). Ask one of the students to read the Beatitudes from Matthew 5:3–12. Then go over the activity's directions and allow time for the students to rate themselves on how well they are doing living out each Beatitude. Suggest they use a simple scale like the following: *Very Well—Well—Not So Well.* Allow time for the students to complete their ranking. Afterward, suggest that they pray for the grace to improve the way they are living out any Beatitude they ranked as *Not So Well*. Finally, tell them that they will discover more about living the Beatitudes later in this chapter.
- Move on to read Jesus' words from Matthew 5:14–16 on page 213. Then direct attention to the activity's two concluding questions. Read both aloud. Ask the students to recall the story of the boy and the light shining through the stained glass windows (from Chapter 8). Help them recall that saintliness is letting the light of Christ shine through. Then have the students write their responses to the two questions from page 213 in their journals. Afterward, encourage them to let their light shine by sharing what they have written.

Discipleship Means Following Jesus and His Teachings (pages 212-216)

- Write the following on the board: **Disciple = Pupil, Friend, and Follower**. Go through each of the senses of discipleship:
    - *Pupil*—Remind the students that Jesus was called "rabbi." Ask them what "rabbi" means. (*teacher*) Point out that Jesus was seen as a unique and powerful rabbi/teacher by friend and foe alike. Ironically, the last word the Apostle Judas spoke to Jesus was "rabbi." Before moving on, see to it that the students understand that being a disciple means accepting and analyzing Jesus' teachings.

- *Friend*—Have the students read John 15:12–15. Then write the following quotation from Thomas à Kempis on the board: **"If thou art willing to suffer no adversity, how wilt thou be the friend of Christ?"** Note the qualities of friendship listed on page 214 of the text.
- *Follower*— Have the students look up and read 1 Peter 3:15: "Always be ready to give an explanation to anyone who asks you for a reason for your hope." Note that we should be ready to talk about the foundation of our faith. Call attention to the definition of follower in the text ("one who imitates Jesus' example and works to spread his message and work").

- Then write the following quotation from Pope St. Gregory the Great on the board: **"Whatsoever one would understand what he hears must hasten to put into practice what he has heard."**
- Go on to point out that being a disciple of Jesus thus means becoming an evangelist; and that means "walking the talk," that is, putting Jesus' teachings into action.

intellectually and analyze thoroughly his teachings

- a *friend* of Jesus, one who enters into a personal relationship with him. It is a relationship marked by intimacy, generosity, availability, sacrifice, concern, and, above all else, mutual love
- *follower* of Jesus, one who imitates his example and works to spread his message and work. This is what it means to *evangelize*, a word that means, "to preach the Gospel." A disciple, therefore, is an *evangelist*, one who preaches Jesus to others in word and deed.

In all three senses, a disciple of Jesus must be concerned about putting into practice specific commands that the Lord gave to us. For example, at the end of the Sermon on the Mount, Jesus said,

> Not everyone who says to me, "Lord, Lord," will enter the kingdom of heaven, but only the one who does the will of my Father in heaven. Many will say to me on that day, "Lord, Lord, did we not prophesy in your name? Did we not drive out demons in your name? Did we not do mighty deeds in your name?" Then I will declare to them solemnly, "I never knew you. Depart from me, you evildoers." Everyone who listens to these words of mine and acts on them will be like a wise man who built his house on rock. The rain fell, the floods came, and the winds blew and buffeted the house. But it did not collapse; it had been set solidly on rock. And everyone who listens to these words of mine but does not act on them will be like a fool who built his house on sand. The rain fell, the floods came, and the winds blew and buffeted the house. And it collapsed and was completely ruined. (Mt 7:21–27)

Lip service is not enough for discipleship. Our faith must be backed up with concrete deeds—doing the Father's will as revealed by his Son, Jesus Christ.

Similarly, note that Jesus calls us to be his friends. Discipleship is about relationship. We are not out on an island enduring the difficulties of being Christian by ourselves. You may be teased or mocked for living out Jesus' teachings and for professing your belief in him. But you can count on Jesus sharing this experience with you as a *friend*:

> As the Father loves me, so I also love you. Remain in my love. If you keep my commandments, you will remain in my love, just as I have kept my Father's commandments and remain in his love. I have told you this so that my joy may be in you and your joy may be complete. This is my commandment: love one another as I love you. No one has greater love than this, to lay down one's life for one's friends. You are my friends if you do what I command you. I no longer call

For Enrichment

Radical Discipleship

> Christians are not distinguished from the rest of humankind by country or speech or customs; the fact is, they nowhere settle in cities of their own; they use no peculiar language; they cultivate no eccentric mode of life. . . . Yet, while they settle in both Greek and non-Greek cities, as each one's lot is cast, and conform to the customs of the country in dress, diet, and mode of life in general, the whole tenor of their way of living stamps it as worthy of admiration and contrary to expectation. . . . They dwell in their own countries, but only as sojourners; they bear their share in all things as citizens, and they endure all hardships as strangers. Every foreign country is a fatherland to them, and every fatherland is foreign. They marry like all other men and they beget children; but they do not cast away their offspring. They have their meals in common, but not their wives. . . . They spend their days on earth, but hold citizenship in heaven. They obey the established laws, but in their private lives go beyond the law. They are reviled, and they bless; they are insulted, and they respect. They love all and are persecuted by all. . . . They are poor and enrich many. . . . In a word, what the soul is in the body, the Christians are in the world. . . . Such is the important post which God has assigned them, and it is not lawful for them to desert it.

—Epistle of Mathetes to Diognetus

WHO WERE THE APOSTLES?

The word *disciple* means "apprentice, student, learner, and follower." As you know, from among the disciples Jesus selected his Twelve Apostles to help him in his work. The term *apostle* comes from a Greek word that means "to send." The number of Apostles was the same as the number of tribes of Israel, a symbolic number that suggests Jesus came to preach his message to Israel first.

Jesus selected the Twelve after a night of prayer on the mountain. Most of the Apostles were humble, lower-class people, but they were skilled at various crafts or trades. To them, Jesus was like a rabbi or teacher of his time. He expected them to learn carefully from his words and actions so that they could pass his message on to others.

Here is some background information on the Twelve Apostles:

- *Peter*, Simon, was a fisherman. Jesus named him Peter, which means "rock." He was the leader of the Apostles. He is mentioned in the New Testament more than any other person other than Jesus. Peter was the first to declare Jesus' identity.
- *Andrew*, also a fisherman, was Peter's brother. John's Gospel reports that Andrew was Jesus' first disciple and that he encouraged Peter to come to Jesus.
- *James, son of Zebedee*, was a fisherman who came to Jesus with his brother John. James became the leader of the local church in Jerusalem after the Resurrection. Herod Agrippa beheaded him in AD 44.
- *John, son of Zebedee*, may be the so-called "beloved disciple" of John's Gospel. He was the source of the Fourth Gospel and the letters named after him.
- *Philip*, from Bethsaida, asks Jesus at the Last Supper to show the Apostles the Father, to which Jesus replies: "Whoever who has seen me has seen the Father" (Jn 14:9).
- *Bartholomew* is probably the same person as the Nathanael mentioned in John's Gospel. Bartholomew means "son of Thalmai" and may have been Nathanael's surname.
- *Matthew* is probably the same person as Levi. He was a tax collector by profession.
- *Thomas* is called "the Twin" in John's Gospel. He would not believe that Jesus had risen from the dead until he saw him. Tradition holds that he preached in India, where he was martyred.
- *James, son of Alphaeus*, is called James the younger in Mark's Gospel, perhaps to distinguish himself from James, Zebedee's son.
- *Simon the Zealot* is identified for the group of revolutionaries who worked to overthrow Roman rule in Palestine through violent means. By following Jesus, Simon had to give up these notions since Jesus is the "Prince of Peace."
- *Judas, son of James*, is also known as Jude. Matthew and Mark call him Thaddeus, probably a surname, so as not to confuse him with Judas Iscariot, the traitor.
- *Judas Iscariot* is called a traitor by each of the Gospels. He betrayed Jesus for thirty pieces of silver, and when he realized the magnitude of what he did, he hung himself.

- Finally, summarize the senses of discipleship by telling the students that to be a disciple of Jesus means having:
  - the knowledge of what to say and skill in how to say it (by being Jesus' pupil)
  - a relationship with God that is worth telling about (by being Jesus' friend)
  - the right attitude, that is, a desire to spread the Gospel in word and deed (by being a follower/evangelist)
- Check the students' understanding of discipleship by inviting them to write a short essay on what it means to be a disciple. Have them include two to three examples of noteworthy disciples that they know in their personal lives or examples of the great saints of the Church. After they have completed the assignment, collect them and check for proper understanding of the elements of discipleship that have been covered so far in this chapter.
- Ask the students to share what comes to mind when they hear the words "obey" or "obedience." List ideas on the board. Note any negative connotations. Then write the following quotation from St. Teresa of Avila on the board: "**I know the power obedience has of making things easy which seem impossible**." Call attention to the text section "What Does Jesus Ask of Us?" (page 216). Point out that when Jesus commands us to obey, he is simply asking us *to love*. Stress that Jesus lived and died not merely to make real love possible, but to make it abundantly available to all who are willing to be his disciples.

- Go on to explain that Christian love is all about action, not talk. Emphasize that Jesus is love *in person*. For him, love is all about self-sacrifice not self-aggrandizement or self-fulfillment. Yet, loving in this sacrificial way *will* fulfill us. In fact, it will fill us to the full with God's love. This is the sort of love that makes the world go round and makes life worth living. This is the sort of love that Jesus both gives to us and then commands of us. As Jesus' disciples, we are called to be filled with this divine love and so become incandescent in thought, word, and deed. Then, like Christ, we too can become "love in person." (*Note:* Tell the students that they will be learning more about what it means to obey Jesus' commands in subsequent lessons.)
- Before concluding the lesson, see if the students can name the Twelve Apostles. Then have the students turn to the feature "Who Were the Apostles?" (page 215). Remind the students that "apostle" comes from the Greek *apostello*, "to send forth." Have the students to read the brief summaries about each Apostle. Then, have them draw a small picture or icon of each Apostle with a symbol to remind them of something about that person. For example, they might draw Matthew holding money (taxes) in his hands to remind them that he was a tax collector.

> you slaves, because a slave does not know what his master is doing. I have called you friends, because I have told you everything I have heard from my Father. It was not you who chose me, but I who chose you and appointed you to go and bear fruit that will remain, so that whatever you ask the Father in my name he may give you. This I command you: love one another. (Jn 15:9–17)

To be a friend of Jesus is a wonderful privilege beyond any other human relationship. But as in all friendships, give-and-take is required. Jesus has given us everything: our lives, our talents, our friendships, our families, our material blessings, and eternal Salvation. In return, he wants us to love and to do what he commands. He also tells us we will remain in his love if we keep his commandments and that we are his friends if we do what he commands.

This theme of obeying Jesus' commands is repeated yet again in the element of evangelization, crucial to being a disciple. In the final verses of the Gospel of Matthew, Jesus commissions the Apostles to be evangelists:

> All power in heaven and on earth has been given to me. Go, therefore, and make disciples of all nations, baptizing them in the name of the Father, and of the Son, and of the holy Spirit, teaching them to observe all that I have commanded you. And behold, I am with you always, until the end of the age. (Mt 28:18–20)

An evangelist must preach Christ's message and invite others to become his disciples *and* also to teach them to observe all his commandments.

What Does Jesus Ask of Us?

What does Jesus command? What are his teachings that we must put into practice? Love certainly is at the heart of his teaching. In his invitation to be his friends in John's Gospel, he calls us to love others as he loved us. Also, when questioned by a lawyer about what is the greatest of all commandments, Jesus repeated the teaching that appears in the Old Testament.

> [Jesus] said to him, "You shall love the Lord, your God, with all your heart, with all your soul, and with all your mind. This is the greatest and the first commandment. The second is like it: You shall love your neighbor as yourself. The whole law and the prophets depend on these two commandments." (Mt 22:36–40)

In effect, this teaching summarized the Ten Commandments (Ex 20:1–17). The first three commandments concern love of God; the last seven deal with love of neighbor. Disciples of Jesus live the Ten Commandments and observe the other teachings Jesus gives to us, including the Beatitudes and his command to look out for the needs of the poor. Details about following Jesus in these ways are outlined in the next sections.

For Review

1. What are the three senses of what it means to be a disciple of Jesus?
2. Cite at least two Gospel passages that indicate that discipleship involves obedience to Jesus' commands.

For Reflection

What does it mean for *you* to love others as Jesus loved you?

Following Jesus' Commands

In the Sermon on the Mount Jesus reminded his listeners that he did not come to abolish the Mosaic Law: "Amen I say to you, until heaven and earth

For Review Answers (page 216)

1. To become Jesus' pupil, friend, and follower.
2. Answers may include Matthew 22:36–40; John 15:9–17; Matthew 7:21–27; Mark 12:28–31; and Luke 10:25–28.

Discipleship: Following in the Footsteps of Jesus 217

Holy Trinity Chapel, rebuilt in 1934 on the summit of Mount Sinai, where Moses received the Ten Commandments, Egypt.

pass away, not the smallest letter or the smallest part of a letter will pass from the law" (Mt 5:18). Jesus later said to the rich young man, "If you wish to enter into life, keep the commandments" (Mt 19:17).

However, Jesus was the only one who could fulfill the Law perfectly. He gave God's interpretation of the Law, summarized in the Beatitudes. We are called to both keep the Ten Commandments and to incorporate the Beatitudes into our lives as disciples of Christ.

Ten Commandments (CCC, 2052-2557)

The first three commandments show us how to love the Lord our God with our whole heart, soul, strength, and mind (Lk 10:27). The last seven commandments show us how to love our neighbor as we love ourselves. St. Paul teaches this important truth:

> The commandments, "You shall not commit adultery; you shall not kill; you shall not steal; you shall not covet," and whatever other commandment there may be, are summed up in this saying, (namely) "You shall love your neighbor as yourself." (Rom 13:9)

Explanation of the individual commandments and the message of Paul's teaching follows.

I. I am the Lord your God: you shall not have strange Gods before me.

The first commandment teaches us to make God central in our lives. We do so when we exercise the theological virtues of faith, hope, and charity. We practice faith and hope by believing and trusting in God's Divine Revelation, mercy, and promises of eternal Salvation. We also show our faith when we worship God and share our Christian beliefs with others. We practice charity when we give heartfelt love to God and other people.

Chapter 9: Discipleship: Following in the Footsteps of Jesus—Lesson 2

Bell Ringers

- Ask the students to offer their responses to the first two For Review questions on page 216 (answers are on page 238 of this text). Be sure to allow the students to ask any other questions they may have.
- Write on the board the following quotation from the famous Lutheran German theologian Dietrich Bonhoeffer: "**Christianity without discipleship is always Christianity without Christ**." Invite the students to discuss what they discovered about Christian love being love in action.
- Move on and introduce this lesson by talking about rules, boundaries, directions, instructions, guidelines, etc., with the students. Use questions like the following to facilitate discussion:
  - Have you ever tried to assemble a model or bake a cake without following instructions? How did it turn out? What mood were you in as you worked?
  - Why do you think we say the ball is "dead" when we step out of bounds while playing basketball or soccer or football?
  - Would a painting such as the *Mona Lisa* still be the *Mona Lisa* if the canvas had no borders, no boundaries?
  - Do you think rules in a family, in a school, in a country are important? Why or why not?
- After the discussion, the students should be better able to appreciate that without rules, boundaries, or guidelines, life would, at best, be arbitrary and at worst, be chaotic and clearly no fun.

Lesson 2 Objectives

The students will:

- discuss the necessity of rules in life.
- list the Ten Commandments.
- list examples of virtues and sins connected to each of the Ten Commandments.
- create stories about young disciples that incorporate real-life applications of each of the Ten Commandments.

Lesson 2 Preview

In this lesson the students study the Ten Commandments to discover that they are a code for discipleship living, not simply a set of negative imperatives. The students see how the first three commandments remind us of our relationship duties to God. The fourth through the tenth commandments speak to our relationships and duties toward one another. The law of the Gospel does not overthrow the Ten Commandments; it completes them. Jesus teaches us that loving God and loving neighbor are two sides of the same coin. Because God who is love has first favored us with love, we are called and empowered to return the favor to God, our neighbor, and ourselves.

Teaching Approaches

Following Jesus' Commands—Ten Commandments (pages 216-223)

- Begin looking at the Ten Commandments by writing the following Scripture references on the board: **Exodus 20:1–17** and **Deuteronomy 5:6–21**. Have a student read each reference aloud. Afterward, remind the students that until God gave Moses the Ten Commandments, the Israelites were a motley crew. The Ten Commandments (the Sinai covenant) made the Israelites *a people* with common values. In the Sinai covenant, God agreed to be Israel's God, and the people agreed to keep the Ten Commandments. These rules transformed a collection of individuals into a holy community. The Commandments help the People of God know God's will, and they lay out guidelines for us to follow as we strive to remain faithful to God.
- Call on different students to read the passages aloud from their Bibles: Psalm 19:8–11; Psalm 119:17–20; and Psalm 119:97–100. Afterward, point out that in each Scripture passage, the psalmist *rejoices* in the Law of God. Explain that the Israelites did not see the Commandments as restraints. Rather, they experienced them as release from floundering in faith to following in faith.
- Point out that the Commandments are all imperatives: "thou shall" and "thou shall not." Explain that one reason the Commandments may have taken this form is that the author of the Torah knew that imperatives are easier to pass on and to remember than declaratives. For example, it's easier for a parent to warn a child "Hot! Don't touch the stove!" than it is to explain and remember the properties of combustion and their effect on human skin. Go on to tell the teens that although most of the commandments are negative imperatives, they all can be "translated" into positive statements that help us live faithful lives.
- Distribute copies of Chapter 9, Handout 1, "Understanding the Ten Commandments." Using their textbooks have them write in the columns next to each commandment all of the requirements and forbidden sins that apply to each commandment. Invite them to use the handout for the following activity as a reference but also to add notes they may have missed.
- Use an "on the spot" format to discuss the Ten Commandments. Have volunteers be on the spot for each of the commandments. Ask the "on the spot" student two or three questions related to the commandment, drawing on the material presented in the

218 Jesus Christ: Source of Our Salvation

The first commandment requires us to practice the *virtue of religion*, which gives God what is his just due simply because he is God. We practice this virtue through adoration, prayer, works of sacrifice, and keeping our promises and vows. When we adore God, we humbly thank him for his generosity to us. When we pray to God, we lift our minds and hearts in praise, thanksgiving, sorrow, petition, and intercession. When we join our works of self-denial to Jesus' sacrifice on the cross, we make our lives pleasing to God. Finally, by practicing the virtue of religion, we are able to keep the promises we make in the Sacraments of Baptism, Confirmation, Holy Orders, and Matrimony and any special vows we make to God like the **evangelical counsels** of poverty, chastity, and obedience.

The first commandment turns us away from sins against faith like *heresy* (false teaching against the faith), *apostasy* (denial of Christ), and *schism* (a break in union with the pope by refusing to accept his Christ-given authority). It also teaches us to avoid sins against hope like *presumption* (holding that a person can save himself without God's help or personal conversion) and *despair*, which says that God will not or cannot forgive a person of his or her sins. Also, the first commandment condemns sins against charity—like the refusal to accept God's love—ingratitude, and spiritual laziness. The worst sin of all is hatred of God; its cause is pride.

Also, the plain words of the commandment condemn the many forms of atheism that deny God's existence. They also condemn the worship of false gods, that is, idolatry, which also includes the worship of Satan and making gods out of things like money, prestige, power, sex, and so forth. *Superstition*, *divination* (seeking to discover the occult—what is hidden), *sorcery* (attempts to tame occult powers), *irreligion* (disrespect for God's loving care by tempting God), *sacrilege* (disrespecting the sacraments and sacred things, places, or persons specially consecrated to God), and *simony* (the buying or selling of spiritual things) are all violations of the first commandment and against the respect and adoration due our loving God alone.

II. You shall not take the name of the Lord your God in vain.

God's name is holy. When we honor God's holy name through praise, reverence, and adoration, we are honoring the One behind the name. This is true also when we reverence the name of Jesus Christ, the Blessed Mother, and the saints.

When we are baptized "in the name of the Father and of the Son and of the Holy Spirit," our own names are also sanctified. We become the Lord's disciples with tremendous dignity. Catholics are often named for a **patron saint** whose life can inspire them and who prays for them in Heaven. Praying the Sign of the Cross helps remind us of our dignity

evangelical counsels
Vows of personal poverty, chastity understood as lifelong celibacy, and obedience to the demands of the community being joined that those entering the consecrated life profess.

patron saint
Saints that are chosen as special intercessors or protectors for our lives.

domestic Church
A name for the Christian family. In the family, parents and children exercise their priesthood of the baptized by worshipping God, receiving the sacraments, and witnessing to Christ and the Church by living as faithful disciples.

Lesson 2 Homework

1. Tell the students to write out their answers to the first nine For Review questions on page 225.
2. Call attention to the feature "Delving Deeper into the Commandments" on page 224. Have the students complete two of the listed assignments.
3. Direct the students to read "Following Jesus' Commands—Live the Beatitudes" (pages 223–225) in preparation for their next lesson.

Background Information

The Commandments express the implications of belonging to God through the establishment of the covenant. Moral existence is a response to the Lord's loving initiative. It is the acknowledgement and homage given to God and a worship of thanksgiving. It is cooperation with the plan God pursues in history.

—*Catechism of the Catholic Church*, **2062**

and that we belong to a loving God who enables us to be called a *Christian*, a disciple of Jesus Christ.

The second commandment forbids any wrong use of God's name or the names of Jesus, Mary, or any saint. It teaches us to keep our promises, for example, when we take an oath, and always to be true to our word. *Perjury* is seriously wrong because it dishonors God's holy name by calling on God to witness to a lie. Blasphemy is also seriously wrong—a sin that can never be justified. *Blasphemy*—any thought, word, or act that expresses contempt for God, Christ, the Church, saints, or holy things—also greatly dishonors God.

III. Remember to keep holy the Lord's day.

The third commandment recalls two Old Testament truths: God rested after the work of creation and God gave the Chosen People the Sabbath day as a sign of the covenant that he made with them after the Exodus. The Israelites understood that this commandment was intended for them to praise God for his works of creation and to thank him for his saving works on their behalf.

Catholics honor this commandment by celebrating the Eucharistic liturgy on Sunday, the day of our Lord's Resurrection. Christ's Paschal Mystery brought a new creation for all humanity. This is why we obey Jesus' command to break bread in his name by worshipping, praising, and thanking God for the gift of his Son and the gift of eternal Salvation. Catholics are required to attend Mass on Sundays and holy days of obligation to express, celebrate, and deepen their unity in Christ. The Eucharist is the heart of our life; it both celebrates and creates our unity in Christ Jesus. It proclaims to others that we belong to Christ and are members of his Body, the Church.

We also sanctify this day by avoiding unnecessary work and business activities. Sunday is a day to spend time with our families, reading, enjoying God's creation, serving others, and refreshing our minds, hearts, and spirits.

IV. Honor your father and your mother.

You have probably heard the expression, "Charity begins at home." There is truth to this statement because if we cannot learn to love our family members, how can we learn to love others? The family is the basic unit of society. In it a husband and wife marry freely as equals to show love to each other and to participate with God in the procreation and education of children. The family is also the **domestic Church**, a community of faith, hope, and charity that teaches virtue, love, and respect. The family mirrors the love and unity of the Blessed Trinity.

The fourth commandment calls on parents to respect their children as persons of dignity and value. Parents are to provide a loving home, see to their children's education, and raise them to be responsible adults who look out for the needs of others. Parents must always show unconditional love and affection to their children. In doing so, they model God's love.

Children, for their part, show their appreciation for the gift of life by respecting and honoring their parents throughout their lives. Children must obey their parents as long as they live in their home and honor and care for their aged parents. Brothers and

Extending the Lesson

Examination of Conscience

The Ten Commandments offer guidelines for behavior and teach us how to love. They can be used effectively in preparation for the Sacrament of Reconciliation. Invite the students to read through the Ten Commandments slowly and write down ways they may have fallen short of the requirements or participated in some of the sinful actions associated with each of the commandments. Invite a local priest to hear confessions during class or use this activity in preparation for a school Penance service during Advent or Lent.

text. Use whatever questions you wish, including definitions of the various sins listed in each section. Likewise, feel free to use any or all of the questions given below for each listed commandment. For each commandment, devise questions of your own design to help the students apply the commandments to the things they see happening around them. You may also wish to invite students to create questions in preparation for this activity. Have them write questions on a half-sheet of paper or note card, and give the questions to you to use.

Be sure to have more than one student (at least two) "on the spot" for each commandment. An easy way to change the student on the spot is to allow the departing students to choose his or her replacement according to a guideline such as choosing someone of the opposite sex or with different colored eyes, etc.

- I. I, the Lord, am your God. You shall not have other gods besides me.
  - What are some "other gods" people your age feel tempted to put before God today? (*Make sure the students recognize that God must be first in our lives. We must not allow celebrities, money, pleasure, or even knowledge to take God's place and become false gods.*)
  - How can practicing our religion help us keep this commandment?
- II. You shall not take the name of the Lord, your God, in vain.
  - Why are false oaths, blasphemy, and cursing violations of the second commandment? (*All do not really intend to address or speak accurately about God.*)
  - What do you think the commandment says about speaking proudly of your faith and even sharing it with others?
  - How might living up to this commandment affect the way we treat people of a different culture or people who do not share our beliefs?
  - What are some "positive opposites" to the sins listed in this section? (*praise, reverence, and adoration*)

Before moving on, make sure the students understand why false oaths, blasphemy, perjury, cursing, and any use of God's name in an irreverent way violates the second commandment. Finally, tell the students that faith in God should make a difference in how we speak, act, and live.

- III. Remember to keep holy the Sabbath day.

- What two Old Testament truths does the third commandment recall? (*God rested from creation; God gave the Sabbath as a gift and sign of the covenant.*)
- Why does God deserve our worship? (*for creation and our Salvation*)
- Besides going to Mass, what other activities might someone your age engage in to keep Sunday holy? (*Just about anything that means doing good for yourself so that God is honored by your choices.*)
- Do you think it would be beneficial if more stores and businesses were closed on Sundays, as they once were? Why or why not?

Remind the students that God favored us first. Our worship simply returns the favor. Then, before moving on, ask the students to jot on a piece of paper everything they can remember doing on the previous Sunday. Direct them to note the activities on their list that they do nearly every Sunday and those they believe help to refresh them and prepare them for the coming week. Take a few moments to discuss the results, noting all those things that mark Sunday as a special kind of day.

- IV. Honor your father and your mother.
    - What does it mean to call the family a "domestic church"?
    - In what specific ways do you do you honor and respect your parents? Your teachers? The clergy? Civil authority?
    - Do these people also show respect for you? If so, in what ways?
- V. You shall not kill.
    - Besides murder and the taking of innocent life, what else does this commandment forbid?
    - Do you think cliques that reject others because they're unpopular violate this commandment? Why or why not?
    - How about bullying others? Does this run contrary to the value of this commandment?
    - Do you think there is any such thing as a "just war"?
    - Do you think capital punishment violates the fifth commandment?
    - What are some ways we respect our own lives?

220 Jesus Christ: Source of Our Salvation

chastity
The moral virtue that enables people to integrate their sexuality into their stations in life.

sisters must also treat each other with respect and love.

The fourth commandment also requires that we respect and obey proper Church and other authority figures like teachers, police, employers, and leaders. However, obedience is not absolute. If, for example, civil laws contradict God's teaching, we must choose God's law over it, even if our actions lead to personal suffering.

V. You shall not kill.

God is the source of life and the final goal of all human life. The fifth commandment demands that we respect life from the first moment of conception until natural death. All persons have great dignity because everyone is created in God's image and likeness. Because of these truths, direct abortion, either willed as a means or an end, gravely violates the fifth commandment. Everyone has the right to life, a right that does not have to be earned. At the other end of the life spectrum, intentional euthanasia and assisted suicide are serious crimes against life and attacks on humanity. They can never be justified.

The fifth commandment outlaws murder, that is, the deliberate killing of human beings. Murder often results from anger and hate and leads to serious wrongdoings like kidnapping, hostage taking, torture, and horrific acts of terrorism. Suicide gravely contradicts love of self, rejects God's dominion over life and death, and violates the virtues of justice, hope, and charity.

The Church teaches that society *must* always use bloodless means to defend against unjust aggressors, if possible. In the case of capital punishment, the Church teaches that today public safety and order can be achieved in many ways without recourse to the death penalty. "The cases in which the execution of the offender is an absolute necessity are very rare, if not practically non-existent" (*CCC*, 2267).

Although legitimate governments have the right to participate in just wars, once engaged in a war, the combatants must follow the moral law by protecting noncombatants and by using the minimum force necessary. The use of nuclear weapons can *never* be justified. And the arms race and the selling of arms is sinful; their cost seriously harms poor people by diverting valuable resources from assisting those in need.

Cloning, nontherapeutic genetic manipulation, medical experimentation on embryos, and other immoral medical procedures that do not conform to the natural law also violate the fifth commandment. So does scandal, which is an attitude or act that helps lead others to commit evil, for example, encouraging someone to take illegal and harmful drugs. Scandal is a grave offense when it leads others to sin mortally.

We show respect for our own lives by eating healthy food, getting proper exercise and rest, using our minds to grow, and avoiding harmful substances like drugs and practices like reckless driving. We also show respect for

life when we defend the rights of others, especially the weak and defenseless in our midst, so they can live with dignity.

VI. You shall not commit adultery. IX. You shall not covet your neighbor's wife.

In his Apostolic Letter *On the Christian Family in the Modern World*, Pope John Paul II wrote about the vocation of men and women:

> God created man in his own image and likeness: calling him to existence through love, he called him at the same time for love. God is love and in himself he lives a mystery of personal loving communion. Creating the human race in His own image and continually keeping it in being, God inscribed in the humanity of man and woman the vocation, and thus the capacity and responsibility, of love and communion. Love is therefore the fundamental and innate vocation of every human being.

The sixth and ninth commandments both teach us how to use our sexuality in accord with God's plan. God gave this gift to married couples so that they can share their love and cooperate with God in bringing forth new life. These commandments direct us to do so responsibly by exercising the virtues of chastity, purity, and modesty.

Chastity helps us integrate our sexuality with all aspects of who we are. It helps us live with self-control according to our station in life. The virtues of *purity* and *modesty* help us to combat lust, the vice of a disordered craving for or enjoyment of sexual pleasures. Purity attunes our minds and hearts to God's holiness. Modesty refuses to unveil what should remain covered. It helps us be decent in the clothes we wear and to display respectful attitudes when talking about sex. All three of these virtues strengthen us to work for wholesomeness in society and combat a sex-saturated culture that demeans humans, turning them into objects for enjoyment.

Acts contrary to God's intention for marriage include *adultery* (a married person having sexual relations with a nonspouse), *divorce* (against Christ's command that marriage should last until death separates the couple), *polygamy* (having several spouses), *incest* (engaging in sexual relations with close relatives), the *sexual abuse* of children and adolescents, and *free unions* (living together without exchanging marriage vows).

Birth control is also contrary to God's intent for the true meaning of sexual intercourse: that each act of sexual love-making should be open to the two ends of marriage—the *unitive,* that is, the bonding of husband and wife as lifelong partners, and the *procreative*, that is, the cooperating with God in bringing new life into the world. Therefore, each act of sexual intercourse should be open to both purposes of marriage: the sharing of life and mutual love. In planning their families, couples must use

- In what other ways do we "kill" others' spirits?
- What groups in our community are working to support life?
- How can people your age defend the lives and rights of others?

Stress that all life comes from God, thus all life is sacred. We must honor life and what is essential for life: justice and peace.

- VI. You shall not commit adultery, and IX. You shall not covet your neighbor's wife.

Before calling a student "on the spot," instruct the students to write on pieces of scrap paper any questions they may have about the issues covered under the heading of these commandments. Collect the questions and refer to them as you cover the material on these commands.

- What are some of the sins against this commandment?
- Does the portrayal of sexuality in the media help or hinder efforts to abide by these two commandments? Explain.
- According to these commandments, where can sexual love be shared?
- What are some of the virtues that help us obey these commands?
- Does our society help or hinder us in living out these two commandments? Explain.
- In addition to divorce, what are some other sins against marriage?
- How might working for sexual equality help us live out the tenth commandment?

Make sure the students understand that the Church teaches that there are two purposes of marriage and sexual intercourse: it is *unitive* and *procreative*. Marriage is *unitive* in that it brings to people in an unbreakable bond of marriage. It is *procreative* in that the Sacrament of Matrimony allows two people to share in God's creative power through sexual intercourse. Parents are also responsible for the proper raising and educating of their children. (*Note:* Depending on the nature of your students, you may wish to engage them in further discussion regarding the pressures they face regarding sexual activity.)

- VII. You shall not steal, and X. You shall not covet anything that belongs to your neighbor.

- What are some sins against this commandment?
- What does "covet" mean? To what does being covetous lead?
- What is your most treasured possession? Why?
- How important is it to you that others respect your possessions?
- How are goofing off on the job or cheating at school related to stealing?

Explain that the seventh and tenth commandments call us to be good and faithful stewards and to live lives marked by justice and mercy, to respect what belongs to others, and to share what we have with those in need. Theses commands also require us to act with fairness and justice and exhibit compassion for the poor.

- VIII. You shall not bear false witness against your neighbor.
  - What is the focus of this command? (*truth-telling*)
  - What are the sins of detraction and calumny? (ask for examples)
  - What are some sins against this commandment?
  - Why is gossiping so damaging to others?
  - What's wrong with bragging about yourself? Bragging about others?
  - What are some ways a government can lie to or manipulate its citizens?

Remind the students that bearing false witness means more than lying. It means destroying someone's reputation; jumping to conclusions about others; talking about others' faults, even if the faults are true; boasting or bragging; and flattery, if we use it to manipulate people.

- Invite the students to get into groups. Give them some time to write a script for a skit about a real-life scenario that teenagers might confront that includes at least five of the Ten Commandments. After they have been given sufficient time to plan for the skit, invite each group to perform it for the class. Afterward, ask each group to share how the scenario required each of the commandments they chose. To ensure that each member of the groups took part in the planning of the skit, have each student write a brief paragraph about

222 Jesus Christ: Source of Our Salvation

moral and natural methods that are open to both life and love.

The respectful and moral use of our sexual faculties forbid the following actions that are often the result of lust:

- *Masturbation*, which is the deliberate stimulation of the sexual organs to gain sexual pleasure.
- *Fornication*, which is sexual intercourse engaged in by unmarried people. It seeks pleasure without responsibility and the unconditional love found only in the bond of marriage.
- *Pornography*, which depersonalizes sex.
- *Prostitution*, which debases those who sell their bodies. It is also seriously sinful for those who pay prostitutes for sex.
- *Rape*, which is always a seriously evil and violent act.
- *Homosexual acts*, which contradict God's intention of male-female bonding in a stable, permanent relationship of marriage.

VII. You shall not steal.
X. You shall not covet anything that belongs to your neighbor.

Jesus said: "Take care against all greed, for though one may be rich, one's life does not consist of possessions" (Lk 12:15). These two commandments teach us to be good stewards of our material possessions (see also pages 227–229). God created the goods of creation for everyone's benefit. We have the right to private possessions, but we must use them responsibly. The virtue of temperance teaches us that we should not let our belongings become our god or become slaves to them. The virtue of justice teaches us to respect the property rights of others and to share our wealth, especially with those who are needy.

The first Beatitude highlights how we should be poor in spirit. Poverty of spirit centers our hearts on God who is the true source of all happiness; it is the key to overcoming greed, avarice, and envy. With the help of the Holy Spirit, we can resist the temptation to acquire and consume—the message sold to us by our contemporary society as the path to happiness and contentment.

The seventh and tenth commandments forbid theft, which is the taking of someone's property against his or her reasonable will; business fraud; the paying of unjust wages; price fixing; corruption; shoddy work; tax evasion; forgery; vandalism; broken promises and contracts; and similar sins. In all cases, if one is guilty of any of these sins, he or she must make restitution.

The tenth commandment warns us that we should not covet, that is, crave unjustly the belongings of others. Covetousness leads to immoral attitudes like *greed* (the desire to amass great wealth), *avarice* (the seeking of wealth and the power that comes from it), and *envy* over another's possessions. These sinful attitudes can lead to immoral actions like theft, robbery, and fraud.

For Enrichment

A Confounding and Compassionate Vision

The Beatitudes confound us. We wonder how the poor, the sorrowing, the down-and-out, or the persecuted can be blessed. The Beatitudes reverse what we consider important. Jesus insists that in the world of God's blessings, the marginalized have the center stage, the meek inherit, and peacemakers are God's children, not traitors to the state. The Beatitudes describe a world in which showing mercy, seeking God, taking insults, hungering for justice, and grieving for loved ones bring blessings among us. The Beatitudes possess a holistic perspective. They offer a vision of wholeness that leaves no one out. They pave the way for the people of God to usher in the coming of the God's Kingdom.

Discipleship: Following in the Footsteps of Jesus 223

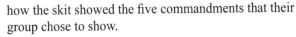

These commandments also require that we be just in our dealings with others, both individuals and with the communities in which we live. We must especially look out for the needs of the poor. This is true for individuals and for nations that have been blessed with many resources and benefits. The virtue of solidarity recognizes that we all are members of the same human family and that out of friendship and charity we must share our resources and wealth.

VIII. You shall not bear false witness against your neighbor.

Truth-telling is the focus of the eighth commandment. Truth is a matter of justice. Being truthful for Christians is a superb way to witness to Jesus Christ who is the Way, the Truth, and the Life. Jesus himself said, "Let your 'Yes' mean 'Yes,' and your 'No' mean 'No.' Anything more is from the evil one" (Mt 5:37).

Being truthful leads to respect for others, their reputations, and their right to privacy. Giving false praise, gossiping, bragging, and outright lying destroy the integrity and honesty of a person. Lying is contrary to God's gift of speech, the purpose of which is telling the truth. Lies can be mortally sinful and cause great harm to others.

The eighth commandment also forbids giving false witness in a trial and perjury (lying under oath). These are serious sins because they lead to the suffering of innocent people or to their unfair punishment. Rash or snap judgments are also wrong because they misjudge a person's blameworthiness for some action. A follower of Christ is called to counteract the tendency to misjudge by always putting a positive interpretation on another's thoughts, words, and deeds. Two other sins against the eighth commandment are *detraction*, which reveals the faults of someone without a good reason, and *calumny*, that is, spreading lies about another. These two sins do great damage to a person's reputation, thereby offending both justice and charity.

Cheating, a violation of honesty, is also a sin against this commandment. Cheating is often commonly practiced in school settings today, often with the response by those who cheat that "everyone is doing it." Even if this were true, cheating would remain a sin against the eighth commandment.

Societal institutions are also bound to be truthful. Governmental agencies and the entertainment industries must be responsible, resisting efforts at propaganda or promoting immoral behavior. Citizens and consumers of information have the right to the truth that comes from freedom, justice, and solidarity.

Live the Beatitudes (CCC, 1718-1724; 1728-1729)

The Beatitudes, summarized below, teach us how to love God and neighbor in a Christ-like way. The Beatitudes are recorded in the Sermon on the Plain (Luke 6:20–26) and Matthew 5:3–12. They complete the promises that God made to Abraham, reveal a path to true happiness, and teach the attitudes disciples of Jesus should possess in order to reach their eternal destiny of union with Christ.

Blessed are the poor in spirit, for theirs is the Kingdom of Heaven.

When we are poor in spirit, we recognize that all we have and all we are is a pure gift from God. We depend on him, the Source of all. We show our appreciation by using our gifts for others.

Blessed are they who mourn, for they shall be comforted.

We are to mourn over the injustices and evils committed against God and people who are in need. Our sorrow over their fate should lead us to help those who suffer and be Jesus' consoling presence to comfort them. We should also mourn for our own sins and the harm they cause others.

Lesson 3 Objectives

The students will:

- list and describe the meaning of each of the Beatitudes.
- consider how well they are living the Beatitudes.
- identify where they see the Beatitudes in their lives and the lives of their peers.

Lesson 3 Preview

In this lesson, the students examine the Beatitudes. They discover how these "blessings" are signs of the Kingdom of God that show us how to find true happiness and to act as disciples of Jesus by loving God and neighbor in a Christ-like way.

how the skit showed the five commandments that their group chose to show.

- Conclude by explaining that the Ten Commandments proclaim God's law and reveal God's love. They are binding on all people, in all places, for all time. Jesus revealed their true inner spirit when he taught the Law of Love. The Holy Spirit and the graces the Spirit brings give us the strength to observe and live the commandments.

Chapter 9: Discipleship: Following in the Footsteps of Jesus—Lesson 3

Bell Ringers

- Ask the students to offer their responses to the first nine For Review questions on page 225 (answers are on page 246 of this text). Be sure to allow the students to ask any other questions they may have.
- Collect the students' work on two of the assignments in the feature "Delving Deeper into the Commandments" on page 224. Evaluate and return them to the students with comments to help them further understand what they have read and written.
- Have the students recall their brief discussion on the Beatitudes from this chapter's first lesson. Ask:
  - What does "beatitude" mean? (*blessing* or *happiness*)
  - How does the Gospel define happiness? (*as the coming of the Kingdom of God*)
  - Why did Jesus give us the Beatitudes? (*to show us what we ought to be doing and how we ought to be living in order to assure the Kingdom's coming*)

Teaching Approaches

Following Jesus' Commands—Live the Beatitudes (pages 223-225)

- Have the students open their Bibles to Matthew 5:3–12 and read the Beatitudes. Point out that Jesus calls these "blessings," even though many would not want to be like any of the people Jesus describes. The Beatitudes reverse what we consider to be important.
- Go through the Beatitudes, one at a time, discussing each one:

- *Blessed are the poor in spirit, for theirs is the kingdom of heaven.* Tell the students that poverty provides a deeper motivation for understanding, welcoming, and caring for the needs of others. Poverty helps us understand what happiness (beatitude) is. People who are "poor in spirit" know they need God. They recognize they cannot save themselves and that life and grace are gifts. Ask:
  - If you feel that you need God, do you let God know? Why or why not?
  - Are you willing to be self-giving for the sake of others?
- *Blessed are they who mourn, for they will be comforted.* Ask:
  - Can you share about a time your sorrow after a loss helped you reach out to another in a similar situation?
  - Has someone helped you deal with sorrow?
- *Blessed are the meek, for they shall inherit the earth.* Explain that the meek are not the wimpy. Rather, they are people who recognize that they cannot really possess people or creation. The meek recognize that things are blessings, so they are humble and helpful. Ask:

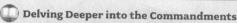

Blessed are the meek, for they will inherit the land.

A meek person is humble, gentle, patient, and compassionate, just like Jesus. The gift of meekness helps us to know the most appropriate time to feel and express anger.

Blessed are they who hunger and thirst for righteousness, for they shall be satisfied.

Jesus' disciples desire to put God's righteous will into action by working tirelessly with the help of the Holy Spirit to grow in holiness, justice, and truth. Hungering for righteousness also means acting on behalf of others, especially those who are suffering.

Blessed are the merciful, for they will be shown mercy.

God showed mercy by sending his Son to forgive our sins and win for us eternal life. He asks us to imitate him by forgiving others, even our enemies. Disciples of Jesus do not hold grudges. By showing compassion, they reveal the merciful God who loves everyone.

Blessed are the clean of heart, for they shall see God.

Those who are clean of heart are single-minded and undivided in their commitment to God. As other Christs, they look on other people with love and acceptance and recognize their unique value. Jesus' disciples have

evangelization Sharing the Good News. Evangelization involves proclaiming the Gospel in such a way that people's hearts and lives are changed.

Delving Deeper into the Commandments

Choose and complete two of the following assignments.

1. Write a list of ten commandments applicable for parents. Write another list of ten commandments applicable for teens. Show both lists to your parents and ask them to write their comments in the margins for each list.
2. Read the United States Catholic Bishops' *Pastoral Plan for Pro-Life Activities*. Report on five public policy positions the bishops recommend for us to build a culture of life. See: www.usccb.org/prolife/pastoralplan.shtml#rededication.
3. Air Force Code: "I will not lie, cheat, or steal, nor will I tolerate anyone who does." How would this code work at your school? Write your response.
4. Examine some popular, general-interest magazines like *People*. Note some of the feature articles to discover how they might be promoting sexual sins that are contrary to the sixth commandment. Examine the ads to find symbols that are selling sex or appealing to the vice of lust. Report your findings.

For Review Answers for Questions 1-9 (page 225)

1. Answers will vary.
2. Answers may include atheism, apostasy, heresy, schism, presumption, despair, superstition, sorcery, divination, idolatry, sacrilege, irreligion, simony.
3. Catholics should celebrate the Eucharistic liturgy on Sunday and holy days of obligation, avoid unnecessary business activities and work, and spend time with family, refreshing mind, heart, and spirit.
4. Answers may include murder, euthanasia, abortion, suicide, war, capital punishment, cloning, scandal, etc.
5. Chastity helps us integrate our sexuality with other aspects of who we are. Purity and modesty help us combat lust by turning our hearts to God's holiness and helping us keep covered what should be covered.
6. The two purposes of marriage are the bonding of husband and wife in love (unitive) and the cooperation with God in bringing new life into the world (procreative).
7. Answers will vary but may include theft, covetousness, envy, avarice, fraud, corruption, forgery, etc.
8. A disciple is called to witness to truth as a matter of justice; Jesus is himself *the* Truth (Mt 5:37); false witness violates the truth, is unjust, and, in effect, denies Jesus.
9. Calumny is spreading lies about another; detraction is revealing the faults of another without a good reason (*gossip is often laden with calumny and detraction*).

their priorities in the right order: union with the Lord is the prime goal in life.

Blessed are the peacemakers, for they will be called children of God.
We are members of the same family, brothers and sisters in Christ. Fighting and arguing leads to dissension and disunity. Jesus' followers must work to settle disputes, root out violence, and show compassion through forgiveness, always in imitation of the Prince of Peace.

Blessed are they who are persecuted for the sake of righteousness, for theirs is the Kingdom of Heaven.
Ultimately to be a follower of Jesus means to pick up the cross. In doing so, disciples of Christ are often misunderstood, mocked, and abused. Some may even have to witness by offering their lives as martyrs. Though the world may reject us for preaching and living the Gospel, our Lord will never abandon us. He promises eternal happiness:

> Blessed are you when they insult you and persecute you and utter every kind of evil against you (falsely) because of me. Rejoice and be glad, for your reward will be great in heaven. Thus they persecuted the prophets who were before you. (Mt 5:11–12)

For Review

1. How do the first three commandments show love for God?
2. Name five sins that are contrary to the first commandment.
3. How should a Catholic keep the Lord's Day holy?
4. Discuss three major violations of the fifth commandment that are common in today's world.
5. How do the virtues of chastity, purity, and modesty combat the vice of lust?
6. What are the two purposes of marriage?
7. List three sins that the seventh and tenth commandments forbid.
8. Why is false witness contrary to being a disciple of Christ?
9. Define *calumny* and *detraction*.
10. Name and briefly explain each of the Beatitudes.

For Reflection

What values form your character? If someone said you were a person of high ethical character, what qualities would they be talking about?

More Requirements of Discipleship

When Christ had accomplished his work of our Salvation, the Holy Spirit was sent to his disciples in the Church that they might continue to work for the Salvation of all. It is our mission as called for by Jesus in Matthew 28:19–20 to go out to all the nations and make them disciples of all. This is another essential element of discipleship—**evangelization**. We can effectively share the Good News only when we are good stewards of our own God-given talents and gifts. These essential elements of discipleship are explored in the next sections.

A Disciple of Jesus Is an Evangelist

Before ascending to Heaven, Jesus called on his disciples to be evangelists, to go forth and make disciples of all the nations. The word *evangelist*

- Of all the things you *have*, what do you really *need*? What are you willing to "let go of" to be able to help other people?
- Are you willing to refrain from self-gratification and to recognize that you are connected to a community that is bigger than you?

◦ *Blessed are they who hunger and thirst for righteousness, for they shall be satisfied.* Ask the students to name people who they believe to be "righteous." List names on the board. Explain that those who hunger and thirst for righteousness are people whose greatest desire is to do what God asks of them. These are folk who crave goodness, whose eyes are on the prize. Ask:

- What is the most important thing in your life? What would you do to get it?
- How well do you understand that God—not stuff, money, or even health—is the only thing worth hungering after?

◦ *Blessed are the merciful, for they will be shown mercy.* Ask:

- Who is calling you to be merciful? Can you show mercy by standing up for someone who is being bullied or by talking to kids who are outside the "in crowd"?
- Do you forgive even when you do not have to?

For Review Answer for Question 10 (page 225)

10. Answers may include:
    - *Poor in spirit*—Poverty allows people to recognize their need for God.
    - *They who mourn*—Mourning leads us to help others and be Jesus' consoling presence.
    - *The meek*—Being humble and patient allows us to know when to feel and express anger.
    - *They who hunger and thirst for righteousness*—Disciples grow in holiness and act on behalf of others who are suffering.
    - *The merciful*—By showing compassion, disciples reveal the merciful God who loves everyone.
    - *The clean of heart*—Jesus' disciples have their priorities in the right order: union with God is the primary goal.
    - *The peacemakers*—Jesus' disciples work together to settle disputes, make peace, and show compassion through forgiveness.
    - *They who are persecuted for the sake of righteousness*—Discipleship requires self-sacrifice even to the point of death on a cross.

- Are you present to those who need you when you could choose otherwise?

◦ *Blessed are the clean of heart, for they will see God.* Explain that the clean of heart are people who see beyond "surface" things. They focus on others to get to the heart of the matter. Ask:

- What kind of "house cleaning" does your heart need? Do you need to let go of a grudge? Clean up your language? Stop gossip? Refuse to spread rumors?
- Who do you know who sees that there is more to *you* than meets the eye?

◦ *Blessed are the peacemakers, for they will be called children of God.* Point out to the students that the term "peacemaker" appears here and nowhere else in the entire Bible. Jesus wants us to know that those who make peace are mending the tears in the social fabric. Suggest to the students that a powerful way for them to be peacemakers is to do what Jesus did—forgive others. Ask:

- How do you react to an offense or a perceived offense? Do you lash out? Do you go for retribution or for reconciliation? (*Challenge the students to commit to offering forgiveness to someone who has wronged them.*)
- How did you feel the last time someone forgave you? (*Emphasize that forgiveness brings release, wipes out retribution, and creates peace.*)
- What are some specific ways you can be a peacemaker in your family? In your school? Among your friends?

◦ *Blessed are they who are persecuted for the sake of righteousness, for theirs in the kingdom of heaven.* Remind the students that Jesus not only preached the Beatitudes, he lived them, and that cost him his life. Down through the ages, it has also cost his followers their lives. Ask:

- If you were accused, brought to court, and tried for being a Christian, would you be convicted? Would you be *willing* to be convicted?

• Divide the class into eight small groups. Assign one Beatitude to each group. (*Note:* That means assigning the final Beatitude [Mt 5:11–12]—see page 225 in the text—to one of the groups.) Have the groups list ways in which they see their peers honoring the Beatitude: that is, mourning, being merciful, acting as peacemakers, etc. Then ask the teens to list ways their peers are not honoring the Beatitude: ways teens ignore what

comes from the Greek for "good news." An evangelist, therefore, is one who shares with other people the Good News, that is, the Gospel of Jesus Christ, "baptizing them in the name of the Father, and of the Son, and of the holy Spirit, teaching them to observe all that I have commanded you" (Mt 28:20).

How can you best evangelize, that is, spread the gospel to others? Consider a way St. Francis of Assisi approached evangelization on one occasion. Francis asked one of his young monks to join him to go into the town to preach. The young monk was thrilled to be chosen to accompany Francis, and joined him enthusiastically. They walked through the main streets, turned into alleys, made their way into the outlying huts, eventually working their way back to the monastery. As they approached the gate, the young monk reminded the great saint, "But, Father, you have forgotten. We went to town to preach."

Francis replied, "We have preached. We were preaching while we were walking. Many people saw us and observed our behavior. It was thus that we have preached our morning sermon. It is of no use to walk anywhere to preach unless we preach everywhere we walk."

This story reminds us of another saying of St. Francis, "Preach the Gospel always and, if necessary, use words."

Similarly, in his address to the youth of Brazil, Pope Benedict XVI challenged Catholic youth with these words:

> I send you out . . . on the great mission of evangelizing young men and women who have gone astray in the world like sheep without a shepherd. Be apostles of youth. Invite them to walk with you, to have the same experience of faith, hope, and love; to encounter Jesus so that they may feel truly loved, accepted, able to realize their full potential. May they too discover the sure ways of the commandments, and, by following them, come to God.

Pope Benedict's point is that living the commandments is an excellent way to evangelize. He encouraged young people to be free and responsible people; to make the family a center of peace and joy; to promote life; and to protect the elderly. He also encouraged youth to make their work holy by carrying it out with skill and diligence. For students, of course, this means working hard at studies to develop one's talents and to prepare for a life of service to family and community.

In addition, the Pope's words call teens and young adults to build a more just and fraternal society by respecting laws, avoiding hatred and violence, being honest, and giving Christian example in every relationship. Yet another way to bring Christ's Gospel to others is to respect the institution of marriage. The Holy Father reminds us that when a couple falls in love, they should practice the virtue of chastity by refraining from sexual relations until marriage. Imagine what a powerful witness to Jesus Christ the sacrifice, self-control, and patience involved in living a chaste life would be if practiced by teens. It would provide a great Christian witness to your peers who are bombarded with messages of sexual indulgence that are contrary to God's will

Lesson 3 Homework

1. Have the students write out their answer to the tenth and final For Review question on page 225.
2. Have the students read "More Requirements of Discipleship" (pages 225–229) in preparation for their next lesson.
3. Remind the students to continue working on their Ongoing Assignments.

Background Information

The Beatitudes depict the countenance of Jesus Christ and portray his charity. They express the vocation of the faithful associated with the glory of his Passion and Resurrection; they shed light on the actions and attitudes characteristic of the Christian life; they are the paradoxical promises that sustain hope in the midst of tribulations; they proclaim the blessings and rewards already secured, however dimly, for Christ's disciples. . . .

—*Catechism of the Catholic Church*, **1717**

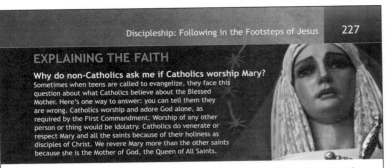

EXPLAINING THE FAITH

Why do non-Catholics ask me if Catholics worship Mary?
Sometimes when teens are called to evangelize, they face this question about what Catholics believe about the Blessed Mother. Here's one way to answer: you can tell them they are wrong. Catholics worship and adore God alone, as required by the First Commandment. Worship of any other person or thing would be idolatry. Catholics do venerate or respect Mary and all the saints because of their holiness as disciples of Christ. We revere Mary more than the other saints because she is the Mother of God, the Queen of All Saints.

for sexual sharing in a committed marriage open to both life and love.

This short summary of Pope Benedict XVI's address emphasizes the need for young people to live upright, moral lives as a mark of discipleship and evangelization. Like St. Francis of Assisi, the pope emphasizes that actions speak louder than words. You do not have to stand on street corners to preach the Gospel. Your life preaches the Gospel. You should always be prepared to share your faith. For example:

- When asked why you act the way you do, you can respond simply that your Catholic faith inspires you to live a Christ-like life.
- Study your Catholic faith so that you are able to explain it. Strive to pay attention in religion classes. Seek answers to questions you do not know. Learn where to find answers to tough questions. Familiarize yourself with the *Catechism of the Catholic Church*. Read the Bible on a regular basis.
- Invite a friend who does not attend Mass regularly to come to Mass with you. Evangelizing involves not only reaching out to non-Catholics but also to lukewarm or nonpracticing Catholics.
- In talking with others about hot-button issues, for example, abortion, do not be afraid to share Church teaching on the subject. Sometimes people have never heard the truth about the great moral issues of the day. You can be a witness to the truth.
- It is acceptable and good to pray in public. A simple bowing of your head and thanking God for the food you are about to eat in a restaurant can be a powerful but quiet and effective witness to your faith.

A Disciple of Jesus Is a Good Steward

A steward is a person who carefully and responsibly manages something that is entrusted to his or her care. Disciples of Jesus are called to stewardship because everything we have is a gift from God, and God wants us to share what we have been given. To be a good steward as Jesus' disciple means that we must share our time, talents, and treasures with others.

Sharing our gifts is also an act of love, following the example of God the Father who gave us the gift of his Son who won for us eternal life. Jesus gives us the gift of the Holy Spirit who is always present to us to show us God's love and goodness. In Baptism, Christ calls us to share in his **common priesthood**, that is, to show his presence in the world. Our Baptism also gives us the vocation of being a prophet so that we can speak the truth with courage and calls us to Christ's kingly role of serving others with love. The Sacrament of Confirmation increases

Lesson 4 Objectives

The students will:

- discover ways to be an evangelist.
- critique the common image of an evangelist.
- understand that stewardship is a requirement of the evangelist.
- explain what it takes to be a steward.

Lesson 4 Preview

In this lesson, the students discuss how evangelism is lived out—in acts of caring stewardship. Many students will associate evangelism with preaching, especially by televangelists. Reassure them that being an evangelist means more than just preaching words; it means living an exemplary life.

should cause them to mourn; the ways they refuse mercy and choose violence over peace, etc. (*Note:* If necessary, remind the students that they are to list general ways of behaving, not the actions of specific individuals.)

- Have each group choose a spokesperson to share lists with the class. While the groups are sharing, invite dialogue about the issues the lists raise.
- Direct the students to return to their original seats. Have available old newspapers and magazines and art materials (scissors, glue, tape, markers, paper, etc.). Direct the students to use headlines, photos, and articles from the newspapers and magazines to create a collage illustrating the Beatitude they were assigned earlier. Consider playing a recording of a Beatitudes hymn such as "Blest Are They" by David Haas or "Beatitudes" by the Dameans.
- When the students finish, allow them to present their work to the class. Post the completed collages in the classroom.

Chapter 9: Discipleship: Following in the Footsteps of Jesus—Lesson 4

Bell Ringer

- Ask the students to offer their response to the tenth and final For Review question on page 225. (See page 247 of this text for answer.) Take time to discuss any other questions or concerns the students may have.

Teaching Approaches

More Requirements of Discipleship (pages 225-229)

- Write the word **evangelization** on the board. Invite the students to write down whatever comes to mind when they see the word. Ask them to share their responses and write them on the board. Discuss any common elements in their responses, particularly those that stress *preaching*.
- Draw attention to its definition in the text (page 224) as well as to how the text defines *evangelist*, viz., "one who shares the Good News." See how this definition compares to their responses on the board.
- Although the students will be familiar with the Great Commission, have them open their Bibles to Matthew 28:16–20 and read it again. Then note on the board

the tasks of discipleship the Great Commission entails:

- **proclaim the Good News (evangelization)**
- **baptize**
- **teach others to follow Jesus' commands (the Great Commandment: love God and love neighbor as self)**

- Have the students turn to the section Primary Source Quotations on page 235. Call attention to the passage from *Lumen Gentium* (the "Dogmatic Constitution on the Church") and have the students read it. Note how the Council Fathers echo and explain the challenge of the Great Commission.
- Go on to ask: How did St. Francis of Assisi describe preaching the Good News (evangelizing)? (*Preach the Gospel always, and, if necessary, use words.*) Discuss with the students the ways they can preach the Gospel without using words.
- Tell the students that Pope Benedict XVI also calls young people to be evangelists and walk the talk. Call on one of the students to read aloud the pope's challenge to youth (on page 226).
- Point out the five ways the pope counsels young people to follow as they evangelize (page 227): (1) live, (2) study, (3) invite, (4) share, (5) pray. Take some time to discuss these methods. Encourage the students to talk about any that they see as being difficult. Then, read aloud the following quotation, which also comes from the same address of Pope Benedict XVI to the youth of Brazil:

> My appeal to you today, young people . . . is this: do not waste your youth. Do not seek to escape from it. Live it intensely. . . . You, young people, are not just the future of the Church and of humanity, as if we could somehow run away from the present. . . . The Church needs you, as young people, to manifest to the world the face of Jesus Christ, visible in the Christian community. Without this young face, the Church would appear disfigured.

- In their journals, invite students to write about teens that they know are evangelists. What do they do with their lives that show that they are evangelists? Afterward, discuss the common characteristics as a class.
- Draw students' attention to the description of the 2007 pastoral letter, "Stewardship and Teenagers: The Challenge of Being a Disciple," on pages 228–229. Go

228 Jesus Christ: Source of Our Salvation

common priesthood
The priesthood of the faithful. Christ has made the Church a "kingdom of priests" who share in his priesthood through the Sacraments of Baptism and Confirmation.

ministerial priesthood
The priesthood of Christ received in the Sacrament of Holy Orders. Its purpose is to serve the common priesthood by building up and guiding the Church in the name of Christ.

in us the gifts of the Holy Spirit so that we can live our priestly, prophetic, and kingly vocation. And the Eucharist gives us the strength to live as Christ's disciples amidst the struggles of daily life. Based on the common priesthood, the **ministerial priesthood** is another way of participation in the mission of Christ. This ministry is conferred in the Sacrament of Holy Orders. It is directed at unfolding the baptismal grace of all Christians.

Jesus is our guide, model, and friend in the life of discipleship. Praying to and developing our friendship with him help us to live our vocation to be good stewards. Meeting him in the Sacrament of Penance gives us the graces to start anew when we have fallen short of being the good stewards of the gifts we have been given. In addition, reading the Bible, learning the Church's social teaching and her powerful message of respect for all of life, and talking to adults whom we trust and admire are three other ways to find inspiration and support for living as faithful stewards and disciples of Jesus Christ.

In the 2007 pastoral letter "Stewardship and Teenagers: The Challenge of Being a Disciple," the United States Catholic bishops list four practical ways teens can love others through responsible stewardship. They are:

- *Share your time.* Visit people who are alone, especially those who are isolated due to age or sickness. Teach what you know to a neighbor or younger sibling. Be present with the people in your life, especially your family. Offer to help. Practice saying yes.
- *Share your talents.* No one else can do exactly what you do. Whether it be singing, cooking, drawing, or playing sports, your talents are for sharing with others. When used generously, the good they provide is immeasurable. Seek opportunities to participate in your parish or faith community as a greeter, altar server, lector, extraordinary minister of Holy Communion, or assistant in the religious education program.

Lesson 4 Homework

1. Assign the four For Review questions on page 229.
2. Encourage the students to begin wrapping up work on their chosen Ongoing Activities.
3. Refer the students to the information on Catholics' devotion to Mary in the feature Explaining the Faith.
4. Have the students read "Putting Discipleship into Practice" (pages 229–233) in preparation for their next lesson.

- *Share your treasure.* The cost of a movie ticket or a pizza can contribute maybe more than you know to help prevent a childhood disease or build a house for someone with nowhere to live. Part of your allowance or paycheck can help your parish provide more services for its community. Decide to give a certain percentage of money at your parish each week. As you live with this decision, you will grow into a lifelong habit of generosity.
- *Share your tradition.* Embrace the rites and sacraments of the Church as beautiful gifts of God, to be appreciated, loved, and shared. Invite a friend to come to Mass with you. Pray for others, both people in your life and those in need throughout the world. Consider what plans God has for you. Whatever his call, it will require the ultimate gift of yourself—through marriage and family, or through the priesthood or consecrated life.

This pastoral letter reminds us that it *is* possible to imitate Christ and to be his disciple by being a good steward. Participation in the sacraments, especially the Eucharist, is crucial as is daily prayer.

For Review

1. What is an evangelist?
2. What are three ways a Catholic teenager can be an evangelist?
3. Define *stewardship*.
4. List three ways a Catholic teenager can be a good steward.

For Reflection

What are your three strongest talents? Write how you can use each of them to be a good steward. Resolve to put one of your gifts into good use in the coming week.

Putting Discipleship into Practice

Love is a central theme in Jesus' teaching to his disciples. Love is the main "job" of Christian discipleship. Time and again, Jesus challenges us to love others. For example:

- "Do to others as you would have them do to you" (Lk 6:31).
- "I give you a new commandment: love one another. As I have loved you, so you also should love one another" (Jn 13:34).
- "But to you who hear I say, love your enemies, do good to those who hate you, bless those who curse you, pray for those who mistreat you" (Lk 6:27–28).

Most challenging is Jesus' command for us to forgive even our *enemies*. Forgiveness can be tough at times, but it is an essential quality of love. Jesus taught us to ask for God's forgiveness in the Lord's Prayer, but he also told us that we must forgive others, too. Jesus said,

> If you forgive others their transgressions, your heavenly Father will forgive you. But if you do not forgive others, neither will your Father forgive your transgressions. (Mt 6:14–15)

Furthermore, our forgiveness should have no limits. Just as God forgives us when we ask for forgiveness, so we should forgive those who have hurt us.

> If your brother sins, rebuke him; and if he repents, forgive him. And if he wrongs you seven times in one day and returns to you seven times saying, "I am sorry," you should forgive him. (Lk 17:3–4)

Love Requires Self-Denial

To love others requires that we put the needs of others before our own needs. It often means saying no to our own wishes and desires for ourselves,

For Review Answers (page 229)

1. An evangelist is one who shares the Gospel with others.
2. Answers will vary but should mention three of the following ways: through living, studying, inviting, sharing, praying.
3. Stewardship is carefully and responsibly managing something that has been entrusted to one's care.
4. By sharing with others his/her time, treasure, talent, and tradition.

on to tell the students that being Jesus' disciple means not only being an evangelist but a steward as well. Write the term **stewardship** on the board. Explain that it entails sharing our time, talents, treasure, and tradition with others. Distribute copies of Chapter 9, Handout 2, "No One Else Can Do What God Is Calling *You* to Do." Spend a few moments discussing each of these ways of stewardship. After addressing each way, have the students complete the corresponding section on Handout 2.

- *Time.* Tell the students that time is probably our most valuable commodity. We can never really possess it. We can spend time or waste it, but never really save it. We can conquer, own, and even transcend things or space. But time conquers, owns, and transcends us. Likewise, it is in time that God comes to us and we encounter God. That's why time is so precious and why sharing time—being present with others in time—is crucial to stewardship.
  - Interestingly, teenagers do much better in volunteering time. According to a poll in *USA Today* (Sept. 2009), 56 percent of teens give of their time to others, while only 46 percent of adults volunteer their time.
- *Talent.* Call attention to the opening paragraph on Handout 1. Stress that each of us has talents that God wants us to use in specific ways. Assure students that their talents—even if imperfect—are of great value and that by using and sharing these talents they will give joy to the world. Encourage them to take a tip from nature: the woods would be a very silent place if no birds sang except those who sang best. Then, hand back to them the paper plates listing the gifts that they and their classmates believe they possess (from Chapter 8, Lesson 4). Suggest they draw on that list to help them determine their best talents, and then complete the writing activity on the handout.
- *Treasure.* Write the following amount on the board: **$114**. Explain that teens with part-time jobs have an average of $114 per week of disposable income. Since most teens live at home, this is a sizeable amount. Stewardship calls us to share a portion of our treasure with those in need. In fact, according to Jesus, how we spend our money determines what sort of people we become. Jesus says that what we do with our treasures affects our hearts. It determines who we are inside. It determines what sort of people we become—bighearted or tightfisted.

- *Tradition.* Ask the students to name traditions that are important to their family. Afterward, point out that traditions are not remembrances of the past, but guideposts for the future. They give us both roots and wings. For example, we celebrate Eucharist to take our place at the table in the Upper Room and at the foot of the Cross, as well as to nourish ourselves as we work for the future completion of God's Kingdom. Have the students write about how they might share their tradition.

- Conclude discussion on stewardship by making the following points:
  - Write the following on the board: **Good stewards are caretakers**. The good steward is someone who takes care of whatever it is that he or she has been entrusted with and puts it to good use.
  - Write the following on the board: **Good stewards are Eucharistic people**. Help the students recognize that stewards understand they have received something of value from God and in return they love God, themselves, and their neighbors.

- Finally, tell the students that stewardship demands discernment and prayer. Call attention to the prayer on the bottom of the handout. Encourage the students to offer this prayer regularly to help them continue to discover, develop, and share their talents.

a form of death to self-centeredness or self-denial. This means, in Jesus' words, to "take up our crosses," probably the most challenging task of Christian discipleship:

> Then Jesus said to his disciples, "Whoever wishes to come after me must deny himself, take up his cross, and follow me. For whoever wishes to save his life will lose it, but whoever loses his life for my sake will find it. What profit would there be for one to gain the whole world and forfeit his life? Or what can one give in exchange for his life? For the Son of Man will come with his angels in his Father's glory, and then he will repay everyone according to his conduct. (Mt 16:24–27)

Dying to self by picking up a cross is, paradoxically, the way to full and complete life. By loving, we find true life. We discover eternal life by giving up a life of self-centeredness. If we are generous to Jesus by being generous to others, then we will be rewarded. Jesus promises this:

> Give and gifts will be given to you; a good measure, packed together, shaken down, and overflowing, will be poured into your lap. For the measure with which you measure will in return be measured out to you. (Lk 6:38)

Christ insists on love, forgiveness, and generosity, and he tells us we are capable of doing all these things because God first loved us, forgives our sins, and has displayed incredible generosity by giving us the gift of life, health, talents, friends, and countless other gifts. The way we show our love for God is by loving others. The link between the two is ironclad:

> We love because he first loved us. If anyone says, "I love God," but hates his brother, he is a liar; for whoever does not love a brother whom he has seen cannot love God whom he has not seen. This is the commandment we have from him: whoever loves God must also love his brother. (1 Jn 4:19–21)

Love Requires Care for the Poor

Jesus identified with the poor and ministered to them. For example, he reminded his dinner host that he should take care to invite the poor, the crippled, the lame, and the blind to his banquet. Jesus promised: "Blessed indeed will you be because of their inability to repay you. For you will be repaid at the resurrection of the righteous" (Lk 14:14). He also told the parable of Lazarus and the Rich Man (Lk 16:19–31) to emphasize that how we treat the hungry, the poor, and the outcast will determine our eternal destiny.

Furthermore, he told his disciples that we will be judged based on how we have loved others, especially the poor. At the Last Judgment, the question our Lord will put to us is not "How popular were you?" nor "How much money did you make?" nor "What were your grades?" nor "How good an

Chapter 9: Discipleship: Following in the Footsteps of Jesus—Lesson 5

Lesson 5 Objectives

The students will:

- discover the connection between love and forgiveness.
- recognize that real love requires self-denial.
- understand that love demands care for the poor and outcast.
- examine the danger of wealth and greed.
- critique the definition of love as a warm feeling.

Lesson 5 Preview

Discipleship demands not only sharing talents, but also practicing self-sacrifice and self-denial. In this lesson, the students begin to appreciate what it takes to live as a disciple.

Bell Ringer

- Ask the students to offer their responses to the four For Review questions on page 229 (answers are on page 251 of this text). Take time to discuss any other questions or concerns the students may have.

Teaching Approaches

Putting Discipleship into Practice (pages 229-233)

- Write on the board the following quotation from Pope John Paul II:

> **"God is love and in himself he lives a mystery of personal loving communion. . . . Love is therefore the fundamental**

athlete were you?" but "How did you take care of those in need—your brothers and sisters?" This is one true way of judging what kind of disciple you are. Consider how Jesus describes how we are to be judged from Matthew 25:

> When the Son of Man comes in his glory, and all the angels with him, he will sit upon his glorious throne, and all the nations will be assembled before him. And he will separate them one from another, as a shepherd separates the sheep from the goats. He will place the sheep on his right and the goats on his left. Then the king will say to those on his right, "Come, you who are blessed by my Father. Inherit the kingdom prepared for you from the foundation of the world. For I was hungry and you gave me food, I was thirsty and you gave me drink, a stranger and you welcomed me, naked and you clothed me, ill and you cared for me, in prison and you visited me." Then the righteous will answer him and say, "Lord, when did we see you hungry and feed you, or thirsty and give you drink? When did we see you a stranger and welcome you, or naked and clothe you? When did we see you ill or in prison, and visit you?" And the king will say to them in reply, "Amen, I say to you, whatever you did for one of these least brothers of mine, you did for me." Then he will say to those on his left, "Depart from me, you accursed, into the eternal fire prepared for the devil and his angels. For I was hungry and you gave me no food, I was thirsty and you gave me no drink, a stranger and you gave me no welcome, naked and you gave me no clothing, ill and in prison, and you did not care for me." Then they will answer and say, "Lord, when did we see you hungry or thirsty or a stranger or naked or ill or in prison, and not minister to your needs?" He will answer them, "Amen, I say to you, what you did not do for one of these least ones, you did not do for me." And these will go off to eternal punishment, but the righteous to eternal life. (Mt 25:31–46)

In his "Letter to the Rulers of People," St. Francis of Assisi wrote these wise words, words that can speak to each of Jesus' followers:

> Keep a clear eye toward life's end. Do not forget your purpose and destiny as God's creature. What you are in his sight is what you are and nothing more. Remember that when you leave this earth, you can take with you nothing that you have received—fading symbols of honor, trappings of power—but only what you have given: a full heart enriched by honest service, love, sacrifice, and courage.

God the Father sees all of us as his precious children. For this reason, we are to treat all people—especially the poor and outcasts who need our care the most—as brothers and sisters in Christ. The one sure way we can determine what kind of disciple we are is by how we fulfill this command of Jesus: respond to the least of these in your midst.

Lesson 5 Homework

1. Assign the three For Review questions on page 233.
2. Tell the students to read over the Chapter Quick View section on pages 234–236 and to review the chapter's Main Ideas. Have the students write out any remaining questions they may have and bring them to the next session.
3. Remind the students to be ready to hand in their three completed Ongoing Assignments at their next session.

and innate vocation of every human being."

—Pope John Paul II, *Familiaris Consortio*, 11

- Note the examples of Jesus challenging us to love as listed in the text (page 229). Being a disciple means sharing even when we do not want to share, when we least can afford to share, and when the person in need of our gift is the last person we wish to serve.
- Write the word **forgiveness** on the board. Ask if any of the students witnessed an act of forgiveness over the past week—in their families, among their friends, even in a movie or TV program. Invite them to write these acts down in their journals. If these acts are not too personal, have them share them with the class.
- Underline the word **forgiveness** on the board. Ask, "When was the last time you sought forgiveness from another? What were the results?" (*Accept all replies, no matter whether the results were positive or negative.*)
- Remind the students that forgiveness is not logical. It flies in the face of the ethic of reprisal and retaliation ("an eye for an eye"). When Jesus came preaching, "Love your enemies, and pray for those who persecute you" (Mt 5:44), he was speaking a new language and overturning that old ethic. Ask, "What kind of God is Jesus revealing here?" (*Accept all reasonable replies, making sure the students recognize that Jesus reveals a God who refuses to retaliate or demand retribution.*)
- Put the following quotation from St. Gregory the Great on the board:

  "The more a sinner's heart is consumed by the fire of love, the more fully is the rust of sin consumed."

- Tell the students that what Jesus and St. Gregory are telling us is that love and forgiveness are gifts to be passed on to others. There is no room in the Christian heart for hate. Our hearts need to be big enough to say, "I forgive."
- Pose the question, "How big is your heart?" Drive home the question by pointing out that most of us are able to forgive the person who says, "I'm sorry." But what about all the people who hurt us and do not ask forgiveness? What about the friend who is spreading rumors about us? What about the bully who picks on us, or the clique at school that excludes us? What about the classmate whose dress, language, and music

offend us? What are we to do about these people? Jesus says, "Forgive."

- Have the students read Luke 23:33–34. Point out that no one was asking for forgiveness. No one sought pardon for nailing Jesus to the Cross. No one promised to give up sinful ways. Yet Jesus tendered forgiveness.
- Tell the students that forgiveness and non-exclusive love are so important for Jesus because loving forgiveness is total medicine. It is not some suspended sentence ("You're okay for now, but later on you'll pay!"); it is absolute restoration. Forgiveness pardons the past and restores the future.
- Move on by calling attention to the title of the text section "Love Requires Self-Denial" (page 229). Ask the students to offer some examples of loving self-denial: for example, parents forgoing a night out to use the money saved for their children; someone missing a party to help you study for a test in a class in which you are struggling; and so on.
- Have the students read Mark 8:34–37. Note that Jesus is making it clear that discipleship—living out the Great Commission—*costs*. Jesus says that those who would become his disciples would suffer for his sake. Emphasize this by having one of the students read aloud John 15:20–21. Then, to stress that Jesus guarantees that his disciples will have to shoulder the cross, have the students read the passage from the Gospel of Matthew on page 231. Finally, to drive home this point, relate the following story about the sculptor Auguste Rodin (famous for *The Thinker*):

  > One day, Rodin came upon a large, carved crucifix beside a road. The artist instantly loved the piece and insisted on having it for himself. He purchased it and had it carted back to his house. Unfortunately, the cross was too big. It wouldn't fit in the dwelling. So, Rodin knocked down the walls, raised the roof, and rebuilt his home around the cross.

  This is precisely what Jesus calls his disciples to do.

- Help the students recognize that loving God cannot be accomplished in the abstract, but only in the flesh. And the way to love God in the flesh is to deny ourselves, build our lives around the Cross, and love others.
- Direct attention to the text section "Love Requires Care for the Poor" (pages 230–231). Have the students reread the story of the Final Judgment (Mt 25:31–46). Then discuss the meaning of the story in relation to discipleship. Ask: What does this story tell us about disciples?

Love Requires that We Avoid Greed

One of the reasons it is so difficult to follow Jesus' command to love is that humans can be trapped by greed. Consider these three sayings of Jesus:

- "No servant can serve two masters. He will either hate one and love the other, or be devoted to one and despise the other. You cannot serve God and mammon" (Lk 16:13).
- "Amen, I say to you, it will be hard for one who is rich to enter the kingdom of heaven. Again I say to you, it is easier for a camel to pass through the eye of a needle than for one who is rich to enter the kingdom of God" (Mt 19:23–24).
- "For where your treasure is, there also will your heart be" (Lk 12:34).

Mammon is the false god of riches and money. If money, possessions, power, and prestige become our top priorities in life, we lose sight of God. Because wealth has the tendency to blind us to God and his will, Jesus said it is hard for the rich to get to Heaven. When the Apostles heard this teaching, they were astonished. They asked Jesus if anyone, then, could be saved. Jesus replied, "For human beings this is impossible, but for God all things are possible" (Mt 19:26). We must be good stewards of all the wealth and graces we are given by God. And when we do share with others, we must do so sincerely and without calling attention to ourselves. In the Sermon on the Mount, Jesus said to his disciples:

> When you give alms, do not blow a trumpet before you, as the hypocrites do in the synagogues and in the streets to win the praise of others. Amen, I say to you, they have received their reward. But when you give alms, do not let your left hand know what your right is doing, so that your almsgiving may be secret. And your Father who sees in secret will repay you. (Mt 6:2–4)

Performing acts of kindness without fanfare, and especially for needy people, is a sure sign that wealth does not control us but that we control it and use if for the good of others.

In summary, the key element of discipleship is to love. We are able to love because God loves us first and the Holy Spirit empowers us to love. Love demands sacrifice and carrying a cross. Love means forgiving others. Love means concrete deeds

Kindness Ideas

Check out the HelpOthers.org website. Click on the "Kindness Ideas" link and read about different ways you can perform some charitable act. Good starting places to consider are these subtopics:

- Help the Homeless
- Reach Out to the Homebound
- Crafts of Kindness
- Healing Kindness
- Connect with Seniors

Pick a kindness practice, or one similar to it, that appeals to you and resolve to put it into action within the next week. In your journal, write a short summary of the project and how you felt doing it.

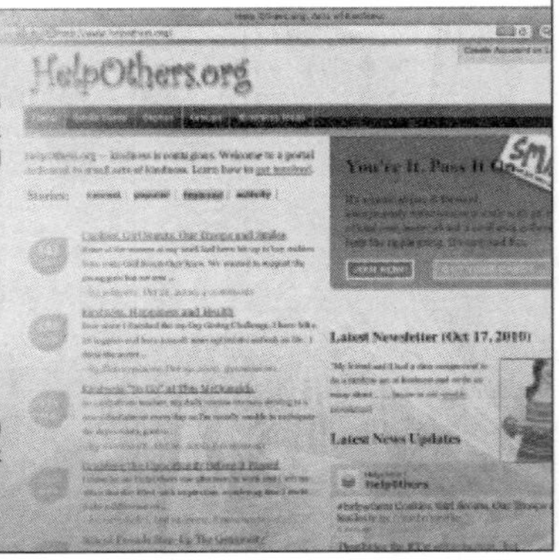

performed for others. Love means being wary of greed. Love means responding to the needs of the poor and outcast. When we love in the name of Christian discipleship, we can make the words of the Zimbabwe pastor our own:

> I won't give up, shut up, let up, until I have stayed up, stored up, prayed up, paid up, preached up, for the cause of Christ. I am a disciple of Jesus. I must go till he comes, give till I drop, preach till all know, and work till he stops me. And, when he comes for his own, he will have no problem recognizing me.

For Review

1. What is the connection between love and forgiveness?
2. What is a major criterion of how we will be judged?
3. What is the spiritual danger of having too much wealth?

For Reflection

"I am what I am in God's sight and nothing more." What does this statement mean to you? What does God see in you?

Act of Love

Pray this traditional prayer. As an additional assignment, use the prayer as a centerpiece for an art project. You may wish to depict in symbols or collage form people who are your neighbors, the injured, and all who are in need of your prayer.

> O my God, I love you above all things, with my whole heart and soul, because you are all good and worthy of all my love. I love my neighbor as myself for the love of you. I forgive all who have injured me, and I ask pardon of all whom I have injured. Amen.

WHAT DOES JESUS SAY ABOUT GREED?

Read the Parable of the Rich Fool, Luke 12:13-21. Answer the following questions:

- What is greed? List other areas of life besides the accumulation of material wealth that greed can affect.
- Is it more likely for a rich person or a poor person to be greedy? Explain your answer.
- How do we become rich before God?

Read the parable of the Rich Man and Lazarus, Luke 16:19-31.

- What images does Jesus use to suggest that the rich man is rich and Lazarus is poor?
- Specifically, why is the rich man punished?
- Is it difficult or easy to give to the poor? Explain.

For Review Answers (page 233)

1. We cannot love without being willing and able to forgive those who have harmed us, for we will be forgiven in the same way we forgive others.
2. We'll be judged according to whether we reached out with love with *real and concrete action* to the poor/outcast: the hungry, the thirsty, the stranger, the naked, the sick, the prisoner.
3. The danger is replacing God with money and, therefore, barring our entrance into God's Kingdom.

- Emphasize that God's concern is whether we have reached out with love, not in the abstract, but in very *real and concrete action* to the poor; that is, to the hungry, the thirsty, the stranger, the naked, the sick, the prisoner. Stress to the students that those whom the judge welcomes into the Kingdom did not simply think loving thoughts about the poor. They gave them food, drink, welcome, visits, and personal presence. They *noticed* when others were alone, or absent, or out of control, or out of a job, or out of a home, or out of sorts, or out of friends—and they came running to help. Those who were condemned did not even notice.
- List the following references to the Book of Psalms on the board: **9:18; 12:5; 22:26; 35:10; 72:12; 113:7; 140:12.** Call on different students to look up and read aloud each one. Then have the students turn to Primary Source Quotations on page 235 and read the quotations by St. Angela Merici and Bl. Luis Guanella. Afterward, direct attention to the question that follows (on page 235): "Who are people who are poor or outcast in your community who can use your love?" Have the students determine what they can do to actively show these people their concern and love.
- Move on to the section "Love Requires that We Avoid Greed" (page 232–233). Go over the three sayings of Jesus listed in the text.
- Remind the students that Jesus had pity for those who were attached to wealth, for he knew that when it came to what we treasure most, a lot is at stake in who or what heads the list. If wealth or anything other than God is at the top, then we have our priorities out of order. Why? Because not only can every other thing disappear in a moment, but more importantly, no person or no amount of wealth can secure our admittance into the Kingdom of God.
- Draw the students' attention to the feature, "What Does Jesus Say about Greed?" on page 233. Give them the opportunity to read each parable on their own and then write their responses in their journals. Afterward, discuss their responses as a class.
- Distribute copies of Chapter 9, Handout 3, "Easy Essays." Explain that the quotation that heads the handout as well as the two short essays are by Peter Maurin who, along with Dorothy Day, founded the Catholic Worker Movement. Maurin penned a number of short articles, which he called "Easy Essays," in order to "entice people into more profound study regarding the rich Christian tradition and radical ways of living the Gospel." Along with Dorothy Day, Maurin strove to live out the Beatitudes as a disciple

of Christ by setting up Houses of Hospitality to help feed, clothe, and comfort the poor.

- Call on different students to read each of the essays. Challenge the students to consider and discuss what Maurin's words might mean for living as faithful disciples of Christ.
- Draw attention to the paragraph on page 232 of the text that begins, "In summary, the key element to discipleship is love." Point out how the paragraph lists the demands of love, and in so doing, beautifully sums up the thrust of this chapter. Direct the students to list the five "demands of love" in the spaces provided on Handout 3. (*sacrifice and carrying a cross; forgiving others; concrete deeds performed for others; being wary of greed; responding to the needs of the poor and outcast*)
- The demands of love should uproot the common understanding of love. Ask the students to respond to the following sentence (write it on the board): **Love requires us to have a warm feeling for God and others.** Discuss their responses and ask them to share what they learned in this lesson that refutes this statement.
- While the students are working, put on the board a copy of the Steward's Prayer (from Chapter 9, Handout 2):

God, show me what you want me to do today;
guide me where you want me to do it,
point out when you want me to do it
And teach me how to get it done.

- Conclude this lesson by leading the students in praying the Steward's Prayer.

Chapter 9: Discipleship: Following in the Footsteps of Jesus—Review Lesson

Bell Ringers

- Ask the students to offer their responses to the three For Review questions on page 233 (answers are on page 255 of this text).
- Collect the Ongoing Assignments for Chapter 9. Allow time for any students who prepared Assignment #6 as a video or audio spot to present it to the class. Likewise, allow time for students who completed Assignment #8 (PowerPoint presentation) to present it.

234 Jesus Christ: Source of Our Salvation

Chapter 9 Quick View

Main Ideas

- Being a disciple of Jesus takes dramatic commitment, even to the possibility of giving up one's life. (p. 214)
- A disciple is a pupil, friend, and follower of Jesus. (pp. 212–214)
- Jesus tells us that we will remain in his love if we keep his commands. (pp. 216–217)
- Jesus did not abolish the Law of the Old Testament; he fulfilled it. We are called to keep the Ten Commandments. (pp. 216–217)
- The first three commandments concern how we can love God with our whole heart, soul, strength, and mind. (pp. 217–219)
- The first commandment requires us to practice the virtue of religion. (p. 217)
- The second commandment forbids any wrong use of God's name or the names of Jesus and the saints. (p. 218)
- The third commandment requires us to keep Sunday holy, especially by celebrating the Eucharist. (p. 219)
- The last seven commandments show us how to love our neighbor as we love ourselves. (pp. 219–223)
- The fourth commandment calls parents and children to respect one another. (p. 219)
- The fifth commandment outlaws killing; we show our respect for life by eating healthy food, exercising, getting proper rest, and avoiding harmful substances. (p. 220)
- The sixth and ninth commandments both teach how to use sexuality in accord with God's plan. (pp. 220–221)
- The seventh and tenth commandments require justice in our dealings with others, both individuals and communities. (p. 222)
- The eighth commandment demands that both individuals and societies are truthful in their relationships with others. (p. 223)
- Incorporating the Beatitudes into our lives is also a key part of being a disciple of Christ. They teach attitudes we should make a part of our lives. (pp. 223–225)
- Another essential element of discipleship is to evangelize, that is, to share the Good News with others through our words and actions. (pp. 225–226)
- To be a good evangelist we must also practice stewardship. (pp. 227–228)
- Putting discipleship into practice means that we first, last, and always are loving of God and neighbor. (pp. 229–230)
- The greatest challenge of loving is often forgiving even our enemies. (p. 230)
- Love requires self-denial, that we care for the poor, and that we avoid greed. (pp. 230–231)

Terms, People, Places

Match the following terms with the definitions below.

A. domestic Church
B. evangelization
C. common priesthood
D. patron saints
E. evangelical counsels
F. chastity

1. Special vows we make to God.
2. People Catholics are often named for; they often inspire us and pray for us.
3. A community of faith that mirrors the love of the Blessed Trinity.
4. A virtue that helps us live with self-control according to our station in life.
5. A call given at Baptism that asks us to demonstrate Christ's presence in the world.
6. Proclaiming the Gospel so that people's hearts are changed.

Review Lesson Objectives

The students will:

- review Chapter 9 in preparation for the chapter test.
- join in prayer together.

Terms, People, Places Answers (page 234)

1. E
2. D
3. A
4. F
5. C
6. B

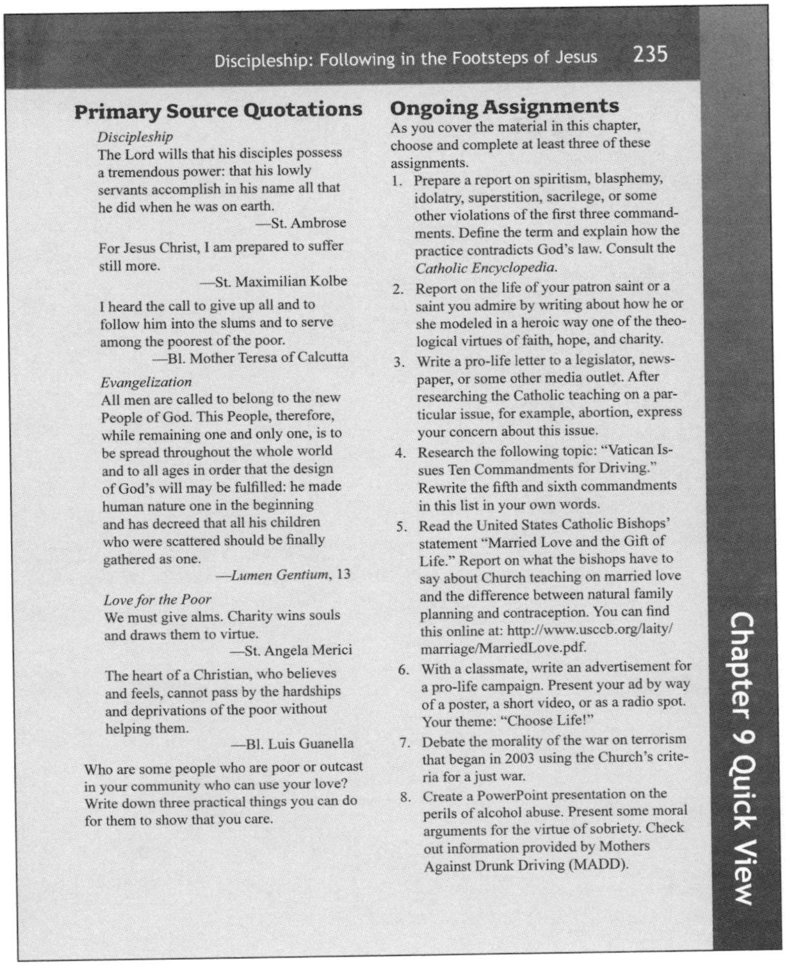

Discipleship: Following in the Footsteps of Jesus 235

Primary Source Quotations

Discipleship

The Lord wills that his disciples possess a tremendous power: that his lowly servants accomplish in his name all that he did when he was on earth.
—St. Ambrose

For Jesus Christ, I am prepared to suffer still more.
—St. Maximilian Kolbe

I heard the call to give up all and to follow him into the slums and to serve among the poorest of the poor.
—Bl. Mother Teresa of Calcutta

Evangelization

All men are called to belong to the new People of God. This People, therefore, while remaining one and only one, is to be spread throughout the whole world and to all ages in order that the design of God's will may be fulfilled: he made human nature one in the beginning and has decreed that all his children who were scattered should be finally gathered as one.
—*Lumen Gentium*, 13

Love for the Poor

We must give alms. Charity wins souls and draws them to virtue.
—St. Angela Merici

The heart of a Christian, who believes and feels, cannot pass by the hardships and deprivations of the poor without helping them.
—Bl. Luis Guanella

Who are some people who are poor or outcast in your community who can use your love? Write down three practical things you can do for them to show that you care.

Ongoing Assignments

As you cover the material in this chapter, choose and complete at least three of these assignments.

1. Prepare a report on spiritism, blasphemy, idolatry, superstition, sacrilege, or some other violations of the first three commandments. Define the term and explain how the practice contradicts God's law. Consult the *Catholic Encyclopedia*.
2. Report on the life of your patron saint or a saint you admire by writing about how he or she modeled in a heroic way one of the theological virtues of faith, hope, and charity.
3. Write a pro-life letter to a legislator, newspaper, or some other media outlet. After researching the Catholic teaching on a particular issue, for example, abortion, express your concern about this issue.
4. Research the following topic: "Vatican Issues Ten Commandments for Driving." Rewrite the fifth and sixth commandments in this list in your own words.
5. Read the United States Catholic Bishops' statement "Married Love and the Gift of Life." Report on what the bishops have to say about Church teaching on married love and the difference between natural family planning and contraception. You can find this online at: http://www.usccb.org/laity/marriage/MarriedLove.pdf.
6. With a classmate, write an advertisement for a pro-life campaign. Present your ad by way of a poster, a short video, or as a radio spot. Your theme: "Choose Life!"
7. Debate the morality of the war on terrorism that began in 2003 using the Church's criteria for a just war.
8. Create a PowerPoint presentation on the perils of alcohol abuse. Present some moral arguments for the virtue of sobriety. Check out information provided by Mothers Against Drunk Driving (MADD).

Chapter 9 Quick View

Review Lesson Homework

1. Complete any unfinished Ongoing Assignments.
2. Reread Chapter 9.
3. Study for the Chapter 9 Test.

Teaching Approaches

Chapter Quick View (pages 234–236)

- Remember, this section is provided for the students to review the chapter material. Although it is helpful for the students simply to read and study the list of Main Ideas, more creative use of the list might help the students retain the information. For example, provide copies of the list with some of the key words and/or phrases blocked out. Use this as a quiz to help students evaluate areas they need to study more carefully or as a simple study sheet.
- Invite anyone who had further questions about the Chapter 9 Main Ideas section on page 234 to ask them now. Invite other class members to offer answers. Clarify any remaining confusion.
- Call attention to Terms, People, Places on page 234. Use the section as a vocabulary study tool by having the students match the terms to their correct definition (answers are on page 256 of this text).
- Take some time to go over any material the students may have overlooked in their review or that you feel needs more attention.
- Be sure to provide some quiet time for the students to study on their own. If students have additional questions, invite them to approach you privately while their classmates study.

Prayer Service

- Gather the students in a circle around a cross or crucifix. Have meditative music playing.
- Lead the students in praying St. Ignatius of Loyola's "Prayer for Generosity" (on page 236).
- Afterward, sing or play a recording of a discipleship themed hymn, such as "Anthem" by Tom Conry, or "Take Up Your Cross" by David Haas.

Chapter 9 Test Lesson

Teaching Approaches

- Allow sufficient time for the students to work on the Chapter 9 Test (starting on page 291 of the TWE and also online at www.avemariapress.com). Collect tests as the students finish.

Test Lesson Homework

1. Read the following text sections of Chapter 10: "An Invitation to Prayer" (pages 240–241) and "Defining Prayer" (pages 241–242).
2. Examine the Chapter 10 Ongoing Assignments on page 263.
3. Have the students check with their parents to discover what their (the students) first words were.

Chapter 9 Quick View

236 Jesus Christ: Source of Our Salvation

9. Read the United States Catholic Bishops' statement titled "Stewardship and Teenagers: The Challenge of Being a Disciple." You can find it on the United States Conference of Catholic Bishops' website: www.usccb.org/bishops/StewardshipTeens.pdf.

Prayer

St. Ignatius of Loyola (1491–1556), the founder of the Society of Jesus—popularly known as the Jesuits—spent a year in prayer and meditation after being wounded from a battle while serving as a Basque knight. He read about the lives of Jesus and the saints and decided to serve the Kingdom of God. He wrote the following prayer that has served as inspiration for Jesuits and others in the years since.

Prayer for Generosity
Lord, teach me to be generous.
Teach me to serve you as you deserve;
to give and not to count the cost;
to fight and not to heed the wounds;
to toil and not to seek for rest;
to labor and not to ask for any reward,
save that of knowing that I do your will.
Amen.

- *Reflection*: What is God's will for you?
- *Resolution*: Serve Jesus in the coming week by serving a particular person at home and at school.

Chapter 9 Test Answers

Part 1: Fill in the Blanks. (2 points each)

1. Peter 2. Thomas 3. patron 4. Francis 5. chastity 6. family 7. steward 8. Apostle 9. Matthew 10. detraction

11, 12, 13 & 14. time; treasure; talent; tradition 15. Andrew 16. calumny 17. Judas Iscariot

18 & 19. presumption; first 20, 21 & 22. pupil; friend; follower 23. justice 24. idolatry

25. Evangelist 26. common

Part 2: Lists and Explanations. (1 point for each item named correctly and 1 point for each item explained correctly)

- List the Ten Commandments. For five of the commandments, describe some specific sins that are forbidden by them. *Note:* Allow variations in wording, but not in numbering. (**15 points possible**)
    1. I am the Lord your God: You shall not have strange gods before me. (*heresy, apostasy, schism, presumption, despair, superstition, divination, sorcery, irreligion, sacrilege, simony*)
    2. You shall not take the name of the Lord your God in vain. (*perjury, blasphemy*)
    3. Remember to keep holy the Lord's day. (*skipping Mass*)
    4. Honor your father and your mother. (*disobeying parents, disrespect toward siblings and other family members, disobeying other authority figures*)
    5. You shall not kill. (*murder, suicide, improper use of military force, cloning, taking drugs*)

Discipleship: Following in the Footsteps of Jesus 237

Chapter 9 Quick View

Chapter 9 Test Answers continued

6. You shall not commit adultery. (*adultery, divorce, polygamy, incest, sexual abuse, free unions, masturbation, fornication, pornography, prostitution, rape, homosexual acts*)
7. You shall not steal. (*theft, business fraud, paying unjust wages, price fixing, corruption, shoddy work, tax evasion, forgery, vandalism, greed, avarice, envy*)
8. You shall not bear false witness against your neighbor. (*gossiping, bragging, lying, detraction, calumny, cheating*)
9. You shall not covet your neighbor's wife. (*adultery, divorce, polygamy, incest, sexual abuse, free unions, masturbation, fornication, pornography, prostitution, rape, homosexual acts*)
10. You shall not covet anything that belongs to your neighbor. (*theft, business fraud, paying unjust wages, price fixing, corruption, shoddy work, tax evasion, forgery, vandalism, greed, avarice, envy*)

- List the eight Beatitudes and explain how you can live out four of them in your life today. *Note:* Accept all legitimate applications of the Beatitudes. (**12 points possible**)
  1. Blessed are the poor in spirit, for theirs is the kingdom of heaven.
  2. Blessed are they who mourn, for they shall be comforted.
  3. Blessed are the meek, for they will inherit the land.
  4. Blessed are the merciful, they will be shown mercy.
  5. Blessed are the clean of heart, for they shall see God.

Chapter 9 Test Answers continued

6. Blessed are the peacemakers, for they will be called children of God.
7. Blessed are they who are persecuted for the sake of righteousness, for theirs is the Kingdom of Heaven.
8. Blessed are you when they insult you and persecute you and utter every kind of evil against you (falsely) because of me. Rejoice and be glad, for your reward will be great in heaven.

- Name the two purposes of marriage. (**4 points possible**)
  1. The unitive—the bonding of husband and wife in love.
  2. The procreative—the cooperation with God in bringing about new life.
- List the Twelve Apostles. (**12 points possible**)
  - Peter
  - Andrew
  - James son of Zebedee
  - John son of Zebedee
  - Philip
  - Bartholomew
  - Matthew
  - Thomas
  - James son of Alphaeus
  - Simon the Zealot
  - Judas son of James
  - Judas Iscariot

Part 3: Discipleship Essay. (5 points)
Answers should include any of the following concepts:

- Disciples are pupils, friends, and followers of Jesus.
- Disciples follow the Ten Commandments and therefore love God and their neighbor as themselves.
- Disciples live the Beatitudes.
- Disciples are evangelists in both word and deed.
- Disciples practice stewardship.
- Disciples show love by self-denial, service to the poor, and avoidance of greed.

Chapter 10: Prayer in the Life of a Disciple of Jesus Christ

Introduction

He prayeth best, who loveth best
All things both great and small;
For the dear God who loveth us,
He made and loveth all.

—Samuel Taylor Coleridge,
The Rime of the Ancient Mariner

Prayer is an act of love, and, therefore, a radically human activity, the activity of acknowledging who and whose we are. Prayer is the heartbeat of the Christian and an essential element of discipleship.

In this final chapter, the students discover some absolutely crucial elements of prayer:

- It is a relationship that requires both quality and quantity time.
- It is not some extra thing we do, but the essential thing we do so that we can do extra things.
- It is not dependent upon positive feelings.
- It requires listening more than speaking, responding more than asking, and silence more than words.
- It empowers us both to be aware of and to grow from God's action in human life.

In their first lesson, the students examine how prayer involves them in a relationship with the Divine. The *Catechism of the Catholic Church* describes prayer as "the living relationship of the children of God with their Father who is good beyond measure" (*CCC*, 2565). The students discover that prayer allows us to appreciate and become more and more open to the generosity of God. In their investigation of the many benefits of prayer, the students discover that prayer is the oxygen of the Christian.

The second lesson provides the students with a "how-to map" of prayer's mechanics. Prayer is a gift and a skill. We can learn how to pray, and we can learn how to get better at it. The students look at various expressions of prayer, try out new ways of prayer, write their own prayers, and then set and commit themselves to a rhythm of prayer.

Christians are heirs to a rich history of prayer. Our praying tradition has roots that reach deep into the Old Testament and identify us with a people who walk with God. In their third lesson, the students examine prayer in the Old Testament and discover some of those roots. As they go on to examine prayer in the New Testament, the students learn that Jesus did not cut those ancient roots but grew out of them, blossoming as the perfect pray-er. Finally, the students examine how the Church continues the rich tradition of using Scripture in its prayer and liturgy.

In the fourth lesson, the students look closely at two powerful prayers for discipleship: the Lord's Prayer and the Hail Mary. The students examine the Lord's Prayer line-by-line. There, they discover the Gospel in a nutshell. The information provided in the text follows that information so skillfully presented in the *Catechism of the Catholic Church*. Since Mary the mother of Jesus is the praying person whose faith and humility flawlessly embody the human response to God's inbreaking, the students look to the Hail Mary as the prayer to use when seeking help on how best to follow her Son.

Advance Preparations

Prepare or have on hand:

For Lesson 1

- Corrected copies of the Chapter 9 Test
- Bibles

Chapter Objectives

To help the students:

- define prayer as a response to God's call and an opportunity to develop a relationship to the Divine.
- describe some of the benefits of prayer.
- practice various expressions of prayer: vocal, meditative, and mental.
- identify the six forms of prayer.
- discover models of prayer in both the Old and New Testaments.
- discover the numerous ways we, as the Church, pray with the Scriptures.
- investigate and understand the various parts of the Lord's Prayer and the Hail Mary.

For Lesson 2

- Bibles
- Copies of Chapter 10, Handout 1, "Meditating on the Scriptures"
- An icon for the students to view (optional)
- Copies of Chapter 10, Handout 2, "Litany of the Saints"
- Copies of Chapter 10, Handout 3, "Novena to Saint Joseph"

For Lesson 3

- Bibles
- A reference to the Gospel reading for the day on which you present this lesson. (*Note*: One place to find it is at www.usccb.org/nab.)

For Lesson 4

- Bibles
- Copies of Chapter 10, Handout 4, "Mary's Prayer"
- A recording of Franz Schubert's "Ave Maria" and player (optional)

For the Chapter 10 Review Lesson

- Audio-visual equipment needed to view slide show and PowerPoint presentations
- Candle and matches
- A recording of a discipleship themed hymn, such as "Anthem" by Tom Conry or "The Love of the Lord" by Michael Joncas and player (optional)
- Copies of the students' prayer booklets

For the Chapter 10 Test Lesson

- Copies of the Chapter 10 Test (starting on page 291 of the TWE and also online at www.avemariapress.com)

Chapter 10 Handouts

- Handout 1, Meditating on the Scriptures—The students meditate.
- Handout 2, Litany of the Saints—The students examine and pray the litany of the saints.
- Handout 3, Novena to Saint Joseph—The students pray a novena prayer to St. Joseph.
- Handout 4, Mary's Prayer—The students pray the Hail Mary in Latin, English, and Spanish.

Chapter 10: Prayer in the Life of a Disciple of Jesus Christ—Lesson 1

Bell Ringers

- Distribute the students' corrected Chapter 9 Tests. Go over the test, using it as a means to review the previous chapter. Address any remaining questions or concerns the students may have.
- Introduce this lesson by inviting the students to share the first prayer or prayers they learned as children. Then discuss:
  - Who taught you the prayer?
  - Do you still use the prayer?
  - Has the way you pray changed since you were a child? How?
  - What is your favorite prayer or way of praying today? Explain why.

Teaching Approaches

An Invitation to Prayer (pages 240–241)

- Ask one of the students to read aloud the passage from Matthew 7 on page 240. Point out that Jesus couches this invitation to prayer in the context of a loving relationship; namely, the love between a parent and child.
- Go on to call on different students to summarize the prayer examples from Mother Teresa and the grandmother and grandchild. Then discuss their reactions to these stories. Ask the students to explain the meaning of the stories and how it might apply to their lives.
- Emphasize that both examples speak to how our God "answers" prayer. Explain that a caring parent knows that not everything a child requests is a gift that is good for that particular child. A loving parent knows when to say yes and when to say no. Finally, while the wise and loving parent gives only "good things" to us (Mt 7:11), those things are not always everything we say we *want*, but they are always everything that we *need*.
- Direct the students to complete the activity, "Self-Evaluation on Prayer" (page 240) and write their responses to the three follow-up questions. Then, have the students share their responses with a partner or in small groups.

An Invitation to Prayer

Prayer is essential to the life of a disciple of Jesus Christ. In the Sermon on the Mount, Jesus instructs us:

> Ask and it will be given to you; seek and you will find; knock and the door will be opened to you. For everyone who asks, receives; and the one who seeks, finds; and to the one who knocks, the door will be opened. Which one of you would hand his son a stone when he asks for a loaf of bread, or a snake when he asks for a fish? If you then, who are wicked, know how to give good gifts to your children, how much more will your heavenly Father give good things to those who ask him. (Mt 7:7–11)

Prayer is powerful. A famous story told about Bl. Mother Teresa of Calcutta points this out. One day, a novice who was in charge of the kitchen came to Mother Teresa and told her that they had no flour to make the food necessary to feed three hundred other novices who were returning for lunch. Mother Teresa instructed the young nun to go to the chapel where she was to pray to Jesus, telling him they had no food. The novice did as she was instructed. Ten minutes later, a man came to the door of the convent and told Mother Teresa that the teachers in the city schools were going on strike and that he had seven thousand lunches that he did not know what to do with. He asked her, "Can you use them?"

Mother Teresa had profound faith and trust that the Lord would provide—and he did. The heavenly Father provides for the needs of his children.

Self-Evaluation on Prayer

Evaluate how frequently you do each of the following prayer experiences. Then write your response to the questions that follow.

- celebrate the Eucharistic liturgy
- read the Bible
- ask God to heal sick relatives and friends
- talk to Jesus as with a friend
- ask God for help in studies or other activities
- recite formal prayers like the Lord's Prayer and the Hail Mary
- ask for God's help when tempted to sin
- think about Jesus and how he would act in certain situations
- say prayers before and after meals
- examine my conscience before going to sleep
- pray the Rosary
- try to figure out questions by asking the Holy Spirit for insight
- praise God for the beauty in creation
- read spiritual books
- thank God for all the gifts he has given, including my friends
- ask Jesus to help see his presence in others
- ask God for forgiveness after sinning
- think about God
- adore Jesus while visiting him in the Blessed Sacrament
- listen to music that helps me think of God's beauty or greatness

Questions

1. How do you define prayer?
2. Which of these prayer experiences do you do the most? the least?
3. Which of these experiences has brought you the greatest peace and satisfaction? Why do you think that is so?

Lesson 1 Objectives

The students will:

- review Chapter 9.
- share their first prayers and first words.
- evaluate their personal prayer habits.
- recall different definitions of prayer.
- define prayer as a response to God's inbreaking and as a relationship to the Divine.
- list some of the benefits of prayer.

Lesson 1 Preview

In this lesson, the students discover that prayer is a personal stance toward God. It is how we enrich and cement our relationship with the Divine. Prayer is not our efforts to wrangle divine favors from a pinch-penny God in order to fill in the gaps of our personalities. Rather, prayer is the way we strive to respond and open ourselves to the overwhelming generosity of God.

Prayer in the Life of a Disciple of Jesus Christ 241

Another story about prayer has a different result. It involves a grandmother who was helping her granddaughter with a homework assignment. However, the child was upset because she had misplaced her favorite doll. Finally, she asked her grandmother if they could kneel down together to ask God to help find the doll. Of course, the grandmother said yes. They both knelt down, closed their eyes, and offered a silent prayer. Then the girl sat down and completed the homework assignment.

The next day, the grandmother asked her granddaughter if she found her doll. "No," she replied, "but I am not thinking about my doll today."

We have Jesus' Word that our heavenly Father will give good things to us. Sometimes God answers our prayers exactly the way we hope that he would, like in the case of Bl. Mother Teresa. At other times, God tells us to be patient and to look for other answers. Perhaps God was trying to teach the little girl patience but also the value of detachment—that possessions are not all that important. Still other times God might say no to our requests because he is answering a much deeper need in our hearts, giving us a more valuable gift that will make us a better person and a better disciple of his Son.

For Reflection

When was a time that prayer helped you the most?

Defining Prayer (*CCC*, 2558-2567; 2590; 2623-2649)

God the Father calls each of us into a vital relationship with him through Jesus Christ in the Holy Spirit. Prayer is a powerful means to grow in union with Jesus. He told us to pray always without becoming weary (Lk 18:1). St. Paul repeated Jesus' advice when he wrote, "Pray without ceasing" (1 Thes 5:17). Along the same lines, St. Frances Cabrini (1850–1917), the first American citizen to be canonized, wrote:

> We must pray without tiring, for the salvation of mankind does not depend on material success; nor on sciences that cloud the intellect. Neither does it depend on arms and human industries, but on Jesus alone.

Prayer is our response to the God who seeks us. As the *Catechism of the Catholic Church* puts it, prayer is a "vital and personal relationship with the living and true God" (*CCC*, 2558). The Holy Spirit enables us to pray. In humility, we approach our loving Father who desires only good things for us, which he grants to us through his Son, Jesus Christ.

The *Catechism* further defines prayer as "the living relationship of the children of God with their Father who is good beyond measure, with his Son Jesus Christ, and with the Holy Spirit" (*CCC*, 2565). Think of prayer, then, as a *relationship*, a coming together with God the Father who is our Abba; with Jesus Christ, our Savior, brother, and friend; and with the Holy Spirit, our Comforter and Helper, who dwells in our hearts. When we pray, we become more aware of who we are as adopted children of our loving God. Prayer brings us into unity with our loving Triune God.

Great saints have also given us excellent definitions of prayer. For example, St. John Damascene said prayer is "the raising of one's mind and heart to God." St. Augustine remarked, "True prayer is nothing but love." St. Thérèse of Lisieux observed, "For me, prayer is a surge of the heart; it is a simple look turned toward heaven, it is a cry of recognition and of love, embracing both trial and joy."

St. Clement defined prayer as "conversation with God." St. Teresa of Avila also pictured prayer this way when she recommended that we think of prayer as a journey with our invisible God, a

Lesson 1 Homework

1. Direct the students to write out their answers to the two For Review questions on page 242.
2. Assign the For Reflection question on page 242.
3. Ask the students to turn to the Ongoing Assignments on page 263. Have them choose three of the listed assignments to complete prior to the conclusion of this chapter. Tell the students the assignments are due on the day they gather for their chapter review.
4. Tell the students to read "How to Pray" (pages 242–250) in preparation for their next lesson.

For Review Answers (page 242)

1. Answers will vary but should include some mention of a relationship with God.
2. Answers will vary but should include examples of the benefits from page 242 of the text.

Defining Prayer (pages 241-242)

- Read aloud the first sentence in this text section: "God the Father calls each of us into a vital relationship with him through Jesus Christ in the Holy Spirit." Stress that God invites us to become part of the divine relationship—the Trinity, the divine "family"—and prayer is our RSVP to that invitation.
- Note how the text points out that both the Scriptures and the saints (St. Frances Cabrini) urge persistence in prayer. Likewise, from another religious tradition, the Buddha said, "The greatest prayer is patience." To illustrate the importance of patience and persistence, use an example like the following:

  > A stonecutter may hammer away at a rock a hundred times without so much as a crack showing in it. Yet, at the hundred and first blow, the rock splits in two. It was not the one blow that did it, but all that had gone before.

- Emphasize that for those of us who call ourselves Christians, prayer—not social justice, not evangelization, not catechesis—is our primary task. We must receive before we can give, commune before we can communicate, and be converted before we can convert. Tell the students to turn to the section Primary Source Quotations on pages 262–263 and read aloud the quotation from St. John Chrysostom: "Nothing is equal to prayer; for what is impossible it makes possible, what is difficult, easy." Then, note that Dr. Martin Luther King Jr. seems to echo Chrysostom when he said, "To be a Christian without prayer is no more possible than to be alive without breathing."
- Tell the students that like exercise, prayer is hard but healthy, and that like healthy exercise, which may begin by being hard, it becomes easy over time. Stress that there is no substitute for it. Good works, self-sacrifice, almsgiving, all have their place, but they cannot stand in for prayer. That is why we dare not make prayer simply something extra in our lives. It must be an essential.
- Call attention to the first sentence of this section's second text paragraph: "Prayer is our *response* to the God who seeks us" [*emphasis added*]. Have the students underline the sentence. Stress here how God makes the first move. God calls and invites. We respond. Prayer, then, is a *response* to our experience of God's inbreaking.
- Drive home this point by inviting the students to share what their first words were as infants (see homework assignment from the Chapter 9 Test Lesson). Note

how many are "da-da" or "ma-ma" or variations. Point out that no matter what our first words were, they were our *response* to the communication—the invitation—of a loving parent(s). And that response strengthened the relationship bonds among us. The same is true of prayer.

- Go on to note how the *Catechism of the Catholic Church* calls prayer a *relationship*—a relationship that links us to the Trinity and to one another. Emphasize that our praying shapes us into people of prayer, people who yearn for a personal relationship with the triune God and who are anxious to respond to God's inbreaking with our best efforts.
- Have the students find in their textbooks the definitions of prayer offered by the saints. List them on the board. Invite the students to tell which they like best.
- Have the students list the "Benefits of Prayer" (page 242) as a class. Invite the students to name any other benefits they have experienced. Conclude by noting how each benefit contributes to our becoming whole and holy, and deepens our relationship with God. Tell the students that like any relationship, our relationship with God is strengthened by regular communication.
- Invite the students to participate in a mock advertising campaign for their Church. Tell them that they are responsible for creating advertisements that include the definition and benefits of prayer. They can create

EXPLAINING THE FAITH

Do my prayers affect God? For example, can they get God to change his mind?
Prayer brings together two great mysteries. The first is of an eternally loving God who knows all that was, all that is, and all that ever will be. The second involves the mystery of our own free will, which enables us to accept or reject God's invitation to love.

When we pray, we are praying to a loving God who has known our prayers for all eternity. Thus, when we pray, we are not telling God anything new. Nor do we exercise any power over him, for example, the power to persuade him to change his mind about something. In fact, it is the Holy Spirit who first inspired us to pray. As a result of knowing and inspiring our prayers from all eternity, God had included them in his plan for the world. Furthermore, the very prayers that God knew we would ask have been answered! Therefore, prayer does not change God. Prayer changes us.

companion who walks next to us along the path of life. Prayer is turning to the Father and talking and listening to him as in a friendly conversation. Just as friendships thrive on conversation, so will regular conversations with our loving God give us the strength to live according to his will.

Benefits of Prayer

Certainly, though, we can say that prayer has many benefits:

- *Prayer contributes to our sense of self-worth.* In prayer we get in touch with who we are as God's child, discovering God's infinite love for us.
- *Prayer leads to happiness*, helping us discover that our restless hearts can find true happiness, not in possessions or fame, but in our relationship with Jesus Christ.
- *Prayer changes us* by making us more loving, by showing us God's will for us and what we must do to follow Christ more closely.
- Just like water helps plants grow, *prayer helps nourish in us virtues* like faith, hope, charity, humility, sensitivity to other people, compassion, and a desire to work for God's kingdom.
- *Prayer energizes, calms, and renews.*
- *Prayer heals* because we meet the Divine Physician who touches our hurting hearts and forgives our sins.
- *Prayer helps relieve anxiety* by helping us heed Jesus' teaching not to worry about everyday cares because our heavenly Father is looking out for us.

Prayer has many benefits, but the greatest is that *prayer deepens our relationship with the Triune God* who loves us beyond what we can imagine. This chapter examines prayer as a central component for the life of a disciple of Jesus Christ.

For Review

1. Give a definition of prayer. Explain its meaning.
2. What is the greatest benefit of prayer?

For Reflection

Write your own personal definition of prayer.

How to Pray

Prayer is an act of love, a personal response to God's love for us. We show this love when we pray to God the Father, our loving Abba who is the source of our life. We show our love when we pray to Jesus Christ, our Lord and Savior, asking for his friendship and

Extending the Lesson

Since many young people have questions/problems surrounding prayer's genuineness and/or meaningfulness, consider making the following points:

- First of all, because prayer is responding to God from the heart, we tend to think that if our heart does not overflow with praise or gratitude for God's presence, then our prayer is phony. Remind the students that prayer never happens apart from life. Life is painful as well as joyful, frustrating as well as fulfilling, so prayer is more than pouring out the fullness of our hearts to God. Prayer is finding the way to God whether our hearts are full or empty. Jesus knew this. That is why he prayed at times of fullness and emptiness.
- A second danger about believing that the heart can pray by itself is equating prayer's worth with how it makes us *feel*. Too often, we tend to judge the worth of prayer according to how meaningful it feels to us. Too often, we expect prayer to engage our full attention and provoke an immediate response of our emotions. When this does not happen, we think our prayer is meaningless, dull, and not from the heart. However, if the immediate response of the emotions is the only criterion available for calling something personal and meaningful, then almost everything we do is meaningless and not from the heart. Assure the students that this is not to say that prayer does not engage us emotionally, because it does. However, it does so only now and then, briefly, and usually unpredictably. Point out to the teens that what prayer does consistently, however, is to nurture the expression of religious affections: wonder, awe, and joy, longing or need, and gratitude.

Prayer in the Life of a Disciple of Jesus Christ 243

help. We show our love when we pray to the Holy Spirit, the interior teacher of Christian prayer, asking for his guidance and strength to live a Christ-like life.

We also show our love when we pray in union with our Blessed Mother. She is the greatest saint. Her openness and example serve as a model of how to cooperate with the graces the Holy Spirit showers on us.

Most Catholics learn how to pray from parents, teachers, parish priests, and other believers whose example inspires them. Common to the lessons are some teachings of saints who have made prayer part of their daily lives. The following "6 Ps" make up good preliminary steps for a rich prayer life:

1. *Place.* One good rule: find a special place to pray where you can calm yourself, put yourself in God's presence, and focus your attention. Consider the following: your bedroom, a special corner in your house where you may light a **votive candle**, the school chapel or parish church, in your car with the radio off, or on a regular walking route outside where you can focus some time on prayer.
2. *Period of Time.* Prayer can take place any time, but it is good to carve out a scheduled part of the day for prayer. For example:
   - first thing in the morning or last thing at night
   - before or after a meal
   - ten minutes during a free period at school
   - between homework assignments

   Catholics set aside one hour a week to worship at the Sunday Eucharist and on holy days of obligation.
3. *Posture.* You can be more alert and relaxed while praying with a suitable posture. Some people pray best when standing or walking, some while sitting upright in a chair, others by

votive candle
A prayer candle typically placed before a statue of Jesus or the Virgin Mary that is lit for a prayer intention.

Lesson 2 Objectives

The students will:

- apply the "6 Ps" to their personal prayer lives.
- list and describe the three expressions of prayer.
- list and describe the six forms of prayer.
- practice meditative prayer.
- create prayers using the three expressions and six forms of prayer.
- list and describe some traditional Catholic prayers.

Lesson 2 Preview

In this lesson, the students discover more about prayer, particularly its expressions and forms. Be ready to devote at least two class periods to the material. Likewise, do your best to arrange the classroom to be a suitable prayer environment or arrange a space outside of the classroom for prayer.

a written advertisement for newspapers, written ads for online-sponsored links, banner advertisements for webpages, jingles, radio spots, TV commercials, etc. You may allow them to work individually or in groups. Grade their projects based on understanding of the content of this lesson and creativity.

- Before dismissing the students, write on the board the following quotation from the Danish philosopher/theologian Søren Kierkegaard: **"Prayer does not change God, but it changes him who prays."** Then call attention to the feature Explaining the Faith on page 242. Go through it with the students. Conclude by noting that prayer does not change God. It changes us. While prayer may not change *things* for us, it does change *us* for things.

Chapter 10: Prayer in the Life of a Disciple of Jesus Christ—Lesson 2

Bell Ringers

- Ask the students to offer their responses to the two For Review questions on page 242 (answers are on page 263 of this text). Be sure to allow the students to ask any other questions they may have.
- Call attention to the section Primary Source Quotations on pages 262–263 and read aloud the quotations from St. Thérèse of Lisieux and St. Rose of Viterbo on the meaning of prayer. Then have the students share their personal definitions of prayer (from For Reflection on page 242). Discuss.

Teaching Approaches

How to Pray (pages 242-250)

- Write on the board the following quotation from the author Corrie ten Boom:

  > **"Don't pray when you feel like it. Have an appointment with the Lord and keep it. A man is powerful on his knees."**

- Go over the "6 Ps" with the students. Stress that these seemingly mundane steps can help us pray even when we do not feel like it. In fact, whether or not we feel like praying, or whether or not we receive an emotional dividend from our prayer, God is with us. God is speaking within us, accepting us as we are, and inviting us to respond. Tell the students that like an artist who aspires to create a painting or an athlete who aspires to win a contest, the person who aspires to respond to God's inbreaking needs disciplines like the "6 Ps."
- Encourage the students to share how they could put these steps into practice in their own lives. First invite them to journal about these possibilities; then have them share their responses as a class.
- Have the students turn to the text section "Prayer Expressions" on pages 245–246. Summarize the various ways we can pray:
    - *Vocal or Spoken Prayer*: This sort of prayer is following the lead of Jesus when he prayed the Lord's Prayer. Vocal prayer may be done by an individual or by a group. When we pray *together*, we give wider utterance to our shared faith, which, in turn, strengthens our relationship to one another as well as to God.

244 Jesus Christ: Source of Our Salvation

lectio divina
Literally, "divine reading." This is a prayerful way to read the Bible or any other sacred writings.

kneeling, still others (like St. Ignatius of Loyola) by lying on their backs. As you begin your prayer in whatever posture you choose, it helps to inhale and exhale slowly, letting the cares of the day drain away.

4. *Presence.* You can begin your prayer time by recalling basic truths like these: God is always present to us. He loves us beyond what we can imagine. He has showered us with the gift of life and so many other gifts. Reminding yourself of these truths will help you approach God with humility and with grateful hearts. You can enter your prayer realizing that the Holy Spirit himself has led us to spend time with our loving God, a special time of trust and companionship with the one who holds us in the palm of his hand. Being present to God in prayer is itself a prayer.
5. *Passage.* There are many ways to pray, as this chapter will point out. One time-honored and sure way to pray is to select a passage from Scripture and then meditate on it. Known as **lectio divina** (see page 245), this is a wonderful way to allow the Lord to speak to your heart.
6. *Persistence.* Amid the distractions of daily life, regular prayer can be tough. It is sometimes described as a battle because when we pray, we are fighting against ourselves, our surroundings, and Satan who tries to turn us away from our prayer. But you should remember the words of St. Padre Pio: "Prayer is the best weapon we have. It is a key to opening God's heart."

Distractions in prayer caused by a wandering mind, an overactive imagination, or external noises are normal. You can counteract them by gazing at a crucifix, holy picture or icon, or by

Lesson 2 Homework

1. Go over the For Reflection (page 250) with the students. Note how the pope is asking young people—in addition to regular communal worship at the Eucharist—to set aside a daily time, place, and duration for prayer. Stress that as disciples of Jesus—i.e., his pupils, friends, and followers—we need to spend both *quality and quantity time* with him. Direct the students to complete the exercise by responding in their journals.
2. Assign the seven For Review questions on page 250.
3. Tell the students to read "Praying with Sacred Scripture" (pages 250–255) in preparation for their next lesson.
4. Remind the students to continue working on their chosen Ongoing Assignments.

lighting a candle to help keep your attention on God. You can call on the Holy Spirit to focus your attention. Repeatedly reciting a prayer-word or -phrase like "Abba," "Lord Jesus," "Come, Holy Spirit," or "Jesus help me" can help drive away distractions.

Jesus is pleased that we want to pray, even if we are distracted or do not think much is going on. In prayer, we are present to the Lord, and he appreciates the time we spend with him. If our prayer is united to Jesus, he will give us much more than we are asking for. His love will touch us, despite our restless minds. He will give us the Holy Spirit who strengthens us and changes us into other Christs. In the battle to pray, we should always remember that any effort we make to try to pray is itself a prayer. The next sections focus on several forms, expressions, and practices of prayer.

Prayer Expressions (CCC, 2700-2719; 2721-2724)

Recall an earlier definition of prayer as conversation with God. Conversation involves talking, where we take our concerns and requests to God. As a wise person once said, "If we want to walk with God, we must talk to God." Vocal prayer—using spoken words—is one way to pray. But we must listen to God as well, cherishing moments of silence when we can hear God speak to us. This can take place in meditation or in mental prayer leading to contemplation.

When we slow down and put ourselves in God's presence, we hear our Lord speak to us through our intellects, feelings, imaginations, wills, and memories. For example, he can put new ideas into our minds, ideas that teach us how to be more loving persons. He can calm our troubled emotions by strengthening our faith and trust that he will take care of us. He can inspire our imaginations by helping us visualize how we solve in a new way a troubled relationship. He can strengthen our wills to do the right thing when we face temptation. And he can heal our bad memories that might be troubling us or remind us of all the good things he has done for us.

Christian prayer is heartfelt, expressing itself as vocal prayer, meditation, and mental prayer.

Vocal Prayer

When we express our prayer vocally in words we are doing what Jesus himself did when he taught the Our Father. When we say our prayers aloud with others, we can strengthen our spiritual relationships with them. The Church has a rich tradition of vocal prayer. For example, this prayer of St. Francis de Sales (1562–1627) is intended for daily recitation:

> My God, I give you this day.
> I offer You, now, all of the good
> that I shall do and I promise to accept,
> for love of You,
> all of the difficulty that I shall meet.
> Help me to conduct myself during this day
> in a manner pleasing to You.
> Amen.

Meditation

Meditation is prayerful reflection, especially on the Word of God found in Sacred Scripture. When we meditate, we "tune into God." We actively use our thoughts, emotions, imaginations, and desires to think about God's presence in the world and in our lives. We meditate to gain a greater knowledge and love of the Lord so that we may better serve him.

Throughout the history of the Church, there have developed different types of *spiritualities* that teach us how to pray and to live like Christ in our daily lives. St. Teresa of Avila, St. Ignatius of Loyola, and St. Francis de Sales are examples of great Catholic saints who teach us how to use the Bible, especially the Gospels, when we meditate. In addition, we can also meditate on the writings of the saints, the events in our world, and the action of God in our own lives. Lectio divina is an example of a meditation on Scripture.

- Have the students pray the prayer of St. Francis de Sales (on page 245).
- Ask for other examples of vocal prayer.

- *Meditation*: This prayer expression focuses us on the presence of God, enabling us to "tune in to God." Point out that while using the Scriptures is perhaps the primary way to meditate, we can, as the text states (page 245) "meditate on the writings of the saints, the events in our world, and the action of God in our own lives." Tell the students that the Catholic monk and writer Thomas Merton wrote:

> Learn how to meditate on paper. Drawing and writing are forms of meditation. Learn how to contemplate works of art. Learn how to pray in the streets or in the country. Know how to meditate not only when you have a book in your hand but when you are waiting for a bus or riding in a train.

- *Mental Prayer*: This prayer focuses our attention on Jesus, allowing us to speak to him silently from the depths of our souls.
    - Note the definition of "contemplation" and the example from St. John Vianney.
    - Tell the students that the word "contemplation" comes from the Latin and means simply "taking time with." In contemplation, we make room for and spend time with God—no words, no thoughts; we simply let go and rest in God.
- To help the students better understand meditative prayer, have them recall their experience of meeting and getting to know a friend. Then have them devise and present impromptu skits or pantomimes showing how they would welcome a new person into their group or home. Ask the students to imagine that this person eventually becomes a friend.
- After the skits/pantomimes are presented, discuss the *process* of initiating and growing in relationship. Bring out the following points:
    - The stranger is greeted and welcomed.
    - Introductory conversation usually takes the form of small talk. This eases the new member into the group and initiates the process of being present to one another.

contemplation
Wordless prayer whereby a person's mind and heart rest in God's goodness and majesty.

contrition
Heartfelt sorrow and aversion for sins committed along with the intention of sinning no more. Contrition is the most important act of penitents, necessary for receiving the Sacrament of Penance.

Eucharist
The source and summit of Christian life, the Eucharist is one of the Sacraments of Initiation. The word *eucharist* comes from a Greek word that means "thankful." The Eucharist commemorates the Last Supper, at which Jesus gave his Body and Blood in the form of bread and wine, and the Lord's sacrificial Death on the cross.

Mental Prayer

Mental prayer usually centers on Jesus. We might converse with him or reflect on one of the mysteries of his life, for example, his Passion and Crucifixion. Sometimes mental prayer can lead to **contemplation**, a form of silent, wordless prayer where we simply rest in the presence of our all-loving God. St. John Vianney told of a simple peasant who described contemplative prayer. The peasant sat daily in front of our Blessed Lord present in the tabernacle. He explained, "I look at him and he looks at me." Contemplative prayer is silently being in God's presence, gazing on him with hearts full of love. In this type of prayer, we seek Christ, give ourselves to the will of the Father, and place ourselves under the guidance of the Holy Spirit. When praying this way, we empty our minds of thoughts and images and simply allow the divine presence to penetrate our being. We do not have to do anything at all. If you are able to pray this way, you have been given a great gift from God.

Prayer Forms (CCC, 2623-2643)

The way we express our prayer may be in several forms. These have been revealed in both Sacred Tradition and Sacred Scripture and are normative for Christian people. They are as follows:

- *Blessing.* We bless God because he first blesses us, that is, he showers his graces on us. Blessing is a response to God's gifts.
- *Adoration.* When we adore God, we humbly acknowledge that he is the loving Creator of everything. Adoration glorifies the God who made us. All blessings flow from him.
- *Petition.* Petition or supplication is asking God to provide what we need—materially or spiritually. Jesus told us to petition God for the coming of the Kingdom and to ask for the gift of the Holy Spirit, the source of all gifts (see Luke 11:9–13). The Holy Spirit enables us to live Christ-like lives. **Contrition** is a special type of petition in which we ask our merciful Father to forgive our sins. A model of contrition is the tax collector who began his prayer with, "Oh God, be merciful to me a sinner" (Lk 18:13).

  Like we so often do in our own prayer, Jesus asked his Father for many things. For example, he prayed that Simon not be tempted. And at the Last Supper, Jesus prayed to his Father that we, his disciples, would always remain in the truth and stay united to him.
- *Intercession.* Intercessory prayer is a special form of petition; it is prayer that we make to God on behalf of others. Jesus Christ is our High Priest who is always offering prayer on our behalf. Our Lord calls on us to pray for each other. He also asks us to pray for our enemies. We can do this because, as Christ's disciples, we can join our prayers to Jesus. It is an honor when friends and relatives ask us to pray for them. It is a special privilege to be able to petition Christ on their behalf.

Intercessory prayer is a wonderful example of Christian mercy and love-in-action. Praying for others at Mass or reciting a Rosary on their behalf are two examples of intercessory prayer and ways to show Christian compassion and love.

- *Thanksgiving*. Everything we have and everything we are is a pure gift from God. Think of the gift of your life, friends, health, the friendship of Jesus who has saved you, and the Holy Spirit who dwells within and showers his gifts on you. God deserves our constant thanks. The Psalmist tells us, "Give thanks to the Lord who is good, whose love endures forever!" (Ps 107:1). In truth, every breath we take is an opportunity to thank God. The Gospels record an example of Jesus expressing his gratitude to the Father when he raised Lazarus from the dead:

  > Father, I thank you for hearing me. I know that you always hear me; but because of the crowd here I have said this, that they may believe that you sent me. (Jn 11:41–42)

  The **Eucharist** (a word which means "to give thanks") is a very special prayer of thanksgiving. At Mass, we bless, adore, praise, and thank God for all the blessings he has given to us. We express our sorrow, ask for forgiveness, and petition God for all the good things we and others need to live our lives fully. When we receive Holy Communion, Christ lives in us and unites us to God and all our Christian brothers and sisters by the power of the Holy Spirit. At Eucharist, Christ allows us to participate in his own thanksgiving to the Father.

- *Praise*. Praise is the form of prayer that acknowledges that God is God. We praise God and give him glory because he is so good, gracious, loving, and saving. He deserves our love, blessing, adoration, and praise for his own sake. The Holy Spirit helps us praise God, enabling us to have faith in Jesus Christ and to call God Abba. True praise of God includes no selfish motive because we take joy in our loving God alone. Many of the Psalms praise, adore, and bless God. Jesus himself praised the Father for revealing his will to the humble and lowly:

  > At that very moment he rejoiced (in) the holy Spirit and said, "I give you praise, Father, Lord of heaven and earth, for although you have hidden these things from the wise and the learned you have revealed them to the childlike. Yes, Father, such has been your gracious will." (Lk 10:21)

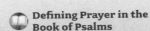

Defining Prayer in the Book of Psalms

Read any three Psalms and identify the kind of prayer taking place in the Psalm. Quote the verses and explain how they fit the definition of one of the prayer forms listed above.

- As the relationship grows and deepens over time, conversation centers on matters of importance as friends want to know and be known.
- As the relationship grows, even silence is a comfortable experience.
- With care and attention, the process of growing in relationship remains open to new and deeper experiences.

- Ask students to give examples of vocal prayer that they have performed. For example, they may cite times when they prayed for something from God, said grace before meals, or recited prayers written by the saints. They might also provide examples of spontaneous prayers that they or others have prayed out loud to God. Have the students practice vocal prayer by inviting them to get into groups to create prayers that the class could say. Pray with these prayers immediately after they complete the assignment or save them for another time.

- Explain that using meditation is a perfect way to grow in relationship to God. Have the students spend the remainder of this class period—or more if necessary—practicing a form of meditative prayer. Arrange to provide an environment where the students will be undisturbed. Distribute copies of Chapter 10, Handout 1, "Meditating on the Scriptures." Tell the students to follow the steps outlined on the handout to aid their meditation. Invite them to work with more than one Scripture passage. Direct them to record their experiences in their journals.
- Mental prayer (contemplative prayer) is the most challenging expression of prayer for most people today. Teens live busy lives and rarely have the opportunity to experience silence, let alone silence with God. Set aside some time during class to give the students the opportunity to be silent and meditate on the mystery of God. You may consider taking the class to the school chapel (if possible), outside the building, or some other place outside of the classroom.
- Write the following *forms* of prayer on the board: **blessing, adoration, petition, intercession, thanksgiving, praise** (see pages 246–247). Ask volunteers to offer a definition and example in their own words for each form. See if the students can give an example of Jesus engaging in each of the forms.

Traditional Catholic Prayer Practices

Church history and Tradition offer several other ways for Catholics to pray. Some examples are listed below.

Icons

Icons are often described as "windows to heaven," where God can touch us here on earth. They are religious images painted by artists who seek to be God's channel, allowing God's spirit to guide the brush.

In Greek, the term *icon* means "image." When we pray before icons, we put ourselves in the presence of the holy person or enter into the religious mystery that is portrayed.

One example of an icon is the Enthroned Madonna (994), located in the Hagia Sophia Museum, in Istanbul, Turkey. Hagia Sophia was first built as a great Byzantine basilica by the Emperor Justinian between 532 and 537. It was the largest cathedral in the world for more than one thousand years.

When you pray with an icon, you gaze at the image coming into the presence of, for example, the Blessed Mother. Gaze at the icon. Thank the Blessed Mother for giving her child to the world. Pray to Jesus and ask him to bless you.

Prayer before the Blessed Sacrament

Keeping a holy hour or spending some time visiting our Lord in the **Blessed Sacrament** is another way to pray. A holy hour is a devotion that commemorates our Lord's vigil in the Garden of Gethsemane when he asked his disciples to stay awake and pray (Mk 14:32–39). Many parishes celebrate the **Forty Hours' Devotion**, where the Holy Sacrament is exposed continuously and the faithful are invited to come spend some time with Jesus. The Blessed Sacrament is contained in a tabernacle in a church or chapel. A sanctuary lamp is a sign of his presence.

MORE WAYS TO PRAY

Variety is the spice of life, even in our prayer life. Use your imagination in praying to God. One idea is to compose short prayers by choosing a word (or several words) that is somehow related to all the letters of the alphabet. Here are some examples:

A Almighty Father, I adore you. Make me an ambassador of your love.

C Christ, my friend. Help me be a worthy child of your Father. Give me courage and conviction to carry my cross.

G Glory to God the Father. Glory to God the Son. Glory to God the Holy Spirit. Gracious God grant us your good gifts.

L Lord, Jesus Christ, Lamb of God, I love you. You light up my life. Help me listen to you, my leader.

S Spirit of God, give me, a sinner, strength to live a Christian life.

Another idea is to write a letter to God the Father or to Jesus. Write the letter as you would to a person you love very much, a person who loves you immeasurably in return. Be honest and direct. Speak of your love, your concerns, what is bothering you, what brings you joy.

You might also try writing a letter to *you* from God's perspective. Ask the Holy Spirit for guidance. Imagine God telling you of his love for you, his mercy, his compassion, his understanding. Allow him to address your hurts and concerns.

Keep your letters. Refer to them from time to time to see how your relationship with God has grown. Reflect on how he has been a part of your life.

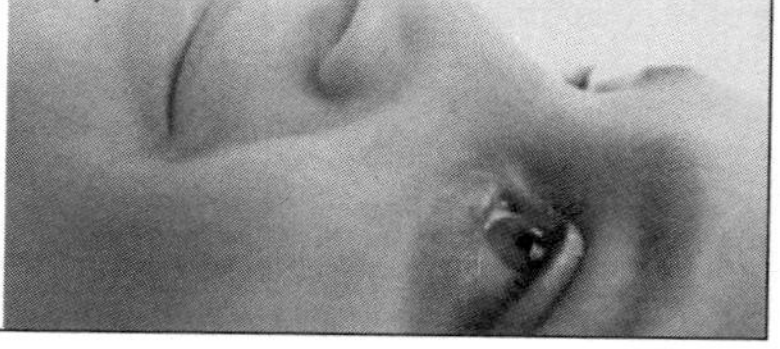

When we are before the Blessed Sacrament we can recite short prayers, read a Gospel passage, enter into a conversation with our Lord, or simply sit in his presence, adoring him and thanking him for his many gifts. Make a point to visit Jesus in the Blessed Sacrament in your school chapel or parish church. You might also wish to come to the Sunday Mass fifteen minutes early (or stay a few minutes after Mass) to pray before the Lord.

Litanies

Jesus taught us to pray fervently, continually, and with perseverance. A **litany** is a popular way to pray because it can help us to remain persistent and focused in prayer. The Greek root of the word *litany* is "to ask in earnest."

Litanies contain a series of prayers both invocations (asking) and responses: for example, "Holy Mother of God . . . pray for us." Litanies can be either communal or private. Popular litanies are the Litany of the Blessed Virgin Mary, the Litany of the Sacred Heart, the Litany of St. Joseph, and the Litany of the Saints.

Novenas

Novena comes from the Latin word for nine. It refers to the time Mary and the Apostles spent in prayer between the Ascension of Jesus and the descent of the Holy Spirit on Pentecost Sunday. Novenas are prayed over nine days, either privately or publicly, to obtain special graces or to petition for particular intentions.

Jesus Prayer

Prayers can be short, as brief as one sentence. A famous one-line prayer is the famous **Jesus Prayer**: "Lord Jesus Christ, Son of God, have mercy on me, a sinner." This faith-filled prayer acknowledges the divinity of Jesus as both Lord and Son of God. He is the Christ, the anointed one of God, who has brought us Salvation. The prayer acknowledges that we are sinners and in need of Christ's forgiveness. You can recite the Jesus Prayer repeatedly for a period of time, concentrating on each word as you slowly inhale and exhale. It is a marvelous prayer of faith and petition to Jesus Christ, our Savior.

You can pray other one-line prayers on many different occasions. For example, when you offer a prayer at the beginning of a task, that task itself can become a prayer. If you say, "Lord, I offer you the work I am about to do preparing this PowerPoint presentation," your effort becomes a prayer. Here are some other examples of one-line prayers:

- Jesus, my friend and Savior, I love you.

Blessed Sacrament
"A name given to the Holy Eucharist, especially the consecrated elements reserved in the tabernacle for adoration, or for the sick" (*CCC*, 1330).

Forty Hours' Devotion
A prayer devotion made for forty continuous hours in which the Blessed Sacrament is exposed. It begins with a Solemn Mass of Exposition, which concludes with the exposition of the Blessed Sacrament and a procession. The forty hours models the time that Jesus spent in the tomb from Death to his Resurrection.

litany
From the Latin word *letania*, meaning "prayer or supplication," a litany is a form of prayer used in liturgies that includes prayers with responses.

Jesus Prayer
A prayer that may have originated with the Desert Fathers in the fifth century, it is a short, formulaic prayer that is said repeatedly.

Trying Out Ways to Pray

During the next week, try praying using a litany or novena. And the end of your prayer time, write your reaction and reflections to praying using the form you chose.

- Call attention to the activity "Defining Prayer in the Book of Psalms" (page 247). Allow time for the students to find three Psalms, to identify what *form* of prayer they believe each is, and then to share and discuss their findings with the class. If you wish, play recordings of different psalms while the students work.
- Allow time for the students to write one prayer for each of the six forms of prayer. Tell the students that the prayers should be original and in their own words. If time prohibits them from completing their work, allow the students to finish their writing as part of their homework. Collect the prayers, put them together in a booklet, and make a copy of the booklet for each student. At the end of the chapter (and this course), present each student with a copy of this booklet.
- Call attention to the text section "Traditional Catholic Prayer Practices" (pages 248–250). Summarize these traditional offerings of prayer as avenues that the Church presents us. Note that this variety allows us to find a prayer practice that suits us best, and it enables us to spice up our prayer life now and then with new ways of prayer.
- If possible, have an example of an icon for the students to view. Distribute copies of Chapter 10, Handout 2, "Litany of the Saints" and Handout 3, "Novena to Saint Joseph." Pray each prayer with the students. Then point out the feature "Trying Out Ways to Pray" on page 249. Encourage the students to use the litany and novena on the handouts or to choose from the websites listed in the text to pray with during the next week.

- Go over the section "More Ways to Pray" (page 248) with the students. Then direct the students to write short prayers similar to those in the text by using the letters of their first name. For example: "Susan"

  Sacred heart of Jesus, keep me always in your love.
  Under your wings, O God, shelter me.
  Send your Spirit to guard me and keep me safe.
  Almighty Father, in you I place my trust.
  Never let me turn away from your love.

  (*Note:* Include these "name" prayers in the prayer booklet you create—see above.) Also, tell the students to write in their journals the letters—to God and from God—as described in the text.
- Invite the students to show their understanding of the three expressions of prayer and the six forms of prayer by creating matching quizzes. After they have completed the quizzes, have them share with another student. Collect the quizzes to assess understanding. Consider adding the questions to the chapter test.
- Before dismissing the students, challenge them to set a rhythm for prayer in their lives that keeps open the lines of communication between themselves and God.

- Help me, Lord Jesus.
- Jesus, protect me from sin.
- Praise God!
- Mary, Mother of God, pray for me.
- Come, Holy Spirit.
- Holy Spirit, enlighten me.
- Thank you heavenly Father for all the gifts you have given me.
- Thank you, Father, for creating this day.

For Review

1. Discuss three good rules for getting started in prayer.
2. Suggest two ways to handle distractions in prayer.
3. Give an example of a vocal prayer.
4. What is meditation?
5. How might a person enter into mental or contemplative prayer?
6. How does God speak to us in the listening part of prayer?

For Reflection

- Write or share some answers to questions Pope Benedict XVI posed to seminarians and youth in his visit to America in 2008: "Have we perhaps lost something of the art of listening? Do you leave space to hear God's whisper, calling you forth into goodness? Friends, do not be afraid of silence or stillness. Listen to God, adore him in the Eucharist. Let his word shape your journey as an unfolding of holiness."
- After listing several special gifts you have been given, compose your own prayer of thanksgiving.
- After reflecting on your sins, compose your own Act of Contrition.
- Note the following in your journal:
  - An ideal time for you to pray on a regular basis
  - A good place for you to pray
  - A comfortable prayer position for you
  - A good way for you to remind yourself of God's presence
  - A prayer-word or phrase that helps you refocus and handle distractions in prayer

Praying with Sacred Scripture (*CCC*, 2567-2589, 2653-2654)

Sacred Scripture is a rich source for prayer. Many prayers Catholics hold dear to their hearts come directly from the Bible or are partly based on Scriptural passages or events. These include prayers said at Mass, Psalms and canticles, and familiar popular prayers like the Our Father, Hail Mary, and the Angelus. Scripture tells of many people who prayed faithfully, both from the Old and New Testaments. The greatest model of prayer is Jesus himself. Finally, Scripture offers instructions on how to pray. Again, Jesus' lessons on how to pray are timeless.

A constant theme in Scripture is that God's relationship with his people is one of prayer. On the one hand, God constantly seeks us. On the other hand, our hearts, although weakened by sin, seek him. Sacred Scripture reveals that God always initiates the process. When humans respond to his invitation, prayer takes place. Prayer is God's gift to us.

Prayer in the Old Testament

There are many models of prayer in the Old Testament. For example, the patriarch Abraham heard

For Review Answers (page 250)

1. Students may mention any three of the "6 Ps" of prayer: place, period of time, posture, presence, passage, and persistence.
2. Answers will vary but should reflect suggestions found on pages 244–245 of the text.
3. Answers will vary but may include reciting prayers of the saints, petitions, grace before meals, and other spontaneous prayers.
4. Answers should reflect an understanding that meditation is a way of prayerful reflection that allows us to tune into God.
5. Answers may include adoration of the Blessed Sacrament, silence, listening rather than speaking, waiting rather than thinking, etc.
6. Answers will vary as with their experiences of God in prayer.

God's voice, responded to his invitation, and obeyed him. He did so even during the difficult times that came his way. Moses was on intimate terms with God, conversing with him "face to face, like a man with his friend" (Ex 33:11). Because of this close relationship, Moses was bold enough to intercede for his people, asking God to be merciful and guide them to the Promised Land. Moses' intercession for the Chosen People prefigured the intercession of Jesus Christ, the High Priest, who came to save us.

Led by kings, priests, and prophets, the Chosen People prayed in the Temple before the Ark of the Covenant. King David, along with other authors, composed the Psalms. Inspired by the Holy Spirit, these marvelous prayers comforted individuals and the community. These prayer-poems, quoted and prayed by Jesus himself, have appeal for all ages. Originally sung in the Temple and later in local synagogues, on pilgrimages, and in family and personal settings, the Psalms capture human emotions like joy and awe before God's creation. They express confidence and trust in a loving God, complaints at the sorrows that befall us, and thanksgiving and praise for a generous, creative God. The Church embraces the Psalms, using them in every Mass and in the **Liturgy of the Hours** (see page 254). She recommends them to us as a time-honored way to learn prayer.

The Old Testament prophets also derived great strength from prayer. They talked to God, interceded for the people, and proclaimed God's Word

to their brothers and sisters. Elijah, the father of the prophets and the one who appeared with Moses at the time of Jesus' Transfiguration, is an example of a man of faith whose prayers God answered. For example, the Lord God enabled Elijah to bring a child back to life (1 Kgs 17:7–24). After he so fervently prayed, "Answer me, O Lord, answer me" (1 Kgs 18:37), Elijah helped the people return to faith on Mount Carmel.

Liturgy of the Hours
The official daily prayer of the Church; also known as the Divine Office. The prayer offers prayers, Scripture, and reflections at regular intervals throughout the day.

Lesson 3 Objectives

The students will:

- recall the models of prayer in both the Old and New Testaments.
- appreciate the variety and steadfastness of Jesus' prayer.
- recognize that prayer was a way of life for Jesus.
- summarize what Jesus taught about prayer.
- describe the numerous ways we, as Church, pray the Scriptures, especially the Divine Office/Liturgy of the Hours.
- practice *lectio divina.*
- categorize Scripture passages as the forms of prayer.

Chapter 10: Prayer in the Life of a Disciple of Jesus Christ—Lesson 3

Bell Ringers

- Ask the students to offer their responses to the seven For Review questions on page 250 (answers are on page 272 of this text). Be sure to allow the students to ask any other questions they may have.
- Review the previous lesson by making the following points:
    - Prayer is more a *reply* to God's inbreaking than it is a *plea* for that inbreaking.
    - Prayer does not beseech God's generosity. Rather, God summons our generosity in word and work harmonized.
    - Trying to validate prayer by its effects—that is, whether or not we get what we ask for—is missing the point that prayer itself is an effect more than a cause. Rather than releasing grace, prayer flows from grace.
    - In conclusion, our concern should not be in what prayer will produce so much as how resonant it is with God's work and our own in the world. As Jesus said, "Seek first the kingdom (of God) and his righteousness, and all these things will be given you besides" (Mt 6:33).
- Invite one or more of the students to lead the class in prayer. Afterward, ask them to explain what expressions and forms of prayer they used.

Teaching Approaches

Praying with Sacred Scripture (pages 250-255)

- Call attention to the text section "Prayer in the Old Testament (pages 250–251). Point out:
    - how Abraham responded with such great faith to God's inbreaking
    - how Moses' prayer was so intimate

Lesson 3 Preview

This lesson helps the students look to the Scriptures as a rich treasure of prayer. Be sure to allow adequate time for the students to look up the Scripture passages suggested in this guide. Likewise, be flexible in order to give the students quiet time to practice Scriptural prayer. Consider scheduling more than one class period in order to cover the material presented in this lesson.

   - how the Psalms—which speak so powerfully of our need to respond to God with blessing, adoration, petition, intercession, thanksgiving, and praise—are the *prayer book* of the Bible
   - how the prayer of the prophets called God's people back to correct worship and correct attitude before God

- Next, list on the board the Old Testament passages below. Have the students find and read the passages. After each, take a few moments to talk about the passage: what the prayer is about, what emotions the prayer expresses, and the prayer's results. Focus on why the pray-ers pray (the need to be in touch with God) and how God responds.
   - **Genesis 12:1–5**
   - **Genesis 15:1–6**
   - **Genesis 18:20–32**
   - **Exodus 15:1–4, 11–13**
   - **Exodus 33:11–20**
   - **2 Samuel 22:1–4, 26–31, 47–51**
   - **Psalm 14**
   - **Psalm 17**
   - **Psalm 30**
   - **1 Kings 17:17–22**
- Have the students write their own psalm. Suggest they base their work on any Psalm they want. If you wish, suggest the following as good examples: Psalm 8; Psalm 51; Psalm 61; Psalm 139; Psalm 150. Allow time for the students to write. Afterward, share psalms. Collect the psalms, make copies, and include them in the prayer booklet you are making for the students (see Lesson 2).
- Go on to summarize the material in the section "Prayer in the New Testament" (pages 252–254). Begin by inviting the students to offer examples of when, where, and why Jesus prayed. Note the variety and consistency of Jesus' prayer. For example:
   - before beginning his ministry
   - before calling his Apostles
   - when dying on the Cross
   - after performing miracles (e.g., the multiplication of loaves and fishes)
   - to discover the Father's will
   - to offer praise and thanks to the Father
   - to petition God (e.g., the agony in the garden)

252 Jesus Christ: Source of Our Salvation

Prayer in the New Testament

We learn best about prayer by contemplating Jesus himself in prayer and then by following his instructions on how to pray. Jesus learned prayer from his Mother and from the Jewish tradition. However, as the eternal Son of God, Jesus' prayer also came from who he was. This is why, at the age of twelve, he said to his parents in the Temple, "I must be in my Father's house" (Lk 2:49).

The Gospels give many examples of Jesus at prayer. For example, after his baptism in the Jordan River, Jesus went to the desert for a forty-day retreat to pray in preparation for his ministry. Jesus also prayed before making important decisions like selecting the Apostles. After performing his first miracles of healing, Jesus withdrew to pray. Likewise, after performing the miracle of the loaves and fishes, Jesus dismissed the crowd and his followers and withdrew to a hill to pray. Also, the night before Peter confessed Jesus to be the Messiah, Jesus prayed.

LEARN FROM THE MASTER

We can learn much about prayer from Jesus' own example at prayer as well as from his specific teachings on how to pray. Read the following passages that contain Jesus' teaching about prayer. For each, briefly summarize the point he is making.

- Matthew 5:44
- Matthew 6:5-8
- Matthew 18:19-20
- Matthew 21:21-22
- Mark 11:23-25
- Luke 11:5-13
- Luke 18:1
- Luke 18:10-14
- John 14:13
- John 15:7

Jesus went to a mountain to pray at the time of the Transfiguration when Peter, James, and John were privileged to see the glory of the Risen Lord. At the Last Supper, Jesus offered the great Priestly Prayer, interceding on our behalf as he asked for us to be one with him so that we can witness to God's love and Salvation. After the Last Supper, Jesus took the Apostles to the Garden of Gethsemane where he prayed over his impending Death on the cross. The content of this prayer reveals that Jesus, like us, was fearful at the thought of death. Yet he prayed, "Father, if you are willing, take this cup away from me; still, not my will but yours be done" (Lk 22:42). Jesus' prayer of *petition* to be spared suffering and death led to a prayer of *submission*, of following the will of his Father. Finally, Jesus prayed on the cross: asking God to forgive those who put him to death; reciting Psalm 22 ("My God, my God why have you forsaken me?"), and committing his spirit to God at the moment of death.

Jesus also taught his disciples how to pray. For example, in the Sermon on the Mount, he told them to pray simply, confidently, and with forgiveness in their hearts. He gave them the words of the Lord's Prayer (see pages 255–259). In Luke's Gospel he told them to pray constantly and with faith that their prayers will be answered.

The New Testament tells of other great models for prayer. The Blessed Mother (see pages 259–261) is referenced in Acts 1:14 praying with the Apostles in the Upper Room, awaiting the coming of the Holy Spirit on Pentecost Sunday. When the Holy Spirit descended on Jesus' disciples, Mary was with them as they "devoted themselves to the teaching of the Apostles and to the communal life, to the breaking of the bread and to the prayers" (Acts 2:42). Prayer was essential to the life of the new Christians.

The New Testament letters attributed to St. Paul reveal him as a man of prayer. Paul praised God for blessings bestowed and for people who joined him in his ministry. Time and again, Paul petitioned God on behalf of the people to whom he preached

Learn from the Master Answers (page 252)

- Matthew 5:44—Pray for enemies.
- Matthew 6:5–8—Don't make a spectacle of prayer.
- Matthew 18:19–20—Pray with others.
- Matthew 21:21–22—Make your prayer in faith.
- Mark 11:23–25—Wrap your prayer in trust and make your prayer with forgiveness for others.
- Luke 11:5–13—Be bold and persistent in prayer.
- Luke 18:1—Pray always; don't give up on prayer.
- Luke 18:10–14—Be humble in your prayer.
- John 14:13—Pray in Jesus' name.
- John 15:7—Stay close to Jesus and his words and your prayer will bear fruit.

Faithful Disciple

ST. BENEDICT

St. Benedict founded the famous monastery of Monte Cassino around the year 520. From this community, Benedict wrote a famous *rule* for monks that was to become the monastic rule for the Western Church.

What can St. Benedict's ancient rule teach us about prayer? After Christianity was legalized and Christians were no longer regularly martyred for their faith, **monasticism** was the most extreme form of Christian witness. From every age, there have been Christians who have felt drawn to a single-minded devotion to God in prayer, solitude, and communal living. In the early centuries, some men and women withdrew from everyday life to go to the desert to be alone with God. There they prayed, fasted, read and meditated on the Scriptures, and performed other various works of penance and sacrifice. They were known as hermits.

Before long, hermits saw an advantage of gathering with others to live the same type of lifestyle in community. Monasteries were formed so that these men and women could share the burden of providing for food, shelter, and protection and could then devote more time to prayer. Benedict was a monk who founded an early monastic community and drew up a rule of life for the monks to live by.

Benedict attempted to seek a balance among three things: public prayer at set times throughout the day (called the "work of God"), the regular reading and meditation on the Bible (called "divine reading"), and manual work for the physical support of the whole monastery.

monasticism
A style of Christian life that stresses communal living and communal worship along with private prayer, silence, poverty, chastity, and obedience.

Benedict's motto was *ora et labora*, "pray and work." By doing this faithfully, those who live a monastic life grow in deeper union with God. Monastic life also provides a strong statement about God's Kingdom. The witness of the monk says, "We are dedicated to the coming of God's Kingdom without being attached to the passing things of this world." The monk's witness—codified by St. Benedict—calls us to question what we are doing and helps us to look more seriously at our own levels of commitment to God.

Lesson 3 Homework

1. Assign the four For Review questions on page 255.
2. Have the students read "Two Special Prayers for Jesus' Disciples" (pages 255–261) and the two quotations regarding the Lord's Prayer in the section Primary Source Quotations (page 263) in preparation for their next lesson.
3. Remind the students to continue working on their chosen Ongoing Assignments.

  - to intercede to the Father on behalf of others
  - as a faithful Jew: in daily prayer (the *Shema*, the *Benedictions*, the *Kaddish*), weekly in the synagogue, at religious festivals

- Emphasize that prayer was actually *a way of life* for Jesus. Like breathing, prayer was a regular, rhythmic habit for him that he taught his disciples to imitate.
- List on the board the following references to Jesus and prayer. Have the students determine which form of prayer—blessing, adoration, petition, intercession, thanksgiving, or praise—each represents.
  - **Luke 10:21–22** (praise)
  - **John 11:41–42** (thanksgiving/praise)
  - **John 17** (intercession)
  - **Luke 18:1–5** (petition)
- Invite the students to consider which of these forms of prayer (blessing, adoration, petition, intercession, thanksgiving, or praise) they find themselves praying most. Discuss their responses as a class. Challenge them to try other forms of prayer in their personal prayer lives.
- Direct the students to complete the activity "Learn from the Master" on page 252. When they finish, share and check responses (answers are on page 274 of this text).
- Have the students read the account of the Annunciation and Mary's prayerful response in Luke 1:26–55. Point out how Mary's prayer perfectly embodies the fullness of Israel's trust and reliance on God as well as the universal human response to God's inbreaking. Note how Mary's prayer is grounded in faith, hope, and love.
- Have the students read Romans 15:5–6, 13 and Ephesians 1:1–23.
  - Point out how Paul's prayer in Romans asks God to grant the gifts of perseverance, encouragement, and hope—gifts all Christians require not only to become pray-ers but also to follow Christ in every way.
  - Draw particular attention to verse 18 in the passage from Ephesians ("may the eyes of [your] hearts be enlightened"). Stress that Paul's prayer is asking God to help us "see"—deep in our hearts—the Good News for the hope and immeasurable treasure that it is, and just how great is the powerful hand reaching to save us.

- Call attention to the text section "The Church Prays with Sacred Scripture" (pages 254–255). Note in the text the numerous ways we, as Church, pray the Scriptures. Then on the board, write the phrase **Liturgy of the Hours/Divine Office.** Tell the students that the *Constitution on the Sacred Liturgy* calls the Liturgy of the Hours or Divine Office "the public prayer of the Church" and the "source of piety and nourishment for personal prayer" (*Constitution on the Sacred Liturgy*, 90). Go on to explain that the Second Vatican Council reaffirmed the valued tradition that all the faithful should be included in the Church's daily praise and urged that all Christians join in communal prayer, at least at times, as the regular and "normal" way of daily worship. Note that many parishes today are once again celebrating daily morning and evening prayer. Ask the students:
  - Do any people in your parish gather daily for morning and evening prayer?
  - When do members of your parish gather for other kinds of communal prayer apart from the Eucharist?
  - Have you ever taken part in such prayer?
- Provide students with the opportunity to pray the Liturgy of the Hours. Consider using the following websites to help you lead them in these prayers:

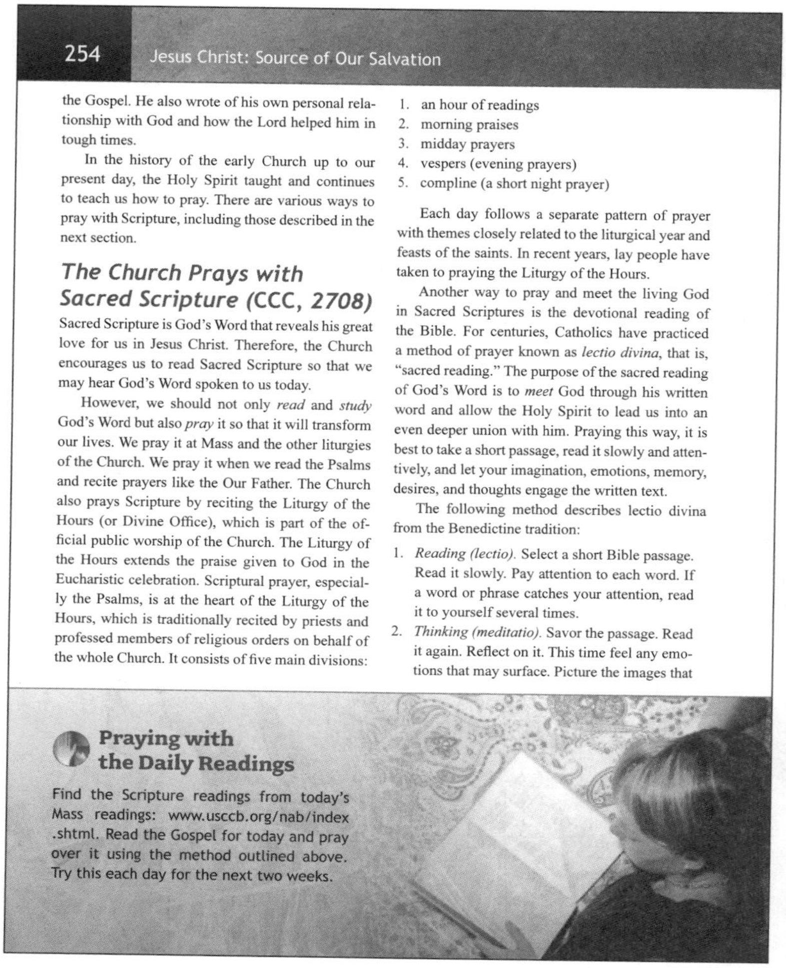

254 Jesus Christ: Source of Our Salvation

the Gospel. He also wrote of his own personal relationship with God and how the Lord helped him in tough times.

In the history of the early Church up to our present day, the Holy Spirit taught and continues to teach us how to pray. There are various ways to pray with Scripture, including those described in the next section.

The Church Prays with Sacred Scripture (CCC, 2708)

Sacred Scripture is God's Word that reveals his great love for us in Jesus Christ. Therefore, the Church encourages us to read Sacred Scripture so that we may hear God's Word spoken to us today.

However, we should not only *read* and *study* God's Word but also *pray* it so that it will transform our lives. We pray it at Mass and the other liturgies of the Church. We pray it when we read the Psalms and recite prayers like the Our Father. The Church also prays Scripture by reciting the Liturgy of the Hours (or Divine Office), which is part of the official public worship of the Church. The Liturgy of the Hours extends the praise given to God in the Eucharistic celebration. Scriptural prayer, especially the Psalms, is at the heart of the Liturgy of the Hours, which is traditionally recited by priests and professed members of religious orders on behalf of the whole Church. It consists of five main divisions:

1. an hour of readings
2. morning praises
3. midday prayers
4. vespers (evening prayers)
5. compline (a short night prayer)

Each day follows a separate pattern of prayer with themes closely related to the liturgical year and feasts of the saints. In recent years, lay people have taken to praying the Liturgy of the Hours.

Another way to pray and meet the living God in Sacred Scriptures is the devotional reading of the Bible. For centuries, Catholics have practiced a method of prayer known as *lectio divina*, that is, "sacred reading." The purpose of the sacred reading of God's Word is to *meet* God through his written word and allow the Holy Spirit to lead us into an even deeper union with him. Praying this way, it is best to take a short passage, read it slowly and attentively, and let your imagination, emotions, memory, desires, and thoughts engage the written text.

The following method describes lectio divina from the Benedictine tradition:

1. *Reading (lectio).* Select a short Bible passage. Read it slowly. Pay attention to each word. If a word or phrase catches your attention, read it to yourself several times.
2. *Thinking (meditatio).* Savor the passage. Read it again. Reflect on it. This time feel any emotions that may surface. Picture the images that

Praying with the Daily Readings

Find the Scripture readings from today's Mass readings: www.usccb.org/nab/index.shtml. Read the Gospel for today and pray over it using the method outlined above. Try this each day for the next two weeks.

For Review Answers (page 255)

1. Answers should refer to Abraham, Moses, David, the Psalms, Elijah, and the other prophets.
2. Jesus is a model for prayer in the way he prayed during important times of his life: as a child, after his baptism, during his ministry, and at the time of his Death.
3. The Liturgy of the Hours is part of the official public worship of the Church and consists of an hour of readings, morning praises, midday prayers, evening prayers (vespers), and night prayer (compline).
4. The five steps for praying *lectio divina* are: read, think, pray, contemplate, resolve.

Background Information

Prayer in the New Covenant

In the New Covenant, prayer is the living relationship of the children of God with their Father who is good beyond measure, with his Son Jesus Christ and with the Holy Spirit. The grace of the Kingdom is "the union of the entire holy and royal Trinity . . . with the whole human spirit." Thus, the life of prayer is the habit of being in the presence of the thrice-holy God and in communion with him. This communion of life is always possible because, through Baptism, we have already been united with Christ. Prayer is Christian insofar as it is communion with Christ and extends throughout the Church, which is his Body. Its dimensions are those of Christ's love.

—*Catechism of the Catholic Church*, **2565**

arise from your imagination. Pay attention to any thoughts or memories the passage might call forth from you.

3. *Prayer (oratio).* Reflect on what the Lord might be saying to you in this passage. Talk to him as you would to a friend. Ask him to show you how to respond to his word. How can you connect this passage to your daily life? How does it relate to the people you encounter every day? Might there be a special message in this Scripture selection just for you? Pay attention to any insights the Holy Spirit might send you.
4. *Contemplation (contemplatio).* Sit in the presence of the Lord. Imagine him looking on you with great love in his heart. Rest quietly in his presence. There is no need to think here, just enjoy your time with him as two friends would who quietly sit on a park bench gazing together at a sunset.
5. *Resolution.* Take an insight that you gained from your "sacred reading" and resolve to apply it to your life. Perhaps it is simply a matter of saying a simple prayer of thanks. Perhaps it is to be more patient with someone in your life. Let the Word the Holy Spirit spoke to you come alive in your life.

Through the power of the Holy Spirit, Christ prays alongside of us. We can be confident that our prayers are heard because Jesus constantly intercedes for us.

For Review

1. Name two examples of prayer from the Old Testament.
2. How is Jesus a model for prayer?
3. What is the Liturgy of the Hours?
4. Name the five steps for praying lectio divina.

For Reflection

- What is a passage from the Old Testament that inspires you to prayer?
- List four adjectives that describe Jesus as the model pray-er.

Two Special Prayers for Jesus' Disciples

The Lord's Prayer, the Our Father, holds the preeminent position among all Christian prayers. From the earliest centuries until today, the Lord's Prayer has been used in the liturgy of the church—in all the sacraments, especially the Eucharist. The early Church prayed the Lord's Prayer three times a day. It remains a part of our daily prayer. No one had dared to address the almighty Creator with the intimate term of address—Father, or more properly "Daddy"—until Jesus invited his followers to do so.

Next to the Lord's Prayer, the Hail Mary is a favorite Catholic prayer. The first part of the prayer comes from Luke's Gospel where he records the greeting of the angel Gabriel (Lk 1:28) and that of Mary's cousin, Elizabeth (Lk 1:42). The second part of the prayer asks Mary to intercede for us.

More information about the Lord's Prayer and the Hail Mary follows.

The Lord's Prayer (CCC, 2759-2865)

Jesus taught his disciples the Lord's Prayer, the perfect Christian prayer and, in the words of Church Father Tertullian, "a summary of the whole Gospel." It is recorded in Matthew 6:9–15 and Luke 11:1–4. The context in Matthew's Gospel is the Sermon on the Mount where Jesus teaches his disciples how to pray. He tells them that they are to be authentic when they pray. They should not be insincere like

- www.universalis.com
- www.ebreviary.com
- http://divineoffice.org

- Tell the students that in addition to *communal* praying of the Scriptures, the Church also encourages us to pray the Scriptures as individuals. Write the phrase ***lectio divina*** on the board. Explain that it means "divine or holy reading." Then call attention to "Praying with the Daily Readings" on page 254. On the board, write the reference to the day's Gospel reading (find it at www.usccb.org/nab). Then have the students pray the Gospel by following the five steps of *lectio divina* as outlined in the text on pages 254–255. List the steps on the board:

  1. read
  2. think
  3. pray
  4. contemplate
  5. resolve

  If you wish, play soothing music as the students pray.

- Afterward, briefly go over the material on St. Benedict and his rule in the feature "Faithful Disciple: St. Benedict" (page 253). Ask the students to list the challenges of the monastic life. Discuss some of the benefits of living a monastic life as well.

Background Information

The Divine Office

The Divine Office or Liturgy of the Hours developed during the early days of the Church, mainly in monastic settings. The form used today was established as early as the sixth century. The structure for each of the hours is similar:

- morning prayer (*lauds*)
- prayer during the day:
  - before noon (*terce*)
  - during the day—midday (*sext*)
  - after noon (*none*—pronounced "non")
- evening prayer (*vespers*)
- office of readings (*matins*)
- night prayer (*compline*)

The Second Vatican Council called for a renewal of the Liturgy of the Hours and urged all Christians to be afforded the opportunity to take part in this ancient prayer.

> By tradition going back to early Christian times, the divine office is devised so that the whole course of the day and night is made holy by the praises of God. Therefore, when this wonderful song of praise is rightly performed by priests and others who are deputed for this purpose by the Church's ordinance, or by the faithful praying together with the priest in the approved form, then it is truly the voice of the bride addressed to her bridegroom; it is the very prayer which Christ himself, together with his body, addresses to the Father.
>
> —*Constitution on the Sacred Liturgy*, **84**

- Conclude the lesson by inviting the students to join in a prayer of adoration, the Glory Be.

Chapter 10: Prayer in the Life of a Disciple of Jesus Christ—Lesson 4

Bell Ringers

- Have the students share their responses to the four For Review questions on page 255 (answers are on page 276 of this text). Be sure to allow the students to ask any other questions they may have.
- Tell the students to form small groups of four or five. Direct each group to develop a letter that asks the local city mayor to make a change(s) that the small group thinks will benefit people their age. Explain that the letter should include the following sections: (1) greeting, (2) mentioning positive things about the mayor and his or her efforts on behalf of the city/town, (3) the concerns the group wants to bring to the mayor's attention, and (4) closing remarks—a sentence or two. Allow 5–10 minutes for the small groups to draft their letters.
- Ask the spokesperson from each group to present its letter to the class. See to it that each letter is composed of the four sections mentioned above.

Teaching Approaches

Two Special Prayers for Jesus' Disciples (pages 255-261)

- Refer the students to the two quotations on the Lord's Prayer in the section Primary Source Quotations (page 263). Ask:
    - Why does St. Thomas Aquinas call the Lord's Prayer the "most perfect of prayers"? (*It tells us what to desire as well as how and when to ask for what we desire.*)
    - What does St. Augustine say about the Lord's Prayer? (*It sums up the whole of Scripture.*)

256 Jesus Christ: Source of Our Salvation

the hypocrites who like to show off when they pray so that others will think they are holy and devout. Jesus further instructs his disciples to pray privately and that it is not necessary to use a lot of words like pagans who babble magical incantations trying to get God to do their will. Rather, Jesus' disciples must keep their prayers simple and pray with faith-filled and forgiving hearts. Jesus then teaches them the words of this perfect prayer:

Our Father in heaven,
hallowed be your name,
your kingdom come,
your will be done,
on earth as in heaven.
Give us today our daily bread;
and forgive us our debts,
as we forgive our debtors;
and do not subject us to the final test,
but deliver us from the evil one.
(Mt 6:9–13)

Luke intended his Gospel for Gentile-Christians. Unlike the Chosen People, Gentiles lacked a strong tradition of prayer. The context of Jesus' teaching the Lord's Prayer in Luke's Gospel stresses Jesus' own example of praying. Recall again that Jesus prayed all the time: for example, after his baptism, before choosing the Apostles, in the Temple and synagogues, on a mountain during the Transfiguration, in Gethsemane, and on the cross. There simply can be no better teacher of prayer than Jesus, so the disciples asked him how they should pray. Luke records Jesus' words as:

Father, hallowed be your name,
your kingdom come.
Give us each day our daily bread
and forgive us our sins
for we ourselves forgive everyone in debt to us,
and do not subject us to the final test.
(Lk 11:2–4)

Luke adds two parables of Jesus that stress important attitudes we should have when we pray (Lk 11:5–13). The first parable tells of a friend who comes knocking at the door at midnight for some bread. Jesus says that despite the late hour, the friend will respond to the request—if not out of friendship—then certainly out of repeated and relentless requests. The point Jesus makes is clear: be persistent in prayer. Never stop praying. Why? Jesus assures us, "And I tell you, ask and you will receive; seek and you will find; knock and the door will be opened to you" (Lk 11:9–10). A second parable explains that just as a human father will give his children what is good for them (in the parable, wholesome food), how much more will our heavenly Father give us what is good for us: that is, the Holy Spirit, spiritual food that gives us eternal life.

The following sections review each part of the Lord's Prayer: the address to our heavenly Father and seven petitions.

Our Father

Jesus is God's only Son who reveals his Father to us. He invites us to address God as Father, that is, Abba in the Aramaic language Jesus spoke. *Abba* is the word children use of their fathers, stressing an intimate, close, personal, dependent relationship. This address tells us that God is a gracious, all-good, and all-loving Father whom we can approach

Lesson 4 Objectives

The students will:

- explain the meaning of various parts of the Lord's Prayer.
- appreciate the importance of the Lord's Prayer to the life of the Church.
- explain the meaning of the Hail Mary.

Lesson 4 Preview

This lesson examines prayers that are probably very familiar to the students. They may be so familiar, in fact, that their importance may be overlooked. Help the students recognize how these two prayers are essential elements in our ongoing efforts to become better disciples of the Lord. Praying these two great orations may be all we need to sustain us on the way of discipleship.

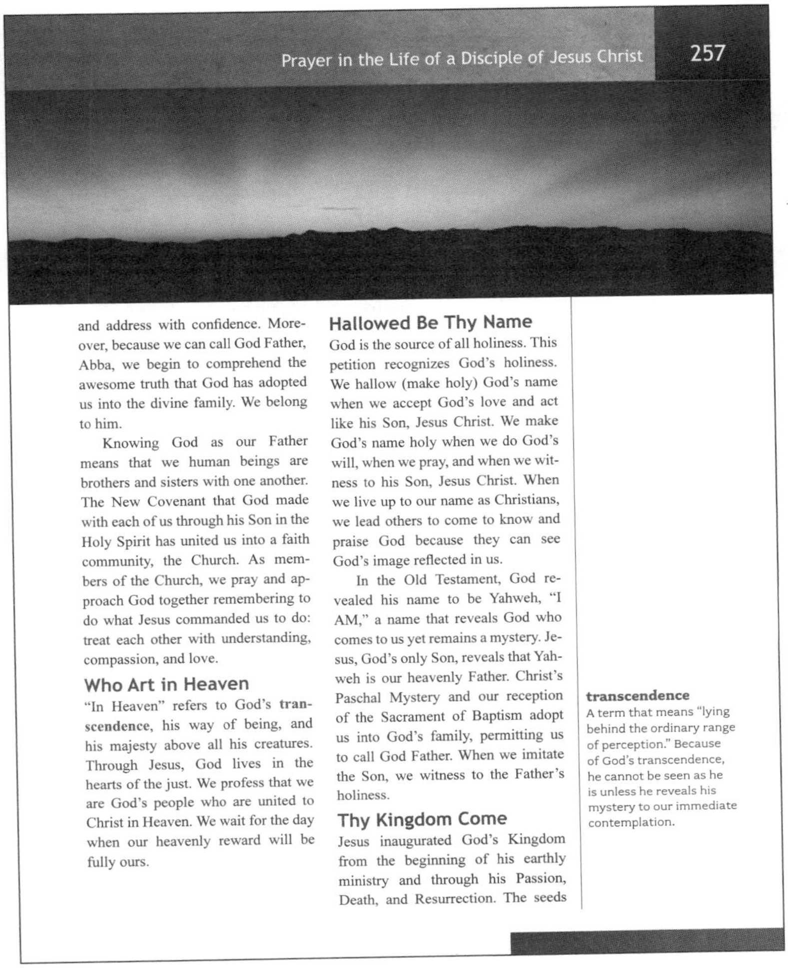

Prayer in the Life of a Disciple of Jesus Christ 257

and address with confidence. Moreover, because we can call God Father, Abba, we begin to comprehend the awesome truth that God has adopted us into the divine family. We belong to him.

Knowing God as our Father means that we human beings are brothers and sisters with one another. The New Covenant that God made with each of us through his Son in the Holy Spirit has united us into a faith community, the Church. As members of the Church, we pray and approach God together remembering to do what Jesus commanded us to do: treat each other with understanding, compassion, and love.

Who Art in Heaven

"In Heaven" refers to God's **transcendence**, his way of being, and his majesty above all his creatures. Through Jesus, God lives in the hearts of the just. We profess that we are God's people who are united to Christ in Heaven. We wait for the day when our heavenly reward will be fully ours.

Hallowed Be Thy Name

God is the source of all holiness. This petition recognizes God's holiness. We hallow (make holy) God's name when we accept God's love and act like his Son, Jesus Christ. We make God's name holy when we do God's will, when we pray, and when we witness to his Son, Jesus Christ. When we live up to our name as Christians, we lead others to come to know and praise God because they can see God's image reflected in us.

In the Old Testament, God revealed his name to be Yahweh, "I AM," a name that reveals God who comes to us yet remains a mystery. Jesus, God's only Son, reveals that Yahweh is our heavenly Father. Christ's Paschal Mystery and our reception of the Sacrament of Baptism adopt us into God's family, permitting us to call God Father. When we imitate the Son, we witness to the Father's holiness.

Thy Kingdom Come

Jesus inaugurated God's Kingdom from the beginning of his earthly ministry and through his Passion, Death, and Resurrection. The seeds

transcendence
A term that means "lying behind the ordinary range of perception." Because of God's transcendence, he cannot be seen as he is unless he reveals his mystery to our immediate contemplation.

- Lead the class in praying the Lord's Prayer.
- Go on to point out that we find the Lord's Prayer in both the Gospel of Matthew and the Gospel of Luke. Note that Matthew's version is the one with which we are most familiar. Remind the students that Matthew was writing for a Jewish audience, which possessed a strong tradition of prayer, so he places the prayer in the context of the Sermon on the Mount, where Jesus teaches *what* to pray for. Luke, writing for a non-Jewish audience, which had almost no tradition of prayer, has Jesus' disciples asking Jesus *how* to pray.
- Have the students reread both versions of the prayer from Matthew and Luke as listed on page 256. Ask them to mention the similarities and the differences they notice in the two.
- Review with the students the key parts of the Lord's Prayer as presented on pages 256–259 of the text. Sum up by pointing out how the Lord's Prayer reveals the following essential points:
  - God is our Father; we are his children.
  - God is transcendent.
  - God is the source of all holiness.
  - God's Kingdom is already here, but not yet fully established.
  - God's will is done through our loving action in the world.

Lesson 4 Homework

1. Direct the students to write out their responses to the four For Review questions on page 261. Also, refer them to the two challenges made in the For Reflection section (page 261).
2. Remind the students to be ready to hand in their chosen Ongoing Assignments (page 263) at their next session.
3. Have the students read through the Chapter Quick View on pages 262–264. If they have any questions, tell them to write them out and bring them to the next session.

- God is present in the Eucharist and we are called to feed the hungry.
- As God forgives, so must we forgive even our enemies.
- God grants us the strength to overcome difficulties.
- God has won a great victory over evil. We ask for God's protection from further evil.

- Afterward, ask the students to recall the letters they wrote at the beginning of the lesson. Ask, "What do those letters and the Lord's Prayer have in common?" (*They both contain greetings, a statement of praise, and petitions/requests.*) Emphasize that when we pray the Lord's Prayer, we are bringing a letter of petition to God—we greet God, offer praise, and then ask for what we need. Take a moment to point out that neither this nor any other prayer of petition *makes* God care about us. God *already* cares about us beyond our imagining. Rather than mustering God's generosity on our behalf, the prayer musters our generosity in word and work harmonized. When we pray the Lord's Prayer, we are not so much asking for what it will produce, as we are seeking to make our efforts at discipleship resonant with God's work in the world.

of the Kingdom are present now in the Church because Jesus has saved and redeemed us. The Lord has set a structure in place in the Church that will remain until the Kingdom is fully achieved. It is God's will that a reign of peace and justice, of truth and service, be advanced in the world. However, God's Kingdom is "not yet" fully established until the Lord comes again at the end of the world—a day when our Savior will transform all of creation into its fullness. Until that day, under the guidance of the Holy Spirit, we should live, experience, and work for the Kingdom right now through our participation in the Church.

We pray for Christ's return and the final coming of God's Kingdom when there will perfect righteousness, peace, and joy. To pray for the coming of God's Kingdom means to join Jesus in his work: to feed the hungry and give drink to the thirsty, to welcome the stranger, to clothe the naked, to visit the sick and imprisoned, and to respond to the needs of all who come into our lives, especially those Jesus called the "least of these."

Thy Will Be Done on Earth as It Is in Heaven

To do the Father's will is to join our will to his Son's and to his ongoing work of Salvation by loving others and responding to the least in our midst. For this to happen, we need the assistance of the Holy Spirit to help us overcome our own selfishness and strengthen us to live as faithful disciples of Jesus Christ—disciples who proclaim and witness in their lives the teachings of our Lord.

Give Us This Day Our Daily Bread

When we ask for bread, we are requesting what bread represents—both material and spiritual goods and blessings that are necessary for life: food, shelter, clothing; friendship, love, and companionship. We pray for Jesus' Real Presence in the Eucharist. He is the Bread of Life, "the Word of God and the Body of Christ" (*CCC*, 2861), whom we receive in Holy Communion.

Praying for *our* daily bread also challenges us to remember the needs of others, especially those of hungry and poor people. This petition also reminds Christ's followers of their duty to share the Bread of Life by preaching the Gospel to others in both word and deed. In this petition, we are also praying for the fullness of God's material and spiritual blessings that will be ours in Heaven.

And Forgive Us Our Trespasses as We Forgive Those Who Trespass against Us

It is difficult to ask for and extend forgiveness. To do so we must humbly acknowledge that we are sinners and that we need the Holy Spirit to help us repent of our selfishness and turn to a life of love and service. We need Jesus' help to turn our selfish ways to a more loving life of service. We confess that we need help on our journey to the Father.

Jesus teaches that for God's forgiveness to penetrate our hearts we must in turn forgive others, even our enemies. In the Sermon on the Mount Jesus teaches, "Blessed are the merciful, for they will be shown mercy" (Mt 5:7). The gift of God's forgiveness must be shared with others. Extending forgiveness is an invitation to love. It is also a superlative way to imitate Jesus who, on the cross, forgave his executioners. We cannot call ourselves Christians and children of the Father without sharing the

Background Information

Mary's Prayer

Beginning with Mary's unique cooperation with the working of the Holy Spirit, the Church developed her prayer to the holy Mother of God, centering it on the person of Christ manifested in his mysteries.

Hail Mary [or Rejoice, Mary]. The greeting of the angel Gabriel opens this prayer. It is God himself who, through his angel as intermediary, greets Mary. Our prayer dares to take up this greeting to Mary with the regard God had for the lowliness of his humble servant and to exult in the joy he finds in her.

Full of grace, the Lord is with thee: These two phrases of the angel's greeting shed light on one another. Mary is full of grace because the Lord is with her. The grace with which she is filled is the presence of him who is the source of all grace. "Rejoice . . . O Daughter of Jerusalem . . . the Lord your God is in your midst" (Zep 3:14, 17a). Mary, in whom the Lord himself has just made his dwelling, is the daughter of Zion in person, the ark of the covenant, the place where the glory of the Lord dwells. She is "the dwelling of God . . . with men" (Rv 21:3). Full of grace, Mary is wholly given over to him who has come to dwell in her and whom she is about to give to the world.

Blessed art thou among women and blessed is the fruit of thy womb, Jesus: After the angel's greeting, we make Elizabeth's greeting our own. "Filled with the Holy Spirit," Elizabeth is the first in the long succession of generations who have called Mary "blessed" (Lk 1:41, 48) "Blessed is she who believed . . ." (Lk 1:45). Mary is "blessed among women" because she believed in the fulfillment of the Lord's word. . . .Mary, because of her faith, became the mother of believers, through whom all nations of the earth receive him who is God's own blessing: Jesus, the "fruit of thy womb."

forgiveness that we ourselves have been so graciously given.

And Lead Us Not into Temptation

Trials inevitably come our way. What we pray for in this petition is that we have the strength to overcome any difficulties that might steer us away from a Christian life of service.

We also pray to God that he not allow us to take the path that leads to sin. We pray to remain in his grace until the very end of our lives. Prayer helps us to resist what leads us to sin and gives us strength to overcome difficulties in living a Christian life. We ask the Holy Spirit to shower us with gifts like fortitude, watchfulness, perseverance, and hearts that can tell the difference between trials that strengthen us spiritually and temptations that lead to sin and death.

But Deliver Us from Evil

In union with the saints, we ask God to show forth the victory that Christ has already won over Satan. We pray that the Father will deliver us from Satan's snares, including the temptations that a godless society presents to us. We petition God to keep us from the evil of accidents, illness, violence, and natural disasters. We pray that God will help us reject any cooperation in unjust, prejudicial, and selfish actions. We pray that we never be put in a situation where we might be tempted to deny our loving Father.

Finally, we pray with the Holy Spirit and all God's people—the Communion of Saints—for the Lord's Second Coming when we will be free forever from the snares of the Evil One.

The Hail Mary (CCC, 2673-2679; 2682)

The Blessed Mother has a unique role in Salvation History. Her faith-filled cooperation with the Holy Spirit serves as a model for all Christians. Throughout history, the Church has prayed in communion with the Virgin Mary "to magnify with her the great things the Lord has done for her, and to entrust supplications and praises to her" (*CCC*, 2682). The Hail Mary, one of the most popular prayers for Catholics, expresses both of these aims. The meaning of the various phrases of this beloved prayer follows.

Hail Mary, Full of Grace

The Angel Gabriel greeted Mary this way, signifying that she was full of grace, without sin, and in blessed union with God who dwelled within her. The *Catechism of the Catholic Church* teaches: "She was, by sheer grace, conceived without sin as the most humble of creatures, the most capable of welcoming the inexpressible gift of the almighty" (*CCC*, 722).

The Lord Is with Thee

Out of his infinite goodness, God chose Mary, preserved her from all sin, and filled her with grace. In freedom, Mary responded to God's blessings by always loving and serving him with total devotion.

Blessed Art Thou among Women

Mary's cousin, Elizabeth, greeted Mary this way when she went to visit Elizabeth to help her before

- Write the following on the board: **faith and humility**. Tell the students that these two words pinpoint the essential qualities of prayer—a response to God's inbreaking, made in faith and with deep humility. Explain:
  - *Faith*—Praying with faith means trusting that God will act on our behalf *and* in our best interests. In other words, God's response may be different from the one we expect. Nevertheless, it will be the response that is best for us.
  - *Humility*—Praying with humility means recognizing our position before God as one of creature before the Creator, as the recipient of grace before the giver of grace.
- Tell the students that these qualities are precisely those Mary the mother of Jesus exhibited in her prayer.
- Have the students read the account of the Annunciation in Luke 1:26–38. Call attention to verse 38: "Mary said, 'Behold, I am the handmaid of the Lord. May it be done to me according to your word.'" Point out how Mary's words demonstrated great *faith*, trusting that God would work through her, even though she did not fully understand how.

Background Information continued

Holy Mary, Mother of God: With Elizabeth we marvel, "And why is this granted me, that the mother of my Lord should come to me?" Because she gives us Jesus, her son, Mary is Mother of God and our mother; we can entrust all our cares and petitions to her: she prays for us as she prayed for herself: "Let it be to me according to your word" (Lk 1:38). By entrusting ourselves to her prayer, we abandon ourselves to the will of God together with her: "Thy will be done."

Pray for us sinners, now and at the hour of our death: By asking Mary to pray for us, we acknowledge ourselves to be poor sinners and we address ourselves to the "Mother of Mercy," the All-Holy One. We give ourselves over to her now, in the Today of our lives. And our trust broadens further, already at the present moment, to surrender "the hour of our death" wholly to her care. May she be there as she was at her son's death on the cross. May she welcome us as our mother at the hour of our passing to lead us to her son, Jesus, in paradise.

—*Catechism of the Catholic Church*, **2676–2677**

- Direct the students to read Luke 1:39–55. Explain that Mary's great prayer (the Magnificat) also reveals her *humility*. Mary credits God for all the wondrous things that have happened and will happen to her and through her. Point out that Mary's prayer teaches us to show faith and humble gratitude to God, the source of all blessings.
- Discuss the Hail Mary with the students. Begin by distributing copies of Chapter 10, Handout 4, "Mary's Prayer," which includes the Hail Mary in Latin, English, and Spanish. If possible, play a recording of Franz Schubert's version of the "Ave Maria." Have the students follow along using the Latin version of the prayer on the handout.
- Go on to review with the students the key parts of the Hail Mary as presented on pages 259–260 of the text. (*Note:* See also the material from the *Catechism of the Catholic Church* in the Background Information section of this lesson.) Begin by pointing out how the prayer has its roots in the angel's greeting to Mary (Lk 1:28) and in Elizabeth's greeting to her (Lk 1:42). Explain that the Church later added the final petition ("Holy Mary, Mother of God, pray for us sinners, now and at the hour of our death").

giving birth to John the Baptist (Lk 1:42). Elizabeth rightly acknowledged that Mary has a unique role in Salvation History. She is the Mother of God whom we honor above all others. Mary is "blessed among women" because she believed that God's Word would be fulfilled in her.

Blessed Is the Fruit of Thy Womb, Jesus

Elizabeth proclaimed this blessing after her son, John the Baptist, leaped in her womb in the presence of the Son of God whom Mary was carrying in her own womb. The Holy Spirit inspired Elizabeth to bless Mary for her faith in accepting God's Word that she was to be the Mother of God. Elizabeth is greatly honored and humbled that the Mother of God should come to visit her (Lk 1:43).

Holy Mary, Mother of God

This phrase acknowledges that Mary is the Mother of God because she gave birth to Jesus who is both true God and true man. The Council of Ephesus (431) defined the dogma that Mary is indeed *Theotokos* ("Birth-giver of God"). We can entrust all of our causes and petitions to Mary. She prays for us as she once prayed for herself: "May it be done to me according to your word" (Lk 1:38).

Pray for Us Sinners

We acknowledge ourselves as sinners and ask our Blessed Mother to intercede for us. Mary is the Mother of God and the Mother of the Church, so she cares deeply about all of her children. Just as she interceded for the couple who ran out of wine at the wedding feast of Cana, our Blessed Mother will intercede for us by taking our concerns and us to her Son. The love of our Blessed Mother knows no bounds, far exceeding the love of even our own earthly mothers. Another Marian prayer, the Memorare reminds us that "never was it known that anyone who fled to your protection, implored your help, or sought your intercession was left unaided." This is why we can confidently pray to Mary and be assured that our prayers will be heard and that in her mercy she will answer them by taking them to her Son.

Now and at the Hour of Our Death

Mary lived a faith-filled life. She witnessed the crucifixion of her Son. She knew firsthand the agonies of death and abandonment. She remained with Jesus through his Death and rejoiced in his Resurrection. In this petition, we ask her to remain with us to the very end and help us on our journey to her Beloved Son and our heavenly Father, especially at the loneliest time of our lives: the moment of our death.

It is reported that St. Francis Xavier (1506–1552) called to Jesus for mercy on his deathbed and then whispered, "O Virgin Mother of God, remember me." Similarly, Bl. Kateri Tekakwitha (ca. 1656–1680), an Algonquin Indian, died with these words on her lips: "Jesus, I love you! Jesus! Mary!" We, too, are encouraged to surrender to Mary's care at the "hour of our death" that she might lead us to her Son, Jesus, in paradise.

Prayer, especially in union with the Blessed Mother, helps us to grow closer to Jesus, our Savior, and to live lives of Christian discipleship. This message serves as a good summary for this chapter and this course. As you continue your studies, may you grow ever closer to your Lord both in knowledge and in love. Concerning your future, remember the words of St. Pio of Pietrelcina (1887–1968): "Pray, hope, and don't worry." And take to heart the words of an old Irish blessing:

May the road rise up to meet you.
May the wind always be at your back.
May the sun shine warm upon your face,
and rains fall soft upon your fields.
And until we meet again,
May God hold you in the palm of his hand.

For Review

1. Discuss two points Jesus makes in Matthew's Gospel about how his disciples should pray.
2. What is the point of the two parables in Luke's Gospel following Jesus' teaching of the Lord's Prayer?
3. Briefly discuss the meaning of each phrase of the Lord's Prayer.
4. Briefly explain the meaning of the Hail Mary.

For Reflection

- Recite five decades of the Rosary. Offer the Rosary for a special intention for someone who has asked you for your prayers.
- How can you be "daily" bread for someone close to you? For a classmate?

- Before concluding, make the following points about why we pray to Mary:
  - First, our faith in the Communion of Saints assures us that those who are in God's presence intercede for us. Mary, the Mother of God in Heaven, surely has her Son's ear.
  - Secondly, Jesus gave Mary to the Church as our mother (see John 19:26–27); thus, as our mother, she loves us and gladly brings our prayers to her Son.
- End this session by praying the Hail Mary or the entire Rosary as a class.

For Review Answers (page 261)

1. Answers will vary but should reflect Jesus' injunctions to be authentic and humble (simple).
2. Luke stresses the importance of persistence in prayer and trust in God's compassionate care for us.
3. Although answers will vary, students should be able to describe the meanings as outlined on pages 256–259 of the text.
4. Although answers will vary, students should be able to describe the meanings as outlined on pages 259–261 of the text.

Chapter 10: Prayer in the Life of a Disciple of Jesus Christ—Review Lesson

Bell Ringers

- Ask the students to offer their responses to the four For Review questions on page 261 (answers are on page 283 of this text).
- Collect the Ongoing Assignments for Chapter 9. Allow time for any students who prepared Assignment #8 (PowerPoint presentation) to present it to the class.

Teaching Approaches

Chapter Quick View (pages 262-264)

- Use the Main Ideas section to review key points. Go through the ideas with the class, having the students refer back to the chapter pages listed in the text.
- Continue the review by going over some or all of the For Review questions from the chapter. If you wish, use a game format. Divide the class into teams. Call on a representative from a team to answer a question. If the representative has difficulty, allow him or her to get help from the team. Award five points for an individual's correct response, two points if the person needed help.
- Invite anyone who had further questions about the Chapter 10 Main Ideas section on page 262 to ask them now. Invite other class members to offer answers. Clarify any remaining confusion.
- Call attention to Terms, People, Places on page 262. Use the section as a vocabulary study tool. Have the students complete the sentences with the correct terms (answers are on page 284 of this text). Then, go on to quiz the students on the remaining terms, asking for a definition of each.
- Take some time to go over any material the students may have overlooked in their review or that you feel needs more attention.
- As time allows, invite various students who handed in written Ongoing Assignments reports to share their information with the group.
- Be sure to provide some quiet time for the students to study on their own. If students have additional questions, invite them to approach you privately while their classmates study.

262 Jesus Christ: Source of Our Salvation

Chapter 10 Quick View

Main Ideas

- Prayer is essential to the life of a disciple. (p. 240)
- There are several definitions of prayer. One way to think of it is a *relationship* with God: Father, Son, and Holy Spirit. (pp. 241–242)
- The greatest benefit of prayer is that it deepens our relationship with the Triune God. (p. 242)
- Prayer is an act of love that can be enhanced by following "6 Ps": place, period of time, posture, presence, passage, and persistence. (pp. 243–244)
- Christian prayer expresses itself as vocal prayer, meditation, and mental prayer. (pp. 243–244)
- Expressions of prayer may be in several forms that are revealed in both Sacred Tradition and Sacred Scripture, including: blessing, adoration, petition, intercession, thanksgiving, and praise. (p. 245)
- Other ways for Catholics to pray are with icons, before the Blessed Sacrament, and by reciting litanies, novenas, and the Jesus Prayer. (pp. 248–249)
- Sacred Scripture is also a rich source of prayer; there are many models of prayer in both the Old Testament and New Testament. (p. 250)
- The Church prays with Sacred Scripture, especially in the Liturgy of the Hours, and also through practice of a prayer method called *lectio divina* or "sacred reading." (pp. 251–255)
- Two special Catholic prayers are the Our Father and the Hail Mary. (pp. 255–256)
- The Our Father has been called "a summary of the whole Gospel." (pp. 256–259)
- The Hail Mary helps the Church remain in communion with the Virgin Mary, "to magnify the great things the Lord has done for her." (pp. 259–261)

Terms, People, Places

Complete each sentence by choosing the correct answer from the list of terms below. You will not use all of the terms.

Blessed Sacrament
contemplation
contrition
Eucharist
Forty Hours' Devotion
Jesus Prayer
lectio divina
litany
Liturgy of the Hours
monasticism
transcendence
votive candle

1. Spending some time before the Lord in the ___________ is another way to pray. Often, this practice is connected with an inter-parish celebration of ___________.
2. After Christians were no longer regularly being martyred for their faith, ___________ became the most extreme form of Christian witness.
3. Mental prayer often leads to ___________.
4. You may wish to keep a ___________ in the area you have chosen as a special prayer space.
5. The petition "in Heaven" in the Our Father refers to God's ___________.

Primary Source Quotations

Meaning of Prayer

For me, prayer means launching out of the heart toward God; a cry of grateful love from the crest of joy or the trough of despair: it is a vast, supernatural force that opens out my heart, and binds me close to Jesus.

—St. Thérèse of Lisieux

Prayer reveals to souls the vanity of earthly goods and pleasures. It fills them

Review Lesson Objectives

The students will:

- review Chapter 10 in preparation for the chapter test.
- join in prayer together.

Terms, People, Places Answers (page 262)

1. Blessed Sacrament and Forty Hours' Devotion
2. monasticism
3. contemplation
4. votive candle
5. transcendence

with light, strength, and consolation, and gives them a foretaste of the calm bliss of our heavenly home.

—St. Rose of Viterbo

Necessity of Prayer
Nothing is equal to prayer; for what is impossible it makes possible, what is difficult, easy.

—St. John Chrysostom

Those who pray are certainly saved; those who do not pray are certainly damned.

—St. Alphonsus Liguori

The Lord's Prayer
The Lord's Prayer is the most perfect of prayers. . . . In it we ask, not only for all the things we can rightly desire, but also in the sequence that they should be desired. This prayer not only teaches us to ask for things, but also in what order we should desire them.

—St. Thomas Aquinas

Run through all the words of the holy prayers [in Scripture], and I do not think that you will find anything in them that is not contained and included in the Lord's Prayer.

—St. Augustine

Ongoing Assignments

As you cover the material in this chapter, choose and complete at least three of these assignments.

1. Research several prayers of saints. Transcribe into your prayer journal two of the most meaningful prayers that you found.
2. Read Isaiah 43:1–3. Write a short reflection about what it might mean for us today.
3. Look up each Gospel passage below. Write the names of the places where Jesus prayed. Then write and describe six places where you pray.
    - Luke 5:16
    - Luke 6:12
    - Mark 14:32
    - Matthew 21:12–13
    - John 17:1
    - Luke 23:34, 46
4. Read each Gospel passage below. Summarize Jesus' teaching on prayer in your own words. Rate how difficult each teaching is for you to follow in your own life.
    - Matthew 6:6–8
    - Luke 11:9–13
    - Matthew 21:21–22
    - Luke 11:5–8
    - Mark 11:25
    - Matthew 18:18–20
5. Write about or share an oral presentation about a friend, religion teacher, religious, or relative who is a model of prayer for you.
6. Translate and transcribe the Lord's Prayer in a foreign language you are studying.
7. Recite the Litany to the Sacred Heart of Jesus. Report on the history of this devotion.
8. Create a PowerPoint presentation to illustrate the Lord's Prayer. Choose appropriate visuals to accompany the text of the prayer.
9. Make a list of "daily bread" that you need to live a full, happy, holy, and healthy life. Consider these categories:
    - physical needs
    - psychological needs
    - spiritual needs

Prayer

St. Thomas Aquinas (ca. 1225–1274), one of the Church's most brilliant thinkers, is the patron saint of students. He composed the following prayer for students:

Prayer before Study
Creator of all things,
true source of light and wisdom,
origin of all being,
graciously let a ray of your light penetrate

Chapter 10 Quick View

Prayer Service

- Gather the students, with their books, in a circle around a lighted candle.
- Lead the students in praying St. Thomas Aquinas' "Prayer before Study" on pages 263–264.
- Then, play a hymn of discipleship such as "Anthem" by Tom Conry or "The Love of the Lord" by Michael Joncas as you present each student with a copy of the prayer booklet containing their prayers and psalms (see Lesson 2). As you give each booklet, say something like the following: "(Name of student), receive this book of prayers; may it serve as your guide as you strive to become a better disciple of the Lord."
- Conclude by sharing a sign of peace.

Review Lesson Homework

1. Point out the Reflection and Resolution on page 264. Encourage the students to follow both.
2. Complete any unfinished Ongoing Assignments.
3. Reread Chapter 10.
4. Study for the Chapter 10 Test.

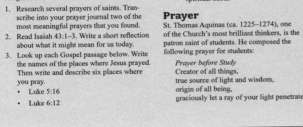

Chapter 10 Test Lesson

Teaching Approaches

- Allow sufficient time for the students to work on the Chapter 10 Test (starting on page 291 of the TWE and also online at www.avemariapress.com). Collect tests as the students finish.

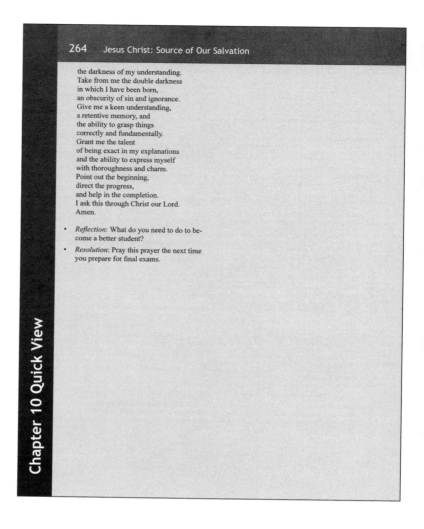

Chapter 10 Quick View

the darkness of my understanding.
Take from me the double darkness
in which I have been born,
an obscurity of sin and ignorance.
Give me a keen understanding,
a retentive memory, and
the ability to grasp things
correctly and fundamentally.
Grant me the talent
of being exact in my explanations
and the ability to express myself
with thoroughness and charm.
Point out the beginning,
direct the progress,
and help in the completion.
I ask this through Christ our Lord.
Amen.

- *Reflection*: What do you need to do to become a better student?
- *Resolution*: Pray this prayer the next time you prepare for final exams.

Chapter 10 Test Answers

Part 1: True or False. (2 points each)

1. F 2. F 3. T 4. T 5. F 6. F 7. T 8. F 9. T 10. T 11. T 12. T 13. F 14. F 15. T

Part 2: Identifying the Forms of Prayer. (3 points each)

1. thanksgiving 2. intercession 3. praise 4. adoration 5. blessing 6. petition

Part 3: Brief Answers. (6 points each)

1. Answers will vary, but refer to page 242 of the text.
2. The three *expressions* of prayer are vocal prayer, meditative prayer, and mental prayer. Descriptions will vary, but compare with pages 245–246 of the text.
3. The six *forms* of prayer are: blessing, adoration, petition, intercession, thanksgiving, praise. Descriptions will vary, but compare with pages 246–247 of the text.
4. The "6 Ps" of a good prayer life are: place, period of time, posture, presence, passage, and persistence. Descriptions will vary, but compare with pages 243–244 of the text.
5. Answers should show an understanding of the Lord's Prayer based on pages 256–259 of the text.
6. Answers may include Abraham, Moses, David, the Psalms, or the prophets.

Chapter 10 Quick View

Chapter 10 Test Answers continued

7. Answers will vary but may include the following:
   - before beginning his ministry
   - before calling his Apostles
   - when dying on the Cross
   - after performing miracles (e.g., the multiplication of loaves and fishes)
   - to discover the Father's will
   - to offer praise and thanks to the Father
   - to petition God (e.g., the agony in the garden)
   - to intercede to the Father on behalf of others
   - as a faithful Jew: in daily prayer (the *Shema*, the *Benedictions*, the *Kaddish*), weekly in the synagogue, at religious festivals

Part 4: Essay. (10 points)

Lectio divina consists of five parts:

- Read—Slowly read a short Bible passage.
- Think—Reflect on the passage.
- Pray—Reflect on what the Lord might be saying to you in this passage.
- Contemplate—Rest in the Lord's presence.
- Resolve—Apply an insight from the prayer to your life.

Appendix

Catholic Handbook for Faith

General Introduction

Jesus Christ: Source of Our Salvation provides an overview of Salvation History culminating in Christ's Paschal Mystery. To supplement this study, the Catholic Handbook for Faith (pages 266–290 of the Student Text) offers an appendix of prayers, creeds, timelines, lists, and other features to stimulate further knowledge and interest among your students.

Throughout this course, you may find that the text encourages the students to ask certain questions about Catholic practice today. You may also find the opportunity to pray certain traditional prayers not included in the main body of the text. The Catholic Handbook for Faith is designed to give you easy-to-find answers to these questions. It is meant to be a supplemental resource that may be used whenever needed.

Teaching Approaches

Instead of just telling the students to memorize certain prayers or dates, there are a number of creative ways that you could help the students learn the Handbook material. Among those are the following:

- *Crossword Puzzles.* Assign the material to be learned and direct the students to make up crossword puzzles with clues. Then have them exchange puzzles with a partner and work to answer them.
- *Individual or Team Games.* Drill the students on certain material in the Handbook by having them play a game based on TV game shows like *Hollywood Squares* or *Jeopardy!* Divide the students into teams to make up questions/answers about the Handbook material that are then presented to the "contestants."
- *Reflection Essays or Journal Entries.* Have the students reflect and write about their understanding of a single passage from a creed or prayer such as the Apostles' Creed or Our Father. You may also wish to have the students write about how they might put the passage into practice in daily life.
- *Pop Quizzes.* Give the students a short, objective pop quiz regarding certain material in the Handbook. Use one of the following formats: fill in the blanks, complete the sentences, or matching.
- *Artistic Creations.* Have the students draw/paint a picture or mural that expresses one part of a creed or prayer. You may also wish to have the students draw symbols for certain patron saints. Have the students explain to the class what a certain prayer or creed means to them.
- *Creative Writing.* Have the students rewrite a creed or prayer in their own words (e.g., as a poem, rap, song, or choral reading).
- *Small-Group Discussions.* Have the students form small groups to discuss what a certain creed or prayer means to them.
- *Slide Shows or PowerPoint Presentations.* Have the students put together a visual presentation to illustrate a certain creed or prayer.
- *Puppet Shows, Skits, or Mime.* Have students retell main events in the life of a saint through homemade puppets, small-group skits, or mime.
- *Research.* Send the students to the Internet or library to find out about the history and origin of a certain creed or prayer.
- *Music.* Have the students compose (or learn) and sing a musical version of a certain prayer, belief, or creed.

Whatever teaching method you use, try to make the learning process interesting and meaningful rather than dull and routine. Help the students internalize the values and beliefs found in this Handbook as a basis for the rest of their lives as Catholics.

Reproducible Pages

Name ____ Date ____________________

Contemplating Compassion

Compassion is that which makes the heart of the good move at the pain of others.
It crushes and destroys the pain of others.

—The Buddha

Compassion is the desire that moves the individual self to widen the scope
of its self-concern to embrace the whole of the universal self.

—Arnold Toynbee

Compassion is the radicalism of our time.

—The Dalai Lama

Kindness gives to another. Compassion knows no "other."

—Anonymous

Compassion is the keen awareness of the interdependence of all things.

—Thomas Merton

Compassion is not sentiment but is making justice and doing works of mercy.

—Matthew Fox

♦♦♦♦♦♦♦♦♦♦♦♦♦♦♦♦

Our Definition of Compassion

Name ______________________________ Date ______________

Why O Why O Why-O?

Why doesn't glue stick to the inside of the bottle?

Why is the word "abbreviation" so long?

Why don't sheep shrink when it rains?

Why isn't "phonetic" spelled the way it sounds?

Why do we drive on parkways and park on driveways?

Why isn't "palindrome" spelled the same way backward?

Why are there flotation devices under airplane seats instead of parachutes?

Why is the third hand on a watch called a second hand?

Why is the time of the day with the slowest traffic called the rush hour?

Why do "fat chance" and "slim chance" mean the same thing?

Why isn't there mouse-flavored cat food?

Why do they report power outages on TV?

If the world is smaller, why do postal rates keep going up?

If necessity is the mother of invention, why does so much unnecessary stuff get invented?

♦♦♦♦♦♦♦♦♦♦♦♦♦♦♦♦

Millions saw the apple fall, but Newton was the only one who asked why.

—Bernard Baruch, Financier and Presidential Advisor

♦♦♦♦♦♦♦♦♦♦♦♦♦♦♦♦

My Biggest WHY Question

____

____

____

____

____

____

Name ______________________________ Date ______________

Sources of the Pentateuch

	J - Yahwist	E - Elohist	D - Deuteronomist	P - Priestly
God's Name	Yahweh	Elohim	Yahweh	Elohim
Place of Origin	Southern Kingdom (Judah)	Northern Kingdom (Israel)	Northern Kingdom (Schechem/Jerusalem)	Babylonian Exile
Probable Date	950 BC	850 BC	650 BC	400 BC
Emphasis/Theme	God's Promises to Patriarchs	Prophecy/Covenants	Morality/ Living the Law	Temple Worship and concerns of priests serving in the Temple
Overall Contribution	Provided a basic outline for the Pentateuch.	Combined J and E.	Highlighted obedience as the response to God's grace.	Offered a coherent framework for the Pentateuch.

Name ______________________________ Date ______________

Chapter 1 Test

Part 1: Matching. Write the letter of the correct definition in the blank near its term. **(3 points each)**

1. _____ Sacred Tradition
2. _____ Pentateuch
3. _____ Salvation History
4. _____ Primeval History
5. _____ Sacred Scripture

A. The story of God's saving actions on our behalf.

B. The inspired Word of God; the written record of God's Revelation.

C. A Greek word meaning "five scrolls." It is used to refer to the first five books of the Bible.

D. The living transmission of the Church's Gospel message found in the Church's teaching, life, and worship.

E. Stories or myths about the origins of the earth, humans, other creatures, languages, and cultures.

Part 2: True or False. Mark **T** if the statement is true. Mark **F** if the statement is false. **(3 points each)**

1. _____ The first creation story portrays God with human qualities.
2. _____ In reading Scripture, it is important to understand the literary forms used by the human author.
3. _____ God's free gift of self-communication is called Redemption.
4. _____ The word *tradition* means "ancient truths."
5. _____ A myth is a truth told concretely.
6. _____ The authority to interpret God's Word authentically belongs to the Magisterium.
7. _____ God created humans to adopt us into the divine family and share eternal life with us.
8. _____ The first creation story was a powerful assault on polytheism.
9. _____ The Church holds that religious truth and scientific truth are always in contradiction.
10. _____ We know what God has revealed through the gift of the Deposit of Faith.
11. _____ Catholics are encouraged to interpret Scripture entirely on their own.
12. _____ The Yahwist source of the Pentateuch is the oldest of the sources.
13. _____ The Pentateuch was composed mostly by Moses.
14. _____ In the second creation account, both males and females are created at the same time.
15. _____ Occasionally the Scriptures do not show the truth.
16. _____ The words "Let us make man in our image, after our likeness" (Gn 1:26) suggest the activity of the Holy Trinity in creation.
17. _____ Second Isaiah linked the theme of creation and Salvation to encourage the Hebrew people who were in exile in Babylon.
18. _____ The Book of Proverbs personifies wisdom, declaring it God's helper in the act of creation.
19. _____ The Priestly source of the Pentateuch stresses the importance of Temple ceremonies.

Part 3: Fill in the Blanks. Choose from the following words to fill in the blanks. **(3 points each)**

exegesis	Holiness	Justice	Mystery	pantheism
Pentateuch	philosophy	polytheism	Torah	

1. ________________ People who practiced ____ thought that God and nature were one and the same.
2. ________________ ____ is the name of the first five books of the Old Testament that comes from the word meaning "law."
3. ________________ ________________ The second creation account teaches that Adam and Eve were born in a state of Original ____ and Original ____, meaning they shared in the Divine Life.
4. ________________ The investigation of truth and principles of human reason is called ____.
5. ________________ God showed his great compassion for us through the Paschal ____.

Part 4: Essays.

1. List and describe three literary forms of the Old Testament. **(6 points)**

2. Write a definition of the word "compassion" and give two real-life examples of the term. **(3 points)**

3. Compare the two creation accounts in the book of Genesis. Write about at least two differences. Then, discuss how these creation accounts compare to other accounts of creation in the Bible (Isaiah, Psalms, Proverbs, the New Testament letters, or the Gospel of John). **(4 points)**

Name ______________________________ Date ______________

The Exultet

Rejoice, heavenly powers! Sing choirs of angels!
Exult, all creation around God's throne!
Jesus Christ, our King is risen!
Sound the trumpet of salvation!

Rejoice, O earth, in shining splendor,
radiant in the brightness of your King!
Christ has conquered! Glory fills you!
Darkness vanishes for ever!

Rejoice, O Mother Church! Exult in glory!
The risen Savior shines upon you!
Let this place resound with joy,
echoing the mighty song of all God's people!

It is truly right that with full hearts and minds and voices we should praise the unseen God, the all-powerful Father,
and his only Son, our Lord Jesus Christ.

For Christ has ransomed us with his blood,
and ***paid for us the price of Adam's sin***
to our eternal Father!

This is our Passover feast,
When Christ, the true Lamb, is slain,
whose blood consecrates the homes of all believers.

This is the night,
when first you saved our fathers:
you freed the people of Israel from their slavery,
and led them dry-shod through the sea.

This is the night, when the pillar of fire destroyed the darkness of sin.

This is the night,
when Christians everywhere,
washed clean of sin and freed from all defilement, are restored to grace and grow together in holiness.

This is the night,
when Jesus broke the chains of death
and rose triumphant from the grave.

What good would life have been to us
had Christ not come as our Redeemer?

Father, how wonderful your care for us!
How boundless your merciful love!
To ransom a slave you gave away your Son.

O happy fault, O necessary sin of Adam,
which gained for us so great a Redeemer!

Most blessed of all nights,
chosen by God to see Christ rising
from the dead!

Of this night scripture says:
"The night will be as clear as day:
it will become my light, my joy."

The power of this holy night dispels all evil,
washes guilt away,
restores lost innocence,
brings mourners joy;
it casts out hatred, brings us peace,
and humbles earthly pride.

Night truly blessed,
when heaven is wedded to earth
and we are reconciled to God!

Therefore, heavenly Father,
in the joy of this night,
receive our evening sacrifice of praise,
your Church's solemn offering.

Accept this Easter candle,
a flame divided but undimmed,
a pillar of fire that glows to the honor of God.

Let it mingle with the lights of heaven
and continue bravely burning
to dispel the darkness of this night!

May the Morning Star which never sets
find this flame still burning:
Christ, that Morning Star,
who came back from the dead,
and shed his peaceful light on all mankind,
your Son, who lives and reigns
for ever and ever. Amen.

Name ________________________________ Date ______________

Prophetic Voices

Amos 2:6-7

What is Amos's attitude toward the rich?

____

____

Amos 5:21, 23-24

What does Amos say about religious formalism?

____

____

Jeremiah 13:20

From whence does Jeremiah say doom is approaching?

____

____

Ezekiel 7:1-4, 26-27

Put Ezekiel's frightening warning in your own words.

____

____

____

____

Ezekiel 34:11-15 and John 10:11-18

How do these two passages compare? Do you think Jesus had Ezekiel in mind when he was speaking?

____

____

____

____

♦♦♦♦♦♦♦♦♦♦♦♦♦♦♦♦

My Prophetic Voice

____

____

____

____

____

Name ______________________________ Date ______________

Isaiah x 3

1. Isaiah (First Isaiah): Chapters 1-39

- Authored by Isaiah of Jerusalem who preached during the biblical golden age of prophecy (eighth century BC).
- Themes: repentance (Is 1:16–18) and warnings of approaching disaster (Is 5:1–7).
- Promises a future of peace (Is 9:5–6) and the coming of Immanuel (Is 7:14).

2. Second Isaiah: Chapters 40-55

- Written by an anonymous prophet (sometimes referred to as Isaiah of Babylon) during the time of the Babylonian Exile.
- Themes: comfort (Is 40:1–5); consolation (Is 49:15–16a); promise of a great future (Is 45:6b).
- Contains a series of four "Servant Songs" detailing the mission of the servant who not only suffers on behalf of the people but also offers them hope.
    - Is 42:1–7
    - Is 49:1–6
    - Is 50:4–9
    - Is 52:13–53:12

3. Third or Trito-Isaiah: Chapters 56-66

- Authored by a disciple(s) of Second Isaiah who depicts himself as a herald of good news—an evangelist—to the poor, bringing healing, freedom, release, favor, and vindication (Is 61:1–2).
- Themes: hope (Is 60:15) and universal salvation (Is 56:7).
- Addressed to a post-exilic people laboring to rebuild their lives—their country, their capital, and their Temple—it assures them that God is with them and so encourages them to be joyful (Is 62:2–5).

♦♦♦♦♦♦♦♦♦♦♦♦♦♦♦♦

"The Golden Passional"

Martin Luther declared that the Fourth Servant Song (Is 52:13–53:12) should be written on gold and lettered in diamonds, thus rendering the passage the title "The Golden Passional." Read and reflect on the song in its entirety. Then note three ways you feel it relates to the suffering of Jesus.

1. ______________________________

2. ______________________________

3. ______________________________

Name ______________________________ Date ______________

Chapter 2 Test

Part 1: True or False. Mark **T** if the statement is true. Mark **F** if the statement is false. **(3 points each)**

1. _____ The sign of the covenant between Noah and his descendants was circumcision.
2. _____ The first king of the Israelites was Saul.
3. _____ The Israelites built a golden calf because they were angry with God for making them wander in the desert.
4. _____ There was a real historical event behind the story of the Fall of Adam and Eve.
5. _____ Jesus was the Suffering Servant prophesied in the Old Testament.

Part 2: Fill in the Blanks. Choose from the following words to fill in the blanks. **(3 points each)**

Abraham	Amos	Cain	concupiscence	covenant	Decalogue	Ezekiel	Holiness	idolatry
Isaiah	Jeremiah	judges	Justice	myth	Pentecost	Protoevangelium	rainbow	Tower of Babel

1. _______________ The Israelites often fell into ____ by worshipping false gods.
2. _______________ ____ is often called the "father of faith."
3. _______________ A ____ is a story whose main purpose is to express a great truth or insight into reality.
4. _______________ A ____ is a binding promise between God and humankind in which God pledges enduring love and asks for such love in return.
5. _______________ ____ is the inclination to do what we know is not right.
6. _______________ The Apostles spoke in many languages and were understood by all present—an event we call ____.
7. _______________ ____ prophesied that the new covenant would be written on the people's hearts.
8. _______________ Original ____ means that humans were created to share in God's own life.
9. _______________ The ____ is the sign of the Noah covenant.
10. _______________ The main purpose of the____ story is that we should not put our faith in human triumphs; God is in charge, not us.
11. _______________ The ____ were tribal chieftains who served as military leaders for Israel, settled disputes, and called the people back to God.
12. _______________ The ____ is the summary of the Torah.
13. _______________ ____ means "first gospel."
14. _______________ Original ____ meant that humans would not die or experience suffering or pain.
15. _______________ ____ prophesied about dry bones.
16. _______________ The Servant Songs are found in the Book of the Prophet ____.
17. _______________ ____ is known for saying, "Am I my brother's keeper?"
18. _______________ ____ is considered the prophet of social justice.

Part 3: Brief Answers. (3 points each)

1. List the names of the three angels mentioned by name in the Bible.

2. Why did Adam and Eve eat from the Tree of Knowledge of Good and Evil?

3. What is natural law?

4. List three of the consequences of Original Sin.

5. List the three basic human drives and needs expressed in the Ten Commandments.

6. What is the role of the biblical prophet?

7. List three promises made by God in the covenant with Abraham.

Part 4: Essay. (10 points)

Jesus' coming was foretold in the Old Testament Scriptures. Support this statement with at least three examples from the Old Testament.

Name ______________________________ Date ______________

Hope

Hope is the word which God has written on the brow of every man.

—Victor Hugo

The history of the Hebrew people is surely a history of hope. While small in number, the Hebrew people survived overwhelming odds and accomplished impossible things. They held fast to hope no matter their condition—in captivity, in wandering, and in exile. Why? Because they continued to believe in the covenant promises God had made with them. They trusted that God would act on their behalf and fulfill all those promises. The psalmist shares the strength that hope gave to the Hebrews:

> Hallelujah!
> Praise the Lord, my soul; I shall praise the Lord all my life,
> sing praise to my God while I live.
> I put no trust in princes, in mere mortals powerless to save. . . .
> Happy those whose help is Jacob's God, whose hope is in the Lord, their God,
> The maker of heaven and earth, the seas and all that is in them,
> Who keeps faith forever, secures justice for the oppressed,
> gives food to the hungry.
> The Lord sets prisoners free; the Lord gives sight to the blind.
> The Lord raises up those who are bowed down; the Lord loves the righteous.
> The Lord protects the stranger, sustains the orphan and the widow,
> but thwarts the way of the wicked.
> The Lord shall reign forever, your God, Zion, through all generations!
> Hallelujah!
> —Psalm 146:1-3, 5-10

- What were some of the covenant promises God made to the Hebrews?
- What was the Hebrews' greatest hope?

♦♦♦♦♦♦♦♦♦♦♦♦♦♦♦♦♦

St. Augustine said, "Of the three theological virtues, hope is the greatest."

- Faith puts us in touch with God.
- Love unites us with the goodness of God.
- Hope places us on the path toward God.

♦♦♦♦♦♦♦♦♦♦♦♦♦♦♦♦♦

Hope sees the invisible, feels the intangible, and achieves the impossible.
Hope is a passion for the impossible.

- What seems impossible for you?
- Describe how hope energizes you to reach for the impossible and to make a difference.

Name ______________________________ Date ________________

An Act of Hope

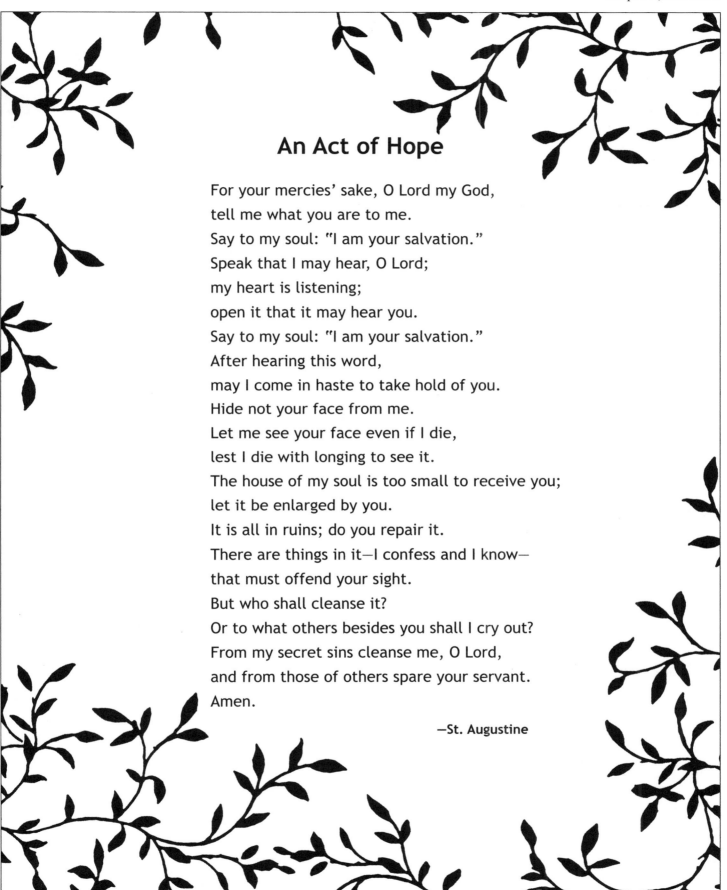

For your mercies' sake, O Lord my God,
tell me what you are to me.
Say to my soul: "I am your salvation."
Speak that I may hear, O Lord;
my heart is listening;
open it that it may hear you.
Say to my soul: "I am your salvation."
After hearing this word,
may I come in haste to take hold of you.
Hide not your face from me.
Let me see your face even if I die,
lest I die with longing to see it.
The house of my soul is too small to receive you;
let it be enlarged by you.
It is all in ruins; do you repair it.
There are things in it—I confess and I know—
that must offend your sight.
But who shall cleanse it?
Or to what others besides you shall I cry out?
From my secret sins cleanse me, O Lord,
and from those of others spare your servant.
Amen.

—St. Augustine

Name ____ Date ____________________

The Gospels

Author	Written At	Audience	Jesus Portrayed As	Begins With
Mark	Rome	Persecuted Gentiles	Suffering Messiah	
John	Ephesus	Jews and Gentiles	Life-Giving Messiah	
Matthew	Antioch	Jewish-Christians	Teaching Messiah	
Luke	Greece	Poor Gentile-Christians	Merciful Messiah	

♦♦♦♦♦♦♦♦♦♦♦♦♦♦♦♦

Unique Elements in Matthew

- Does Jesus' genealogy move from **present to past** or **past to present**? (*Circle the correct answer.*)
- Matthew presents Jesus as a descendant of ____________________ and ____________________.
- Matthew traces Jesus' genealogy through which human parent?
- An angel appears to which of Jesus' parents?
- Who gives Jesus his name and what does that name mean?
- According to Matthew, what's lighting up the night sky?
- According to Matthew, who are the first to visit the child Jesus?
- Why does the Holy Family leave Bethlehem and where do they go?
- With what Old Testament figure does Matthew compare Jesus?

Name ______________________________ Date ______________

The House of Christmas

There fared a mother driven forth
Out of an inn to roam;
In the place where she was homeless
All men are at home.
The crazy stable close at hand,
With shaking timber and shifting sand,
Grew a stronger thing to abide and stand
Than the square stones of Rome.

For men are homesick in their homes,
And strangers under the sun,
And they lay on their heads in a foreign land
Whenever the day is done.
Here we have battle and blazing eyes,
And chance and honour and high surprise,
But our homes are under miraculous skies
Where the yule tale was begun.

A Child in a foul stable,
Where the beasts feed and foam;
Only where He was homeless
Are you and I at home;
We have hands that fashion and heads that know,
But our hearts we lost—how long ago!
In a place no chart nor ship can show
Under the sky's dome.

This world is wild as an old wives' tale,
And strange the plain things are,
The earth is enough and the air is enough
For our wonder and our war;
But our rest is as far as the fire-drake swings
And our peace is put in impossible things
Where clashed and thundered unthinkable wings
Round an incredible star.

To an open house in the evening
Home shall men come,
To an older place than Eden
And a taller town than Rome.
To the end of the way of the wandering star,
To the things that cannot be and that are,
To the place where God was homeless
And all men are at home.

—G. K. Chesterton

Name ______________________________ Date ______________

What Are the Gospels?

First of all, what the Gospels *are not*. They are not simple biographies that invite us to read about Jesus and admire him. The Gospels summon us to pay attention to him, to believe in him, and to follow him.

The Gospels are. . .

- proclamations of Good News
- encounters with that Good News—Jesus himself
- challenges to believe

Read each of the Gospel passages below.

- Describe what image the evangelist uses to portray Jesus.
- Express the Good News.
- Then, describe how the person in the passage responded to Jesus.

Mark 1:40-42

Image of Jesus & the Good News

____

____

Response of the healed man

____

____

Luke 10:38-42

Image of Jesus & the Good News

____

____

Response of Mary

____

____

Mark 8:27-30

Image of Jesus & the Good News

____

____

Response of Peter

____

____

♦♦♦♦♦♦♦♦♦♦♦♦♦♦♦♦

Jesus challenged his listeners to believe and to make a commitment. Today, the Gospels continue to challenge us to believe in Jesus and to follow him. Read each of the Gospel passages below.

- Describe what you think it challenges you to believe about Jesus.
- Finally, describe how you could meet that challenge.

John 20:24-29

The challenge

____

____

My response

____

____

Luke 6:37-42

The challenge

____

____

My response

____

____

Name ____ Date ____________________

Chapter 3 Test

Part 1: True or False. Mark **T** if the statement is true. Mark **F** if the statement is false. **(2 points each)**

1. _____ John the Baptist's parents, Zechariah and Elizabeth, resemble Abraham and Sarah in the Old Testament.
2. _____ The Gospels serve as fairly accurate biographies of Jesus.
3. _____ John the Baptist was seen as the new Isaiah.
4. _____ Matthew's Gospel records the journey of Joseph and Mary from Bethlehem to Egypt.
5. _____ Jesus was born around the year AD 4–6.
6. _____ Luke's Gospel reports that the first people to visit the child Jesus were shepherds.
7. _____ Reference to the magi and the star of Bethlehem may be found in Luke.
8. _____ In Matthew's Gospel it is Joseph who gives Jesus his name.
9. _____ Jesus' announcement that he was the Messiah received a favorable welcome from those in his hometown.
10. ____ Jesus' birth without Original Sin is called the Immaculate Conception.
11. ____ The Feast of the Epiphany celebrates Jesus' manifestation as the Messiah to all nations.
12. ____ Jesus' ability to resist the temptations of the devil arose from his divine nature.
13. ____ The doctrine of the virgin birth is known as the Immaculate Conception.
14. ____ Mary's response to Elizabeth's greeting is known as the Angelus.
15. ____ John's Gospel does not contain an infancy narrative.
16. ____ Matthew's genealogy is concerned with telling the reader that Jesus is the fulfillment of Jewish hopes.
17. ____ To some extent shepherds were seen as outcasts in Jesus' time.
18. ____ God's Word becoming a human being is known as the Paschal Mystery.
19. ____ The central theme of Jesus' preaching is the coming of the Kingdom of God.
20. ____ Luke wrote for Gentile-Christians.
21. ____ Mark's Gospel begins with a prophecy about a messenger coming to prepare the Messiah's way.
22. ____ John baptized in the Jordan River because it was a symbol of Jewish freedom.
23. ____ Jesus' circumcision signified his incorporation into the Jewish people.
24. ____ John called Jesus the Lamb of God.
25. ____ The earliest of the four Gospels is Matthew.
26. ____ The angel Raphael appeared to Mary.

Part 2: Matching. Write the letter of the correct term in the blank near its definition. **(2 points each)**

1. ______ A word that literally means "ransom."
2. ______ The process of God's reconciling and renewing all things through Jesus and God's will being done on earth as in heaven.
3. ______ A name for Jesus that means "God is with us."
4. ______ The dogma that God's Son assumed a human nature in order to save us from our sins.
5. ______ A meeting place for study and prayer.

A. Emmanuel
B. Incarnation
C. Redemption
D. synagogue
E. Kingdom of God

Part 3: Fill in the Blanks. (2 points each)

1. ________________ The Gospel of ____ was probably written last after the other three Gospels.
2. ________________ The Gospel of ____ was likely used as a source for two other Gospels.
3. ________________ John the Baptist led an ____ life, meaning he lived a life of poverty and self-denial.

Part 4: Short Answers. (3 points each)

1. Name and briefly explain three of the four purposes of the Incarnation discussed in this chapter.

2. Name three theological truths that were revealed by Jesus' baptism.

3. What were the three things that the devil used to tempt Jesus in the desert?

4. Which three sacraments were referenced in Jesus' miracle at the wedding feast of Cana?

Part 5: Essays. Respond to the following. **(10 points each)**

1. Each of the Gospels begins in a different way. Briefly describe the beginning of each of the Gospels, then discuss their differences, particularly between Matthew and Luke.

2. All of the Evangelists hoped to show a strong connection between the Old Testament and the life of Christ. Describe at least three examples of connections between the Old Testament and the opening chapters of the four Gospels.

Name ______________________________ Date ______________

The Measure of Success

Success. People dress for it, pray for it, work for it, cheat for it, and sometimes die for it. But what is it? And how do we measure it? Circle any of the following terms that you feel are measures of success. Then add four terms of your own.

talent	beauty	brains	ambition	money
luck	satisfaction	great clothes	friendship	power
winning	popularity	fame	possessions	peace of mind
competitiveness	______	______	______	______

Name four people you believe to be successful. For each person you name, tell why.

I think ______________________ is successful because ______________________

I think ______________________ is successful because ______________________

I think ______________________ is successful because ______________________

I think ______________________ is successful because ______________________

Are you a success? Why or why not?

Name ______________________________ Date ______________

Definitely Different Viewpoints

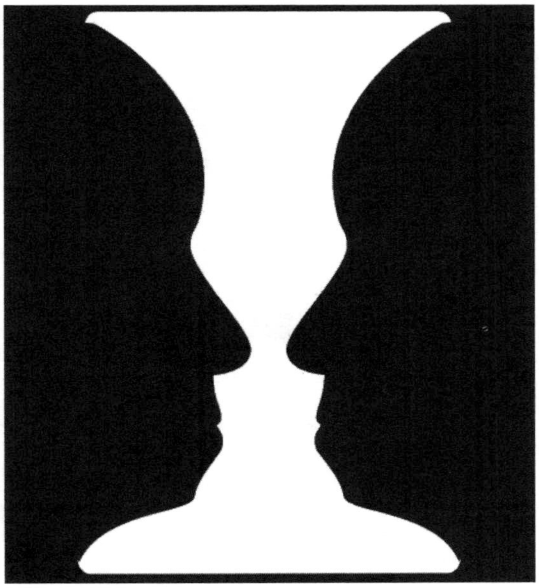

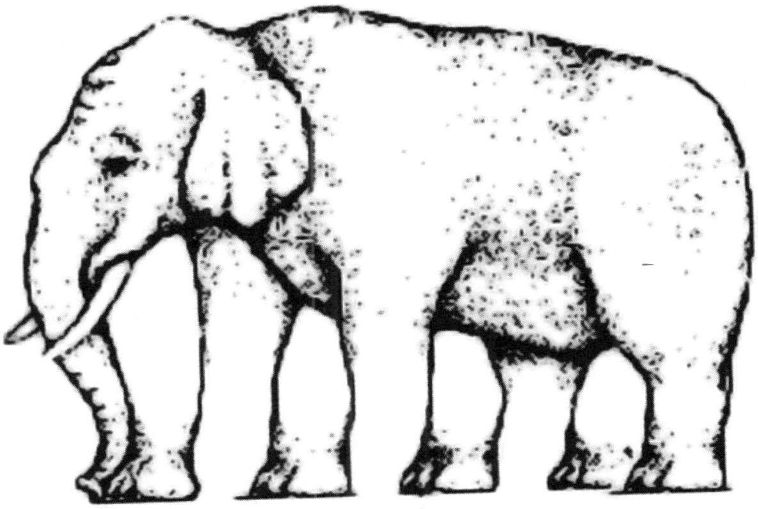

Name ______________________________ Date ______________

I See Myself . . .

Dear ____________________,

And God Sees Me . . .

I believe in people, people like ____.
(*your name*)

I believe that they, one by one and all together . . .

Name ______________________________ Date ______________

Works, Wonders, and Signs

Jesus' miracles . . .

I. Serve as signs of the Kingdom of God.
II. Attest to Jesus' mission = To free us from sin.
III. Invite us to believe.
IV. Prefigure his victory (in his Paschal Mystery) over Satan, sin, and death.

♦♦♦♦♦♦♦♦♦♦♦♦♦♦♦♦

Types of Jesus' Miracles

Physical Healings—power over ______________________________

Two examples: ______________________ and ______________________

Exorcisms—power over ______________________________

Two examples: ______________________ and ______________________

Nature Miracles—power over ______________________________

Two examples: ______________________ and ______________________

Raisings from Death—power over ______________________________

Two examples: ______________________ and ______________________

♦♦♦♦♦♦♦♦♦♦♦♦♦♦♦♦

Friend Jesus,
Please, here's what you can do for me . . .

____

____

____

____

____

♦♦♦♦♦♦♦♦♦♦♦♦♦♦♦♦

Friend Jesus,
Please, here's what I can do for you . . .

____

____

____

____

____

Name ______________________________ Date ______________

Chapter 4 Test

Part 1: Fill in the Blanks. Choose from the following words to fill in the blanks. **(2 points each)**

Beatitudes	belief	bread	comparison	Golden Rule	Jerusalem	Jesus	Levi
miracles	Mount	mustard	Passover	Plain	prejudice	repentance	Rome
Samaritan	Sanhedrin	Transfiguration	Trinity	wheat	wine	yeast	Zacchaeus

1 & 2. ________________ ________________ Parables of the ____ seed and the ____ in the dough represent the present and future dimensions of the Kingdom of God.

3. ________________ The parable of the ____ and weeds revealed that only God can decide who will be punished as evildoers and who will be rewarded in Heaven.

4 & 5. ________________ ________________ Jesus presented the Beatitudes in the Sermon on the ____ in Matthew and in the Sermon on the ____ in Luke.

6 & 7. ________________ ________________ Jesus' messages and actions threatened both the religious authority of the ____ and the imperialist power of ____.

8 & 9. ________________ ________________ Jesus said that entrance into the Kingdom required ____ and ____ in the Good News.

10. ________________ The ____ are proclamations of God's grace.

11. ________________ The Beatitudes call us to go beyond the ____.

12. ________________ The word "parable" derives from a Greek term meaning ____.

13 & 14. ________________ ________________ Jesus was criticized for associating with tax collectors like ____ and ____.

15. ________________ Matthew 25 makes it clear that if we exclude anyone from God's Kingdom, we are, in fact, excluding ____.

16. ________________ At the ____, the glory of God incarnate in the Son was displayed.

17. ________________ ____ are powerful signs of God's presence and action on our behalf.

18. ________________ The Transfiguration reveals the ____.

19. ________________ Luke sets the account of the Last Supper in the context of the ____.

20 & 21. ________________ ________________ At the Last Supper Jesus identified himself with the ____ and ____.

22. ________________ The parable of the Good ____ teaches us that we should love our neighbor, even our enemies.

23. ________________ Jesus knew that as a prophet he had to die in ____.

24. ________________ Many people have ____, or unsubstantiated or pre-formed judgments about individuals or groups based on race, gender, etc.

Part 2: True or False. Mark **T** if the statement is true. Mark **F** if the statement is false. **(2 points each)**

1. _____ Jesus was accused of the crime of blasphemy.

2. _____ The outwardly religious have a better chance of entering the Kingdom of God than the poor or sinners.

3. _____ Jesus is really present in the consecrated bread and wine at Mass.

4. _____ All three synoptic authors use the term "Kingdom of God."

5. _____ The parable of the tenants is an allegory.

6. _____ The Transfiguration revealed that Jesus was the Son of God.

7. _____ Parables are events that the laws of nature cannot explain.

8. ______ The parable of the Prodigal Son is about a winner and a loser.

9. ______ The Gospel of John calls Jesus' miracles signs or works.

10. _____ Moses and Abraham appeared with Jesus at his Transfiguration.

11. _____ All Twelve Apostles were present at the Transfiguration.

12. _____ Before the Transfiguration, Peter confessed that he thought Jesus was Elijah.

Part 3: Essays. Respond to the following.

1. How would you describe the Kingdom of God? State *three* teachings about the Kingdom of God and support each one with a parable that Jesus used to reveal this message. (**6 points**)

2. What did Jesus require of his disciples? Explain at least *two* requirements from the Sermon on the Plain. (**2 points**)

3. Name the *four* types of miracles Jesus performed and provide the name or brief description of at least one example of each type of miracle. (**8 points**)

4. Describe at least *two* connections between the Jewish Passover and the Last Supper. (**2 points**)

Part 4: Interpreting a Parable. Read the following parable and provide an interpretation of it, noting what the items in the parable represent and what the parable says about the Kingdom of God. (**10 points**)

> What woman having ten coins and losing one would not light a lamp and sweep the house, searching carefully until she finds it? And when she does find it, she calls together her friends and neighbors and says to them, "Rejoice with me because I have found the coin that I lost." In just the same way, I tell you, there will be rejoicing among the angels of God over one sinner who repents. (Lk 13:8–10)

Name ______________________________ Date ________________

Jesus on Trial

Prosecution	Defense

Possible Witnesses

In the space provided, write why the witness believes Jesus should or should not be executed.

Pilate—

Sanhedrin—

All Sinners—

Witness #_____—

Witness #_____—

Witness #_____—

Opening Argument

Witnesses Question

Prosecution Witnesses	Defense Witnesses

Closing Argument

Name ______________________________ Date ______________

Elements of the Passions

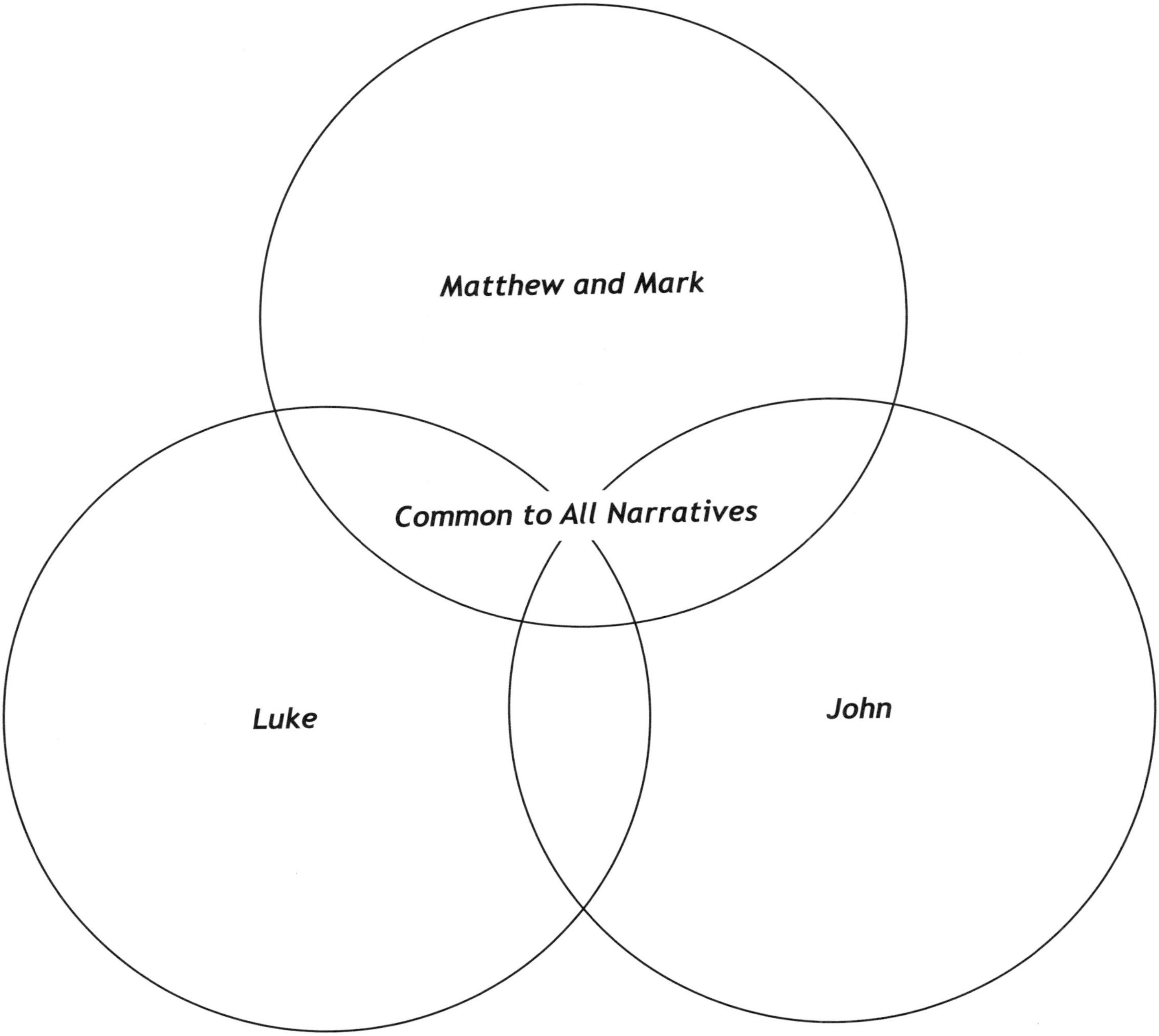

Name ______________________________ Date ______________

Jesus' Way of the Cross

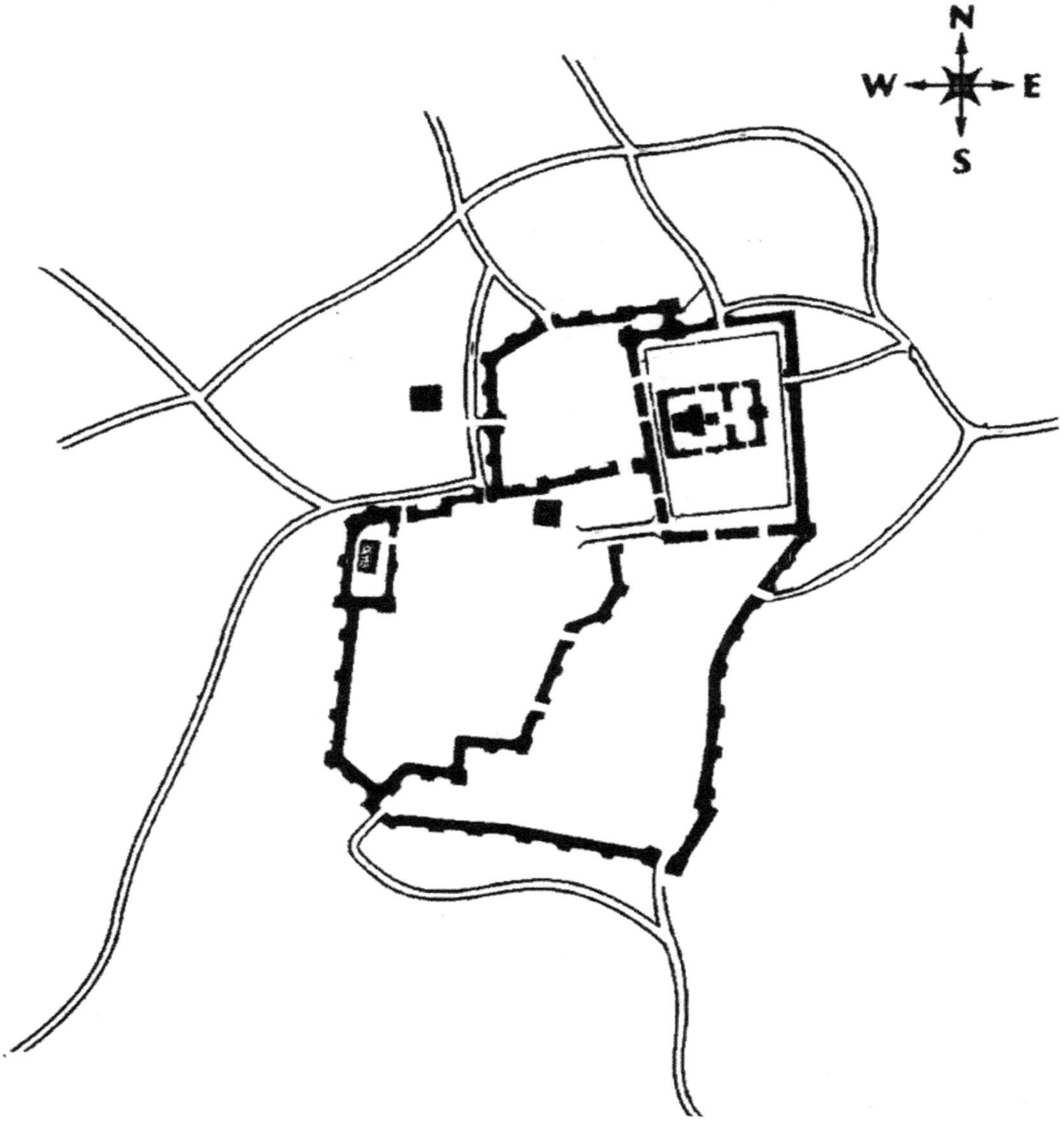

1. Label the following:

Temple
Golgotha
Garden of Gethsemane
Upper Room
Joseph Caiaphas's residence
Way of the Cross
Mount of Olives
Fortress of Antonia
Kidron Valley
Herod Antipas's palace

2. Number the places on the map in the order that Jesus went there.

Name ______________________________ Date ______________

The Memorare

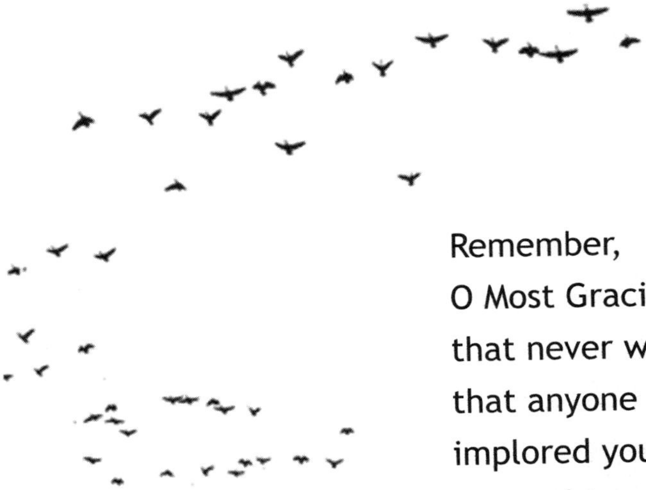

Remember,
O Most Gracious Virgin Mary,
that never was it known
that anyone who fled to your protection,
implored your help,
or sought your intercession,
was left unaided.
Inspired by this confidence,
I fly unto you,
O Virgin of Virgins, my Mother;
to you do I come,
before you I stand,
sinful and sorrowful.
O Mother of the Word Incarnate,
despise not my petitions,
but in your mercy,
hear and answer me.
Amen.

Name ____ Date ____________________

Chapter 5 Test

Part 1: True or False. Mark **T** if the statement is true. Mark **F** if the statement is false. **(2 points each)**

1. _____ The Sanhedrin found Jesus guilty of blasphemy but brought him to Pilate with a charge of sedition.
2. _____ Jesus chose to die to identify with us and to conquer sin and death on our behalf.
3. _____ Maximilian Kolbe voluntarily sacrificed his life so that another might live.
4. _____ Jesus did not choose to die.
5. _____ In crucifixion, the victim usually died due to suffocation.
6. _____ Jesus' driving out the moneychangers from the Temple demonstrated his authority over Israel's religious practices and challenged the entire sacrificial system.
7. _____ The Death of Jesus was not part of God's salvific plan.
8. _____ Crucifixion was the traditional form of Jewish capital punishment.
9. _____ The Eucharist is a memorial of Jesus' sacrifice on the Cross.
10. ____ Jesus was sentenced to death by the Sanhedrin.
11. ____ The chief priest and other members of the Sanhedrin had an economic and religious interest in the Temple.
12. ____ Jesus died for our sins; therefore, we all bear responsibility for his Death.
13. ____ Both Pilate and the Jewish leaders who opposed Jesus regarded him as a threat to their authority.
14. ____ The passion narratives of Mark and Matthew stress elements of abandonment and vindication.
15. ____ The passion narratives include relatively few references to Old Testament prophecies.
16. ____ Maximilian Kolbe was a priest.
17. ____ God the Father sent his Son to die on the Cross out of anger for human sin.
18. ____ Matthew's passion narrative describes Jesus in control of the events.
19. ____ The Sadducees were jealous of Jesus and saw him as a threat to the civil order (the status quo) and to their authority as religious leaders.
20. ____ Jesus' anointing at Bethany was a sign that the woman who anointed him recognized him as the Christ.
21. ____ Luke's passion narrative centers on Jesus' compassion.
22. ____ The tearing of the Temple veil symbolizes the end of the Old Covenant.
23. ____ All but one of Jesus' disciples standing by him at the Cross were women.
24. ____ Christ was Jesus' last name.
25. ____ Mary was the first and most faithful disciple of her son, Jesus.
26. ____ Pilate was a cruel and ruthless Roman governor.

Part 2: Fill in the Blanks. (2 points each)

1. ________________ Jesus entered Jerusalem riding on a ____.

2. ________________ Joseph ____ was the high priest at the time of Jesus' crucifixion.

3. ________________ Jesus celebrated ____ with the Apostles at the Last Supper.

4. ________________ Jesus prayed in agony in the Garden of ____.

5. ________________ Jesus was crucified at ____.

6. ________________ ____ of Cyrene was pressed into the service of carrying the Cross for Jesus.

7. ________________ ____ of Arimathea wrapped Jesus in clean linen and had him placed in a tomb.

8. ________________ Pilate had Jesus' charge posted on the Cross. The abbreviation of the charge is INRI, which stands for ____.

9. ________________ Many members of the Jewish religious leaders called the ____ were Sadducees.

10. ________________ Maximilian Kolbe is considered a ____ because his death bore witness to the truth of his faith.

11. ________________ The High Priest was the only person allowed to enter the ____.

12. ________________ To blame the Jews today for Jesus' Death is called ____.

Part 3: Brief Answers. Respond to the following.

1. Who is to blame for the Death of Jesus and why did they wish to crucify Jesus? (Choose two people/groups) (**4 points**)

2. Describe three specific connections that the writers of the Gospels made between the passion narratives and the Old Testament (Exodus, Psalms, Isaiah, Amos, Zechariah). (**6 points**)

3. Name at least four common elements shared by all four passion narratives. (**4 points**)

4. Name at least two elements of the passion narratives that are unique to Matthew/Mark, Luke, and John. (**6 points**)

5. Why would God the Father allow Jesus, his only begotten Son, to suffer and die? (**4 points**)

Name ______________________________ Date ______________

Eureka!

Mackerel
Trout
Tuna
Z
Z
Bass
Z Z Z
Shark
Herring

waltz
foxtrot
mambo
tango

wise

(1) ____________________ (2) ____________________ (3) ____________________

Under

foot pole foot pole
foot pole foot pole
a foot pole foot pole
foot pole foot pole
foot pole foot pole

(4) ____________________ (5) ____________________ (6) ____________________

(7) TIASTITCHME

____

(8) To give others a sporting chance, the king has decreed that no tenors may attend the royal dance. Obviously, the dance is a ______________________________.

(9) Supply missing letters, and find a winged proverb: a-i-d-n-h-h-n-i-w-r-h-w-i-t-e-u-h

(10)
Brahms
Bach
Chopin
Mozart
Beethoven
Liszt

____

Name ______________________________ Date ______________

Resurrection Reflections

If Christ Rose Not Again

If it be all for naught, for nothingness
At last, why does God make the world so fair?
Why spill this golden splendor out across
The western hills, and light the silver lamp
Of eve? Why give me eyes to see, and soul
To love so strong and deep? Then, with a pang
This brightness stabs me through, and wakes within
Rebellious voice to cry against all death?
Why set this hunger for eternity
To gnaw my heartstrings through, if death ends all?
If death ends all, then evil must be good,
Wrong must be right, and beauty ugliness.
God is a Judas who betrays His Son,
And with a kiss, damns all the world to hell,—
If Christ rose not again.

—Unknown soldier, killed in World War I*

Descending Theology: The Resurrection

From the far star points of his pinned extremities,
cold inched in—black ice and squid ink—
till the hung flesh was empty.
Lonely in that void even for pain,
he missed his splintered feet,
the human stare buried in his face.
He ached for two hands made of meat
he could reach to the end of.
In the corpse's core, the stone fist
of his heart began to bang
on the stiff chest's door, and breath spilled
back into that battered shape. Now
it's your limbs he comes to fill, as warm water
shatters at birth, rivering every way.

—Mary Karr**

**Masterpieces of Religious Verse*, James Dalton Morrison, ed., New York: Harper & Bros., 1948, 205.
****Poetry* Magazine, January 2006.

Name ______________________________ Date ______________

Resurrection Consequences—The 4 Cs

Confirms: The Resurrection confirms all Christ's works and teaching.

- Christ's Identity, Works, and Teachings

  John 8:28

  ____

  ____

Completes: The Resurrection, following Christ's sacrifice on the Cross, accomplished our Salvation.

- Our Salvation

  1 Peter 2:24

  ____

  ____

Confers: The Resurrection gives new life, justifies us in God's grace, and adopts us into the divine family.

- New Life and Justification

  John 3:16–17

  ____

  ____

  ____

  ____

- Adoption into God's Family

  John 1:12

  ____

  ____

Creates: Through the power of the Holy Spirit, Christians participate in the life, suffering, Death, and Resurrection of Jesus.

- A New Future

  John 11:25–26

  ____

  ____

  ____

  ____

Name ______________________________ Date ______________

On the Feast of Pentecost

Father of light,
from whom every good gift comes,
send your Spirit into our lives
with the power of a mighty wind,
and by the flame of your wisdom
open the horizons of our minds.
Loosen our tongues to sing your praise
in words beyond the power of speech,
for without your Spirit
we could never raise our voices in words of peace
or announce the truth that Jesus is Lord,
who lives with you
and the Holy Spirit,
one God,
for ever and ever.
Amen.

—Opening Prayer for the Feast of Pentecost

Name ______________________________ Date ______________

Chapter 6 Test

Part 1: True or False. Mark **T** if the statement is true. Mark **F** if the statement is false. **(2 points each)**

1. _____ The original ending of the Gospel of Mark is Mk 16:8.
2. _____ All of the Gospels mention that Mary Magdalene came to the empty tomb.
3. _____ Paul gives us the earliest account of the Paschal Mystery.
4. _____ All of the Gospels agree that there were two angels in Jesus' empty tomb.
5. _____ The Apostles' Creed professes that after Christ died, he immediately went to Heaven.
6. _____ Thomas was told by Jesus to place his hand in Jesus' side and his fingers in the nail holes of Jesus' hands to prove he had risen.
7. _____ No Gospel account reports anyone seeing how the Resurrection happened.
8. _____ *Kerygma* means the service we are called to render to others.
9. _____ All four Gospels agree that women were the first to arrive at the tomb.
10. ____ The women visited Jesus' tomb on a Monday.
11. ____ In John's Gospel, Jesus gives his disciples the Gift of the Holy Spirit on Easter Sunday.
12. ____ Jesus appears to Thomas only in the Gospel of Luke.
13. ____ We can call Jesus' Ascension a true homecoming.
14. ____ Only Matthew's Gospel tells us why guards were posted at Jesus' tomb.
15. ____ The disciples at Emmaus recognized Jesus in the breaking of the bread.
16. ____ Jesus' body did not decay in the tomb like normal bodies.
17. ____ Many elements of the *kerygma* can be found in the sermons of St. Peter.
18. ____ The most special way we encounter Jesus alive today is in the Eucharist.
19. ____ When Mary Magdalene recognized Jesus in the garden, she called him "Master."
20. ____ The beloved disciple believed in the Resurrection after seeing the discarded burial clothes.
21. ____ Peter was the first person to witness the empty tomb according to all the Gospels.
22. ____ No verifiable evidence exists that indicates the Resurrection was a real, historical event.
23. ____ The account of Jesus appearing to his followers by the seaside was probably added to John's Gospel by one of his disciples.
24. ____ The Gospel writers went to great pains to harmonize their Resurrection appearance accounts.
25. ____ Jesus' appearance to the two men on the road to Emmaus is depicted in the Gospel of John.
26. ____ The "disciple whom Jesus loved" is only mentioned in the Gospel of Mark.

Part 2: Fill in the Blanks. (2 points each)

1. ________________ The ____ is the core teaching about Jesus Christ as Savior and Lord.
2. ________________ Paschal ____ was what the Israelites were commanded to eat as a part of the Passover celebration.

3. ________________ Many Jews today still read the ____, a collection of rabbinical teachings collected after the destruction of the Temple in AD 70.

4. ________________ Catholics meet the Risen Lord during Sunday liturgies in the ____.

5. ________________ The "beloved disciple" or the "disciple whom Jesus loved" is traditionally considered to be ____.

6. ________________ The ____ of Jesus refers to the time when his glorified body took its rightful place in heaven.

7. ________________ The ____ of the Blessed Virgin refers to the time when Mary's body and soul were taken up into heavenly glory.

8. ________________ The word ____ comes from the Latin word that means "learner" and was used often to describe Jesus' followers.

9. ________________ The Last ____ is the last day when Christ will come again to fully establish God's Kingdom.

10. ________________ The ____ is the innermost or spiritual part of a person and lives on eternally.

Part 3: Six "3s." Respond to the following. **(3 points each)**

1. Cite three similarities between the longer ending of Mark and the other three Gospels.

2. Name three consequences of the Resurrection (three of the "4 Cs").

3. Name three sacraments and how we encounter the Risen Christ in them.

4. Cite three pieces of evidence that the Resurrection was a historical event.

5. List three characteristics of Christ's risen body.

6. List three benefits of receiving Holy Communion.

Part 4: Essay. Respond to the following. **(10 points)**

1. Some people deny that Jesus rose from the dead. If you were to encounter such a person, write down the argument you would make with supporting evidence for the reality of Christ's Resurrection. Also include one argument against the Resurrection and refute it with evidence.

Name ______________________________ Date ______________

The Eucharist—A Meal of Friendship

Each of us is a friend of Jesus. For that, we give thanks. For that, we are a "Eucharistic" people. We remember Jesus and celebrate his friendship with us whenever we:

- Gather
- Share stories and Good News
- Share a meal together
- Promise—and keep our promise—to go forth bringing the friendship of Jesus to others.

♦♦♦♦♦♦♦♦♦♦♦♦♦♦♦♦

Describe how these four actions of the Eucharist strengthen your friendship with Jesus and the Church community as well.

We gather.

We share stories and good news.

We share a meal together.

We promise—and keep our promise—to go forth bringing the friendship of Jesus to others.

Name ______________________________ Date ______________

Death—Then What?

particular judgment

↓

(Purgatory → Heaven) OR (Hell)

↓

Second Coming of Christ

↓

Resurrection of the Body

↓

General Resurrection

↓

Kingdom fulfilled

Particular Judgment

God's justice is not ours.

God's justice has nothing to do with vindictiveness.

The many choices we have made in life—choices that turn us toward or away from God and neighbor— are the bases of judgment.

Purgatory

a transitory state of purification

Heaven

a permanent state of lasting love

Hell

a permanent state of unrepented sin, separation, and total loneliness

Second Coming of Christ (Parousia)

Resurrection of the Body

General Judgment

A time to . . .

____

____

(Luke 21:28)

The Kingdom of God Fulfilled

Name ______________________ Date ______________

Prayer for a Happy Death

by President Corazon C. Aquino

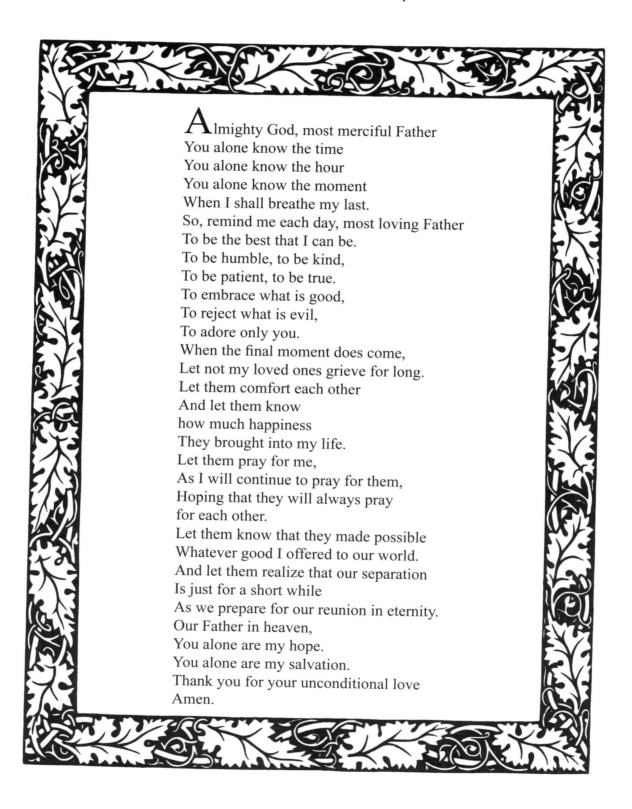

Almighty God, most merciful Father
You alone know the time
You alone know the hour
You alone know the moment
When I shall breathe my last.
So, remind me each day, most loving Father
To be the best that I can be.
To be humble, to be kind,
To be patient, to be true.
To embrace what is good,
To reject what is evil,
To adore only you.
When the final moment does come,
Let not my loved ones grieve for long.
Let them comfort each other
And let them know
how much happiness
They brought into my life.
Let them pray for me,
As I will continue to pray for them,
Hoping that they will always pray
for each other.
Let them know that they made possible
Whatever good I offered to our world.
And let them realize that our separation
Is just for a short while
As we prepare for our reunion in eternity.
Our Father in heaven,
You alone are my hope.
You alone are my salvation.
Thank you for your unconditional love
Amen.

Name ______________________________ Date ______________

Chapter 7 Test

Part 1: Fill in the Blanks. Choose from the following words to fill in the blanks. **(2 points each)**

Anointing of the Sick	Baptism	Beatific Vision	belief	Communion of Saints		Confirmation
conversion	eschatology	Gehenna	grace	Hades	Heaven	hell
Holy Orders	Incarnation	Kingdom of God	Matrimony	Parousia	Paschal Mystery	
Penance	Purgatory	repentance	sacrament			

1. ______________ ____ is a transitional state of purification in which the imperfect person encounters the perfection of God.
2. ______________ The ____ shows us that human beings are, indeed, images of the Divine, and sisters and brothers of the Son of God himself.
3. ______________ In the Sacrament of ____, we share the gift of Jesus, God's own Spirit, who enables us to call God "Father."

4 & 5. ______________ ______________ Each ____ is a means of ____, allowing us to experience the presence of Christ at various moments of our lives.

6. ______________ The ____ refers to the process of God's reconciling and renewing all things through his Son, and God's will being done on earth as it is in Heaven.
7. ______________ ____ is the study and teaching about the "last things."
8. ______________ In the sacrament of ____, we are marked with the Sign of the Cross; named "Christians," friends of Jesus; and are reborn as brothers and sisters of the Lord.
9. ______________ People who die after freely and definitively separating themselves from God most likely will spend eternity in ____.

10 & 11. ______________ ______________ In the sacraments at the Service of Communion (____ and ____), Jesus grants us the grace to act as a friend to others and welcome others into the circle of Jesus' friends.

12 & 13. ______________ ______________ The two prerequisites for belonging to God's Kingdom are ____ and ____.

14 & 15. ______________ ______________ Jesus referred to Hell as the fires of ____ and ____ where the rich man suffered.

16. ______________ The Eucharist commemorates the ____ by celebrating Jesus' Death, Resurrection, and Ascension.
17. ______________ Jesus' arriving in glory at his Second Coming is also known as the ____ or the Last Days.

18 & 19. ______________ ______________ In the Sacraments of ____ and ____, Jesus reaches out to us as a forgiving, reconciling, and healing friend.

20. ______________ ____ is home; it is where we are loved and are loving forever.
21. ______________ Seeing God "face to face," or the ____, is the source of our eternal happiness and final union with the Triune God for eternity.
22. ______________ The ____ is composed of the people of the Church on earth, in Heaven, and in Purgatory.

Part 2: True or False. Mark **T** if the statement is true. Mark **F** if the statement is false. **(2 points each)**

1. _____ The creation of the earth was *the* masterpiece of God's creation.
2. _____ We experience the Incarnation in the sacraments.
3. _____ People in Purgatory can never go to Hell.
4. _____ Confirmation celebrates our rebirth into the Church.
5. _____ God always intended for humankind to be destined for death.
6. _____ The study of the last things is called cosmology.

7. ______ The particular judgment refers to Christ's Second Coming.

8. ______ The manifestation of God's love for us in the flesh is called the Annunciation.

9. ______ We first receive the Spirit in the Sacrament of Baptism.

10. ______ After we die, our bodies stay on earth forever and our souls go to Heaven.

11. ______ God condemns people to Hell because of anger for their disobedience.

12. ______ It is pointless to pray for the dead since they have already been judged by God.

13. ______ A person who has committed enough venial sins will be condemned to hell.

14. ______ People with mortal sin have lost sanctifying grace.

15. ______ The Liturgy of the Word includes Scripture readings and the homily.

Part 3: Short Answers. Respond to the following. **(3 points each)**

1. List three fruits of the Holy Spirit.

2. List three differences between the particular and the General Judgment.

Part 4: After Death. (10 total points)

List the following in the order in which they could occur:

1. ______ A. death
2. ______ B. Fulfillment of the Kingdom of God
3. ______ C. Heaven, Hell, or Purgatory
4. ______ D. Second Coming of Christ
5. ______ E. Last or General Judgment
6. ______ F. particular judgment

Part 5: Take-Home Essay. You will be awarded **up to 10 points** for your work on the following essay.

How do the seven sacraments celebrate the wonders of our Salvation? Write an essay on the significance of the sacraments and their relationship to the Incarnation, Paschal Mystery, and Salvation.

Name ____ Date ____________________

Saintliness

Your Birthright

God created man in his image; in the divine image he created him; male and female he created them. God blessed them . . . then God looked at everything he had made, and he found it very good.

—Genesis 1:27–28, 31

Your Vocation

Our fundamental vocation is the vocation to holiness/saintliness, that is, the perfection of charity. Holiness is the greatest testimony of the dignity conferred on a disciple of Christ and the basic charge entrusted to all the sons and daughters of the Church.

—Pope John Paul II, *The Lay Members of Christ's Faithful People, On the Vocation and the Mission of the Lay Faithful in the World*, 16

Your Life-Long Task

Saintliness is not simply a state in which God invites us to dwell, but a task God asks us to undertake. "Each one . . . according to his own gifts and duties must steadfastly advance along the way of a living faith, which arouses hope and works through love."

—Vatican II, *Dogmatic Constitution on the Church*, 41

Your Challenge

Young people of every continent, do not be afraid to be the saints of the new millennium! Be contemplative, love prayer; be coherent with your faith and generous in the service of your brothers and sisters, be active members of the Church and builders of peace.

—Pope John Paul II, World Youth Day, 2000

Your Reaction

____

____

____

____

____

____

____

____

____

____

____

____

____

Name ______________________________ Date ______________

The Four Faces of Justice

Commutative justice calls for fundamental fairness in all agreements and exchanges between individuals or private social groups. It demands respect for the equal human dignity of all persons in economic transactions, contracts, or promises. For example, workers owe their employers diligent work in exchange for their wages. Employers are obligated to treat their employees as persons, paying them fair wages in exchange for the work done and establishing conditions and patterns of work that are truly human.

—National Conference of Catholic Bishops,
Economic Justice for All, 69

Distributive justice requires that the allocation of income, wealth, and power in society be evaluated in light of its effects on persons whose basic material needs are unmet. The Second Vatican Council stated: "The right to have a share of earthly goods sufficient for oneself and one's family belongs to everyone." If persons are to be recognized as members of the human community, then the community has an obligation to help fulfill these basic needs unless an absolute scarcity of resources makes this strictly impossible.

—National Conference of Catholic Bishops,
Economic Justice for All, 70

Legal justice means recognizing that the more closely the world comes together, the more widely do people's obligations transcend particular groups and extend to the whole world. This will be realized only if individuals and groups practice moral and social virtues and foster them in social living. Then, under the necessary help of divine grace, there will arise a generation of new women and men, the molders of new humanity.

—Pope Paul VI,
Constitution on the Church in the Modern World, 30

Social justice implies that persons have an obligation to be active and productive participants in the life of society and that society has a duty to enable them to participate in this way.

—National Conference of Catholic Bishops,
Economic Justice for All, 71

All human beings, therefore, are ends to be served by the institutions that make up the economy, not means to be exploited for more narrowly defined goals. Human personhood must be respected with a reverence that is religious. When we deal with each other, we should do so with the sense of awe that arises in the presence of something holy and sacred. For that is what human beings are: we are created in the image of God (Gn 1:27).

—National Conference of Catholic Bishops,
Economic Justice for All, 28

Name ____ Date ____________________

Just or Unjust?

For each statement, mark **J** if you think it's just, **U** if unjust. Be ready to explain your decisions.

_______ Providing parking places for "Handicapped Only."

_______ Establishing a military draft for men but not for women.

_______ Giving students with learning disabilities more time than "normal" students to finish homework and tests.

_______ Making convicted and released sex offenders register with police, and publishing their addresses on the Internet.

_______ Requiring all students to say the words "under God" in the Pledge of Allegiance.

A Self-Evaluation

Do you consider yourself a just person? Find out. Mark each statement **T** (True) or **F** (False).

_______ I treat other people the way I want to be treated.

_______ I am generally open-minded and reasonable.

_______ I try always to play by the rules.

_______ I think it's impossible to treat everyone fairly.

_______ I take advantage of people.

_______ I treat people with equanimity and impartiality.

_______ I consider how my actions affect others.

_______ I feel obliged to contribute to the common good.

_______ I think life is basically unfair and that there's not much anyone can do about it.

I think I am/am not a just person because

____

____

____

____

____

____

____

____

____

____

____

Name _______________________________________ Date ____________________

I Think Faith Is Like . . .

Each dual statement contains options that could complete the phrase "I think faith is like . . ." For each statement, circle the option with which you identify most.

a search for truth	- - - - - - - -	truth discovered
hanging on	- - - - - - - -	letting go
simple	- - - - - - - -	complicated
a sure bet	- - - - - - - -	risky business
sunshine	- - - - - - - -	clouds
chicken soup	- - - - - - - -	Buffalo wings
a sprint	- - - - - - - -	a marathon
a question	- - - - - - - -	an answer
a valley	- - - - - - - -	a mountain
mashed potatoes	- - - - - - - -	jalapeño peppers
defeat	- - - - - - - -	triumph
giving	- - - - - - - -	receiving
a leap	- - - - - - - -	a decision
useful	- - - - - - - -	useless
relaxed	- - - - - - - -	stressed
morning	- - - - - - - -	evening
special	- - - - - - - -	ordinary
dangerous	- - - - - - - -	safe

Describe a time your faith helped you overcome an obstacle.

____

____

____

____

____

____

If your faith in God was the basis for a TV show, what would it be called?

____

____

____

____

____

____

Name ______________________________ Date ______________

Measuring Up to Love

How well do you measure up to love? For each statement circle how well you believe you're doing.

I am caring and patient in my dealings with others.

Not at all Not so well Well More than Well Perfectly

I strive to be kind to all I meet.

Not at all Not so well Well More than Well Perfectly

I am never envious of others.

Not at all Not so well Well More than Well Perfectly

I am not possessive when it comes to my friendships.

Not at all Not so well Well More than Well Perfectly

I am concerned, first of all, for the well-being of friends and loved ones.

Not at all Not so well Well More than Well Perfectly

I never lose my cool.

Not at all Not so well Well More than Well Perfectly

I am always willing to give the benefit of the doubt to those who disagree with me.

Not at all Not so well Well More than Well Perfectly

I am not envious of others' success or good fortune.

Not at all Not so well Well More than Well Perfectly

I don't hold grudges.

Not at all Not so well Well More than Well Perfectly

I refuse to gossip or talk behind the backs of others.

Not at all Not so well Well More than Well Perfectly

I am willing to put the needs of others before my own.

Not at all Not so well Well More than Well Perfectly

I am making an effort to learn to love those who dislike me.

Not at all Not so well Well More than Well Perfectly

I'm serious about making Jesus the love of my life.

Not at all Not so well Well More than Well Perfectly

♦♦♦♦♦♦♦♦♦♦♦♦♦♦♦♦

God does not love you because you are good.
You are good because God loves you.

Name ____ Date ____________________

Chapter 8 Test

Part 1: True or False. Mark **T** if the statement is true. Mark **F** if the statement is false. (**2 points each**)

1. _____ The conscience is a voice in our head that tells us what to do.
2. _____ Everyone is called to be a saint.
3. _____ St. Thomas Aquinas calls prudence "right reason in action."
4. _____ Fortitude is a virtue that helps us think and judge carefully before acting so we can make wise choices and do things well.
5. _____ Actual graces are gifts given to individuals to help the Church grow.
6. _____ For Jesus, love requires self-denial.
7. _____ Sanctifying grace enables us to turn from sin and to follow Jesus on the way to holiness.
8. _____ A charism is a habitual and firm disposition to do good.
9. _____ Justification is possible through actual grace.
10. ____ Grace is a gift we earn by being holy people.
11. ____ Traditionally there are seven fruits of the Holy Spirit.
12. ____ A vice is a bad habit that inclines us to do evil rather than good.
13. ____ The human virtues are also called moral virtues.
14. ____ Human reason enables us to recognize God's voice, which urges us to do good and avoid what is evil.

Part 2: Matching. Write the letter of the correct term in the blank near its definition. You may use some terms twice. (**2 points each**)

1. _____ the virtues on which all other virtues "hinge"
2. _____ feeding the hungry, clothing the naked, visiting the sick and imprisoned, sheltering the homeless, and burying the dead
3. _____ counsel the doubtful, instruct the ignorant, admonish the sinner, comfort the sorrowful, forgive injuries, bear wrongs patiently, and pray for the living and the dead
4. _____ prudence, justice, fortitude, and temperance
5. _____ faith, hope, and charity
6. _____ virtues that are bestowed on us at Baptism
7. _____ wisdom, understanding, knowledge, counsel, fortitude, piety, and fear of the Lord
8. _____ a word that means "call"
9. _____ the name for the special gifts the Holy Spirit gives to individual Christians (includes the gifts of the Holy Spirit)

Part 2: Matching (continued). (2 points each)

1. ______ equated with common sense and wisdom
2. ______ makes it possible for us to totally commit to God
3. ______ abstinence, sobriety, and chastity
4. ______ giving due to God and neighbor
5. ______ allows us to desire the Kingdom of Heaven and happiness in eternal life
6. ______ "mother of all virtues"; lasts for eternity
7. ______ courage to conquer fears

A. Faith
B. Hope
C. Charity
D. Prudence
E. Justice
F. Fortitude
G. Temperance

Part 3: Brief Answers. Respond to the following.

1. List and briefly describe the three sources of morality. **(6 points)**

2. List and describe four types of grace. **(8 points)**

3. Name four types of justice and briefly explain the meaning of each. **(8 points)**

4. Describe at least three ways we can strengthen the virtue of faith. **(6 points)**

5. List and describe three steps we can take for conscience formation. **(6 points)**

6. List and describe three Gifts of the Holy Spirit. **(6 points)**

Name ______________________________ Date ______________

Understanding the Ten Commandments

The Commandments	Requirements and Virtues	Forbidden Sins
I. I am the Lord your God: you shall not have strange gods before me.		
II. You shall not take the name of the Lord your God in vain.		
III. Remember to keep holy the Lord's day.		
IV. Honor your father and your mother.		
V. You shall not kill.		
VI. You shall not commit adultery.		
VII. You shall not steal.		
VIII. You shall not bear false witness against your neighbor.		
IX. You shall not covet your neighbor's wife.		
X. You shall not covet anything that belongs to your neighbor.		

Name ____ Date ____________________

No One Else Can Do What God Is Calling *You* to Do

When thinking about the future, we generally ask ourselves,
"What do I want to do?"
But have you ever asked yourself,
"What does God want me to do?"

While we share with others the mission described in Matthew 28, each of us has a *specific* personal mission, a life work that is more than a career or a job or even what "I want to do." God has entrusted each of us with a unique set of talents, skills, virtues, and spiritual gifts, and God wants us to use them in a *particular* way over our lifetime. This is what stewardship is all about.

In their pastoral letter on stewardship, the United States Conference of Catholic Bishops wrote: "A Christian steward is one who receives God's gifts gratefully, cherishes and tends them in a responsible and accountable manner, shares them in justice and love with others, and returns them with increase to the Lord."

Stewardship = Sharing Time, Talent, Treasure, and Tradition

Time: Name two specific ways you will share your time with others.

1.

2.

Talent: These are my three best talents and how I think I can share them.

1.

2.

3.

Treasure: I commit to share ___________ percent of my personal income with my parish.

Tradition: How can you share your tradition?

The Steward's Prayer

God, show me **what** you want me to do today;
guide me **where** you want me to do it,
point out **when** you want me to do it
And teach me **how** to get it done.

Name ______________________________ Date ______________

Easy Essays

"What we give to the poor for Christ's sake is what we carry with us when we die."

♦♦♦♦♦♦♦♦♦♦♦♦♦♦♦♦

Rich and Poor

There is a rub
between the rich
who like to get richer
and the poor
who don't like
to get poorer.
The rich,
who like
to get richer
turn to the Church
to save them
from the poor
who don't like
to get poorer.
But the Church
can only tell the rich
who like
to get richer,
"Woe to you rich,
who like to get richer,
if you don't help the poor
who don't like to get poorer."

Better and Better Off

The world would be better off
if people tried to become better.
And people would become better
if they stopped trying to become better off.
For when everybody tries to become better off
nobody is better off.
But when everybody tries to
become better,
everybody is better off.
Everybody would be rich
if nobody tried to become richer.
And nobody would be poor
If everybody tried to be the poorest.
And everybody would be what
he ought to be
if everybody tried to be
what he wants the other fellow to be.

♦♦♦♦♦♦♦♦♦♦♦♦♦♦♦♦

Love Demands . . .

1. ______________________________
2. ______________________________
3. ______________________________
4. ______________________________
5. ______________________________

Name ____ Date ____________________

Chapter 9 Test

Part 1: Fill in the Blanks. Choose from the following words to fill in the blanks. (**2 points each**)

Andrew	Apostle	calumny	chastity	common	detraction	Evangelist	family	first
follower	Francis	friend	idolatry	Judas Iscariot	justice	Matthew	patron	Peter
presumption	pupil	steward	talent	Thomas	time	tradition	treasure	

1. ________________ Jesus named this Apostle ____, which means "rock."
2. ________________ The Apostle ____, who was called "the Twin" in John's Gospel, would not believe that Jesus had risen from the dead until he saw him.
3. ________________ ____ saints are chosen as special intercessors or protectors for our lives.
4. ________________ St. ____ is credited with saying, "Preach the Gospel always and, if necessary, use words."
5. ________________ The virtue of ____ helps us integrate sexuality with all aspects of who we are.
6. ________________ The ____ is also called the Domestic Church.
7. ________________ A ____ is one who carefully and responsibly manages something that has been entrusted to his or her care.
8. ________________ The word ____ means "one who is sent forth."
9. ________________ ____ was probably a tax collector.
10. ________________ The sin of ____ is to reveal the faults of someone without good reason.

11, 12, 13 & 14. ________________ ________________ ________________ ________________ Being a steward means sharing our ____, ____, ____, and ____ with others.

15. ________________ John's Gospel reports that ____ was the first disciple.
16. ________________ Spreading lies about another person is called ____.
17. ________________ ____ betrayed Jesus for thirty pieces of silver.

18 & 19. ________________ ________________ Believing you can save yourself without God's help is the sin of ____, which violates the ____ Commandment.

20, 21 & 22. ________________ ________________ ________________ According to the three senses of discipleship, a disciple is a ____, ____, and ____.

23. ________________ The virtue of ____ teaches us to respect the rights of others.
24. ________________ Worshiping something other than the true God, like money, is called ____.
25. ________________ An ____ is someone who shares the Good News with others.
26. ________________ The ____ priesthood of the faithful suggests that all baptized members of the Church are priests.

Part 2: Lists and Explanations. You will receive 1 point for each item named correctly and 1 point for each item explained correctly.

- List the Ten Commandments. For five of the commandments, describe some specific sins that are forbidden by them. (**15 points possible**)
- List the eight Beatitudes and explain how you can live out four of them in your life today. (**12 points possible**)
- List and explain the two purposes of marriage. (**4 points possible**)
- List the Twelve Apostles. (**12 points possible**)

Part 3: Discipleship Essay. (5 points)

What does it take to be a disciple? Write an essay describing what it takes to be a disciple according to the teachings of Jesus.

Name ______________________________ Date ______________

Meditating on the Scriptures

✷ ***Choose*** a Scripture passage from the list below. Mark it in the Bible so that you can easily turn to it when the time comes.

✷ ***Quiet*** yourself inside and outside. Be still and allow the cares of the day to dissipate. Breathe slowly. Notice your breathing. Relax your body so that your mind can focus. Sit with your back straight, hands in lap, eyes closed.

✷ ***Realize*** that God is present to you. Ask the Holy Spirit to guide you in your prayer.

✷ ***Read*** your chosen Scripture passage slowly and reflectively.

✷ ***Imagine*** yourself into the passage. Picture what is happening. What do you see, smell, taste, hear? What is Jesus like? What is he saying and doing? If he is telling a story, do you identify with any of its characters? What does Jesus reveal about God? How is he affecting others? What does the passage say to you?

✷ ***Meditate***. What is the theme of the passage? Pause to talk to the Lord. Allow him to speak to you through the reading. Share with him your deepest thoughts. Ask forgiveness for your failings. If distractions come your way, return to the Scripture passage. Take your time. Just as you would enjoy quiet moments with a friend, enjoy these moments with Jesus.

✷ ***Pay Attention***. Ask yourself, "What is the Lord saying to me? What message is there in this passage for my life?"

✷ ***Conclude***. Thank God for being present to you. Resolve to do something concrete as a result of your meditation. For example, you may want to forgive someone who hurt you, or ask another for forgiveness.

Scripture Passages

Call of the Apostles (Lk 5:1–11)
Feeding of the 5,000 (Jn 6:1–13)
Calming of the storm (Mk 4:35–41)
Miracle at Cana (Jn 2:1–12)
Emmaus (Lk 24:13–35)
The Good Samaritan (Lk 10:25–37)
Treasure and the Pearl (Mt 13:44–46)
Laborers in the Vineyard (Mt 20:1–16)
Prodigal Son (Lk 15:11–32)
Temptation in the Desert (Mt 4:1–11)

Name ______________________________ Date ______________

Litany of the Saints

Lord, have mercy

Lord, have mercy

Christ, have mercy

Christ, have mercy

Lord, have mercy

Lord, have mercy

Response: *pray for us*

Holy Mary, Mother of God,

Saint Michael,

Holy angels of God,

Saint John the Baptist,

Saint Joseph,

Saint Peter and Saint Paul,

Saint Andrew,

Saint John,

Saint Mary Magdalene,

Saint Stephen,

Saint Ignatius of Antioch,

Saint Lawrence,

Saint Perpetua and Saint Felicity,

Saint Agnes,

Saint Gregory,

Saint Augustine,

Saint Athanasius,

Saint Basil,

Saint Martin,

Saint Benedict,

Saint Francis and Saint Dominic,

Saint Francis Xavier,

Saint John Vianney,

Saint Catherine,

Saint Teresa of Jesus,

(*other names of saints may be added*)

All holy men and women,

Response: *Lord, save your people*

Lord, be merciful,

From all evil,

From every sin,

From everlasting death,

By your coming as man,

By your death and rising to new life,

By your gift of the Holy Spirit,

Response: *Lord, hear our prayer*

Be merciful to us sinners,

Guide and protect your holy Church,

Keep the pope and all the clergy in faithful service to your Church,

Bring all peoples together in trust and peace,

Strengthen us in your service,

Jesus, Son of the living God,

Christ, hear us.

Christ, hear us.

Lord Jesus, hear our prayer.

Lord Jesus, hear our prayer.

Let us pray:
God of our ancestors who set their hearts on you, of those who fell asleep in peace, and of those who won the martyrs' crown: we are surrounded by these witnesses as by clouds of incense. Count us in the communion of all the saints; keep us always in their good and blessed company. In their midst, we make every prayer through Christ who is our Lord forever and ever.

Amen.

Name ____ Date ____________________

Novena to Saint Joseph

Say the following prayer for nine days for anything you may desire. Then let go and let God. Trust that whatever is the outcome of your novena is truly what is best for you in accordance with God's will.

O Saint Joseph, whose protection is so great, so strong, so prompt before the throne of God, I place in you all my interests and desires.

O Saint Joseph, assist me by your powerful intercession and obtain for me from your Divine Son all spiritual blessings through Jesus Christ, Our Lord; so that having engaged here below your heavenly power, I may offer my thanksgiving and homage to the most loving of Fathers.

O Saint Joseph, I never weary contemplating you and Jesus asleep in your arms; I dare not approach while he reposes near your heart. Press him close in my name and ask him to hold me close when I draw my dying breath. Amen.

O Saint Joseph, hear my prayers and answer my petitions. (*Mention your intention.*)

O Saint Joseph, pray for me.

Name ______________________________ Date ________________

Mary's Prayer

Ave Maria,
gratia plena,
Dominus tecum.
Benedicta tu in mulieribus,
et benedictus fructus ventris tui, Iesus.
Sancta Maria, Mater Dei,
ora pro nobis peccatoribus, nunc
et in hora mortis nostrae.
Amen.

♦♦♦♦♦♦♦♦♦♦♦♦♦♦♦♦

Hail, Mary,
full of grace
the Lord is with thee.
Blessed art thou among women,
and blessed is the fruit of thy womb, Jesus.
Holy Mary, Mother of God,
pray for us sinners, now
and at the hour of our death.
Amen.

♦♦♦♦♦♦♦♦♦♦♦♦♦♦♦♦

Dios te salve, María,
llena eres de gracia,
el Señor es contigo.
Bendita tú eres entre todas las mujeres,
y bendito es el fruto de tu vientre, Jesús.
Santa María, Madre de Dios,
ruega por nosotros, pecadores, ahora
y en la hora de nuestra muerte.
Amen.

Name ______________________________ Date ______________

Chapter 10 Test

Part 1: True or False. Mark **T** if the statement is true. Mark **F** if the statement is false. (**2 points each**)

1. _____ *Eucharist* comes from the Greek word meaning "to give praise."

2. _____ Contrition is a special type of adoration.

3. _____ When mental prayer leads to a silence or resting in the presence of God, it is called contemplation.

4. _____ The form of prayer that we make on behalf of others is called intercession.

5. _____ The form of prayer that asks God for help or favors is called prayer of contemplation.

6. _____ The Forty Hours Devotion is made of forty continuous hours of praying the Divine Office.

7. _____ The monastic life consists of communal living and worship, private prayer, work, silence, poverty, chastity, and obedience.

8. _____ *Lectio divina* includes a number of litanies to the saints.

9. _____ Mary's prayer was grounded in humility and faith.

10. ____ The Lord's Prayer has been called "a summary of the whole Gospel."

11. ____ The *Catechism of the Catholic Church* calls prayer a relationship that links us to the Trinity and to one another.

12. ____ A novena is prayed every day for nine days.

13. ____ Praying with icons is a form of idolatry.

14. ____ The Divine Office is also called *lectio divina*.

15. ____ The first part of the Hail Mary is from the New Testament.

Part 2: Identifying the Forms of Prayer. Identify each form of prayer below. (**3 points each**)

1. ____________________ "Give thanks to the Lord, who is good, whose love endures forever. Let the house of Israel say: God's love endures forever." (Psalm 118:1–2)

2. ____________________ "Holy Mary, Mother of God, pray for us sinners now and at the hour of our death."

3. ____________________ "I love you, Lord, my strength, Lord, my rock, my fortress, my deliverer, my God, my rock of refuge, my shield, my saving horn, my stronghold! Praise be to the Lord, I exclaim!" (Psalm 18:2–3a)

4. ____________________ "O Godhead hid, devoutly I adore thee, who truly art within the forms before me; to thee my heart I bow with bended knee, as failing quite in contemplating thee." (St. Thomas Aquinas)

5. ____________________ "I will extol you, my God and king; I will bless your name forever. Every day I will bless you." (Psalm 145:1–2a)

6. ____________________ "Abba, Father, all things are possible with you. Take this cup away from me, but not as I will but what you will." (Mark 14:36)

Part 3: Brief Answers. Respond to the following. (**6 points each**)

1. List six benefits of prayer.

2. List and briefly describe the three expressions of prayer.

3. List and briefly describe the six forms of prayer.

4. List the "6 Ps" of a good prayer life. Briefly describe two.

5. Explain the meaning of each phrase of the Lord's Prayer.

6. List three models of prayer in the Old Testament and tell how they exemplified a good life of prayer.

7. Name at least three times when Jesus prayed.

Part 4: Essay. Respond to the following. (**10 points**)

Describe how to pray *lectio divina*.